MANAGEMENT OF

INFORMATION SECURITY

Second Edition

MANAGEMENT OF

INFORMATION SECURITY

Second Edition

Dr. Michael E. Whitman, CISSP

Herbert J. Mattord, CISSP
Kennesaw State University

COURSE TECHNOLOGY
CENGAGE Learning

Australia • Brazil • Japan • Korea • Mexico • Singapore • Spain • United Kingdom • United States

COURSE TECHNOLOGY
CENGAGE Learning™

Management of Information Security

Michael E. Whitman, Ph.D., CISSP and Herbert J. Mattord, M.B.A., CISSP

Acquisitions Editor: Maureen Martin

Product Manager: Kate Hennessy

Developmental Editor: Lynne Raughley

Content Product Managers: Aimee Poirier, Philippa Lehar

Editorial Assistant: Erin Kennedy

Marketing Specialist: Vicki Ortiz

Print Buyer: Julio Esperas

Compositor: GEX Publishing Services

For product information and technology assistance, contact us at **Cengage Learning Customer & Sales Support, 1-800-354-9706**

For permission to use material from this text or product, submit all requests online at **cengage.com/permissions**
Further permission questions can be emailed to **permissionrequest@cengage.com**

ISBN-13: 978-1-4239-0130-3
ISBN-10: 1-4239-0130-4

Course Technology Cengage Learning
25 Thomson Place
Boston, Massachusetts, 02210
USA

Cengage Learning is a leading provider of customized learning solutions with office locations around the glode, including Singapore, the United Kingdom, Australia, Mexico, Brazil and Japan. Locate your office at: **international.cengage.com/region**

Cengage Learning products are represented in Canada by Nelson Education, Ltd.

For your lifelong learning solutions, visit **course.cengage.com**

Visit our corporate website at **cengage.com**

Printed in Canada
2 3 4 5 6 7 8 9 12 11 10 09 08

To Rhonda, Rachel, Alex, and Meghan: thank you for your loving support.
—MEW

To Frances Godwin, my mother, who taught me that anything is possible.
—HJM

TABLE OF CONTENTS

As global networks continue to expand, the interconnections among them become ever more vital to the smooth operation of commerce, now dependent on communication and computing systems. However, escalating attacks on information systems and the success of criminal attackers illustrate the weaknesses in current information technologies and the need for heightened information system security.

To secure current systems and networks, organizations must draw on the pool of current information security practitioners. These same organizations will count on the next generation of professionals to have the correct mix of skills and experiences to develop more secure computing environments in the future. Students of technology must learn to recognize the threats and vulnerabilities present in existing systems. They must also learn how to design and develop the secure systems that will address these threats in the future.

The purpose of this textbook is to fulfill the need for a quality academic textbook in the discipline of Information Security Management. While there are dozens of quality publications on information security and assurance for the practitioner, there are few textbooks that provide the student with a focus on information security management. Specifically, those in disciplines such as Information Systems, Criminal Justice, Political Science, and Accounting Information Systems must understand the foundations of management of information security and the development of managerial strategy for information security. The underlying tenet of this textbook is that information security in the modern organization is a management problem, and not one that technology alone can answer; it is a problem that has important economic consequences and for which management is accountable.

Approach

The book provides a management overview of information security and a thorough treatment of the administration of information security. It can be used to support course delivery for information security driven programs targeted at Information Technology students, as well as IT management and technology management curricula aimed at business or technical management students.

Certified Information Systems Security Professionals Common Body of Knowledge— Because the authors are Certified Information Systems Security Professionals (CISSP), the CISSP knowledge domains have had an influence in the design of the text. Although care was taken to avoid producing another CISSP study guide, the authors' backgrounds have resulted in a treatment that ensures that much of the CISSP Common Body of Knowledge (CBK), especially in the area of management of information security, has been integrated into the text to some degree.

Chapter Scenarios—Each chapter opens with a short story that follows the same fictional company as it encounters various information security issues. The final part of each chapter is a conclusion to the scenario and offers a few discussion questions to round out each scenario. These questions give the student and the instructor an opportunity to discuss the issues that underlay the content.

Viewpoints—An essay from an information security practitioner or academic is included in each chapter. These sections provide a range of commentary that illustrate interesting topics or share personal opinions, giving the student a wider view on the topics in the text.

Offline Boxes—These sections highlight interesting topics and detailed technical issues, allowing the student to delve more deeply into certain topics.

Hands-On Learning—At the end of each chapter, students will find a Chapter Summary and Review Questions, as well as Exercises and Case Exercises, which give them the opportunity to examine the information security arena outside the classroom. Using the Exercises, the student can research, analyze, and write to reinforce learning objectives and deepen their understanding of the text. With the Case Exercises, students use professional judgment, powers of observation, and elementary research to create solutions for simple information security scenarios.

Author Team

Michael Whitman and Herbert Mattord have jointly developed this text to merge knowledge from the world of academic study with practical experience from the business world.

Michael Whitman, Ph.D., CISSP is a Professor of Information Systems in the Computer Science and Information Systems Department at Kennesaw State University, Kennesaw, Georgia, where he is also the Coordinator of the Bachelor of Science in Information Security and Assurance and the Director of the KSU Center for Information Security Education and Awareness (*infosec.kennesaw.edu*). He and Herbert Mattord are the authors of *Principles of Information Security*, *Principles of Incident Response and Disaster Recovery, Readings and Cases in the Management of Information Security*, and *The Hands-On Information Security Lab Manual*, all from Thomson Course Technology. Dr. Whitman is an active researcher in Information Security, Fair and Responsible Use Policies, Ethical Computing, and Information Systems Research Methods. He currently teaches graduate and undergraduate courses in Information Security, Local Area Networking, and Data Communications. He has published articles in the top journals in his field, including *Information Systems Research*, the *Communications of the ACM*, *Information and Management*, the *Journal of International Business Studies*, and the *Journal of Computer Information Systems*. He is an active member of the Information Systems Security Association, the Computer Security Institute, the Association for Computing Machinery, and the Association for Information Systems.

Herbert Mattord, M.B.A. CISSP completed 24 years of IT industry experience as an application developer, database administrator, project manager, and information security practitioner in 2002. He is currently a full-time Professor on the faculty at Kennesaw State University. He and Michael Whitman are the authors of *Principles of Information Security, Principles of Incident Response and Disaster Recovery, Readings and Cases in the Management of Information Security*, and *The Hands-On Information Security Lab Manual* all from Thomson Course Technology. During his career as an IT practitioner, he has been an adjunct professor at Kennesaw State University; Southern Polytechnic State University in Marietta, Georgia; Austin Community College in Austin, Texas; and Texas State University: San Marcos. He currently teaches undergraduate courses in Information Security, Data Communications, Local Area Networks, Database Technology, Project Management, and Systems Analysis & Design. He is the coordinator for the department's Certificate in Information Security and Assurance, and is also an active member of the Information Systems Security Association and the Association for Computing Machinery. He was formerly the Manager of Corporate Information Technology Security at Georgia-Pacific Corporation, where much of the practical knowledge found in this and his earlier textbook was acquired. Herb is currently pursuing a Ph.D. in Information Systems at Nova Southeastern University.

OVERVIEW

Chapter 1—Introduction to the Management of Information Security

The opening chapter establishes the foundation for understanding the field of information security by explaining the importance of information technology and identifying who is responsible for protecting an organization's information assets. Students learn the definition and key characteristics of information security, as well as the differences between information security management and general management.

Chapter 2—Planning for Security

This chapter explains the importance of planning and describes the principal components of organizational planning and information security system implementation planning.

Chapter 3—Planning for Contingencies

This chapter describes the need for contingency planning and explores the major components. It illustrates how to create a simple set of contingency plans using business impact analysis, and how to prepare and execute a test of those plans.

Chapter 4—Information Security Policy

This chapter defines information security policy and describes its central role in a successful information security program. Research has shown that there are three major types of information security policy; the chapter explains what goes into each type, and demonstrates how to develop, implement, and maintain various types of information security policies.

Chapter 5—Developing the Security Programs

Chapter 5 explores the various organizational approaches to information security and provides an explanation of the functional components of the information security program. Students learn how to plan and staff an organization's information security department based on the size of the organization and other factors, as well as how to evaluate the internal and external factors that influence the activities and organization of an information security program. The chapter also identifies and describes the typical job titles and functions performed in the information security program, and concludes with an exploration of the creation and management of a security education, training, and awareness program.

Chapter 6—Security Management Models and Practices

This chapter describes the components of the dominant information security management models, including U.S. government-sanctioned models, and discusses how to customize them for a specific organization's needs. Students learn how to implement the fundamental elements of key information security management practices and gain an understanding of emerging trends in the certification and accreditation of U.S. federal IT systems.

Chapter 7—Risk Assessment: Identifying and Assessing Risk

Chapter 7 defines risk management and its role in the organization, and demonstrates how to use risk management techniques to identify and prioritize risk factors for information assets. The risk management model presented here assesses risk based on the likelihood of adverse events and the effects on information assets when events occur. The chapter concludes with a brief discussion on how to document the results of the risk identification process.

Chapter 8—Risk Management: Controlling Risk

This chapter presents essential risk mitigation strategy options and opens the discussion on controlling risk. This includes identifying risk control classification categories, using existing conceptual frameworks to evaluate risk controls, and formulating a cost-benefit analysis. Students learn how to maintain and perpetuate risk controls. As an alternative to the approach presented in the early parts of the chapter, the OCTAVE and Microsoft methods of managing risk are discussed.

Chapter 9—Protection Mechanisms

Chapter 9 introduces students to the world of technical risk controls by exploring access control approaches, including authentication, authorization, and biometric access controls as well as firewalls and the common approaches to firewall implementation. The technical control approaches for dial-up access, intrusion detection systems, and cryptography are also covered.

Chapter 10—Personnel and Security

This chapter expands on the discussion of the skills and requirements for information security positions introduced in Chapter 5. It explores the various information security professional certifications, and identifies which skills are encompassed by each. The second half of the chapter explores the implementation of information security constraints—used to control employee behavior and prevent misuse of information—on an organization's human resources processes.

Chapter 11—Law and Ethics

In this chapter, students learn about the legal environment and its relationship to information security. The chapter describes the major national and international laws that affect the practice of information security, as well as the role of culture in ethics as it applies to information security.

Chapter 12—Information Security Project Management

The final chapter covers project management within the discipline of information security. It provides basic project management techniques as well as guidance on applying project management principles to an information security program.

Appendix—NIST SP 800-26, Security Self-Assessment Guide for Information Technology Systems and ISO 17799:2005 Overview

The appendix reproduces an essential security management model from the NIST library and provides an overview of ISO/IEC 17799:2005.

INSTRUCTOR RESOURCES

A variety of teaching tools have been prepared to support this textbook and offer many options to enhance the classroom learning experience:

Electronic Instructor's Manual—The Instructor's Manual includes suggestions and strategies for using this text, such as advice for lecture topics. The Instructors Manual also includes answers to the review questions and suggested solutions to the exercises at the end of each chapter.

Figure Files—Figure files allow instructors to create their own presentations using figures taken from the text.

PowerPoint Presentations—This book comes with Microsoft PowerPoint slides for each chapter. These are included as a teaching aid for classroom presentation, to make available to students on the network for chapter review, or to be printed for classroom distribution. Instructors can add their own slides for additional topics they introduce to the class.

Lab Manual—Thomson Course Technology has produced a lab manual written by the authors that can be used to provide technical hands-on exercises in conjuction with this book. (*Hands-On Information Security Lab Manual, Second Edition* ISBN 0-619-21631-X). Contact your Thomson Course Technology sales representative for more information.

Readings and Cases—Thomson Course Technology also produced a text titled *Readings and Cases in the Management of Information Security* (ISBN 0-619-21627-1) by the authors, which also makes an excellent text companion. Contact your Thomson Course Technology sales representative for more information.

Curriculum Model for Programs of Study in Information Security and Assurance—In addition to the texts authored by this team, a curriculum model for programs of study in Information Security and Assurance is available from the Kennesaw State University Center for Information Security Education and Awareness (http://infosec.kennesaw.edu). This document provides details on designing and implementing security coursework and curricula in academic institutions, as well as guidance and lessons learned from the authors' perspective.

ExamView®—ExamView®, the ultimate tool for objective-based testing needs, is a powerful objective-based test generator that enables instructors to create paper, LAN, or Web-based tests from test banks designed specifically for their Thomson Course Technology text. Instructors can utilize the ultra-efficient QuickTest Wizard to create tests in less than five minutes by taking advantage of Thomson Course Technology's question banks, or customize their own exams from scratch.

ACKNOWLEDGMENTS

The authors would like to thank their families for their support and understanding for the many hours dedicated to this project, hours taken, in many cases, from family activities. Special thanks to Carola Mattord, doctoral candidate in English at Georgia State University. Her reviews of early drafts and suggestions for keeping the writing focused on the students resulted in a more readable manuscript.

Reviewers

We are indebted to the following individuals for their respective contributions of perceptive feedback on the initial proposal, the project outline, and the chapter-by-chapter reviews of the text:

- Denise Padavano, Peirce College

- Nick LaManna, New England Institute of Technology

- Marcus Rogers, Purdue University

- Joseph Sherif, California State University, Fullerton

Special Thanks

The authors wish to thank the Editorial and Production teams at Thomson Course Technology. Their diligent and professional efforts greatly enhanced the final product:

- Kate Hennessy, Product Manager

- Lynne Raughley, Developmental Editor

- Maureen Martin, Acquisitions Editor

- Marisa Taylor and Philippa Lehar, Content Product Managers

In addition, several professional and commercial organizations and individuals have aided the development of the textbook by providing information and inspiration, and the authors wish to acknowledge their contribution:

- The Human Firewall Council

- NetIQ Corporation

- The viewpoint authors:
  - Morgan Alexander-LeStat
  - Henry Bonin
  - George Hulme
  - Lee Imrey
  - Steve Kahan
  - Eng-Kiat Koh
  - Chris Pick
  - Bruce Schneier
  - Krizi Trivisani
  - Todd Tucker

- Steven Kahan

- Charles Cresson Wood

- Our colleagues in the Department of Computer Science and Information Systems, Kennesaw State University

- Professor Merle King, Chair of the Department of Computer Science and Information Systems, Kennesaw State University

Our Commitment

The authors are committed to serving the needs of the adopters and readers. We would be pleased and honored to receive feedback on the textbook and its supporting materials. You can contact us through Thomson Course Technology at mis@course.com.

FOREWORD

By Charles Cresson Wood

Over the last 25 years that I've worked in the information security field, I've had an opportunity to perform risk assessments for over 130 different organizations around the world. No matter how large the organization, no matter how well-respected the organization, and no matter how high-tech the public's view of the organization, in all cases I find that management doesn't take information security seriously enough. In part this is because information security is still a relatively new field, and we don't yet understand many things about it. In part this is because top management often doesn't know much, and doesn't care to know much, about information systems technology, and in part this is because top management has been making traditional trade-off decisions, where security loses when up against other objectives such as low cost, increased speed, user-friendliness, time to market with a new product, etc.

Over the last few decades, times have changed dramatically, except top management, in most cases, hasn't yet appreciated how different things are. For example, consider the case of Arthur Andersen, once one of the largest and most highly-respected public accounting firms in the world. Andersen did some auditing and consulting work for Enron, now a discredited and largely defunct energy trading concern. A U.S. government Securities & Exchange Commission investigation into Enron's accounting practices caused certain Andersen employees to destroy documents that might have been relevant to the investigation. Aside from the fact that Andersen staff may have been involved in "cooking the books" along with Enron accounting staff, there was a major misunderstanding about the document destruction policy at Andersen. Certain staff believed they were doing the right thing when they destroyed thousands of pounds of Enron documents. Of course, document destruction is an important part of the information security field. If these staff members had received much better training about this document destruction policy, Andersen might still be in existence today. So here we have a misunderstanding about, and a lack of adequate training in, information security, leading to the downfall of one the world's finest accounting firms. Nonetheless, at most organizations today, top management still erroneously believes that information security is a relatively unimportant issue not worthy of considerable top management attention.

Additionally, consider a recent poll conducted by Harris Interactive, which indicated that fully 79% of the American public believes that their personal information will be shared with other organizations without their permission. Apparently Americans don't believe businesses and government agencies when they publish privacy policies. Americans think these policies are just "window dressing," or something to please the auditors and regulators. What we have here is a major trust problem, where customers don't believe what businesses and government agencies say about the handling of private data. This is indicative of a serious failure on the part of these organizations; they have failed to convince customers that they will dutifully respect privacy rights. At the same time, an earlier study performed by the same organization (then called Louis Harris Associates) indicated that the take-up or adoption rate for new electronic services such as Internet business would double when adequate privacy safeguards were added. In other words, customers will be twice as likely to place an order online if they feel comfortable that their personal information will be adequately protected. Yet top management often doesn't allocate sufficient resources to information security, for instance by establishing a Chief Privacy Officer, and the net result is that sales suffer. Top management so often doesn't appreciate how doing a good job in the information security realm will lead to a variety of tangible business benefits like competitive advantage. If being able to double the level of sales isn't important to top management, what is?

Information security now needs to be recognized as a regular part of every modern organization. People need to have information security in their job descriptions, departments need to have information security in their mission statements, and outsourcing firms need to have information security in their contracts. Every personal computer needs to be outfitted with a virus detection software package, a personal firewall, a spam filter, and related security software. End users need to be trained about information security; for instance, they need to be told what to do when their machine is infected with a computer virus. End users are now on the front line of the information security war. And a war it is, because new, more complex, and more aggressive ways to compromise information systems security are being developed every day.

Information security cannot be something that is left to the technologists within the Information Technology department. End users, for example, must deal with telephone callers seeking to get information through what is called social engineering. Also known as masquerading or spoofing, this technique involves leading users to believe that the caller is somebody other than who they really are. A caller could say they were from the IT department, that they need to have the user's user-ID and fixed password in order to correct a problem with the network. While it may sound unbelievable, unless they are told not to divulge such information, studies have shown that a large percentage of the user population will simply reveal their user-ID and password.

Everybody who comes into contact with sensitive, valuable, or critical information needs to know about information security. This means that the janitor needs to know how to dispose of confidential documents that may have been thrown away in the trash. This means that the temporary staff person who is answering the telephone at the front desk needs to know what information he or she can divulge to outsiders. This means that outsourcing firms must know how to respond to a hacker break-in so that losses are minimized, so that the subscribing organization's good reputation is maintained, and so that the subscribing firm's business activity can proceed without undue interruption. In other words, information security must be approached with a team of individuals, all consistently using the same approaches to security, each with their own special part to play.

In this context, I welcome this newly revised textbook to train our future leaders. Every person working in modern businesses or government agencies will need to know some practical information about information security. If they cover information security at all, too many of the current college classes get bogged-down in the technology. While the technology is interesting, it is an overview, a holistic perspective, that is needed so that future leaders can understand the importance of and the ways to use information security. Information security is multi-disciplinary, multi-departmental, and increasingly multi-organizational in its scope. Future business leaders must appreciate how information security fits in with the other activities performed by the organizations where they will work.

The need for this information security knowledge gets more pressing every year. The U.S. Federal Bureau of Investigation teams up with the Computer Security Institute every year to do a survey about computer crime. One of the most recent surveys indicated that quantified losses due to computer crime were up 42% over the year before (apparently this still isn't serious enough to get many top managers to pay attention). Yet still 50% of the respondents to this survey don't have something as simple as a policy informing them where they should report violations and incidents. If workers at an organization don't even know to whom and when they should report a violation or an incident, then there is no chance that management will know what is really happening when it comes to information security. If management doesn't know what's happening, then there will be no hope that they will be able to adequately manage the problem. In the interests of adequately managing this problem, this book helps by talking about best practices that can help management figure out what's happening, and from there, determine the best way to address the problems.

Charles Cresson Wood, CISA, CISSP, CISM
Independent Information Security Consultant
Sausalito, California

## CHAPTER 1

INTRODUCTION TO THE MANAGEMENT OF INFORMATION SECURITY

QUOTE

If this is the information superhighway, it's going through a lot of bad, bad neighborhoods.

Dorian Berger, 1997

One month into her new job at Random Widget Works, Inc. (RWW), Iris Majwabu left her office early one afternoon to attend a meeting of the Information Systems Security Association (ISSA). Her new position was a promotion from her previous assignment at RWW as an information security risk manager.

This occasion marked Iris's first ISSA meeting. With a mountain of pressing matters on her cluttered desk, Iris didn't know why she was making it a priority. She sighed. As the first Chief Information Security Officer (CISO) to be named at RWW, she already spent many hours in business meetings, followed by long hours at her desk as she pressed on in defining her new position at the firm.

In the ISSA meeting room she saw Charley Moody, her supervisor from a company she used to work for, Sequential Label and Supply (SLS). Charley had been promoted to CIO of SLS almost a year ago.

"Hi, Charley," she said.

"Hello, Iris." They shook hands warmly. "Congratulations on your promotion. How are things going in your new position?"

"So far," she replied, "things are going well—I think."

Charlie noticed her hesitancy. "You think?" he said. "Okay, tell me what's going on."

Iris explained. "I am struggling to get a consensus from the management team about the problems that we have. I'm told that information security is a priority, but everything is in disarray. Any ideas that are brought up, especially my ideas, are chopped to bits before they're even considered by management. There's no established policy covering our information security needs, and it seems that we have little hope of getting one approved. The information security budget covers my salary plus funding for one technician in the network department. The IT managers act like I'm a waste of their time, and they don't seem to take security issues as seriously as I do. It's like trying to drive a herd of cats!"

Charley thought for a moment, and then said, "I've got some ideas that may help. We should talk more, but not now; the meeting is about to start. Here's my number—call me tomorrow and we'll arrange to get together for coffee."

LEARNING OBJECTIVES

Upon completion of this material, you should be able to:

- Recognize the importance of the manager's role in securing an organization's use of information technology, and understand who is responsible for protecting an organization's information assets
- Know and understand the definition and key characteristics of information security
- Know and understand the definition and key characteristics of leadership and management
- Recognize the characteristics that differentiate information security management from general management

INTRODUCTION

In today's global markets, business operations are enabled by technology. From boardroom to mailroom, businesses make deals, ship goods, track client accounts, and inventory company assets, all through the implementation of systems made possible by information technology (IT). IT enables the storage and transportation of information—often a company's most valuable resource—from one business unit to another. But what happens if the vehicle breaks down, even for a little while? Business deals fall through, shipments are lost, and company assets become even more vulnerable to threats from both inside and outside the firm. In the past, the business manager's response to this possibility was to proclaim, "We have technology people to handle technology problems." This remark might have been valid in the days when technology was confined to the climate-controlled rooms of the data center and information processing was centralized. In the last 20 years, however, technology has permeated every facet of the business environment. Businesses now move when employees move from office to office or from city to city or even office to home. Since businesses have become more fluid, the concept of *computer security* has evolved into the idea of *information security*. Because this new concept covers a broader range of issues, from the protection of data to the protection of human resources, information security is no longer the sole responsibility of a small, dedicated group of professionals in the company. It is now the responsibility of every employee, and especially managers.

Astute business managers increasingly recognize the critical nature of information security as the vehicle by which the organization's information assets are secured. In response to this growing awareness, businesses are creating new positions to solve the newly perceived problems. The emergence of technical managers, like Iris in the opening scenario of this chapter, allows for the creation of professionally managed information security teams whose main objective is the protection of information assets.

Organizations must realize that information security funding and planning decisions involve more than just technical managers, such as information security managers or members of the information security team. Rather, the process should involve three distinct groups of decision makers, or **communities of interest**:

- Information security managers and professionals
- IT managers and professionls
- Nontechnical general business managers and professionals

Through a process of constructive debate, these three professional groups work to find consensus on an overall plan to protect the organization's information assets.

The communities of interest fulfill the following roles:

- The **information security community** protects the organization's information assets from the many threats they face.
- The **information technology community** supports the business objectives of the organization by supplying and supporting IT appropriate to the business' needs.
- The nontechnical **general business community** articulates and communicates organizational policy and objectives and allocates resources to the other groups.

Working together, these communities of interest make collective decisions about how to secure an organization's information assets most effectively. As the discussion in this chapter's opening scenario between Iris and Charley suggests, managing a successful information security program takes time, resources, and a lot of effort by all three communities within the organization. Each community of interest must understand that information security is about risk: identifying, measuring, and mitigating—or, at a minimum, documenting—the risk of operating information assets. It is up to the leadership of each of the communities of interest to identify and support initiatives for controlling the risks faced by the organization's information assets. But to make sound business decisions concerning the security of information assets, managers must understand the concept of information security, the roles professionals play within that field, and the issues an organization faces in a fluid global business environment.

WHAT IS SECURITY?

Understanding the technical aspects of information security requires that you know the definitions of certain IT terms and concepts. This knowledge enables you to engage in more effective communication with the IT and information security communities.

In general, **security** is defined as "the quality or state of being secure—to be free from danger."[1] To be secure is to be protected from adversaries or other hazards. National security, for example, is a system of multilayered processes that protects the sovereignty of a state, its assets, resources, and people. Achieving an appropriate level of security for an organization also depends on the implementation of a multilayered system. Security is often achieved by means of several strategies usually undertaken simultaneously or used in combination with one another. While each strategy has its own focus and builds on its own specializations, the various strategies share many common elements. From a management perspective, each must be properly planned, organized, staffed, directed, and controlled. Examples of the specialized areas of security include the following:

- **Physical security**, which encompasses strategies to protect people, physical assets, and the workplace from various threats including fire, unauthorized access, or natural disasters
- **Operations security**, which focuses on securing the organization's ability to carry out its operational activities without interruption or compromise
- **Communications security**, which encompasses the protection of an organization's communications media, technology, and content, and its ability to use these tools to achieve the organization's objectives
- **Network security**, which addresses the protection of an organization's data networking devices, connections, and contents, and the ability to use that network to accomplish the organization's data communication functions

Each of these areas contributes to the information security program as a whole. This textbook bases its definition of information security on the standards published by the Committee on National Security Systems (CNSS), formerly known as the National Security Telecommunications and Information Systems Security Committee (NSTISSC).

Information security (InfoSec) is the protection of information and its critical elements, including the systems and hardware that use, store, and transmit that information, through the application of policy, training and awareness programs, and technology. Figure 1-1 shows that information security includes the broad areas of information security management (the topic of this book), computer and data security, and network security. At the heart of the study of information security is the concept of policy (discussed in detail in Chapter 4). Policy, awareness, training, education, and technology are vital concepts for the protection of information and for keeping information systems from danger.

NSTISSC Security Model

The CNSS document NSTISSI No. 4011 *National Training Standard for Information Security (InfoSec) Professionals* (see *http://www.nsa.gov/ia/academia/cnsstesstandards.cfm*) presents one comprehensive model of information security. The CNSS security model, also known as the McCumber Cube after its developer, John McCumber, is rapidly becoming the standard for many aspects of the security of information systems. This

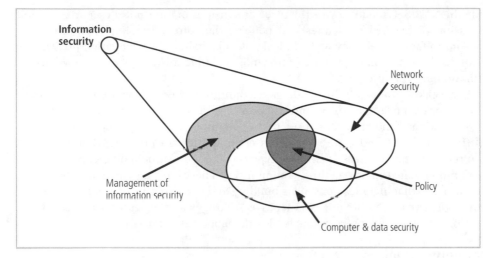

FIGURE 1-1 Components of Information Security

model, illustrated in Figure 1-2, shows the three dimensions central to the discussion of information security. If we extend the relationship among the three dimensions represented by the axes shown in the figure, we end up with a 3 × 3 × 3 cube with 27 cells. Each cell represents an area of intersection among these three dimensions that must be addressed to secure information systems. When using this model to design or review any information security program, you must make sure that each of the 27 cells is properly addressed by each of the three communities of interest. For example, the cell representing the intersection between the technology, integrity, and storage areas is expected to include controls or safeguards addressing the use of *technology* to protect the *integrity* of information while in *storage*. Such a control might consist of a host intrusion detection system (HIDS), which alerts the security administrators when a critical file is modified.

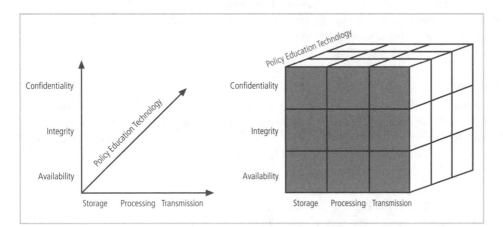

FIGURE 1-2 NSTISSC Security Model

While the NSTISSC model covers the three dimensions of information security, it omits any discussion of detailed guidelines and policies that direct the implementation of controls. And in fact, merely having technical controls, policies, or education programs in place is inadequate. The main purpose of this model is to identify gaps in the coverage of an information security program.

Another weakness of using this model is encountered when it is viewed from a single perspective. For example, the HIDS control that was described earlier addresses only the needs and concerns of the information security community, leaving out the needs and concerns of the broader IT and general business communities. In practice, thorough risk reduction requires that controls of all three types (policy, education, and technical) be created and communicated among all three communities. These controls can come about only through a process that includes consensus building and constructive conflict to reflect the balancing act that each organization faces as it designs and executes an information security program. Later chapters of this book will elaborate on these issues.

Key Concepts of Information Security

To better understand the management of information security, you must become familiar with the key characteristics of information that make it valuable to an organization. The **C.I.A. triangle**, which is the basis of the CNSS model of information security, has been the industry standard for computer security since the development of the mainframe.

The C.I.A. triangle is founded on three desirable characteristics of information —confidentiality, integrity, and availability—that are as important today as they were when first put forth. However, present-day needs have made these three concepts alone inadequate because they are limited in scope and cannot encompass the constantly changing environment of the IT industry. Threats to these three characteristics of information have evolved into a vast collection of potential dangers, including accidental or intentional damage, destruction, theft, unintended or unauthorized modification, or other misuses from human or other threats. This new environment of constantly evolving threats has necessitated the development of a more robust model of the characteristics of information. The updated model addresses the complexities of the current information security environment and the rapidly changing modern IT industry. The C.I.A. triangle, therefore, has expanded into a more comprehensive list of critical characteristics of information, covered later in this chapter.

Confidentiality

Confidentiality of information ensures that only those with sufficient privileges and a demonstrated need may access certain information. When unauthorized individuals or systems can view information, confidentiality is breached. To protect the confidentiality of information, a number of measures are used, including:

- Information classification
- Secure document storage
- Application of general security policies
- Education of information custodians and end users
- Cryptography (encryption)

Confidentiality is closely related to another key characteristic of information, privacy (discussed later in this chapter). The complex relationship between these two characteristics is examined in detail in Chapter 11. In an organization, confidentiality of information is especially important for personal information about employees, customers, or patients. People expect that an organization will closely guard such information. Whether the organization is a federal agency, a commercial enterprise, or a nonprofit charity, problems arise when organizations disclose confidential information. Disclosure can occur either deliberately or by mistake. For example, confidential information could be mistakenly e-mailed to someone *outside* the organization rather than *inside* the organization. Or perhaps an employee discards a document containing critical information without destroying it. Or maybe a hacker successfully breaks into an internal database of a Web-based organization and steals sensitive information about clients, such as names, addresses, or credit card information.

Integrity

Integrity is the quality or state of being whole, complete, and uncorrupted. The integrity of information is threatened when it is exposed to corruption, damage, destruction, or other disruption of its authentic state. Corruption can occur while information is being entered, stored, or transmitted.

Many computer viruses and worms, for example, are designed to corrupt data. For this reason, the key method for detecting an integrity failure of a file system from an attack by a virus or worm is to look for changes in one file's state as indicated by the file's size, or in a more advanced operating system, the file's hash value (discussed later in this section) or checksum.

The corruption of a file, however, does not always result from deliberate attacks. Faulty programming or even noise in the transmission channel or media can cause data to lose its integrity. For example, a low voltage state in a signal carrying a digital bit (a one or zero) can cause the receiving system to record the data incorrectly.

To compensate for internal and external threats to the integrity of information, systems employ a variety of error control techniques, including redundancy bits and check bits. During each transmission, algorithms, hash values, and error-correcting codes ensure the integrity of the information. Data that has not been verified in this manner is retransmitted or otherwise recovered.

As noted earlier, one way to ensure information integrity is by means of **file hashing**—the use of a special algorithm that evaluates the bits in a file and then computes a single representative number called a hash value; that is, essentially converting a variable length input into a fixed length output, typically ranging from 56 to 256 bits. The **hash value**—the value resulting from a hashing calculation—is different for each combination of bits. If the computer system performs the same hashing algorithm on the file and arrives at a different number than the file's recorded hash value, then the file has been compromised. Because information is of little or no value or use if its integrity cannot be verified, information integrity is a cornerstone of information security.

Availability

Availability is the characteristic of information that enables user access to information without interference or obstruction and in a useable format. A *user* in this definition may be either a person or another computer system. Availability does not imply that the information is accessible to *any* user; rather, it means availability to *authorized* users.

To understand this concept more fully, consider the contents of a library—in particular, research libraries that require identification for access to the library as a whole or to certain collections. Library patrons must present the required identification before accessing the collection. Once patrons are granted access, they expect to be able to locate and access resources in the appropriate languages and formats.

Privacy

The information that is collected, used, and stored by an organization is intended only for the purposes stated to the data owner at the time it was collected. This definition of **privacy** does not focus on freedom from observation (the meaning usually associated with the word), but rather means that information will be used only in ways known to the person providing it. Many organizations collect, swap, and sell personal information as a commodity. It is now possible to collect and combine information on individuals from separate sources, which has yielded detailed databases whose data might be used in ways not agreed to, or even communicated to, the original data owner. Many people have become aware of these practices and are looking to government for protection of their privacy.

Identification

An information system possesses the characteristic of **identification** when it is able to recognize individual users. Identification is the first step in gaining access to secured material, and it serves as the foundation for subsequent authentication and authorization. Identification and authentication are essential to establishing the level of access or authorization that an individual is granted. Identification is typically performed by means of a user name or other ID.

Authentication

Authentication occurs when a control provides proof that a user possesses the identity that he or she claims. Examples include the use of cryptographic certificates to establish Secure Sockets Layer (SSL) connections, or the use of cryptographic hardware devices—for example, hardware tokens provided by companies such as SecurID and Authenx—to confirm a user's identity.

Authorization

After the identity of a user is authenticated, a process called **authorization** provides assurance that the user (whether a person or a computer) has been specifically and explicitly authorized by the proper authority to access, update, or delete the contents of an information asset. An example of this control is the activation and use of access control lists and authorization groups in a networking environment. Another example is a database authorization scheme to verify that the user of an application is authorized for specific functions such as read, write, create, and delete.

Accountability

The characteristic of **accountability** exists when a control provides assurance that every activity undertaken can be attributed to a named person or automated process. For example, audit logs that track user activity on an information system provide accountability.

A successful information security program combines the conceptual elements described above to reduce risk to its information assets. The art of accomplishing meaningful reductions in risk requires communication and cooperation among all three communities of interest. In other words, securing information technology can be achieved only through careful management and dynamic leadership.

WHAT IS MANAGEMENT?

To effectively manage the information security process, you must understand certain core principles of management. In its simplest form, **management** is the process of achieving objectives using a given set of resources. A **manager** is a member of the organization assigned to marshal and administer resources, coordinate the completion of tasks, and handle the many roles necessary to complete the desired objectives. A manager has many roles to play within organizations, including the following:

- **Informational role**: Collecting, processing, and using information that can affect the completion of the objective
- **Interpersonal role**: Interacting with superiors, subordinates, outside stakeholders, and other parties that influence or are influenced by the completion of the task
- **Decisional role**: Selecting from among alternative approaches, and resolving conflicts, dilemmas, or challenges

The Difference Between Leadership and Management

The distinction between a leader and a manager arises in the execution of organizational tasks.

The leader influences employees so that they are willing to accomplish objectives. He or she is expected to *lead by example* and demonstrate personal traits that instill a desire in others to follow. In other words, leadership provides purpose, direction, and motivation to those who follow.

By comparison, a manager administers the resources of the organization. He or she creates budgets, authorizes expenditures, and hires employees. This distinction between a leader and a manager is important because leadership may not always be a function of a manager, and nonmanagers are often assigned to leadership roles. Many times, however, managers fulfill both the role of manager and leader.

Characteristics of a Leader

What makes a good leader? The U.S. military uses the following list of 14 leadership traits as a teaching tool for its officer corps to identify potential leaders:

1. Bearing—maintaining professional carriage and appearance
2. Courage—proceeding in the face of adversity
3. Decisiveness—making and expressing decisions in a clear and authoritative manner
4. Dependability—performing and completing tasks in a reliable and predictable manner
5. Endurance—withstanding mental, physical, and emotional hardship
6. Enthusiasm—displaying sincere interest in and exuberance for the accomplishment of tasks
7. Initiative—identifying and accomplishing tasks in the absence of specific guidance
8. Integrity—being of sound moral fiber, and good ethical worth
9. Judgment—using sound personal decision making to determine effective and appropriate solutions
10. Justice—being impartial and fair in exercising authority
11. Knowledge—possessing a base of information gained through experience or education
12. Loyalty—expressing open support and faithfulness to one's organization and fellow employees
13. Tact—dealing with a situation without undue personal bias or creating offense
14. Unselfishness—performing duties by placing the welfare of others and the accomplishment of the mission first

The private sector typically uses a shorter list of such traits, such as drive, desire to lead, honesty and integrity, self-confidence, cognitive ability, and knowledge of the business.

The U.S. military also provides an action plan for the improvement of an individual's leadership abilities:

1. Know yourself and seek self-improvement.
2. Be technically and tactically proficient.
3. Seek responsibility and take responsibility for your actions.
4. Make sound and timely decisions.
5. Set the example.
6. Know your [subordinates] and look out for their well-being.
7. Keep your subordinates informed.
8. Develop a sense of responsibility in your subordinates.
9. Ensure the task is understood, supervised, and accomplished.
10. Build the team.
11. Employ your [team] in accordance with its capabilities.

A key characteristic of a leader is concern for subordinates as well as strong motivation for accomplishing organizational objectives. A characteristic of leadership is the exhibition of the principles of *be...know...and do....*

As a leader you must *be* a person of strong and honorable character, *be* committed to professional ethics, *be* an example of individual values, and *be* able to resolve complex ethical dilemmas. You must *know* the details of your situation, the standards to which you work, yourself, human nature, and your team. You must *do* by providing purpose, direction, and motivation to your teams.

Behavioral Types of Leaders

There are three basic behavioral types of leaders: the *autocratic*, the *democratic*, and the *laissez-faire*.

Autocratic leaders reserve all decision-making responsibility for themselves, and are more *"do as I say"* types of managers. Such a leader typically issues an order to accomplish a task, and does not usually seek or accept alternative viewpoints.

The democratic leader works in the opposite way, typically seeking input from all interested parties, requesting ideas and suggestions, and then formulating a position that can be supported by a majority. Each of these two diametrically opposed positions has both strengths and weaknesses. The autocratic leader can be more efficient in that he or she is not constrained by the necessity to accommodate alternative supporting viewpoints. The democratic leader can be the less efficient because valuable time can be spent in discussion and debate when planning for the task. By contrast, the autocratic leader can also be the less effective if the knowledge possessed by the leader is less than sufficient for the task. The democratic leader can be more effective when dealing with very complex topics and those in which subordinates have strongly held opinions.

The laissez-faire leader is also known as the *"laid-back"* leader. While both autocratic and democratic leaders tend to be action-oriented, the laissez-faire leader often sits back and allows the process to develop as it goes, only making minimal decisions to avoid bringing the process to a complete halt.

Effective leaders function with a combination of these styles, shifting approaches as situations warrant. For example, depending on the circumstances, a leader will solicit input when the situation permits, make autocratic decisions when immediate action is required, or allow the operation to proceed if it is progressing in an efficient and effective manner.

Characteristics of Management

The management of tasks leading to the accomplishment of any objective requires certain basic skills. These skills are referred to as management characteristics, functions, principles, or responsibilities. Two basic approaches to management exist:

- Traditional management theory uses the core principles of planning, organizing, staffing, directing, and controlling (POSDC).
- Popular management theory categorizes the principles of management into planning, organizing, leading, and controlling (POLC).

The following discussion uses POLC to examine the skills that managers must employ when dealing with tasks. Figure 1-3 shows an overview of these elements and illustrates how the elements are conceptually related.

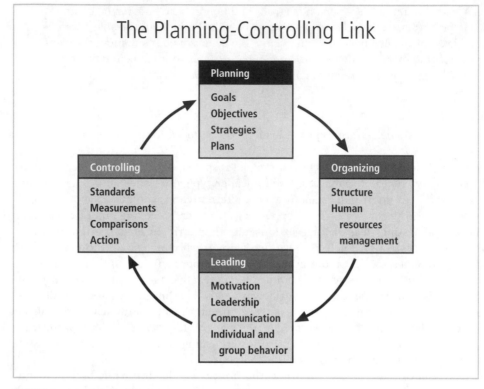

FIGURE 1-3 The Planning-Controlling Link[2]

Planning

The process that develops, creates, and implements strategies for the accomplishment of objectives is called **planning**. Several different approaches to planning are examined more thoroughly in later chapters and throughout this book. The three levels of planning are:

- *Strategic planning* occurs at the highest levels of the organization and for a longer period of time, usually five or more years.
- *Tactical planning* focuses on production planning and integrates organizational resources at a level below the entire enterprise and for an intermediate duration (such as one to five years).
- *Operational planning* focuses on the day-to-day operations of local resources, and occurs in the short or immediate term.

As Iris indicates in the opening of this chapter, lack of planning causes confusion and frustration among managers and staff.

The general approach to planning begins with the creation of strategic plans for the entire organization. The resulting plan is then divided up into planning elements appropriate for each major business unit of the organization. These business units in turn create business plans that meet the requirements of the overall organizational strategy. The plans are communicated to mid-level managers so that they can create tactical plans at their levels. Supervisors use the tactical plans to create operational plans that guide the day-to-day operations of the organization. To better understand the planning process, an organization must thoroughly define its goals and objectives. While the exact definition varies depending on context, the term **goal** refers to the end result of a planning process—for example, the goal line in football. The term **objective** refers to an intermediate point that allows us to measure progress toward the goal—a first down, using the football analogy. If you accomplish all objectives in a timely manner, then you are likely to accomplish your goal.

By itself, the management of the planning function within an organization encompasses an entire field of study. It involves understanding how to plan and relies on an integral understanding of project management. Project management is the management of all aspects of a project from inception, through organization and start-up, task completion, and eventual wrap-up. It involves the entire suite of activities necessary to ensure that the project is accomplished with the appropriate application of resources, including time, money, and staff. Project management is discussed in detail in Chapter 12.

Organizing

The principle of management dedicated to the structuring of resources to support the accomplishment of objectives is called **organization**. It includes structuring departments and their associated staff, the storage of raw materials to facilitate manufacturing, and the information to aid in the accomplishment of the task. Recent definitions of organization include staffing, because organizing people so as to maximize their productivity is not substantially different than organizing time, money, or equipment.

Organizing tasks requires determining what is to be done, in what order, by whom, by which methods, and according to what timeline. These activities are typically considered a part of project management, and are discussed in later chapters of this book. Defining organizational units and establishing departmental responsibilities and reporting relationships among staff may be outside the authority of any individual manager. What may be within a manager's domain are the creation of project teams and internal departments, and the assignment of specific staff to specific positions. The selection and retention of security personnel, and the role of the information security department in the selection and retention of other personnel, is covered in Chapters 5 and 10.

Leading

As noted earlier, **leadership** encourages the implementation of the planning and organizing functions. It includes supervising employee behavior, performance, attendance, and attitude. Leadership generally addresses the direction and motivation of the human resource.

Controlling

Monitoring progress toward completion, and making necessary adjustments to achieve desired objectives, requires the exercise of **control**. In general, the control function assures the organization of the validity of the plan. The manager ensures that sufficient progress is made, that impediments to the completion of the task are resolved, and that no additional resources are required. Should the plan be found invalid in light of the operational reality of the organization, the manager takes corrective action. The controlling function also determines what must be monitored as well as applies specific **control tools** to gather and evaluate information.

Four categories of control tools exist:

- *Information control tools* affect organizational communications, which is the flow of information throughout the entire organization, whether manual or automated.
- *Financial control tools* guide the expenditure of monetary resources, including total cost of ownership (TCO), return on investment (ROI), and cost-benefit analysis (CBA), along with the ordinary and expected budget process. The use of budgets as financial controls, as developed in planning, directly affects all operational functions. Project management brings a specific focus to certain financial controls that measure progress and performance. Being *on time* and *under budget* are two important controls used to regulate the progress of a project.
- *Operational control tools* evaluate the efficiency and effectiveness of business processes. The use of graphical control tools, such as PERT, Gantt charts, and process flow, along with others discussed in Chapter 12, regulate the function of projects and operations.
- *Behavioral control tools* regulate the efficiency and effectiveness of human resources; they include supervision, performance evaluations, and discipline. Supervision refers to the immediate oversight, guidance, and instruction of employees. Performance evaluations are the periodic assessment of general job performance. Discipline is the method by which the manager deals with unapproved behavior.

Each of these tool categories relies on the use of cybernetic control loops, often called negative feedback. They all use performance measurements, comparison, and corrective action, as illustrated in Figure 1-4. In this figure, the cybernetic control process begins with a measurement of actual performance, which is then compared to the expected standard of performance as determined by the planning process. If the standard is being met, the process is allowed to continue toward completion. If an acceptable level of performance is not being met, either the process is corrected to achieve satisfactory results, or the expected level of planned performance is redefined.

Understanding the four core principles discussed above enables managers to focus their energies and efforts in the right direction, using tried-and-true management methods. Ultimately, management success is measured by how a manager solves problems.

Solving Problems

All managers face problems in the course of the organization's day-to-day operation. Whether a problem is low or high profile, the same basic process can be used to solve it. Time pressures often constrain decision making when problems arise, however. The process of gathering and evaluating the necessary facts may be beyond available capabilities. Nevertheless, the methodology described in the following steps can be used as a basic blueprint for resolving many operational problems.

Step 1: Recognize and Define the Problem   The most frequent flaw in problem solving is failing to define the problem completely. Begin by clearly identifying exactly which problem needs to be solved. For example, if Iris receives complaints at RWW about the receipt

15

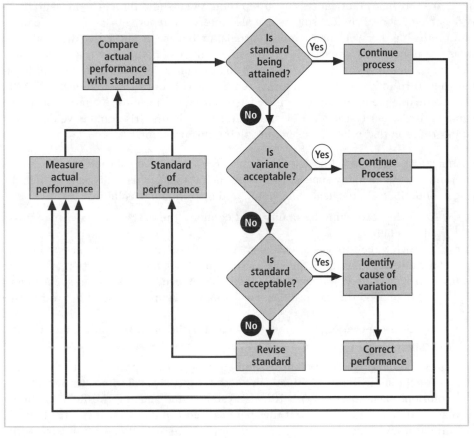

FIGURE 1-4 The Control Process

of a large number of unsolicited commercial e-mails (also known as spam), she must first determine whether the complaints are valid. Are employees receiving unsolicited spam, or have they signed up for notifications and mailing lists?

Step 2: Gather Facts and Make Assumptions To understand the background and events that shape the problem, a manager can gather facts about the organizational, cultural, technological, and behavioral factors that are at the root of the issue. He or she can then make assumptions about the methods that are available to solve the problem. For example, by interviewing several employees, Iris might determine that they are receiving a large quantity of unsolicited e-mail. She might also determine that each of these employees has accessed approved vendor support sites, which require an e-mail sign-in process. In such a case, Iris would suspect that the problem of excessive e-mail is, in fact, the result of employees providing their company e-mail addresses, which are being improperly used by the site owners.

Step 3: Develop Possible Solutions The next step is to begin formulating possible solutions. Managers can use several methods to generate ideas. One of these is brainstorming, a process where a number of individuals air as many ideas as possible in a short time,

Introduction to the Management of Information Security

without regard for their practicality. The group then reviews and filters the ideas to identify any feasible options. Problem solvers can also interview experts, or perform research into solutions using the Web, magazines, journals, or books. In any case, the goal is to develop as many solutions as possible. In the preceding example, once Iris locates the source of the spam e-mails, she can speak with the e-mail server and firewall administrators, and then turn to her Certified Information Systems Security Professional (CISSP) reading list. She might contact several of her friends from the local ISSA chapter, as well as spend time surfing security-related Web sites. After a few hours, Iris could have dozens of pages of information that might be useful in solving this problem.

Step 4: Analyze and Compare Possible Solutions   Each proposed solution must be examined and ranked as to its likely success in solving the problem. This analysis may include reviewing economic, technological, behavioral, and operational feasibilities.

- To review economic feasibility, you compare the costs and benefits of possible solutions.
- To review technological feasibility, you address the organization's ability to acquire the technology needed to implement a candidate solution.
- To review behavioral feasibility, you assess a candidate solution according to the likelihood that subordinates will adopt and support a solution, rather than resisting it.
- To review operational feasibility, you assess the organization's ability to integrate a candidate solution into its current business processes.

Using these methods, you can compare and contrast various proposals. In the spam example, Iris might immediately eliminate any overly expensive solutions, throw out some technical solutions incompatible with RWW's systems, and narrow the field to three alternatives: (1) do nothing, and accept the spam as a cost of doing business; (2) have the e-mail administrator change the users' accounts; or (3) have the firewall administrator filter access to and traffic from the spam sites. Iris could then discuss these alternatives with all administrators involved. Each solution is feasible, is inexpensive, and does not negatively affect RWW's overall operations.

Step 5: Select, Implement, and Evaluate a Solution   Once a solution is chosen and implemented, you must evaluate it to determine its effectiveness in solving the problem. It is important to monitor the chosen solution carefully so that if it proves ineffective, it can be cancelled or altered quickly. In Iris's case, she might decide to implement the firewall filters to reduce the spam, as most of it comes from a few common sources. She might also decide to require the affected employees to attend an e-mail security policy training program, where they can be reminded of the importance of controlling when and where they release company e-mail addresses. In addition, these employees might be required to submit periodic reports regarding the status of the e-mail problem.

VIEWPOINT

Information Security: On the Cusp of a Management Evolution

By Steve Kahan, Vice President of Marketing and Product Management, The Planet

The field of information security is today in the midst of a transformation. Until recently, the industry has been dominated by technical experts responding to technical issues as they provide information services, and confined to areas of computer and network operations. It is now evolving quickly into a management discipline that gets board-room attention—one that involves managing people and processes, as well as technology. This evolution is the result of several major changes in our global, Internet-connected environment.

Information security breaches and the damage they cause have risen dramatically in the past few years. Computer security vulnerabilities and reported attacks more than double annually. It has been estimated that the worldwide financial impact of such activities reached $13.2 billion in 2001 alone. We are also seeing a surge of new government regulations covering all kinds of industries and aimed at setting standards for cyber security and privacy. The increase in security breaches, along with these new regulations, have spurred an increase in internal audits among private and public organizations worldwide seeking to comply with regulatory requirements and leading practices.

Security professionals are recognizing that technology alone cannot solve the problem of securing our nation's vital information assets. An increasing number of academic programs are focusing on information security, and books, such as this one, are beginning to articulate and codify the discipline of information security management.

Outside of the academic world, efforts by organizations, such as the Human Firewall Council, a public awareness campaign of the Information Systems Security Association, have helped raise the awareness and visibility of security management issues. The term "human firewall" refers to the idea that the people within an organization, if made aware and properly educated, will support information security efforts and form a layer of protection (much like a firewall) to prevent and deter threats to a company's critical information assets. Through the Human Firewall's Security Management Index and Security Awareness Index surveys and reports, we have begun to provide the measurements necessary to feed the growth of information security as a management discipline. This is an exciting time to be involved in the study and practice of information security management. As a reader and a participant in the evolution of information security, you are among the pioneers setting the standards that will guide security professionals in the years to come.

PRINCIPLES OF INFORMATION SECURITY MANAGEMENT

As noted earlier, information security management is one of the three communities of interest functioning in most organizations. As part of the management team, it operates like all other management units by using the common characteristics of leadership and management discussed earlier in this chapter. However, the goals and objectives of the information security management team differ from those of the IT and general management communities in that they are focused on the secure operation of the organization. Because information security management is charged with taking responsibility for a specialized program, certain characteristics of its management are unique to this community of interest. These unique features extend the basic characteristics of general leadership and management and, as such, form the basis for the balance of this book.

The extended characteristics of information security are known as the six *P*s. Each is defined and examined briefly here.

Planning

Planning in InfoSec management is an extension of the basic planning model discussed earlier in this chapter. Included in the InfoSec planning model are activities necessary to support the design, creation, and implementation of information security strategies, as they exist within the IT planning environment.

The business strategy is translated into the IT strategy, which is in turn converted into the InfoSec strategy. For example, the CIO uses the IT objectives gleaned from the business unit plans to create the organization's IT strategy. The IT strategy then informs the planning efforts for each IT functional area. Depending on the location of the InfoSec function in the organization, the IT strategy may be used for information security planning when the CISO gets involved with the CIO or other executives to develop the strategy to the next lower level.

The CISO then works with the appropriate security managers to develop operational security plans. These security managers consult with security technicians to develop tactical security plans. Each of these plans is usually coordinated across the IT functions of the enterprise and placed into a master schedule for implementation. The overall goal is to create plans that support long-term achievement of the overall organizational strategy.

If all goes as planned, the entire collection of tactical plans results in accomplishment of operational goals, and the entire collection of operational goals results in accomplishment of subordinate strategic goals; this helps to meet the strategic goals and objectives of the organization as a whole.

Several types of InfoSec plans exist, including incident response planning, business continuity planning, disaster recovery planning, policy planning, personnel planning, technology rollout planning, risk management planning, and security program planning including education, training, and awareness. Each of these plans has unique goals and objectives, and each benefits from the same organized methical approach. These planning areas are discussed in detail in later chapters of this book.

Another basic planning consideration unique to InfoSec is locating the InfoSec department within the organization structure. This topic is discussed in Chapter 5.

Policy

The set of organizational guidelines that dictates certain behavior within the organization is called **policy**. In InfoSec, there are three general categories of policy:

- *Enterprise information security policy* (EISP) sets the tone for the InfoSec department and the InfoSec climate across the organization. This policy is developed within the context of the strategic IT plan. The CISO typically drafts the program policy, which is usually supported and signed by the CIO or the CEO.

- *Issue-specific security policies* (ISSP) are sets of rules that define acceptable behavior within a specific technology, such as e-mail or Internet usage.
- *System-specific policies* (SysSPs) are technical and/or managerial in nature and control the configuration and/or use of a piece of equipment or technology. For example, an access control list (ACL) is an SysSP that defines the accesses permitted for the specified device.

Programs

Programs are the operations conducted within InfoSec, which are specifically managed as separate entities. A security education training and awareness (SETA) program is one such entity. SETA programs provide critical information to employees to either improve their current level of security knowledge or maintain it. Other programs that may emerge include a physical security program, complete with fire, physical access, gates, guards, and so on. Each organization may have one or more security programs that must be managed.

Protection

The protection function is executed via a set of risk management activities, including risk assessment and control, as well as protection mechanisms, technologies, and tools. Each of these mechanisms represents some aspect of the management of specific controls in the overall information security plan.

People

People are the most critical link in the information security program. As discussed in the Viewpoint section, it is imperative that managers continuously recognize the crucial role that people play in the information security program. This area of InfoSec includes security personnel and the security of personnel, as well as aspects of the SETA program mentioned earlier.

Project Management

The final component is the application of thorough project management discipline to all elements of the information security program. Whether the task is to roll out a new security training program or to select and implement a new firewall, it is important that the process be managed as a project. This effort involves identifying and controlling the resources applied to the project, as well as measuring progress and adjusting the process as progress is made toward the goal.

Chapter Summary

- In today's global markets, business operations are enabled by technology.

- Since businesses and technology have become more fluid, the concept of computer security has been replaced by the concept of information security.

- From an information security perspective, organizations often contain three communities of interest: information security managers and professionals, IT managers and professionals, and nontechnical managers and professionals.

- Security is achieved via many routes, with several approaches usually undertaken singly or used in combination with one another. Specialized areas of security include:

  - Physical security

  - Personal security

  - Operations security

  - Communications security

  - Network security

- The C.I.A. triangle is based on three desirable characteristics of information: confidentiality, integrity, and availability.

- The CNSS (formerly the NSTISSC) presents a comprehensive model of information security that is rapidly becoming the evaluation standard for many aspects of the security of information systems.

- In its simplest form, management is the process of achieving objectives by using resources.

- The important distinction between a leader and a manager is that a leader influences employees so that they are willing to accomplish objectives, whereas a manager creates budgets, authorizes expenditures, and hires employees.

- The U.S. military uses a list of 14 leadership traits as a teaching tool for its officer corps, while the private sector typically uses a shorter list of such traits.

- Key characteristics of a leader are concern for employees as well as strong motivations for accomplishing organizational objectives.

- There are three basic behavioral types of leaders: the autocratic, the democratic, and the laissez-faire.

- Basic management skills are sometimes referred to as management characteristics, functions, principles, or responsibilities.

- The traditional approach to management theory uses the core principles of planning, organizing, staffing, directing, and controlling (POSDC).

- One approach to management theory categorizes the principles of management into planning, organizing, leading, and controlling (POLC).

- The process that develops, creates, and implements strategies for the accomplishment of objectives is called planning. There are three levels of planning: strategic, tactical, and operational.

- The principle of management dedicated to the structuring of resources to support the accomplishment of objectives is called organization.

- Leadership includes supervising employee behavior, performance, attendance, and attitude.

- Exercising control involves monitoring progress toward completion and making necessary adjustments to achieve the desired objectives.

- Problem solving is a multistep process that involves defining the problem, developing and analyzing possible solutions, and then selecting, implementing, and evaluating the best solution.

- Information security management operates like all other management units, but the goals and objectives of the InfoSec management team are different in that they focus on the secure operation of the organization.

Review Questions

1. A globally interconnected commercial world has emerged from the technical advances that created the Internet. Has its creation increased or decreased the need for organizations to maintain secure operation of their systems? Why?

2. Which trend in IT has eliminated the "we have technology people to handle technology problems" approach as a method for securing systems?

3. List and describe an organization's three communities of interest that engage in efforts to solve InfoSec problems. Give two or three examples of who might be in each community.

4. What is the definition of security? How is a secure state usually achieved?

5. List and describe the specialized areas of security.

6. What is the definition of information security? What essential protections must be in place to protect information systems from danger?

7. What is the C.I.A. triangle? Define each of its component parts.

8. Why is the C.I.A. triangle significant? Is it widely referenced?

9. Describe the CNSS security model. What are its three dimensions?

10. What is the definition of privacy as it relates to information security? How is this definition of privacy different from the everyday definition? Why is this difference significant?

11. Define the InfoSec processes of identification, authentication, authorization, and accountability.

12. What is management and what is a manager? What roles do managers play as they execute their responsibilities?

13. Are leadership and management similar? How are they different?

14. List and describe the behavioral types of leadership. Are they usually found in their pure form?

15. What are the characteristics of management based on the popular approach to management? Define each characteristic.

16. What are the three types of general planning? Define each.

17. List and describe the four categories of control tools.

18. List and describe the five steps of the general problem-solving process.

19. List and describe the extended characteristics of information security management.

20. Define project management. Why is project management of particular interest in the field of information security?

Exercises

1. Using a Web browser and search engine, find the Web site of the Committee on National Security Systems (CNSS), formerly the National Security Telecommunications and Information Systems Security Committee (NSTISSC). Locate the documentation library and browse the index. Which one or two documents would be of most interest to a security administrator? A CISO?

2. Think of an organization that uses information technology, but would not need to provide for information security on those systems. Describe that environment and explain why information security is not a factor for that organization.

3. Assume that a security model is needed for the protection of information in your class. Using the CNSS model, examine each of the cells and write a brief statement on how you would address the components represented in that cell.

4. Consider the information stored in your personal computer. Do you, at this moment, have information stored in your computer that is critical to your personal life? If that information became compromised or lost, what effect would it have on you?

5. Using the Web, identify the senior executive officer, the chief information officer, and the chief information security officer for your school or your current employer. Note that some organizations may use different titles for these personnel, so look for the closest approximate that can be found.

Case Exercises

Charley and Iris made an appointment to meet for a working lunch the next week. Charley sat down the day before the meeting to jot down his thoughts about good advice for Iris.

1. Based on your reading of the chapter and what you now know about the issues, list at least three things Iris could do.

2. Among the items listed in your advice to Iris, which one is the most important? Why?

Endnotes

[1] Merriam-Webster. "security." Merriam-Webster Online. [Cited 1 February 2002]. Available from the World Wide Web at http://www.m-w.com/cgi-bin/dictionary.

[2] From the lecture notes of Dr. Louis Jourdan, Clayton College and State University. [Cited April 15, 2003]. Available from the World Wide Web at http://business.clayton.edu/ljourdan/mgmt3101ic/.

## CHAPTER 2

PLANNING FOR SECURITY

QUOTE
You got to be careful if you don't know where you're going, because you might not get there.
—Yogi Berra

Iris was a little uneasy. While this wasn't her first meeting with Mike Edwards, the Chief Information Officer, it was her first planning meeting. Around the table, the other IT department heads were chatting, drinking their coffee. Iris stared at her notepad, where she had carefully written "Strategic Planning Meeting" and nothing else.

Mike entered the room followed by his assistants. Stan, his lead executive assistant, was loaded down with stacks of copied documents, which he and the other assistants began handing out around the table. Iris took her copy and scanned the title: Random Widget Works, Inc., Strategic Planning Document, Information Technology Division, FY 2008–2012.

Mike began, "As you know, it's annual planning time again. You just got your copies of the multiyear IT strategic plan. Last month you each received your numbered copy of the company strategic plan." Iris remembered the half-inch-thick document she had carefully read and then locked in her filing cabinet.

Mike continued, "I'm going to go through the IT vision and mission statements, and then review the details of how the IT plan will allow us to meet the objectives articulated in the strategic plan. In 30 days you'll submit your draft plans to me for review. Don't hesitate to come by to discuss any issues or questions."

Later that day, Iris dropped by Mike's office to discuss her planning responsibilities. This duty was not something he had briefed her about yet. Mike apologized, "I'm sorry, Iris. I meant to spend some time outlining your role as security manager. I'm afraid I can't do it this week; maybe we can start next week, by reviewing some key points I want you to make sure are in your plan."

The next day Iris had lunch with Charley Moody.

After they ordered, Iris said, "We just started on our strategic planning project and I'm developing a security strategic plan. You know, I've never worked up one of these from scratch before. Got any good advice on what to look for?"

Charley responded, "Sure. Actually, I have something for you in my car that might help."

After they finished lunch, the pair went out to the parking lot. Inside Charley's trunk were two cardboard boxes, marked "BOOKS." He opened one and rummaged around for a few seconds. "Here," he said, handing her a textbook.

Iris read the title out loud, "*Strategic Planning.*"

"This one is from a planning seminar I did a while back. I have a later edition, but there really isn't much difference between the two. I was cleaning out some of my redundant books. I was going to donate these to the library book sale. It's yours if you want it. It might help with your planning project."

Charley closed the trunk and said, "Read over the first few chapters—that'll give you the basics. Then sit down with your planning documents from corporate management and from IT. For each goal stated by the CEO and CIO, think about what your department needs to do to meet it. Write up how you think the company as a whole, and your team in particular, can satisfy that objective. Then go back and describe the resources you'll need to make it happen."

Iris asked, "That's it?"

Charley shook his head. "There's more to it than that, but this will get you started. Once you've got that done, I can share some of what I know about how to frame your plans and format them for use in the planning process."

LEARNING OBJECTIVES

Upon completion of this material, you should be able to:

- Identify the roles in organizations that are active in the planning process
- Grasp the principal components of information security system implementation planning in the organizational planning scheme

- Differentiate between strategic organization information security planning and specialized contingency planning
- Identify and specify the unique considerations and relationships between specialized contingency planning

INTRODUCTION

Chapter 1 discussed information security management within the context of general management, covering many of the elements of management as they apply to information security. The broader subject of *planning* delves more deeply into organizational planning and the process of planning for information security. This subject is divided into two chapters (see Figure 2-1). This chapter examines organizational planning, specifically, the process of planning for information security. Chapter 3 covers a very important topic in information security planning—contingency planning—in greater detail.

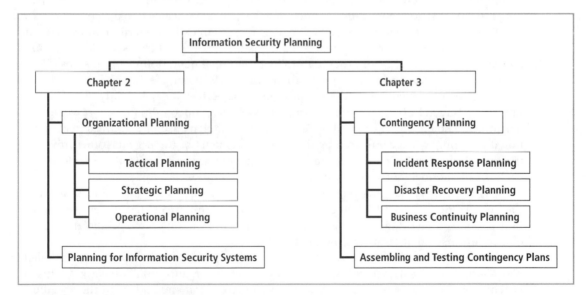

FIGURE 2-1 Information Security and Planning

It is difficult to overstate the essential nature of planning in business and organizational management. In a setting where there are continual constraints on resources, both human and financial, good planning enables an organization to make the most out of the resources at hand. While Chief Information Security Officers (CISOs) and other information security managers can generate an urgent response to an immediate threat, they are well advised to ensure the long-term viability of the information security program by utilizing a portion of the resources allocated through routine planning. However, some organizations spend too much time, money, and human effort on planning with too little return to justify their investment. Each organization must balance the benefits of the chosen degree of planning effort against the costs of the effort.

THE ROLE OF PLANNING

Planning usually involves many interrelated groups and organizational processes. The groups involved in planning represent the three communities of interest discussed in Chapter 1; they may be internal or external to the organization, and can include employees, management, stockholders, and other outside stakeholders. Among the other factors that affect planning are the physical environment, the political and legal environment, the competitive environment, and the technological environment.

Planning done by members of the information security community of interest uses the same processes as planning for the general management and IT management communities of interest. Because the information security community of interest seeks to influence the whole organization, an effective information security planner should know how the organizational planning process works so that participation in this process can yield measurable results. Before we can explore the positioning of information security within an organization's planning processes, however, we must first define the concept of organizational planning.

Planning is the dominant means of managing resources in modern organizations. It entails the enumeration of a sequence of actions intended to achieve specific goals during a defined period of time, and then controlling the implementation of these steps. Planning provides direction for the organization's future. Without specific and detailed planning, organizational units would attempt to meet objectives independently, with each unit being guided by its own initiatives and ideas. Such an uncoordinated effort will not only fail to meet objectives, but will also result in an inefficient use of resources. Organizational planning, when conducted by the various segments of the organization, provides a uniform script that increases efficiency and reduces waste and duplication of effort by each organizational unit within the individual communities of interest.

Organizational planning should be undertaken by using a top-down process in which the organization's leadership chooses the direction and initiatives that the entire organization should pursue. Initially, the organizational plan contains few specific detailed objectives; instead, it outlines general objectives.

The primary goal of the organizational planning process is the creation of detailed plans—that is, systematic directions on how to meet the organization's objectives. This task is accomplished with a process that begins with the general and ends with the specific.

PRECURSORS TO PLANNING

To implement effective planning, an organization's leaders should first have developed positions that explicitly state the organization's ethical, entrepreneurial, and philosophical perspectives. In recent years, the critical nature of the first of these perspectives—the ethical perspective—has come sharply into focus. Events such as the widely publicized problems at Enron and WorldCom, among others, illustrate the importance of an organization having solid and well-articulated ethical underpinnings. While ethical failures of this magnitude are, one hopes, exceptional, many organizations have begun to review critically the documents that establish their ethical foundations.

When an organization's stated positions do not match the demonstrated ethical, entrepreneurial, and philosophical approaches of its management teams, the developmental plan, which is guided by its mission statement, vision, values, and strategy, becomes unmanageable.

Values Statement

The first position that management must articulate is found in the **values statement**. The trust and confidence of stakeholders and the public are important factors for any organization. By establishing a formal set of organizational principles and qualities in a values statement, as well as benchmarks for measuring behavior against these published values, an organization makes its conduct and performance standards clear to its employees and the public. The quality management movement of the 1980s and 1990s amply illustrated that organizations with strong values can earn greater loyalty from customers and employees.

Microsoft has a formal employee mission and values statement published on its Web site, as shown in Figure 2-2.

Integrity, honesty, passion, and respectfulness are significant parts of Microsoft's corporate philosophy. A values statement for RWW might take the following form:

> RWW values commitment, honesty, integrity, and social responsibility among its employees, and is committed to providing its services in harmony with its corporate, social, legal, and natural environments.

Vision Statement

The second underpinning of organizational planning is the **vision statement**. In contrast to the mission statement, which expresses what the organization is, the vision statement expresses what the organization wants to become. Vision statements should therefore be ambitious; after all, they are meant to express the aspirations of the organization and to serve as a means for visualizing its future. In other words, the vision statement is the best-case scenario for the organization's future. Many organizations mix or combine the vision statement and the mission statement. RWW's vision statement might be:

> Random Widget Works will be the preferred manufacturer of choice for every business's widget equipment needs, with an RWW widget in every machine they use.

This is a very bold, ambitious vision statement. Even though it may not seem very realistic, vision statements are not meant to be probable, only possible. The vision statement is a concise statement of where the organization wants to go.

FIGURE 2-2 Microsoft's Mission and Values Statement

Mission Statement

The **mission statement** explicitly declares the business of the organization and its intended areas of operations. It is, in a sense, the organization's identity card. For example:

> Random Widget Works Inc. designs and manufactures quality widgets and associated equipment and supplies for use in modern business environments.

Not the 12-page sleeping pill you expected? A mission statement should be concise, should reflect both internal and external operations, and should be robust enough to remain valid for a period of four to six years. Simply put, the mission statement must explain *what* the organization does and for *whom.*

Many organizations encourage or require each division or major department—including the information security department—to generate its own mission statement. These mission statements can be as concise as the example provided, and express a general commitment to the importance of the confidentiality, integrity, and availability of information; or they can provide a more detailed description of the function of the information security department, as shown in the following example. This mission statement appears in *Information Security Roles and Responsibilities Made Easy.*

> The Information Security Department is charged with identifying, assessing, and appropriately managing risks to Company X's information and information systems. It evaluates the options for dealing with these risks, and works with departments throughout Company X to decide upon and then implement controls that appropriately and proactively respond to these same risks. The Department is also responsible for developing requirements that apply to the entire organization as well as external information systems in which Company X participates (for example, extranets) [these requirements include policies, standards, and procedures]. The focal point for all matters related to information security, this Department is ultimately responsible for all endeavors within Company X that seek to avoid, prevent, detect, correct, or recover from threats to information or information systems.
>
> These threats include, but are not limited to:
>
> - Unauthorized access to information
> - Unauthorized use of information
> - Unauthorized disclosure of information
> - Unauthorized diversion of information
> - Unauthorized modification of information
> - Unauthorized destruction of information
> - Unauthorized duplication of information
> - Unavailability of information.[1]

The mission statement is the follow-up to the vision statement. If the vision statement states where we want to go, the mission statement describes how we want to get there. Taken together, the mission, vision, and values statements provide the philosophical foundation for planning and guide the creation of the strategic plan.

STRATEGIC PLANNING

Strategy, or **strategic planning**, lays out the long-term direction to be taken by the organization. Strategic planning guides organizational efforts, and focuses resources toward specific, clearly defined goals, in the midst of an ever-changing environment.

As you learned in Chapter 1, a clearly directed strategy flows from top to bottom, and a systematic approach is required to translate it into a program that can inform and lead all members of the organization. As shown in Figure 2-3, strategic plans formed at the highest levels of the organization are translated into more specific strategic plans for intermediate layers of management. These plans are then converted into tactical planning for supervisory managers and eventually provide direction for the operational plans undertaken by the nonmanagement members of the organization. This multilayered approach encompasses two key objectives: general strategy and overall strategic planning. First, general strategy is translated into specific strategy; second, overall strategic planning is translated into lower-level tactical and operational planning. Each of these steps is discussed next.

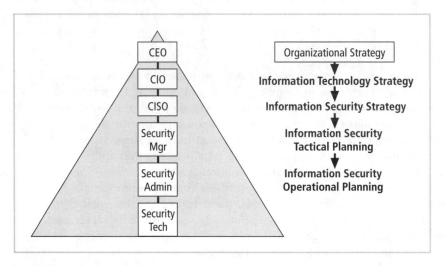

FIGURE 2-3   Top-Down Strategic Planning

Creating a Strategic Plan

After an organization develops a general strategy, it must create an overall strategic plan by extending that general strategy into specific strategic plans for major divisions. Each level of each division translates those objectives into more specific objectives for the level below. For example, a CEO might develop the following general statement of strategy:

> Providing the highest quality health care service in the industry.

To execute this broad strategy and turn the general statement into action, the executive team (sometimes called the C-level of the organization, as in CEO, COO, CFO, CIO, and so on) must first define individual responsibilities. For example, the Chief Information Officer (CIO) might translate the previous general statement into this more specific statement:

> Providing high-level health care information service in support of the highest quality health care service in the industry.

The Chief Operations Officer (COO) might derive a different strategic goal, which focuses more on his or her specific responsibilities:

> Providing the highest quality medical services.

The CISO might translate the CIO's goal as follows:

> Ensuring that health care information services are provided securely and in conformance with all state and federal information processing, information security, and privacy statutes, including HIPPA compliance.

The translation of goals from the strategic level to the next lower level is perhaps more art than science. It relies on the executive's ability to know and understand the strategic goals of the entire organization, to know and appreciate the strategic and tactical abilities of each unit within the organization, and to negotiate with peers, superiors, and subordinates. This mix of skills helps to achieve the proper balance in articulating goals that fall within performance capabilities.

Planning Levels

Once the organization's overall strategic plan is translated into strategic goals for each major division or operation, the next step is to translate these strategies into tasks with specific, measurable, achievable, and time-bound objectives. Strategic planning then begins a transformation from general, sweeping statements toward more specific and applied objectives. Strategic plans are used to create tactical plans, which are in turn used to develop operational plans. Figure 2-4 illustrates the various planning levels discussed in this section.

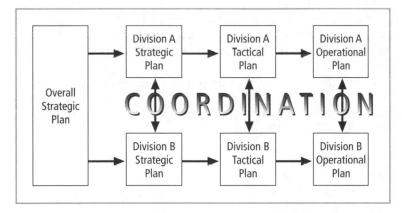

FIGURE 2-4 Planning Levels

Tactical planning has a more short-term focus than strategic planning, usually one to three years. It breaks down each applicable strategic goal into a series of incremental objectives. Each objective should be specific and ideally will have a delivery date within a year. Budgeting, resource allocation, and personnel are critical components of the tactical plan. Although these components may be discussed in general terms at the strategic planning level, they are crucial at the tactical level because they must be in place before the tactical plan can be translated into the operational plan. Tactical plans often include project plans and resource acquisition planning documents (such as product specifications), project budgets, project reviews, and monthly and annual reports.

Because tactical plans are often created for specific projects, some organizations no longer call this process tactical planning; instead, they refer to it as project planning or intermediate planning. The CISO and the security managers use the tactical plan to organize, prioritize, and acquire resources necessary for the major projects and to provide support for the overall strategic plan.

Managers and employees use operational plans, which are derived from the tactical plans, to organize the ongoing, day-to-day performance of tasks. An operational plan includes clearly identified coordination activities that span department boundaries, communications requirements, weekly meetings, summaries, progress reports, and associated tasks. These plans are carefully designed to reflect the organizational structure, with each subunit, department, or project team conducting its own operational planning and reporting components. Frequent communication and feedback from the teams to the project managers and/or team leaders and then up to the various management levels will make the planning process as a whole more manageable and successful.

For example, operational planning within information security may encompass such objectives as the selection, configuration, and deployment of a firewall, or the design and implementation of a security education, training, and awareness (SETA) program. Each of these tasks needs effective tactical planning that covers its entire development life cycle.

Planning and the CISO

The first priority of the CISO and the information security management team should be the structure of a strategic plan. While each organization may have its own format for the design and distribution of a strategic plan, the fundamental elements of planning are the same for all types of enterprises. There are a number of excellent text, trade, and reference books on strategic planning, and the serious information security manager is encouraged to explore this topic.

Following is a brief outline showing the basic structure of a strategic plan.

What are the elements of a strategic plan?
Introduction by the President of the Board or CEO

I. Executive Summary
II. Mission Statement and Vision Statement
III. Organizational Profile and History
IV. Strategic Issues and Core Values
V. Program Goals and Objectives
VI. Management/Operations Goals and Objectives
VII. Appendices (optional) [strengths, weaknesses, opportunities, and threats (SWOT) analyses, surveys, budgets, etc.][2]

You have already learned about some of the components in the above outline. Those areas not previously discussed are very straightforward, such as the organizational profile, history, and appendices; they originate in studies conducted by the organization or highlight information about the environment in which the organization operates. These supplements may help the organization to identify new directions or eliminate directions that are less profitable than anticipated. Information security planners can consult studies such as the CSI/FBI survey, the Threats to Information Security study (described in detail later in this chapter), the Human Firewall Council's Security Management and Security Awareness Indices, and internal risk assessments to help identify trends of interest or relevance to the organization. These documents are key resources that can identify areas of concern that should be addressed by the information security strategic plan.

Some additional tips for planning follow:

1. Create a compelling vision statement that frames the evolving plan and acts as a magnet for people who want to make a difference.
2. Embrace the use of a balanced scorecard approach, which demands the use of a balanced set of measures and cause-and-effect thinking.
3. Deploy a draft of a high-level plan early and ask for input from stakeholders in the organization.
4. Make the evolving plan visible.
5. Make the process invigorating for everyone.
6. Be persistent.
7. Make the process continuous.
8. Provide meaning.
9. Be yourself.
10. Lighten up and have some fun.[3]

VIEWPOINT

Planning for Security

By Eng-Klat Koh, Products & Alliances, Encentuate

With an increasing number of applications in the enterprise and more access modes available, organizations now face the opposing challenges of providing convenient access while tightening security, creating a huge dichotomy for their IT departments. A survey of over 700 information security practitioners by the Computer Security Institute revealed that over 71% of them had been attacked, with combined reported losses of $130 million.[4] Losses due to virus attacks accounted for more than $42 million of the losses. The number of reported computer breaches increased over a thousand times from 1999 to 2005.[5] Clearly, this issue is a growing problem that shows no sign of abating.

Good security requires a comprehensive defense, encompassing infrastructure, process, and people. Many organizations focus only on infrastructure defense—but that leaves the other avenues wide open for attack. It is important that you address all aspects of total defense; if you don't, your vulnerabilities will be exploited.

Infrastructure security requires that enterprises protect all points of access, not just the perimeter. Many enterprises focus on perimeter defense, but this approach assumes that the enterprise perimeter is well defined, which unfortunately, is no longer true. Just as virus protection has to extend to all enterprise end-points, so must security. In addition, the best firewalls and perimeter defense cannot stop what appears to be a legitimate user from gaining access. To counter these threats, enterprises need to strengthen

continued

security at the application layers where the value-at-risk is the highest. For this reason, identity and access management is now considered central to good infrastructure security. Identity and access management should be deployed at all enterprise end-points to counter the disappearing perimeter problem, and to ensure users are strongly authenticated and access can be tracked across all end-points. Figure 2.5 shows the key identity and access management functions that should be available at the enterprise end-points, including the ability to centrally manage those end-points.

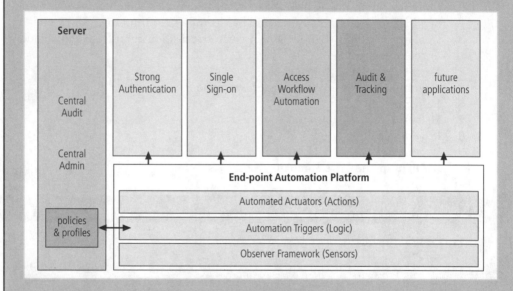

FIGURE 2-5 End-point Identity and Access Management

Good infrastructure security needs to be augmented with good security processes and policies. For starters, enterprises should have well-established and well-communicated policies. A good policy should have the the following characteristics:

- It should clearly identify the assets to be protected
- It should clearly identify the required security measures and the responsibilities of each user group
- It should clearly identify who is responsible for implementing, monitoring, and funding the security initiatives
- It should include a training policy for employee awareness... It is important not only to raise awareness of security policies, but also to ensure that employees—especially those charged with implementing security initiatives—are well trained.

Finally, enterprises should recognize that the weakest link in the security chain is probably their own employees. Employees are susceptible to user errors and social attacks.

continued

A good security plan should include good infrastructure protection via end-point identity and access management systems, good and well communicated policies, and adopt user-centric designs. In a recent Computer Technology Industry Association survey, more than 63% of computer breaches could be traced to human errors.[6] Unfortunately many security solutions are extremely difficult to use; the very systems designed to protect access often end up slowing legitimate users. Faced with the choice between higher security or lower user productivity, businesses and users often consciously bypass security. A good security solution should be user-centric; ideally raising user productivity and convenience while enhancing security and compliance. Fortunately, the new generation of end-point identity and access management solutions often include significant automation capabilities that not only enhance security compliance, but automate the process of compliance. Figure 2.5 presents more details.

Ultimately, security is only as good as the weakest link. When planning for security, enterprises have to adopt total defense, or risk being attacked. Eighty percent protection is just not good enough.

PLANNING FOR INFORMATION SECURITY IMPLEMENTATION

The CIO and CISO play important roles in translating overall strategic planning into tactical and operational information security plans. Depending on the information security function's placement within the organizational chart (discussed in detail in Chapter 5), the roles of the CIO and the CISO may differ. Most commonly, the CISO directly reports to the CIO.[7] In that case, the CIO charges the CISO and other IT department heads with creating and adopting plans that are consistent and supportive of the entire organizational strategy. The CIO must also ensure that the various IT functional areas in the organization provide broad support for the plan, and that no areas are omitted or ignored.

The CISO (also called the Chief Security Officer or CSO, Director of Information Security, or Information Security Manager) plays a more active role in the development of the planning details than does the CIO. Consider the job description for the Information Security Department Manager from *Information Security Roles and Responsibilities Made Easy*:

- Creates a strategic information security plan with a vision for the future of information security at Company X (utilizing evolving information security technology, this vision meets a variety of objectives such as management's fiduciary and legal responsibilities, customer expectations for secure modern business practices, and the competitive requirements of the marketplace)
- Understands the fundamental business activities performed by Company X and, based on this understanding, suggests appropriate information security solutions that uniquely protect these activities
- Develops action plans, schedules, budgets, status reports, and other top management communications intended to improve the status of information security at Company X[8]

Once the organization's overall strategic plan has been translated into IT and information security departmental objectives by the CIO, and then further translated into tactical and operational plans by the CISO, the implementation of information security can begin.

Implementation of information security can be accomplished in two ways: bottom-up or top-down. These two basic approaches are illustrated in Figure 2-6.

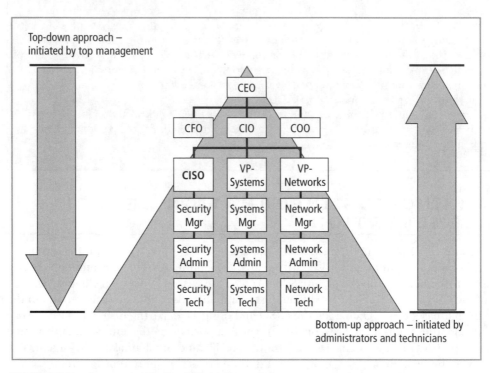

FIGURE 2-6 Approaches to Security Implementation

The **bottom-up approach** might begin as a grass-roots effort in which systems administrators attempt to improve the security of their systems. The key advantage of this approach is that it utilizes the technical expertise of the individual administrators, who work with the information systems on a daily basis. System and network administrators possess in-depth knowledge that can greatly enhance the state of information security in the organization. These professionals know and understand many of the threats to their systems and the mechanisms needed to protect them successfully. Unfortunately, this approach seldom works, as it lacks a number of critical features, such as coordinated planning from upper management, coordination between departments, and the provision of sufficient resources.

The **top-down approach**, in contrast, features strong upper-management support, a dedicated champion, usually assured funding, a clear planning and implementation process, and the ability to influence organizational culture. High-level managers provide resources; give direction; issue policies, procedures, and processes; dictate the goals and expected outcomes of the project; and determine who is accountable for each of the required actions. The most successful top-down approach also incorporates a formal development strategy referred to as the systems development life cycle.

For any top-down approach to succeed, high-level management must buy into the effort and provide their full support to all departments. Such an initiative must have a **champion**—ideally, an executive with sufficient influence to move the project forward, ensure that it is properly managed, and push for its acceptance throughout the organization. Typically, the champion of a far-reaching information security program is the CIO or another senior executive such as the Vice President of Information Technology (VP-IT). Without this high-level support, many mid-level administrators fail to dedicate enough resources to the project or dismiss it as a low priority.

Involvement and support of end users is also critical to the success of this type of effort. Because the process and outcome of the initiative most directly affect these individuals, they must be included in the information security planning process. Key end users should be assigned to developmental teams, known as **joint application development** teams (JAD). A successful JAD must be able to survive employee turnover; that is, it should not be vulnerable to changes in personnel. For this reason, the processes and procedures must be documented and integrated into organizational culture. They must be adopted *and promoted* by the organization's management. These attributes are seldom found in projects that begin as bottom-up initiatives.

The success of information security plans can be enhanced by using the processes of system analysis and design, a discipline that is an integral part of most academic curricula in the field of information technology. The following sections provide a brief treatment of this topic, but are not designed to replace a more thorough study of the discipline.

Introduction to the Security Systems Development Life Cycle

In general, a **systems development life cycle (SDLC)** is a methodology for the design and implementation of an information system in an organization. A **methodology** is a formal approach to solving a problem based on a structured sequence of procedures. Using a methodology ensures a rigorous process and increases the likelihood of achieving the desired final objective. Organizations often reuse a successful methodology as they gain experience with it. This tried-and-true approach is combined with sound project management practices to develop key project milestones, allocate resources, select personnel, and perform the tasks needed to accomplish a project's objectives. Sometimes the SDLC is used to develop custom applications or to manage the integration or deployment process of a purchased package solution. A variation of this methodology, used to create a comprehensive security posture, is called the security systems development life cycle (SecSDLC).

System projects may be initiated in response to specific conditions or combinations of conditions. The impetus to begin an SDLC-based project may be **event-driven**—that is, a response to some event in the business community, inside the organization, or within the ranks of employees, customers, or other stakeholders. Alternatively, it could be **plan-driven**—that is, the result of a carefully developed planning strategy. Either way, once an organization recognizes the need for a project, the use of a methodology can ensure that development proceeds in an orderly, comprehensive fashion. At the end of each phase, a **structured review** or *reality check* takes place, during which the team and its management-level reviewers decide whether the project should be continued, discontinued, outsourced, or postponed until additional expertise or organizational knowledge is acquired.

An approach that makes use of six phases in a traditional waterfall model SDLC will illustrate the SecSDLC in the sections that follow. The phrase *waterfall model* indicates that the work products of each phase fall into the next phase to serve as its starting point. While the SecSDLC may differ from the traditional SDLC in several specific activities, the overall methodology is the same. The SecSDLC process involves the identification of specific threats and the risks that they represent, and the subsequent design and implementation of specific controls to counter those threats and assist in the management of the risk. The process turns information security into a coherent program rather than a series of responses to individual threats and attacks. Figure 2-7 shows the phases in the SecSDLC.

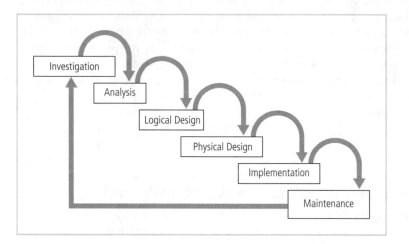

FIGURE 2-7   Phases of the SecSDLC

Investigation in the SecSDLC

The investigation phase of the SecSDLC begins with a directive from upper management specifying the process, outcomes, and goals of the project, as well as its budget and other constraints. Frequently, this phase begins with the affirmation or creation of security policies on which the security program of the organization is or will be founded. Teams of managers, employees, and consultants are assembled to analyze problems, define their scope, specify goals and objectives, and identify any additional constraints not covered in the enterprise security policy. (A more complete treatment of information security policy is presented in Chapter 4.) Finally, an organizational feasibility analysis determines whether the organization has the resources and commitment to conduct a successful security analysis and design.

It is unfortunate, but many information security projects are initiated in response to a significant security breach within an organization. While these circumstances may not be the ideal conditions under which to begin work on an organization's information security posture, the SecSDLC team should emphasize that improvement is now under way.

Analysis in the SecSDLC

In the analysis phase, the documents from the investigation phase are studied. The development team created during the investigation phase conducts a preliminary analysis of existing security policies or programs, along with documented current threats and associated controls. This phase also includes an analysis of relevant legal issues that could affect the design of the security solution. Increasingly, privacy laws are a major consideration when making decisions about information systems that manage personal information. Recently, many state legislatures have made illegal certain computer-related activities that were once unregulated, so a detailed understanding of these issues is vital.

The risk management task also begins in this stage. Risk management is the process of identifying, assessing, and evaluating the levels of risk facing the organization—specifically, the threats to the organization's security and to the information stored and processed by the organization. Ponder the words of the famous Chinese General Sun Tzu:

> If you know the enemy and know yourself, you need not fear the result of a hundred battles. If you know yourself but not the enemy, for every victory gained you will also suffer a defeat. If you know neither the enemy nor yourself, you will succumb in every battle.[9]

You begin the analysis process by getting to know your enemy. In information security, the enemy is the threats and attacks that your systems face as they provide services to your organization and its customers.

To better understand the analysis phase of the SecSDLC, you should know something about the kinds of threats facing organizations in the modern, connected world of information technology. In this context, a **threat** is a category of objects, persons, or other entities that represents a constant danger to an asset. While each enterprise's categorization of threats will almost certainly vary, threats are relatively well researched and consequently fairly well understood. To better understand the numerous threats facing an organization, a scheme has been developed to group threats by their respective activities. This model consists of 12 general categories that represent real and present dangers to an organization's information and systems. The following sections, and Table 2-1, identify and describe each of these 12 categories of risk.

Acts of Human Error or Failure.   This category includes acts performed without intent or without malicious purpose. When people use information systems, sometimes mistakes happen. Inexperience, improper training, the making of incorrect assumptions, and other circumstances can cause these problems.

Compromises to Intellectual Property.   The owner of intellectual property has the right to control proprietary ideas, as well as their tangible or virtual representation. Information about an organization's intellectual property can be of great interest to its competitors and can be accidentally or deliberately disseminated to those outside the organization.

Deliberate Acts of Espionage or Trespass.   This threat covers a well-known and broad category of electronic and human activities that can breach the confidentiality of information. When an unauthorized individual gains access to information that an organization is trying to protect, the act is categorized as a deliberate act of espionage or trespass.

Deliberate Acts of Information Extortion.   Information extortion occurs when an attacker or formerly trusted insider steals information from a computer system and then demands compensation for its return or for an agreement to not disclose the information. This practice is common in credit card number theft.

Deliberate Acts of Sabotage or Vandalism.   This threat originates with an individual or group of individuals who intend to sabotage deliberately the operations of a computer system or business, or who perform acts of vandalism either to destroy an asset or damage the image of the organization. These threats can range from petty vandalism by employees to Web page defacement by outside persons or groups.

Deliberate Acts of Theft.   Theft is the illegal taking of another's property, whether physical, electronic, or intellectual.

Deliberate Software Attacks.   Deliberate software attacks occur when an individual or group designs software—often called malicious code or software, or malware—to attack a vulnerable system. Some of the more common types of malicious code are viruses, worms, Trojan horses, logic bombs, and back doors.

Deviations in Quality of Service by Service Providers.   This category includes situations in which a product or service is not delivered as expected. The organization's information system depends on the successful operation of many interdependent support systems, including power grids, telecommunications networks, parts suppliers, service vendors, and even the janitorial staff and garbage haulers.

The threat of irregularities from power utilities is common. When they occur they can lead to several types of power fluctuations:

- A voltage levels spike (a momentary increase)
- A surge (a prolonged increase)
- A momentary low voltage or sag
- A more prolonged drop in voltage, called a brownout
- A complete loss of power for a moment, called a fault
- A more lengthy loss, known as a blackout

Forces of Nature.   Forces of nature (known as *force majeure*) or acts of God pose some of the most dangerous threats imaginable because they can occur with very little warning. They include fire, flood, earthquake, and lightning, as well as volcanic eruption and insect infestation.

Technical Hardware Failures or Errors.   Technical hardware failures or errors occur when a manufacturer distributes equipment containing a known or unknown flaw. These defects can cause the system to perform outside of expected parameters, resulting in unreliable service or lack of availability.

Technical Software Failures or Errors.   This category of threats comes from software with known or unknown hidden faults. These faults may range from bugs to untested failure conditions.

Technological Obsolescence.   When the infrastructure becomes antiquated or outdated, it leads to unreliable and untrustworthy systems that may be difficult to maintain without extensive investment of resources.

TABLE 2-1   Threats to Information Security[10]

Categories of threat	Examples
1. Acts of human error or failure	Accidents, employee mistakes
2. Compromises to intellectual property	Piracy, copyright infringement
3. Deliberate acts of espionage or trespass	Unauthorized access and/or data collection
4. Deliberate acts of information extortion	Blackmail of information disclosure
5. Deliberate acts of sabotage or vandalism	Destruction of systems or information
6. Deliberate acts of theft	Illegal confiscation of equipment or information
7. Deliberate software attacks	Viruses, worms, macros, denial-of-service
8. Deviations in quality of service from service providers	Power and WAN service issues
9. Forces of nature	Fire, flood, earthquake, lightning
10. Technical hardware failures or errors	Equipment failure
11. Technical software failures or errors	Bugs, code problems, unknown loopholes
12. Technological obsolescence	Antiquated or outdated technologies

The preceding list of threats may be manifested as attacks against the assets of the organization. An **attack** is an act or event that exploits a vulnerability. It is accomplished by a **threat agent**—or specific instance of a threat—that damages or steals an organization's information or physical asset. An **exploit** is a technique or mechanism used to compromise an information asset. A **vulnerability** is an identified weakness of a controlled information asset—the absence of controls, or the controls in place are no longer effective. A technical attack may involve the use of an exploit to achieve the compromise of a controlled system, whereas a nontechnical attack may involve natural events or less sophisticated approaches. The following list outlines some types of technical attacks:

- Back doors: A feature left behind by system designers or maintenance staff or installed by malicious code.
- Brute force: The application of computing and network resources to try every possible combination of values to compromise a control, to read encrypted data, or to crack a password.
- Buffer overflow: An application error that occurs when more data is sent to a buffer than it can handle.

- Denial-of-service (DoS) and distributed denial-of-service (DDoS): The transmission of a large number of connection or information requests to a target, thereby blocking other, legitimate traffic. When multiple systems are organized into a simultaneous attack, it is categorized as a DDoS.
- Dictionary: An attempt to narrow the field of possible password values by selecting specific accounts as targets and/or using a list of common values (the dictionary) with which to guess, rather than simply trying random combinations.
- DNS cache poisoning: The replacement of legitimate information in a DNS server with a Web site or other Internet location the attacker wants the user to view; also known as a redirect attack.
- Hoaxes: Reports of threats or attacks that are not true that result in a waste of time and resources.
- Mail bombing: The routing of large quantities of e-mail to the target.
- Malicious code: The execution of viruses, worms, Trojan horses, and active Web scripts with the intent to destroy, steal, or deny access to information.
- Man-in-the-middle: Also known as a TCP hijacking attack. The commandeering of a network connection session, so that an attacker can read and perhaps modify the data transferred in that connection.
- Password crack: An attempt to reverse-calculate or guess a password. Password attacks include dictionary attacks, brute force attacks, and man-in-the-middle attacks (see specific attacks elsewhere in this list).
- Phishing: A specialized social engineering attack in which the attacker uses an e-mail or forged Web site to attempt to extract personal information from a user.
- Sniffer: A program or device that can monitor data traveling over a network.
- Social engineering: The use of social skills to convince people to reveal access credentials or other valuable information.
- Spam: Unsolicited commercial e-mail, the electronic equivalent of junk mail.
- Spear phishing: A targeted social engineering attack in which the attacker crafts an individualized letter or e-mail to attempt to extract personal information from an unsuspecting user.
- Spoofing: A technique used to gain unauthorized access to computers, whereby the intruder sends network-level messages to a computer with an IP address indicating that the message is coming from a trusted host.
- Timing: An attack that enables an attacker to extract secrets maintained in a security system by observing the time it takes the system to respond to various queries.

The last step in knowing the enemy is to find some method of prioritizing the risk posed by each category of threat and its related methods of attack. This can be done by adopting threat levels from an existing study of threats or by creating your own categorization of threats for your environment based on scenario analyses.

To manage risk, you must identify and assess the value of your information assets. This iterative process must include a classification and categorization of all elements of an organization's systems: people, procedures, data and information, software, hardware, and networking elements. As you assign each organizational asset to a category, you can pose certain questions to help develop the weighting criteria for an information asset valuation or impact evaluation:

- Which information asset is the most critical to the success of the organization?
- Which information asset generates the most revenue?
- Which information asset has the highest profitability?
- Which information asset would be the most expensive to replace?
- Which information asset would be the most expensive to protect?
- Which information asset would be the most embarrassing or cause the greatest liability if revealed?

The list should include enough categories to allow for various priority levels, because the next step is to rank the components based on criteria driven by the categorization. In addition, the categories must be comprehensive (i.e., all information assets must fit somewhere) and mutually exclusive (i.e., each asset must fall into only one category). For example, if an organization has a public key infrastructure certificate authority (a software application that provides cryptographic key management services), it could be placed in the asset list as "Software, Application" or "Software, Security" using purely technical standards. In this case, it should be placed as "Software, Security" because this kind of software, which is part of the security infrastructure, must be carefully protected. It is more important to have a comprehensive set of categories than a mutually exclusive set, as it may be difficult to avoid overlapping categories entirely.

The next challenge in the analysis phase is to review each information asset for each threat it faces and create a list of vulnerabilities. As indicated earlier, vulnerabilities are specific avenues that threat agents can exploit. They represent the "chinks in the armor" of the information asset—a flaw or weakness in an information asset, a security procedure, or a control that could be exploited either accidentally or on purpose to breach security.

As the analysis phase continues, the next task is to assess the relative risk for each of the information assets via a process called **risk assessment** or **risk analysis**. Risk assessment assigns a comparative risk rating or score to each specific information asset. While this number does not mean anything in absolute terms, it is useful in gauging the relative risk introduced by each vulnerable information asset and allows us to make comparative ratings later in the risk control process. Risk assessment is covered in detail in Chapter 7.

Risk management is the part of the analysis phase that identifies vulnerabilities in an organization's information systems and takes carefully reasoned steps to assure the confidentiality, integrity, and availability of all components in the organization's information system. Risk management is covered in detail in Chapter 8.

Design in the SecSDLC

The SecSDLC design phase actually consists of two distinct phases: the logical design and the physical design. In the logical design phase, team members create and develop the blueprint for security, and they examine and implement key policies that influence later decisions. At this stage, critical contingency plans for incident response are developed. Next, a feasibility analysis determines whether the project should continue in-house or should be outsourced.

In the physical design phase, team members evaluate the technology needed to support the security blueprint, generate alternative solutions, and agree on a final design. The security blueprint may be revisited to keep it synchronized with the changes needed when the physical design is completed. Criteria for determining the definition of successful solutions are also prepared during this phase, as are designs for physically securing the technological solutions. At the end of this phase, a feasibility study should determine the readiness of the organization for the proposed project, and then the champion and users should be presented with the design. At that point, the interested parties have a chance to approve (or not approve) the project before implementation begins.

During the logical and physical design phases, a security manager may seek to use established security models to guide the design process. Security models provide frameworks for ensuring that all areas of security are addressed; organizations can adapt or adopt a framework to meet their own information security needs. A number of information security frameworks have been published. One good source of framework documents is the Computer Security Resource Center of the National Institute for Standards and Technology (NIST; http://csrc.nist.gov). These documents, which are publicly available at no charge, have withstood the test of time and have been broadly reviewed by government and industry professionals. Other references include *Information Technology—Code of Practice for Information Security Management,* which was originally published as the British Standard BS 7799. This code of practice was adopted as an international standard by the International Organization for Standardization (ISO) and the International Electrotechnical Commission (IEC) as ISO/IEC 17799 in 2000 as a framework for information security, and updated as ISO/IEC 17799: 2005. A revised version of the British Standard, has also been formally adopted by the ISO/IEC and released as ISO/IEC 27001:2005 Information technology—Security techniques—Information security management systems—Requirements to bring it into compliance with the international revisions included in the ISO/IEC 17799 standard. These documents can be purchased from http://www.iso.org/iso/en/prods-services/ISOstore/store.html. A good place to start collecting information about these standards is at the NIST FAQ page found at http://csrc.nist.gov/publications/secpubs/otherpubs/reviso-faq-110502.pdf.

One of the design elements (or redesign elements, in the case of some projects) of the information security program is the organization's information security policy. The meaning of the term "security policy" differs depending on the context in which it is used. Governmental agencies, for example, discuss security policy in terms of national security and interaction with foreign states. In another context, a security policy can be part of a credit card agency's method of processing credit card numbers. In general, a security policy consists of a set of rules that protects an organization's assets. An **information security policy** provides rules for the protection of the information assets of an organization. As stated in Chapter 1, the task of the information security program is to protect the *confidentiality, integrity, and availability* of information and information systems, whether in transit, storage, or processing. This task is accomplished by applying policy, education and training programs, and technology. Management must define three types of security policies, based on the NIST Special Publication 800-14: general or enterprise information security policy, issue-specific security policies, and systems-specific security policies. Each of these is covered in detail in Chapter 4.

Another integral part of the information security program to be designed is the **security education, training, and awareness (SETA)** program. The responsibility of the CISO, the SETA program is a control measure designed to reduce accidental security breaches by employees. As mentioned earlier, employee errors represent one of the top threats to information assets; for this reason, it is well worth expending resources to develop programs to combat this problem. SETA programs are designed to supplement the general information security education and training programs that are already in place. Good practice dictates that the systems development life cycle includes user training during the implementation phase. Employee training should be managed to ensure that all employees are trained properly.

The SETA program consists of three elements: security education, security training, and security awareness. An organization may not be capable of or willing to undertake all three of these elements, so it may outsource them to local educational institutions. The purpose of SETA is to enhance security by the following means:

> 1) Improving awareness of the need to protect system resources; 2) developing skills and knowledge so computer users can perform their jobs more securely; and 3) building in-depth knowledge, as needed, to design, implement, or operate security programs for organizations and systems.[11]

As the design phase continues, attention turns to the design of the controls and safeguards used to protect information from attacks by threats. The terms **control** and **safeguard** are often used interchangeably. There are three categories of controls: managerial controls, operational controls, and technical controls.

Managerial controls cover security processes that are designed by the strategic planners and performed by security administration of the organization. They set the direction and scope of the security process and provide detailed instructions for its conduct. Management controls address the design and implementation of the security planning process and security program management. These controls also address risk management and security controls reviews (discussed in detail in Chapters 7 and 8). Management controls further describe the necessity and scope of legal compliance and the maintenance of the entire security life cycle.

Operational controls deal with the operational functionality of security in the organization. They cover management functions and lower-level planning, such as disaster recovery and incident response planning. In addition, these controls address personnel security, physical security, and the protection of production inputs and outputs. Operational controls also provide structure to the development of education, training, and awareness programs for users, administrators, and management. Finally, they address hardware and software systems maintenance and the integrity of data.

Technical controls address those tactical and technical issues related to designing and implementing security in the organization. Here the technologies necessary to protect information are examined and selected. Whereas operational controls address specific operational issues, such as developing controls and integrating them into the business functions, technical controls address the specifics of technology selection and the acquisition (make or buy) of certain technical components, including logical access controls, such as those related to identification, authentication, authorization, and accountability. Technical controls also address the development and implementation of audit trails for accountability and cryptography to protect information in storage and transit. Finally, they cover the classification of assets and users, so as to facilitate the authorization levels needed.

To the expanded categories used to classify the SecSDLC system components, we add another dimension to represent the sensitivity and security priority of the data and the devices that store, transmit, and process the data. Examples of such data classifications include confidential data, internal data, and public data. The opposite of the data classification scheme is the personnel security clearance structure, which identifies the level of information individuals are authorized to view based on their "need to know."

Another element of the design phase is the creation of essential preparedness documents. Managers in the IT and information security communities are usually called on to provide strategic planning to assure the organization of continuous information systems availability. In addition, managers of the organization must be ready to act when an attack occurs. Plans for handling attacks, disasters, or other types of incidents go by various names: business continuity plans, disaster recovery plans, incident response plans, or just contingency plans. In large, complex organizations, each of these named plans may represent separate but related planning functions, differing in scope, applicability, and design. In a small organization, the security administrator (or systems administrator) may have one simple plan, which consists of a straightforward set of media backup and recovery strategies, and a few service agreements from the company's service providers. The sad reality is that many organizations have a level of planning that is woefully deficient.

Incident response, disaster recovery, and business continuity planning are all components of contingency planning. **Contingency planning (CP)** is the entire planning conducted by the organization to prepare for, react to, and recover from events that threaten the security of information assets in the organization and to provide for the subsequent restoration to normal business operations. Organizations need to develop disaster recovery plans, incident response plans, and business continuity plans as subsets of the overall CP. **Incident response planning (IRP)** is the planning process associated with the identification, classification, response, and recovery from an incident. **Disaster recovery planning (DRP)** is the planning process associated with the preparation for and recovery from a disaster, whether natural or human-made. **Business continuity planning (BCP)** is the planning process associated with ensuring that critical business functions continue if a catastrophic incident or disaster occurs. These critical building blocks of response planning are presented in Chapter 3.

As the design phase progresses, attention turns to **physical security**, which addresses the design, implementation, and maintenance of countermeasures intended to protect the physical resources of an organization. Physical resources include people, hardware, and the supporting system elements and resources associated with the management of information in all its states—transmission, storage, and processing. Many technology-based controls can be circumvented if an attacker gains physical access to the devices being controlled. For example, when employees fail to secure a server console, the operating system running on that computer becomes vulnerable to attack. Some computer systems are constructed in such a way that it is easy to steal the hard drive and the information it contains. As a result, physical security should receive as much attention as logical security in the security development life cycle. For further discussions on the dimension of physical security, consult one of the many fine text, trade, or reference books on the subject.

Implementation in the SecSDLC

The SecSDLC implementation phase is similar to the corresponding phase of the traditional SDLC. Security solutions are acquired (made or bought), tested, implemented, and retested. Personnel issues are evaluated, and specific training and education programs are conducted. Finally, the entire tested package is presented to upper management for final approval.

The information security systems software or application systems selection process is not appreciably different from that for general IT needs. Vendors should be provided with detailed specifications, and they should in turn provide detailed information about products and costs. As in IT system implementation, it is essential to establish clear specifications and rigorous test plans to assure a high-quality implementation.

Perhaps the most important element of the implementation phase is the management of the project plan. Project management is a process that underlies all phases of the SecSDLC. The execution of the project plan proceeds in three steps:

1. Planning the project
2. Supervising the tasks and action steps within the project plan
3. Wrapping up the project plan

The project plan can be developed in any number of ways. Each organization must determine its own project management methodology for IT and information security projects. Whenever possible, information security projects should follow the organizational practices of project management. If your organization has not established clearly defined project management practices, the following pages supply general guidelines on recommended practices. Project management and its relationship to information security are described in detail in Chapter 12.

Information security is a field with a vast array of technical and nontechnical requirements. For this reason, the project team should include individuals who are experienced in one or multiple requirements of both the technical and nontechnical areas. Many of the same skills needed to manage and implement security are needed to design it. Members of the development team fill the following roles:

- The champion: A senior executive who promotes the project and ensures its support, both financially and administratively, at the highest levels of the organization.
- The team leader: A project manager—perhaps a departmental line manager or staff unit manager—who understands project management, personnel management, and information security technical requirements.
- Security policy developers: Individuals who understand the organizational culture, existing policies, and requirements for developing and implementing successful policies.
- Risk assessment specialists: Individuals who understand financial risk assessment techniques, the value of organizational assets, and the security methods to be used.
- Security professionals: Dedicated, trained, and well-educated specialists in all aspects of information security from both technical and nontechnical standpoints.
- Systems administrators: Individuals with the primary responsibility for administering the systems that house the information used by the organization.

- End users: The individuals whom the new system will most directly affect. Ideally, a disparate group of users from various departments and levels, and with varying degrees of technical knowledge, will assist the team in applying realistic controls in ways that do not disrupt the essential business activities they seek to safeguard.

Just as each potential employee and each potential employer look for the best fit during the hiring process, so each organization should thoroughly examine its options when staffing the information security function. When implementing information security in an organization, many human resource issues must be addressed. First, the entire organization must decide how to position and name the security function within the organization. Second, the information security community of interest must plan for the proper staffing (or adjustments to the staffing plan) for the information security function. Third, the IT community of interest must understand how information security affects every role in the IT function and adjust job descriptions and documented practices accordingly. Finally, the general management community of interest must work with the information security professionals to integrate solid information security concepts into the personnel management practices of the organization as a whole.

It takes a wide range of professionals to support a diverse information security program. Because a good security plan is initiated from the top down, senior management is the key component and vital force driving the successful implementation of an information security program. To develop and execute specific security policies and procedures, additional administrative support is required. Finally, technical expertise is necessary to implement the details of the security operation.

The various roles and the titles used to easily refer to them have already been used in this textbook. Until now, an approximate definition for these roles has been adequate. At this point, however, more precise descriptions of the professionals involved in information security are warranted.

- **The Chief Information Officer (CIO)** is the senior technology officer responsible for aligning the strategic efforts of the organization into action plans for the information systems or data-processing division of the organization.
- **The Chief Information Security Officer (CISO)**, sometimes called the Chief Security Officer, Security Manager, Director of Information Security, or a similar title, is responsible for the assessment, management, and implementation of securing the information in the organization.
- **Security Managers** are accountable for ensuring the day-to-day operation of the information security program, accomplishing the objectives identified by the CISO, and resolving issues identified by technicians.
- **Security Technicians** are technically qualified individuals tasked to configure firewalls and intrusion detection systems (commonly referred to as IDSs), implement security software, diagnose and troubleshoot problems, and coordinate with systems and network administrators to ensure that security technology is properly implemented.
- **Data Owners** are responsible for the security and use of a particular set of information.

- **Data Custodians** work directly with data owners and are responsible for the storage, maintenance, and protection of the information.
- **Data Users** are systems users who work with the information to perform their daily jobs supporting the mission of the organization. Everyone in the organization is responsible for the security of data, so data users are included here as individuals with an information security role.

The various roles and players in information security implementation across the organization are presented in depth in Chapter 10.

Many organizations look for job applicants who have professional certifications so that they can more easily identify these individuals' proficiency. Unfortunately, most existing certifications are relatively new and not fully understood by hiring organizations. The certifying bodies continue to work diligently to educate the business community on the value and qualifications of their certificate recipients. Employers are trying to understand the match between certifications and the position requirements, and the candidates are trying to gain employment based on their newly received certifications.

Considered the most prestigious certification for security managers and CISOs, the Certified Information Systems Security Professional (CISSP) is one of two certifications offered by the International Information Systems Security Certification Consortium (ISC)2; see http://www.isc2.org. The Systems Security Certified Practitioner (SSCP) is the other.

The System Administration, Networking and Security Organization, better known as SANS (www.sans.org), developed a series of technical security certifications in 1999, known as the GIAC (www.giac.org). At that time, no technical certifications existed. Anyone who wanted to work in the technical security field could obtain only networking or computing certifications, such as the Microsoft Certified Systems Engineer (MCSE) or Certified Novell Engineer (CNE) certification. Today, the GIAC family of certifications can be pursued independently or combined to earn the comprehensive certification, GIAC Security Engineer (GSE). Like the SSCP, the GIAC Information Security Officer (GISO) is an overview certification that combines basic technical knowledge with understanding of threats, risks, and best practices.

The Security Certified Professional (SCP) certification (www.securitycertified.net) provides two tracks: Security Certified Network Professional (SCNP) and Security Certified Network Architect (SCNA). Both are designed for the security technician and have dominant technical components; the latter certification also emphasizes authentication principles.

CompTIA (www.comptia.com), the company that established the first vendor-neutral professional IT certifications, the A+ series, has recently defined the body of knowledge required for its next certification. The Security+ certification is similar to the Network+ certification and to many others in its focus on key skills necessary to perform security without being tied to a particular software or hardware vendor package.

A newer certification that is gaining in recognition and respect is the Certified Information Security Manager (CISM) offered by the Information Systems Audit and Control Association (ISACA). This organization also offers the Certified Information Systems Auditor (CISA), which also has several security-related components. ISACA promotes this certification for auditing, networking, and security professionals.

A thorough discussion of information security industry certification approaches and programs is provided in Chapter 10.

Maintenance in the SecSDLC

The maintenance and change phase, though last, is perhaps most important, given the flexibility and persistence of many of the threats facing the modern organization. Today's information security systems need constant monitoring, testing, modifying, updating, and repairing. Traditional applications systems that are developed within the framework of the SDLC are not designed to anticipate a vicious attack that requires some degree of application reconstruction as a normal course of operation. In security, the battle for stable, reliable systems is a defensive one. As new threats emerge and old threats evolve, the information security profile of an organization requires constant adaptation to prevent threats from successfully penetrating sensitive data.

Once the information security program is implemented, it must be operated, properly managed, and kept up-to-date by means of established procedures. If the program is not adjusting adequately to the changes in the internal or external environment, it may be necessary to begin the cycle again. The CISO determines whether the information security group can adapt adequately and maintain the information security profile of the organization, or whether the macroscopic process of the SecSDLC must start anew to redevelop a fundamentally different information security profile. It is less expensive and more effective when an information security program is able to deal with change. Even when an information security program is adapting and growing, those processes of maintenance and change mirror the overall process of the SecSDLC, differing only in scope. As deficiencies are found and vulnerabilities pinpointed, projects to maintain, extend, or enhance the program follow the SecSDLC steps. Therefore, for maintenance, the steps include investigation, analysis, design, and implementation.

While a systems management model is designed to manage and operate systems, a maintenance model is intended to complement a systems management model and focus organizational effort on system maintenance. Figure 2-8 presents one recommended approach for dealing with information security maintenance. The recommended maintenance model consists of five subject areas or domains, as described in the following sections.

External Monitoring. The objective of external monitoring within the maintenance model shown is to provide early awareness of new and emerging threats, threat agents, vulnerabilities, and attacks, thereby enabling the creation of an effective and timely defense.

Internal Monitoring. The primary goal of internal monitoring is to maintain an informed awareness of the state of all of the organization's networks, information systems, and information security defenses. This status must be communicated and documented, especially the status of the parts of information systems that are connected to the external network.

Planning and Risk Assessment. The primary objective of planning and risk assessment is to keep a wary eye on the entire information security program. This is achieved in part by identifying and planning ongoing information security activities that further reduce risk. Also, the risk assessment group identifies and documents risks introduced by both IT projects and information security projects. Furthermore, it identifies and documents risks that may be latent in the present environment.

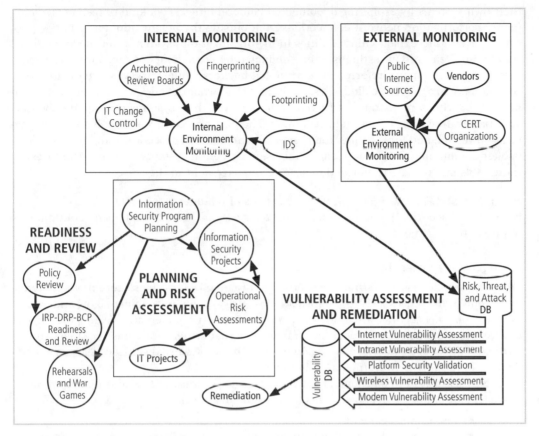

FIGURE 2-8   Maintenance Model

Vulnerability Assessment and Remediation.   The primary goal of vulnerability assessment and remediation is the identification of specific, documented vulnerabilities and their timely remediation. This is accomplished by:

- Using documented vulnerability assessment procedures to safely collect intelligence about networks (internal and public-facing), platforms (servers, desktops, and process control), dial-in modems, and wireless network systems;
- Documenting background information and providing tested remediation procedures for the reported vulnerabilities; and
- Tracking, communicating, and reporting to management the itemized facts about the discovered vulnerabilities and the success or failure of the organization to remediate them.

Vulnerability assessment involves the physical and logical assessment of the vulnerabilities present in both information security and related nonsecurity systems. This analysis is most often accomplished with penetration testing. In **penetration testing**, security personnel simulate or perform specific and controlled attacks to compromise or disrupt their own systems by exploiting documented vulnerabilities. This kind of testing is commonly performed on network connections from outside the organization, as security personnel attempt to exploit vulnerabilities in the organization's system from the attacker's standpoint. Penetration testing is often conducted by consultants or outsourced contractors, who are commonly referred to as **white-hat hackers**, **ethical hackers**, **tiger teams**, or **red teams**. What they are called is less important than what they do, which is critical. Information security administrators who have not looked at their systems through the eyes of an attacker are failing to maintain readiness. The best procedures and tools to use in penetration testing and other vulnerability assessments are the procedures and tools of the hacker community. Fortunately, many intrusion detection systems spot the signatures of these tools and can alert information security management to their use.

Readiness and Review.   The primary objectives of readiness and review are to keep the information security program functioning as designed and, it is hoped, continuously improve it over time.

Systems Management Model

One maintenance issue that must be settled in the SecSDLC is the selection of a systems management model. To assist the information security community in managing and operating the ongoing security program, a systems management model must be adopted. In general, systems management models are frameworks that structure the tasks of managing a particular set of activities or business functions. The framework discussed below is a modification of the ISO network management model.

The ISO network management model provides structure to the administration and management of networks and systems by covering five areas:

- Fault management
- Configuration and change management
- Accounting and auditing management
- Performance management
- Security program management

In its original form, the ISO model is not directly applicable to the management of an information security program, but it can be modified to reflect the various administrative tasks in most information security programs. The five areas of the ISO model in a security management are discussed in the following sections.

Fault Management.   In the ISO model, fault management involves identifying, tracking, diagnosing, and resolving faults in the system. Information security fault management involves identifying faults in the applied information security profile and then addressing them. Another aspect of fault management is the monitoring and resolution of user complaints.

Configuration and Change Management.   Configuration management is the administration of various components involved in the security program. Change management is the administration of changes in the strategy, operation, or components of the information security program. Both configuration and change management administration focus on making technical as well as nontechnical changes. Technical changes affect the technology implemented to support security in the hardware, software, and data components; nontechnical changes affect procedures and people.

Accounting and Auditing Management.   The next category in the ISO security management model involves chargeback accounting and systems monitoring. Chargeback accounting happens when organizations internally charge their departments for system use. While chargebacks are seldom used today, certain kinds of resource usage are commonly tracked—such as those on a computing system (e.g., a server or a desktop computer) or human effort-hours—to recover IT costs from non-IT units of the organization. Accounting management involves monitoring the use of a particular component of a system. In networking, this monitoring may simply determine which users are using which resources. However, in security, it may be easy to track which resources are being used but difficult to determine who is using them. At that point, accounting management begins to overlap with performance management (discussed below). With accounting management you begin to determine optimal points of systems use as indicators for upgrade and improvement.

Auditing is the process of reviewing the use of a system not to determine its performance, but rather to determine whether misuse or malfeasance has occurred.

Performance Management.   Because many information security technical controls are implemented on common IT processors, they are affected by the same factors as most computer-based technologies. It is therefore important to monitor the performance of security systems and their underlying IT infrastructure to determine whether they are effectively and efficiently doing the job for which they were intended. Some information security control systems, such as Internet usage monitors that look for inappropriate utilization of Internet resources, operate as pass-by devices.

Security Program Management.   Once an information security program is functional, it must be operated and managed. The ISO five-area framework provides some structure for a management model, but it focuses on ensuring that various areas are addressed, rather than guiding the actual conduct of management. To assist in the actual management of information security programs, a formal management standard can provide some insight into the processes and procedures needed. It could be based on the BS7799/ISO17799 model or the NIST models described earlier in this chapter.

Comparing the SDLC and the SecSDLC

Table 2-2 summarizes the steps performed in both the SDLC and the SecSDLC. Since SecSDLC is based on the SDLC, the steps in the cycles are similar, and those common to both cycles are identified in the second column. The third column shows the security issues unique to the SecSDLC.

TABLE 2-2 SDLC and SecSDLC Phase Summary

	Steps common to the SDLC and the SecSDLC	Steps unique to the SecSDLC
Phase 1: Investigation	• Outline project scope/goals • Estimate costs • Evaluate existing resources • Analyze feasibility	• Define project process and goals and document them in the program security policy
Phase 2: Analysis	• Assess current system against plan developed in Phase 1 • Develop preliminary system requirements • Study integration of new system with existing system • Document findings and update feasibility analysis	• Analyze existing security policies and programs • Analyze current threats and controls • Examine legal issues • Perform risk analysis
Phase 3: Logical Design	• Assess current business needs against plan developed in Phase 2 • Select applications, data support, and structures • Generate multiple solutions for selection of best • Document findings and update feasibility analysis	• Develop security blueprint • Plan incident response actions • Plan business response to disaster • Determine feasibility of continuing and/or outsourcing the project
Phase 4: Physical Design	• Select technologies to support solutions developed in Phase 3 • Select the best solution • Decide whether to make or buy components • Document findings and update feasibility analysis	• Select technologies needed to support security blueprint • Develop definition of successful solution • Design physical security measures to support technological solutions • Review and approve project
Phase 5: Implementation	• Develop or buy software • Order components • Document system • Train users • Update feasibility analysis • Present system to users • Test system and review performance	• Buy or develop security solutions • At end of phase, present tested package to management for approval
Phase 6: Maintenance	• Support and modify system for its useful life • Test periodically for compliance with business needs • Upgrade and patch as necessary	• Constantly monitor, test, modify, update, and repair to respond to changing threats

Chapter Summary

- Planning is central to the management of any organization.

- Planning is based on the preparation, application, and control of a sequence of action steps to achieve specific goals.

- To develop and implement effective planning, documents representing the philosophical, ethical, and entrepreneurial perspectives of the company are first created—namely, the mission statement, the vision statement, the values statement, and strategy.

- Security can begin either as a grass-roots effort (a bottom-up approach) or with plans formulated by senior management (a top-down approach).

- The systems development life cycle (SDLC) is a methodology for the design and implementation of an information system in an organization. A methodology is a formal approach to solving a problem based on a structured sequence of procedures.

- Using a methodology ensures a rigorous process and increases the likelihood of achieving the desired final objective.

- The process of phased system development described by the traditional SDLC can be adapted to support the specialized implementation of a security project by using the security systems development life cycle (SecSDLC). The fundamental process is the identification of specific threats and the risks that they represent to the organization, followed by the design and implementation of specific controls to counter those threats and assist in the management of the risks.

- The investigation phase of the SecSDLC begins with a directive from upper management, dictating the process, outcomes, and goals of the project, as well as its budget and other constraints.

- In the analysis phase, the team examines existing security policies or programs, along with documented current threats and associated controls. This phase also includes an analysis of relevant legal issues that could affect the design of the security solution. Risk management begins in this stage as well. Risk management is the process of identifying, assessing, and evaluating the levels of risk facing the organization—specifically, threats to the organization's security and to the information stored and processed by the organization.

- Analysis begins with knowing your enemy. In information security, the enemy consists of threats and attacks that your systems face.

- The design phase includes two distinct phases: the logical design and the physical design. In the logical design phase, blueprints for security are created, and key policies that influence later decisions are examined and implemented. In the physical design phase, the security technology needed to support this blueprint is evaluated, alternative solutions are generated, and a final design is determined.

- The maintenance and change phase, though last, is perhaps most important, given the flexibility and persistence of many of the threats facing the modern organization. Once the information security program is implemented, it must be operated and properly managed through the establishment of procedures. Additional procedures are needed to keep the organization safe as change occurs.

Review Questions

1. Describe the essential parts of planning. How does the existence of resource constraints affect the need for planning?

2. What are the three common layers of planning? How do they differ?

3. Who are the stakeholders? Why is it important to consider their views when planning?

4. What is a mission statement? Why is it important? What does it contain?

5. What is a vision statement? Why is it important? What does it contain?

6. What is a values statement? Why is it important? What does it contain?

7. What is strategy?

8. Describe top-down strategic planning. How does it differ from bottom-up strategic planning? Which is usually more effective in implementing security in a large, diverse organization?

9. Describe the planning role of the CISO. How does that role differ from the planning role of the CIO?

10. How does the SecSDLC differ from the more general SDLC?

11. What is the primary objective of the SecSDLC? What are its major steps, and what are the major objectives of each step?

12. What is a threat in the context of information security? How many categories of threats exist as presented in this chapter?

13. What is the difference between a threat and an attack?

14. How can a vulnerability be converted into an attack? What label would we give to the entity that performs this transformation?

15. What name is given to an attack that makes use of viruses and worms? What name is given to an attack that does not actually cause damage other than wasted time and resources?

16. What questions might be asked to help identify and classify information assets? Which is the most useful question in the list?

17. What name is given to the process of assigning a comparative risk rating to each specific information asset? What are the uses of such a rating?

18. What term is used to describe the provision of rules intended to protect the information assets of an organization?

19. What term is used to describe the control measure that reduces security incidents among members of the organization by familiarizing them with relevant policies and practices in an ongoing manner?

20. What are the three categories of information security controls? How is each used to reduce risk for the organization?

Exercises

1. Using a Web search engine, find an article from a reputable source published within the past six months that reports on the relative risk that comes from inside the organization as opposed to risk that comes from external sources. If the article notes that this relative risk is changing, how is it changing and to what does the article attribute the change?

2. Using a Web search engine, find five examples of corporate vision statements, corporate mission statements, and corporate goals. Do these examples express concern for the security of corporate information?

3. Search your institution's published documents, including its Web pages. Locate its mission statement, vision statement, and strategic goals. Identify any references to information security. Also look for any planning documents related to information security.

4. Using a Web browser, go to http://gocsi.com. Search for the link offering a free copy of the latest CSI/FBI study. Summarize the key points and bring your summary to class to discuss with your fellow students.

5. Go to the library and search through recent newspaper articles about your area. How many examples of threats to information security can you find in the last week?

Case Exercises

During the Random Widget's CIO strategic planning meeting...

CIO Mike Edwards discussed and expanded on the details of how the IT division would enable RWW to achieve each of its strategic goals. As he was finishing his review of the document, Mike made a crucial point: "Make sure you don't let this planning document get out. These documents are not to leave the building."

Iris asked, "Shouldn't they be labeled 'Confidential' then?"

"What do you mean, Iris?" Mike asked.

Iris replied, "I've been working on a data classification scheme for RWW along with the systems administrators. We have a draft that uses three data classification levels for the company. Every piece of information in the company is categorized as 'Confidential,' 'Sensitive,' or 'Public.' This document should be clearly labeled 'Confidential' to prevent it from being released by mistake."

After a moment's thought Mike exclaimed, "Excellent! Please send copies of the draft data classification scheme to all department heads immediately." He turned to Stan, his assistant, and said, "Please have new covers that label this plan as 'Confidential' prepared by noon today, and have one of your people replace each cover with the revised, properly marked cover before the end of business today."

1. Create definitions of "Confidential," "Sensitive," and "Public" for RWW. Develop a list of examples of documents that should be labeled with each classification.

2. Design a labeling scheme (cover sheet, stamp, or other format) to associate with this classification system.

Endnotes

[1] Charles Cresson Wood. *Information Security Roles and Responsibilities Made Easy.* Houston, TX: PentaSafe, 2002:46.

[2] Michael Allison and Jude Kaye. *Strategic Planning for Nonprofit Organizations.* Accessed March 19, 2003 from www.nonprofitgeorgia.org/faq-planning.html.

[3] Brian Ward. *Planning as Doing.* Accessed October 30, 2006 from http://www.refresher.com/!bwplanning.html.

[4] 2005 CSI/FBI Computer Crime and Security Survey. Accessed July 1, 2006 from www.gocsi.com.

[5] CERT. In: A survey of digital security. *The Economist,* Oct. 26–Nov. 1, 2002.

[6] John Leyden. *The Register.* Accessed March 19, 2003 from www.theregister.co.uk/content/55/29827.htm.

[7] Charles Cresson Wood. *Information Security Roles and Responsibilities Made Easy.* Houston, TX: PentaSafe, 2002:96.

[8] Charles Cresson Wood. *Information Security Roles and Responsibilities Made Easy.* Houston, TX: PentaSafe, 2002:58

[9] Sun Tzu. *The Art of War.* Trans. by Samuel B. Griffith. Oxford, UK: Oxford University Press, 1988.

[10] Michael Whitman. Enemy at the gates: threats to information security. *Communications of the ACM,* August 2003, pp. 91–95.

[11] National Institute of Standards and Technology. *An Introduction to Computer Security: The NIST Handbook.* SP 800–12, 1995.

## CHAPTER 3

PLANNING FOR CONTINGENCIES

QUOTE

Things which you do not hope happen more frequently than things which you do hope.
— Plautus

A week after the strategic planning meeting, Iris was just finishing a draft of the information security strategic plan. Satisfied with her progress thus far, she activated the calendar on her computer and began reviewing her schedule, hoping to find a good day and time to meet with Mike about contingency planning. During their last luncheon, her friend Charley had warned her not to let too much time pass before addressing the issue again. She knew he was right. It simply was not a good idea to put off discussing such an important project until the end of the month, as Mike had suggested during last week's strategic planning meeting. Having a plan in place in case of an emergency just made good business sense, even if it was not perceived as a high priority by many of her management peers.

Suddenly, the building's fire alarm went off. Heart pumping, Iris left her office. With or without a contingency plan, it was her responsibility to assess this situation as quickly and as safely as possible. Was there an incident? A disaster? Or was it simply a false alarm? As she quickly moved down the line of cubicles, Iris called for everyone who had not yet left the floor to leave by way of the nearest exit. Then she rushed to the floor's fire control panel, which was located in the elevator lobby. A blinking light showed that one heat-sensitive sprinkler head had been activated. Iris waited a moment to see whether any other blinking lights came on. None did, but the existing light stayed on. It seemed that she was dealing with an incident, and not a disaster.

Iris headed down the hall to the place shown on the fire panel where the sprinkler had been triggered. She turned the corner, and saw Harry and Joel from the accounting department in the break station, which was right next to their offices. Harry was inspecting what had once been the coffeepot, while Joel held a fire extinguisher. Both were wet and irritated. The room smelled of scorched coffee and was filled with smoke. To her relief, there was no fire.

"Is everyone all right?" she asked.

"Yeah," Harry replied, "but our offices are a mess. There's water everywhere."

Joel shook his head in disgust. "What a time for this to happen. We were just finishing the quarterly reports, too."

"Never mind that. The important thing is that you're both okay. You guys need to make a trip home so you can get changed . . . ."

Iris was interrupted by Mike Edwards, who had just joined them. "What happened?" he asked.

Iris shrugged. "It's a minor incident, Mike, everything's under control. The fire department will be here any minute."

"Incident? Incident?" Joel said in dismay as he pointed at his desk, where steam rose from his soaked CPU, and a pile of drenched reports littered the floor. "This isn't an incident. *This is a disaster*!"

LEARNING OBJECTIVES

Upon completion of this material, you should be able to:

- Recognize the need for contingency planning
- Articulate the major components of contingency planning
- Create a simple set of contingency plans, using business impact analysis
- Prepare and execute a test of contingency plans
- Explain the unified contingency plan approach

INTRODUCTION

Chapter 2 introduced the topic of planning and provided some specifics about planning for the organization in general and for the information security program in particular. This chapter focuses on planning for unexpected events, when the use of technology is disrupted and business operations can come to a standstill. Because technology drives business, planning for an unexpected event usually involves managers from both the information technology and information security communities of interest, who analyze the entire technological infrastructure of the organization under the mission statement and current organizational objectives. But, for a plan to gain the support of all members of the organization, it must also be sanctioned and actively supported by the general business community of interest.

The need to have a plan in place that systematically addresses how to identify, contain, and resolve an unexpected event was identified in the earliest days of information technology. The latest modification to the approaches taken toward these issues is noted in the 1998 NIST Special Publication 800-18, *Guide for Developing Security Plans for Information Technology Systems*. It advises that when an unexpected event occurs, "Procedures are required that will permit the organization to continue essential functions if information technology support is interrupted."[1] Some organizations—particularly federal agencies for national security reasons—are charged by law or other mandate to have such procedures in place at all times.

Business organizations of various sizes should also prepare for the unexpected. In general, a business organization's ability to weather losses caused by an unexpected event depends on proper planning and execution of such a plan; without a workable plan, an unexpected event can cause severe damage to an organization's information resources and assets from which it may never recover. As noted by The Hartford insurance company: "On average, over 40% of businesses that don't have a disaster plan go out of business after a major loss like a fire, a break-in, or a storm."[2] In 1991, for instance, national news outlets reported that two key executives of the Bruno's supermarket chain, Angelo and Lee Bruno, were killed in a plane crash. While it will never be known for certain, the steady growth of the firm since its founding during the Great Depression seems to have reversed course at that point. The fortunes of the company declined and it went through bankruptcy in 2000. Although the brand continues in a few southern markets, the business as it operated before the crash no longer exists. The development of a plan for handling unexpected events should be a high priority for all managers. That plan should take into account the possibility that key members of the organization will not be available to assist in the recovery process.

WHAT IS CONTINGENCY PLANNING?

The overall process of preparing for unexpected events is called **contingency planning (CP)**. CP is the process by which the information technology and information security communities of interest position their respective organizational units to prepare for, detect, react to, and recover from events that threaten the security of information resources and assets, both human and natural. The main goal of CP is to restore normal modes of operation with minimal cost and disruption to normal business activities after an unexpected event—in other words, to make sure things get back to the way they were within a reasonable period of time. Ideally, CP should ensure the continuous availability of information systems to the organization even in the face of the unexpected.

CP consists of four major components:

- Business impact analysis (BIA)
- Incident response plan (IR plan)
- Disaster recovery plan (DR plan)
- Business continuity plan (BC plan)

The BIA, a preparatory activity common to both CP and risk management, is covered in Chapters 7 and 8. It helps the organization determine which business functions and information systems are the most critical to the success of the organization. The IR plan focuses on the immediate response to an incident. Any unexpected event is treated as an incident, unless and until a response team deems it to be a disaster. Then the DR plan, which focuses on restoring operations at the primary site, is invoked. If operations at the primary site cannot be quickly restored—for example, when the damage is major or will affect the organization's functioning over the long term—the BC plan occurs concurrently with the DR plan, enabling the business to continue at an alternate site, until the organization is able to resume operations at its primary site or select a new primary location.

Depending on the size and business philosophy of an organization, information technology and information security managers can either (1) create and develop these four CP components as one unified plan or (2) create the four separately in conjunction with a set of interlocking procedures that enable continuity. Typically, larger, more complex organizations create and develop the CP components separately, as the functions of each component differ in scope, applicability, and design. Smaller organizations tend to adopt a one-plan method, consisting of a straightforward set of recovery strategies.

Ideally, the CIO, systems administrators, CISO, and key IT and business managers should be actively involved during the creation and development of all CP components, as well as during the distribution of responsibilities among the three communities of interest. The elements required to begin the CP process are a planning methodology; a policy environment to enable the planning process; an understanding of the cause and effects of core precursor activities, known as the BIA; and access to financial and other resources, as articulated and outlined by the planning budget. Each of these is explained in the sections that follow. Once formed, the **contingency planning management team (CPMT)** begins developing a CP document using the following process:

1. Develop the contingency planning policy statement: A formal department or agency policy provides the authority and guidance necessary to develop an effective contingency plan.
2. Conduct the BIA: The BIA helps to identify and prioritize critical IT systems and components. A template for developing the BIA is also provided [in NIST Special Publication 800-34] to assist the user.
3. Identify preventive controls: Measures taken to reduce the effects of system disruptions can increase system availability and reduce contingency life cycle costs.
4. Develop recovery strategies: Recovery strategies ensure that the system may be recovered quickly and effectively following a disruption.
5. Develop an IT contingency plan: The contingency plan should contain detailed guidance and procedures for restoring a damaged system.
6. Plan testing, training, and exercises: Testing the plan identifies planning gaps, whereas training prepares recovery personnel for plan activation; both activities improve plan effectiveness and overall agency preparedness.
7. Plan maintenance: The plan should be a living document that is updated regularly to remain current with system enhancements.[3]

Four teams of individuals are involved in contingency planning and contingency operations:

- The *CP team* collects information about information systems and the threats they face, conducts the business impact analysis, and then creates the contingency plans for incident response, disaster recovery, and business continuity. The CP team often consists of a coordinating manager and representatives from each of the other three teams.

  The CP team should include the following personnel:

  - Champion: As with any strategic function, the CP project must have a high-level manager to support, promote, and endorse the findings of the project. This **champion** could be the CIO, or ideally the CEO/President.
  - Project manager: A champion provides the strategic vision and the linkage to the power structure of the organization, but does not manage the project. A **project manager**—possibly a mid-level manager or even the CISO—leads the project, putting in place a sound project planning process, guiding the development of a complete and useful project, and prudently managing resources.
  - Team members: The **team members** should be the managers or their representatives from the various communities of interest: business, information technology, and information security. Business managers supply details of their activities and insight into those functions critical to running the business. Information technology managers supply information about the at-risk systems and provide information for the BIA and documenation technical content for IRP, DRP, and BCP. Information security managers oversee the security planning and provide information on threats, vulnerabilities, attacks, and recovery requirements. A representative from the legal affairs or corporate counsel's office helps keep all planning steps within legal and contractual boundaries. A member of the corporate communications department makes sure the crisis management and communications plan elements are consistent with the needs of that group.
- The *incident response team* manages and executes the IR plan by detecting, evaluating, and responding to incidents.
- The *disaster recovery team* manages and executes the DR plan by detecting, evaluating, and responding to disasters, and by reestablishing operations at the primary business site.
- The *business continuity team* manages and executes the BC plan by setting up and starting off-site operations in the event of an incident or disaster.

As indicated earlier, in larger organizations these teams are distinct entities, with non-overlapping membership, although the latter three teams have representatives on the CP team. In smaller organizations, the four teams may include overlapping groups of people.

As illustrated in the opening scenario of this chapter, many organizations' contingency plans are woefully inadequate. CP often fails to receive the high priority necessary for the efficient and timely recovery of business operations during and after an unexpected event. The fact that many organizations do not place an adequate premium on CP does not mean that it is unimportant, however. The Computer Security Resource Center

(CSRC) at the National Institute for Standards and Technology (NIST) describes the need for this type of planning as follows:

> These procedures (contingency plans, business interruption plans, and continuity of operations plans) should be coordinated with the backup, contingency, and recovery plans of any general support systems, including networks used by the application. The contingency plans should ensure that interfacing systems are identified and contingency/disaster planning coordinated.[4]

As you learn more about CP, you may notice that it shares certain characteristics with risk management and the SecSDLC methodology. Many information technology and information security managers are already familiar with these processes; they can readily adapt their existing knowledge to the CP process.

COMPONENTS OF CONTINGENCY PLANNING

As noted earlier, CP includes four major components: the business impact analysis, and incident response, disaster recovery, and business continuity plans. Whether an organization adopts the one-plan method or the multiple-plan method with interlocking procedures, each of these CP components must be addressed and developed in its entirety. The following sections describe each component in detail, and discusses when and how each should be used. They also consider how to determine which plan is best suited for the identification, containment, and resolution of any given unexpected event. Figure 3-1 depicts the major project modules performed during contingency planning efforts.

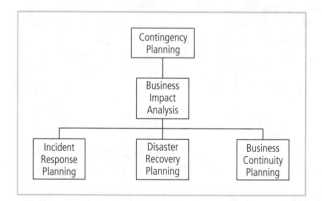

FIGURE 3-1 Contingency Planning Hierarchies

Business Impact Analysis

The **business impact analysis (BIA)**, the first phase in the CP process, provides the CP team with information about systems and the threats they face. The BIA is a crucial component of the initial planning stages, as it provides detailed scenarios of the effects that each potential attack could have on the organization.

One of the fundamental differences between a BIA and the risk management processes discussed in Chapters 7 and 8 is that risk management focuses on identifying the threats, vulnerabilities, and attacks to determine which controls can protect the information. The BIA assumes that these controls have been bypassed, have failed, or have otherwise proved ineffective, and that the attack succeeded.

The CP team conducts the BIA in the following stages, which are shown in Figure 3-2 and described in the sections that follow:

1. Threat attack identification and prioritization
2. Business unit analysis
3. Attack success scenario development
4. Potential damage assessment
5. Subordinate plan classification

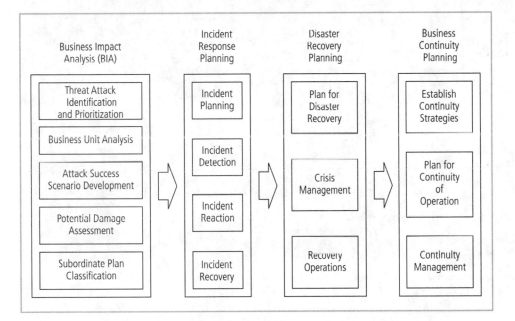

FIGURE 3-2 Major Tasks In Contingency Planning

Threat Attack Identification and Prioritization

An organization that has followed the SecSDLC outlined in Chapter 2, and the risk management process described in Chapters 7 and 8, will have already identified and prioritized threats facing it. To conduct the BIA, these organizations simply update the threat list and add one piece of information, the attack profile.

An **attack profile** is a detailed description of the activities that occur during an attack. The example attack profile shown in Table 3-1 includes preliminary indications of the attack, as well as the actions taken and the outcome. Such a profile must be developed for every serious threat that the organization faces, whether natural or human-made, deliberate or accidental. This document is useful in later planning stages to provide indicators of attacks. It is used here to determine the extent of damage that could result to a business unit if the attack were successful.

TABLE 3-1 Example Attack Profile

Date of analysis:	*June 23, 2008*
Attack name/description:	*Malicious code via e-mail*
Threat/probable threat agents:	• *Vandalism/script kiddies* • *Theft/experienced hacker*
Known or possible vulnerabilities:	• *Emergent weakness in e-mail clients* • *Inappropriate actions by employees, contractors, and visitors using e-mail clients* • *Emergent weakness in e-mail servers or gateways*
Likely precursor activities or indicators:	*Announcements from vendors and bulletins*
Likely attack activities or indicators of attack in progress:	• *E-mail volume measurements may show variances* • *Unusual system failures among clients* • *Unusual system failures among servers* • *Notification from e-mail recipients who may be ahead of us in attack life cycle*
Information assets at risk from this attack:	*All connected systems due to blended attack model now prevalent*
Damage or loss to information assets likely from this attack:	• *Denial-of-service for some clients almost certain* • *Denial-of-service for servers possible* • *Possible losses of data depending on nature of attack*
Other assets at risk from this attack:	*None likely*
Damage or loss to other assets likely from this attack:	*None likely*
Immediate actions indicated when this attack is under way:	• *Disconnect e-mail gateway(s)* • *Update e-mail gateway filtering patterns and apply* • *Update and distribute client filtering patterns* • *Isolate all infected servers* • *Isolate all infected clients* • *Begin server recovery actions for infected servers* • *Begin client recovery actions for infected clients*
Follow-up actions after this attack was successfully executed against our systems:	*Review pattern update timing and procedure to assure adequacy*
Comments:	*None at this time*

Business Unit Analysis

The second major BIA task is the analysis and prioritization of business functions within the organization. Each business department, unit, or division must be independently evaluated to determine how important its functions are to the organization as a whole. For example, recovery operations would probably focus on the IT department and network operation before turning to the personnel department's hiring activities. Likewise, recovering a manufacturing company's assembly line is more urgent than recovering its maintenance tracking system. This is not to say that personnel functions and assembly line maintenance are not important to the business, but unless the organization's main revenue-producing operations can be restored quickly, other functions are irrelevant.

Attack Success Scenario Development

Once the threat attack profiles have been developed and the business functions prioritized, the BIA planning team must create a series of scenarios depicting the effects of an occurrence of each threat on each prioritized functional area. This step can be a long and detailed process, as such occurrences may have implications for many functions. Attack profiles should include scenarios depicting a typical attack, including its methodology, indicators of an attack, and broad consequences. Once the attack profiles are completed, the business function details can be integrated with the attack profiles. Then **attack success scenarios** with more detail are added to the attack profile, including alternative outcomes—best, worst, and most likely. This level of detail allows planners to address each possibility in turn.

Potential Damage Assessment

From these detailed scenarios, the BIA planning team must estimate the cost of the best, worst, and most likely outcomes by preparing an **attack scenario end case**. This allows the organization to identify what must be done to recover from each possible case. (At this time the team does not attempt to determine how much to spend on the protection of business units—this issue is analyzed during risk management). The costs include accounting for the time required by the response team members to perform the required actions—described in the following sections—to effectively recover from any incident or disaster. These cost estimates can persuade management representatives throughout an organization of the importance of planning and recovery efforts.

Subordinate Plan Classification

Once the potential damage has been assessed, and each scenario and attack scenario end case has been evaluated, a subordinate plan must be developed or identified from among existing plans already in place. Some of these related plans may already be part of standard operating procedures, such as file recovery from backup. Other strategies may be in place as part of existing DR or BC plans. Because most attacks are not disastrous and therefore fall into the category of incident response, the BIA planning team will likely develop a number of subordinate plans that are meant to be used exclusively at the incident level. Scenarios that do qualify as disastrous are likely addressed in the DR plan or BC plan.

Each attack scenario end case is categorized as disastrous or not. The difference between the two classifications reflects whether the organization is able to take effective action during the event to combat the attack's effects. Attack end cases that are disastrous find members of the organization waiting out the attack and planning to recover from it after the attack ends. In a typical disaster recovery operation, the lives and welfare of the employee are the highest priority, since most disasters involve fires, floods, hurricanes, tornadoes, and the like. Other disasters might include the following events as a sample of the many possible disaster that could arise:

- Electrical blackouts affecting a city or region
- Attacks on service providers that result in a loss of communications to the organization (either telephone or Internet)
- Massive, malicious-code attacks that sweep through the organization before they can be contained

Incident Response Plan

The **incident response plan (IR plan)** comprises a detailed set of processes and procedures that anticipate, detect, and mitigate the effects of an unexpected event that might compromise information resources and assets. **Incident response planning (IRP)** is therefore the preparation for such an event. In CP, an unexpected event is called an **incident**. An incident occurs when an attack (natural or human-made) affects information resources and/or assets, causing actual damage or other disruptions. **Incident response (IR)**, then, is a set of procedures that commence when an incident is detected. IR must be carefully planned and coordinated because organizations heavily depend on the quick and efficient containment and resolution of incidents. The IR plan is usually activated when an incident causes minimal damage—according to criteria set in advance by the organization—with little or no disruption to business operations.

Incident Response Policy

Prior to the development of each plan outlined in this chapter, the CP team should work to develop the policy environment to enable the BIA process and, and to provide specific policy guidance to authorize the creation of each of the planning components (IR, DR, BC). These policies provide guidance on the structure of the subordinate teams and the philosophy of the organization, and assist in the structuring of the plan. As the planning committee forms a **security incident response team (SIRT)**, key SIRT representatives join the IR planning committee in the development of policy to define the operations of the team, articulate the organizational response to various types of incidents, and advise end users on how to contribute to the effective response of the organization, rather than contributing to the problem at hand. You will learn more about SIRT's roles and composition later in this section.

The incident response policy is similar in structure to other policies used by the organization. Just as the enterprise information security policy defines the information security roles and responsibilities for the entire enterprise, the incident response policy defines the roles and responsibilities for incident response for the SIRT and others who will be mobilized in the activation of the plan. The *Computer Security Incident Handling Guide* from the National Institute on Standards and Technology (NIST SP 800-61) identifies the following as key components of a typical IR policy:[5]

- Statement of management commitment
- Purpose and objectives of the policy
- Scope of the policy (to whom and what it applies and under what circumstances)

- Definition of information security incidents and their consequences within the context of the organization
- Organizational structure and delineation of roles, responsibilities, and levels of authority; should include the authority of the incident response team to confiscate or disconnect equipment and to monitor suspicious activity, and the requirements for reporting certain types of incidents
- Prioritization or severity ratings of incidents
- Performance measures (as discussed in Chapter 6)
- Reporting and contact forms

IR policy, like all policies, must gain the full support of top management and be clearly understood by all affected parties. It is especially important to gain the support of those communities of interest that will be required to alter business practices or make changes to their information technology infrastructures. For example, if the SIRT determines that the only way to stop a massive denial-of-service attack is to sever the organization's connection to the Internet, they should have a signed document locked in an appropriate filing cabinet preauthorizing such action. This ensures that the SIRT is performing authorized actions, and protects both the SIRT members and the organization from misunderstanding and potential liability.

Incident Response Plan: Getting Started

The scenario at the beginning of this chapter depicts an incident and not a disaster, despite Joel's declaration otherwise. By now, it should be clear why a technology manager, like Iris, must become involved in assessing the damage to two drenched accounting offices and the break room. Because the incident at RWW was determined by Iris to have caused minimal damage, a corresponding IR plan would have been activated, if RWW had a properly developed IR plan. If the fire had spread beyond the break room, triggered the sprinkler systems throughout the building, and caused employee injuries, then an IR plan (even if RWW had one) would not have been adequate to deal with the situation. Instead, it would be necessary to initiate the DR plan and the BC plan, both of which are discussed later in this chapter.

When one of the threats that were identified in Chapter 2 turns into a valid attack, it is classified as an information security incident, but only if it has all of the following characteristics:

- It is directed against information assets.
- It has a realistic chance of success.
- It threatens the confidentiality, integrity, or availability of information resources and assets.

The prevention of threats and attacks has been intentionally omitted from this discussion because guarding against such possibilities is primarily the responsibility of the information security department, which works with the rest of the organization to implement sound policy, effective risk controls, and ongoing training and awareness programs. It is important to understand that *IR is a reactive measure, not a preventive one*.

The responsibility for creating an organization's IR plan usually falls to the CISO. With the aid of other managers and systems administrators on the CP team, the CISO should select members from each community of interest to form an independent IR team, which executes the IR plan. The roles and responsibilities of the members of the IR team should be clearly documented and communicated throughout the organization. The IR plan also includes an alert roster, which lists certain critical agencies to be contacted during the course of an incident.

Using the multistep CP process discussed in the previous section as a model, the CP team can create the IR plan. During this planning process the IR procedures take shape. For every incident scenario, the CP team creates three sets of incident-handling procedures:

1. During the incident: The planners develop and document the procedures that must be performed during the incident. These procedures are grouped and assigned to individuals. Systems administrators' tasks differ from managerial tasks, so members of the planning committee must draft a set of function-specific procedures.

2. After the incident: Once the procedures for handling an incident are drafted, the planners develop and document the procedures that must be performed immediately after the incident has ceased. Again, separate functional areas may develop different procedures.

3. Before the incident: The planners draft a third set of procedures, those tasks that must be performed to prepare for the incident. These procedures include details of the data backup schedules, disaster recovery preparation, training schedules, testing plans, copies of service agreements, and BC plans, if any. At this level, the BC plan could consist of just additional material on a service bureau that stores data off-site via electronic vaulting, with an agreement to provide office space and lease equipment as needed.

Figure 3-3 presents an example of pages from the IR plan that support each of these phases. Once these sets of procedures are clearly documented, the IR portion of the IR plan is assembled and the critical information as outlined in these planning sections is recorded.

Preparing to Plan

Planning for an incident and the responses to it require a detailed understanding of the information systems and the threats they face. The BIA provides the data used to develop the IR plan. The IR planning team seeks to develop a series of predefined responses that will guide the team and information security staff through the incident response steps. Predefining incident responses enables the organization to react to a detected incident quickly and effectively, without confusion or wasted time and effort.

The execution of the IR plan typically falls to the SIRT. As noted previously, the SIRT is a subset of the IR team and is composed of technical and managerial information technology and information security professionals prepared to diagnose and respond to an incident. In some organizations the SIRT may simply be a loose or informal association of IT and InfoSec staffers who would be called up if an attack was detected on the organization's information assets. In other, more formal implementations, the SIRT (also referred to as a computer SIRT or CSIRT), is a set of policies, procedures, technologies, people, and

Before an Attack

Users
1. Don't put suspicious diskettes in your system. Check your system before b
2. Don't download free games system without authorizatic Services department.
3. Don't open attachments in Make sure all attachments party by confirming the orig
4. Don't forward messages th warn others of a virus or th

Technology Services
1. Ensure virus protection soft properly configured, and up
2. Automate whenever possib Provide awareness and trai users on proper use of the antivirus software.

After an Attack

Users
1. Scan your computer thoroughly for any additional viruses.
2. Review e-mail (TITLES ON REOPEN attachments) fo
3. Write down everything yc before you detected the v
4. Verify that your antivirus definitions are up-to-date

Technology Services
1. Conduct an incident reco
2. Interview all users detect
3. Verify that all systems an definitions are up-to-date
4. Reconnect quarantined u
5. Brief all infected users or procedures.
6. File the incident recovery Notify all users that this of virus has been detecte antivirus software and de

During an Attack

Users
1. If your antivirus software detects an attack, it will delete the virus or quarantine the file that carries it. Record any messages that your antivirus software displays and notify Technology Services immediately.
2. If your computer begins behaving unusually or you determine that you have contracted a virus through other means, turn your computer off immediately, by pulling the plug. Notify Technology Services immediately.

Technology Services
1. If users begin reporting virus attacks, record the information provided by the users.
2. Temporarily disconnect those users from the network at the switch.
3. Begin scanning all active systems for that strain of virus.
4. Deploy a response team to inspect the users' system.

FIGURE 3-3   Incident Response Planning

data put in place to prevent, detect, react, and recover from an incident that could potentially damage the organization's information. At some level, every member of an organization is a member of the SIRT, since every action they take can cause or avert an incident.

The SIRT should be available for contact by anyone who discovers or suspects that an incident involving the organization has occurred. One or more team members, depending on the magnitude of the incident and availability of personnel, then handles the incident. The incident handlers analyze the incident data, determine the impact of the incident, and act appropriately to limit the damage to the organization and restore normal services. Although the SIRT may have only a few members, the team's success depends on the participation and cooperation of individuals throughout the organization.

The SIRT consists of professionals who are capable of handling the information systems and functional areas affected by an incident. For example, imagine a firefighting team responding to an emergency call. Rather than responding to the fire as individuals, each member of the team has a specific role to perform, so that the team acts as a unified body that assesses the situation, determines the appropriate response, and coordinates the response. Similarly, each member of the IR team must know his or her specific role, work in concert with other team members, and execute the objectives of the IR plan.

Incident Detection

The challenge for every IR team is determining whether an event is the product of routine systems use or an actual incident. **Incident classification** is the process of examining a possible incident, or **incident candidate**, and determining whether it constitutes an actual incident. Classifying an incident is the responsibility of the IR team. Initial reports from end users, intrusion detection systems, host- and network-based virus detection software, and systems administrators are all ways to track and detect incident candidates. Careful training in the reporting of an incident candidate allows end users, help desk staff, and all security personnel to relay vital information to the IR team. Once an actual incident is properly identified, members of the IR team can effectively execute the corresponding procedures from the IR plan.

A number of occurrences signal the presence of an incident candidate. Unfortunately, these same events can result from an overloaded network, computer, or server, and some are similar to the normal operation of these information assets. Other incident candidates mimic the actions of a misbehaving computing system, software package, or other less serious threat. To help make the detection of actual incidents more reliable, D. L. Pipkin has identified three categories of incident indicators: possible, probable, and definite.[6]

Possible Indicators.   The following four types of incident candidates are considered *possible* actual incidents:

1. Presence of unfamiliar files: Users might discover unfamiliar files in their home directories or on their office computers. Administrators might also find unexplained files that do not seem to be in a logical location or owned by an authorized user.

2. Presence or execution of unknown programs or processes: Users or administrators might detect unfamiliar programs running, or processes executing, on office machines or network servers.

3. Unusual consumption of computing resources: For example, consumption of memory or hard disk space might suddenly spike or fall. Many computer operating systems, including Windows, Linux, and UNIX variants, allow users and administrators to monitor CPU and memory consumption. Most computers also have the ability to monitor hard drive space. In addition, servers maintain logs of file creation and storage.

4. Unusual system crashes: Computer systems can crash. Older operating systems running newer programs are notorious for locking up or spontaneously rebooting whenever the operating system is unable to execute a requested process or service. You are probably familiar with systems error messages such as "Unrecoverable Application Error," "General Protection Fault," and the infamous Windows NT "Blue Screen of Death." However, if a computer system seems to be crashing, hanging, rebooting, or freezing more frequently than usual, the cause could be an incident candidate.

Probable Indicators.   The four types of incident candidates described below are *probable* indicators of actual incidents:

1. Activities at unexpected times: If traffic levels on the organization's network exceed the measured baseline values, an incident candidate is probably present. If this activity surge occurs when few members of the organization are at work, this probability becomes much higher. Similarly, if systems are accessing drives, such as floppy and CD-ROM drives, when the end user is not using them, an incident may also be occurring.

2. Presence of new accounts: Periodic review of user accounts can reveal an account (or accounts) that the administrator does not remember creating or that are not logged in the administrator's journal. Even one unlogged new account is an incident candidate. An unlogged new account with root or other special privileges has an even higher probability of being an actual incident.

3. Reported attacks: If users of the system report a suspected attack, there is a high probability that an attack has occurred, which constitutes an incident. The technical sophistication of the person making the report should be considered.

4. Notification from IDS: If the organization has installed and correctly configured a host- or network-based intrusion detection system (IDS), then notification from the IDS indicates that an incident might be in progress. However, IDSs are seldom configured optimally and, even when they are, tend to issue many false positives or false alarms. The administrator must then determine whether the notification is real or is the result of a routine operation by a user or other administrator.

Definite Indicators.   The five types of incident candidates described below are *definite* indicators of an actual incident. That is, they clearly signal that an incident is in progress or has occurred. In these cases, the corresponding IR must be activated immediately.

1. Use of dormant accounts: Many network servers maintain default accounts, and there often exist accounts from former employees, employees on a leave of absence or sabbatical without remote access privileges, or dummy accounts set up to support system testing. If any of these accounts begins accessing system resources, querying servers, or engaging in other activities, an incident is almost certain to have occurred.

2. Changes to logs: The smart systems administrator backs up system logs as well as system data. As part of a routine incident scan, systems administrators can compare these logs to the online versions to determine whether they have been modified. If they have, and the systems administrator cannot determine explicitly that an authorized individual modified them, an incident has occurred.

3. Presence of hacker tools: Network administrators sometimes use system vulnerability and network evaluation tools to scan internal computers and networks to determine what a hacker can see. These tools are also used to support research into attack profiles. All too often, however, they are used by employees, contractors, or outsiders with local network access to hack into

systems. To combat this problem, many organizations explicitly prohibit the use of these tools without written permission from the CISO, making any unauthorized installation a policy violation. Most organizations that engage in penetration-testing operations require that all tools in this category be confined to specific systems, and that they not be used on the general network unless active penetration testing is under way.

4. Notifications by partner or peer: If a business partner or another connected organization reports an attack from your computing systems, then an incident has occurred.

5. Notification by hacker: Some hackers enjoy taunting their victims. If an organization's Web pages are defaced, it is an incident. If an organization receives an extortion request for money in exchange for its customers' credit card files, an incident is in progress.

Occurrences of Actual Incidents. When the following actual incidents are confirmed, the corresponding IR must be immediately activated:

1. Loss of availability: Information or information systems become unavailable.
2. Loss of integrity: Users report corrupt data files, garbage where data should be, or data that just looks wrong.
3. Loss of confidentiality: You are notified of sensitive information leaks, or information you thought was protected has been disclosed.
4. Violation of policy: If organizational policies addressing information or information security have been violated, an incident has occurred.
5. Violation of law or regulation: If the law has been broken and the organization's information assets are involved, an incident has occurred.

Incident Response

Once an actual incident has been confirmed and properly classified, the IR plan moves from the detection phase to the reaction phase.

The steps in IR are designed to stop the incident, mitigate its effects, and provide information for the recovery from the incident. In the incident response phase, a number of action steps taken by the SIRT and others must occur quickly and may take place concurrently. An effective IR plan prioritizes and documents these steps to allow for efficient reference in the midst of an incident. These steps include notification of key personnel, assignment of tasks, assignment of tasks, and documentation of the incident.

Notification of Key Personnel. As soon as the SIRT determines that an incident is in progress, the right people must be notified in the right order. Most response organizations, such as firefighters or the military, maintain an alert roster for all emergencies. An **alert roster** is a document containing contact information on the individuals to be notified in the event of an actual incident.

There are two ways to activate an alert roster: sequentially and hierarchically. A **sequential roster** requires that a contact person call each and every person on the roster. A **hierarchical roster** requires that the first person call designated people on the roster, who in turn call designated other people, and so on. Each approach has both advantages and disadvantages. The hierarchical system is quicker because more people are calling at the same time, but the message can become distorted as it is passed from person to person. The sequential system is more accurate, but slower because a single contact person provides each responder with the message.

The **alert message** is a scripted description of the incident and consists of just enough information so that each responder, SIRT or otherwise, knows what portion of the IR plan to implement without impeding the notification process. It is important to recognize that not everyone is on the alert roster—only those individuals who must respond to a specific actual incident. As with any part of the IR plan, the alert roster must be regularly maintained, tested, and rehearsed if it is to remain effective.

During this phase other key personnel not on the alert roster, such as general management, must be notified of the incident as well. This notification should occur only after the incident has been confirmed, but before media or other external sources learn of it. Among those likely to be included in the notification process are members of the legal, communications, and human resources departments. In addition, some incidents are disclosed to the employees in general, as a lesson in security, and some are not, as a measure of security. Furthermore, other organizations may need to be notified if it is determined that the incident is not confined to internal information resources, or if the incident is part of a larger-scale assault. For example, during Mafiaboy's distributed denial-of-service attack on multiple high-visibility Web-based vendors in late 1999, many of the target organizations reached out for help. In general, the IR planners should determine in advance whom to notify and when, and should offer guidance about additional notification steps to take as needed.

Documenting an Incident.   As soon as an incident has been confirmed and the notification process is under way, the team should begin to document it. The documentation should record the *who, what, when, where, why,* and *how* of each action taken while the incident is occurring. This documentation serves as a case study after the fact to determine whether the right actions were taken and if they were effective. It also proves, should it become necessary, that the organization did everything possible to prevent the spread of the incident. Legally, the standards of due care may offer some protection to the organization should an incident adversely affect individuals inside and outside the organization, or other organizations that use the target organization's systems. Incident documentation can also be used as a simulation in future training sessions on future versions of the IR plan.

Incident Containment Strategies.   One of the most critical components of IR is stopping the incident or containing its scope or impact. Incident containment strategies vary depending on the incident, and on the amount of damage caused. Before an incident can be stopped or contained, however, the affected areas must be identified. Now is not the time to conduct a detailed analysis of the affected areas; those tasks are typically performed after the fact, in the forensics process. Instead, simple identification of what information and systems are involved determines the containment actions to be taken. Incident containment strategies focus on two tasks: stopping the incident and recovering control of the affected systems.

The SIRT can stop the incident and attempt to recover control by means of several strategies. If the incident originates outside the organization, the simplest and most straightforward approach is to disconnect the affected communication circuits. Of course, if the organization's lifeblood runs through that circuit, this step may be too drastic; if the incident does not threaten critical functional areas, it may be more feasible to monitor the incident and contain it another way. One approach used by some organizations is to apply filtering rules dynamically to limit certain types of network access. For example, if a threat agent is attacking a network by exploiting a vulnerability in the Simple Network Management Protocol (SNMP), then applying a blocking filter for the commonly used IP ports for that vulnerability will stop the attack without compromising other services on the network. Depending on the nature of the attack and the organization's technical capabilities, ad hoc controls can sometimes gain valuable time to devise a more permanent control strategy. Other containment strategies include the following:

- Disabling compromised user accounts
- Reconfiguring a firewall to block the problem traffic
- Temporarily disabling the compromised process or service
- Taking down the conduit application or server—for example, the e-mail server
- Stopping all computers and network devices

Obviously, the final strategy is used only when all system control has been lost, and the only hope is to preserve the data stored on the computers so that operations can resume normally once the incident is resolved. The SIRT, following the procedures outlined in the IR plan, determines the length of the interruption.

Consider the chapter-opening scenario again. What if, instead of a fire, the event had been a virus attack? And what if the key incident response personnel had been home sick, on vacation, or otherwise not there? Think how many people in your class or office are not there on a regular basis. Many businesses involve travel, with employees going off-site to meetings, seminars, training, vacations, or other diverse requirements. In considering these possibilities, the importance of preparedness becomes clear. Everyone should know how to handle an incident, not just the CISO and systems administrators.

Incident Escalation.   An incident may increase in scope or severity to the point that the IR plan cannot adequately handle it. An important part of knowing how to handle an incident is knowing at what point to escalate the incident to a disaster, or to transfer the incident to an outside authority such as law enforcement or another public response unit. Each organization will have to determine, during the business impact analysis, the point at which an incident is deemed a disaster. These criteria must be included in the IR plan. The organization must also document when to involve outside responders, as discussed in other sections. Escalation is one of those things that once done cannot be undone, so it is important to know when and where it should be used.

Incident Recovery

Once the incident has been contained, and system control has been regained, incident recovery can begin. As in the incident response phase, the first task is to inform the appropriate human resources. Almost simultaneously, the SIRT must assess the full extent of the damage so as to determine what must be done to restore the systems. Each individual involved should begin recovery operations based on the appropriate incident recovery section of the IR plan.

The immediate determination of the scope of the breach of confidentiality, integrity, and availability of information and information assets is called **incident damage assessment**. Incident damage assessment can take days or weeks depending on the extent of the damage. The damage can range from minor (a curious hacker snooped around) to severe (hundreds of computer systems infected by a worm or virus). System logs, intrusion detection logs, configuration logs, and other documents, as well as the documentation from the incident response, provide information on the type, scope, and extent of damage. Using this information, the SIRT assesses the current state of the information and systems, and compares it to a known state. Individuals who document the damage from actual incidents must be trained to collect and preserve evidence, in case the incident is part of a crime or results in a civil action.

Once the extent of the damage has been determined, the recovery process begins. This process involves the following steps:[7]

- Identify the vulnerabilities that allowed the incident to occur and spread. Resolve them.
- Address the safeguards that failed to stop or limit the incident, or were missing from the system in the first place. Install, replace, or upgrade them.
- Evaluate monitoring capabilities (if present). Improve detection and reporting methods, or install new monitoring capabilities.
- Restore the data from backups. The IR team must understand the backup strategy used by the organization, restore the data contained in backups, and then use the appropriate recover processes from incremental backups or database journals to recreate any data that was created or modified since the last backup.
- Restore the services and processes in use. Compromised services and processes must be examined, cleaned, and then restored. If services or processes were interrupted in the course of regaining control of the systems, they need to be brought back online.
- Continuously monitor the system. If an incident happened once, it could easily happen again. Hackers frequently boast of their exploits in chat rooms and dare their peers to match their efforts. If word gets out, others may be tempted to try the same or different attacks on your systems. It is therefore important to maintain vigilance during the entire IR process.
- Restore the confidence of the members of the organization's communities of interest. Management, following the recommendation from the SIRT, may want to issue a short memorandum outlining the incident, and assuring all that the incident was handled and the damage was controlled. If the incident was minor, say so. If the incident was major or severely damaged systems or data, reassure users that they can expect operations to return to normal as soon as possible. The objective of this communication is to prevent panic or confusion from causing additional disruption to the operations of the organization.

Before returning to its routine duties, the SIRT must conduct an **after-action review (AAR)**. The after-action review entails a detailed examination of the events that occurred from first detection to final recovery. All key players review their notes and verify that the IR documentation is accurate and precise. All team members review their actions during the incident and identify areas where the IR plan worked, did not work, or should improve. This exercise allows the team to update the IR plan. The AAR can serve as a training case for future staff. It also brings the SIRT's actions to a close.

Law Enforcement Involvement

When an incident violates civil or criminal law, it is the organization's responsibility to notify the proper authorities. Selecting the appropriate law enforcement agency depends on the type of crime committed. The Federal Bureau of Investigation (FBI), for example, handles computer crimes that cross state lines as well as investigates terrorism and cyber-terrorism, which can include attacks against businesses and other organizations. The U.S. Secret Service examines crimes involving U.S. currency, counterfeiting, credit cards, and identity theft. The U.S. Treasury Department has a bank fraud investigation unit, and the Securities and Exchange Commission has investigation and fraud control units as well. However, the heavy case loads of these agencies means that they typically prioritize those incidents that affect the national critical infrastructure or that have significant economic impact. The FBI Web site, for example, states that the FBI Computer Intrusion Squad:

> ... pursues the investigation of cyber-based attacks, primarily unauthorized access (intrusion) and denial-of-service, directed at the major components of this country's critical information, military, and economic infrastructures. Critical infrastructure includes the nation's power grids and power-supply systems, transportation control systems, money transfer and accounting systems, defense-related systems, and telecommunications networks. Additionally, the Squad investigates cyber attacks directed at private industry and public institutions that maintain information vital to national security and/or the economic success of the nation.[8]

In other words, if the crime is not directed at or does not affect the national infrastructure, the FBI may not be able to assist the organization as effectively as state or local agencies can. However, in general, if a crime crosses state lines, it becomes a federal matter. The FBI may also become involved at the request of a state agency, if it has the resources to spare.

Each state, county, and city in the United States has its own law enforcement agencies. These agencies enforce all local and state laws and handle suspects and security crime scenes for state and federal cases. Local law enforcement agencies rarely have computer crimes task forces, but the investigative (detective) units are quite capable of processing crime scenes and handling most common criminal violations, such as physical theft or trespassing, damage to property, and the apprehension and processing of suspects in computer-related crimes.

Involving law enforcement agencies has both advantages and disadvantages. Such agencies are usually much better equipped to process evidence than a business. Unless the security forces in the organization have been trained in processing evidence and computer forensics, they may do more harm than good when attempting to extract information that can lead to the legal conviction of a suspected criminal. Law enforcement agencies are also prepared to handle the warrants and subpoenas necessary when documenting a case. They are adept at obtaining statements from witnesses, affidavits, and other required documents. For all these reasons, law enforcement personnel can be a security administrator's greatest allies in prosecuting a computer crime. It is therefore important to become familiar with the appropriate local and state agencies before you have to make a call announcing a suspected crime. Most state and federal agencies sponsor awareness programs, provide guest speakers at conferences, and offer programs such as the FBI's InfraGard program (www.infragard.net), currently assigned to the Department of Homeland Security's Cyber Division. These agents clearly understand the challenges facing security administrators.

The disadvantages of law enforcement involvement include possible loss of control of the chain of events following an incident, including the collection of information and evidence, and the prosecution of suspects. An organization that wants simply to reprimand or dismiss an employee should not involve a law enforcement agency in the resolution of an incident. Additionally, the organization may not hear about the case for weeks or even months due to heavy caseloads or resource shortages. A very real issue for commercial organizations when involving law enforcement agencies is the taking of equipment vital to the organization's business as evidence. Assets can be removed, stored, and preserved to prepare the criminal case. Despite these difficulties, if the organization detects a criminal act, it has the legal obligation to notify the appropriate law enforcement officials. Failure to do so can subject the organization and its officers to prosecution as accessories to the crimes or for impeding the course of an investigation. It is up to the security administrator to ask questions of law enforcement agencies to determine when each agency should be involved, and specifically which crimes will be addressed by each agency.

Disaster Recovery Plan

The next vital part of contingency planning is disaster recovery planning. The IT community of interest, under the leadership of the CIO, is often made responsible for disaster recovery planning, including aspects that are not necessarily technology-based.

Disaster recovery planning (DRP) entails the preparation for and recovery from a disaster, whether natural or human-made. In some cases, actual incidents detected by the IR team may escalate to the level of disaster, and the IR plan may no longer be able to handle the effective and efficient recovery from the loss. For example, if a malicious program evades containment actions and infects and disables many or most of an organization's systems and its ability to function, the **disaster recovery plan (DR plan)** is activated. Sometimes events are by their nature immediately classified as disasters, such as an extensive fire, flood, damaging storm, or earthquake.

As you learned earlier in this chapter, the CP team creates the DR plan. In general, a disaster has occurred when either of two criteria is met: (1) the organization is unable to contain or control the impact of an incident or (2) the level of damage or destruction from an incident is so severe that the organization cannot quickly recover from it. The distinction between an incident and a disaster may be subtle. The CP team must document in the DR plan whether an event is classified as an incident or a disaster. This determination is critical because it determines which plan is activated. The key role of a DR plan is defining how to reestablish operations at the location where the organization is usually located.

You learned earlier in this chapter about a planning process recommended by NIST that uses seven steps. In the broader context of organizational contingency planning, these steps form the overall CP process. These steps are used again here within the narrower context of the DRP process:

1. Develop the DR planning policy statement: A formal department or agency policy provides the authority and guidance necessary to develop an effective contingency plan.

2. Review the BIA: The BIA was prepared to help to identify and prioritize critical IT systems and components. A review of what was discovered is an important step in the process.

3. Identify preventive controls: Measures taken to reduce the effects of system disruptions can increase system availability and reduce contingency life cycle costs.

4. Develop recovery strategies: Thorough recovery strategies ensure that the system can be recovered quickly and effectively following a disruption.

5. Develop the disaster recovery plan document: The plan should contain detailed guidance and procedures for restoring a damaged system.

6. Plan testing, training, and exercises: Testing the plan identifies planning gaps, whereas training prepares recovery personnel for plan activation; both activities improve plan effectiveness and overall agency preparedness.

7. Plan maintenance: The plan should be a living document that is updated regularly to remain current with system enhancements.

The DR team, led by the business manager designated as the DR team leader, begins with the development of the DR policy. The policy presents an overview of an organization's philosophy on the conduct of disaster recovery operations and serves as the guide for the development of the DR plan. The DR policy itself may have been created by the organization's CP team and handed down to the DR team leader. Alternatively, the DR team may be assigned the role of developing the DR policy. In either case, the disaster recovery policy contains the following key elements:

- Purpose: The purpose of the disaster recovery program is to provide for the direction and guidance of any and all disaster recovery operations. In addition, the program provides for the development and support of the disaster recovery plan. In everyday practice those responsible for the program must also work to emphasize the importance of creating and maintaining effective disaster recovery functions. As with any major enterprise-wide policy effort, it is important for the disaster recovery program to begin with a clear statement of executive vision.

- Scope: This section of the policy identifies the organizational units and groups of employees to which the policy applies. This clarification is important if the organization is geographically dispersed or is creating different policies for different organizational units.

- Roles and responsibilities: This section of the DR policy identifies the roles and responsibilities of the key players in the disaster recovery operation. It can include a delineation of the responsibilities of the executive management down to the individual employee. Some sections of the DR policy may be duplicated from the organization's overall contingency planning policy. In smaller organizations, this redundancy can be eliminated, as many of the functions are performed by the same group.

- Resource requirements: An organization can allocate specific resources to the development of disaster recovery plans here. While this may include directives for individuals, it can be separated from the previous section for emphasis and clarity.

- Training requirements: This section defines and highlights the training requirements for the units within the organization and the various categories of employees.
- Exercise and testing schedules: This section stipulates the testing intervals of the DR plan, as well as the type of testing and the individuals involved.
- Plan maintenance schedule: This section states the review and update intervals of the plan, and identifies who is involved in the review. It is not necessary for the entire DR team to be involved, but the review can be combined with a periodic test of the DR plan as long as the resulting discussion includes areas for improvement for the plan.
- Special considerations (such as information storage and maintenance).

Disaster Classification

A DR plan can classify disasters in a number of ways. The most common method is to separate natural disasters, such as those described in Table 3-2, from human-made disasters. *Acts of terrorism,* including cyber-terrorism or hactivism, *acts of war,* and *acts of man* that may begin as incidents and escalate into disasters are all examples of human-made disasters.

Another way of classifying disasters is by speed of development. **Rapid-onset disasters** occur suddenly, with little warning, taking the lives of people and destroying the means of production. Rapid-onset disasters may be caused by earthquakes, floods, storm winds, tornadoes, or mud flows. **Slow-onset disasters** occur over time and gradually degrade the capacity of an organization to withstand their effects. Hazards causing these disaster conditions typically include droughts, famines, environmental degradation, desertification, deforestation, and pest infestation.[9]

TABLE 3-2 Acts of God and Their Effects on Information Systems

Fire	Damages the building housing the computing equipment that constitutes all or part of the information system. Also encompasses smoke damage from the fire and water damage from sprinkler systems or firefighters. Can usually be mitigated with fire casualty insurance or business interruption insurance.
Flood	Can cause direct damage to all or part of the information system or to the building that houses all or part of the information system. May also disrupt operations by interrupting access to the buildings that house all or part of the information system. Can sometimes be mitigated with flood insurance or business interruption insurance.

TABLE 3-2 Acts of God and Their Effects on Information Systems (continued)

Earthquake	Can cause direct damage to all or part of the information system or, more often, to the building that houses them. May also disrupt operations by interrupting access to the buildings that house all or part of the information system. Can sometimes be mitigated with specific casualty insurance or business interruption insurance, but is usually a specific and separate policy.
Lightning	Can directly damage all or part of the information system or its power distribution components. Can also cause fires or other damage to the building that houses all or part of the information system. May also disrupt operations by interrupting access to the buildings that house all or part of the information system as well as the routine delivery of electrical power. Can usually be mitigated with multipurpose casualty insurance or business interruption insurance.
Landslide or mudslide	Can damage all or part of the information system or, more likely, the building that houses them. May also disrupt operations by interrupting access to the buildings that house all or part of the information system as well as the routine delivery of electrical power. Can sometimes be mitigated with casualty insurance or business interruption insurance.
Tornado or severe windstorm	Can directly damage all or part of the information system or, more likely, the building that houses them. May also disrupt operations by interrupting access to the buildings that house all or part of the information system as well as the routine delivery of electrical power. Can sometimes be mitigated with casualty insurance or business interruption insurance.
Hurricane or typhoon	Can directly damage all or part of the information system or, more likely, the building that houses them. Organizations located in coastal or low-lying areas may experience flooding (see previous page). May also disrupt operations by interrupting access to the buildings that house all or part of the information system as well as the routine delivery of electrical power. Can sometimes be mitigated with casualty insurance or business interruption insurance.
Tsunami	Can directly damage all or part of the information system or, more likely, the building that houses them. Organizations located in coastal areas may experience tsunamis. May also cause disruption to operations by interrupting access or electrical power to the buildings that house all or part of the information system. Can sometimes be mitigated with casualty insurance or business interruption insurance.

TABLE 3-2   Acts of God and Their Effects on Information Systems (continued)

Electrostatic discharge (ESD)	Can be costly or dangerous when it ignites flammable mixtures and damages costly electronic components. Static electricity can draw dust into clean-room environments or cause products to stick together. The cost of ESD-damaged electronic devices and interruptions to service can range from a few cents to millions of dollars for critical systems. Loss of production time in information processing due to the effects of ESD is significant. While not usually viewed as a threat, ESD can disrupt information systems and is not usually an insurable loss unless covered by business interruption insurance.
Dust contamination	Can shorten the life of information systems or cause unplanned downtime.

Planning for Disaster

To plan for disaster, the CP team engages in scenario development and impact analysis, along the way categorizing the level of threat that each potential disaster poses. When generating a disaster recovery scenario, start first with the most important asset—people. Do you have the human resources with the appropriate organizational knowledge to restore business operations? Organizations must cross-train their employees to ensure that operations and a sense of normalcy can be restored. In addition, the DR plan must be tested regularly so that the DR team can lead the recovery effort quickly and efficiently. Key elements that the CP team must build into the DR plan include the following:

1. Clear delegation of roles and responsibilities: Everyone assigned to the DR team should be aware of his or her duties during a disaster. Some team members may be responsible for coordinating with local services, such as fire, police, and medical personnel. Some may be responsible for the evacuation of company personnel, if required. Others may be assigned to simply pack up and leave.

2. Execution of the alert roster and notification of key personnel: These notifications may extend outside the organization to include the fire, police, or medical services mentioned earlier, as well as insurance agencies, disaster teams such as those of the Red Cross, and management teams.

3. Clear establishment of priorities: During a disaster response, the first priority is always the preservation of human life. Data and systems protection is subordinate when the disaster threatens the lives, health, or welfare of the employees or members of the community. Only after all employees and neighbors have been safeguarded can the disaster recovery team attend to protection of other organizational assets.

4. Procedures for documentation of the disaster: Just as in an incident response, the disaster must be carefully recorded from the onset. This documentation is used later to determine how and why the disaster occurred.

5. Action steps to mitigate the impact of the disaster on the operations of the organization: The DR plan should specify the responsibilities of each DR team member, such as the evacuation of physical assets or making sure that all systems are securely shut down, to prevent further loss of data.

6. Alternative implementations for the various systems components, should primary versions be unavailable: These components include stand-by equipment, either purchased, leased, or under contract with a disaster recovery service agency. Developing systems with excess capacity, fault tolerance, auto-recovery, and fail-safe features facilitates a quick recovery. Something as simple as using Dynamic Host Control Protocol (DHCP) to assign network addresses instead of using static addresses can allow systems to regain connectivity quickly and easily without technical support. Networks should support dynamic reconfiguration; restoration of network connectivity should be planned. Data recovery requires effective backup strategies as well as flexible hardware configurations. System management should be a top priority. All solutions should be tightly integrated and developed in a strategic plan to provide continuity. Piecemeal construction can result in a disaster after the disaster, as incompatible systems are unexpectedly thrust together.

A number of options are available to an organization to protect their information and assist in getting operations up and running quickly:

- Traditional data backups: The use of a combination of on-site and off-site tape drive or hard drive backup methods, in a variety of rotation schemes. Because the backup point is sometime in the past, recent data is potentially lost. Most common data backup schemes involve random array of independent disks (RAID) or disk-to-disk-to-tape methods.

- Electronic vaulting: The bulk batch-transfer of data to an off-site facility. This transfer is usually conducted via leased lines or secure Internet connections. The receiving server archives the data as it is received. Some disaster recovery companies specialize in **electronic vaulting** services.

- Remote journaling: The transfer of live transactions to an off-site facility. **Remote journaling** differs from electronic vaulting in two ways: (1) only transactions are transferred, not archived data; and (2) the transfer takes place online and in much closer to real time. While electronic vaulting is akin to a traditional backup, with a dump of data to the off-site storage, remote journaling involves online activities on a systems level, much like server fault tolerance, where data is written to two locations simultaneously.

- Database shadowing: The storage of duplicate online transaction data, along with the duplication of the databases at the remote site on a redundant server. **Database shadowing** combines electronic vaulting with remote journaling, by writing multiple copies of the database simultaneously in two separated locations.

As part of DR plan readiness, each employee should have two types of emergency information cards in his or her possession at all times. The first lists personal emergency information—the person to notify in case of an emergency (next of kin), medical conditions, and a form of identification. The second comprises a set of instructions on what to do in the event of an emergency. This snapshot of the DR plan should contain a contact number or hotline for calling the organization during an emergency, emergency services numbers (fire, police, medical), evacuation and assembly locations (storm shelters, for example), the name and number of the disaster recovery coordinator, and any other needed information.

Crisis Management

The DR plan must also include reference to another process that many organizations plan for separately—**crisis management**, or the action steps that affect the people both inside and outside the organization that are taken during and after a disaster. The DR team works closely with the crisis management team to assure complete and timely communication during a disaster. According to Gartner Research, the crisis management team is responsible for managing the event from an enterprise perspective and covers the following major activities:

- Supporting personnel and their loved ones during the crisis
- Determining the event's impact on normal business operations and, if necessary, making a disaster declaration
- Keeping the public informed about the event and the actions being taken to ensure the recovery of personnel and the enterprise
- Communicating with major customers, suppliers, partners, regulatory agencies, industry organizations, the media, and other interested parties[10]

The crisis management team should establish a base of operations or command center near the site of the disaster as soon as possible. It should include individuals from all functional areas of the organization to facilitate communications and cooperation. The crisis management team is charged with two key tasks:

1. Verifying personnel status: Everyone must be accounted for, including individuals who are on vacations, leaves of absence, and business trips.
2. Activating the alert roster: Alert rosters and general personnel phone lists are used to notify individuals whose assistance may be needed, or to simply tell employees not to report to work until the disaster is over.

The crisis management team should plan an approach for releasing information in the event of a disaster, and should perhaps even have boilerplate scripts prepared for press releases. Advice from Lanny Davis, former counselor to President Bill Clinton, is very clear. When beset by damaging events, tell the whole story as soon as possible directly to the affected audience. This can be summed up with the pithy statement, "Tell it early, tell it all, tell it yourself," which is the subtitle of Davis's memoir.[11]

Responding to the Disaster

When a disaster strikes, actual events can at times overwhelm even the best of DR plans. To be prepared, the CP team should incorporate a degree of flexibility into the plan. If the physical facilities are intact, the DR team should begin the restoration of systems and data to work toward full operational capability. If the organization's facilities are destroyed, alternative actions must be taken until new facilities can be acquired. When a disaster threatens the viability of an organization at the primary site, the disaster recovery process becomes a business continuity process, which is described in detail later in this chapter.

VIEWPOINT

Counterattack

By Bruce Schneier, CTO, BT Counterpane

Counterattacks must be an idea whose time has come, because they are being talked about everywhere. The entertainment industry has floated a bill that would give it the ability to break into other people's computers if it suspects copyright violation. Several articles have been written about automated law enforcement, where both governments and private companies use computers to automatically find and target suspected criminals. And Tim Mullen and other security researchers are talking about "strike back," where the victim of a computer assault automatically attacks the perpetrator.

The common theme here is vigilantism: citizens and companies taking the law into their own hands and going after their assailants. Viscerally, it has a certain appeal. But it's a horrible idea, and one that society after society has eschewed.

Our society does not give us the right of revenge, and wouldn't work very well if it did. Our laws give us the right to justice, in either the criminal or civil context. Justice is all we can expect if we want to enjoy our constitutional freedoms, personal safety, and an orderly society.

Anyone accused of a crime deserves a fair trial. He deserves the right to defend himself, the right to face his accuser, the right to an attorney, and the right to be held innocent until proven guilty.

Vigilantism flies in the face of these rights. It punishes people before they have been found guilty. An angry mob lynching a suspected murderer is wrong, even if that person is actually guilty. The Motion Picture Association of America (MPAA) disabling a computer because its owner is suspected of copying a movie is wrong, even if the movie *was* copied. Revenge is a basic human desire, but revenge becomes justice only if carried out by the state.

And the state has more motivation to be fair. The Recording Industry Association of America (RIAA) sent a cease-and-desist letter to an Internet service provider (ISP) asking it to remove certain files that were the copyrighted works of George Harrison. The RIAA simply Googled for the string "harrison" and went after everyone who turned up. Vigilantism is wrong because the vigilante could be wrong. The goal of a state legal system is justice; the goal of the RIAA was expediency.

Strike-back systems are much the same. The idea is that if a computer is attacking yours—sending you viruses, acting as a DDoS zombie, and so on—you can forcibly shut that computer down or remotely install a patch. Such an action might be satisfying in many ways, but it's legally and morally wrong.

Imagine you're a homeowner, and your neighbor has some kind of device on the outside of his house that makes noise. A lot of noise. All day and all night. Enough noise that any reasonable person would claim it to be a public nuisance. Even so, it is not legal for you to take matters into your own hands and stop the noise.

continued

Destroying property is not a recognized remedy for stopping a nuisance, even if it is causing you real harm. Your remedies are to (1) call the police and ask them to turn the noise off, break it, or insist that the neighbor turn it off or (2) sue the neighbor and ask the court to enjoin him from using that device (unless the noise problem can be fixed) and award you damages for your aggravation. Vigilante justice is simply not an option, no matter how right you believe your cause to be.

This is law, not technology, so there are all sorts of shades of gray. Factors to consider when assessing the morality or legality of an action are the interests at stake in the original attack; the nature of the property, liberty, or personnel threatened by the counterattack; the risk of being wrong; and the availability and effectiveness of other measures. The RIAA bill is at one extreme because copyright is a limited property interest, and there is a great risk of wrongful deprivation of use of the computer, and of the user's privacy and security. A strike-back attack that disables a dangerous Internet worm is perhaps more justifiable. Clearly this is something that the courts will have to sort out.

In 1789, the Declaration of the Rights of Man and of the Citizen said the following: "No person shall be accused, arrested, or imprisoned except in the cases and according to the forms prescribed by law. Anyone soliciting, transmitting, executing, or causing to be executed any arbitrary order shall be punished." And also: "As all persons are held innocent until they shall have been declared guilty, if arrest shall be deemed indispensable, all harshness not essential to the securing of the prisoner's person shall be severely repressed by law."

Neither the interests of systems administrators on the Internet nor the interests of companies like Disney should be allowed to trump these rights.

Business Continuity Plan

Business continuity planning (BCP) ensures that critical business functions can continue if a disaster occurs. Unlike the DR plan, which is usually managed by the IT community of interest, the **business continuity plan (BC plan)** is most properly managed by the CEO of an organization. The BC plan is activated and executed concurrently with the DR plan when the disaster is major or long term and requires fuller and complex restoration of information and IT resources. If a disaster has rendered the current business location unusable, there must be a plan to allow the business to continue to function. While the BC plan reestablishes critical business functions at an alternate site, the DR plan team focuses on the reestablishment of the technical infrastructure and business operations at the primary site. Not every business needs such a plan, or such facilities. Some small companies or fiscally sound organizations may be able simply to cease operations until the primary facilities are restored. Manufacturing and retail organizations, however, depend on continued operations for revenue. Thus, these entities must have a BC plan in place so as to relocate operations quickly with minimal loss of revenue.

BC is an element of contingency planning, and it is best accomplished using a repeatable process or methodology. A well-regarded reference document, NIST Special Publication 800-34, *Contingency Planning Guide for Information Technology Systems*,[12] includes guidance for planning for incidents, disasters, and situations calling for business continuity. The approach used in that document has been adapted for BC use here.

The first step in all contingency efforts is the development of policy; the next step is to plan. In some organizations these are considered corequisite operations where development of policy is a function of planning, while in others policy comes before planning and is a separate process. In this text, the BC policy is developed prior to the BC plan; and the development of both are part of BC planning. The NIST approach used in SP 800-34 defines a seven-step process used to develop and maintain a viable contingency planning program. The steps from the NIST approach have been adapted here for the BC planning process:

1. Develop the BC planning policy statement: A formal organizational policy provides the authority and guidance necessary to develop an effective continuity plan. As with any enterprise-wide policy process, it is important to begin with the executive vision.
2. Review the BIA: The BIA helps to identify and prioritize critical IT systems and components.
3. Identify preventive controls: Measures taken to reduce the effects of system disruptions can increase system availability and reduce continuity life cycle costs.
4. Develop relocation strategies: Thorough relocation strategies ensure that critical system functions may be recovered quickly and effectively following a disruption.
5. Develop the continuity plan: The continuity plan should contain detailed guidance and procedures for restoring a damaged system.
6. Plan testing, training, and exercises: Testing the plan identifies planning gaps, whereas training prepares recovery personnel for plan activation; both activities improve plan effectiveness and overall agency preparedness.
7. Plan maintenance: The plan should be a living document that is updated regularly to remain current with system enhancements.

BC Planning Policy Statement

BC planning begins with the development of the BC policy, which reflects the organization's philosophy on the conduct of business continuity operations and serves as the guiding document for the development of BC planning. The BC team leader might receive the BC policy from the CP team, or might guide the BC team in developing one. The BC policy contains the following key sections:

- Purpose: What is the purpose of the business continuity program? To provide the necessary planning and coordination to facilitate the relocation of critical business functions should a disaster prohibit continued operations at the primary site.
- Scope: This section identifies the organizational units and groups of employees to which the policy applies. This is especially useful in organizations that are geographically dispersed, or that are creating different policies for different organizational units.
- Roles and responsibilities: This section identifies the roles and responsibilities of key players in the business continuity operation, from executive management down to individual employees. In some cases, sections may be

duplicated from the organization's overall contingency planning policy. For smaller organizations, this redundancy can be eliminated because many of the functions are performed by the same group of individuals.

- Resource requirements: Organizations can allocate specific resources to the development of business continuity plans. Although this may include directives for individuals, it can be separated from the roles and responsibilities section for emphasis and clarity.

- Training requirements: This sections specifies the training requirements for the various employee groups.

- Exercise and testing schedules: This section stipulates the frequency of BC plan testing, and can include both the type of exercise or testing and the individuals involved.

- Plan maintenance schedule: This section specifies the procedures and frequency of BC plan reviews, and identifies the personnel who will be involved in the review. It is not necessary for the entire BC team to be involved; the review can be combined with a periodic test of the BC (as in a talk-through) as long as the resulting discussion includes areas for improvement for the plan.

- Special considerations: As described earlier, in extreme situations the DR and BC plans overlap. Thus, this section provides an overview of the information storage and retrieval plans of the organization. While the specifics do not have to be elaborated in this document, at a minimum the plan should identify where more detailed documentation is kept, which individuals are responsible, and any other information needed to implement the strategy.

You may have noticed that this structure is virtually identical to that of the disaster recovery policy and plans. The processes are generally the same, with minor differences in implementation.

The identification of critical business functions and the resources to support them is the cornerstone of the BC plan. When a disaster strikes, these functions are the first to be reestablished at the alternate site. The CP team needs to appoint a group of individuals to evaluate and compare the various alternatives and to recommend which strategy should be selected and implemented. The strategy selected usually involves an off-site facility, which should be inspected, configured, secured, and tested on a periodic basis. The selection should be reviewed periodically to determine whether a better alternative has emerged or whether the organization needs a different solution.

Many organizations with operations in New York City had their business continuity efforts (or lack thereof) tested critically on September 11, 2001. Similarly, organizations located in the Gulf Coast region of the United States had their BCP effectiveness tested during the 2005 hurricane season. When these organizations considered how much business continuity they wanted to have, they were faced with establishing two design parameters for their BC planning process: the recovery time objective and the recovery point objective. The **recovery time objective (RTO)** is the amount of time that passes before an infrastructure is available once the need for BC is declared. Reducing RTO requires mechanisms to shorten start-up time or provisions to make data available online at a failover site. The **recovery point objective (RPO)** is the point in the past to which the recovered applications and data at the alternate infrastructure will be restored. In database terms, this is the amount of data loss that will be experienced as a result of the resumption at the alternate site. Reducing RPO requires mechanisms to increase the synchronicity of data replication between production systems and the backup implementations for those systems.

Continuity Strategies

A CP team can choose from several strategies in its planning for business continuity. The determining factor is usually cost. In general, three exclusive-use options exist:

- Hot site: A **hot site** is a fully configured computer facility, with all services, communications links, and physical plant operations. It duplicates computing resources, peripherals, phone systems, applications, and workstations. Essentially, this duplicate facility needs only the latest data backups and the personnel to function. If the organization uses one of the data services listed in the following sections, a hot site can be fully functional within minutes. Not surprisingly, it is the most expensive alternative available. Other disadvantages include the need to provide maintenance for all the systems and equipment at the hot site, as well as physical and information security. However, if the organization requires a 24/7 capability for near real-time recovery, the hot site is the optimal strategy.

- Warm site: A **warm site** provides many of the same services and options as the hot site, but typically software applications are not included or are not installed and configured. It frequently includes computing equipment and peripherals with servers but not client workstations. A warm site offers many of the advantages of a hot site at a lower cost. The disadvantage is that it requires several hours—perhaps days—to make a warm site fully functional.

- Cold site: A **cold site** provides only rudimentary services and facilities. No computer hardware or peripherals are provided. All communications services must be installed after the site is occupied. A cold site is an empty room with standard heating, air conditioning, and electrical service. Everything else is an added cost option. Despite these disadvantages, a cold site may be better than nothing. Its primary advantage is its low cost. The most useful feature of this approach is that it ensures an organization has floor space should a widespread disaster strike, but some organizations are prepared to struggle to lease new space rather than pay maintenance fees on a cold site.

There are also three shared-use contingency options:

- Timeshare: A **timeshare** operates like one of the three sites described above, but is leased in conjunction with a business partner or sister organization. It allows the organization to provide a disaster recovery/business continuity option, while reducing its overall costs. The primary disadvantage is the possibility that more than one timeshare participant might need the facility simultaneously. Other disadvantages include the need to stock the facility with the equipment and data from all organizations involved, the complexity of negotiating the timeshare with the sharing organizations, and the possibility that one or more parties might exit the agreement or sublease their options. Operating under a timeshare is much like agreeing to colease an apartment with a group of friends. One can only hope that the organizations remain on amicable terms, as they all could potentially gain physical access to each other's data.

- Service bureau: A **service bureau** is a service agency that provides a service for a fee. In the case of disaster recovery/continuity planning, this service is the provision of physical facilities in the event of a disaster. Such agencies also frequently provide off-site data storage for a fee. Contracts with service bureaus can specify exactly what the organization needs under what circumstances. A service agreement usually guarantees space when needed; the service bureau must acquire additional space in the event of a widespread disaster. In this sense, it resembles the rental car provision in a car insurance policy. The disadvantage is that service contracts must be renegotiated periodically and rates can change. It can also be quite expensive.

- Mutual agreement: A **mutual agreement** is a contract between two organizations in which each party agrees to assist the other in the event of a disaster. It stipulates that each organization is obligated to provide the necessary facilities, resources, and services until the receiving organization is able to recover from the disaster. This arrangement can be a lot like moving in with relatives or friends—it does not take long for an organization to wear out its welcome. Many organizations balk at the idea of having to fund (even in the short term) duplicate services and resources. Still, mutual agreements between divisions of the same parent company, between subordinate and senior organizations, or between business partners may be a cost-effective solution when both parties to the agreement have a mutual interest in each other's continued operations and both have similar capabilities and capacities.

In addition to these six basic strategies, some specialized alternatives are available, such as a **rolling mobile site** configured in the payload area of a tractor/trailer, or externally stored resources, such as a rental storage area containing duplicate or older equipment. These alternatives are similar to the Pre-positioning of Overseas Material Configured to Unit Sets (POM-CUS) sites of the Cold War era, in which caches of materials to be used in the event of an emergency or war were stored. An organization might arrange with a prefabricated building contractor for immediate, temporary facilities (mobile offices) on-site in the event of a disaster.

Timing and Sequence of CP Elements

As indicated earlier, the IR plan focuses on immediate response, but if the incident escalates into a disaster, the IR plan may give way to the DR plan and BC plan, as illustrated in Figure 3-4. The DR plan typically focuses on restoring systems after disasters occur, and therefore is closely associated with the BC plan. The BC plan occurs concurrently with the DR plan when the damage is major or long term, requiring more than simple restoration of information and information resources, as illustrated in Figure 3-5.

Some experts argue that the three planning components (the IR, DR, and BC plans) of CP are so closely linked that they are indistinguishable. In fact, each has a distinct place, role, and planning requirement. Furthermore, each component (IR, DR, and BC) comes into play at a specific time in the life of an incident. Figure 3-6 illustrates this sequence and

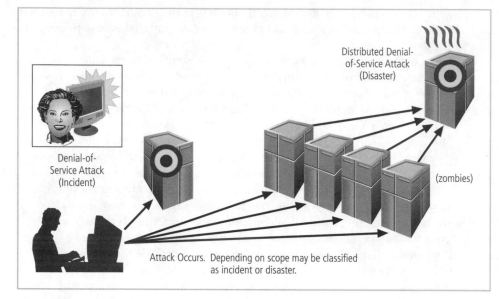

FIGURE 3-4   Incident Response and Disaster Recovery

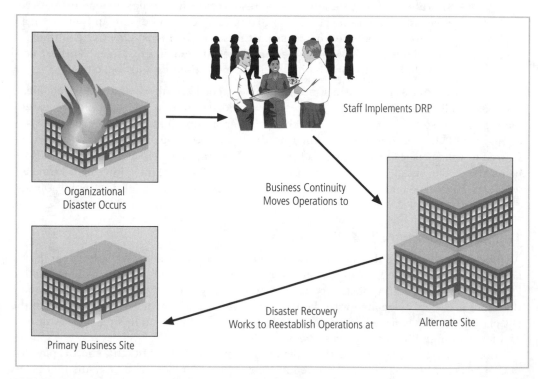

FIGURE 3-5   Disaster Recovery and Business Continuity Planning

shows the overlap that may occur. How the plans interact and the ways in which they are brought into action are discussed in the sections that follow.

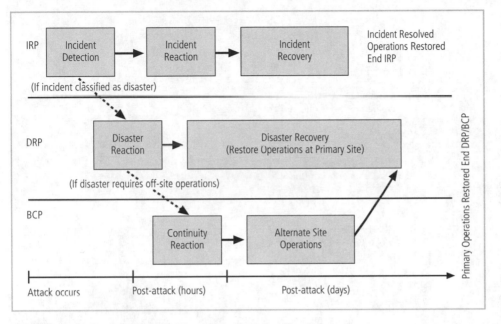

FIGURE 3-6   Contingency Planning Implementation Timeline

BUSINESS RESUMPTION PLANNING

Because the DR and BC plans are closely related, most organizations prepare the two at the same time, and may combine them into a single planning document called the **business resumption plan (or BR plan)**. Such a comprehensive plan must be able to support the reestablishment of operations at two different locations—one immediately at an alternate site, and one eventually back at the primary site. Therefore, although a single planning team can develop the BR Plan, execution of the plan requires separate execution teams.

The planning process for the DR plan should be tied to, but distinct from, the IR plan. As noted earlier in the chapter, an incident may escalate into a disaster when it grows dramatically in scope and intensity. It is important that the three planning development processes be so tightly integrated that the reaction teams can easily make the transition from incident response to disaster recovery and business continuity planning.

One useful resource is the Business Continuity Plan template provided by the Federal Agency Security Practices section of the CSRC at NIST (http://fasp.nist.gov/). Although it is labeled as a contingency plan, this Web page provides a template business resumption plan in the form of a joint DR/BC plan, complete with instructions designed for Department of Justice (DOJ)–related agencies. The instructions specifically describe the approach taken for the template, allowing easy conversion to suit many public and private organizations. Table 3-3 provides the table of contents for this document.

TABLE 3-3 Contingency Plan Template

Contents	
1.	Executive Summary
2.	Introduction
	2.1 Purpose
	2.2 Scope
	2.3 Plan Information
3.	Contingency Plan Overview
	3.1 Applicable Provisions and Directives
	3.2 Objectives
	3.3 Organization
	3.4 Contingency Phases
	3.4.1 Response Phase
	3.4.2 Resumption Phase
	3.4.3 Recovery Phase
	3.4.4 Restoration Phase
	3.5 Assumptions
	3.6 Critical Success Factors and Issues
	3.7 Mission-Critical Systems/Applications/Services
	3.8 Threats
	3.8.1 Probable Threats
4.	System Description
	4.1 Physical Environment
	4.2 Technical Environment
5.	Plan
	5.1 Plan Management
	5.1.1 Contingency Planning Workgroups
	5.1.2 Contingency Plan Coordinator
	5.1.3 System Contingency Coordinators
	5.1.4 Incident Notification
	5.1.5 Internal Personnel Notification
	5.1.6 External Contact Notification
	5.1.7 Media Releases
	5.1.8 Alternate Site(s)

TABLE 3-3 Contingency Plan Template (continued)

Contents

Source: (http://csrc.nist.gov/fasp/FASPDocs/contingency-plan/contingencyplan-template.doc)

Sample Disaster Recovery Plan

Figure 3-7 shows another example of what may be found in a disaster recovery plan. This document provides a sample disaster recovery plan adapted from one provided by the Texas State Library and Archives State and Local Records Management Division.[13]

EXAMPLE DISASTER RECOVERY PLAN

1. Name of agency_____

2. Date of completion or update of the plan_____

3. Agency staff to be called in the event of a disaster:

    Disaster Recovery Team:

    Name: Numbers: Position:

    _____
    _____
    _____

    Building Maintenance_____

    Building Security_____

    Legal Advisor_____

    Note below who is to call whom upon the discovery of a disaster (Telephone Tree):

4. Emergency services to be called (if needed) in event of a disaster:

    Service: Contact Person: Number:

    Ambulance_____

    Carpenters_____

    Data Processing Backup_____

    Electrician_____

    Emergency Management Coordinator_____

    Exterminator_____

    Fire Department_____

    Food Services_____

    Locksmith_____

    Plumber_____

    Police_____

    Security Personnel (extra)_____

    Software Vendor_____

    Temporary Personnel_____

    Utility Companies:

    Electric_____

    Gas_____

    Water_____

    Others:

FIGURE 3-7   Sample Disaster Recovery Plan

5. Locations of in-house emergency equipment and supplies (attach map or floor plan with locations marked):

Batteries_____

Badges (employee identification)_____

Camera /Film_____

Cut-off Switches and Valves:

    Electric_____

    Gas_____

    Water_____

Sprinkler System (if separate)_____

Extension Cords (heavy-duty)_____

Fire Extinguishers_____

Flashlights_____

Ladders_____

Mops/Sponges/Buckets/Brooms_____

Nylon Monofilament_____

Packing Tape/String/Sissors_____

Paper Towels (white)_____

Plastic Trash Bags_____

Rubber Gloves_____

Transistor Radio (battery powered)_____

3

6. Sources of off-site equipment and supplies (if maintained on-site, note location):

Item: Contact/Company: Number:

Cellular Phone_____

Dehumidifiers_____

Drying Space_____

Dust Masks_____

Fans_____

Fork Lift_____

Freezer/Wax Paper_____

Freezer Space/Refrigeration Truck_____

Fungicides_____

Generator (portable)_____

Hard Hats_____

Pallets_____

Plastic Milk Crates_____

Pumps (submersion)_____

Rubber Boots_____

Safety Glasses_____

Trash Can (all sizes)_____

Vacuum/Freeze Drying Facilities_____

    Waterproof Clothing_____

    Wet-Dry Vacuum_____

4

7. Salvage Priority List:

Attach a copy of the records retention schedule identifying all vital/essential records series. The location and record medium of the preservation duplicate for each vital records series should be noted.

It is also very helpful if other records series are reviewed to determine their priority for salvage should a disaster occur. The following questions can be helpful in determining priorities:

1. Can the records be replaced? At what cost?
2. Would the cost of replacement be less or more than restoration of the records?
3. How important are the records to the agency?
4. Are the records duplicated elsewhere?

To simplify this process, priorities may be assigned as follows:

1. Salvage at all costs.
   (example, records that are historically valuable or non-vital records that are important to agency operations and very difficult to recreate)

2. Salvage if time and resources permit.
   (example, records that are less important to the agency or somewhat easier to recreate)

3. Dispose of as part of general cleanup.
   (example, records that do not need to be salvaged because they are convenience copies and the record copy is at another location)

8. Agency Disaster Recovery Procedures:

Attach a list of specific procedures to be followed in the event of a disaster in you agency, including responsibilities of in-house recovery team members.

9. Follow-up Assessment:

A written report, including photographs, should be prepared after recovery and attached to a copy of the disaster plan. The report should note the effectiveness of the plan, and should include an evaluation of the sources of supplies and equipment, and of any off-site facilities used.

(Adapted from *Basic Guidelines for Disaster Planning in Oklahoma*)

5

FIGURE 3-7 Sample Disaster Recovery Plan (continued)

The plan has nine major sections, each of which is outlined below. Many organizations—particularly ones with multiple locations and hundreds of employees—would find this plan too simple. Nevertheless, the basic structure provides a solid starting point for any organization.

1. Name of agency: The first section identifies the department, division, or institution to which this particular plan applies. This identification is especially important in organizations that are large enough to require more than one plan.

2. Date of completion or update of the plan and the date of the most recent test.

3. Agency staff to be called in the event of a disaster: This roster should be kept current; it will not help the organization to have a list of employees who are no longer with the company. This section should also identify key support personnel, such as building maintenance supervisors, physical security directors, legal council, and the starting points on the alert roster. A copy of the alert roster (also known as the telephone tree) should be attached.

4. Emergency services to be called (if needed) in event of a disaster: While dialing 911 will certainly bring police, fire, and ambulance services, the organization may have equally pressing needs for emergency teams from the gas, electric, and water companies. This section should also list electricians, plumbers, locksmiths, and software and hardware vendors.

5. Locations of in-house emergency equipment and supplies: This section should include maps and floor plans with directions to all critical in-house emergency materials, including shut-off switches and valves for gas, electric, and water. Directions to key supplies including first aid kits, fire extinguishers, flashlights, batteries, and a stash of office supplies should also be provided. It is a good idea to place a disaster pack on every floor in an unlocked closet or readily accessible location. These items should be inventoried and updated as needed.

6. Sources of off-site equipment and supplies: These items include contact sources for mobile phones, dehumidifiers, industrial equipment, such as forklifts and portable generators, and other safety and recovery components.

7. Salvage priority list: While the IT director may have just enough time to grab the last on-site backup before darting out the door in the event of a fire, most likely additional materials can be salvaged if recovery efforts permit. In this event, recovery teams should know what has priority. This list should specify whether to recover hard copies or if the effort should be directed toward saving equipment. Similarly, it specifies whether the organization should focus on archival records or recent documents. The plan should include the locations and priorities of all items of value to the organization. When determining priorities, ask questions such as: Are these records archived elsewhere (i.e., off-site), or is this the only copy? Can these records be reproduced if lost, and if so, at what cost? Is the cost of replacement more or less than the cost of the value of the materials? It may be useful to create a simple rating scheme for materials. Data classification labels can be adapted to include disaster recovery information. For example, some records may be labeled "Salvage at all costs," "Salvage if time and resources permit," or "Do not salvage."

8. Agency disaster recovery procedures: This very important section outlines the specific assignments given to key personnel, including the disaster recovery team, to be performed in the event of a disaster. If these duties differ by type of disaster, it may be useful to create multiple scenarios, each listing the duties and responsibilities of the parties involved. It is equally important to make sure that all personnel identified in this section have a copy of the DRP stored where they can easily access it, and that they are familiar with their responsibilities.

9. Follow-up assessment: The final section details what is to be accomplished after disaster strikes—specifically, what documentation is required for recovery efforts, including mandatory insurance reports, required photographs, and the after-action review format.

TESTING CONTINGENCY PLANS

Very few plans are executable as initially written; instead, they must be tested to identify vulnerabilities, faults, and inefficient processes. Once problems are identified during the testing process, improvements can be made, and the resulting plan can be relied on in times of need. Five strategies[14] can be used to test contingency plans:

- Desk check: The simplest kind of validation involves distributing copies of the appropriate plans to all individuals who will be assigned roles during an actual incident. Each of these people performs a **desk check** by reviewing the plan and creating a list of correct and incorrect components. While not a true test, this strategy is a good way to review the perceived feasibility and effectiveness of the plan.

- Structured walk-through: In a **structured walk-through**, all involved individuals walk through the steps they would take during an actual event. This exercise can consist of an on-site walk-through, in which everyone discusses their actions at each particular location and juncture, or it may be more of a "talk-through" or "chalk talk," in which all involved individuals sit around a conference table and discuss in turn their responsibilities as the incident unfolds.

- Simulation: In a **simulation**, each person works individually, rather than in a group setting, to simulate the performance of each task. The simulation stops short of performing the actual physical tasks required, such as installing the backup data or disconnecting a communications circuit. The major difference between a walk-through and a simulation is that individuals work on their own tasks and are responsible for identifying the faults in their own procedures.

- Parallel testing: In **parallel testing**, individuals act as if an actual incident occurred, and begin performing their required tasks and executing the necessary procedures, without interfering with the normal operations of the business. Great care must be taken to ensure that the procedures performed do not halt the operations of the business functions, thereby creating an actual incident.

- Full interruption: In **full-interruption** testing, the individuals follow each and every procedure, including the interruption of service, restoration of data from backups, and notification of appropriate individuals. This exercise is often performed after normal business hours in organizations that cannot afford to disrupt or simulate the disruption of business functions. Although full-interruption testing is the most rigorous testing strategy, it is unfortunately too risky for most businesses.

At a minimum, organizations should conduct periodic walk-throughs (or chalk talks) of each of the CP component plans. Failure to update these plans as the business and its information resources change can erode the team's ability to respond to an incident, or possibly cause greater damage than the incident itself. If this sounds like a major training effort, note that the author Richard Marcinko, a former Navy SEAL, provides a few relevant statements to motivate teams:[15]

- The more you sweat in training, the less you bleed in combat.
- Training and preparation hurts.
- Lead from the front, not the rear.
- You don't have to like it; just do it.
- Keep it simple.
- Never assume.
- You are paid for your results, not your methods.

One often-neglected aspect of training is cross-training. In a real incident or disaster, the people assigned to particular roles are often not available. In some cases, alternate people must perform the duties of personnel who have been incapacitated by the disastrous event that triggered the activation of the plan. The testing process should train people to take over in the event that a team leader or integral member of the execution team is unavailable.

CONTINGENCY PLANNING: FINAL THOUGHTS

Just as in all organizational efforts, iteration results in improvement. A formal implementation of this methodology is continuous process improvement (CPI). Each time the organization rehearses its plans, it should learn from the process, improve the plans, and then rehearse again. Each time an incident or disaster occurs, the organization should review what went right and what went wrong. Through the ongoing evaluation and improvement, the organization continues to move forward, and continually improves upon the process, so that it can strive for an even better outcome.

Chapter Summary

- Planning for unexpected events is usually the responsibility of managers from both the information technology and information security communities of interest.

- For a plan to be seen as valid by all members of the organization, it must be sanctioned and actively supported by the general business community of interest.

- Some organizations are required by law or other mandate to have CP procedures in place at all times, but all business organizations should prepare for the unexpected.

- Contingency planning (CP) is the process by which the information technology and information security communities of interest position their organizations to prepare for, detect, react to, and recover from events that threaten the security of information resources and assets, both human and artificial.

- CP is made up of four major components: The data collection and documentation process known as the business impact analysis (BIA), the incident response (IR) plan, the disaster recovery (DR) plan, and the business continuity (BC) plan.

- Organizations can either create and develop the three planning elements of the CP process (the IR, BC, and DR plans) as one unified plan, or they can create the three elements separately in conjunction with a set of interlocking procedures that enable continuity.

- To ensure continuity during the creation of the CP components, a seven-step CP process is used:

  1. Develop the contingency planning policy statement
  2. Conduct the Business Impact Analysis
  3. Identify preventive controls
  4. Develop recovery strategies
  5. Develop an IT contingency plan
  6. Plan testing, training, and exercises
  7. Plan maintenance

- Four teams of individuals are involved in contingency planning and contingency operations: The business impact analysis data collection and documenation team, the contingency planning team, the incident response team, and the disaster recovery team.

- The incident response plan is a detailed set of processes and procedures that plan for, detect, and resolve the effects of an unexpected event on information resources and assets.

- For every scenario identified, the CP team creates three sets of procedures—for before, during, and after the incident—to detect, contain, and resolve the incident.

- Incident classification is the process by which the IR team examines an incident candidate and determines whether it constitutes an actual incident.

- Three categories of incident indicators are used: possible, probable, and definite.

- Possible indicators include the presence of unfamiliar files, the presence or execution of unknown programs or processes, the unusual consumption of computing resources, and unusual system crashes.

- Probable indicators include activities at unexpected times, the presence of new accounts, reported attacks, and notification from an IDS.

- Definite indicators include use of dormant accounts, changes to logs, the presence of hacker tools, notifications by partner or peer, and notification by hacker.

- When any one of the following happens, an actual incident is in progress: Loss of availability, loss of integrity, loss of confidentiality, violation of policy, or violation of law.

- When an actual incident violates civil or criminal law, the organization must notify the proper authorities for further action. Selecting the appropriate law enforcement agency depends on the type of crime committed.

- Disaster recovery planning encompasses preparation for handling and recovering from a disaster, whether natural or human-made.

- The DRP must include crisis management, the action steps taken during and after a disaster.

- Business continuity planning ensures that critical business functions continue if a catastrophic incident or disaster occurs. Business continuity plans can include provisions for hot sites, warm sites, cold sites, timeshares, service bureaus, and mutual agreements.

- The CP team should include a champion, a project manager, and team members.

- Business impact analysis (BIA) entails an investigation and assessment of the effects that various attacks can have on the organization.

- All plans must be tested to identify vulnerabilities, faults, and inefficient processes. Five testing strategies can be used to test contingency plans: Desk check, structured walk-through, simulation, parallel testing, and full-interruption testing.

Review Questions

1. What is the name for the broad process of planning for the unexpected? What are its primary components?

2. Which two communities of interest are usually associated with contingency planning? Which community must give authority to ensure broad support for the plans?

3. What percentage of businesses that do not have a disaster plan go out of business after a major loss, according to The Hartford insurance company?

4. List the seven-step CP process as defined by the NIST. Why is it the recommended standard approach to the process?

5. List and describe the four teams that perform the planning and execution of the CP plans and processes. What is the primary role of each?

6. Define the term *incident* as used in the context of IRP. How is it related to the concept of incident response?

7. List and describe the three criteria used to determine whether an actual incident is occurring.

8. List and describe the three sets of procedures used to detect, contain, and resolve an incident.

9. List and describe the four IR planning steps.

10. List and describe the actions that should be taken during an incident response.

11. What is an alert roster? What is an alert message? Describe the two ways they can be used.

12. List and describe several containment strategies given in the text. On which two tasks do they focus?

13. What is an incident damage assessment? What is it used for?

14. What criteria should be used when considering whether or not to involve law enforcement agencies during an incident?

15. What is a disaster recovery plan, and why is it important to the organization?

16. List and describe two rapid-onset disasters. List and describe one slow-onset disaster. How would you respond differently to the two types of disasters?

17. What is a business continuity plan, and why is it important?

18. What is a business impact analysis and what is it used for?

19. Why should continuity plans be tested and rehearsed?

20. Which types of organizations might use a unified continuity plan? Which types of organizations might use the various contingency planning components as separate plans? Why?

Exercises

1. Using a Web search engine, search for the terms "disaster recovery" and "business continuity." How many responses do you get for each term? Note how many companies do not distinguish between the two.

2. Go to csrc.nist.gov. Under "Publications," search for Special Publication (SP) 800-34 Contingency Planning Guide for Information Technology Systems, June 2002. Download and review this document. Summarize the key points for an in-class discussion.

3. Using a Web search engine, visit one of the popular disaster recovery/business continuity sites such as www.disasterrecoveryworld.com/, www.drj.com/, www.drie.org/, www.drii.org/, or csrc.nist.gov. Search for the terms "hot site," "warm site," and "cold site." Do the descriptions provided match those of the text? Why or why not?

4. Using the format provided in the text, design an incident response plan for your home computer. Include actions to be taken if each of the following events occur:
   - Virus attack
   - Power failure
   - Fire
   - Burst water pipe
   - ISP failure

   What other scenarios do you think are important to plan for?

5. Look for information on incident response on your institution's Web site. Does your institution have a published plan? Identify the areas in an academic institution's contingency planning that might differ from those of a "for-profit" institution.

Case Exercises

...Iris tried not to smile. She explained, "Of course, it isn't technically a disaster, but I understand what you mean. How much information is lost?"

Joel looked at her in dismay. "Lost? All of it! We had just saved the report and sent it to the department print server!"

Iris asked, "Where did you save it—to your local drive or to the department share?"

Joel tried to remember. "I think it was to the G: drive. Why?"

"Well, the G: drive is on a machine at the end of the hall, which doesn't have a water-based fire suppression system. It's probably fine. And if you did save it to your local drive, there's about an 80% chance we can get it anyway. I doubt the water damaged the hard drive itself." Iris continued, "We were lucky this time. If the fire had spread to the next room, the paper file storage could have been destroyed."

1. Extrapolate on the case. At what point could this incident have been declared a disaster? What would Iris have done differently if it had?

2. Identify the procedures that Joel could have taken to minimize the potential loss in this incident. What would he need to do different in the event of a disaster, if anything?

Endnotes

[1] NIST. *Special Publication 800-18: Guide for Developing Security Plans for Information Technology Systems.* December 1998. Accessed May 13, 2003 from csrc.nist.gov/publications/nistpubs/800-18/Planguide.doc, p. 31.

[2] *Why You Need a Disaster Recovery Plan.* Accessed May 13, 2003 from sb.thehartford.com/reduce_risk/disaster_recovery.asp.

[3] M. Swanson, A. Wohl, L. Pope, T. Grance, J. Hash, R. Thomas. *Contingency Planning Guide for Information Technology Systems*, NIST Special Publication 800-34. Accessed June 13, 2005, from csrc.nist.gov/publications/nistpubs/800-34/sp800-34.pdf.

[4] NIST. *Special Publication 800-18: Guide for Developing Security Plans for Information Technology Systems.* December 1998. Accessed May 13, 2003 from csrc.nist.gov/publications/nistpubs/800-18/Planguide.doc, p. 31.

[5] Tim Grance, Karen Kent, and Brian Kim. *Computer Security Incident Handling Guide*, Special Publication SP 800-61 (National Institute of Standards and Technology, 2004).

[6] Donald L. Pipkin. *Information Security: Protecting the Global Enterprise.* Upper Saddle River, NJ: Prentice Hall PTR, 2000:256.

[7] Donald L. Pipkin. *Information Security: Protecting the Global Enterprise.* Upper Saddle River, NJ: Prentice Hall PTR, 2000:285.

[8] Federal Bureau of Investigation. *Technology Crimes (San Francisco).* Available from the World Wide Web at http://www.fbi.gov/contact/fo/sanfran/sfcomputer.htm.

[9] International Federation of Red Cross and Red Crescent Societies. *Disaster Preparedness Training Programme.* Accessed March 1, 2003 from www.ifrc.org/what/dp/manual/introdp.pdf.

[10] Roberta Witty. What is crisis management? *Gartner Online*, September 19, 2001. Accessed June 26, 2002 from security1.gartner.com/story.php.id.152.jsp.

[11] Lanny J. Davis. *Truth to Tell: Tell It Early, Tell It All, Tell It Yourself: Notes from My White House Education*. New York: Free Press, May 1999.

[12] M. Swanson, et al. *Contingency Planning Guide for Information Technology Systems*, NIST Special Publication 800-34. Accessed July 13, 2005 from csrc.nist.gov/publications/nistpubs/800-34/sp800-34.pdf.

[13] Texas State Library and Archives State and Local Records Management Division. *Example Disaster Recovery Plan*. Accessed May 21, 2003 from www.tsl.state.tx.us/slrm/disaster/recovery_plan.pdf.

[14] Ronald L. Krutz and Russell Dean Vines. *The CISSP Prep Guide: Mastering the Ten Domains of Computer Security*. New York: John Wiley and Sons, 2001:288.

[15] Richard Marcinko and John Weisman. *Designation Gold*. New York: Pocket Books, 1998:preface.

CHAPTER **4**

INFORMATION SECURITY POLICY

QUOTE

Each problem that I solved became a rule which served afterwards to solve other problems.
René Descartes

Iris was returning from lunch when she ran into Susan Weinstein, one of RWW's senior account executives, who was accompanied by a man whom Iris did not know. Susan introduced him as Bob Watson, a prospective client. As they were chatting, Iris noticed Bob's distracted demeanor and Susan's forced smile and unusually stiff manner.

We didn't get the account, Iris realized.

A few minutes later, she saw why the meeting between RWW's account executive and prospective client did not go well. In the cubicle across the hall from Susan's office, two programmers were having lunch. Tim had his feet propped up on the desk. In one hand was a half-eaten hamburger; in the other, he held several playing cards. John had made himself comfortable by taking off his shoes. Next to his elbow was an open cup of coffee, which he had placed in the open tray of the PC's CD-ROM drive. On the desk between the two employees was a small pile of coins.

Iris went into her office and pulled the company's policy manual off the shelf. She was already familiar with RWW's policies, but for the steps she had in mind, she needed specifics. But RWW's policy and procedure manual did not contain policies about alerting employees to meetings with prospective clients, or eating and drinking in the workplace, or specifics about practices that supported data protection and other information security necessities.

Before Iris left that evening, she typed up her notes and scheduled an early morning meeting with her boss, Mike Edwards. As she left for home, she thought, *I think that Tim and John playing cards and eating in their office may have cost us a new account. I'll suggest to Mike that it's time for us to set up a policy review committee.*

LEARNING OBJECTIVES

Upon completion of this material, you should be able to:

- Define information security policy and understand its central role in a successful information security program
- Recognize the three major types of information security policy and know what goes into each type
- Develop, implement, and maintain various types of information security policies

INTRODUCTION

The previous chapters of this book explained the relevance and role of information security in the modern organization (Chapter 1) and described the various planning activities that can augment the effectiveness of an organization's information security programs (organizational planning in Chapter 2 and contingency planning in Chapter 3). This chapter focuses on information security policy: what it is, how to write it, how to implement it, and how to maintain it.

The success of any information security program lies in policy development. In 1989, the National Institute of Standards and Technology (NIST) addressed this point in Special Publication SP 500-169, *Executive Guide to the Protection of Information Resources*:

> The success of an information resources protection program depends on the policy generated, and on the attitude of management toward securing information on automated systems. You, the policy maker, set the tone and the emphasis on how important a role information security will have within your agency. Your primary responsibility is to set the information resource security policy for the organization with the objectives of reduced risk, compliance with laws and regulations and assurance of operational continuity, information integrity, and confidentiality.[1]

Policy is the essential foundation of an effective information security program. As stated by Charles Cresson Wood, in his widely referenced book *Information Security Policies Made Easy*,

The centrality of information security policies to virtually everything that happens in the information security field is increasingly evident. For example, system administrators cannot securely install a firewall unless they have received a set of clear information security policies. These policies will stipulate the type of transmission services that should be permitted, how to authenticate the identities of users, and how to log security-relevant events. An effective information security training and awareness effort cannot be initiated without writing information security policies because policies provide the essential content that can be utilized in training and awareness material.[2]

WHY POLICY?

A quality information security program begins and ends with policy. Properly developed and implemented policies enable the information security program to function almost seamlessly within the workplace. Although information security policies are the least expensive means of control to execute, they are often the most difficult to implement. Policy controls cost only the time and effort that the management team spends to create, approve, and communicate them, and that employees spend integrating the policies into their daily activities. Even when the management team hires an outside consultant to assist in the development of policy, the costs are minimal compared to the other forms of control, especially technical controls.

Some basic rules must be followed when shaping a policy:

- Policy should never conflict with law.
- Policy must be able to stand up in court, if challenged.
- Policy must be properly supported and administered.

Consider some of the facts that were revealed during the Enron scandal. The management team at Enron Energy Corporation was found to have lied about the organization's financial records, specifically about reported profits. The management team was also accused of a host of dubious business practices, including concealing financial losses and debts. The depth and breadth of the fraud was so great that tens of thousands of investors lost significant amounts of money and at least one executive committed suicide rather than face criminal charges. One of the company's accounting firms, the once well-respected Arthur Andersen, contributed to the problem by shredding literally tons of financial documents. Andersen's auditors and MIS consultants claimed that this shredding of working papers was Andersen's established policy. The former chief auditor from Andersen was fired after an internal probe revealed that the company shredded these documents, and deleted e-mail messages related to Enron, with the intent to conceal facts from investigators. He pleaded guilty to obstruction of justice, which carries a maximum sentence of 10 years in prison. While recent events in the Enron matter leave the final disposition of the case in doubt, the concept remains valid—an organization must conform to its own policy and that policy must be consistently applied.

Following a policy that conflicts with law is a criminal act. In the Enron/Andersen scandal, managers, employees, and others affiliated with Enron and Andersen went to jail claiming they were simply following policy. Since the policy as written did not violate any laws, they might have been able to use it as a defense if they had been consistently following that policy prior to the incidents in question. Andersen's document retention policy originally stated that staff must keep working papers for six years before destroying them. But client-related files, such as correspondence or other records, were only kept "until not useful." Managers and individual partners keeping such material in client folders or other files should "purge" the documents, the policy stated. But in cases of threatened litigation, Andersen staff must not destroy "related information." A subsequent change to the documentation retention policy at Andersen was interpreted as a mandate to shred all but the most essential working papers as soon as possible, unless destruction was precluded by an order for legal discovery. The shredding began right after Andersen management found out that Enron was to be investigated for fraudulent business practices, which pointed toward an intent to cover the firm's tracks, and those of its business partners. The shredding policy was a problem because it was not consistently applied—members of the Andersen organization assigned to the Enron project could not demonstrate that they followed the policy routinely, but only when it enabled them to shred incriminating documents.

Policy is often difficult to implement. The following guidelines may help in the formulation of information technology (IT) policy as well as information security policy.

1. All policies must contribute to the success of the organization.
2. Management must ensure the adequate sharing of responsibility for proper use of information systems.
3. End users of information systems should be involved in the steps of policy formulation.[3]

Policy must be tailored to the specific needs of the organization. While it is an admirable goal for policies to be complete and comprehensive, the existence of too many policies or policies that are too complex can cause confusion and possibly demoralize employees.

One implementation model that emphasizes the role of policy in an information security program is the **bull's-eye model**. Because it provides a proven mechanism for prioritizing complex changes, the bull's-eye model has become widely accepted among information security professionals. In this model, issues are addressed by moving from the general to the specific, always starting with policy. That is, the focus is on systemic solutions instead of individual problems. Figure 4-1 illustrates the four layers of the bull's-eye model:

1. Policies—the outer layer in the bull's-eye diagram
2. Networks—the place where threats from public networks meet the organization's networking infrastructure; in the past, most information security efforts have focused on networks, and until recently information security was often thought to be synonymous with network security
3. Systems—computers used as servers, desktop computers, and systems used for process control and manufacturing systems
4. Applications—all applications systems, ranging from packaged applications, such as office automation and e-mail programs, to high-end enterprise resource planning (ERP) packages, to custom application software developed by the organization

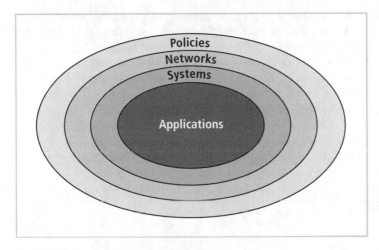

FIGURE 4-1   The Bull's-eye Model

Whether via the use of the bull's-eye model or any other methodology, until sound and usable IT and information security policy is developed, communicated, and enforced, no additional resources should be spent on controls.

Charles Cresson Wood summarizes the need for policy as follows:

> ...policies are important reference documents for internal audits and for the resolution of legal disputes about management's due diligence [and] policy documents can act as a clear statement of management's intent...[4]

Policy, Standards, and Practices

Policy is generally defined as a plan or course of action, as of a government, political party, or business, intended to influence and determine decisions, actions, and other matters. Policy represents the formal statement of the organization's managerial philosophy, in the case of our focus, the organization's information security philosophy. The traditional communities of interest described in previous chapters use policy to express their views regarding the security environment of the organization. This policy then becomes the basis or planning, management, and maintenance of the information security profile. Once policies are designed, created, approved, and implemented, the technologies and procedures that are necessary to accomplish them can be designed, developed, and implemented. In other words, policies comprise a set of rules that dictate acceptable and unacceptable behavior within an organization. Policies direct how issues should be addressed and technologies should be used. Policies should not specify the proper operation of equipment or software—this information should be placed in other documentation called standards, procedures, practices, and guidelines.

Policies must also specify the penalties for unacceptable behavior and define an appeals process. For example, an organization might prohibit the viewing of inappropriate Web sites at the workplace. To execute this policy, the organization must implement a set of standards that clarify and define exactly what is inappropriate in the workplace and to what degree the organization will act to stop the inappropriate behavior. A **standard** is a more detailed statement of what must be done to comply with policy. In the implementation of such an inappropriate-use policy, the organization might create a standard that all inappropriate content will be blocked and then list the material that is considered inappropriate. Later in the process, technical controls and their associated procedures might be established such that the network blocks access to pornographic Web sites. **Practices**, **procedures**, and **guidelines** explain how employees are to comply with policy. Figure 4-2 illustrates the relationship among policies, standards, and practices.

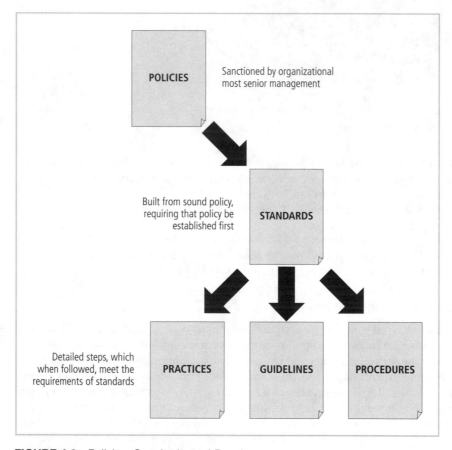

FIGURE 4-2 Policies, Standards, and Practices

To produce a complete information security policy, management must define three types of information security policies. These three types are based on NIST Special Publication 800-14, which outlines the requirements of writing policy for senior managers. (This document, which is discussed in greater detail later in this chapter, is recommended for professionals involved in creating policy and can be found at http://csrc.nist.gov/publications/nistpubs/800-14/800-14.pdf.) The three types of policy are as follows:

- Enterprise information security program policy
- Issue-specific security policies
- System-specific security policies

Each of these policy types is found in most organizations. The usual procedure is to first create the enterprise information security policy—the highest level of policy. After that, general security policy needs are met by developing issue- and system-specific policies. The three types of policy are described in detail in the following sections.

ENTERPRISE INFORMATION SECURITY POLICY

An **enterprise information security policy (EISP)**—also known as a security program policy, general security policy, IT security policy, high-level information security policy, or more simply, information security policy—sets the strategic direction, scope, and tone for all of an organization's security efforts. The EISP assigns responsibilities for the various areas of information security, including maintenance of information security policies and the practices and responsibilities of end users. In particular, the EISP guides the development, implementation, and management requirements of the information security program, which must be met by information security management, IT development, IT operations, and other specific security functions.

The EISP must directly support the organization's vision and mission statements. It must also be defensible if legal challenges to it arise. It is an executive-level document, drafted by the CISO in consultation with the CIO. Usually two to ten pages long, the EISP shapes the security philosophy in the IT environment. The EISP does not typically require frequent or routine modification, unless the strategic direction of the organization changes.

Integrating an Organization's Mission and Objectives into the EISP

The EISP plays a number of vital roles, not the least of which is to state the importance of information security to the organization's mission and objectives. As demonstrated in the organizational and information security planning processes discussed in Chapter 2, information security strategic planning derives from the IT strategic policy, which is itself derived from the organization's strategic planning. Unless the EISP directly reflects this association, the policy will likely become confusing and counterproductive.

How can the EISP be crafted to reflect the organization's mission and objectives? Suppose that an academic institution's mission statement promotes academic freedom, independent research, and the relatively unrestricted pursuit of knowledge. This institution's EISP should reflect great tolerance for the use of organizational technology, a commitment to protecting the intellectual property of the faculty, and a degree of understanding for study delving into what could be called esoteric areas. The EISP should not contradict the organizational mission statement. For example, if the academic institution's mission statement supports the unrestricted pursuit of knowledge, then the EISP should not restrict access to pornographic Web sites or specify penalties for such access. Such a policy would directly contradict the academic institution's mission statement.

EISP Elements

Although the specifics of EISPs vary from organization to organization, most EISP documents should include the following elements:

- An overview of the corporate philosophy on security
- Information on the structure of the information security organization and individuals who fulfill the information security role
- Fully articulated responsibilities for security that are shared by all members of the organization (employees, contractors, consultants, partners, and visitors)
- Fully articulated responsibilities for security that are *unique to each role* within the organization

The components of a good EISP are shown in Table 4-1.[5]

TABLE 4-1   Components of the EISP

Component	Description
Statement of Purpose	Answers the question, "What is this policy for?" Provides a framework that helps the reader to understand the intent of the document. Can include text such as the following. "This document will: • Identify the elements of a good security policy • Explain the need for information security • Specify the various categories of information security • Identify the information security responsibilities and roles • Identify appropriate levels of security through standards and guidelines This document establishes an overarching security policy and direction for our company. Individual departments are expected to establish standards, guidelines, and operating procedures that adhere to and reference this policy while addressing their specific and individual needs."[6]
Information Technology Security Elements	Defines information security. For example: "Protecting the confidentiality, integrity, and availability of information while in processing, transmission, and storage, through the use of policy, education and training, and technology..."[7] This section can also lay out security definitions or philosophies to clarify the policy.
Need for Information Technology Security	Provides information on the importance of information security in the organization and the obligation (legal and ethical) to protect critical information whether regarding customers, employees, or markets.
Information Technology Security Responsibilities and Roles	Defines the organizational structure designed to support information security within the organization. Identifies categories of individuals with responsibility for information security (IT department, management, users) and their information security responsibilities, including maintenance of this document.
Reference to Other Information Technology Standards and Guidelines	Lists other standards that influence and are influenced by this policy document, perhaps including relevant laws (federal and state) and other policies.

Example EISP Components

Charles Cresson Wood, the author of *Information Security Policy Made Easy*, includes a sample high-level information security policy in his book. Table 4-2 shows the specific components of this model, which, when integrated into the framework described in Table 4-1, provide detailed guidance for the creation of an organization-specific EISP. In his EISP version, Wood also provides justification for each policy statement and the target audience, information that would not typically be included in the policy document itself.

TABLE 4-2 Information Security Policy (EISP) Document Elements

1.	Protection of Information	
	Policy:	Information must be protected in a manner commensurate with its sensitivity, value, and criticality.
	Commentary:	This policy applies regardless of the media on which information is stored, the locations where the information is stored, the systems technology used to process the information, or the people who handle the information. This policy encourages examining the ways information flows through an organization. The policy also points to the scope of Information Security management's work throughout, and often even outside, an organization.
	Audience:	Technical staff
2.	Use of Information	
	Policy:	Company X information must be used only for the business purposes expressly authorized by management.
	Commentary:	This policy states that all nonapproved uses of Company X information are prohibited.
	Audience:	All
3.	Information Handling, Access, and Usage	
	Policy:	Information is a vital asset and all accesses to, uses of, and processing of Company X information must be consistent with policies and standards.
	Commentary:	This policy sets the context for a number of other information security policies. Such a statement is frequently incorporated into the first set of policies and summary material oriented toward users and members of the top management team. It is necessary for these people to appreciate how information has become a critical factor of production in business. This policy motivates the need for information security measures and to create a new understanding of the importance of information systems in organizations.
	Audience:	All
4.	Data and Program Damage Disclaimers	
	Policy:	Company X disclaims any responsibility for loss or damage to data or software that results from its efforts to protect the confidentiality, integrity, and availability of the information handled by computers and communications systems.

TABLE 4-2 Information Security Policy (EISP) Document Elements (continued)

Commentary:	This policy notifies users that they cannot hold Company X liable for damages associated with management's attempts to secure its system.
Audience:	End users
5. Legal Conflicts	
Policy:	Company X information security policies were drafted to meet or exceed the protections found in existing laws and regulations, and any Company X information security policy believed to be in conflict with existing laws or regulations must be promptly reported to Information Security management.
Commentary:	This policy creates a context for the requirements specified in an information security policy document. Sound policies go beyond laws and regulations, or at least ensure that an organization will meet the requirements specified by laws and regulations. This policy acknowledges support for laws and regulations, and expresses an intention to stay in compliance with existing laws and regulations. The policy is suitable for both internal information security policies and those made available to the public.
Audience:	End users
6. Exceptions to Policies	
Policy:	Exceptions to information security policies exist in rare instances where a risk assessment examining the implications of being out of compliance has been performed, where a standard risk acceptance form has been prepared by the data owner or management, and where this form has been approved by both Information Security management and Internal Audit management.
Commentary:	Management will be called upon to approve certain exceptions to policies. This policy clarifies that exceptions will be granted only after a risk acceptance form has been completed, signed, and approved. The form should include a statement where the data owner or management takes responsibility for any losses occurring from the out-of-compliance situation. The existence of such a form provides an escape value that can be used to address those situations where users insist on being out of compliance with policies. It is desirable to make all out-of-compliance situations both known and documented. This means that if there were to be a loss that occurred as a result of the situation, management could demonstrate to a judge or jury that it was aware of the situation, examined the risks, and decided to waive the relevant policy or standard.
Audience:	Management
7. Policy Nonenforcement	
Policy:	Management's nonenforcement of any policy requirement does not constitute its consent.
Commentary:	This policy notifies policy statement readers that they should not expect out-of-compliance conditions to be continued only because management has not yet enforced the policy. This policy eliminates any claim that local management may state that an out-of-compliance condition should remain as it is because the condition has been in existence for a considerable period of time.

Audience:	End users

8.   Violation of Law

Policy:	Company X management must seriously consider prosecution for all known violations of the law.
Commentary:	This policy encourages the prosecution of abusive and criminal acts. While a decision to prosecute will be contingent on the specifics of the case, management should not dismiss prosecution without review. This policy may be important in terms of communicating to those would-be perpetrators of abusive or criminal acts. Many computer crimes are not prosecuted and perpetrators often know this, expecting victim organizations to terminate them and suppress the entire affair.
Audience:	Management

9.   Revocation of Access Privileges

Policy:	Company X reserves the right to revoke a user's information technology privileges at any time.
Commentary:	This policy notifies users that they jeopardize their status as authorized users if they engage in activities that interfere with the normal and proper operation of Company X information systems, that adversely affect the ability of others to use these information systems, or that are harmful or offensive to others. For example, crashing the system could be expected to be harmful to other users, and would subject the perpetrator to disciplinary action including privilege revocation. The policy attempts to broadly describe an ethic for computing. Rather than specifying all of the adverse things that people could do, such as crashing a system, this policy is discreet and at a high level. This policy may give management latitude when it comes to deciding about privilege revocation.
Audience:	End users

10.   Industry-Specific Information Security Standards

Policy:	Company X information systems must employ industry-specific information security standards.
Commentary:	This policy requires systems designers and other technical staff to employ industry-standard controls. For example, in banking, encryption systems should use industry-specific systems for key management. Other industry-specific controls are relevant to the medical services industry, the aerospace and defense community, and other industry groups.
Audience:	Technical staff

11.   Use of Information Security Policies and Procedures

Policy:	All Company X information security documentation, including, but not limited to, policies, standards, and procedures, must be classified as "Internal Use Only," unless expressly created for external business processes or partners.

TABLE 4-2 Information Security Policy (EISP) Document Elements (continued)

Commentary:	This policy prevents workers from disclosing to outsiders the specifics of how Company X secures its information and systems. These details may be used to compromise Company X information and systems.
Audience:	All

Review and Evaluation

1. Security Controls Enforceability

Policy:	All information systems security controls must be enforceable prior to being adopted as a part of standard operating procedure.
Commentary:	Controls that are not enforced have a tendency to become useless. For example, if management has a policy about clean desks by locking up all sensitive materials after work, and it is not enforced, then employees quickly learn to ignore the policy. This policy is intended to require management to review the enforcement of controls, an issue that may not occur before adopting a control. A definition of the word "enforceable" may be advisable in some instances. For a control to be enforceable, it must be possible for management to clearly determine whether staff is in compliance with the control, and whether the control is effectively doing its intended job. The policy is purposefully vague about what constitutes standard operating procedure. This permits the policy to apply to a wide variety of circumstances, regardless of whether the control is documented, specific to a certain department, or used in an experimental way. In some instances, this policy may require the control designers to add a monitoring mechanism that reports on the status of the control. For example, encryption boxes from some vendors have lights that indicate that they are working, as they should.
Audience:	Management and technical staff

Source: Charles Cresson Wood. *Information Security Policies Made Easy*, 9th ed. NetIQ Corporation, 2003: 31–34. Used with permission.

The formulation of program policy in the EISP establishes the overall information security environment. As noted earlier, any number of specific issues may require policy guidance beyond what can be offered in the EISP. The next level of policy document, the issue-specific policy, delivers this needed specificity.

ISSUE-SPECIFIC SECURITY POLICY

A sound **issue-specific security policy (ISSP)** provides detailed, targeted guidance to instruct all members of the organization in the use of a process, technology, or system that is used by the organization. The ISSP should begin by introducing the organization's fundamental technological philosophy. It should assure members of the organization that its purpose is not to establish a foundation for administrative enforcement or legal prosecution, but rather to provide a common understanding of the purposes for which an employee can and cannot use the technology. Once this understanding is established, employees are free to use the technology without seeking approval for each type of use. This type of policy serves to protect both the employee and the organization from inefficiency and ambiguity.

The ISSP can sometimes become a confusing policy document. Its structure allows for more detailed elements than those found in higher-level policy documents like the EISP. While it is true that an ISSP may have some elements of a procedure included, its intent is to act as a readily accessible standard for compliance to the more broadly defined policies established in the EISP. We will later see that the system-specific policy document is even more procedural in some cases.

An effective ISSP accomplishes the following:

- It articulates the organization's expectations about how its technology-based system should be used.
- It documents how the technology-based system is controlled and identifies the processes and authorities that provide this control.
- It indemnifies the organization against liability for an employee's inappropriate or illegal use of the system.

An effective ISSP is a binding agreement between parties (the organization and its members) and shows that the organization has made a good-faith effort to ensure that its technology will not be used in an inappropriate manner. Every organization's ISSP has three characteristics:

- It addresses specific technology-based systems.
- It requires frequent updates.
- It contains an issue statement explaining the organization's position on a particular issue. [8]

An ISSP may cover many topics, including:

- Use of electronic mail
- Use of the Internet and the World Wide Web
- Incident response
- Disaster planning and/or business continuity planning
- Specific minimum configurations of computers to defend against worms and viruses
- Prohibitions against hacking or testing organization security controls
- Home use of company-owned computer equipment
- Use of personal equipment on company networks
- Use of telecommunications technologies (fax, phone)
- Use of photocopying equipment

While many other issue-specific policies in the organization, such as those described in the opening scenario, may fall outside the responsibility of information security, representatives of the information security unit can serve on policy committees and advise other departments in the creation and management of their policies.

Components of the ISSP

Table 4-3 describes the typical ISSP components. Each of these components is, in turn, discussed in the sections that follow. The specific situation of the particular organization dictates the exact wording of the security procedures as well as issues not covered within these general guidelines.

TABLE 4-3 Framework for Issue-Specific Security Policies

1. Statement of Purpose

   a. Scope and Applicability

   b. Definition of Technology Addressed

   c. Responsibilities

2. Authorized Uses

   a. User Access

   b. Fair and Responsible Use

   c. Protection of Privacy

3. Prohibited Uses

   a. Disruptive Use or Misuse

   b. Criminal Use

   c. Offensive or Harassing Materials

   d. Copyrighted, Licensed, or Other Intellectual Property

   e. Other Restrictions

4. Systems Management

   a. Management of Stored Materials

   b. Employer Monitoring

   c. Virus Protection

   d. Physical Security

   e. Encryption

5. Violations of Policy

   a. Procedures for Reporting Violations

   b. Penalties for Violations

6. Policy Review and Modification

   a. Scheduled Review of Policy

   b. Procedures for Modification

7. Limitations of Liability

   a. Statements of Liability

   b. Other Disclaimers

Source: Michael E. Whitman, Anthony M. Townsend, and Robert J. Alberts. Considerations for an effective telecommunications-use policy. *Communications of the ACM*, June 1999, 42(6):101–109.

Statement of Purpose

The ISSP should begin with a clear statement of purpose that outlines the scope and applicability of the policy. It should address the following questions: What purpose does this policy serve? Who is responsible and accountable for policy implementation? What technologies and issues does the policy document address?

Authorized Uses

This section of the policy statement explains who can use the technology governed by the policy and for what purposes. Recall that an organization's information systems are the exclusive property of the organization, and users have no particular rights of use. Each technology and process is provided for business operations. This section defines "fair and responsible use" of equipment and other organizational assets, and it addresses key legal issues, such as protection of personal information and privacy. The policy makes any use for any purpose not explicitly identified a misuse of equipment. When it is management's intention to allow some selective, extra-organizational uses, such as using company systems and networks for noncommercial personal e-mail, that use must be allowed for in the policy.

Prohibited Uses

While the previous section specifies what the issue or technology *can* be used for, this section outlines what it *cannot* be used for. Unless a particular use is clearly prohibited, the organization cannot penalize employees for it. For example, the following actions might be prohibited: personal use, disruptive use or misuse, criminal use, offensive or harassing materials, and infringement of copyrighted, licensed, or other intellectual property.

In some organizations, that which is not permitted is prohibited; while in others, that which is not prohibited is permitted. In either case, be sure to state clearly the assumptions and then spell out the exceptions. The organization's stance will make a difference in how the topic of usage is addressed. Some organizations will use the approach given here that explicitly states what is allowed and prohibited. Other organizations might want to be less explicit, and might combine the Authorized and Prohibited Uses sections into a single section titled Appropriate Uses.

Systems Management

This section focuses on the users' relationships to systems management. A company may want to issue specific rules regarding the use of e-mail and electronic documents, and storage of those documents, as well as guidelines about authorized employer monitoring, and the physical and electronic security of e-mail and other electronic documents. The Systems Management section should specify users' and systems administrators' responsibilities, so that all parties know what they are accountable for.

Violations of Policy

This section specifies the penalties and repercussions of violating the usage and systems management policies. Penalties should be laid out for each type or category of violation.

This section should also provide instructions on how to report observed or suspected violations, either openly or anonymously, because some employees may fear that powerful individuals in the organization could retaliate against someone who reports violations. Anonymous submissions are often the only way to convince individual users to report the unauthorized activities of other, more influential employees.

Policy Review and Modification

Every policy should contain procedures and a timetable for periodic review. This section should outline a specific methodology for the review and modification of the ISSP, so as to ensure that users always have guidelines that reflect the organization's current technologies and needs.

Limitations of Liability

The final section offers a general statement of liability or a set of disclaimers. If an individual employee is caught conducting illegal activities with organizational equipment or assets, management does not want the organization to be held liable. Therefore, if employees violate a company policy or any law using company technologies, the company will not protect them and the company is not liable for their actions, assuming that the violation is not known or sanctioned by management.

Implementing the ISSP

A number of approaches for creating and managing ISSPs are possible. Three of the most common are described here:

- Create a number of independent ISSP documents, each tailored to a specific issue.
- Create a single comprehensive ISSP document that covers all issues.
- Create a modular ISSP document that unifies policy creation and administration, while maintaining each specific issue's requirements. This approach results in a modular document with a standard template for structure and appearance, in which certain aspects are standardized, while others—including much of the content—are customized for each issue. The end result is several independent ISSP documents, all derived from a common template and physically well managed and easy to use.

Table 4-4 describes the advantages and disadvantages of each approach.

TABLE 4-4 ISSP Approaches

Approach	Advantages	Disadvantages
Individual Policy	Clear assignment to a responsible department Written by those with superior subject matter expertise for technology-specific systems	Typically yields a scattershot result that fails to cover all of the necessary issues Can suffer from poor policy dissemination, enforcement, and review

TABLE 4-4 ISSP Approaches (continued)

Approach	Advantages	Disadvantages
Comprehensive Policy	Well controlled by centrally managed procedures assuring complete topic coverage Often provides better formal procedures than when policies are individually formulated Usually identifies processes for dissemination, enforcement, and review	May overgeneralize the issues and skip over vulnerabilities May be written by those with less complete subject matter expertise
Modular Policy	Often considered an optimal balance between the individual ISSP and the comprehensive ISSP approaches Well controlled by centrally managed procedures, assuring complete topic coverage Clear assignment to a responsible department Written by those with superior subject matter expertise for technology-specific systems	May be more expensive than other alternatives Implementation can be difficult to manage

The recommended approach is the modular policy because it offers a balance between issue orientation and policy management. The policies generated via this approach are individual modules, each created and updated by the individuals who are responsible for a specific issue. These individuals report to a central policy administration group that incorporates these specific issues into an overall policy.

VIEWPOINT

Information Security Policies: Turning People into the First Line of Defense

By Chris Pick, Vice President, Market Strategy, NetIQ Solutions by Attachmate

In my career as a security professional, I served as an information security consultant for Ernst and Young for many years and wrote hundreds of policies for organizations in almost every market around the world. Typically, these policies are collected as printed documents in a rather large, three-ring binder that sits imposingly on the shelf. And that's the problem with most security policies. Too many policies simply stay on the shelf gathering dust—never making an impact on what actually happens in the day-to-day operations of an organization.

continued

SYSTEM-SPECIFIC SECURITY POLICY

While an EISP is a high-level policy, and an ISSP is a policy document that may contain procedural elements, both are formalized as written documents readily identifiable as policy. The system-specific security policies (SysSPs) sometimes have a different look and may, in fact, seem like procedures to some readers. SysSPs often function as standards or procedures to be used when configuring or maintaining systems—for example, to configure and operate a network firewall. Such a document could include a statement of managerial intent; guidance to network engineers on selecting, configuring, and operating firewalls; and an access control list that defines levels of access for each authorized user. Note that the policy framework ensures that the creation and use of an ISSP or SysSP is enabled by the EISP policy position on those topic areas.

SysSPs can be separated into two general groups, managerial guidance and technical specifications, or they may combine these two types of SysSP content into a single policy document, as in the preceding example.

Managerial Guidance SysSPs

A managerial guidance SysSP document is created by management to guide the implementation and configuration of technology as well as to address the behavior of people in the organization in ways that support the security of information. For example, while the specific configuration of a firewall belongs in the technical specifications SysSP, the process of constructing and implementing the firewall must follow guidelines established by management. An organization might not want its employees to have access to the Internet via the organization's network, for instance; in that case, the firewall has to be implemented according to this rule.

Firewalls are not the only area that may require SysSPs. Any technology that affects the confidentiality, integrity, or availability of information must be assessed to evaluate the trade-off between improved security and restrictions.

SysSPs can be developed at the same time as ISSPs, or they can be prepared in advance of their related ISSPs. Before management can craft a policy informing users what they can do with the technology and how they may do it, it might be necessary for system administrators to configure and operate the system. Some organizations may prefer to develop ISSPs and SysSPs in tandem, so that operational procedures and user guidelines are created simultaneously.

Technical Specifications SysSPs

While a manager may work with a systems administrator to create managerial policy as described in the preceding section, the system administrator may in turn need to create a different type of policy to implement the managerial policy. For example, an ISSP may require that user passwords be changed quarterly; a systems administrator can implement a technical control within a specific application to enforce this policy. The screen shots in Figure 4-3 illustrate network operating systems configured to implement a password change requirement.

There are two general methods of implementing such technical controls: access control lists and configuration rules.

Access Control Lists

Access control lists (ACLs) include the user access lists, matrices, and capability tables that govern the rights and privileges of users. ACLs can control access to file storage systems, object brokers, or other network communications devices. A **capability table** specifies which subjects and objects that users or groups can access; in some systems, capability tables are called user profiles or user policies. These specifications frequently take the form of complex matrices, in which assets are listed along the column headers, while users are listed along the row headers. The resulting matrix would then contain ACLs in columns for a particular device or asset, while a row would represent the capability table for a particular user.

The Microsoft Windows 2003 and Novell Netware families of systems translate ACLs into configuration sets that administrators can use to control access to their systems. The level of detail and specificity (often called granularity) may vary from system to system,

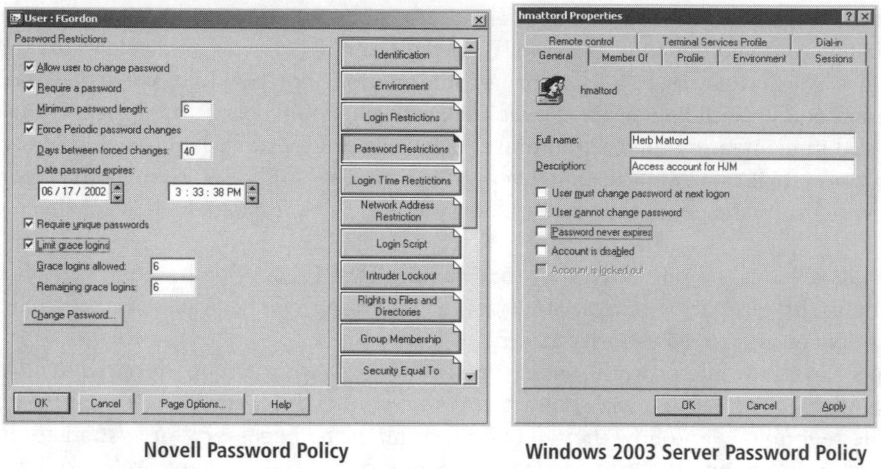

Novell Password Policy	Windows 2003 Server Password Policy

FIGURE 4-3 Password SysSP

but in general ACLs enable administrations to restrict access according to user, computer, time, duration, or even a particular file. This range gives a great deal of control to the administrator. In general, ACLs regulate the following aspects of access:

- *Who* can use the system
- *What* authorized users can access
- *When* authorized users can access the system
- *Where* authorized users can access the system from
- *How* authorized users can access the system

Restricting *who* can use the system requires no explanation. To restrict *what* users can access—for example, which printers, files, communications, and applications—administrators assign user privileges, such as the following:

- Read
- Write
- Execute

This list is not exhaustive, but contains some key ACL privilege types. Figures 4-4 and 4-5 show how the ACL security model has been implemented by Linux and Microsoft operating systems, respectively.

Configuration Rules

Configuration rules are configuration codes that guide the execution of the system when information is passing through it. Rule-based policies are more specific to the operation of a system than ACLs are, and they may or may not deal with users directly. Many security systems require specific configuration scripts that dictate which actions to perform on

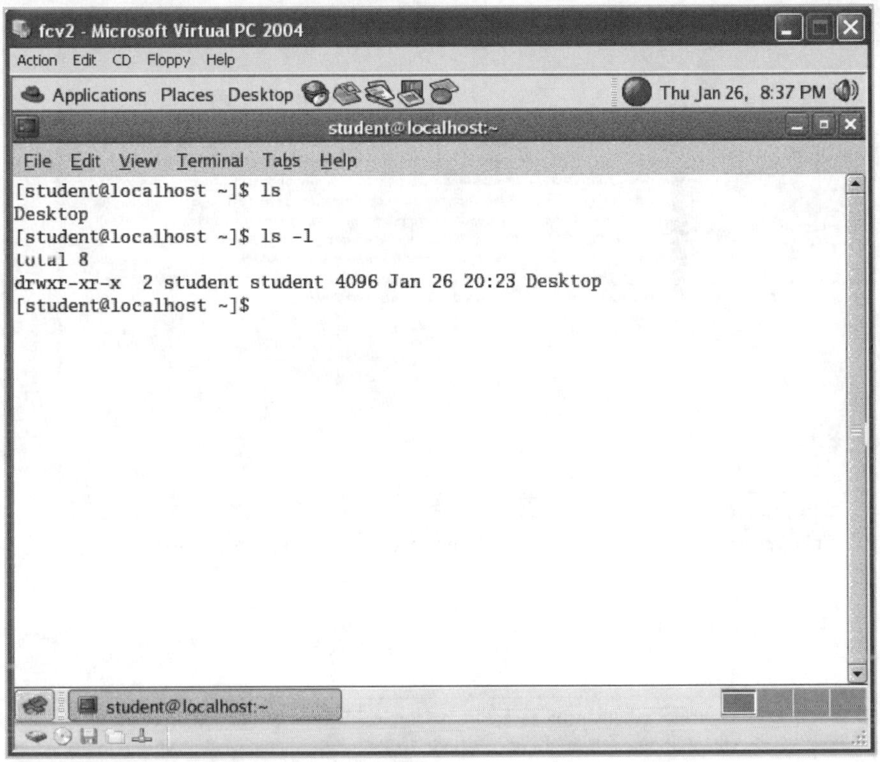

```
fcv2 - Microsoft Virtual PC 2004                          [_][□][X]
Action  Edit  CD  Floppy  Help

Applications  Places  Desktop  🌐🖥🐢💾🐢         Thu Jan 26,  8:37 PM 🔊
                        student@localhost:~                 [_][□][X]
File  Edit  View  Terminal  Tabs  Help
[student@localhost ~]$ ls
Desktop
[student@localhost ~]$ ls -l
total 8
drwxr-xr-x  2 student student 4096 Jan 26 20:23 Desktop
[student@localhost ~]$
```

FIGURE 4-4 Linux ACL

each set of information they process. Examples include firewalls, intrusion detection systems (IDSs), and proxy servers. Figures 4-6 and 4-7 show how this security model has been implemented by Checkpoint in a firewall rule set and by Tripwire in an IDS rule set, respectively.

Combination SysSPs

Many organizations create a single document that combines elements of both the management guidance SysSP and the technical specifications SysSP. While this document can be somewhat confusing to the users of the policies, it is very practical to have the guidance from both perspectives in a single place. Such a document should carefully articulate the required actions as the procedures are presented.

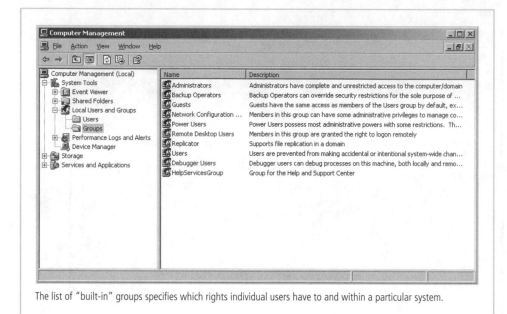

The list of "built-in" groups specifies which rights individual users have to and within a particular system.

FIGURE 4-5 Windows XP ACL

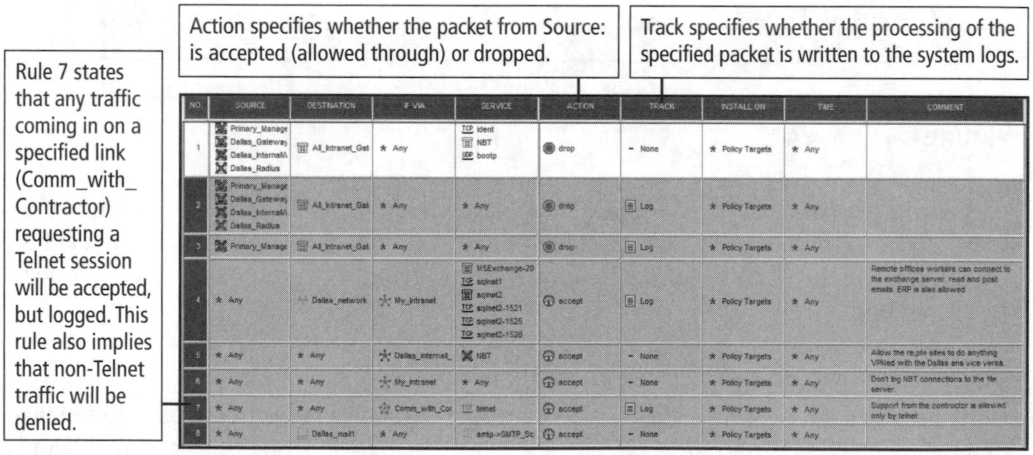

Action specifies whether the packet from Source: is accepted (allowed through) or dropped.

Track specifies whether the processing of the specified packet is written to the system logs.

Rule 7 states that any traffic coming in on a specified link (Comm_with_ Contractor) requesting a Telnet session will be accepted, but logged. This rule also implies that non-Telnet traffic will be denied.

FIGURE 4-6 Firewall Configuration Rules

```
###################################################################### #
# This Policy was created by the Tripwire Policy Resource Center      # #
# Created on: Mon Mar 25 21:54:27 GMT 2002                           # #
#       Copyright (C) 2001, Tripwire Inc. Reprinted with permission  #
###################################################################### #
@@section global
SYSTEMDRIVE="C:" ;
BOOTDRIVE="C:" ;
SYSTEMROOT="C:\\Winnt" ;
PROGRAMFILES="C:\\Program Files" ;
IE5="C:\\Program Files\\Plus!\\Microsoft Internet" ;
# Email Recipients # #
SIG_HIGHEST_MAILRECIPIENTS  = "Administrator" ;
SIG_HIGH_MAILRECIPIENTS     = "Administrator" ;
SIG_MED_MAILRECIPIENTS      = "Administrator" ;
SIG_LOW_MAILRECIPIENTS      = "Administrator" ;
# Security Levels # #
SIG_LOW      = 33 ;      # Non-critical files that are of minimal security impact
SIG_MED      = 66 ;      # Non-critical files that are of significant security impact
SIG_HIGH     = 100 ;     # Critical files that are significant points of vulnerability
SIG_HIGHEST  = 1000 ;    # Super-critical files.  Mostly used for the TCB section.
@@section NTFS
{
 rulename = "IE 5.01 Registry keys",
 severity = $ (SIG_HIGHEST),
 emailto  = $ (SIG_HIGHEST_MAILRECIPIENTS),
 recurse  = true
}
{
 $ (HKLM_CCS_SM_CBadApps)                        -> $ (REG_SEC_HIGHEST) ;
 $ (HKLM_CRYPT)                                  -> $ (REG_SEC_HIGHEST) ;
 $ (HKLM_CRYPTINIT)                              -> $ (REG_SEC_HIGHEST) ;
 $ (HKLM_CRYPTMSG)                               -> $ (REG_SEC_HIGHEST) ;
 $ (HKLM_CRYPTSIGN)                              -> $ (REG_SEC_HIGHEST) ;
 $ (HKLM_EventSystem)                            -> $ (REG_SEC_HIGHEST) ;
 $ (HKLM_SW_IE_Setup)                            -> $ (REG_SEC_HIGHEST) ;
 $ (HKLM_WHM)                                    -> $ (REG_SEC_HIGHEST) ;
 $ (HKLM_WIE)                                    -> $ (REG_SEC_HIGHEST) ;
 $ (HKLM_WIE_TNF_Setup)                          -> $ (REG_SEC_HIGHEST) ;
 $ (HKLM_WMM)                                    -> $ (REG_SEC_HIGHEST) ;
}
#          Snippet Name: A Nimda Virus Rule                          # #
#         Snippet Author: support@tripwire.com                       # #
#        Snippet Version: 1.0.0                                      # #
#                Nimda#                                              # #
@@section NTFS
{
 rulename = "Nimda File Scan",
 Severity = 100
}
{
 $ (SYSTEMROOT)\ZaCker.vbs -> $ (IgnoreNone);
 $ (SYSTEMROOT)\MixDaLaL.vbs -> $ (IgnoreNone);
 $ (SYSTEMDIR)\ZaCker.vbs -> $ (IgnoreNone);
 $ (SYSTEMDIR)\MixDaLaL.vbs -> $ (IgnoreNone);
}
```

This section defines which security levels are to be used and who is to be notified if that level file is modified.

This section looks for unauthorized modifications to Internet Explorer Registry edits, most likely due to virus or hacker efforts.

This section defines the rules necessary to detect and react to the Nimda virus.

FIGURE 4-7 IDS Configuration Rules

GUIDELINES FOR EFFECTIVE POLICY

How policy is developed and implemented can help or hinder its usefulness to the organization. In general, policy is only enforceable if it is properly designed, developed, and implemented using a process that assures repeatable results. One effective approach has six stages: development, dissemination (distribution), review (reading), comprehension (understanding), compliance (agreement), and uniform enforcement. Thus, for policies to be effective, they must be properly:

1. Developed using industry-accepted practices
2. Distributed or disseminated using all appropriate methods
3. Reviewed or read by all employees
4. Understood by all employees
5. Formally agreed to by act or assertion
6. Uniformly applied and enforced

We will examine each of these stages in the sections that follow.

Developing Information Security Policy

It is often useful to view policy development as a two-part project. In the first part of the project, policy is designed and developed (or, as in the case of an outdated policy, redesigned and rewritten), and in the second part, management processes are established to perpetuate the policy within the organization. The former is an exercise in project management, whereas the latter requires adherence to good business practices.

Like any IT project, a policy development or redevelopment project should be well planned, properly funded, and aggressively managed to ensure that it is completed on time and within budget. One way to accomplish this goal is to use a systems development life cycle (SDLC). You are already familiar with a variant of the SDLC, the SecSDLC, from Chapter 2. The following discussion expands the use of the SecSDLC model by discussing the tasks that could be included in each phase of the SecSDLC during a policy development project. You will learn more about project management in the realm of information security in Chapter 12.

Investigation Phase

During the investigation phase the policy development team should attain the following:

- Support from senior management, because any project without it has a reduced chance of success. Only with the support of top management will a specific policy receive the attention it deserves from the intermediate-level managers who must implement it, and from the users who must comply with it.
- Support and active involvement of IT management, specifically the CIO. Only with the CIO's active support will technology area managers be motivated to participate in policy development and support the implementation efforts to deploy it once created.
- Clear articulation of goals.

- Participation of the correct individuals from the communities of interest affected by the recommended policies. Assembling the right team, by ensuring the participation of the proper representatives from the groups that will be affected by the new policies, is very important. The team must include representatives from the legal department, the human resources department, and end users of the various IT systems covered by the policies, as well as a *project champion* with sufficient stature and prestige to accomplish the goals of the project, and a capable project manager to see the project through to completion.

- A detailed outline of the scope of the policy development project, and sound estimates for the cost and scheduling of the project.

Analysis Phase

The analysis phase should produce the following:

- A new or recent risk assessment or IT audit documenting the current information security needs of the organization. This risk assessment should include any loss history, as well as past lawsuits, grievances, or other records of negative outcomes from information security areas.
- The gathering of key reference materials—including any existing policies—in addition to the items noted above. Sometimes policy documents that affect information security will be housed in the Human Resources department as well as the accounting, finance, legal, or corporate security department.

According to Charles Cresson Wood:

> Some who are facing significant time or resource constraints will be tempted to skip the above-mentioned data gathering processes. Whenever data gathering is significantly abbreviated, the likelihood that management will reject the resulting document increases. It is through this data gathering process that management's view of information security can be identified, the policies that already exist, the policies that need to be added or changed, how management enforces policies, the unique vulnerabilities that the organization faces, and other essential background information. If serious consideration has not been given to this background information, it is unlikely that a newly written information security policy will be responsive to the true needs of the organization.[9]

Design Phase

During the design phase the team must create a plan to distribute, and verify the distribution of, the policies. Members of the organization must explicitly acknowledge that they have received and read the policy. Otherwise, an employee can claim never to have seen a policy, and unless the manager can produce strong evidence to the contrary, any enforcement action, such as dismissal for inappropriate use of the Web, can be overturned and punitive damages might be awarded to the former employee. The simplest way to document acknowledgment of a written policy is to attach a cover sheet that states: "I have received, read, understood, and agreed to this policy." The employee's signature and date provides a paper trail of his or her receipt of the policy.

Some situations preclude a formal documentation process. Take, for instance, student use of campus computer labs. Most universities have stringent policies on what students can and cannot do in a computer lab. These policies are usually posted on the Web, in the student handbook, in course catalogs, and in a number of other locations, including bulletin boards in the labs. For the policies to be enforceable, however, some mechanism must be established that records the student's acknowledgment of the policy. This is frequently accomplished with a banner screen that displays a brief statement warning the user that the policy is in place, and that use of the system constitutes acceptance of the policy. The user must then click an OK button or press a key to get past the screen. This method can be ineffective if the acknowledgment screen does not require any unusual action to move past it, however; this kind of acknowledgment screen is often called a *blow-by screen*.

In the past, companies used banners or pop-up windows to display *end-user license agreements (EULAs)*. An EULA, which is usually presented on a screen to the user during software installation, spells out fair and responsible use of the software being installed. At one time, EULAs were typically presented on blow-by screens, with an instruction like "Press any key to agree," so that users could install the software without explicitly agreeing to the restrictions on software use, thus negating the software company's legal claim. Today, most EULA screens require that the user click a button, press a function key, or type words to agree to the terms of the EULA. Similar methods are used on network and computer logins to reinforce acknowledgement of the system use policy. Figure 4-8 provides an example of a EULA screen that requires specific user input.

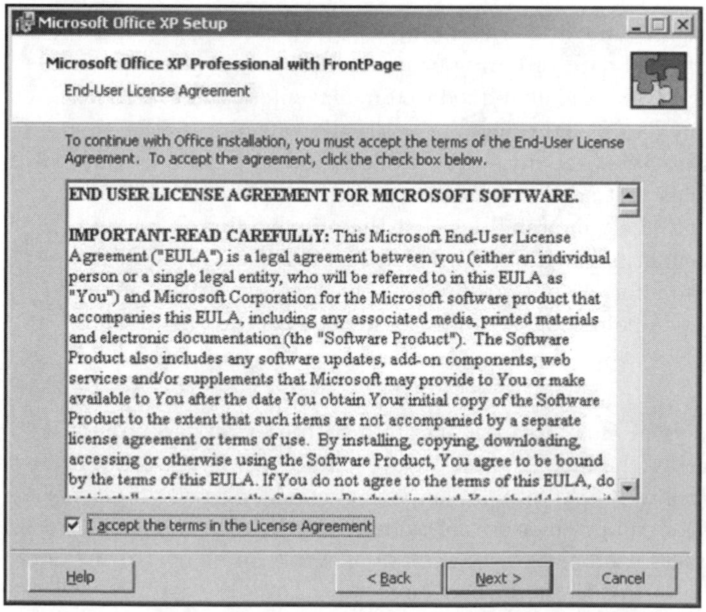

FIGURE 4-8   End User License Agreement for Microsoft Word XP

The design should also include specifications for any automated tool used for the creation and management of policy documents, as well as revisions to feasibility analysis reports based on improved costs and benefits as the design is clarified.

Implementation Phase

In the implementation phase, the policy development team actually writes the policies. This can be a challenging process, but you do not have to come up with a good policy document from scratch. A number of resources are at your disposal, including:

- The Web, where you can search for other, similar policies. The point here is not to advocate wholesale copying of these policies, but rather to encourage you to look for ideas on what should be contained in your policy. For example, dozens of policies available on the Web describe fair and responsible use of various technologies. What you may not find, however, are policies that relate to sensitive internal documents or processes.
- Government sites, such as http://csrc.nist.gov and http://fasp.nist.gov/fasp/, that contain numerous sample policies and policy support documents, including SP 800-12, *An Introduction to Computer Security: The NIST Handbook*. While these policies are typically directed toward or applicable to federal government Web sites, you may be able to adapt some sections to meet your organization's needs.
- Professional literature. Several authors have published books on the subject. Of particular note is Charles Cresson Wood's book *Information Security Policy Made Easy*, which not only provides more than 1,000 pages of policies, but also makes those policies available in electronic format, complete with permission to use them in internal documents. Exercise caution when using such resources, however; it is extremely easy to take large sections of policy and end up with a massive document that is neither publishable nor enforceable.
- Peer networks. Other information security professionals have to write similar policies and implement similar plans. Attend meetings like those offered by the Information Systems Security Association (www.issa.org), and ask your peers.
- Professional consultants. Policy is one area of information security that can certainly be developed in-house. However, if you simply cannot find the time to develop your own policy, then hiring outside consultants may be your last option. Keep in mind that no consultant can know your organization as thoroughly as you do, and the consultant may simply design generic policies that you can then adapt to your specific situation.

During the implementation phase, the policy development team ensures that the policy is prepared correctly, distributed, read, and understood by those to whom it applies, and that those individuals' understanding and acceptance of the policy are documented as described in later sections of this chapter.

Maintenance Phase

During the maintenance phase, the policy development team monitors, maintains, and modifies the policy as needed to ensure that it remains effective as a tool to meet changing threats. The policy should have a built-in mechanism through which users can report problems, preferably anonymously, with the policy.

Policy Distribution

While it might seem straightforward, actually getting the policy document into the hands of employees can require a substantial investment by the organization in order to be effective. The most common alternatives are hard-copy distribution; either directly distributing a copy to the employee or posting the policy in a publicly available location. Posting a policy on a bulletin board or other public area may be insufficient, unless another policy requires the employees to read the bulletin board on a specified schedule (daily, weekly, and so forth). Distribution by internal or external mail still may not guarantee that the individual really receives the document. Unless the organization can prove the policy actually reaches the end users, it cannot be enforced. Unlike in civil or criminal law, ignorance of policy, where policy is inadequately distributed, is considered an acceptable excuse. Distribution of classified policies—those containing confidential internal information, preferably anonymously—requires additional levels of controls, in the labeling of the document, in the dissemination of new policy, and in the collection and destruction of older versions.

Another common method of dissemination is by electronic means–e-mail, intranet, or document management systems. Perhaps the easiest way is to post current and archived versions of policies on a secure intranet in html or pdf (Adobe) form. The organization still must enable a mechanism to prove distribution, such as an auditing log tracking when users access the documents. E-mail as an alternative delivery mechanism has advantages and disadvantages. While it is easy to send a document to an employee, and even track when the employee opens the e-mail, it becomes cumbersome for employees to review inapplicable policies, and the document can quickly fill the e-mail application's storage capacity. Perhaps the best method is electronic policy distribution software, which is described in the section on Automated Tools. Electronic policy management software can not only assist in the distribution of policy documents, but can also support the development and assessment of comprehension.[10]

Policy Reading

Barriers to employees' reading policies can arise from literacy or language issues. A surprisingly large percentage of the workforce is considered functionally illiterate. A 2003 survey conducted by the National Assessment of Adult Literacy (NAAL), a federal agency that works in concert with the U.S. Department of Education, found that 14% of American adults scored "below basic" level in prose literacy.[11] Many jobs do not require literacy skills, for example custodial, groundskeepers, or production line workers. Because such workers can still pose risks to information security, they must be made familiar with the policy, even if it must be read to them. Visually impaired employees also require additional assistance, either through audio versions of the document or large type.

Of the 11 million adults identified as illiterate in the 2003 NAAL survey, 7 million could not answer simple test questions due to pure reading deficiencies, and 4 million could not take the test because of language barriers.[12] The number of non-English speaking residents in the United States continues to climb. However, language challenges are not restricted to those organization with locations in the United States. Multinational organizations also must deal with the challenges of gauging reading levels of foreign citizens. Simple translations of policy documents, while a minimum requirement, necessitate careful monitoring. Translation issues have long created challenges for organizations. For example, a translation error in 1989 resulted in the Nike Corporation running an advertisement showing a Samburu tribesman speaking in his native language, ostensibly echoing the company slogan. What he really says is, "I don't want these. Give me big shoes."[13]

Policy Comprehension

A quote attributed to Confucius states: "Tell me, and I forget; show me, and I remember; let me do and I understand." In the policy arena this means that simply making certain that a copy of the policy gets to employees in a form they can review may not be sufficient to ensure that they truly understand what the policy requires of them. Comprehension is defined as: "the ability to grasp the meaning of material. [Comprehension] may be shown ... to go one step beyond the simple remembering of material, and represent the lowest level of understanding."[14]

To be certain that employees understand the policy, the document must be written at a reasonable reading level, with minimal technical jargon and management terminology. The readability statistics supplied by most productivity suite applications like Microsoft Word can help to determine the reading level of the policy. Figure 4-9 presents the readability statistics for this section.

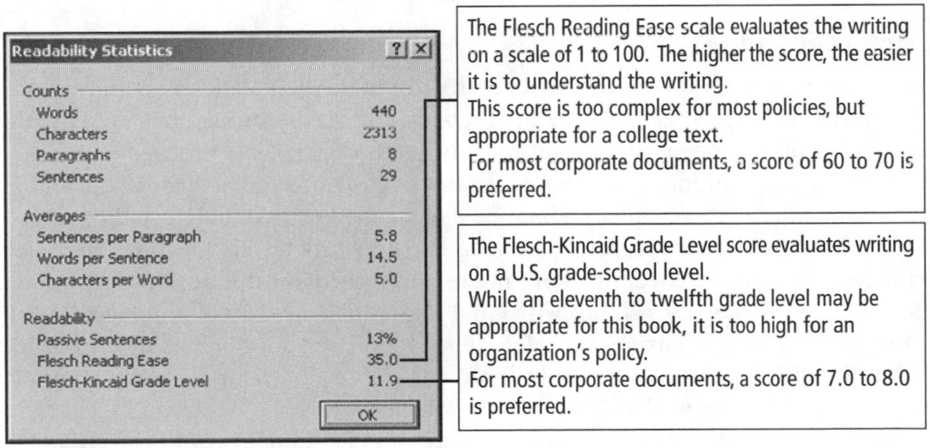

Readability Statistics	? X
Counts	
Words	440
Characters	2313
Paragraphs	8
Sentences	29
Averages	
Sentences per Paragraph	5.8
Words per Sentence	14.5
Characters per Word	5.0
Readability	
Passive Sentences	13%
Flesch Reading Ease	35.0
Flesch-Kincaid Grade Level	11.9
OK	

The Flesch Reading Ease scale evaluates the writing on a scale of 1 to 100. The higher the score, the easier it is to understand the writing.
This score is too complex for most policies, but appropriate for a college text.
For most corporate documents, a score of 60 to 70 is preferred.

The Flesch-Kincaid Grade Level score evaluates writing on a U.S. grade-school level.
While an eleventh to twelfth grade level may be appropriate for this book, it is too high for an organization's policy.
For most corporate documents, a score of 7.0 to 8.0 is preferred.

FIGURE 4-9 Readability Statistics

The next step is to use some form of assessment to gauge how well employees understand the policy's underlying issues. Quizzes and other forms of examination can be employed to assess quantitatively which employees understand the policy by earning a minimum score (i.e., 70%), and which employees require additional training and awareness efforts before the policy can be enforced. Quizzes can be distributed in either hardcopy or electronic formats. The management of employee performance on policy comprehension can be assisted by the electronic policy management systems mentioned earlier.[15]

Policy Compliance

As Michael E. Whitman has written,

> Policies must be agreed to by act or affirmation. Agreement by act occurs when the employee performs an action, which requires them to acknowledge understanding of the policy, prior to use of a technology or organizational resource. Network banners, end-user license agreements, and posted warnings can serve to meet this burden of proof. However, these in and of themselves may not be sufficient. Only through direct collection of a signature or the equivalent digital alternative can the organization prove that it has obtained an agreement to comply with policy, which also demonstrates that the previous conditions have been met of distributed, read, and understood.[16]

What if an employee refuses explicitly to agree to comply with policy? Can the organization deny access to information that an individual needs to do their job? While this situation has not yet been adjudicated in the legal system, it seems clear that failure to agree to a policy is tantamount to refusing to work, and thus may be grounds for termination. Organizations can avoid this dilemma by incorporating policy confirmation statements into employment contracts, annual evaluations, or other documents necessary for the individual's continued employment.

Policy Enforcement

The final component of design and implementation of effective policies is uniform and impartial enforcement. As in law enforcement, policy enforcement must be able to withstand external scrutiny. Because this scrutiny may occur during legal proceedings, for example in a civil suit contending wrongful termination, organizations must establish high standards of due care with regard to policy management. For instance, if policy mandates that all employees wear identification badges in a clearly visible location, and select members of management decided they were not required to follow this policy, any actions taken against other employees will not withstand legal challenges. If an employee is punished, censured, or dismissed as a result of a refusal to follow policy, and is able to demonstrate that the policies are not uniformly enforced or applied, then the organization may find itself facing punitive as well as compensatory damages.

One forward-thinking organization found a way to enlist employees in the enforcement of policy. After the organization had just published a new ID badge policy, the manager responsible for the policy was seen without his ID. One of his employees chided him in jest, saying, "You must be a visitor here, since you don't have an ID. Can I help you?" The manager smiled and promptly produced his ID, along with a $20 bill, which he presented to the employee as a reward for vigilant policy enforcement. Soon, the entire staff was routinely challenging anyone without a badge.[17]

Automated Tools

The need for effective policy management has led to the emergence of a class of software tools that supports policy development, implementation, and maintenance. At the forefront of these tools is the VigilEnt Policy Center (VPC), a centralized policy approval and implementation system. VPC allows policy developers to create policy, manage the approval process with multiple individuals or groups, and distribute approved policy throughout their organizations. VPC assesses readers' understanding of the policy and electronically records reader acknowledgments. Use of VPC reduces or eliminates the need to distribute hard copies of documents that might go unread and to manage multiple policy receipt acknowledgment forms. Tools like VPC keep policies confidential, behind password-protected intranets, and generate periodic reports indicating which employees have and have not read and acknowledged the policies. Figure 4-10 illustrates the VPC methodology.

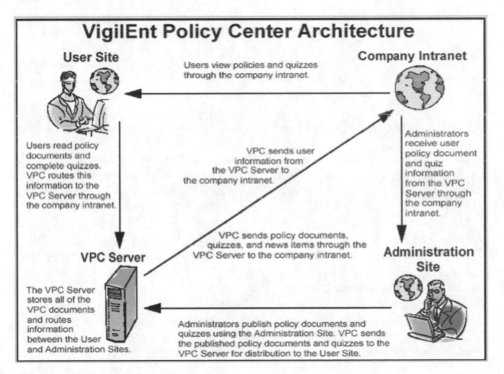

FIGURE 4-10 The VigilEnt Policy Center

When policies are created and distributed without software automation tools, it is often not clear where a policy originated, and which manager approved it. However, with tools such as VPC, the primary manager responsible for the policy has his or her name prominently displayed on the policy, along with the date of approval. This identification can make managers reluctant to implement policies using automated software tools, because it can associate a particular manager with new restrictions or rules. This hesitancy is a difficult hurdle to overcome but can be addressed by evaluating managerial job performance on achieved objectives—in this case, an effective policy process—rather than on the basis that an unobserved failure is a success.

The *Information Securities Policy Made Easy* Approach

The following sections, adapted from and used with permission of the author and publisher of *Information Security Policies Made Easy (ISPME)* referenced earlier,[18] discusses another approach to policy development.

Gathering Key Reference Materials

Information security policies should be largely driven by the nature of the information handled by the organization. One should acquaint him- or herself with the nature of the information handled by the organization. [...] Overviews of internal information systems prepared for top executives, board members, merger and acquisition candidates, and strategic partners also may be useful background to the policy writing effort. Because information systems change so rapidly, available documentation is likely to be outdated. Knowledgeable workers should be interviewed to accurately identify the nature of the information currently being handled by the organization, including what information is sensitive, what information is valuable, and what information is critical.

When developing a set of information security policies, a recent risk assessment or an information technology audit should be referenced that clearly indicates the organization's current information security needs. A loss history documenting the specifics of recent incidents may be helpful in terms of identifying areas in need of further attention. Lawsuits, formal written grievances, and other disputes may identify areas that should be addressed in a policy document. To identify further problem areas, meetings with interested parties such as the in-house legal counsel, the director of Physical Security, the chief information officer, the Internal Audit director, and the director of Human Resources are advised.

To identify the policy areas needing further attention, copies of all other relevant and current organizational policy documents should be collected. Relevant policies include application systems development policies, computer operations policies, computer equipment acquisition policies, human resources policies, information system quality control policies, and physical security policies. If obtainable, policies from other organizations in the same industry can provide useful background information. If the organization is a subsidiary or affiliate of another organization, then the parent organization's policies should be obtained and used as reference material. If the organization is a participant in an electronic data interchange, value-added network, a multi-organizational Internet commerce arrangement, or any other multi-organizational networks, the policies of these networks should be obtained and reviewed.

Another major reason to do a good deal of background research in preparation for policy writing is to ensure that the requirements defined in the policy document are consistent with management's intentions. One of the fastest ways to lose credibility for an information security policy writing effort is to propose a policy that is clearly inconsistent with existing organizational norms. For example, employees at a high-tech company routinely downloaded games from the Internet and played these games on their powerful workstations during breaks and after-hours. Top management knew of and tacitly approved of these activities. At the same time, a published policy indicated that no personal use of the corporation's information systems would be tolerated. This glaring inconsistency caused a large majority of the workers at this company to dismiss the policy document as irrelevant.

Another important reason to spend considerable time on background research is to identify and define the organization's business-related strategic directions. A new or revised policy document needs to be consistent with these strategic directions if top management is going to approve and support the policy. For example, suppose an organization decides it wants to once again centralize its currently decentralized information systems activities. A policy document that stresses many activities to be performed by a group of decentralized information security coordinators would then be inconsistent with management's intentions, and consequently would be unlikely to be approved.

Yet another reason to thoroughly research the current situation before beginning the policy writing process is to identify the internal information systems architecture. An information security policy document should be consistent with and fully support an existing information systems architecture. This is not addressing information security architecture, but an information systems architecture. An information security policy document is typically developed after an information systems architecture is already in place. The development of an information security policy document will permit an information security architecture to be developed. For example, a policy about permissible access through an Internet firewall will enable a security architecture to be specified. It will also enable an appropriate firewall product to be chosen and implemented.[19]

Defining a Framework for Policies

After the above-mentioned reference materials have been collected, a list should be compiled that contains topics to be covered in a new or more comprehensive information security policy document. The first draft of the list should include policies that are intended for immediate adoption and those that are intended for adoption in the future. [...]

Next, an attempt should be made to define the ways in which the organization intends to express information security policies. For example, policies may be placed in a standard operating procedures manual. Alternatively, the director of the Information Security department may periodically issue electronic mail memos summarizing policies. It is common for privacy policies to be posted on the Internet. [...] The channels used to express a policy will determine how the policy should be written. For example, if [...] a policy document will reside on an intranet Web server, then a more graphic and hypertext-linked style is appropriate.

The ways that the organization currently uses or intends to use information security policies should be examined. Policies may be used to guide information system acquisition efforts, drive information technology audit plans, and assist users in securely operating their desktop computers. [...] Defining the uses of policies will identify the audiences to whom policies will be addressed. [...]

Study of the style in which existing policies are written, the use of certain words, the conventional format for documenting policies, the system for numbering and naming policies, and the linkages between policies and other management directives like procedures and standards should be completed.

Preparing a Coverage Matrix

After preparing a rough list of the areas needing attention, and after becoming acquainted with the ways in which the organization expresses and uses policies, the policies found in this guide now can be used. At this point the additional topics to be covered should be evaluated. Review the policy titles or the policies themselves, but skip the accompanying commentaries. [...]

[...] categories should be developed that uniquely respond to the organization's needs. Alternatively, categories reflecting the areas to be addressed may be patterned after an internal audit report or an information security guide that management values. Another way to segment the controls would be broad control objectives such as "avoid," "prevent," "deter," "detect," "mitigate," "recover," and "correct."

At this point, a draft high-level outline reflecting the topics to be addressed should be developed. This outline is best if accompanied by a brief explanation with examples of topics to be covered in each section. The explanation can be only a sentence or two and just enough to provide a preview of the topics included. At this point, distribution of the high-level outline to interested parties is recommended, and the constructive feedback received should then be integrated with the high-level outline.

At this point, a determination must be made of the proper audiences to which these messages are to be addressed. Often policies will be directed at several significantly different audiences because each audience has distinctly different needs. [...]

When more than two audiences will be addressed by separate policy documents, it is recommended that a "coverage matrix" be prepared before actually writing the first draft policy documents. This can be achieved by preparing a separate detailed outline for each of the identified audiences. A coverage matrix is simply an organizational tool to ensure that all the appropriate information security policy messages are presented to all the appropriate audiences. It is a way of looking at the work to be done and can bring order to what otherwise may be a complicated policy writing effort. Once the topics to be communicated have been identified and organized in a coverage matrix, the preparation of policy documents will be relatively easy and straightforward.

A coverage matrix in its simplest form is a two-dimensional table. It can, for instance, use the primary audiences to which the policies are directed as row identifiers, and policy categories as column headings. These policy categories are the major sections appearing in the above-mentioned high-level outline. The cells in the center of the matrix should be filled with reference numbers, each referring to a policy found in this guide and perhaps elsewhere. [...]

[Figure 4-11] provides an example of a matrix that can be developed. The policy numbers appearing in this matrix are placeholders and are deliberately not the result of an analysis. Each organization will need to prepare its own coverage matrix, inserting policy [document names] in the relevant cells to reflect its own unique business and information systems environment.

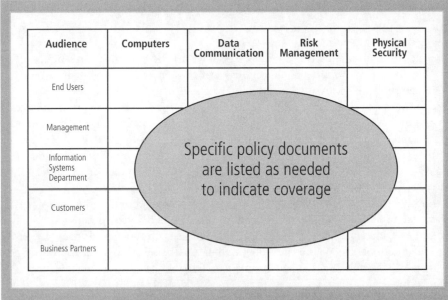

Audience	Computers	Data Communication	Risk Management	Physical Security
End Users				
Management				
Information Systems Department				
Customers				
Business Partners				

Specific policy documents are listed as needed to indicate coverage

FIGURE 4-11   A Sample Coverage Matrix

If the development of this type of a coverage matrix seems too time-consuming, a similar table using broad categories [...] can be prepared.

An alternative approach provides what could be considered a middle ground between a single policy and separate policies for different audiences. In this case, a broad umbrella policy document can apply to all staff, while separate specialized policy documents can be used to address audiences such as information owners, systems developers, telecommuters, and other target audiences. With this approach there is a basic set of rules that applies to everyone, but then there are also special policies that apply only to selected audiences. At larger organizations with intranets, this approach is increasingly common.

In an effort to save time, some people often anticipate there will be only one audience. This one-size-fits-all approach may work for the first few policy statements that an organization issues, but the more sophisticated the information security effort, the less applicable this approach will become. It will often save a significant amount of time if the different audiences are targeted from the beginning of a policy writing effort, rather than having to keep modifying a one-size-fits-all policy that was originally intended to meet the needs of multiple audiences. [...]

Just because there are different audiences for policies does not necessarily imply that there should be different documents. It is possible to have different chapters or sections in an information security manual devoted to different audiences. This approach is attractive because all the policies are then found in one document rather than several. Having all information security policies in a single manual facilitates maintenance and revisions. It is also attractive because individuals often find themselves falling into two or more of the audiences. For example, an individual may be both a general user and a systems developer.

Now the policy numbers should be written directly into the body of the coverage matrix. The process of filling in the body of the coverage matrix often highlights the fact that certain audiences are not being adequately addressed, just as it often indicates that certain areas need additional policies to be truly responsive to the organization's needs. If outlines for policy documents to different audiences were prepared, but no coverage matrix was used, these discrepancies may not have been revealed. [...]

After the overall topics to be covered have been clarified through a coverage matrix, a detailed outline of the soon-to-be-prepared policy documents can be compiled. Depending on the management at the organization, there may be a need to get interested parties to review a detailed outline. If no such review is required, then a detailed outline may not be needed. In this case, using the coverage matrix, the first policy documents can begin to be drafted.

Anyone who noticed a great deal of political uncertainty associated with the policy writing process may wish to prepare a detailed outline and subject it to a review process. While this may delay the process, it ensures that the resulting document is on target and truly responsive to the organization's needs. Where only one audience is being addressed, the coverage matrix can be dispensed with, but a detailed outline is needed. Either a coverage matrix or a detailed outline is important. Without one or the other, weeks of wasted time writing policies on topics that are not needed or not wanted by management are at risk. [...]

After the policy writing process is complete, the coverage matrix, outlines, and related working papers should be saved. In a year or two a revised policy document will probably be needed. It will save a lot of time if the person writing revised policies can consult the original working papers. The coverage matrix and related working papers may also serve as important information in a court case, should there ever be any allegations that management did not seriously think about the risks and the policy messages that needed to be communicated.

Similarly, the working papers should be retained for a year or two because internal and external auditors may wish to review them. Having the working papers in an accessible storage location can also be important if a member of the management team claims that his or her comments were not integrated into the final draft policy document.[20]

Making Critical Systems Design Decisions

Before a final version of a policy document can be published, management often needs to make a number of security-related systems design decisions. Examples of these decisions include the:

- Groups of users [who] will be given Internet access.
- Frequency that they will need access, whether continuous, regular, or occasional.
- Type of access they will need, whether electronic mail, Web surfing, file transfer, remote logon, or chat rooms.
- Type of access control, whether dynamic passwords, fixed passwords, or smart cards.
- Types of user activity that will be monitored, whether files transferred, Web sites visited, or hours per day of usage.

Identification of these and other systems design decisions is ordinarily indirect. Typically a draft policy document that incorporates a number of suggested options will be prepared. Unfortunately, in an effort to expedite the policy writing process, alternative solutions are not highlighted. As a result, management may approve of a policy document incorporating decisions with far-reaching implications, many of which were unappreciated at the time of the approval. This may lead to excessive costs for information security as the initial approaches described in the policy document soon need to be replaced or revised. It may also mean that the policy document needs to be changed much sooner than it otherwise would be. [   ]

In organizations that have been attending to information security for some time, management will have already seriously considered all the necessary fundamental systems design options. In these cases, a policy writing effort will simply involve documenting the decisions already made, and choosing appropriate ways to express these decisions in the form of policies. In these cases, there will be no need for a separate review of the critical systems design issues as discussed above. Instead, the focus can be on the extension of these existing design decisions to new information systems such as extranets, and to new technologies such as new programming languages.

Structuring Review, Approval, and Enforcement Processes

Once the first draft of the information security policy document has been written, a few colleagues should review [it]. After the changes are made in response to feedback from these colleagues, the policy document should be sent to interested internal parties such as Internal Audit management and the Intellectual Property attorney. After a few critical allies have made changes, it is ready for review by the Information Security management committee. The next release of the draft can involve distribution to a much larger body of interested parties—for example, all information owners and all people employed in Information Systems. This review process is advisable because it builds on support from critical players, pre-selling the document to these critical players, and building support from these same critical players. [...] Many review cycles, each with more changes to the policy document, are often necessary. [...]

The final step in the review process is the signature of the general manager, president, chief executive officer, or chairman of the board. A brief message indicating that compliance is expected as a condition of continued employment should be found on the first page of a policy document, or the opening Web page if the policy is posted on an intranet server. This message should be signed by the top executive in a readily visible place so that the reader can have no doubt that the policy document is strongly supported by top management. [...]

An information security management committee is generally composed of representatives from departments within the organization who are interested in information security. [...] In most cases, Information Security management will write a draft version of an information security policy, then submit it to the management committee for review and approval. If the organization does not yet have a management committee, development of an information security policy is an excellent time to propose the formation of such a committee. The committee is generally made up of five to eight individuals who have relevant expertise, who view themselves as influential in the information security area, and who can represent their own department or area of expertise. [...]

In some cases, a separate information security policy development committee is formed. Such a committee could be formed regardless of the existence of an information security management committee. This development committee may be a subcommittee of the management committee. If a development committee is created, it should not actually write the policy. Policies written by committees are often a combination of inconsistent ideas and poorly organized thoughts that never seem to coherently come together into an integrated and understandable document. Instead, the first draft policy should be written by a single technically competent individual who has good writing skills and is familiar with the organization's business activities. [...]

While preparing new information security policies, an adequate enforcement process must exist or soon will exist. If policies cannot be enforced they will, in all probability, not be effective. To have policies that are not enforced may be worse than not having policies at all. This is because the policies may teach workers hypocrisy and tolerance for inappropriate behaviors. Having policies that are not enforced may also lull management into thinking that information security problems have been addressed when the reality is something else. [...]

In advance of the issuance of new policies, ways to achieve compliance should be discussed with the Internal Audit or Information Technology Audit department. [...] Compliance in many instances can be assisted when computerized tools are used to ensure agreements [such as non-disclosure agreements] (NDAs) can be found on an intranet server accessible to all employees. Whenever an NDA is needed, a user can simply print the relevant form found on this server. The ready availability of tools such as this will help users translate information security policies into action. [...]

Enforcement actions are often more effective if workers are aware of what activities would be information security policy violations, and exactly what penalties would be encountered if they were caught. Establishing clear expectations through an information security awareness program is a very important part of an effective and enforceable set of policies. Such awareness programs might, for example, clearly state that business information is the property of Company X, and that it must not be copied, modified, deleted, or used for unintended purposes without management approval.

[...] It should not be the intent to catch people and discipline the offending worker. While punishment should be used for offenders as necessary, it is not the intent of enforcement mechanisms to generate large numbers of out-of-compliance notices. If a large number of people are out of compliance, this is an indication that the policies and related awareness programs have been ineffective. In these situations, the intention behind the policies may need to be communicated more effectively, or the policies may need to be modified to better reflect the organizational culture or prevailing operating circumstances.[21]

Checklist of Steps in the Policy Development Process

This checklist is intended to provide a quick overview of the major steps associated with the development, refinement, and approval of an internal information security policy document. [...]. Many of the following steps can be pursued simultaneously or in an order different than the following:

1. Perform a risk assessment or information technology audit to determine your organization's unique information security needs. These needs must be addressed in a policy document.
2. Clarify what the word "policy" means within your organization so that you are not preparing a "standard," "procedure," or some other related material.
3. Ensure that roles and responsibilities related to information security are clarified, including responsibility for issuing and maintaining policies.
4. Convince management that it is advisable to have documented information security policies.
5. Identify the top management staff who will be approving the final information security document and all influential reviewers.
6. Collect and read all existing internal information security awareness material and make a list of the included bottom-line messages.
7. Conduct a brief internal survey to gather ideas that stakeholders believe should be included in a new or updated information security policy.
8. Examine other policies issued by your organization, such as those from Human Resources management, to identify prevailing format, style, tone, length, and cross-references. The goal is to produce information that conforms with previous efforts.
9. Identify the audience to receive information security policy materials and determine whether [each person will] get a separate document or a separate page on an intranet site.
10. Determine the extent to which the audience is literate, computer knowledgeable, and receptive to security messages. This includes understanding the corporate culture surrounding information security.
11. Decide whether some other awareness efforts must take place before information security policies are issued. For example, one effort might show that information itself has become a critical factor of production.
12. Using ideas from the risk assessment, prepare a list of absolutely essential policy messages that must be communicated. Consult the policy statements as well as the sample policies found in this book.
13. If there is more than one audience, match the audiences with the bottom-line messages to be communicated through a coverage matrix. [...]
14. Determine how the policy material will be disseminated, noting the constraints and implications of each medium of communication. An intranet site is recommended. [...]
15. Review the compliance checking process, disciplinary process, and enforcement process to ensure that they all can work smoothly with the new policy document.
16. Determine whether the number of messages is too large to be handled all at one time, and if so, identify different categories of material that will be issued at different times.

17. Have an outline of topics to be included in the first document reviewed by several stakeholders. An information security management committee is the ideal review board.
18. Based on comments from the stakeholders, revise the initial outline and prepare a first draft. [...]
19. Have the first draft document reviewed by the stakeholders for initial reactions, presentation suggestions, and implementation ideas.
20. Revise the draft in response to comments from stakeholders. Expect this step to [be repeated] several times.
21. Request top management approval on the policy. Changes may be necessary, in which case this step may [be repeated] several times.
22. Prepare extracts of the policy document for selected purposes—for example, for a form signed by users receiving new or renewed user IDs and passwords.
23. Develop an awareness plan that uses the policy document as a source of ideas and requirements.
24. Create a working papers memo indicating the disposition of all comments received from reviewers, even if no changes were made.
25. Write a memo about the project, what you learned, and what needs to be fixed so that the next version of the policy document can be prepared more efficiently, better received by the readers, and more responsive to the unique circumstances facing your organization.
26. Prepare a list of next steps that will be required to implement the requirements specified in the policy document. [These steps] can include the development of an information security architecture, manual procedures documents, and technical information security standards, and acquisition of new products, hiring new technical staff, and other matters.

Next Steps

There are many paths available after an information security policy has been approved. [...] There will typically be many other projects that are initiated as a result of preparing an information security policy document. For example, a policy preparation effort may have illuminated the fact that an existing information security requirement is obsolete.[...]

Post Policies to Intranet or Equivalent. The new document should be placed on the Company X intranet, and links to related documents should be added. Multiple indexes should be prepared so that users can quickly locate material of interest. A key word search facility should be added. Other electronic bulletin board equivalents, such as a Human Resources kiosk, could include the document. [...]

Develop a Self-Assessment Questionnaire. The essential requirements found in the new information security policy document should be extracted and reformatted in the form of a questionnaire. Internal Audit then should issue the questionnaire to department managers. Responses to the questionnaire will highlight those areas where departments are out of compliance and where additional control enhancements are needed. Based on the results of the survey, remedial projects can be proposed. The questionnaire can be used as part of a regular compliance-checking internal audit process. [...]

Develop Revised User ID Issuance Form.   A form is used at many organizations as a way to document management approval prior to the issuance of a user ID. [...] A summary of the critical ideas in the new information security policy document should be included as part of this form along with words such as "the user mentioned below has read and agrees to abide by Company X information security policies as a condition of [his or her] continued use of Company X information systems." All new or reissued user IDs should then be enabled only after the form is signed.

Develop Agreement to Comply with Information Security Policies Form.   A legal document reflecting an agreement by employees to comply with information security policies should be drafted, edited, and later approved by management. This form should be signed by all workers, or at the very least by all newly hired or retained workers. An awareness program should be initiated to publicize the existence of the new policy document and to get signed forms. [...]

Develop Tests to Determine if Workers Understand Policies.   A set of tests or quizzes can be developed to determine if workers understand the essential points covered in an information security policy document. These tests and quizzes can be used to determine what additional training and awareness material needs to be developed and delivered. The tests and quizzes also can be used as gateways to certain privileges. For example, only after a worker passes a test or a quiz will telecommuting privileges be enabled. [...]

Assign Information Security Coordinators.   Many centralized Information Security departments are understaffed and cannot handle all the information security jobs that need to be done. To assist in the implementation of the controls described in the new policy document, decentralized information security coordinators should be assigned. System administrators, systems managers, network managers, and other technical staff often serve in this part-time capacity. Coordinators serve as a local liaison with the central information security group, interpreting policies for a department or division. [...]

Train Information Security Coordinators.   Before the information security coordinators can be expected to do substantive work, they should receive a training course. A half-day course should be developed to acquaint them with the requirements defined in the new information security policy document, existing organizational resources, and the best ways to deal with a variety of problems such as power failures, hacker intrusions, and computer virus infections. A handbook for local information security coordinators is also recommended. [...]

Prepare and Deliver a Basic Information Security Training Course.   A brief training course should be prepared and presented to all employees at Company X. The policy document can be the primary source of ideas for a training and awareness course. A variety of other material, such as the corporate code of conduct, should also be drawn upon when preparing this course. After this course has been presented several times, it can be revamped, then recorded by videotape or computer-based training software. In some instances, separate audiences may need different training courses. Possible audiences include new hires going through orientation, current employees in need of additional training, system administrators, network administrators, and others likely to be designated as information security coordinators, and systems analysts, application programmers, systems-related project managers, systems quality assurance staff, and other technical staff who will not be serving in an information security coordinator capacity. [...]

Develop Application-Specific Information Security Policies. Certain highly sensitive applications will need additional application-specific policies and procedures. Now that the new information security policy document has been prepared, more detailed policies and related requirements for high-risk application systems should be developed. Certain computing environments, not just applications, such as Internet electronic commerce, may warrant more detailed policies and procedures. The conceptual hierarchy described below can be used to describe the linkage between these application-specific documents and the new information security policy. [...]

Develop a Conceptual Hierarchy of Information Security Requirements. The information security area is complex, and this complexity shows up in various documents that define information security requirements. In many organizations, these include standards, guidelines, policies, procedures, and architectures. A general information security policy document should be at the top of a conceptual hierarchy, with application-related information security policy documents falling underneath. Standards, guidelines, procedures, and other documents should be controlled by the general organization-wide information security policy statement. A conceptual hierarchy should indicate when certain documents apply, which documents take precedence when a conflict exists, and which documents are current or outdated. This conceptual hierarchy will be useful for training and awareness purposes, and can be posted to the Company X information security intranet page. [...]

Assign Information Ownership and Custodianship. Management ownership of specific types of information should be assigned according to the requirements defined in the new information security document. After ownership roles have been assigned, custodianship roles should come next. In many instances, these efforts will be a natural transition to the compilation of a corporate data dictionary, an electronic document management system, or a similar project. [...]

Establish an Information Security Management Committee. To supervise the various information security initiatives now under way, a committee should be formed with middle-level managers from each of the major divisions at Company X. This committee will ensure that current and proposed information security activities are consistent with business objectives. The committee will serve as a sounding board for proposals, prior to presenting these same proposals to top management. The committee ordinarily would meet once a quarter, and would not provide any technical assistance to the Information Security department. [...] A mission statement and related details about such a committee can also be found in the book *Information Security Roles and Responsibilities Made Easy.*

Develop an Information Security Architecture Document. Even though the basic rules for information security are specified in a policy document, in most cases there is a need to put together a grand vision for designing secure systems. The larger an organization, the more the need for a document such as this. Complexity is much more of a problem in these organizations. An architecture should specify the controls that will be used now and in the near future, and provide a plan for the migration to controls to be adopted in the near future. Some organizations also use an architecture document as a place to specify certain approved information security products and vendors. An architecture deals with system interfaces, technical standards, and other more technical considerations than a policy document. [...]

Automating Policy Enforcement Through Policy Servers

At many organizations, the complexity of information systems is overwhelming the ability of staff to manage these systems. To deal with this complexity, new expert systems tools are being introduced. [...] An interesting new development [...] is called a policy server. Policy servers take organization-specific policies and code them in a special machine-readable language that then can be accessed by a wide variety of operating systems, access control packages, and network management systems. Examples of these policies or rules include the minimum number of characters in a password, the maximum number of logon attempts before a connection will be severed, and whether attachments to electronic mail files will be passed through firewalls. [...] In the near future, suites of products from a single vendor, and suites from a combination of vendors, will start to perform some of the rationalizing and centralizing tasks of a policy server.

To prepare their organizations for these upcoming developments, consideration should be given to how the policies they develop today will be put into the computer models of tomorrow. Attempts should be made to be as logical and straightforward as possible. Not only will this help the readers understand how to behave when it comes to information security, but it will also help tomorrow's programmers in their efforts to create computer-enforced rules. Attempts also should be made to achieve the most cross-organization, cross-network, cross-system, and cross-platform coordination of information security policies. This will also reduce complexity and permit the organization to more readily adopt new policy enforcement tools.

SP 800-18 Rev. 1: *Guide for Developing Security Plans for Federal Information Systems*

NIST's Special Publication 800-18 Rev. 1 reinforces these approaches to policy management. Because policies are living documents that constantly change and grow, organizations cannot simply create such an important set of documents and then shelve them. Instead, these documents must be properly disseminated (distributed, read, understood, and agreed to) and managed. Good management practices for policy development and maintenance make for a more resilient organization. For example, all policies, including security policies, undergo tremendous stress when corporate mergers and divestitures occur. In these situations changes happen quickly, and employees suffer uncertainty and are faced with many distractions; these stresses can reveal weaknesses in the management of security policies. When two companies come together as one, but still have separate policies, it can be very difficult to implement security controls. Likewise, when one company with unified policies splits into two, the policy needs of both spin-offs change and must be accommodated.

To keep policies current and viable, an individual must be responsible for scheduling reviews, defining review practices and procedures, and ensuring that policy and revision dates are present.

Policy Administrator

Just as information systems and information security projects must have a champion and manager, so must policies. The policy champion and manager is called the policy administrator. Typically, this person is a mid-level staff member who is responsible for the creation, revision, distribution, and storage of the policy. The policy administrator does not necessarily have to be technically oriented. While practicing information security professionals require extensive technical knowledge, policy management and policy administration require only a moderate technical background. The policy administrator solicits input both from the technically adept information security experts and from the business-focused managers in each community of interest. In turn, he or she notifies all affected members of the organization when the policy is modified.

It is rather disheartening when a policy that requires hundreds of staff-hours of development time is inserted into a three-ring binder and then placed on a manager's bookcase to gather dust. A good policy administrator can prevent this by making sure that the policy document and all subsequent revisions to it are appropriately distributed. The policy administrator must be clearly identified on the policy document as the primary contact for providing additional information or suggesting revisions to the policy.

Review Schedule

In a changing environment, policies can retain their effectiveness only if they are periodically reviewed for currency and accuracy, and modified to keep them current. As stated in Chapter 3, to ensure **due diligence**, an organization must demonstrate that it is continually attempting to meet the requirements of the market in which it operates. This applies to both public (government, academic, and nonprofit) and private (commercial and for-profit) organizations. For this reason, any policy document should contain a properly organized schedule of reviews. Generally, a policy should be reviewed at least annually. The policy administrator should solicit input from representatives of all affected parties, management and staff, and then use this input to modify the document accordingly.

Review Procedures and Practices

To facilitate policy reviews, the policy administrator should implement a mechanism by which individuals can easily make recommendations for revisions to the policies and other related documentation. Recommendation methods could include e-mail, office mail, or an anonymous drop box. If the policy is controversial, the policy administrator may feel that anonymous submission of information is the best way to determine the suitability of the policy as perceived by employees. Many employees feel intimidated by management and will hesitate to voice honest opinions about a policy in a more open forum.

Once the policy has come up for review, all comments should be examined and management-approved changes should be implemented. Additional review methods could involve including representative users in the revision process and allowing for direct comment on the revision of the policy. In reality, most policies are drafted by a single responsible individual and are then reviewed, or "signed into law," by a higher-level manager. This method should not preclude the collection and review of employee input, however.

Policy and Revision Date

In some organizations, policies are drafted and published without a date, leaving users of the policy unaware of its age or status. This practice can create problems, including legal ones, if employees are "complying" with an out-of-date policy. Such problems are particularly common in an environment where there is high turnover. Ideally, the policy document should include its date of origin, along with the dates, if any, of revisions. Some policies may need a "sunset clause," particularly if they govern information use for a short-term association with second-party businesses or agencies. The inclusion of such an expiration date prevents a temporary policy from becoming a permanent mistake.

A FINAL NOTE ON POLICY

Lest the reader believe that the only reason to have policies is to avoid litigation, it is important to emphasize their preventive nature. Policies exist first and foremost to inform employees of what is and is not acceptable behavior in the organization. Policy development is meant to improve employee productivity and to prevent potentially embarrassing situations. In a worst-case scenario, an employee could be fired for failure to comply with a policy. If the organization cannot verify that the employee was in fact properly educated on the policy, as described earlier in the chapter, the employee could sue the organization for wrongful termination. Lawsuits cost money, and the organization could be so financially devastated that it has to go out of business. Other employees will then lose their livelihoods, and no one wins.

In reality, most employees inherently want to do what is right. If properly educated on what is acceptable and what is not, they will choose to follow the rules for acceptable behavior. Most people prefer systems that provide fair treatment. If they know the penalties for failure to comply, no outrage will arise when someone is caught misbehaving and the penalties are applied. Knowing what is prohibited, what the penalties are, and how penalties will be enforced is a preventive measure that should free employees to focus on the business at hand.

Chapter Summary

- A quality information security program begins and ends with policy.

- Policy drives the performance of personnel in ways that enhance the information security of an organization's information assets.

- Developing proper guidelines for an information security program is a management problem, not a technical one. The technical aspect of an information security program is merely one part of the entire program and should be dealt with only after management has created relevant policies.

- Although information security policies are the least expensive means of control to execute, they are often the most difficult to implement. Policy controls cost only the time and effort that the management team spends to create, approve, and communicate them, and that employees spend to integrate the policies into their daily activities.

- The information security policy must satisfy several criteria:

  - Policy should never conflict with law.

  - Policy must stand up in court, when it is challenged.

  - Policy must be properly supported and administered.

- Guidelines for the formulation of information security policy are as follows:

  - Policy generators must recognize that all policies contribute to the success of the organization.

  - Management must ensure the adequate sharing of responsibility.

  - End users should be involved in the policy development process.

- A policy is a statement of the organization's position that is intended to influence and determine decisions and actions and that is used to control the actions of people and the development of procedures.

- A policy may be viewed as a set of rules that dictates acceptable and unacceptable behavior within an organization.

- Policies must contain information on what is required and what is prohibited; on the penalties for violating policy; and on the appeal process.

- For a policy to be effective, it must be properly disseminated to those responsible for implementing it.

- Management must define three types of information security policies:

  - Enterprise information security program policy (EISP), which sets the strategic direction, scope, and tone for all security efforts. The EISP must be based on and must support the organization's vision and mission statement.

  - Issue-specific information security policies, which provide guidance to all members of an organization regarding the use of information technology.

  - System-specific information security policies, which guide the management and technical specifications of particular technologies and systems.

Review Questions

1. What is information security policy? Why it is critical to the success of the information security program?

2. Of the controls or countermeasures used to control information security risk, which is viewed as the least expensive? What are the primary costs of this type of control?

3. List and describe the three challenges in shaping policy.

4. List and describe the three guidelines for sound policy, as stated by Bergeron and Bérubé.

5. Describe the bull's-eye model. What does it say about policy in the information security program?

6. Are policies different from standards? In what way?

7. Are policies different from procedures? In what way?

8. For a policy to have any effect, what must happen after it is approved by management? What are some ways to accomplish this?

9. Is policy considered static or dynamic? Which factors might determine this status?

10. List and describe the three types of information security policy as described by NIST SP 800-14.

11. What is the purpose of an enterprise information security program policy (EISP)?

12. What is the purpose of an issue-specific security policy (ISSP)?

13. What is the purpose of a system-specific security program policy (SysSP)?

14. To what degree should the organization's values, mission, and objectives be integrated into the policy documents?

15. List and describe four elements that should be present in the EISP.

16. List and describe three functions that the ISSP serves in the organization.

17. What should be the first component of an ISSP when it is presented? Why? What should be the second major heading, in your opinion? Why?

18. List and describe three common ways in which ISSP documents are created and/or managed.

19. List and describe the two general groups of material included in most SysSP documents.

20. List and describe the three approaches to policy development presented in the chapter. In your opinion, which is better suited for use by a smaller organization, and why? If the target organization were very much larger, which approach would be superior and why?

Exercises

1. Using the Internet, go to the International Information Systems Security Certifications Consortium Web site (www.isc2.org) and look for the information security common body of knowledge (CBK). When you review the list of 10 areas in the CBK, is policy listed? Why do you think this is so?

2. Search your institution's intranet or Web sites for its security policies. Do you find an enterprise security policy? What issue-specific security policies can you locate? Are all of these

policies issued or coordinated by the same individual or office, or are they scattered throughout the institution?

3. Using the policies you located in Exercise 2, use the framework presented in this chapter and evaluate the comprehensiveness of each policy. Which areas are missing?

4. Using the framework presented in this chapter, draft a sample issue-specific security policy for an organization. At the beginning of your document, describe the organization for which you are creating the policy, and then complete the policy using the framework.

5. Search for sample security policies on the Web. Identify five EISP and five ISSP sample policies, and bring them to class. Compare these with the framework presented in this chapter, and comment on the policies' comprehensiveness.

Case Exercises

Prior to the first meeting of the RWW Enterprise Policy Review Committee, Mike and Iris met in Mike's office to formulate a common IT and Information Security approach to the upcoming policy review cycle. Here is part of their conversation:

Mike motioned for Iris to sit down, and then said, "You've convinced me that IT and InfoSec policy are tightly integrated, and that InfoSec policy is critical to the enterprise. I would like you to join me as a member of the Enterprise Policy Review Committee. Okay?"

Iris, who knew how important policy was to her program's success, replied, "Sure. No problem."

Mike continued, "Good. We'll work together to make sure the EISP you've drafted gets equal status with the other top-level enterprise policies and that the second-tier issue and third-tier system policies are also referenced in all other top-level policies, especially those of the HR department."

Iris nodded. Mike went on, "I want you to take the current HR policy document binder and make a wish list of changes you need to be sure we get the right references in place. Let me see your HR policy change plan by the end of the week."

1. If the Enterprise Policy Review Committee is not open to the approach that Mike and Iris want to use for structuring information security policies into three tiers, how should they proceed?

2. Should the CISO (Iris) be assessing HR policies? Why or why not?

Endnotes

[1] C. Helsing, N. Swanson, N, and M. Todd. Special Publication 500-169: *Executive Guide to the Protection of Information Resources*. October 1989. Accessed August 14, 2006 from csrc.nist. gov/publications/nistpubs/500-169/sp500-169.txt.

[2] Charles Cresson Wood. *Information Security Policies Made Easy*, 9th ed. NetIQ Corporation, 2003: 1.

[3] F. Bergeron and C. Bérubé. End users talk computer policy. *Journal of Systems Management*, December 1990; 41(12):14–17.

[4] Charles Cresson Wood. *Information Security Policies Made Easy*, 9th ed. NetIQ Corporation, 2003: 1.

[5] Derived from a number of sources, the most notable of which is www.wustl.edu/policies/infosecurity.html.

[6] Washington State University. *Information Security Policy*. Accessed 4/12/03 from www.wustl.edu/policies/infosecurity.html.

[7] Washington State University. *Information Security Policy*. Accessed 4/12/03 from www.wustl.edu/policies/infosecurity.html.

[8] Washington State University. *Information Security Policy*. Accessed 4/12/03 from www.wustl.edu/policies/infosecurity.html.

[9] Charles Cresson Wood. *Information Security Policies Made Easy*, 9th ed. NetIQ Corporation, 2003: 9.

[10] Michael E. Whitman. "Security Policy: From Design to Maintenance." *Information Security Policies and Strategies—An Advances in MIS monograph.* Goodman, S., Straub, D., & Zwass, V. (eds). Armonk NY: M. E. Sharp, Inc.

[11] National Assessment of Adult Literacy. 2003 Survey Results. Accessed Cited July 21, 2006 from nces.ed.gov/NAAL/index.asp?file=KeyFindings/Demographics/Overall.asp&PageId=16#2.

[12] National Assessment of Adult Literacy. 2003 Survey Results. Accessed July 21, 2006 from nces.ed.gov/NAAL/index.asp?file=KeyFindings/Demographics/Overall.asp&PageId=16#2.

[13] David A. Ricks. *Blunders in International Business*. Cambridge, MA: Blackwell, 1993: 40.

[14] Benjamin S. Bloom, Bertram B. Mesia, and David R. Krathwohl. *Taxonomy of Educational Objectives*. New York: David McKay, 1964.

[15] Michael E. Whitman "Security Policy: From Design to Maintenance." *Information Security Policies and Strategies—An Advances in MIS monograph.* Goodman, S., Straub, D., & Zwass, V. (eds). Armonk NY: M. E. Sharp, Inc.

[16] Michael E. Whitman "Security Policy: From Design to Maintenance." *Information Security Policies and Strategies—An Advances in MIS monograph.* Goodman, S., Straub, D., & Zwass, V. (eds). Armonk NY: M. E. Sharp, Inc.

[17] Michael E. Whitman. "Security Policy: From Design to Maintenance." *Information Security Policies and Strategies—An Advances in MIS monograph.* Goodman, S., Straub, D., & Zwass, V. (eds). Armonk NY: M. E. Sharp, Inc.

[18] Charles Cresson Wood. *Information Security Policies Made Easy*. NetIQ Corporation, 2003: 1. http://www.netiq.com/products/pub/ispme.asp.

[19] Charles Cresson Wood. Information Security Policies Made Easy. NetIQ Corporation, 2003: 1. http://www.netiq.com/products/pub/ispme.asp.

[20] Charles Cresson Wood. Information Security Policies Made Easy. NetIQ Corporation, 2003: 1. http://www.netiq.com/products/pub/ispme.asp.

[21] Charles Cresson Wood. Information Security Policies Made Easy. NetIQ Corporation, 2003: 1. http://www.netiq.com/products/pub/ispme.asp.

5

DEVELOPING THE SECURITY PROGRAM

Iris was looking over the freshly printed first issue of RWW's information security newsletter, *The Paladin*, when Mike Edwards walked into her office.

"What's new, Iris?" he asked.

"See for yourself!" she replied with a grin, as she handed him her latest completed project.

"Very nice," he commented. "How close are you to publication?"

"We've just put it on the intranet, and we're going to run off a few dozen hard copies for our office. That's your copy."

"Thanks!" he said while he scanned the cover article. "What is this disclosure situation all about?"

Mike was referring to the recent state law that mandated very specific definitions and penalties for computer-related crimes such as computer trespassing and theft of computer information. What had caught his attention was the clause providing penalties for the disclosure of some types of personal data such as Social Security numbers and account passwords. The penalties ranged from $500 to $5000 per incident, and even included up to a year in jail.

Mike whistled and said, "We need to talk about this issue at the senior staff meeting. We should get the other departments involved to make sure we don't have any problems complying with this law."

Iris nodded and said, "Maybe someone from corporate legal should be there, too."

"Good idea."

Then Mike asked about the newsletter's listing of information security training sessions. "Where did you get the training staff?" he asked.

"I've been meaning to talk to you about that," Iris said. "I'll teach the classes until my security manager, Tom, can take over. But we should ask the corporate training office about getting some of their staff up to speed on our topics."

"Sounds good. I'll get with Jerry tomorrow after the staff meeting," Mike replied.

LEARNING OBJECTIVES

Upon completion of this material you should be able to:

- Recognize and understand the organizational approaches to information security
- List and describe the functional components of an information security program
- Determine how to plan and staff an organization's information security program based on its size
- Evaluate the internal and external factors that influence the activities and organization of an information security program
- List and describe the typical job titles and functions performed in the information security program
- Describe the components of a security education, training, and awareness program and understand how organizations create and manage these programs

INTRODUCTION

Some organizations use the term "security program" to describe the entire set of personnel, plans, policies, and initiatives related to information security. Others use the term "information security" to refer to the broader context of corporate or physical security plus those areas usually associated with computer, network, or data security. The term **information security program** is used in this book to describe the structure and organization of the effort that strives to contain the risks to the information assets of the organization.

ORGANIZING FOR SECURITY

Among the variables that determine how a given organization chooses to structure its information security program are organizational culture, size, security personnel budget, and security capital budget. The first and most influential of these variables is the organizational culture. If upper management and staff believe that information security is a waste of time and resources, the information security program will remain small and poorly supported. Efforts made by the information security staff will be viewed as contrary to the mission of the organization and detrimental to the organization's productivity. Conversely, where there is a strong, positive view of information security, the information security program is likely to be larger and well supported, both financially and otherwise.

The organization's size and available resources also directly affect the size and structure of the information security program. Organizations with complex IT infrastructures and sophisticated system users are likely to require more information security support. Large, complex organizations may have entire divisions dedicated to information security, including a CISO, multiple security managers, multiple administrators, and many technicians. Such divisions might have specialized staff focusing on specific issues—for example, policy, planning, firewalls, and intrusion detection systems (IDSs). In general, the larger the organization, the larger the information security program. Smaller organizations, by contrast, may have a single security administrator, or they may assign the information security responsibilities to a systems or network administrator.

Another variable is the personnel budget for the information security program. The size of the information security budget typically corresponds to the size of the organization. Although no standard exists for the size of the information security budget and/or the number of security personnel in any given organization, measured industry averages are available. Industry averages vary widely and may be expressed in terms of information security budget per unit of revenue, information security staff per number of total employees in the organization, or as information security budget per unit of IT budget. Determining the industry average in any given case may be a challenge, but the reality is that regardless of the industry average, it is the management of the particular organization that has the most influence over this variable, for better or worse. In general, security programs are understaffed for the tasks they have been assigned. Top security managers must constantly struggle to create policy and policy plans, manage personnel issues, plan training, and keep the administrative and support staff focused on their assigned responsibilities and tasks. According to the article referenced in the following Offline, "Does Size Matter?,"

> ...as organizations get larger in size, their security departments are not keeping up with the demands of increasingly complex organizational infrastructures. Security spending per user and per machine declines exponentially as organizations grow, leaving most handcuffed when it comes to implementing effective security procedures.[1]

Office politics, the economy, and budget forecasts are just some of the factors that cause upper management to juggle with staffing levels. In today's environment, the information security programs in most organizations do not yet receive the support they need to function properly. That situation may change, however, because the current political climate and the many reported events regarding information security breaches are rapidly forcing organizational cultures to view information security as an additional critical function.

Another important variable is the capital and expense budget for physical resources dedicated to information security. This budget includes allocation of offices, computer labs, and testing facilities, as well as the general information security expense budget. Because the information security staff handle confidential information regarding security plans, policies, structures, designs, and a host of other items, it is prudent to provide this group with its own secured physical resources, including office space.

OFFLINE

Does Size Matter?

While many IT professionals may think they would be better off in the big IT departments of nationally renowned organizations, the fact is they may be better off at a smaller organization. Big organizations have large staffs, full-time and part-time security professionals, and more problems than the typical smaller organization. This section defines small, medium, large, and very large organizations, and describes the problems inherent in each and how they are staffed to deal with them.

- The small organization has 10–100 computers. Most small organizations have a simple, centralized IT organizational model, and spend disproportionately more on security, averaging almost 20% of the total IT budget. The typical security staff in this organization is usually only one person (the lone ranger!), if in fact there is a full-time security professional. Much more frequently, information security is an additional duty of one of the IT staffers. However, financially the small organizations, including ones with the smallest budgets, spend more per user than medium- and large-sized organizations. "More than two-thirds [of small organizations] say all or most of their security decisions are guided by management-approved policies, and 57% say that all or most of their responses to incidents were guided by a predefined IR plan."[2]

- The medium-sized organization has 100–1000 computers, and has a smaller budget (averaging about 11% of the total IT budget), about the same security staff, and a larger need than the small organization. The medium-sized organization's security people must rely on help from IT staff to carry out security plans and practices. "Their ability to set policy, handle incidents in a regular manner and effectively allocate resources are, overall, worse than any other group. Considering their size, the number of incidents they recognize is skyrocketing. Some 70% of them had damages from security breaches, a 48% increase over small organizations."[3]

continued

- The large organization has 1000 to 10,000 computers. Organizations of this size have generally integrated planning and policy into the organizational culture; "eight in 10 organizations say at least some of their security decisions are guided by them."[4] Unfortunately, the large organization tends to spend substantially less on security (only about 5% of the total IT budget on average), creating issues across the organization, especially in the "people" areas.
- The very large organization has more than 10,000 computers, and large information security budgets, which grow faster than IT budgets. However, in these multimillion-dollar security budgets, the average amount per user is still less than in any other type of organization. "Where small organizations spend more than $5000 per user on security, very large organizations spend about one-eighteenth of that, roughly $300 per user," or approximately 6% of the total IT budget. The very large organization does a better job in the policy and resource management areas, although "only about a third of organizations in this demographic handled incidents according to an IR plan."[5]

Adapted from Does size matter? by Andrew Briney and Frank Prince as published in *Information Security* magazine September 2002.

Organizing an information security program poses several managerial challenges. Although the size of an organization influences the makeup of its information security program, certain basic functions should occur in every organization, and thus these functions should be included in any budget allocation. Table 5-1 outlines the suggested functions for a successful information security program. These functions are not necessarily performed within the information security department, but they must be performed somewhere within the organization.

TABLE 5-1 Functions Needed to Implement the Information Security Program

Function	Description	Comments
Risk Assessment	Evaluates risk present in IT initiatives and/or systems	Identifies the sources of risk and may offer advice on controls that can reduce risk
Risk Management	Implements or oversees use of controls to reduce risk	Often paired with risk assessment
Systems Testing	Evaluates patches used to close software vulnerabilities and acceptance testing of new systems to assure compliance with policy and effectiveness	Usually part of the incident response and/or risk management functions
Policy	Maintains and promotes information security policy across the organization	Must be coordinated with organization wide policy processes

TABLE 5-1 Functions Needed to Implement the Information Security Program (continued)

Function	Description	Comments
Legal Assessment	Maintains awareness of planned and actual laws and their impact, and coordinates with outside legal counsel and law enforcement agencies	Almost always external to the information security and IT departments
Incident Response	Handles the initial response to potential incidents, manages escalation of actual incidents, and coordinates the earliest responses to incidents and disasters	Often cross-functional and drawn from multiple departments; should include middle management to manage escalation processes
Planning	Researches, creates, maintains, and promotes information security plans; often takes a project management approach to planning as contrasted with strategic planning for the whole organization	Must coordinate with organization wide policy processes
Measurement	Uses existing control systems (and perhaps specialized data collection systems) to measure all aspects of the information security environment	Management relies on timely and accurate statistics to make informed decisions
Compliance	Verifies that system and network administrators repair identified vulnerabilities promptly and correctly	Poses problems for good customer service because it is difficult to be customer focused and to enforce compliance at the same time
Centralized Authentication	Manages the granting and revocation of network and system credentials for all members of the organization	Often delegated to the help desk or staffed in conjunction and colocated with the help desk function
Systems Security Administration	Administers the configuration of computer systems, which are often organized into groups by the operating system they run	Many organizations may have originally assigned all security functions to these groups outside of the information security function; this can be a source of conflict when organizations update their information security program
Training	Trains general staff in information security topics, IT staff in specialized technical controls, and internal information security staff in specialized areas of information security, including both technical and managerial topics	Some or all of this function may be carried out in conjunction with the corporate training department
Network Security Administration	Administers configuration of computer networks, often organized into groups by logical network area (i.e., WAN, LAN, DMZ) or geographic location	Many organizations may have originally assigned some security functions to these groups outside of the information security function, which may require close coordination or reassignment

Function	Description	Comments
Vulnerability Assessment	Locates exposure within information assets so these vulnerabilities can be repaired before weaknesses are exploited	Sometimes called the penetration testing team or the ethical hacking unit; often outsourced to consultant "tiger teams"

Security in Large Organizations

Organizations having more than 1000 devices requiring security management are likely to be staffed and funded at a level that enables them to accomplish most of the functions identified in Table 5-1. Large organizations often create an internal entity to deal with the specific information security challenges they face. Not surprisingly, the security functions and organizational approaches implemented by larger organizations are as diverse as the organizations themselves. Information security departments in such organizations tend to form and re-form internal groups to meet long-term challenges even as they handle day-to-day security operations. Thus, functions are likely to be split into groups in larger organizations; in contrast, smaller organizations typically create fewer groups, perhaps only having one general group representing the whole department.

One recommended approach is to separate the functions into four areas:

1. Functions performed by nontechnology business units outside of the IT area of management control, such as

    - Legal

    - Training

2. Functions performed by IT groups outside of the information security area of management control, such as

    - Systems security administration

    - Network security administration

    - Centralized authentication

3. Functions performed within the information security department as a customer service to the organization and its external partners, such as

    - Risk assessment

    - Systems testing

    - Incident response

    - Planning

    - Measurement

    - Vulnerability assessment

4. Functions performed within the information security department as a compliance enforcement obligation, such as

- Policy

- Compliance/Audit

- Risk management

It remains the CISO's responsibility to see that information security functions are adequately performed somewhere within the organization. As indicated in Figures 5-1 and 5-2, respectively, large and very large organizations typically have dedicated staffs—sometimes large ones—to support the security program. The deployment of full-time security personnel depends on a number of factors, including sensitivity of the information to be protected, industry regulations (as in the financial and health care industries), and general profitability. The more resources the company can dedicate to its personnel budget, the more likely it is to maintain a large information security staff. As shown in Figure 5-1, a typical large organization has on average 1–2 full-time administrator, 3–4 full-time administrators/technicians, and as many as 16 part-time staff members, who have information security duties in addition to their duties in other areas. For example, a systems administrator of a Windows 2003 server may be responsible for maintaining both the server and the security applications running on it. The very large organization, as illustrated in Figure 5-2, may have more than 20 full-time security personnel, and 40 or more individuals with part-time responsibilities.

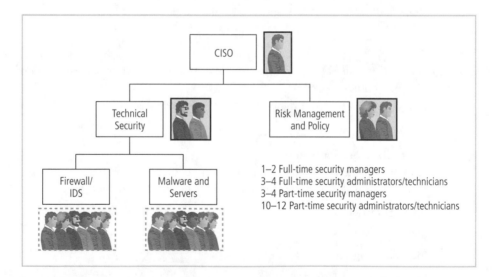

1–2 Full-time security managers
3–4 Full-time security administrators/technicians
3–4 Part-time security managers
10–12 Part-time security administrators/technicians

FIGURE 5-1 Information Security Staffing in a Large Organization

Security in Medium-Sized Organizations

Medium-sized organizations have between 100 and 1000 machines requiring security management. These organizations may still be large enough to implement the multitiered approach to security described previously for large organizations, though perhaps with fewer

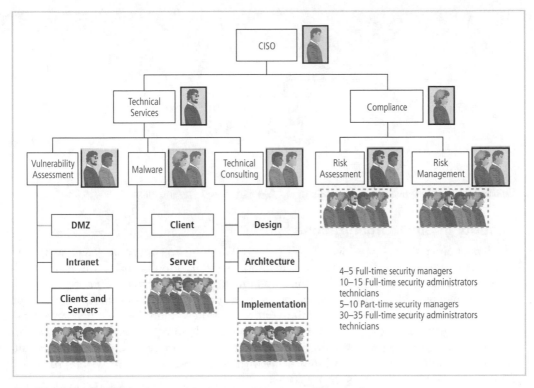

FIGURE 5-2   Information Security Staffing in a Very Large Organization

dedicated groups and more functions assigned to each group. In a medium-sized organization, more of the functional areas from Table 5-1 are assigned to other departments within IT, but outside of the information security department. Also, the central authentication function often gets handed off to systems administration personnel within the IT department.

Medium-sized organizations tend to ignore some of the functions from Table 5-1—in particular, when the information security department cannot staff a certain function and the IT or other department is not encouraged or required to perform that function in its stead. In these cases, the CISO must improve the collaboration among these groups, and must provide leadership in advocating decisions that stretch the capabilities of the organization.

As illustrated in Figure 5-3, the full- and part-time staff of the medium-sized organization is dramatically smaller than that of its larger counterparts. This organization may only have one full-time security person, with perhaps three individuals with part-time information security responsibilities.

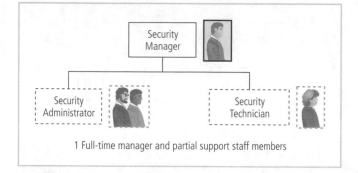

1 Full-time manager and partial support staff members

FIGURE 5-3 Information Security Staffing in a Medium-Sized Organization

Security in Small Organizations

Smaller organizations—those with fewer than 100 systems to supervise—face particular challenges. Information security in the small organization often becomes the responsibility of a *jack-of-all-trades,* a single security administrator with perhaps one or two assistants for managing the technical components. It is not uncommon in smaller organizations to have the systems or network administrators play these many roles. Such organizations frequently have little in the way of formal policy, planning, or security measures, and they usually outsource their Web presence or electronic commerce operations. As a result, the security administrator most often deals with desktop management, virus protection, and local area network security issues.

Because resources in smaller organizations are often limited, the security administrator frequently turns to freeware or *hackerware* to lower the costs of assessing and implementing security. As you will learn in Chapter 9, these tools can be quite effective in both providing access to otherwise unavailable utilities and lowering the total cost of security.

In small organizations, security training and awareness is most commonly conducted on a one-on-one basis, with the security administrator providing advice to users as needed. Any published policies are likely to be issue-specific—for example, on Web and Internet use, and fair-and-responsible use of office equipment. Formal planning, when it happens, is usually part of the IT planning conducted by the Director of Information Systems or CIO.

To their advantage, some observers feel that small organizations avoid some threats precisely because of their small size. The thinking is that hacktivists, hackers, and other threat agents may be less likely to go after smaller companies, opting instead to attack larger, more prestigious targets. Although this questionable strategy has not been proven, it is not wise to gamble the future of the organization on its staying unnoticed. To use an old saying, "There is no security in obscurity."

Threats from insiders are also less likely in an environment where every employee knows every other employee. In general, the less anonymity an employee has, the less likely he or she feels able to get away with mischief, abuse, or misuse of company assets.

The lack of resources available to the smaller organization's security administrators is somewhat offset by the lower risk of becoming a target. Figure 5-4 shows the challenges faced in smaller organizations, which typically have either one individual who has full-time duties in information security or, more likely, one individual who manages or conducts information security duties in addition to those of other functional areas, most likely IT. This individual may have partial supervision of one or two assistants.

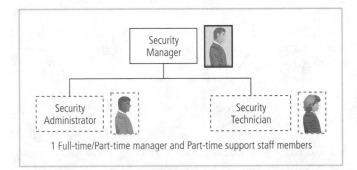

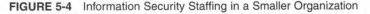

1 Full-time/Part-time manager and Part-time support staff members

FIGURE 5-4   Information Security Staffing in a Smaller Organization

VIEWPOINT

Developing a Security Program

By Krizi Trivisani, CISSP, Director and Chief Security Officer, Information Security Office, The George Washington University.

Getting started can be the hardest part of any journey—especially if you do not have a clear understanding of where to begin or where are you going. Developing an information security program can be an enormous task, and, as with a journey, it helps to have a map of the territory before you start. But it is important to remember that maps can—and do—change over time; thus your program must have a certain amount of flexibility built in. I like to think of my security architecture as living and breathing, able to adapt and change as threats evolve.

When developing a security program for an organization, it is essential to understand your environment, as it will be the biggest influence on how your program will work. The first question to ask is, "What are you trying to protect?" Identifying the data critical to your company's success—customer, financial, student, medical, and so on—will help you establish the "crown jewels" upon which you will focus your protective efforts.

Keep your organization's mission in mind and develop your security program to support it. For example, a bank may restrict access on a "need to know" basis, whereas a university may encourage full access and sharing across its network, save for a protective layer around the central systems required to manage the university itself. Select a security philosophy that works best at combating the challenges your organization faces.

continued

Don't forget about legislation—the things you are required to do must be included in your plan. An alphabet soup of requirements—SOX, HIPAA, FERPA, GLB—is ever-present in security compliance. Make sure you know which ones affect you and take appropriate measures. The excuse "I didn't know we were covered" won't help you in court. Adhering to appropriate industry guidelines will also help you measure and track your program's progress and avoid pitfalls later.

Some organizations still spend more on coffee than they do on security. Completing a risk assessment with a cost-benefit analysis will help you determine where to best apply your scarce resources. The odds are good that you will not have enough money to create one security group that will be responsible for everything. Instead, find out who is doing security-related tasks in the organization and create relationships with them. Often they will be your best advocates, and having representatives from multiple departments will help create widespread security ownership.

Speaking of ownership, who are your stakeholders? Support from upper-level management is crucial to your program's success. The security office must have the proper level of authority and autonomy to protect the crown jewels from threats originating both inside and outside of the organization. Know who the decision makers are, and keep them informed on a regular basis.

Starting a security program also requires a change in culture. Most people resist change, so awareness and involvement should be integral elements in your program. Understand your organization's culture and tailor your efforts appropriately. In addition, look for resources outside of your organization. Some of your best allies may be other people in similar situations. Find other security professionals who are willing to share ideas. Join local chapters and national organizations to network, continue your professional development, and stay abreast of the latest trends.

Sir Winston Churchill once said, "Every day you may make progress. Every step may be fruitful. Yet there will stretch out before you an ever-lengthening, ever-ascending, ever-improving path. You know you will never get to the end of the journey. But this, so far from discouraging, only adds to the joy and glory of the climb."

PLACING INFORMATION SECURITY WITHIN AN ORGANIZATION

In large organizations the information security department is often located within the IT department, headed by the CISO who reports directly to the top computing executive, or CIO. Such a structure implies that the goals and objectives of the CISO and CIO are closely aligned. In reality, this is not always the case. By its very nature, an information security program is sometimes at odds with the goals and objectives of the IT department as a whole. On the one hand, the CIO, as the executive in charge of the organization's technology, manages the efficiency in processing and accessing the organization's information. Anything that limits access or slows information processing directly contradicts the CIO's mission. On the other hand, the CISO functions more like an internal auditor, with the information security department examining existing systems to discover information security faults and flaws in technology, software, and employees' activities and processes. At times, these activities may disrupt the processing and accessing of the organization's information. Because the goals and objectives of the CIO and the CISO may come in conflict, it is not difficult to understand the current movement to separate information security from the IT division.

The vision of separate IT and information security functions is shared by many executives. A 2002 survey conducted by Meta Group found that while only 3% of the consulting firm's clients positioned the information security department outside IT, the clients viewed this positioning as what a forward-thinking organization should do. The article "Where the Chief Security Officer Belongs" perhaps states this point more succinctly: "The people who do and the people who watch shouldn't report to a common manager."[6]

The challenge is to design a reporting structure for the information security program that balances the competing needs of the communities of interest. In many cases, the unit that executes the information security program is shoehorned into the organizational chart in a way that reflects its marginal status, and it may be shuffled from place to place within the organization with little attention paid to how such organizational moves hinder its effectiveness. Organizations searching for a rational compromise will attempt to find a place for the information security program that allows it to balance policy enforcement with education, training, awareness, and customer service needs. This approach can help make information security part of the organizational culture.

There are many ways to position the information security program within an organization. In his book *Information Security Roles and Responsibilities Made Easy*, Charles Cresson Wood has compiled many of the best practices on information security program positioning from many industry groups. His chapter covering this topic, "Reporting Relationships," has been condensed here.

This [area] covers the generally accepted and frequently encountered reporting relationships for an Information Security Department. The pros and cons of twelve options are explored and six reporting relationships are recommended. Because there are many places in the organizational hierarchy where an Information Security Department could be situated, you should review the list of pros and cons for each option, thinking about what is most important in your organization. [...] You should then summarize these considerations in a memo, and after this memo is prepared, you will most likely be leaning in the direction of one of these reporting relationships. At that point in time, a clear and well-justified proposal for an Information Security Department reporting relationship can be formulated.

[...] In successful organizational structures, the Department reports high up in the management hierarchy. Reporting directly to top management is advisable for the Information Security Department Manager [or CISO] because it fosters objectivity and the ability to erceive what's truly in the best interest of the organization as a whole, rather than what's in the best interest of a particular department (such as the Information Technology Department). A highly placed executive in charge of information security will also be more readily able to gain management's attention, and this in turn will increase the likelihood that the Information Security Department will obtain the necessary budget and staffing resources. An Information Security Department that reports high up on the management ladder will also be more readily able to force compliance with certain requirements, such as a standard specifying consistent implementation of certain encryption technology.

In a few progressive organizations, being located high on the management ladder means that the Information Security Department Manager is a Senior Vice President who reports directly to the Chief Executive Officer (CEO). This is, for example, the organizational structure now found at a well-known credit card company. Having an Information Security Manager who reports directly to the CEO may also be appropriate for a short while until major improvements in the information security area have been made. This temporary reporting structure clearly communicates that information security is important and worthy of top management's attention.

Nonetheless, for a medium- to large-scale organization, the most common reporting structure involves one or two levels of management between the Information Security Department Manager and the CEO. In general, the smaller the number of intermediate levels of management, the greater the strategic importance of the information security function. It is important that the distance between the CEO and the Information Security Manager be minimized. [...]

[...] If you are establishing an information security function for the first time, or if a major reorganization is under way, you should seriously think about which middle managers would best serve as the conduit for messages sent to the CEO. Other desirable attributes are:

- Openness to new ideas
- Clout with top management
- Respect in the eyes of a wide variety of employees
- Comfort and familiarity with basic information systems concepts
- Willingness to take a stand for those things that are genuinely in the long-term best interest of the organization

The ideal middle-level manager should report directly to the CEO, or as high up on the organizational hierarchy as possible. The manager's organizational unit will also need a credible day-to-day relationship with, or a strategic tie-in with, the information security function. For example, a Risk and Insurance Management Department would have such a tie-in, but an Assembly Line Operations Department most often would not. The candidates are many, but some common choices are the Executive Vice President Administrative Services, the Legal Department Manager (Chief Legal Officer), and the Chief Information Officer (CIO).

This [section] makes reference to six [figures that illustrate] Options 1 through 6. These six reporting relationships are explored in that sequence. After that, six other options, which are not as frequently encountered, are discussed. The six [figures] are illustrative of real-world organizations and are not in any way meant to be hypothetical or normative. Throughout [...] I have attempted to be descriptive rather than to propose a new paradigm, and in that respect, because these options are based on real-world experience, you can be assured that any one of these six initial options could be effective within your organization. The [figures] are also meant to convey an indication of good practice on which you can rely.

Option 1: Information Technology

In [Figure 5-5], you will note that in this organizational structure the Information Security Department reports to the Information Technology Department. [...] Here the Information Security Department Manager reports directly to the Chief Information Officer (CIO), or the Vice President of Information Systems. In this option, you will find the most common organizational structure. Various statistical studies show that over 50% of organizations use this reporting relationship. This option is desirable because the manager to whom the Information Security Department Manager reports generally has clout with top management, and understands (in broad and general terms) the information systems technological issues. This option is also advantageous because it involves only one manager between the Information Security Department Manager and the Chief Executive Officer (CEO). The option is additionally advisable because the Information Security Department staff, on a day-to-day basis, must spend a good deal of time with the Information Technology Department staff. In that respect, this option is convenient. Nonetheless, this option is flawed because it includes an inherent conflict of interest. When confronted with resource allocation issues, or when required to strike a trade-off, the CIO is likely to discriminate against the information security function. Other objectives such as cost minimization, user friendliness, or time-to-market with a new product or service will likely take precedence over information security. Another drawback of this option involves the implied conclusion that information security is strictly a technological issue, which clearly it is not. Although common, this organizational structure is not as desirable as several of the other options, and for that reason is not particularly recommended.

Note that [Figure 5-5] does not have information security reporting to a Computer Operations Manager, the Management Information Systems Manager, the Information Resources Manager, or some other manager who in turn reports to the CIO or the Vice President of Information Systems. Having an additional level of management also increases the likelihood that messages sent from the Information Security Department to the CEO will be corrupted in transit (the "whisper down the lane" problem). Other reasons not to pursue this organizational structure are covered below in "Option 8: Help Desk."

In [Figure 5-5], you should note that the Information Security Department Manager also has a dotted-line reporting relationship with the Information Security Management Committee. Although they are highly recommended, both this dotted-line relationship and the Committee can be omitted for smaller organizations. A Committee of this nature is a good idea because it provides a sounding board, a management direction-setting body, and a communication path with the rest of the organization. A drawback of using a committee like this is that it may take longer to get management approval for certain initiatives, but the approval that is obtained is likely to be more lasting and more widely distributed throughout the organization.

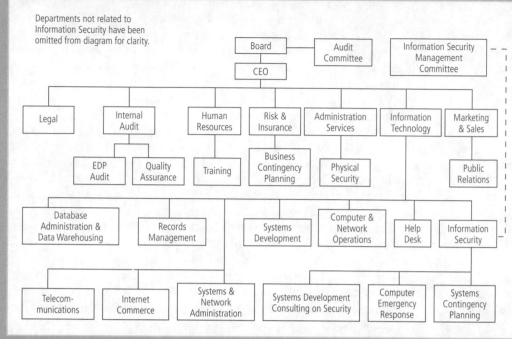

Departments not related to Information Security have been omitted from diagram for clarity.

From *Information Security Roles and Responsibilities Made Easy*, used with permission.

FIGURE 5-5 Wood's Option 1: Information Security Reports to Information Technology Department

Option 2: Security

Another popular option, which again is not necessarily recommended, involves the Information Security Department reporting to the Security Department. In this case, the information security function is perceived to be primarily protective in nature, and therefore comparable to the Physical Security Department as well as the Personnel Security and Safety Department. Where this organizational design prevails, you may occasionally find the Information Security Department is instead referred to as the Information Protection Department. Shown in [Figure 5-6], this approach is desirable because it facilitates communication with others who have both a security perspective and related security responsibilities. This may help with incident investigations as well as reaching practical solutions to problems like laptop computer theft (which involves a combination of physical and information security). This option is also desirable because it brings a longer-term preventive viewpoint to information security activities, which in turn is likely to lower overall information security costs.

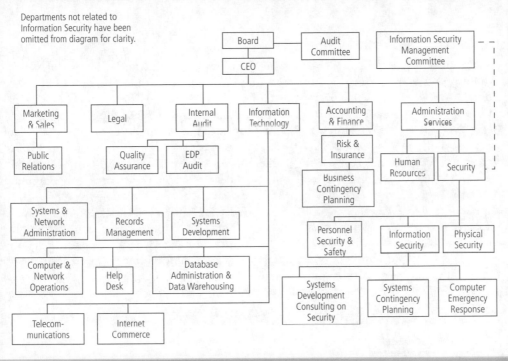

Departments not related to Information Security have been omitted from diagram for clarity.

From *Information Security Roles and Responsibilities Made Easy,* used with permission.

FIGURE 5-6 Wood's Option 2: Information Security Reports to Broadly Defined Security Department

Nonetheless, there are some problems with this structure. Although the information security and physical security functions may at first seem to be philosophically aligned, there is a significant cultural difference between the two. For example, information security staff see themselves as high-tech workers, while physical security staff see themselves as participants in the criminal justice system. These cultural differences may cause someinformation security specialists to feel that it's not appropriate to be managed by a specialist in physical security, which will most often be the background of the Security Department Manager. This option is moreover undesirable because, at most firms, the budget for physical security has not increased much over the last few years, but the budget for information security has rapidly escalated; by combining these two departments under the Security Department umbrella, top management may underestimate the resources that the information security function will need. Option 2 is furthermore undesirable because the Security Department Manager will often lack an appreciation of information systems technology, and so may be a poor communicator with top management. This option is furthermore ill advised because it involves two middle managers in the communication path between the Information Security Department Manager and the CEO. To make it still less appealing, this option is likely to indirectly communicate that the Information Security Department is a new type of police; this perspective will make it more difficult for the Information Security Department to establish consultative relationships with other departments. On balance, this organizational structure is acceptable, but not as desirable as some of the other diagrams described.

Option 3: Administrative Services

Another way to do things, which is a significant improvement over both Options 1 and 2, is shown in [Figure 5-7]. Here the Information Security Department reports to the Administrative Services Department (which may also be called Administrative Support). In this case, the Information Security Department Manager reports to the Administrative Services Department Manager or the Vice President of Administration. This approach assumes that the Information Security Department is advisory in nature (also called a *staff function*), and performs services for workers throughout the organization, much like the Human Resources Department. This option is desirable because there is only one middle manager between the Information Security Department Manager and the CEO. The approach is also advisable because it acknowledges that information and information systems are found everywhere throughout the organization, and that workers throughout the organization are expected to work with the Information Security Department. This option is also attractive because it supports efforts to secure information no matter what form it takes (on paper, verbal, etc.), rather than viewing the information security function as strictly a computer- and network-oriented activity.

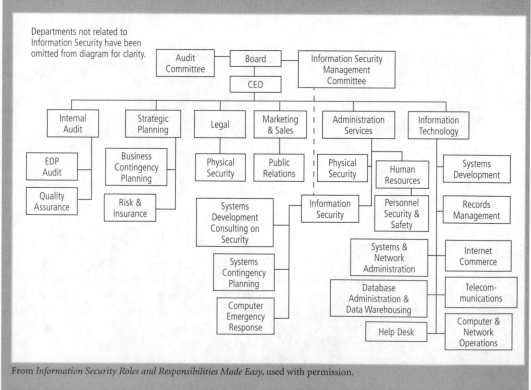

From *Information Security Roles and Responsibilities Made Easy*, used with permission.

FIGURE 5-7   Wood's Option 3: Information Security Reports to Administrative Services Department

In many cases, depending on who fills the Administrative Services Vice President position, this option suffers because the Vice President doesn't know much about information systems technology, and this in turn may hamper his or her efforts to communicate with the CEO about information security. This option may also be ill advised for those organizations that could severely suffer, or even go out of business, if major information security problems were encountered. An Internet merchant (a "dot-com" firm) fits this billing. For these firms, this option doesn't give information security the prominence it deserves, nor does it give it the strategic and long-term focus that information security requires. Thus, with this option, the Information Security Department may be subject to more cost-cutting pressure from top management than it would with Option 4 or 5. On balance, though, for organizations that are not highly information intensive, such as a chain of restaurants, this is a desirable and recommended option.

Option 4: Insurance and Risk Management

[Figure 5-8] shows how the Information Security Department can report to the Insurance and Risk Management Department. With this approach, the Information Security Department Manager would typically report to the Chief Risk Manager (CRM) or the Vice President of Risk and Insurance Management. This option is desirable because it fosters what is often called an integrated risk management perspective. With this viewpoint, a centralized perspective prioritizes and compares all risks across the organization. The application of this idea typically involves assessing the extent of potential losses and the likelihood of losses across all functional departments, including Information Security, Physical Security, Legal, Internal Audit, Customer Relations, Accounting and Finance, etc. The intention is to see the big picture and be able to allocate resources to those departments and risk management efforts that most need these resources. You are strongly urged to foster the integrated risk management viewpoint, even if the current or proposed organizational structure doesn't reflect it, because information security will often be shown to be a serious and largely unaddressed problem area deserving greater organizational resources and greater management attention. Beyond integrated risk management, this option is desirable because it involves only one middle manager between the Information Security Department Manager and the CEO.

The CRM is also likely to be prevention oriented, adopt a longer-term viewpoint, and is able to engage the CEO in intelligent discussions about *risk acceptance* (doing nothing), *risk mitigation* (adding controls), and *risk transfer* (buying insurance). A CRM is also likely to be comfortable thinking about the future and generating scenarios reflecting a number of different possibilities, including information security scenarios such as a denial-of-service (DoS) attack. The CRM, however, is often not familiar with information systems technology, and so may need some special coaching or extra background research from the Information Security Department Manager to make important points with the CEO. Another problem with this approach is that its focus is strategic, and the operational and administrative aspects of information security (such as changing privileges when people change jobs) may not get the attention that they deserve from the CRM. Nonetheless, on balance this is a desirable option and is recommended for organizations that are information intensive, such as banks, stock brokerages, telephone companies, and research institutes.

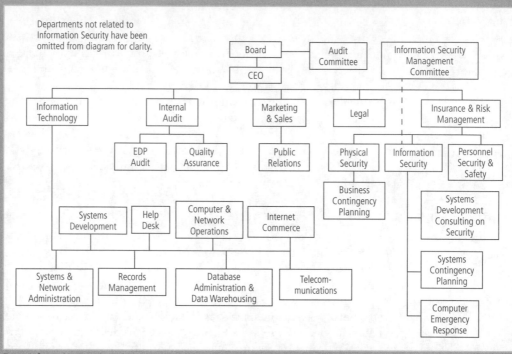

Departments not related to Information Security have been omitted from diagram for clarity.

From *Information Security Roles and Responsibilities Made Easy,* used with permission.

FIGURE 5-8   Wood's Option 4: Information Security Reports to Insurance and Risk Management Department

Option 5: Strategy and Planning

In [Figure 5-9], you will find still another possible organizational structure found in the real world. Here the Information Security Department reports to the Strategy and Planning Department. In this case, the Information Security Department Manager reports directly to the Vice President of Strategy and Planning. This option views the information security function as critical to the success of the organization. This option would be appropriate for an Internet merchant (a "dot-com" enterprise) or a credit card company, both of which are critically dependent on the success of the information security function. This option is desirable because it involves only one middle manager between the Information Security Department Manager and the CEO. It is thus just one step down from the option mentioned at the beginning of this chapter, where the Senior Vice President of Information Security reports directly to the CEO.

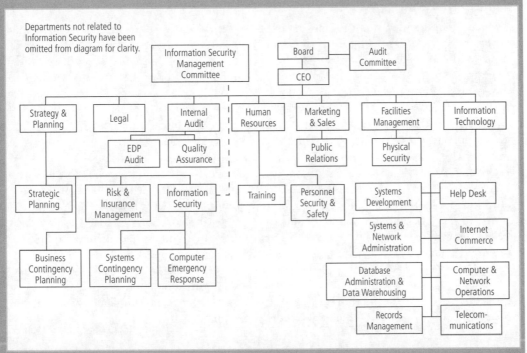

Departments not related to Information Security have been omitted from diagram for clarity.

From *Information Security Roles and Responsibilities Made Easy*, used with permission.

FIGURE 5-9 Wood's Option 5: Information Security Reports to Strategy and Planning Department

Option 5 is desirable because it underscores the need for documented information security requirements (policies, standards, procedures, etc.) that apply to the entire organization. Like Options 3 and 4, this reporting structure also acknowledges the multidepartmental and multidisciplinary nature of information security tasks such as risk analysis and incident investigations. This option is also advisable because the Information Security Department works with others that share a scenario-oriented view of the world (they often ask "what if..." questions). Another desirable aspect of this approach is that it implicitly communicates that information security is very importantly a management and people issue, not just a technological issue.

This same advantage can be a disadvantage if workers in the Information Technology Department consider the staff in the Information Security Department to be management oriented, and out of touch when it comes to the technology (of course, the work of the Information Security Department can clearly communicate that this is a misperception). One problem with this approach is that the focus is strategic, and the operational and administrative aspects of information security (such as changing privileges when people change jobs) may not get the attention that they deserve from the Vice President of Strategy and Planning. On balance, though, this is an advisable reporting relationship for the information security function, and should be something that the Information Department Manager is considering for the long run even if he or she is not proposing it today.

Option 6: Legal

[Figure 5-10] shows an unusual but nonetheless viable and recommended organizational structure. In this case the Information Security Department reports to the Legal Department. This option correctly emphasizes that information is the asset of primary concern, not information systems. This option thus places great emphasis on copyrights, patents, trademarks, and related intellectual property protection mechanisms. As they should, contracts—such as nondisclosure agreements (NDAs) and outsourcing agreements—will also get great attention with this organizational structure. With this option there is also great emphasis on compliance with laws, regulations, and ethical standards (like privacy). Information security is increasingly mandated by law, regulated, and affected by ethical standards, so Option 6 is really an organizational structure for the future. If your organization happens to be in a highly regulated industry, such as credit bureaus or defense contractors, then this organizational structure could be appropriate. This option is desirable because access to top management is provided through only one middle manager—the Legal Department Manager, sometimes called the Chief Legal Officer (CLO). This manager is often quite articulate and credible and often a desirable carrier of Information Security Department messages to the CEO. This reporting structure is also advisable because the members of the Legal Department are comfortable with, and spend a lot of time developing, documentation such as policies and procedures; and documentation showing that the organization is in compliance with the information security standard of due care is increasingly important.

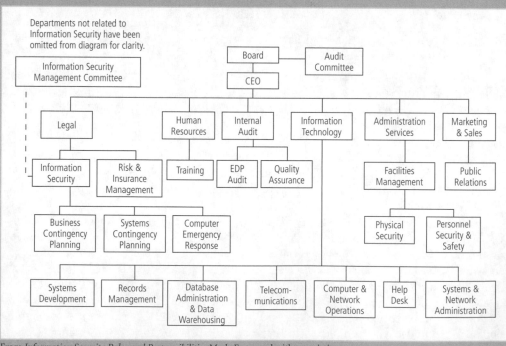

From *Information Security Roles and Responsibilities Made Easy,* used with permission.

FIGURE 5-10 Wood's Option 6: Information Security Reports to Legal Department

On the downside of Option 6 is the potential overemphasis on compliance, with the potential consequential underemphasis on other aspects of information security, such as access control administration. This organizational structure might also inadvertently lead to the Information Security Department doing compliance checking work, which presents a clear conflict of interest (as explained in "Option 7: Internal Audit"). Compliance checking should be performed by an Internal Auditing Department, not the Information Security Department. On balance, though, this organizational structure has much to recommend it, and will probably be encountered in an increasing number of organizations in the years ahead.

Option 7: Internal Audit

Although I have seen it in the real world, the Information Security Department should definitely not report to the Internal Audit Department. In this case, the Information Security Department Manager reports to the Internal Auditing Department Manager. An examination of the mission statement for the Internal Audit Department [...] reveals that Internal Audit is charged with reviewing the work done by other units, including the Information Security Department. If the Information Security Department were to report to the Internal Audit Department, a conflict of interest would exist. Internal Audit would be tempted to exaggerate the good work of the Information Security Department so that the Internal Audit Department as a whole would look good. A controls-oriented Chief Internal Auditor may also be tempted to allocate more resources to an Information Security Department than are realistically warranted, and this in turn could create an undue security burden for the rest of the organization as well as a backlash that could take years to overcome. Reporting to the Internal Audit Department may also be contraindicated because Internal Audit often has adversarial relationships with other departments, and the perspectives that go along with those relationships could be unwittingly transferred to relationships between the Information Security Department and other departments.

On the other hand, one advantage of reporting to the Internal Audit Department is that the Internal Audit Department Manager has a controls perspective and will at least in theory support what an Information Security Department is trying to do. Another reason in favor of reporting to Internal Audit is the tremendous clout that this group has with top management and the Board of Directors. Nothing in this paragraph is meant to discourage the Information Security Department from establishing a close and mutually beneficial working relationship with an Internal Audit Department, and such a good working relationship is characteristic of firms with successful information security efforts.

Just because there is no direct reporting relationship to EDP Audit (or Internal Audit for that matter) doesn't mean it isn't a good idea to have a dotted-line reporting relationship to the Audit Committee on the Board of Directors. This dotted-line relationship is intended to be a periodic reporting relationship as well as a safety valve. Information Security can provide quarterly reports about the status of information security to the Audit Committee. If the Committee doesn't like what they are hearing, they can then redirect the efforts of top managers. Likewise, if top management is relatively unreceptive to the Information Security Department's point of view, Information Security can take its concerns to the Audit Committee. This dotted-line reporting relationship doesn't currently exist in many organizations, but there are many efforts now under way to establish this type of relationship.

Option 8: Help Desk

Another option involves having the Information Security Department report to the Help Desk Department. In this case, the Information Security Department Manager reports to the Help Desk Department Manager. As is the case with reporting into the Internal Audit Department, this option was not presented in a diagram because it is not advised. A Help Desk Department is a lower-level technical group that does not get much top management attention or respect. Likewise, the Help Desk Department generally does not command many resources, and this scarcity of resources may be carried over into the Information Security Department. If the Information Security Department reported to the Help Desk Department, there would be at least two levels of middle management between the Information Security Department Manager and the CEO, and this could further hinder the acquisition of adequate resources. Another reason not to establish an organizational structure like this involves the Help Desk Department's customer focus and service orientation. While this may at first be perceived to be a desirable characteristic, it may also force the Information Security Department to opt for quick response, ease of use, and other objectives besides a high level of security. It could, nonetheless, be advantageous to report to the Help Desk Department in terms of mobilization after a break-in, for example, when it comes time to get a computer emergency response team (CERT) into action. This is because a Help Desk Department is on the front lines, and is often first to hear about a problem. This reporting structure could also be beneficial because the Help Desk Department's trouble ticket system could be directly tied into logs of information security problems. Analysis of these logs could provide the Information Security Department with important insight into problems as they are occurring. On balance, though, this reporting relationship, like reporting relationships to other lower-level departments, is strongly discouraged. Similar remarks could be offered for organizational designs involving the reporting of an Information Security Department into other subgroups within the Information Technology Department. Examples include the Computer Operations Department, the Systems Development Department, and the Records Management Department.

Option 9: Accounting and Finance Through IT

Another option involves the Information Security Department reporting to the Accounting and Finance Department through the Information Technology Department. This option is undesirable for the reasons mentioned under "Option 1: Information Technology" (notably trade-offs with competing objectives). This option is furthermore undesirable because the Information Security Department would be buried deep in the organizational hierarchy, and would be therefore unlikely to get the resources and top management attention that it needs. While the Information Security Department is a staff (advisory service) department like the Accounting and Finance Department, it is growing much more rapidly than the Accounting and Finance Department. Integration with the Accounting and Finance Department may thus conceal this rapid growth rate from top management, which in turn could lead to underfunded information security efforts. Reporting to the Accounting and Finance Department may also cause the needs of the Information Security Department to be lost within, and overshadowed by, the needs of the Accounting and Finance Department. If the Information Security Department is combined with other activities in the Accounting and Finance Department, top management is likely to see the information security function as a back-office operation, and not a strategic issue worthy of top management attention.

Option 10: Human Resources

Still another possibility for the Information Security Department is reporting to the Human Resources Department. [...] There is a certain synergy that could be achieved when the Information Security Department is part of the Human Resources Department; this comes from both groups developing policies that must be followed by workers throughout the organization. For example, the Human Resources disciplinary process is used to deal with those who are not in compliance with information security policies. If the Human Resources Department also handles the staff training function, this synergy can be magnified. Nonetheless, this is generally considered an ill-advised organizational position for the Information Security Department because the Human Resources Department Manager often knows very little about information systems, and is therefore most often not a credible conduit for communications to top management. [...]

Option 11: Facilities Management

Yet another option for the Information Security Department involves reporting to the Facilities Management Department (sometimes called Buildings and Grounds). Since this option is not recommended, no diagram has been provided. This is a rare but occasionally encountered organizational structure that views the information security function as something similar to the building guards who help prevent burglary. With this organizational structure, the Information Security Department is seen by top management as an asset protection function much like the Physical Security Department. [...]

Option 12: Operations

Under this approach, the Information Security Department Manager reports to the Chief Operating Officer (COO). This approach assumes that information security is a line management responsibility, and a topic that all department managers must consider in their day-to-day activities. While it is desirable to emphasize management's responsibilities, it is also true that information security is a staff function, a function that provides advice and guidance to other departments. [...]

Summary of Reporting Relationships

The Information Security Department at many organizations has been an unwelcome stepchild, handed back and forth between various groups, none of which felt as though they were its proper home. [...]

Smaller organizations will want to have a part-time Information Security Coordinator or Information Security Manager. [...] Small to medium-sized organizations will often require at least one full-time person, and medium-sized to large organizations will often require several full-time information security staff. [...] Since so few people are involved, in smaller organizations, the formal designation of a separate department will be considered to be unwarranted. But for all other organizations, no matter where the information security function happens to report, it is desirable to designate a separate department that has been formally recognized by top management. [...][7]

COMPONENTS OF THE SECURITY PROGRAM

The information security needs of any organization are unique to the culture, size, and budget of that organization. Determining the level on which the information security program operates depends on the organization's strategic plan, and in particular on the plan's vision and mission statements. The CIO and CISO should use these two documents to formulate the mission statement for the information security program. Some guidance concerning the formulation of mission statements is provided by Charles Cresson Wood:

> A mission statement is a brief statement of objectives that describes what top management expects from the involved organizational unit. Although a broad-brush overview of activities is often helpful in a mission statement, specifics about these activities should instead appear in [associated] job description[s]. A mission statement should deal with a whole department or similar multi-person organizational unit, and should not talk about the objectives for a specific job title. [...] Likewise, a mission statement should not use any technical language, acronyms, or other jargon that will not be immediately understood by non-technical workers or top management.[8]

Two documents from the National Institute of Standards and Technology (NIST) also provide guidance for developing an information security program. SP 800-14, *Generally Accepted Principles and Practices for Securing Information Technology Systems*,

> ...gives a foundation that organizations can reference when conducting multi-organizational business as well as internal business. Management, internal auditors, users, system developers, and security practitioners [sic] can use the guideline to gain an understanding of the basic security requirements most IT systems should contain. The foundation begins with generally accepted system security principles and continues with common practices that are used in securing IT systems.[9]

The other, and perhaps more important, NIST publication is SP 800-12, *An Introduction to Computer Security: The NIST Handbook*. This manual "provides a broad overview of many of the core topics included in computer [and information] security to help readers understand their computer security needs and develop a sound approach to the selection of appropriate security controls."[10] This handbook includes sections covering many topics, including the following:

- Elements of computer security
- Roles and responsibilities
- Common threats

- Common information security controls
- Risk management
- Security program management
- Contingency planning

Table 5-2 summarizes the essential program elements presented in these two NIST documents.

TABLE 5-2 Elements of a Security Program

Primary Element	Components
Policy	Program Policy, Issue-Specific Policy, System-Specific Policy
Program Management	Central Security Program, System-Level Program
Risk Management	Risk Assessment, Risk Mitigation, Uncertainty Analysis
Life-Cycle Planning	Security Plan, Initiation Phase, Development/Acquisition Phase, Implementation Phase, Operation/Maintenance Phase
Personnel/User Issues	Staffing, User Administration
Preparing for Contingencies and Disasters	Business Plan, Identify Resources, Develop Scenarios, Develop Strategies, Test and Revise Plan
Computer Security Incident Handling	Incident Detection, Reaction, Recovery, and Followup
Awareness and Training	SETA plans, Awareness Projects, and Policy and Procedure Training
Security Considerations in Computer Support and Operations	Help Desk Integration, Defending Against Social Engineering, and Improving System Administration
Physical and Environmental Security	Guards, Gates, Locks and Keys, and Alarms
Identification and Authentication	Identification, Authentication, Passwords, Advanced Authentication
Logical Access Control	Access Criteria, Access Control Mechanisms
Audit Trails	System Logs, Log Review Processes, and Log Consolidation and Management
Cryptography	TKI, VPN, Key Management, and Key Recovery

Source: National Institute of Standards and Technology. *Generally Accepted Principles and Practices for Securing Information Technology Systems*. NIST Publication 800-14. http://csrc.nist.gov/publications/nistpubs/800-14/800-14.pdf.

There is much overlap between the elements of Table 5-2 and the earlier list of functions of an information security program given in Table 5-1. Both resources should be used when reviewing the components of any specific information security program.

INFORMATION SECURITY ROLES AND TITLES

A study of information security positions by Schwartz, Erwin, Weafer, and Briney found that positions can be classified into one of three types: those that *define,* those that *build,* and those that *administer.*

> Definers provide the policies, guidelines, and standards. [...] They're the people who do the consulting and the risk assessment, who develop the product and technical architectures. These are senior people with a lot of broad knowledge, but often not a lot of depth. Then you have the builders. They're the real techies, who create and install security solutions. [...] Finally, you have the people who operate and administrate the security tools, the security monitoring function, and the people who continuously improve the processes. [...] What I find is we often try to use the same people for all of these roles. We use builders all the time [...] If you break your InfoSec professionals into these three groups, you can recruit them more efficiently, with the policy people being the more senior people, the builders being more technical, and the operating people being those you can train to do a specific task.[11]

A typical organization has a number of individuals with information security responsibilities. While the titles used within any specific organization may be different from one organization to the next, most of the job functions fit into one of the following categories:

- Chief Information Security Officer (CISO)
- Security managers
- Security administrators and analysts
- Security technicians
- Security staffers and watchstanders
- Security consultants
- Security officers and investigators
- Help desk personnel

Each of these positions is discussed briefly here and more fully in Chapter 10.

Chief Information Security Officer

The CISO is primarily responsible for the assessment, management, and implementation of the program that secures the organization's information. An article in *CSO Magazine*, "The State of the CISO," reports that the title CISO is only used in about 20% of the organizations surveyed. "The top three titles for this role again [in 2006] are Manager of Security (21%), Director of Security (21%), and Chief Information Security Officer (20%). Those with EVP, Sr. VP or VP of Security titles now account for 10% of respondents (up from 6% in 2004), and those with the title of CSO account for 10% of the survey base."[12] This position may also be called the Security Administrator or other similar title. The creation of the CISO position is still relatively new; 71% of the CISOs who responded to the *CSO Magazine* survey indicated that they were the first person in their organization with a senior security manager title. The average CISO had been in their current position for approximately four and a quarter years.[13]

The CISO usually reports directly to the CIO, although in larger organizations one or more layers of management may separate the two officers. According to the *CSO Magazine* study, "Increasingly, respondents said they report to the CIO or CTO, 38% compared to 29% in 2004. With this increase, other titles the CSO once reported to are becoming less common. This includes the CEO/President, down to 7% from 13%, and the Chief Financial Officer, down to 6% from 9% in last year's study."[14] Figure 5-11 shows the CISO as the senior-most information security role.

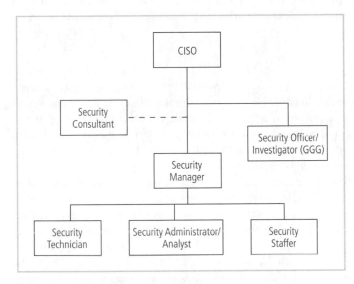

FIGURE 5-11   Information Security Roles

Security Managers

Security managers are accountable for the day-to-day operations of the information security program. They accomplish objectives identified by the CISO, to whom they report as shown in Figure 5-11, and resolve issues identified by technicians, administrators, analysts, or staffers whom they supervise. Managing technology requires an understanding of it, but not necessarily technical mastery in its configuration, operation, and fault resolution. Some team leaders or project managers within the information security community may be responsible for management-like functions, such as scheduling, setting priorities, or administering any number of procedural tasks, but are not necessarily held accountable for making a particular technology function. Accountability for the actions of others is the hallmark of a true manager, and is the criteria which distinguishes actual managers from others without such accountability but whose job titles include the word "manager."

Security Administrators and Analysts

The security administrator is a hybrid of a security technician (see the following section) and a security manager (described in the previous section). Such individuals have both technical knowledge and managerial skill. They are frequently called on to manage the day-to-day operations of security technology, as well as to assist in the development and conduct of training programs, policy, and the like.

The security analyst is a specialized security administrator. In traditional IT, the security administrator corresponds to a systems administrator or database administrator, and the security analyst to a systems analyst. The systems analyst, in addition to performing his or her security administration duties, must analyze and design security solutions within a specific domain (firewall, IDS, antivirus program). Systems analysts must be able to identify users' needs and to understand the technological complexities and capabilities of the security systems they design.

Security Technicians

Security technicians are the technically qualified individuals who configure firewalls and IDSs, implement security software, diagnose and troubleshoot problems, and coordinate with systems and network administrators to ensure that security technology is properly implemented. A security technician is usually an entry-level position; some technical skills are required, however, which can make it challenging for those new to the field as it is difficult to get a job without experience, and experience comes with a job.

Just as in networking, security technicians tend to be specialized, focusing on one major security technology group (firewalls, IDSs, servers, routers, or software), and further specializing in one particular software or hardware package within that group, such as Checkpoint firewalls, Nokia firewalls, or Tripwire IDS. These technologies are sufficiently complex to warrant a high level of specialization. Security technicians who want to move up in the corporate hierarchy must expand their technical knowledge horizontally, gaining an understanding of the general, organizational issues of information security as well as all technical areas.

Security Staffers and Watchstanders

Security staffer is a catchall title that applies to individuals who perform routine watch-standing activities. It includes the people who watch intrusion consoles, monitor e-mail accounts, and perform other routine, yet critical roles that support the mission of the information security department. The role of the watchstander is evolving as it is a relatively new position. Watchstanders are usually entry-level information security professionals responsible for monitoring some aspect of the organization's security posture, whether technical, as in the case of an IDS watchstander, or managerial. They assist with the research and development of security policy, plans, or risk management efforts. In this position new information security professionals have the opportunity to learn more about the organization's information security program before becoming a critical component of its administration.

Security Consultants

The information security consultant is typically an independent expert in some aspect of information security (disaster recovery, business continuity planning, security architecture, policy development, or strategic planning). He or she is usually brought in when the organization makes the decision to outsource one or more aspects of its security program. While it is usually preferable to involve a formal security services company, qualified individual consultants are available for hire.

Security Officers and Investigators

Occasionally, the physical security and information security programs are blended into a single unit. When that occurs, a series of roles are added to the combined program, including security officers and investigators—the guards, gates, and guns (GGG) aspect of security, which is closely related to law enforcement. Physical security professionals comprise a vital component of information security, since physical access trumps logical security.

Help Desk Personnel

An important part of the information security team is the help desk, which enhances the security team's ability to identify potential problems. When a user calls the help desk with a complaint about his or her computer, the network, or an Internet connection, the user's problem may turn out to be related to a bigger problem, such as a hacker, denial-of-service attack, or a virus.

Because help desk technicians perform a specialized role in information security, they need specialized training. These staff members must be prepared to identify and diagnose both traditional technical problems and threats to information security. Their ability to do so may cut precious hours off of an incident response.

IMPLEMENTING SECURITY EDUCATION, TRAINING, AND AWARENESS PROGRAMS

Once the information security program's place in the organization is established, planning for **security education, training, and awareness (SETA)** programs begins. The SETA program is the responsibility of the CISO and is designed to reduce the incidence of accidental security breaches by members of the organization, including employees, contractors, consultants, vendors, and business partners who come into contact with its information assets. As mentioned in Chapter 2, *acts of human error or failure* (known generally as *errors*) are among the top threats to information assets.

Security awareness, training, and education programs offer three major benefits:

- They can improve employee behavior.
- They can inform members of the organization about where to report violations of policy.
- They enable the organization to hold employees accountable for their actions.

Employee accountability is necessary to ensure that the acts of an individual do not threaten the long-term viability of the entire company. When employees recognize that the organization protects itself by enforcing accountability, they will be less likely to view these programs as punitive. In fact, when an organization does not enforce accountability, it increases the risk of incurring a substantial loss that might cause it to fail, putting the entire workforce out of jobs.

SETA programs enhance general education and training programs by focusing on information security. For example, if an organization finds that many employees are using e-mail attachments in an unsafe manner, then e-mail users must be trained or retrained. As a matter of good practice, all systems development life cycles (SDLCs) include user training during both the implementation and maintenance phases. Information security projects are no different; they require initial training programs as systems are deployed and occasional retraining as needs arise.

A SETA program consists of three elements: security education, security training, and security awareness. An organization may not be able or willing to undertake the development of all of these components in-house, and may outsource them to local educational institutions. The purpose of SETA is to enhance security in three ways:

- By building in-depth knowledge, as needed, to design, implement, or operate security programs for organizations and systems
- By developing skills and knowledge so that computer users can perform their jobs while using IT systems more securely
- By improving awareness of the need to protect system resources[15]

Table 5-3 shows the features of security education, training, and awareness within the organization.

TABLE 5-3 Framework of Security Education Training and Awareness

	Awareness	Training	Education
Attribute	"What"	"How"	"Why"
Level	Information	Knowledge	Insight
Objective	Recognition	Skill	Understanding
Teaching Method	Media • Videos • Newsletters • Posters, Inc.	Practical Instruction • Lecture • Case study workshop • Hands-on practice	Theoretical Instruction • Discussion seminar • Background reading
Test Measure	True/False Multiple Choice (identify learning)	Problem Solving (apply learning)	Essay (interpret learning)
Impact Timeframe	Short-term	Intermediate	Long-term

Source: National Institute of Standards and Technology. *An Introduction to Computer Security: The NIST Handbook*. SP 800-12. http://csrc.nist.gov/publications/nistpubs/800-12/.

Security Education

Some organizations may have employees within the information security department who are not prepared by their background or experience for the information security roles they are intended to perform. When tactical circumstances allow and/or strategic imperatives dictate, these employees may be encouraged to use a formal education method. Resources that describe information security training programs include the NIST training and education site at http://csrc.nist.gov/ATE/training_&_education.html, the Virginia Alliance for Security Computing and Networking (VA SCAN) at http://www.vascan.org/toolkit_tt.html, and the National Security Agency (NSA)–identified Centers of Academic Excellence in Information Assurance Education (CAEIAE) at http://www.nsa.gov/ia/academia/caeiae.cfm. Local resources might also provide information and services in educational areas. Local companies and/or educational institutions can be used. For example, Kennesaw State University's Center for Information Security Education and Awareness (http://infosec.kennesaw.edu) provides "information on information security educational opportunities and initiatives in the KSU community. The Center also serves to increase the level of information security awareness in the KSU community."

Information security training programs must address the following issues:

- The information security educational components required of all *information security* professionals
- The general educational requirements that all *information technology* professionals must have

A number of institutions of higher learning, including colleges and universities, provide formal coursework in information security. Unfortunately, a recent review found that the majority of information security or computer security degrees (bachelor's or master's) are, in reality, computer science or information systems degrees that include a few courses in information security. While some programs do offer depth and breadth in information security education, prospective students must carefully examine the curriculum before enrolling. Students planning for careers in information security should review the number of courses offered, as well as the content of those courses.

The general IT educational curriculum needs to prepare students to work in a setting that values a secure and ethical computing environment. As noted by Irvin, Chin, and Frinke in the article "Integrating Security into the Curriculum,"

> An educational system that cultivates an appropriate knowledge of computer security will increase the likelihood that the next generation of IT workers will have the background needed to design and develop systems that are engineered to be reliable and secure.[16]

The need for improved information security education is so great that in May 1998 President Clinton issued Presidential Decision Directive 63, the Policy on Critical Infrastructure Protection. Among other requirements, the directive mandated that the NSA establish outreach programs like the CAEIAE. The CAEIAE program goal is "to reduce vulnerabilities in our National Information Infrastructure by promoting higher education in information assurance, and producing a growing number of professionals with IA expertise."[17] These initiatives are intended to increase not only the number of information security professionals, but also the information security awareness and educational knowledge of all technologists.

Developing Information Security Curricula

Hybrid information technology/security programs have emerged to fill the gap created by the lack of formal guidance from established curricula bodies. Established organizations that have developed and promoted standardized curricula, such as the Association of Computing Machinery (ACM), the Institute of Electrical and Electronics Engineers (IEEE), and the Accreditation Board for Engineering and Technology (ABET), do not have formal information security curricula models. For two-year institutions, however, the National Science Foundation (NSF) and the American Association of Community Colleges sponsored a workshop in 2002 that drafted recommendations for a report entitled *The Role of Community Colleges in Cybersecurity Education.* This report serves as a starting point for community colleges developing curricula in the field. A similar effort is currently underway for four-year institutions, but remains in its infancy.

Any institution designing a formal curriculum in information security must carefully map the expected learning outcomes of the planned curriculum to course learning objectives to establish the body of knowledge to be taught. This knowledge map, which can help potential students assess information security programs, identifies the skills and knowledge clusters obtained by the program's graduates. Graduate-level programs are more complex, and possibly more managerial in nature, depending on the program. At the undergraduate level, program planners examine the areas that graduates are expected to work in, and then define the required skills and knowledge.

Creating a knowledge map can be difficult because many academics are unaware of the numerous subdisciplines within the field of information security, each of which may have different knowledge requirements. For example, a student wanting a managerial focus needs to be educated in policy, planning, personnel administration, and other relevant topics, and thus would want to take courses like the ones for which this textbook is written. In contrast, a student whose interests are more technical would want courses in specific hardware areas such as Windows Network Security, firewalls and IDSs, or remote access and authentication.

Because many institutions have no frame of reference for which skills and knowledge are required for a particular job area, frequently they refer to the certifications offered in that field (certification is discussed in Chapter 10). A managerial program would examine certifications like the CISSP, CISM, or GISO; a technical program would examine the specific GIAC or Security+ certifications. A balanced program takes the best of both programs and then maps the knowledge areas from each specialty area backward to specific courses.

Figure 5-12 shows the complex process of mapping information security positions to the roles they perform, and the corresponding core knowledge requirements of those roles. These roles (defined earlier) must then be carefully mapped to the required knowledge domains. For example, a CISO may need to have a working understanding of all knowledge areas, while a firewall administrator may need true expertise in only one or two areas. The depth of knowledge is indicated by a level of mastery using an established taxonomy of learning objectives or a simple scale such as "understanding ⇒ accomplishment ⇒ proficiency ⇒ mastery."

Once the knowledge areas are identified, common knowledge areas are aggregated into teaching domains, from which individual courses can be created. Courses should be designed so that the student can obtain the required knowledge and skills upon completion of the program. For example, in a program for firewall administrators, an introductory class (to supply understanding) might be followed by a technical security class (to supply accomplishment), which might be followed by a firewall administration class (to supply proficiency and mastery).

The final step is to identify the prerequisite knowledge for each class. Figure 5-13 provides examples of increasingly more technical classes with their knowledge areas and prerequisite requirements.

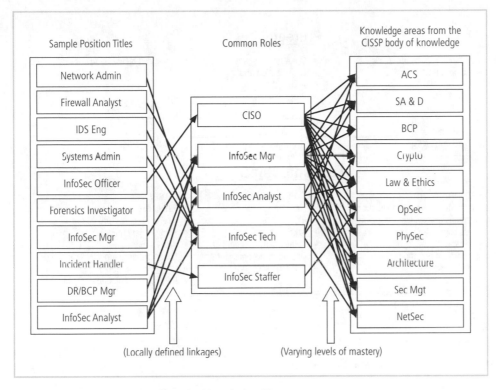

FIGURE 5-12 Information Security Knowledge Map

Security Training

Security training involves providing members of the organization with detailed information and hands-on instruction to enable them to perform their duties securely. Management of information security can develop customized in-house training or outsource all or part of the training program.

Alternatively, organizations can subsidize or underwrite industry training conferences and programs offered through professional agencies such as SANS (www.sans.org), ISC[2] (www.isc2.org), ISSA (www.issa.org), and CSI (www.gocsi.com). Many of these programs are too technical for the average employee, but they may be ideal for the continuing education requirements of information security professionals.

A number of resources can help organizations put together SETA programs. The Computer Security Resource Center at NIST, for example, provides several very useful documents free of charge in its special publications area (http://csrc.nist.gov).

Among the most useful of these documents for information security practitioners and those developing training programs is NIST SP 800-16. This 188-page manual with extensive appendices describes training with an emphasis on training criteria or standards, rather than on specific curricula or content. The training criteria are established according to trainees' role(s) within their organizations, and are measured by their on-the-job performance. This emphasis on roles and results, rather than on fixed content, gives the training requirements flexibility, adaptability, and longevity.[18]

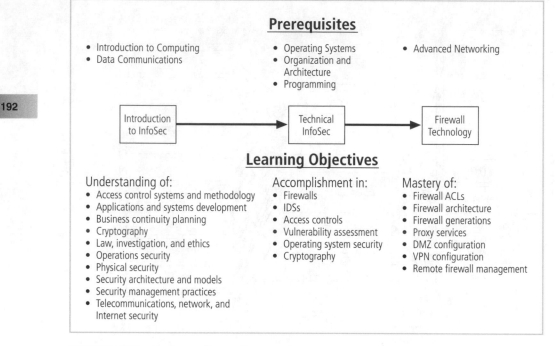

FIGURE 5-13   Technical Course Progression

This approach makes the document a durable and useful guide. Although it is directed toward federal agencies and organizations, its overall approach applies to all kinds of organizations:

> Federal agencies and organizations cannot protect the integrity, confidentiality, and availability of information in today's highly networked systems environment without ensuring that each person involved understands their roles and responsibilities and is adequately trained to perform them.[19]

The Computer Security Act of 1987 requires federal agencies to provide mandatory periodic training in computer security awareness and accepted computer practices to all employees involved with the management, use, or operation of their computer systems. Other federal requirements for computer security training are contained in OMB Circular A-130, Appendix III, and OPM regulations.[20]

Training is most effective when it is designed for a specific category of user. The more closely the training is designed to match specific needs, the more effective it is. Training includes teaching users not only what they should or should not do, but also how they should do it.

There are two methods for customizing training for users. The first is by functional background: general user, managerial user, and technical user. The second is by skill level: novice, intermediate, and advanced. Because traditional training models are accustomed to using skill level as course customization criteria, the more detailed discussion that follows focuses on the development of training by functional area.

Training for General Users

One method of ensuring that policies are read and understood by general users is to provide training on those policies. This strategy allows users to ask questions and receive specific guidance, and it allows the organization to collect the required letters of compliance. These general users also require training on the technical details of how to do their jobs securely, including good security practices, password management, specialized access controls, and violation reporting.

A convenient time to conduct this type of training is during employee orientation. At this critical time, employees are educated on a wide variety of organizational policies and on the expectations that the organization has for its employees. Because employees should have no preconceived notions or established methods of behavior at that point, they are more likely to be receptive to this instruction. This openness is balanced against their lack of familiarity with the systems and/or their jobs, so any particular issues that they might have questions about will not have arisen yet.

Training for Managerial Users

Management may have the same training requirements as the general user, but managers typically expect a more personal form of training, characterized by smaller groups and more interaction and discussion. In fact, managers often resist organized training of any kind. This is another area in which a champion can exert influence. Support at the executive level can convince managers to attend training events, which in turn reinforces the entire training program.

Training for Technical Users

Technical training for IT staff, security staff, and technically competent general users is more detailed than general user or managerial training, and may therefore require the use consultants or outside training organizations. There are three methods for selecting or developing advanced technical training:

- By job category—for example, technical users versus managers
- By job function—for example, accounting versus marketing versus operations functional areas
- By technology product—for example, e-mail client, database

Training Techniques

Good training techniques are as essential to successful training as thorough knowledge of the subject area. As explained by Charles Trepper in his article "Training Developers More Efficiently,"

> Using the wrong method can actually hinder the transfer of knowledge and lead to unnecessary expense and frustrated, poorly trained employees. Good training programs, regardless of delivery method, take advantage of the latest learning technologies and best practices. Recent developments include less use of centralized public courses and more on-site training. Training is often needed for one or a

few individuals, not necessarily for a large group. Waiting until there is a large-enough group for a class can cost companies lost productivity. Other best practices include the increased use of short, task-oriented modules and training sessions, available during the normal work week, that are immediate and consistent. Newer concepts in training also provide students with the training they need when they need it—a practice often called just-in-time training.[21]

Delivery Methods

Selection of the training delivery method is not always based on the best outcome for the trainee. Often other factors—most usually budget, scheduling, and needs of the organization—come first. Table 5-4 lists the most common delivery methods.

TABLE 5-4   Training Delivery Methods

Method	Advantages	Disadvantages
One-on-One: A dedicated trainer works with each trainee on the areas specified.	• Informal • Personal • Customized to the needs of the trainee • Can be scheduled to fit the needs of the trainee	• Resource intensive, to the point of being inefficient
Formal Class: A single trainer works with multiple trainees in a formal setting.	• Formal training plan, efficient • Trainees can learn from each other • Interaction with trainer is possible • Usually considered cost-effective	• Relatively inflexible • May not be sufficiently responsive to the needs of all trainees • Difficult to schedule, especially if more than one session is needed
Computer-Based Training (CBT): Prepackaged software that provides training at the trainees workstation.	• Flexible, no special scheduling requirements • Self-paced, can go as fast or as slow as the trainee needs • Can be very cost-effective	• Software can be very expensive • Content may not be customized to the needs of the organization
Distance Learning/Web Seminars: Trainees receive a seminar presentation at their computers. Some models allow teleconferencing for voice feedback; others have text questions and feedback.	• Can be live, or can be archived and viewed at the trainee's convenience • Can be low- or no-cost	• If archived, can be very inflexible, with no mechanism for trainee feedback • If live, can be difficult to schedule

TABLE 5-4 Training Delivery Methods (continued)

Method	Advantages	Disadvantages
User Support Group: Support from a community of users is commonly facilitated by a particular vendor as a mechanism to augment the support for products or software.	• Allows users to learn from each other • Usually conducted in an informal social setting	• Does not use a formal training model • Centered on a specific topic or product
On-the-Job Training: Trainees learn the specifics of their jobs while working, using the software, hardware, and procedures they will continue to use.	• Very applied to the task at hand • Inexpensive	• A sink-or-swim approach • Can result in substandard work performance until trainee gets up to speed
Self-Study (Noncomputerized): Trainees study materials on their own, usually when not actively performing their jobs.	• Lowest cost to the organization • Places materials in the hands of the trainee • Trainees can select the material they need to focus on the most • Self-paced	• Shifts responsibility for training onto the trainee, with little formal support

Selecting the Training Staff

To provide employee training, an organization can use a local training program, a continuing education department, or another external training agency. Alternatively, it can hire a professional trainer, a consultant, or someone from an accredited institution to conduct on-site training. It can also organize and conduct training in-house using its own employees. This last option should not be undertaken without careful consideration. Effective training requires a special set of skills and abilities. Teaching a class of five or more peers (or subordinates) is very different than offering friendly advice to coworkers.

Implementing Training

While each organization develops its own strategy based on the techniques discussed above, the following seven-step methodology generally applies:

Step 1: Identify program scope, goals, and objectives.
Step 2: Identify training staff.
Step 3: Identify target audiences.
Step 4: Motivate management and employees.
Step 5: Administer the program.
Step 6: Maintain the program.
Step 7: Evaluate the program.

This methodology and the material that follows, is drawn from the NIST document, *SP 800-12 An Introduction to Computer Security: The NIST Handbook.*[22]

Identify Program Scope, Goals, and Objectives The scope of the security training program should encompass all personnel who interact with computer systems. Because users need training that relates directly to their use of particular systems, an organization-wide training program may need to be supplemented by more specific programs targeted at specific groups. Generally, the goal of a security training program is to sustain an appropriate level of protection for computer resources by increasing employee awareness of, and ability to fulfill, computer security responsibilities. More specific goals may need to be established as well. Objectives should be defined to meet the organization's specific goals.

Identify Training Staff   Whether the trainer is an in-house expert or a hired professional, the organization should carefully match the capabilities of the training to the needs of the class. It is also vital that the trainer knows how to communicate information and ideas effectively.

Identify Target Audiences   A security training program that distinguishes between groups of people, presents only the information needed by the particular audience, and omits irrelevant information yields the best results. In larger organizations, some individuals will fit into more than one group. In smaller organizations, it may not be necessary to draw distinctions between groups.

You can divide employees into groups for training as follows:

- By level of awareness. Separating individuals into groups according to level of awareness may require research to determine how well employees follow computer security procedures or understand how computer security fits into their jobs.
- By general job task or function. Individuals may be grouped as data providers, data processors, or data users.
- By specific job category. Many organizations assign individuals to job categories. As each job category generally has different job responsibilities, training for each will necessarily be different. Examples of job categories include general management, technology management, applications development, and security.
- By level of computer knowledge. Computer experts may find a program containing highly technical information more valuable than one covering management issues in computer security. Conversely, a computer novice would benefit more from a training program that presents fundamentals.
- By types of technology or systems used. Security techniques used for each off-the-shelf product or application system usually vary. The users of major applications normally require training specific to that application.

Motivate Management and Employees   To successfully implement an awareness and training program, it is important to gain the *support* of both management and employees. For this reason, consideration should be given to using motivational techniques as part of the SETA program. Motivational techniques should demonstrate to management and employees how participation in the security training program benefits the organization. To motivate managers, for example, make them aware of the potential for losses and the role of training in computer security. Employees must understand how computer security benefits them and the organization and how it relates to their jobs.

Administer the Program   Several important considerations apply when administering the security training program:

- Visibility. The visibility of a security training program plays a key role in its success. Efforts to achieve a highly prominent place in the organization should begin during the early stages of security training program development.
- Training methods. The methods used in the security training program should be consistent with the material presented and should be tailored to the specific audience's needs. Some training and awareness methods and techniques were listed earlier in the "Training Techniques" section.
- Training topics. Topics should be selected based on the audience's requirements.
- Training materials. In general, higher-quality training materials are more favorably received, but are more expensive. To reduce costs, you can obtain training materials from other organizations. Modifying existing materials is usually cheaper than developing them from scratch.
- Training presentation. Presentation issues to consider include the frequency of training (for example, annually or as needed), the length of presentations (for example, 20 minutes for general presentations, one hour for updates, or one week for an off-site class), and the style of presentation (for example, formal, informal, computer-based, humorous).

Maintain the Program   Efforts should be made to keep abreast of changes in computer technology and security requirements. A training program that meets an organization's needs today may become ineffective if the organization begins using a new application or changes its environment, such as by connecting to the Internet. Likewise, an awareness program can become obsolete if laws, organizational policies, or common usage practices change. For example, if an awareness program uses examples from Eudora (a popular e-mail client program) to train employees about a new policy for e-mail usage, when the organization actually uses the e-mail client Outlook, employees may discount the security training program, and by association, the importance of computer security.

Evaluate the Program   Organizations can evaluate their training programs by ascertaining how much information is retained, to what extent computer security procedures are being followed, and the attitudes toward computer security. The results of such an evaluation should help identify and correct problems. Some popular evaluation methods (which can be used in conjunction with one another) are:

- Using trainee evaluations to collect feedback
- Observing how well employees follow recommended security procedures after being trained
- Testing employees on material after it has been covered in training
- Monitoring the number and kind of computer security incidents reported before and after the training program is implemented

Security Awareness

One of the least frequently implemented but most effective security methods is the security awareness program. As noted in the NIST document SP 800-12,

> Security awareness programs: (1) set the stage for training by changing organizational attitudes to realize the importance of security and the adverse consequences of its failure; and (2) remind users of the procedures to be followed.[23]

A security awareness program keeps information security at the forefront of users' minds on a daily basis. Awareness serves to instill a sense of responsibility and purpose in employees who handle and manage information, and it leads employees to care more about their work environment. When developing an awareness program, be sure to:

- Focus on people both as part of the problem and as part of the solution.
- Refrain from using technical jargon; speak the language the users understand.
- Use every available venue to access all users.
- Define at least one key learning objective, state it clearly, and provide sufficient detail and coverage to reinforce the learning of it.
- Keep things light; refrain from "preaching" to users.
- Do not overload users with too much detail or too great a volume of information.
- Help users understand their roles in information security and how a breach in that security can affect their jobs.
- Take advantage of in-house communications media to deliver messages.
- Make the awareness program formal; plan and document all actions.
- Provide good information early, rather than perfect information late.

As Susan Hansche indicates in her article "Designing a Security Awareness Program," good security awareness programs should be

...supported and led by example from management, simple and straightforward, a continuous effort. They should repeat important messages to ensure they get delivered. They should be entertaining, holding the users' interest and humorous where appropriate in order to make slogans easy to remember. They should tell employees what the dangers are (threats) and how they can help protect the information vital to their jobs.[24]

Hansche continues by noting that awareness programs should focus on topics that the employees can relate to, including

...threats to physical assets and stored information, threats to open network environments, [and] federal and state laws they are required to follow, including copyright violations or privacy act information. It can also include specific organization or department policies and information on how to identify and protect sensitive or classified information, as well as how to store, label, and transport information. This awareness information should also address who they should report security incidents to, whether real or suspect.[25]

Employee Behavior and Awareness

Security awareness and security training are designed to modify any employee behavior that endangers the security of the organization's information. By teaching employees how to properly handle information, use applications, and operate within the organization, you minimize the risk of accidental compromise, damage, or destruction of information. By making employees aware of threats to information security, the potential damage that can result from these threats, and the ways that these threats can occur, increase the probability that they will take such threats seriously. By making employees aware of policy, the penalties for failure to comply with policy, and the mechanism by which policy violations are discovered, you reduce the probability that an employee will try to get away with intentional misuse and abuse of information. As noted in Chapter 2, penalties for policy violations are effective only when (1) employees fear the penalty, (2) employees believe they may be caught, and (3) employees believe that, if caught, they will be penalized.

Security training and awareness activities can be undermined, however, if management does not set a good example. Failure of management—especially upper management—to follow organizational policy is quickly mirrored by the actions and activities of all employees. For example, suppose Random Widget Works has a policy that all employees must wear identification badges in a visible location at all times. If, over time, employees observe that senior executives do not wear badges, then soon no one will wear a badge, and attempts to penalize employees for this failure will be compromised. Policy breaches by upper management are always perceived as a lack of support for the policy. For that reason, management must always lead by example.

Employee Accountability

Effective training and awareness programs make employees accountable for their actions. The legal defense *ignorantia legis neminem excusat* (ignorance of the law excuses no one) may not be valid in a criminal courtroom, but it does protect employees who are fighting policy violation penalties in labor disputes, administrative law hearings, or civil court cases. As you learned in Chapter 4, comprehensive and properly disseminated policies enable organizations to require employee compliance. Dissemination and enforcement of policy become easier when training and awareness programs are in place.

Demonstrating **due care** and **due diligence**—warning employees that misconduct, abuse, and misuse of information resources will not be tolerated and that the organization will not defend employees who engage in this behavior—can help indemnify the institution against lawsuits. Lawyers tend to seek compensation from employers, which have more assets than employees, and thus attempt to prove that the alleged conduct was not clearly prohibited by organizational policy, thereby making the organization liable for it.

Awareness Techniques

The NIST document SP 800-12, *An Introduction to Computer Security: The NIST Handbook,* describes the essentials of developing effective awareness techniques:

> Awareness can take on different forms for particular audiences. Appropriate awareness for management officials might stress management's pivotal role in establishing organizational attitudes toward security. Appropriate awareness for other groups, such as system programmers or information analysts, should address the need for security as it relates to their job. In today's systems environment, almost everyone in an organization may have access to system resources and therefore may have the potential to cause harm.
>
> A security awareness program can use many methods to deliver its message, many of them listed in the following section. Awareness is often incorporated into basic security training and can use any method that can change employees' attitudes. Effective security awareness programs need to be designed with the recognition that people tend to practice a *tuning out* process (also known as *acclimation*). For example, after a while, a security poster, no matter how well designed, will be ignored; it will, in effect, simply blend into the environment. For this reason, awareness techniques should be creative and frequently changed.[26]

Developing Security Awareness Components

Many security awareness components are available at low cost, or virtually no cost, except for the time and energy of the developer. Others can be very expensive if purchased externally. Security awareness components include the following items:

- Videos
- Posters and banners
- Lectures and conferences

- Computer-based training
- Newsletters
- Brochures and flyers
- Trinkets (coffee cups, pens, pencils, T-shirts)
- Bulletin boards

Several of these options are discussed in detail in the following sections.

The Security Newsletter   A security newsletter is the most cost-effective method of disseminating security information and news to employees. Newsletters can be disseminated via hard copy, e-mail, or intranet. Newsworthy topics can include new threats to the organization's information assets, the schedule for upcoming security classes, and the addition of new security personnel. The goal is to keep information security uppermost in users' minds and to stimulate them to care about it.

Consider the newsletter model illustrated in Figure 5-14. The components of this sample newsletter are the cover page, the back cover, and the interior.

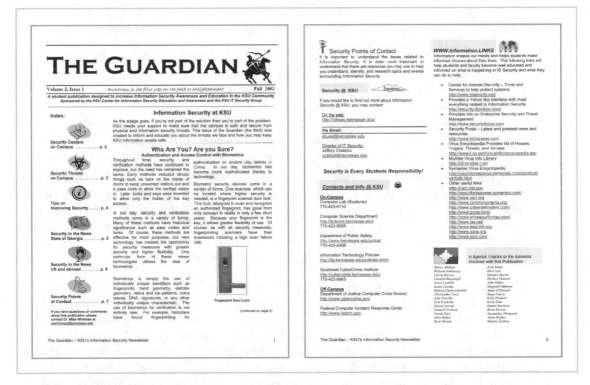

FIGURE 5-14   SETA Awareness Components: Newsletters

The cover should include a nameplate—a banner at the top of the page highlighting the newsletter's title. The title itself should evoke an image of security, such as *The Guardian*, *The Sentinel*, *The Protector*, or *A Higher Plane*. Graphics should be used, but sparingly. Clipart works well, as do company logos or designs. The cover should also contain standard literary denotations such as volume, issue, date, and so on, to allow for archiving, which provides proof of due care and due diligence in the event the process is audited. In addition, a simple index or table of contents should appear on the cover. While each issue's content will be distinct, in most cases the layout is standardized. Developing a template containing just the frame, page numbers, and a common back cover simplifies the creation of newsletters.

The back cover is most often used to provide contact information for information security personnel, the help desk, physical security (law enforcement), and other quick reference items. It might also include editorial and author information.

The newsletter should contain articles of interest, gleaned from information security publications, along with local publications, summaries of policies, security-related activities, and the like. It might also include these items:

- Summaries of key policies (one per issue, to avoid overloading the reader)
- Summaries of key news articles (one or two each at the national, state, and local levels)
- A calendar of security events, including training sessions, presentations, and other activities
- Announcements relevant to information security, such as planned installations, upgrades, or deployment of new technologies or policies
- How-to's, such as
  - How to make sure virus definitions are current
  - How to report an incident
  - How to properly classify, label, and store information
  - How to determine whether e-mail is dangerous
  - How to secure the office before leaving (clean desk policies)
  - How to avoid tailgaters, those who follow other people through controlled entry gates or doors closely to avoid presenting credentials of their own

The form in which the newsletter is published will vary according to organizational needs. Hard copies, especially in color, may be inordinately expensive, even if the institution owns its own reproduction equipment. Larger organizations may prefer to distribute color Portable Document Format (PDF) copies, or even HTML documents via e-mail or intranet. Some companies may choose to create an HTML Web site and e-mail links to users, rather than distributing hard copy or sending attachments.

The Security Poster   A security poster series—which can be displayed in common areas, especially where technology is used—is a simple and inexpensive way to keep security on people's minds. The examples shown in Figure 5-15, along with eight others, were developed in one long afternoon, with the bulk of the time spent looking for the right clipart. Professionally developed graphic posters can be quite expensive, so in-house development may be the best solution (but don't simply copy someone else's work), especially if the organization has the ability to print on poster-sized paper. If not, most copy shops can enlarge letter-sized copies to poster size.

FIGURE 5-15   SETA Awareness Components: Posters

Several keys to a good poster series are:

- Varying the content and keeping posters updated
- Keeping them simple, but visually interesting
- Making the message clear
- Providing information on reporting violations

A variation on the poster series is the screen saver slideshow. Many modern operating systems allow you to create a rotating slideshow, which you can configure as a screen saver.

The Trinket Program   This option is one of the most expensive security awareness programs. Trinkets may not cost much on a per-unit basis, but they can be expensive to distribute throughout an organization. Trinkets are everyday items with specialized security messages printed on them, as shown in Figure 5-16.

Several types of trinkets commonly are used:

- Pens and pencils
- Mouse pads

FIGURE 5-16   SETA Awareness Components: Trinkets

- Coffee mugs
- Plastic cups
- Hats
- T-shirts

Trinket programs can get people's attention at first, but the messages they impart will eventually be lost unless reinforced by other means.

Information Security Awareness Web Site   Organizations can establish Web pages or sites dedicated to promoting information security awareness, like Kennesaw State University's Web site at infosec.kennesaw.edu. As with other SETA awareness methods, the challenge lies in updating the messages frequently enough to keep them fresh. When new information is posted, employees can be informed via e-mail. The latest and archived newsletters can reside on the Web site, along with press releases, awards, and recognitions.

Here are some tips on creating and maintaining an educational Web site:[27]

1. See what's already out there. You do not have to reinvent the wheel. Look at what other organizations have done with their InfoSec awareness Web sites. Determine ownership, as you do not want to infringe on another organization's intellectual property. It is one thing to adopt a good idea; it is another thing to present it as your own. Where necessary, give credit where credit is due. A good rule of thumb is to look at a large number of sites, then design your site from memory using the best things you have seen.

2. Plan ahead. Design the Web site on paper before designing it on the computer. Standardize file naming conventions, file and image locations, and other development components, so that you do not have to recode links or pages because you changed your convention halfway through.

3. Keep page loading time to a minimum. Avoid large images and complex/long pages. Design for the lowest common denominator, typically a 640 × 480 display screen with VGA graphics. Use .jpg graphics wherever possible, as opposed to larger file formats.

4. Appearance matters. Create a themed "look and feel" for the pages, using templates and visually attractive formats. Keep quick links on the side, on the bottom, or in floating palettes.

5. Seek feedback. Ask others to review your work, and accept the best suggestions for improvement. Use statistical measurements to determine which parts of the Web site are used most frequently.

6. Assume nothing and check everything. Verify your standards by using other computers to view the documents. Try out the Web site with multiple browsers, platforms, and systems. Each may claim to use a standardized interpreter, but their idiosyncrasies may yield unexpected results.

7. Spend time promoting your site. Let everyone at the company know it is there. Send notifications when new content is posted. Posting information on a Web site can reduce e-mail traffic.

One final recommendation is to place your Web site on the intranet. You can then include phone numbers and information not generally released to the public, such as notices of breaches and violations, and company policies and procedures for handling problems.

Security Awareness Conference/Presentations   Another means of renewing the information security message is to have a guest speaker or even a mini-conference dedicated to the topic—perhaps in association with International Computer Security Day! Never heard of it? That's not surprising. Even through it's been around since 1988, International Computer Security Day (November 30) is an underpromoted event, much like information security itself. (For more information see the Association for Computer Security Day at www.geocities.com/a4csd/index.html.) If this date does not suit the corporate calendar, you can always choose the semi-annual National Computer Security Days—October 31 and April 4. "First held in 2002, the semi-annual National Cyber Security Days are coordinated with daylight savings in April and October in the U.S. and are intended to raise the public's awareness of cyber-security issues and promote safe online practices."[28]

Guest speakers at this event could discuss vital industry-specific information security issues. The drawbacks: Speakers seldom speak for free, and few organizations are willing to suspend work for such an event, even a half-day conference.

Chapter Summary

- The term "information security program" is used to describe the structure and organization of the effort that contains risks to the information assets of the organization.

- In the largest organizations, specific InfoSec functions are likely to be performed by specialized groups of staff members; in smaller organizations, these functions may be carried out by all members of the department.

- Information security functions should be separated into four areas:

    - Functions performed by nontechnical areas of the organization outside of the information technology area of management control

    - Functions performed by IT groups outside of the information security area of management control

    - Functions performed within the information security department as a customer service to the organization and its external partners

    - Functions performed within the information security department as a compliance enforcement obligation

- Implementation of full-time security personnel will vary depending on a number of industry factors:

    - A typical large organization will have on average 1–2 full-time managers, 3–4 full-time technicians/administrators, and as many as 16 part-time staff members.

    - A very large organization may have more than 20 full-time security personnel and 40 or more individuals with part-time responsibilities.

    - A medium-sized organization may have only one full-time security person and as many as three individuals with part-time responsibilities.

    - Smaller organizations may have either one individual with full-time duties in information security or one individual who is a part-time manager.

- Information security positions can be classified into one of three areas: those that *define,* those that *build,* and those that *administer.*

- The SETA program is the responsibility of the CISO and is designed to reduce the incidence of accidental security breaches.

- SETA programs improve employee behavior and enable the organization to hold employees accountable for their actions.

- Training is most effective when it is designed for a specific category of users. Training includes teaching users not only what they should or should not do, but also how they should do it.

- There are two methods for customizing training for users: by functional background and by level of skill. Training delivery methods include one-on-one, formal classes, computer-based training, distance learning/Web seminars, user support groups, on-the-job training, and self-study (noncomputerized).

- A security awareness program can deliver its message via videotapes, newsletters, posters, bulletin boards, flyers, demonstrations, briefings, short reminder notices at logon, talks, or lectures.

Review Questions

1. What is an information security program?

2. What functions constitute a complete information security program?

3. What organizational variables can influence the size and composition of an information security program's staff?

4. What is the typical size of the security staff in a small organization? A medium-sized organization? A large organization? A very large organization?

5. Where can an organization place the information security unit? Where should (and shouldn't) it be placed?

6. Into what four areas should the information security functions be divided?

7. What are the five roles that an information security professional can assume?

8. What are the three areas of the SETA program?

9. What can influence the effectiveness of a training program?

10. What are some of the various ways to implement an awareness program?

11. Which two documents largely determine the shape of the information security program? Which other documents can assist in this effort?

12. What are the elements of a security program, according to NIST SP 800-14?

13. Information security positions can be classified into what three areas? What are the differences among them?

14. Describe the two overriding benefits of awareness, training, and education.

15. What is the purpose of a SETA program?

16. Which of the SETA program's three elements is the organization best prepared to offer? Which should it consider outsourcing?

17. How does training differ from education? Which is provided to the broader audience with regard to information security?

18. What are the various training program delivery methods?

19. Describe a sample seven-step methodology for implementing training.

20. When developing an awareness program, what priorities should you keep in mind?

Exercises

1. Search for the term "security awareness" on the Internet. Describe the available materials and services.

2. Choose one of the Web sites you found in Exercise 1 that you think might work for a security awareness program at your school. Write a short essay on how you might go about getting that awareness material or service into place on your campus.

3. Get the latest copy of your local Sunday newspaper. Look through the paper and circulars for advertisements for training and education in security- and technology-related areas. What are the costs of the advertised security specific training? Network certification? General computer training?

4. Design five security posters on various aspects of information security, using a graphics presentation program and clipart. Bring the posters to class and discuss the methods you used to develop your materials.

5. Examine your institution's Web site and identify full- and part-time information security jobs. Create an organizational chart showing the reporting structures for these individuals.

Case Exercises

Mike Edwards thanked the attorney from the corporate legal office for his presentation on the newly enacted state computer crime and privacy law, and then asked, "How should we comply and when does it take effect?" The attorney gave a full analysis of RWW's responsibilities.

Mike turned to his staff of department managers and said, "It's important that we comply with the new law. First, however, we need to determine how much it will cost us to comply with the password privacy area. I need from each of you a budget impact analysis that encompasses the effort needed to meet this new requirement."

1. What elements will each department manager have to consider to complete Mike's assignment?

2. How will a privacy law affect an organization like RWW? What other laws also affect privacy in the workplace?

Endnotes

[1] Andrew Briney and Frank Prince. Does size matter? *Information Security*, September 2002, 36–54.

[2] Loc. cit.

[3] Loc. cit.

[4] Loc. cit.

[5] Loc. cit.

[6] M. Hayes. Where the chief security officer belongs. *InformationWeek*, February 25, 2002. Accessed November 22, 2006 from www.informationweek.com/story/showArticle.jhtml?articleID=6500913.

[7] Charles Cresson Wood. *Information Security Roles and Responsibilities Made Easy.* Houston: PentaSafe, 2002: 95–105. Used with permission.

[8] Ibid., p. 45.

[9] National Institute of Standards and Technology. *Generally Accepted Principles and Practices for Securing Information Technology Systems.* NIST Publication 800-14. Accessed November 22, 2006 from csrc.nist.gov/publications/nistpubs/800-14/800-14.pdf.

[10] National Institute of Standards and Technology. *An Introduction to Computer Security: The NIST Handbook.* NIST Publication 800-12, 15. Accessed November 22, 2006 from csrc.nist. gov/publications/nistpubs/800-12/handbook.pdf.

[11] Eddie Schwartz, Dan Erwin, Vincent Weafer, and Andy Briney. Roundtable: InfoSec staffing help wanted! *Information Security Magazine Online,* April 2001. Accessed November 22, 2006 from www.infosecuritymag.com/articles/april01/features_roundtable.shtml.

[12] Julie Hanson. The state of the CISO: The evolving role of the chief security officer 2004–2005. *CSO Magazine,* 2006. Accessed November 22, 2006 from www.csoonline.com/csoresearch/report93.html.

[13] Loc. cit.

[14] Loc. cit.

[15] National Institute of Standards and Technology. *An Introduction to Computer Security: The NIST Handbook.* SP 800-12. Accessed November 22, 2006 from csrc.nist.gov/publications/nistpubs/800-12/.

[16] C. Irvine, S-K. Chin, and D. Frincke. Integrating security into the curriculum. *Computer,* December 1998, 31(12), 25–30.

[17] National InfoSec Education and Training Program (NIETP). Centers of Academic Excellence in Information Assurance Education. Accessed November 22, 2006 from www.nsa.gov/ia/academia/acade00001.cfm.

[18] National Institute of Standards and Technology. *Information Technology Security Training Requirements: A Role- and Performance-Based Model.* Accessed November 22, 2006 from csrc.nist.gov/publications/nistpubs/800-16/800-16.pdf.

[19] Loc. cit.

[20] CIRCULAR NO. A-130 Revised. Office of Management and Budget. Accessed October 27, 2006 from www.whitehouse.gov/omb/circulars/a130/a130trans4.html.

[21] Charles Trepper. Training developers more efficiently. *InformationWeekOnline.* Accessed November 22, 2006 from www.informationweek.com/738/38addev.htm.

[22] National Institute of Standards and Technology. An Introduction to Computer Security: The NIST Handbook. SP 800-12. Accessed November 22, 2006 from csrc.nist.gov/publications/nistpubs/800-12/.

[23] Loc. cit.

[24] Susan Hansche. Designing a security awareness program: Part I. *Information Systems Security,* January/February 2001, 9(6), 14–23.

[25] Loc. cit.

[26] National Institute of Standards and Technology. *An Introduction to Computer Security: The NIST Handbook.* SP 800-12. Accessed November 22, 2006 from csrc.nist.gov/publications/nistpubs/800-12/.

[27] S. Plous. Tips on creating and maintaining an educational Web site. *Teaching of Psychology,* 2000, 27, 63–70.

[28] IWS. "Computer Security Day." Accessed November 22, 2006 from www.iwar.org.uk/comsec/resources/sa-tools/security-awareness-day.htm.

## CHAPTER 6

SECURITY MANAGEMENT MODELS AND PRACTICES

> ### QUOTE
>
> *Security can only be achieved through constant change, through discarding old ideas that have outlived their usefulness and adapting others to current facts.*
>
> William O. Douglas, U.S. Supreme Court Justice (1898–1980)

Iris looked at the mound of documents on her desk. Each one was neatly labeled with its own acronym and number: NIST, ISO, Special Publication, and RFC. Her head was beginning to swim. She had not imagined that it would be quite so difficult to choose a security management model for her review of RWW's ongoing security program. She wanted an independent framework that would allow her to perform a thorough analysis of RWW's program.

She had known that networking with her colleagues was important. But this set of references was a concrete example of the benefits of staying professionally engaged.

Iris was almost finished skimming the stack when she found what she was looking for: a document that contained a self-assessment checklist with page after page of specific items important in the management of information security. She perused the list carefully. Using her Internet connection, Iris downloaded the full document, inserted a few minor changes, made copies for the managers who worked for her, and then scheduled a meeting.

At the meeting, Tom, the risk assessment and policy manager, commented, "Gee, Iris, when did you have time to design this checklist?"

Iris replied, "I didn't. I was lucky enough to find the perfect one for us. I changed just a few items to make it specific enough for our needs." She quickly outlined her plan. Using the checklist, each manager would indicate the progress that RWW had made in that area—specifically, whether policy had been created and, if so, whether it had been integrated into the company culture. Iris explained how to use the forms and noted when she expected the assessment to be complete.

"What happens once we're done?" one manager asked.

"That's when the real work begins," Iris said. "We'll establish priorities for improving the areas that need revision, and sustaining the areas that are satisfactory. Then we'll determine whether we have the resources to accomplish that work; if not, I'll go to the CIO and request more resources."

LEARNING OBJECTIVES

Upon completion of this material, you should be able to:

- Recognize the dominant information security management models, including U.S. government-sanctioned models, and learn how to select from among them and customize them for a specific organization's needs
- Implement the fundamental elements of key information security management practices
- Follow emerging trends in the certification and accreditation of U.S. federal IT systems

INTRODUCTION

The communities of interest that are accountable for the security of an organization's information assets must design a working security plan, and then implement a management model to execute and maintain that plan. This effort may begin with the creation or validation of a security framework, followed by the development of an information security blueprint that describes existing controls and identifies other necessary security controls. The terms *blueprint* and *framework* are closely related. A **framework** is the outline of the more thorough **blueprint**, which sets out the model to be followed in the creation of the design, selection, and the initial and ongoing implementation of all subsequent security controls, including information security policies, security education and training programs, and technological controls.

To generate a security blueprint, most organizations draw on established security models and practices. A **security model** is a generic blueprint offered by a service organization. Some of these models are proprietary, and are only available for high fees; others are relatively inexpensive, such as ISO standards; and some are free. Free models are available from the National Institute of Standards and Technology (NIST) and a variety of other sources. The model you choose must be flexible, scalable, robust, and sufficiently detailed.

Another way to create a blueprint is to look at the paths taken by other organizations. In this kind of *benchmarking,* you follow the recommended practices or industry standards. Benchmarking can provide details on *which* controls should be considered, but it does not provide implementation details that explain *how* controls should be put into action.

One way to select a methodology is to adapt or adopt an existing security management model or set of practices. A number of published information security models and frameworks exist, such as those from government organizations presented later in this chapter. Because each information security environment is unique, you may need to modify or adapt portions of several frameworks—what works well for one organization may not precisely fit another.

SECURITY MANAGEMENT MODELS

Many security management models and practices are available as are the number of consultants who offer them. Among the most accessible places to find a quality security management model are U.S. federal agencies and international organizations. In fact, one of the most popular security management models has been ratified into an international standard. The International Organization for Standardization (ISO) and the International Electrotechnical Commission (IEC) jointly issued International Standard 17799 and its companion document 27001, each of which addresses a related area of security management practice:

- ISO/IEC 17799:2005 *Information technology—Security Techniques—Code of Practice for Information Security Management*
- ISO/IEC 27001 *Information Security Management: Specification with Guidance for Use*

These documents, discussed in detail in the following sections, are proprietary. Organizations wanting to adopt the model must purchase the rights to do so.

Several alternative sources for security management models exist as well. The first and foremost are free documents provided by NIST's Computer Security Resource Center (http://csrc.nist.gov). This site houses many publications, including ones containing models and practices. You learned about some of these publications in earlier chapters of this book. Later in this chapter, you will learn more about the following NIST publications:

- NIST SP 800-12, *Computer Security Handbook*
- NIST SP 800-14, *Generally Accepted Principles and Practices for Securing Information Technology Systems*
- NIST SP 800-18, *Guide for Developing Security Plans for Information Technology Systems*
- NIST SP 800-26, *Security Self-Assessment Guide for Information Technology Systems*
- NIST SP 800-30, *Risk Management Guide for Information Technology Systems*

Three supplemental resources are also discussed in this chapter:

- RFC 2196, *Site Security Handbook*
- Control Objectives for Information and related Technology (COBIT)
- Committee of Sponsoring Organizations of the Treadway Commission (COSO)

ISO/IEC 17799:2005 *Information Technology—Security Techniques—Code of Practice for Information Security Management*

ISO/IEC 17799 is one of the most widely referenced and often discussed security models. It is is based on the British standard *Information Technology—Code of Practice for Information Security Management,* which was originally published as **British Standard 7799**. The British code of practice was adopted as an international standard framework for information security by the ISO and the IEC as **ISO/IEC 17799:2002**. While the details of ISO/IEC 17799 are available only to buyers of the standard, its structure and general organization are well known. For a summary description, see the section of this chapter entitled "The ISO/IEC 17799:2005 Sections."

In 2005, ISO/IEC 17799:2002 was updated to **ISO/IEC 17799:2005** *Information Technology—Security Techniques—Code of Practice for Information Security Management.* The stated purpose of ISO/IEC 17799: 2005 is to establish

> guidelines and general principles for initiating, implementing, maintaining, and improving information security management in an organization. The objectives outlined provide general guidance on the commonly accepted goals of information security management. ISO/IEC 17799:2005 contains recommended practices of control objectives and controls in the following areas of information security management:
>
> - Security policy
> - Organization of information security
> - Asset management
> - Human resources security
> - Physical and environmental security
> - Communications and operations management
> - Access control
> - Information systems acquisition, development, and maintenance
> - Information security incident management
> - Business continuity management
> - Compliance
>
> The control objectives and controls in ISO/IEC 17799:2005 are intended to be implemented to meet the requirements identified by a risk assessment. ISO/IEC 17799:2005 is intended as a common basis and practical guideline for developing organizational security standards and effective security management practices, and to help build confidence in inter-organizational activities.[1]

ISO/IEC 17799:2005 includes a total of 133 possible controls, not all of which must be used by every organization. Part of the security model selection process is to identify which are relevant. Some of the topics include provision of outsourcing, external service delivery, and patch management. Other areas have been modified and improved, including employment termination and mobile/distributed communication. In addition to revising the content itself, the document has also had its "user friendliness" improved, making the standard much more understandable for the average business person or IT professional.

Each section of ISO/IEC 17799:2005 includes four categories of information:

- One or more objectives
- Controls relevant to the achievement of the objectives
- Implementation guidance
- Other information[2]

ISO/IEC 17799:2005 is actually the latest evolution of the original two-volume British Standard BS 7799. BS 7799 offered an overview of the various areas of security and provided information on 127 controls over 10 broad areas. Volume 2 provided information on how to implement Volume 1 and how to set up an Information Security Management Structure (ISMS). Figure 6-1 shows a comprehensive overview of the entire process and Figure 6-2 provides the steps involved in implementation of the standard. In the United Kingdom, these standards, when implemented correctly, are used to obtain the ISMS certification and accreditation, as determined by a BS 7799–certified evaluator. Many countries, including the United States, Germany, and Japan, have not formally adopted ISO/IEC 17799 as national policy, however. Groups within each of these countries claim that the methodology has some fundamental flaws:

- The global information security community has not defined any justification for a code of practice as identified in ISO/IEC 17799.
- ISO/IEC 17799 lacks the necessary measurement precision of a technical standard.[3]
- There is no reason to believe that ISO/IEC 17799 is more useful than any other approach.
- ISO/IEC 17799 is not as complete as other frameworks.
- ISO/IEC 17799 is perceived as having been hurriedly prepared, given the tremendous impact that its adoption could have on industry information security controls.[4]

After all, 17799 is only 115 pages long, with its companion (27001) only 34 pages long. The NIST counterparts' page counts number in the thousands.

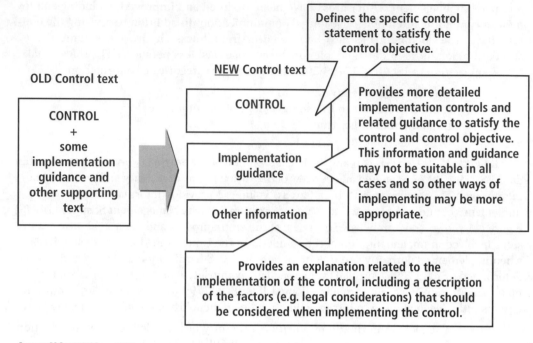

Source: ISO 17799News, 2005

FIGURE 6-1 17799:2005 Usability

With the release of the 2005 version, certain issues may be resolved. Some industry experts predict that the 17799 document will be renumbered to ISO/IEC 27002 to align it more closely with the newest version of its companion document, ISO/IEC 27001. For an overview of the sections of 17799:2005, see the Technical Details box in this chapter.

SANS SCORE and ISO/IEC 17799

One way to determine how closely an organization is complying with ISO 17799 is to use the SANS SCORE (Security Consensus Operational Readiness Evaluation) Audit Checklist, which is based on 17799:2005. This checklist can be downloaded free of charge from *http://www.sans.org/score/ISO_17799checklist2.php*. It provides a mechanism by which an organization can determine its current level of compliance. The Technical Details box that follows provides an overview of the sections of ISO/IEC 17799.

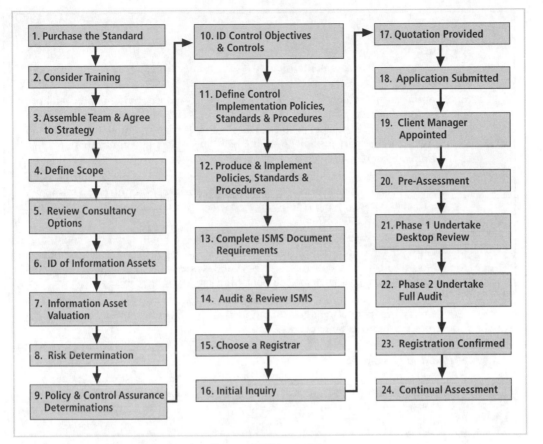

Based on a presentation by David Watson – http://iso17799world.com/auth.htm

FIGURE 6-2 Implementation of ISO/IEC 17799:2000

TECHNICAL DETAILS

ISO/IEC 17799:2005 Sections

The SANS Audit Checklist[5] provides insight into 11 sections of 17799:

1. Security Policy—focusing mainly on information security policy
2. Organization of Information Security—for both the internal organization and external parties
3. Asset Management—including responsibility for assets and information classification

continued

4. Human Resources Security—ranging from controls prior to employment, during employment, to termination or change of employment

5. Physical and Environmental Security—including secure areas and equipment security

6. Communications and Operations Management—incorporating operational procedures and responsibilities, third-party service delivery management, system planning and acceptance, protection against malicious and mobile code, backup, network security management, media handling, exchange of information, electronic commerce services, and monitoring

7. Access Control—focusing on business requirement for access control, user access management, user responsibilities, network access control, operating system access control, application and information access control, and mobile computing and teleworking

8. Information Systems Acquisition, Development and Maintenance—including security requirements of information systems, correct processing in applications, cryptographic controls, security of system files, security in development and support processes, and technical vulnerability management

9. Information Security Incident Management—addressing reporting information security events and weaknesses and management of information security incidents and improvements

10. Business Continuity Management—information security aspects of business continuity management

11. Compliance—including compliance with legal requirements, compliance with security policies and standards, and technical compliance and information systems audit considerations[6]

While the improvements to ISO/IEC 17799 make it an even more relevant information security framework, it is difficult to predict how it will affect small- and medium-sized U.S. organizations. Perhaps only those organizations with European Union customer base will be required to adopt it; however, some indications suggest that this standard may have broader uses within other U.S. organizations.

ISO/IEC 27001:2005: The Information Security Management System

As mentioned earlier, the predecessor to 17799 is BS 7799:1, the companion to that document is BS 7799:2. Part 2 of BS 7799 provides implementation details using a Plan-Do-Check-Act cycle, as described here and shown in Figure 6-3 in abbreviated form:

Plan:
1. Define the scope of the ISMS.
2. Define an ISMS policy.
3. Define the approach to risk assessment.
4. Identify the risks.
5. Assess the risks.
6. Identify and evaluate options for the treatment of risk.

7. Select control objectives and controls.
8. Prepare a Statement of Applicability (SOA).

Do:

9. Formulate a Risk Treatment Plan.
10. Implement the Risk Treatment Plan.
11. Implement controls.
12. Implement training and awareness programs.
13. Manage operations.
14. Manage resources.
15. Implement procedures to detect and respond to security incidents.

Check:

16. Execute monitoring procedures.
17. Undertake regular reviews of ISMS effectiveness.
18. Review the level of residual and acceptable risk.
19. Conduct internal ISMS audits.
20. Undertake regular management review of the ISMS.
21. Record actions and events that impact an ISMS.

Act:

22. Implement identified improvements.
23. Take corrective or preventive action.
24. Apply lessons learned.
25. Communicate results to interested parties.
26. Ensure improvements achieve objectives.[7]

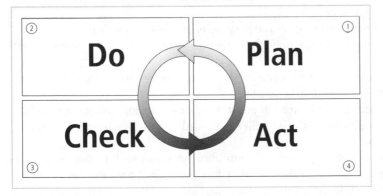

FIGURE 6-3 BS7799:2—Plan-Do-Check-Act

Although Part 2 provides some implementation information, it simply specifies *what* must be done—not *how* to do it. As noted by Gamma Secure Systems, a well-regarded British security consulting firm that has participated in the ISO/IEC 197799 and British Standard 7799 process since they began, "The standard has an appendix that gives guidance on the use of the standard, in particular to expand on the Plan-Do-Check-Act concept. It is important to realize that there will be many Plan-Do-Check-Act cycles within a single ISMS, all operating asynchronously at different speeds."[8]

In 2005, with the release of the latest iteration of ISO/IEC 17799, a version of BS 7799:2 was also updated and codified as **ISO/IEC 27001:2005** *Information Technology— Security Techniques—Information Security Management Systems—Requirements.* This document is the foundation for third-party certification. Its major sections include:

- Introduction
- Scope
- Terms and definitions
- Normative references
- ISMS
- Management responsibility
- Management review
- ISMS improvement

According to ISO, the proposed use of ISO/IEC 27001:2005 is for:

- use within organizations to formulate security requirements and objectives;
- use within organizations as a way to ensure that security risks are managed cost-effectively;
- use within organizations to ensure compliance with laws and regulations;
- use within an organization as a process framework for the implementation and management of controls to ensure that the specific security objectives of an organization are met;
- definition of new information security management processes;
- identification and clarification of existing information security management processes;
- use by the management of organizations to determine the status of information security management activities;
- use by the internal and external auditors of organizations to determine the degree of compliance with the policies, directives, and standards adopted by an organization;
- use by organizations to provide relevant information about information security policies, directives, standards, and procedures to trading partners and other organizations with whom they interact for operational or commercial reasons;
- implementation of business-enabling information security;
- use by organizations to provide relevant information about information security to customers.[9]

ISO/IEC 27001, much like its predecessor BS 7799, is primarily intended to be used by an organization to seek certification. Thus, it serves best as an assessment tool rather than an implementation framework.

NIST Security Models

Other approaches to structuring information security management are described in the many documents available from NIST's Computer Security Resource Center (http://csrc.nist.gov). These documents, which are among the references cited by the U.S. government as reasons not to adopt ISO/IEC 17799 standards, enjoy two notable advantages over many other sources of security information: (1) they are publicly available at no charge and (2) they have been available for some time and thus have been broadly reviewed by government and industry professionals. You can use the NIST SP documents listed earlier, along with the comments provided below, to help you design a custom security framework for your organization's information security program.

NIST Special Publication 800-12

SP 800-12, *Computer Security Handbook,* is an excellent reference and guide for routine management of information security. It provides little guidance, however, on the design and implementation of new security systems; use it as a supplement to gain a deeper understanding in the background and terminology of security. The following excerpt gives an idea of the kind of information found in SP 800-12.

> 800-12 draws upon the OECD's Guidelines for the Security of Information Systems, which was endorsed by the United States. It provides for:
>
> Accountability—The responsibilities and accountability of owners, providers, and users of information systems and other parties [...] should be explicit.
>
> Awareness—Owners, providers, users, and other parties should readily be able, consistent with maintaining security, to gain appropriate knowledge of and be informed about the existence and general extent of measures [...] for the security of information systems.
>
> Ethics—The information systems and the security of information systems should be provided and used in such a manner that the rights and legitimate interest of others are respected.
>
> Multidisciplinary—Measures, practices, and procedures for the security of information systems should take account of and address all relevant considerations and viewpoints. [...]
>
> Proportionality—Security levels, costs, measures, practices, and procedures should be appropriate and proportionate to the value and degree of reliance on the information systems, and to the severity, probability, and extent of potential harm. [...]

Integration—Measures, practices, and procedures for the security of information systems should be coordinated and integrated with each other and other measures, practices, and procedures of the organization so as to create a coherent system of security.

Timeliness—Public and private parties, at both national and international levels, should act in a timely, coordinated manner to prevent and to respond to breaches of security of information systems.

Reassessment—The security of information systems should be reassessed periodically, as information systems and the requirements for their security vary over time.

Democracy—The security of information systems should be compatible with the legitimate use and flow of data and information in a democratic society.[10]

SP 800-12 also lays out NIST's philosophy on security management by identifying 17 controls organized into three categories. These three categories are described below:

The Management Controls section addresses security topics that can be characterized as managerial. They are techniques and concerns that are normally addressed by management in the organization's computer security program. In general, they focus on the management of the computer security program and the management of risk within the organization.

The Operational Controls section addresses security controls that focus on controls that are, broadly speaking, implemented and executed by people (as opposed to systems). These controls are put in place to improve the security of a particular system (or group of systems). They often require technical or specialized expertise and often rely upon management activities as well as technical controls.

The Technical Controls section focuses on security controls that the computer system executes. These controls are dependent upon the proper functioning of the system for their effectiveness. The implementation of technical controls, however, always requires significant operational considerations and should be consistent with the management of security within the organization.[11]

The 17 specific areas of control are discussed in more detail in the section on NIST SP 800-26 later in this chapter.

NIST Special Publication 800-14

NIST SP 800-14, *Generally Accepted Principles and Practices for Securing Information Technology Systems,* describes recommended practices and provides information on commonly accepted information security principles that can direct the security team in the development of a security blueprint. It also describes the philosophical principles that the security team should integrate into the entire information security process, expanding on the components of SP 800-12. Table 6-1 shows the table of contents for NIST SP 800-14.

TABLE 6-1 Table of Contents for NIST SP 800-14, *Generally Accepted Principles and Practices for Securing Information Technology Systems*

TABLE 6-1 Table of Contents for NIST SP 800-14, *Generally Accepted Principles and Practices for Securing Information Technology Systems* (continued)

The more significant points made in NIST SP 800-14 are as follows:

1. *Security supports the mission of the organization.* The implementation of information security is not independent of the organization's mission. On the contrary, *it is driven by it.* An information security system that is not grounded in the organization's mission, vision, and culture is guaranteed to fail. The information security program must support and further the organization's mission, which means that it must include elements of the mission in each of its policies, procedures, and training programs.

2. *Security is an integral element of sound management.* Effective management includes planning, organizing, leading, and controlling activities. Security supports the planning function when information security policies provide input into the organization initiatives, and it supports the controlling function when security controls enforce both managerial and security policies.

3. *Security should be cost-effective.* The costs of information security should be considered part of the cost of doing business, much like the cost of the computers, networks, and voice communications systems. None of these systems generates any profit, and they may not lead to competitive advantages. As discussed in Chapter 5, however, information security should justify its own

costs. Security measures whose costs outweigh their benefits must be rationalized based on other business reasons (such as legal requirements).

4. *Systems owners have security responsibilities outside their own organizations.* Whenever systems store and use information from customers, patients, clients, partners, and others, the security of such data becomes a serious responsibility for the owners of the systems. Also, the owners have the general duty to protect information assets on behalf of all stakeholders of the organization. These stakeholders may include shareholders in publicly held organizations, and the government and taxpayers in the case of public agencies and institutions.

5. *Security responsibilities and accountability should be made explicit.* Policy documents should clearly identify the security responsibilities of users, administrators, and managers. To be legally binding, such documents must be disseminated, read, understood, and agreed to. As described in Chapter 4, ignorance of the law is no excuse, but ignorance of policy can be. Any relevant legislation must also become part of the security program.

6. *Security requires a comprehensive and integrated approach.* As emphasized throughout this book, *security is everyone's responsibility.* Throughout each stage of the SecSDLC, the three communities of interest—information technology management and professionals, information security management and professionals, and the nontechnical general business managers and professionals of the broader organization—should participate in all aspects of the information security program.

7. *Security should be periodically reassessed.* Information security that is implemented and then ignored lacks due diligence and is considered negligent. Security is an ongoing process. To remain effective in the face of a constantly shifting set of threats and a constantly changing user base, the security process must be periodically repeated. Continuous analyses of threats, assets, and controls must be conducted and new blueprints developed.

8. *Security is constrained by societal factors.* Many factors influence the implementation and maintenance of security. Legal demands, shareholder requirements, and even business practices affect the implementation of security controls and safeguards. While security professionals would prefer to isolate information assets from the Internet—the major source of threats to those assets—the business requirements of the organization may preclude this control measure.

Table 6-2 presents the principles for securing information technology systems from NIST SP 800-14. This table serves as a checklist for the blueprint process and provides a method to ensure that all key elements are present in the design of an information security program and that the planning efforts produce a blueprint for an effective security architecture.

Security Management Models and Practices

TABLE 6-2 NIST SP 800-14, *Principles for Securing Information Technology Systems*

Principle 1.	Establish a sound security policy as the "foundation" for the design.
Principle 2.	Treat security as an integral part of the overall system design.
Principle 3.	Clearly delineate the physical and logical security boundaries governed by associated security policies.
Principle 4.	Reduce risk to an acceptable level.
Principle 5.	Assume that external systems are insecure.
Principle 6.	Identify potential trade-offs between reducing risk and increased costs and decreases in other aspects of operational effectiveness.
Principle 7.	Implement layered security (ensure no single point of vulnerability).
Principle 8.	Implement tailored system security measures to meet organizational security goals.
Principle 9.	Strive for simplicity.
Principle 10.	Design and operate an IT system to limit vulnerability and to be resilient in response.
Principle 11.	Minimize the system elements to be trusted.
Principle 12.	Implement security through a combination of measures distributed physically and logically.
Principle 13.	Provide assurance that the system is, and continues to be, resilient in the face of expected threats.
Principle 14.	Limit or contain vulnerabilities.
Principle 15.	Formulate security measures to address multiple overlapping information domains.
Principle 16.	Isolate public access systems from mission-critical resources (e.g., data, processes).
Principle 17.	Use boundary mechanisms to separate computing systems and network infrastructures.
Principle 18.	Where possible, base security on open standards for portability and interoperability.
Principle 19.	Use a common language in developing security requirements.
Principle 20.	Design and implement audit mechanisms to detect unauthorized use and to support incident investigations.
Principle 21.	Design security to allow for regular adoption of new technologies, including a secure and logical technology upgrade process.
Principle 22.	Authenticate users and processes to ensure appropriate access control decisions both within and across domains.
Principle 23.	Use unique identities to ensure accountability.
Principle 24.	Implement least privilege (process of granting the lowest level of access consistent with accomplishing the assigned role).

TABLE 6-2 NIST SP 800-14, *Principles for Securing Information Technology Systems* (continued)

Principle 25.	Do not implement unnecessary security mechanisms.
Principle 26.	Protect information while being processed, in transit, and in storage.
Principle 27.	Strive for operational ease of use.
Principle 28.	Develop and exercise contingency or disaster recovery procedures to ensure appropriate availability.
Principle 29.	Consider custom products to achieve adequate security.
Principle 30.	Ensure proper security in the shutdown or disposal of a system.
Principle 31.	Protect against all likely classes of "attacks."
Principle 32.	Identify and prevent common errors and vulnerabilities.
Principle 33.	Ensure that developers are trained in how to develop secure software.

NIST Special Publication 800-18

NIST SP 800-18, *Guide for Developing Security Plans for Information Technology Systems,* provides detailed methods for assessing, designing, and implementing controls and plans for various-sized applications. It serves as a guide for the activities described in this chapter, and for the overall information security planning process. In addition, this document includes templates for major application security plans. As with any publication of this scope and magnitude, SP 800-18 must be customized to fit the particular needs of the organization. Table 6-3 shows the table of contents for SP 800-18.

TABLE 6-3 Table of Contents for NIST SP 800-18, *Guide for Developing Security Plans for Information Technology Systems*

1. **Introduction**
   1.1 Background
   1.2 Major Application or General Support System Plans
   1.3 Relationship to Other NIST Security Documents
   1.4 Purposes of Security Plans
   1.5 Security Plan Responsibilities
   1.6 Recommended Format
   1.7 Advice and Comment on Plan
   1.8 Audience
   1.9 Organization of Document

2. **System Analysis**
   2.1 System Boundaries
   2.2 Multiple Similar Systems
   2.3 System Category
        2.3.1 Major Applications
        2.3.2 General Support System

TABLE 6-3   Table of Contents for NIST SP 800-18, *Guide for Developing Security Plans for Information Technology Systems* (continued)

3. **Plan Development—All Systems**
    3.1 Plan Control
    3.2 System Identification
        3.2.1 System Name/Title
        3.2.2 Responsible Organization
        3.2.3 Information Contact(s)
        3.2.4 Assignment of Security Responsibility
    3.3 System Operational Status
    3.4 General Description/Purpose
    3.5 System Environment
    3.6 System Interconnection/Information Sharing
    3.7 Sensitivity of Information Handled
        3.7.1 Laws, Regulations, and Policies Affecting the System
        3.7.2 General Description of Sensitivity

4. **Management Controls**
    4.1 Risk Assessment and Management
    4.2 Review of Security Controls
    4.3 Rules of Behavior
    4.4 Planning for Security in the Life Cycle
        4.4.1 Initiation Phase
        4.4.2 Development/Acquisition Phase
        4.4.3 Implementation Phase
        4.4.4 Operation/Maintenance Phase
        4.4.5 Disposal Phase
    4.5 Authorize Processing

5. **Operational Controls**
    5.MA   Major Application—Operational Controls
    5.MA.1 Personnel Security
    5.MA.2 Physical and Environmental Protection
        5.MA.2.1 Explanation of Physical and Environment Security
        5.MA.2.2 Computer Room Example
    5.MA.3 Production, Input/Output Controls
    5.MA.4 Contingency Planning
    5.MA.5 Application Software Maintenance Controls
    5.MA.6 Data Integrity/Validation Controls
    5.MA.7 Documentation
    5.MA.8 Security Awareness and Training

6. **MA Major Application—Technical Controls**
    6.MA.1 Identification and Authentication
        6.MA.1.1 Identification
        6.MA.1.2 Authentication
    6.MA.2 Logical Access Controls (Authorization/Access Controls)
    6.MA.3 Public Access Controls
    6.MA.4 Audit Trails

TABLE 6-3 Table of Contents for NIST SP 800-18, *Guide for Developing Security Plans for Information Technology Systems* (continued)

7. **GSS General Support System—Operational Controls**
    7.GSS.1 Personnel Controls
    7.GSS.2 Physical and Environmental Protection
        7.GSS.2.1 Explanation of Physical and Environment Security
        7.GSS.2.2 Computer Room Example
    7.GSS.3 Production, Input/Output Controls
    7.GSS.4 Contingency Planning (Continuity of Support)
    7 GSS 5 Hardware and System Software Maintenance Controls
    7.GSS.6 Integrity Controls
    7.GSS.7 Documentation
    7.GSS.8 Security Awareness and Training
    7.GSS.9 Incident Response Capability

8. **GSS General Support System—Technical Controls**
    8.GSS.1 Identification and Authentication
        8.GSS.1.1 Identification
        8.GSS.1.2 Authentication
    8.GSS.2 Logical Access Controls (Authorization/Access Controls)
    8.GSS.3 Audit Trails

NIST Special Publication 800-26

NIST SP 800-26, *Security Self-Assessment Guide for Information Technology Systems*, describes 17 areas that span managerial, operational, and technical controls. These 17 areas, which are shown in Table 6-4, form the core of the NIST security management structure.

When working in these areas, be sure to consider the information processed by the system under review and evaluate the need for protective measures. Relate the information processed to each of the three basic information protection requirements (confidentiality, integrity, and availability). In addition, it is often helpful to categorize systems or groups of systems by sensitivity level. Three examples of such categories for sensitive unclassified information are described here:

- High: Extremely grave injury accrues to U.S. interests if the information is compromised; could cause loss of life, imprisonment, or major financial loss, or require legal action for correction
- Medium: Serious injury accrues to U.S. interests if the information is compromised; could cause significant financial loss or require legal action for correction
- Low: Injury accrues to U.S. interests if the information is compromised; would cause only minor financial loss or require only administrative action for correction

TABLE 6-4   Topic Areas Covered in NIST SP 800-26, *Security Self-Assessment Guide for Information Technology Systems*

Management Controls
1. Risk Management
2. Review of Security Controls
3. Life Cycle Maintenance
4. Authorization of Processing (Certification and Accreditation)
5. System Security Plan

Operational Controls
6. Personnel Security
7. Physical Security
8. Production, Input/Output Controls
9. Contingency Planning
10. Hardware and Systems Software
11. Data Integrity
12. Documentation
13. Security Awareness, Training, and Education
14. Incident Response Capability

Technical Controls
15. Identification and Authentication
16. Logical Access Controls
17. Audit Trails

Each of the topics shown in Table 6-4 emerged out of earlier documents and the knowledge and experience of information security professionals.

NIST Special Publication 800-30

NIST SP 800-30, *Risk Management Guide for Information Technology Systems,* provides

> a foundation for the development of an effective risk management program, containing both the definitions and the practical guidance necessary for assessing and mitigating risks identified within IT systems. The ultimate goal is to help organizations to better manage IT-related mission risks.[12]

This guide is designed to help you develop or evaluate the risk management process. It is organized into five chapters, as shown in Table 6-5.

TABLE 6-5   Table of Contents for NIST SP 800-30, *Risk Management Guide for Information Technology Systems*

1. **Introduction**

2. **Risk Management Overview**
   2.1 Importance of Risk Management
   2.2 Integration of Risk Management into SDLC
   2.3 Key Roles

TABLE 6-5 Table of Contents for NIST SP 800-30, *Risk Management Guide for Information Technology Systems* (continued)

3. **Risk Assessment**
   3.1 Step 1: System Characterization
   3.2 Step 2: Threat Identification
   3.3 Step 3: Vulnerability Identification
   3.4 Step 4: Control Analysis
   3.5 Step 5: Likelihood Determination
   3.6 Step 6: Impact Analysis
   3.7 Step 7: Risk
   3.8 Step 8: Control Recommendations
   3.9 Step 9: Results Documentation

4. **Risk Mitigation**
   4.1 Risk Mitigation
   4.2 Risk Mitigation Strategy
   4.3 Approach for Control Implementation
   4.4 Control Categories
   4.5 Cost-Benefit Analysis
   4.6 Residual Risk

5. **Evaluation and Assessment**
   5.1 Good Security Practice
   5.2 Keys For Success

Appendix A   Sample Interview Questions

Appendix B   Sample Risk Assessment Report Outline

Appendix C   Sample Implementation Safeguard Plan Summary Table

Appendix D   Acronyms

Appendix E   Glossary

Appendix F   References

RFC 2196 Site Security Handbook

While the Internet Engineering Task Force (IETF), which is part of the Internet Society, promotes no particular architecture, the Security Area Working Group within the IETF has created RFC 2196, *Site Security Handbook*. (The Security Area Working Group acts as an advisory board for the protocols and areas developed and promoted through the Internet Society.) RFC 2196 provides a good functional discussion of important security issues and an overview of five basic areas of security, along with development and implementation details. It includes chapters on such critical security topics as policies, technical architecture, services, and incident handling. For example, the technical architecture chapter begins by highlighting the importance of security policies, then expands into an examination of services, access controls, and other relevant areas. Table 6-6 presents the table of contents for RFC 2196.

TABLE 6-6   Table of Contents for RFC 2196, *Site Security Handbook*

1. **Introduction**
   1.1 Purpose of this Work
   1.2 Audience
   1.3 Definitions
   1.4 Related Work
   1.5 Basic Approach
   1.6 Risk Assessment

2. **Security Policies**
   2.1 What Is a Security Policy and Why Have One?
   2.2 What Makes a Good Security Policy?
   2.3 Keeping the Policy Flexible

3. **Architecture**
   3.1 Objectives
   3.2 Network and Service Configuration
   3.3 Firewalls

4. **Security Services and Procedures**
   4.1 Authentication
   4.2 Confidentiality
   4.3 Integrity
   4.4 Authorization
   4.5 Access
   4.6 Auditing
   4.7 Securing Backups

5. **Security Incident Handling**
   5.1 Preparing and Planning for Incident Handling
   5.2 Notification and Points of Contact
   5.3 Identifying an Incident
   5.4 Handling an Incident
   5.5 Aftermath of an Incident
   5.6 Responsibilities

6. **Ongoing Activities**

7. **Tools and Locations**

8. **Mailing Lists and Other Resources**

9. **References**

COBIT

Control Objectives for Information and related Technology (COBIT) also provides advice about the implementation of sound controls and control objectives for information security. This document can be used not only as a planning tool for information security, but also as a controls model. COBIT was created by the Information Systems Audit and Control

Association (ISACA), and the IT Governance Institute (ITGI) in 1992. Documentation on COBIT was first published in 1996, and was updated in 1998, 2000, 2003, and most recently in December 2005. According to ISACA:

> COBIT is an IT governance framework and supporting toolset that allows managers to bridge the gap between control requirements, technical issues, and business risks. COBIT enables clear policy development and good practice for IT control throughout organizations. ITGI's latest version—COBIT 4.0—emphasizes regulatory compliance, helps organizations to increase the value attained from IT, enables alignment, and simplifies implementation of the COBIT framework. It does not invalidate work done based on earlier versions of COBIT but instead can be used to enhance work already done based upon those earlier versions. When major activities are planned for IT governance initiatives, or when an overhaul of the enterprise control framework is anticipated, it is recommended to start fresh with COBIT 4.0. COBIT 4.0 presents activities in a more streamlined and practical manner so continuous improvement in IT governance is easier than ever to achieve.[13]

COBIT presents 34 high-level objectives that cover 215 control objectives. The control objectives are categorized into four domains: plan and organize, acquire and implement, deliver and support, and monitor and evaluate. Each of these domains is examined in more detail.

Plan and Organize

This domain covers the *planning and organization* of information technology use, and makes recommendations for achieving organizational goals and objectives through the use of IT. Part of this process is to examine the form IT is to assume in the organization to obtain the best possible results. The high-level controlling objectives for planning and organization are:

PO1	Define a Strategic IT Plan
PO2	Define the Information Architecture
PO3	Determine Technological Direction
PO4	Define the IT Processes, Organization, and Relationships
PO5	Manage the IT Investment
PO6	Communicate Management Aims and Direction
PO7	Manage IT Human Resources
PO8	Manage Quality
PO9	Assess and Manage IT Risks
PO10	Manage Projects

Acquire and Implement

The *acquisition and implementation* domain focuses on specification of requirements, acquisition of needed components, and integration of these components into the organization's systems. It also examines ongoing maintenance and change requirements to extend the usability of the system. The high-level controlling objectives for acquiring and implementing are:

AI1   Identify Automated Solutions
AI2   Acquire and Maintain Application Software
AI3   Acquire and Maintain Technology Infrastructure
AI4   Enable Operation and Use
AI5   Procure IT Resources
AI6   Manage Changes
AI7   Install and Accredit Solutions and Changes

Delivery and Support

The *delivery and support* domain focuses on the functionality of the system and its use to the end user. It also examines the systems applications—including the input, processing, and output components. Efficiency and effectiveness of operations are critical to the system function, and therefore processes that support those operations are also examined. The high-level controlling objectives for delivery and support are:

DS1   Define and Manage Service Levels
DS2   Manage Third-Party Services
DS3   Manage Performance and Capacity
DS4   Ensure Continuous Service
DS5   Ensure Systems Security
DS6   Identify and Allocate Costs
DS7   Educate and Train Users
DS8   Manage Service Desk and Incidents
DS9   Manage the Configuration
DS10   Manage Problems
DS11   Manage Data
DS12   Manage the Physical Environment
DS13   Manage Operations

Monitor and Evaluate

The *monitor and evaluate* domain seeks to examine the alignment between IT systems usage and organizational strategy. This assessment identifies the regulatory requirements for which controls are needed. Monitoring the effectiveness and efficiency of IT systems against the organizational control processes in the delivery and support domain is also a function of this domain. The high-level controlling objectives for monitoring and evaluating are:

ME1   Monitor and Evaluate IT Processes
ME2   Monitor and Evaluate Internal Control
ME3   Ensure Regulatory Compliance
ME4   Provide IT Governance

Although COBIT was designed to be an IT governance structure, it provides a framework to support security requirements and assessment needs. Organizations that incorporate COBIT assessments into their IT governance are better prepared for general information security risk management operations.

COSO

Another controls-based model, the **Committee of Sponsoring Organizations of the Treadway Commission (COSO)**, is a U.S. private-sector initiative, formed in 1985. Its major objective is to identify the factors that cause fraudulent financial reporting and to make recommendations to reduce its incidence. COSO has established a common definition of internal controls, standards, and criteria against which companies and organizations can assess their control systems.[14] COSO helps organizations comply with critical regulations like the Sarbanes-Oxley Act of 2002.

COSO Definitions and Key Concepts

According to COSO, "[i]nternal control is a process, effected by an entity's board of directors, management and other personnel, designed to provide reasonable assurance regarding the achievement of objectives in the following categories:

- Effectiveness and efficiency of operations
- Reliability of financial reporting
- Compliance with applicable laws and regulations"[15]

COSO's key concepts include the following:

- "Internal control is a process. It is a means to an end, not an end in itself.
- Internal control is affected by people. It's not merely policy manuals and forms, but people at every level of an organization.
- Internal control can be expected to provide only reasonable assurance, not absolute assurance, to an entity's management and board.
- Internal control is geared to the achievement of objectives in one or more separate but overlapping categories."[16]

COSO Framework

The COSO framework is built on five interrelated components. Again, while COSO is designed as a framework to describe and analyze internal control systems, part of those internal controls systems are on IT systems that incorporate information security controls. COSO's five components are:

- Control environment—the foundation of all internal control components. Environmental factors include the integrity, ethical values, management's operating style, delegation of authority systems, as well as the processes for managing and developing people in the organization.
- Risk assessment—based on the establishment of objectives, risk assessment assists in the identification and examination of valid risks to objectives, as well as information.

- Control activities—including the policies and procedures to support management directives. These activities occur throughout the organization and include approvals, authorizations, verifications, reconciliations, reviews of operating performance, security of assets, and segregation of duties.
- Information and communication—responsible for the delivery of reports, regulatory, financial, and otherwise. Effective communication should also include third parties and other stakeholders.
- Monitoring—continuous or discrete activities to ensure internal control systems are functioning as expected. Internal control deficiencies detected through these monitoring activities should be reported upstream and corrective actions should be taken to ensure continuous improvement of the system.[17]

SECURITY MANAGEMENT PRACTICES

In information security, two categories of benchmarks are used: standards of due care/due diligence, and recommended practices. Recommended practices include a subcategory of practices—the so-called gold standard—that are generally regarded as "the best of the best."

Standards of Due Care/Due Diligence

For legal reasons, an organization may be compelled to adopt a certain minimum level of security. When organizations adopt minimum levels of security to anticipate a future legal defense, they may need to show that they have done what any *prudent* organization would do in similar circumstances; this is known as a **standard of due care**. Implementing controls at this minimum standard—and maintaining them—demonstrates that an organization has performed **due diligence**. Although some argue that the two terms are interchangeable, the term due diligence encompasses a requirement that the implemented standards continue to provide the required level of protection. Failure to support a standard of due care or due diligence can expose an organization to legal liability, provided it can be shown that the organization was negligent in its application or lack of application of information protection. This is especially important when the organization maintains information about customers, including medical, legal, or other personal data.

The information security protection environment that an organization must maintain can be large and complex. It may therefore be impossible to implement recommended practices in all categories. Based on the budget assigned to the protection of information, it may also be financially impossible to provide security levels on par with those offered by organizations that can spend more money on information security. Information security practices are often viewed relatively; as noted by F. M. Avolio, "Good security now is better than perfect security never."[18]

Some organizations might want to implement the best, most technologically advanced controls available, but for financial or other reasons cannot do so. Ultimately, it is counterproductive to establish costly, state-of-the-art security in one area, only to leave other areas exposed. Instead, organizations must make sure that they have met a reasonable level of security in all areas, and that they have adequately protected all information assets, before improving individual areas to meet the highest standards.

Recommended Security Practices

Security efforts that seek to provide a superior level of performance in the protection of information are referred to as recommended **business practices** or sometimes called *best practices*. Security efforts that are among the best in the industry are termed **best security practices (BSPs)**. These practices balance the need for information access with the need for adequate protection. They seek to provide as much security as possible for information and information systems while simultaneously demonstrating fiscal responsibility and ensuring ready information access. Of course, companies with best practices may not be the best in every area; they may have established an extremely high quality or successful security effort in only one area.

The federal government has established a Web site that allows government agencies to share their best security practices with other agencies (http://fasp.nist.gov). This site developed from the Federal Agency Security Project (FASP)—the result of the Federal Chief Information Officer (CIO) Council's Federal Best Security Practices (BSP) pilot effort to identify, evaluate, and disseminate recommended practices for computer information protection and security. The FASP site contains agency policies, procedures, and practices; the CIO pilot BSPs; and a Frequently Asked Questions (FAQ) section.[19]

While few commercial equivalents exist at this time, many of the BSPs discussed here are applicable to the area of information security in both the public and private sectors. BSPs are organized into the areas shown in Table 6-7, which describes each area and lists examples that can be found on the Web site.

TABLE 6-7 Federal Agency Best Security Practices

Area	Description	Examples
Audit Trail	A record of system activity by system or application processes and by user activity	• Sample Generic Policy • High-Level Procedures for Audit Trails
Authorize Processing (C&A)	A method of assurance of the security of the system	• Certification and Accreditation Documentation Performance Work Summary • Sample Generic Policy and High-Level Procedures for Certification/Accreditation • C&A of Core Financial System for USAID • How to Accredit Information Systems for Operation
Contingency Planning	Strategies for keeping an organization's critical functions operating in the event of disruptions, whether large or small	• Contingency Planning Template • Contingency Planning Template Instructions • Sample Generic Policy and High-Level Procedures for Contingency Plans • Continuity of Operations from the U.S. Treasury

TABLE 6-7 Federal Agency Best Security Practices (continued)

Area	Description	Examples
Data Integrity	Controls used to protect data from accidental or malicious alteration or destruction and to provide assurance to the user that the information meets expectations about its quality and integrity	• How to Protect Against Viruses Using Attachment Blocking • Sample Generic Policy and High-Level Procedures for Data Integrity/Validation
Documentation	Descriptions of the hardware, software, policies, standards, procedures, and approvals related to the system document and formalized description of the system's security controls	• Sample Generic Policy and High-Level Procedures for System Documentation
Hardware and System Software Maintenance	Controls used to monitor the installation of, and updates to, hardware and software to ensure that the system functions as expected and that a historical record is maintained of changes	• Configuration Management Plan • Interim Policy Document on Configuration Management • Sample Generic Policy and High-Level Procedures for Hardware and Application Software Security
Identification and Authentication	Technical measures that prevent unauthorized people (or or unauthorized processes) from entering an IT system	• Creating Strong Passwords • Password Cracking Information • Password Management Standard • Sample Generic Policy and High-Level Procedures for Passwords and Access Forms
Incident Response Capability	The capacity to provide help to users when a security incident occurs in a system	• Computer Incident Response Team Desk Reference • Identification and Authentication on Agency Systems • Computer Virus Incident Report Form • Agency Computer Incident Response Guide • Sample Generic Policy and High-Level Procedures for Incident Response • Developing an Agency Incident Response Process
Life Cycle	IT system life cycles contain five basic phases: initiation, development and/or acquisition, implementation, operation, and disposal	• Sample Generic Policy and High- Level Procedures for Life Cycle Security • Integrating Security into Systems Development Life Cycle

TABLE 6-7 Federal Agency Best Security Practices (continued)

Area	Description	Examples
Logical Access Controls	System-based mechanisms used to designate who or what is to have access to a specific system resource and the type of transactions and functions that are permitted	• Decision Paper on Use of Screen Warning Banner • Sample Warning Banner from the National Labor Relations Board
Network Security	Secure communication capability that allows one user or system to connect to another user or system	• E-Mail Spam Policy • Network Perimeter Security Policy • Securing POP Mail on Windows Clients • How to Deploy Firewalls • Configuration of Technical Safeguards • Network Security Management Policy • How to Secure a Domain Name Server (DNS)
Personnel Security	Human users, designers, implementers, and managers—how they interact with computers and the access and authorities they need to do their jobs	• Policy on Limited Personnel Use of Government Office Equipment • E-mail Policy • Internet Use Policy • Limited Personnel Use of Government Equipment • Nondisclosure Form • Guidelines for Evaluating Information on Public Web Sites • Receipt of Proprietary Information • Sample Generic Policy and High-Level Procedures for Personnel Security • Investigative Requirements for Contractor Employees
Physical and Environment Protection	Measures taken to protect systems, buildings, and related supporting infrastructures against threats associated with their physical environment	• Securing Portable Electronic Media Agency • Sample Generic Policy and High-Level Procedures for Facility Protection
Production, Input/ Output Controls	Covers topics ranging from user help desks to procedures for storing, handling, and destroying media	• Disk Sanitization Procedures • Sample Generic Policy and High-Level Procedures for Marking, Handling, Processing, Storage, and Disposal of Data

TABLE 6-7 Federal Agency Best Security Practices (continued)

Area	Description	Examples
Policy and Procedures	Formally documented security policies and procedures	• Internet Security Policy • Telecommuting and Mobile Computer Security Policy • Sample of Agency Large Service Application (LSA) Information Technology (IT) Security Program Policy • Security Handbook and Standard Operating Procedures for the GSA
Program Management	Overall scope of the program (i.e., policies, and security program plans and guidance)	• IT Security Cost Estimation Guide from the Department of Education • A Summary Guide: Public Law, Executive Orders, and Policy Documents • Position Description for Computer System Security Officer

The Gold Standard

Recommended business practices are not sufficient for organizations that want to implement the most protective, most supportive, yet fiscally responsible standards they can. These organizations strive to achieve the gold standard. As noted earlier, the **gold standard** is a model level of performance that demonstrates industrial leadership, quality, and concern for the protection of information. The implementation of gold-standard security requires a great deal of support, in terms of both financial and personnel resources. While some public information on recommended practices is available, no published criteria for a gold standard exist. In reality, the gold standard is a level of security that is out of reach for most organizations. While many vendors claim to offer a gold standard in one product or service, such assertions are predominantly marketing hype.

Selecting Recommended Practices

Choosing which recommended practices to implement can pose a challenge for some organizations. In industries that are regulated by governmental agencies, government guidelines are in fact requirements that must be met. For other organizations, government guidelines merely serve as excellent sources of information about what steps other organizations are required to take to control information security risks, and can inform their selection of recommended practices.

When considering recommended practices for your organization, ask the following questions:

- Does your organization resemble the identified target organization of the recommended practice? A recommended practice is only useful if your organization is similar to the organization from which it comes.

- Are you in a similar industry as the target? A strategy that works well in manufacturing organizations might have little relevance to a nonprofit organization.
- Do you face similar challenges as the target? If your organization lacks a functioning information security program, a recommended practice target that assumes such a program is in place has value.
- Is your organizational structure similar to the target? A recommended practice proposed for a small office is not applicable to a multinational company.
- Are the resources you can expend similar to those required by the recommended practice? A recommended practice proposal that assumes unlimited funding has limited value if your program must deal with budget constraints.
- Are you in a similar threat environment as the one assumed by the recommended practice? recommended practices that are months or even weeks old may not answer the current threat environment. To see how quickly obsolescence arises, merely consider the recommended practices for Internet connectivity over the past five years.

Another source for recommended practices information is found at the Web site operated by the Computer Emergency Response Team (CERT) at Carnegie Mellon University. The presentation titled "Which Best Practices are Best For Me?" can be found at (http://www.cert.org/archive/pdf/secureit_bestpractices.pdf). This report presents a discussion about a varierty of the security improvement practices that you may find useful. Similarly, Microsoft has published a set of recommended practices in security at its Web site (www.microsoft.com/privacy/safeinternet/security/best_practices/default.htm). Microsoft focuses on seven key tactics:

1. Use antivirus software.
2. Use strong passwords.
3. Verify your software security settings.
4. Update product security.
5. Build personal firewalls.
6. Back up early and often.
7. Protect against power surges and losses.

These resources are but a few of the many public and private organizations that promote solid recommended security practices. Investing a few hours in searching the Web will reveal dozens of other locations that offer additional information. In fact, finding information on security design is the easy part. Sorting through the collected mass of information, documents, and publications, however, can require a substantial investment in time and human resources. The goal is to obtain a clear methodology for creating a framework, which in turn leads to a blueprint that provides specifics on the development of a security system that includes all the necessary components—policy, education and training programs, and technology.

Benchmarking and Recommended Practices Limitations

The biggest barrier to benchmarking in information security is that organizations do not talk to each other. A successful attack is viewed as an organizational failure and is kept secret, insofar as possible. As a consequence, the entire industry suffers because valuable lessons are not recorded, disseminated, and evaluated. Today, however, an increasing number of security administrators are joining professional associations and societies like the Information Systems Security Association (ISSA) and sharing their stories and lessons learned. An alternative to participating in this direct dialog is to publish sanitized versions of attacks on organizations and information in security journals.

Another problem with benchmarking is that no two organizations are identical. Even if two organizations offer products or services in the same market, their size, composition, management philosophies, organizational culture, technological infrastructure, and budgets for security may differ dramatically. Indeed, if they exchange information, they might not be able to apply it to each other's strategies. What organizations seek most are lessons that can help them strategically, rather than information about specific technologies they should adopt. If security were a technical problem, then implementing the same technology would solve the problem regardless of industry or organizational composition. Because it is a managerial and people problem, however, the number and types of variables that affect the security of the organization will likely differ radically in any two organizations.

A third problem is that recommended practices are a moving target. Knowing what was happening a few years ago, which is emphasized in benchmarking, does not necessarily tell you what to do next. While it is true that, in security, those who do not prepare for the attacks of the past will see them again, it is also true that preparing for past threats does not protect you from what lies ahead. Security programs must continually keep abreast of new threats as well as methods, techniques, policies, guidelines, educational and training approaches, and, yes, technologies to combat them.

Baselining

A practice related to benchmarking is baselining. A **baseline** is a "value or profile of a performance metric against which changes in the performance metric can be usefully compared."[20] An example of a baseline is the number of attacks per week that an organization experiences. The initial baseline is taken by measuring the activity over a "typical" period to derive an average weekly value for that metric. In the future, this baseline can serve as a reference point to determine whether the number of attacks is increasing. *Baselining* is the process of measuring against established standards. In information security, it involves the comparison of security activities and events against the organization's future performance. Used in this way, baselining can provide the foundation for internal benchmarking. The information gathered for an organization's first risk assessment becomes the baseline for future comparisons. The next section of this chapter provides a more complete discussion of the use of metrics in information security management.

When baselining, it is useful to have a guide to the overall process. NIST offers a number of publications specifically written to support these activities:

- SP 800-27 Revision A, *Engineering Principles for Information Technology Security (A Baseline for Achieving Security)*, was published in June 2004.
- SP 800-26, *Security Self-Assessment Guide for Information Technology Systems,* November 2001, is discussed elsewhere in this chapter.

- Draft SP 800-26, Rev. 1 NIST DRAFT Special Publication 800-26, Revision 1: *Guide for Information Security Program Assessments and System Reporting Form,* is currently under review.
- Revised NIST SP 800-26 *System Questionnaire with NIST SP 800-53 References and Associated Security Control Mappings,* April 2005, is designed to accompany 800-26.

These documents are available at http://csrc.nist.gov/publications/nistpubs/index.html.

Baselining and researching recommended practices provide less detail for the design and implementation of a security program than does use of a complete methodology. Nevertheless, by baselining and using recommended practices, you can piece together the desired outcome of the security process, then work backward to achieve an effective design.

The Internet Security Task Force (http://www.ca.com/ISTF/recommendations.htm) also provides information on recommended practices. This task force is a collection of parties, both public and private, with a shared interest in the security of the Internet. It provides recommendations for security implementations. Another widely referenced source is CERT (www.cert.org), which promotes a series of security modules. CERT's Web site provides links to practices and implementation that make up a security methodology.

It may be worth your time and money to join professional societies that maintain information on recommended practices for their members. The Technology Manager's Forum (www.techforum.com) bestows annual recommended practice awards in a number of areas, including information security. The Information Security Forum's (www.isfsecuritystandard.com) free publication, *Standard of Good Practice,* outlines information security recommended practices.

Many organizations sponsor seminars and classes on recommended practices for implementing security. For example, the Information Systems Audit and Control Association (www.isaca.com) hosts such seminars on a regular basis. Similarly, the International Association of Professional Security Consultants (www.iapsc.org) has a listing of recommended practices, as does the Global Grid Forum (www.gridforum.org). You can also peruse Web portals for posted security recommended practices. Several free portals dedicated to security maintain collections of practices, such as SearchSecurity.com and NIST's Computer Resources Center.

The Gartner Group published 12 questions as a self-assessment for recommended security practices. The questions are organized into three categories—people, processes, and technology—which loosely map to the managerial, operational, and technical areas of the NIST methodology. The 12 questions are given below:

People

1. Do you perform background checks on all employees with access to sensitive data, areas, or access points?
2. Would the average employee recognize a security issue?
3. Would they choose to report it?
4. Would they know how to report it to the right people?

Processes

5. Are enterprise security policies updated on at least an annual basis, employees educated on changes, and consistently enforced?
6. Does your enterprise follow a patch/update management and evaluation process to prioritize and mediate new security vulnerabilities?
7. Are the user accounts of former employees immediately removed on termination?
8. Are security group representatives involved in all stages of the project life cycle for new projects?

Technology

9. Is every possible route to the Internet protected by a properly configured firewall?
10. Is sensitive data on laptops and remote systems encrypted?
11. Do you regularly scan your systems and networks, using a vulnerability analysis tool, for security exposures?
12. Are malicious software scanning tools deployed on all workstations and servers?[21]

METRICS IN INFORMATION SECURITY MANAGEMENT

Executives often ask the CISO questions like "What will this security control cost?" or "Is it working?" or even more ominous, "Why is this control system of yours not working?" As noted by Gerald Kovacich, "This last question often comes right after a successful [..] attack."[22]

While CISOs sometimes claim that the costs and benefits of InfoSec are impossible to measure, these questions can be answered. To do so requires the design and ongoing use of an InfoSec metrics program.

What Are InfoSec Metrics?

When an organization applies statistical and quantitative approaches of mathematical analysis to the process of measuring the activities and outcomes of the InfoSec program, it is using InfoSec metrics. InfoSec metrics enable organizations to measure the level of effort required to meet the stated objectives of the InfoSec program.

Managing the use of InfoSec metrics requires commitment from the InfoSec management team. This effort will consume resources including people's time, hardware cycles, and perhaps an investment in specialty software. The results of the effort will need to be periodically and consistently reviewed to make sure they remain relevant and useful. Before beginning the process of designing, collecting, and using metrics, the CISO should be prepared to answer the following questions posed by Dr. Kovacich:

- Why should these statistics be collected?
- What specific statistics will be collected?
- How will these statistics be collected?
- When will these statistics be collected?
- Who will collect these statistics?
- Where (at what point in the function's process) will these statistics be collected?[23]

Specifying InfoSec Metrics

The first task in the metrics process is to assess and quantify what will be measured. While InfoSec planning and organizing activities may only require time estimates, you must obtain more detailed measurements for the production level of effort and the project work.

Production level statistics depend greatly on the number of systems and the number of users of those systems. As the number of systems changes and/or the number of users of those systems changes, the expected effort to maintain the same level of service will vary accordingly. Some organizations simply track these two values to measure the service being delivered. Other organizations need more detailed metrics, perhaps including the number of new users added, number of access control changes, number of users removed or deauthorized, number of access control violations, number of awareness briefings, number of systems by type, number of incidents by category (such as virus or worm outbreaks), number of malicious code instances blocked by filter, and many, many other possible measurements.

Collecting project metrics may be even more challenging. Unless the organization is satisfied with a simple tally of who spent how many hours doing which tasks (this is more project management than metrics reporting), some mechanism to link the outcome of each project in terms of loss control or risk reduction to the resources consumed will be needed. This is a nontrivial process and most organizations rely on narrative explanation rather than measurement-driven calculations to justify project expenditures.

Collecting InfoSec Metrics

The prospect of collecting metrics is daunting to some organizations. At larger organizations, merely counting up the number of computing systems may be a time-consuming project. Some thought must go into the processes used for data collection and record keeping. Once the question of what to measure is decided, the how, when, where, and who questions of metrics collection must be answered. Designing the collection process requires thoughtful consideration of the intent of the metric along with a thorough knowledge of how production services are delivered.

Interpreting InfoSec Metrics

In most cases, simply listing the measurements collected does not adequately convey their meaning. For example, a line chart showing the number of malicious code attacks occurring per day may communicate a basic fact, but unless the reporting mechanism can provide the context—for example, the number of new malicious code variants on the Internet in that time period—the metric will not serve its intended purpose. In addition, you must make decisions about how to present correlated metrics—pie, line, bar, scatter, or bar charts—as well as colors to use to denote which kinds of results.

Disseminating InfoSec Metrics

The CISO must also consider to whom the results of the metrics program should be disseminated, and how they should be delivered. Many times the CISO presents these types of reports in personal meetings with key executive peers. It is seldom advisable to broadcast complex and nuanced metrics-based reports to large groups, unless the key points are well established and embedded in a more complete context such as a newsletter or press release.

EMERGING TRENDS IN CERTIFICATION AND ACCREDITATION

In security management, **accreditation** is the authorization of an IT system to process, store, or transmit information. Accreditation is issued by a management official and serves as a means of assuring that systems are of adequate quality. It also challenges managers and technical staff to find the best methods to assure security, given technical constraints, operational constraints, and mission requirements.[24] In the same vein, **certification** is defined as "the comprehensive evaluation of the technical and nontechnical security controls of an IT system to support the accreditation process that establishes the extent to which a particular design and implementation meets a set of specified security requirements."[25] Organizations pursue accreditation or certification to gain a competitive advantage, or to provide assurance or confidence to their customers. Federal systems require accreditation under OMB Circular A-130 and the Computer Security Act of 1987. Accreditation demonstrates that management has determined an acceptable risk level and provided resources to control unacceptable risk levels.

VIEWPOINT

Information System Certification and Accreditation

By Morgan Lestat-Alexander, Systems Architect, Northrop Grumman Information Technology Contractor with the U.S. Centers for Disease Control and Prevention, Division of Shared Services

As a federal agency, the Centers for Disease Control and Prevention (CDC) is required by law to ensure that all of its information systems have been authorized to operate. This authorization is provided through a formal process known as certification and accreditation (C&A). C&A helps to ensure that agency management officials are aware of the risks inherent in the operation of a given system, approve of the current system security controls, and are willing to be held accountable for system breaches, exposure, or loss of service. Under the recently passed Federal Information Security Management Act (FISMA), C&A compliance can also impact federal funding decisions; systems that are not accredited and that cannot demonstrate active security maintenance may lose funding and be subject to suspension or cancellation.

The C&A process for federal agencies is defined by NIST through the institute's special publications framework. The CDC has customized this framework into a life-cycle process specifically designed to support the agency's missions and goals. The result is a set of five major requirements that each system must satisfactorily complete before being authorized to operate:

- System characterization: A complete description of the system, its users, data, dependencies, architecture, components, and purpose

continued

- System security plan: A definition of system security requirements and the controls currently deployed to meet those requirements
- Risk assessment: A formal analysis of the threats, vulnerabilities, and risks inherent in the operation of the system
- Security testing and evaluation: The verification of existing security controls and the technical evaluation of their effectiveness
- Plan of action and milestones: A mitigation plan that tracks identified system weaknesses, planned corrective measures, and progress against remediation goals

When a system achieves accreditation, it enters into a maintenance cycle of monitoring, support, and review. Over time, the needs of the agency and the system users will inevitably change. The underlying technologies that support the system may change, too. The C&A process manages all of these changes through regular periodic testing, change control management, system maintenance, and scheduled reaccreditation.

C&A processes, when used effectively, become living life-cycle management tools that ensure appropriate system security and provide a solid demonstration of an organization's commitment to due care and continued diligence.

Accreditation and certification are not permanent. Just as standards of due diligence and due care require an ongoing maintenance effort, most accreditation and certification processes require reaccreditation or recertification every few years (typically every three to five years). For commentary on this topic, see the Viewpoint feature earlier in this chapter.

SP 800-37: Guidelines for the Security Certification and Accreditation of Federal Information Technology Systems

NIST developed and promotes a System Certification and Accreditation Project designed to achieve three goals:

- Develop standard guidelines and procedures for certifying and accrediting federal IT systems, including the critical infrastructure of the United States.
- Define essential minimum security controls for federal IT systems.
- Promote the development of public- and private-sector assessment organizations and certification of individuals capable of providing cost-effective, high-quality security certifications based on standard guidelines and procedures.

The security certification and accreditation (C&A) initiative offers several specific benefits:

- More consistent, comparable, and repeatable certifications of IT systems
- More complete, reliable information for authorizing officials—leading to better understanding of complex IT systems and their associated risks and vulnerabilities—and, therefore, to more informed decisions by management officials
- Greater availability of competent security evaluation and assessment services
- More secure IT systems within the federal government [26]

Figure 6-4 shows the relationship between the primary publication SP 800-37 and other NIST publications.

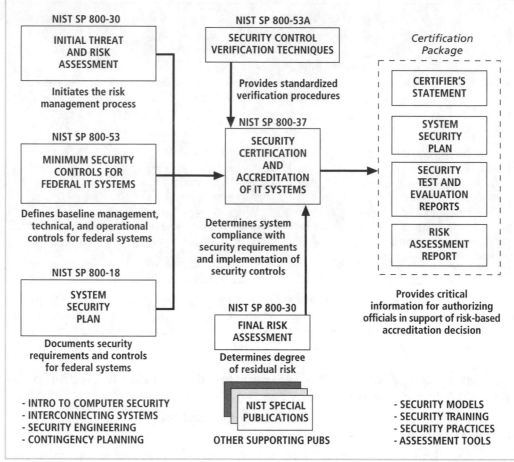

Source: R. Ross and M. Swanson. *Guidelines for the Security Certification and Accreditation of Federal Information Technology Systems. NIST SP 800-53.* October 2002.

FIGURE 6-4 Special Publications Supporting SP 800-37

SP 800-37 focuses on a three-step security controls selection process:[27]

Step 1: Characterize the System

Obtain the following system-related information from the security plan:

- Accreditation boundary for the system and, if appropriate, the proposed decomposition of the system into subsystem coponents
- Criticality/sensitivity of the system (or subsystems, if appropriate) based on levels of concern for confidentiality, integrity, and availability
- External system exposure based on level of concern by system or by subsystem, if appropriate
- Internal system exposure based on level of concern by system or by subsystem, if appropriate

Step 2: Select the Appropriate Minimum Security Controls for the System

- Select minimum security controls from the standard package of basic controls
- Select additional minimum security controls (moderate/high levels), if appropriate, to create a supplemental package of controls based on increased levels of concern for confidentiality, integrity, and/or availability
- Create agency-specific or technology-driven security controls

Step 3: Adjust Security Controls Based on System Exposure and Risk Decisions

- Adjust the selected controls based on internal/external exposure and risk-based decisions; describe the controls in documented, allowable waivers

Systems are classified into one of three security certification levels:[28]

- Security Certification Level 1: The entry-level certification appropriate for low-priority (concern) systems. SCL-1 certifications typically employ agency-directed, independent assessments or basic security reviews of IT systems using questionnaires or specialized checklists, intended to demonstrate proper levels of implementation for these low levels of concern.
- Security Certification Level 2: The mid-level certification appropriate for moderate-priority (concern) systems. SCL-2 certifications call for independent assessments of IT systems building on the verification techniques and procedures from SCL-1 and adding more substantial techniques and procedures, as appropriate.
- Security Certification Level 3: The top-level certification appropriate for high-priority (concern) systems. SCL-3 certifications call for independent assessments of IT systems building on the verification techniques and procedures from SCL-1 and SCL-2 and employing the most rigorous verification techniques, as appropriate.

SP 800-53: Minimum Security Controls for Federal Information Technology Systems

SP 800-53 is the second part of NIST's System Certification and Accreditation Project. Its purpose is to "establish a set of standardized, minimum security controls for IT systems addressing low, moderate, and high levels of concern for confidentiality, integrity, and availability."[29] SP 800-53 derives its information from a number of other federal documents, including NIST SP 800-26, Department of Defense (DoD) Policy 8500, Director of Central Intelligence Directive (DCID) 6-3, ISO/IEC Standard 17799, and General Accounting Office (GAO) Federal Information System Controls Audit Manual (FISCAM).

As in earlier NIST documents (especially SP 800-18), security controls in SP 800-53 are classified into the three familiar general categories of security controls: management, operational, and technical. Each of the three classes addresses various aspects of security topics, including "risk management, system development and acquisition, configuration management, system interconnection, personnel security, security awareness, education, and training, physical and environmental protection, media protection, contingency planning, hardware and system software maintenance, system and data integrity, documentation, incident response capability, identification and authentication, logical access, audit, and communications."[30] New to the C&A criteria is the concept of critical elements, which were initially defined in SP 800-26. Critical elements represent "important security-related focus areas for the system with each critical element addressed by one or more security controls."[31] As technology evolves, so will the set of security controls, requiring additional control mechanisms. Figure 6-5 describes the participants in the certification and accreditation process.

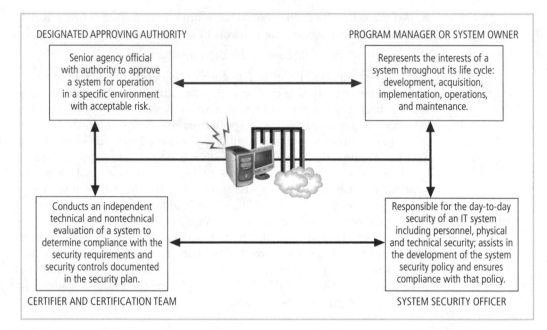

FIGURE 6-5   Participants in the Certification and Accreditation Process

NIST SP 800-53, *Recommended Security Controls for Federal Information Systems*, was published in February 2005. Draft 2 of 800-53, Revision 1 was released for public comment on October 20, 2006.

Chapter Summary

- A security model is a generic blueprint offered by a service organization or institution for other organizations to follow.

- Among the most accessible places to find a quality security management model are U.S. federal agencies and international organizations.

- ISO/IEC 17799:2005, *Information Technology—Security Techniques—Code of Practice for Information Security Management,* originally published as the British Standard BS 7799, provides information security management recommendations to information security professionals.

- ISO/IEC 27001 evolved from BS 7799:2 and picks up where ISO/IEC 17799 leaves off. It provides information on how to implement 17799 and how to set up an Information Security Management Structure (ISMS).

- RFC 2196, *Site Management Handbook,* provides an overview of five basic areas of security with detailed discussions on their development and implementation.

- The National Institute for Standards and Technology (NIST) provides several references that can assist in the design of a security framework.

- SP 800-12, *Computer Security Handbook,* is an excellent reference and guide for the security manager or administrator in the routine management of information security.

- SP 800-14, *Generally Accepted Security Principles and Practices,* provides recommended practices and information on commonly accepted information security principles.

- SP 800-18, *Guide for Developing Security Plans,* lays out the foundation for a comprehensive security blueprint and framework.

- SP 800-26, *Security Self-Assessment Guide for Information Technology Systems,* includes assessment checklists organized into 17 areas that span managerial, operational, and technical controls.

- SP 800-30, *Risk Management for Information Technology Systems,* lays out a foundation for the development of an effective risk management program.

- Due diligence entails the demonstration that the organization is ensuring that the implemented standards continue to provide the required level of protection.

- Security efforts that seek to provide a superior level of information protection are referred to as recommended business practices.

- When considering recommended practices for adoption in your organization, compare your organization to the example practice according to the following criteria: industry, organizational size, organizational structure, resources, and threat environment.

- A baseline is a value or profile of a performance metric against which changes in the performance metric can be usefully compared.

- Metrics are used in the information security management discipline in much the same way they are used elsewhere in the organization, to inform management practices for both planning and operational needs.

- Federal information systems are required to be accredited. NIST is promoting a System Certification and Accreditation Project designed to develop standard guidelines. This consists of three steps:

    Step 1: Characterize the System

    Step 2: Select the Appropriate Minimum Security Controls for the System

    Step 3: Adjust Security Controls Based on System Exposure and Risk Decisions

    Under this project, systems are classified into one of three security certification levels: SCL-1, SCL-2, and SCL-3.

Review Questions

1. What is an information security framework? How does it relate to the information security blueprint?

2. What is a security model? How might an information security professional use such a model?

3. Which international information security standards evolved from the BS 7799 model? What do they include?

4. What is an alternative model to the BS 7799 model (and its successors)? What does it include?

5. What are the sections of ISO/IEC 17799?

6. What is the COBIT? Who is its sponsor? What does it accomplish?

7. Which organization sponsors RFC 2196? What does RFC 2196 provide?

8. What are the two primary advantages of NIST security models?

9. What is the name and purpose of NIST SP 800-12? What resources does it provide?

10. What is the name and purpose of NIST SP 800-14? What resources does it provide?

11. What is the name and purpose of NIST SP 800-18? What resources does it provide?

12. What is the name and purpose of NIST SP 800-26? What resources does it provide?

13. What is the name and purpose of NIST SP 800-30? What resources does it provide?

14. What is COSO and why is it important?

15. What is the standard of due care? How does it relate to due diligence?

16. What is a recommended security practice? What is a good source for finding such recommended practices?

17. What is a gold standard in information security practices? Where can you find published criteria for it?

18. When selecting recommended practices, what criteria should you use?

19. What is benchmarking? What is baselining? How do they differ?

20. Which reference document describes the new initiative for certification and accreditation of federal IT systems?

Exercises

1. Visit the U.S. Postal Service Web site at www.usps.com/cpim/ftp/hand/as805/. Review the content page for this extensive manual. Compare this program to the NIST documents outlined in this chapter. Which areas are similar to those covered in the NIST documents; which areas are different?

2. Compare the ISO/IEC 17799 outline with the NIST documents discussed in this chapter. Which areas, if any, are missing from the NIST documents? Identify the strengths and weaknesses of the NIST programs compared to the ISO standard.

3. Search the Internet for the term "security best practices." Compare your findings to the recommended practices outlined in the NIST documents.

4. Using the list of Generally Accepted System Security Principles, look for examples within your institution that support (or do not support) each principle.

5. What other security models exist? Search the Internet for "security models" and compare your findings to the models described in this chapter.

Case Exercises

Iris sighed as she completed her initial review of her staff's checklist results. She pulled out a notepad and began outlining the projects she foresaw, based on the shortcomings identified via the checklists. She was fortunate to have found a useful model for an information security review of her program.

1. Based on your understanding of the chapter, from which model did Iris draw her checklist?

2. Referring to the section in this chapter regarding recommended practices, what do you think Iris should do next?

Endnotes

[1] ISO. ISO/IEC 17799:2005 *Information Technology—Security Techniques—Code of Practice for Information Security Management*. Accessed August 14, 2006. http://www.iso.org/iso/en/prods-services/popstds/informationsecurity.html.

[2] Praxiom, ISO/IEC 17799:2005 Translated into Plain English. Accessed August 14, 2006. http://www.praxiom.com/iso-17799-intro.htm.

[3] National Institute of Standards and Technology. *Information Security Management, Code of Practice for Information Security Management*. ISO/IEC 17799. December 6, 2001.

[4] National Institute of Standards and Technology. *Information Security Management, Code of Practice for Information Security Management*. ISO/IEC 17799. December 6, 2001.

[5] Thiagarajan, Val SANS Audit Check List—Information Security Management—BS ISO/ IEC 17799:2005. Accessed August 12, 2006. http://www.sans.org/score/ISO_17799checklist.php.

[6] Thiagarajan, Val SANS Audit Check List—Information Security Management—BS ISO/ IEC 17799:2005. Accessed August 12, 2006. http://www.sans.org/score/ISO_17799checklist.php.

[7] T. Humphries. *The Newly Revised Part 2 of BS 7799*. Accessed May 27, 2003. http://www.gammassl.co.uk/bs7799/The%20Newly%20Revised%20Part%202%20of%20BS%207799ver3a.pdf.

8 *How 7799 Works.* Accessed May 27, 2003. http://www.gammassl.co.uk/bs7799/works.html.

9 ISO. ISO 27001:2005. Accessed August 14, 2006. http://www.iso.org/iso/en/CatalogueDetailPage.CatalogueDetail?CSNUMBER=42103&scopelist=PROGRAMME.

10 National Institute of Standards and Technology. *An Introduction to Computer Security: The NIST Handbook.* SP 800-12. October 1995.

11 National Institute of Standards and Technology. *An Introduction to Computer Security: The NIST Handbook.* SP 800-12. October 1995.

12 National Institute of Standards and Technology. *Risk Management Guide for Information Technology Systems.* SP 800-30. January 2002.

13 SOX Online COSO and COBIT Center. Accessed August 14, 2006. http://www.sox-online.com/coso_cobit.html.

14 Wikipedia, the free encyclopedia. Committee of Sponsoring Organizations of the Treadway Commission. Accessed August 12, 2006. http://en.wikipedia.org/wiki/COSO.

15 COSO. COSO Definition of internal control. Accessed August 12, 2006. http://www.coso.org/key.htm.

16 COSO. COSO Definition of internal control. Accessed August 12, 2006. http://www.coso.org/key.htm.

17 Wikipedia: the free encyclopedia. COSO. Accessed August 12, 2006. http://en.wikipedia.org/wiki/COSO.

18 F. M. Avolio. Best practices in network security. *Network Computing,* March 20, 2000.

19 http://fasp.nist.gov.

20 Network Baselining and Performance Management. Network Computing Online. Accessed October 29, 2006. http://www.networkcomputing.com/netdesign/base2.html.

21 Gartner Group. *Enterprise Security Diagnostic: Best Practices.* Accessed May 1, 2003. https://www.garterinfo.com/sec_diagnostic/.

22 Gerald L. Kovacich. *The Information Systems Security Officer's Guide,* 2nd ed. Elsevier Science, 2003: 196.

23 Gerald L. Kovacich. *The Information Systems Security Officer's Guide,* 2nd ed. Elsevier Science, 2003: 197.

24 National Institute of Standards and Technology. *Background.* Accessed May 27, 2003. http://csrc.nist.gov/sec-cert/ca-background.html.

25 National Institute of Standards and Technology. *Background.* Accessed May 27, 2003. http://csrc.nist.gov/sec-cert/ca-background.html.

26 National Institute of Standards and Technology. *Background.* Accessed May 27, 2003. http://csrc.nist.gov/sec-cert/ca-background.html.

27 R. Ross and M. Swanson. *Guidelines for the Security Certification and Accreditation of Federal Information Technology Systems.* NIST SP 800-53. October 2002.

28 R. Ross and M. Swanson. *Guidelines for the Security Certification and Accreditation of Federal Information Technology Systems.* NIST SP 800-53. October 2002.

29 National Institute of Standards and Technology. *Security Controls.* Accessed May 27, 2003. http://csrc.nist.gov/sec-cert/ca-controls.html.

30 National Institute of Standards and Technology. *Security Controls.* Accessed May 27, 2003. http://csrc.nist.gov/sec-cert/ca-controls.html.

31 National Institute of Standards and Technology. *Security Controls.* Accessed May 27, 2003. http://csrc.nist.gov/sec-cert/ca-controls.html.

CHAPTER **7**

RISK MANAGEMENT: IDENTIFYING AND ASSESSING RISK

> **QUOTE**
>
> *Once we know our weaknesses, they cease to do us any harm.*
>
> G. C. (Geog Christoph) Lichtenberg (1742–1799) German physicist, philosopher

Iris Majwabu and Mike Edwards sat side by side on the short flight to the nearby city where the RWW board of directors audit committee was meeting that afternoon. The two had been invited to present RWW's IT risk management program to the committee. The board's concerns stemmed from a recent briefing by the National Association of Corporate Directors, which focused on trends affecting the potential liability of board members in the area of information security in general and risk management in particular.

After the plane leveled off, Mike pulled out his copy of the presentation he planned to give that afternoon. He and Iris had been working on it for at least two weeks, and each knew the slides by heart. Iris was along to assist with the question-and-answer period that would follow Mike's presentation.

"They're not going to be happy campers when you're done," said Iris.

"Nope. They are likely to be a little unhappy. The CEO is worried about how they'll respond, and about what might come up at the full board meeting next month," Mike said. "I'm afraid the disconnection between IT and Internal Audit in this briefing may have some unexpected consequences."

Iris considered what she knew about the weaknesses of the internal audit department's approach to the company's non-IT assets. Where Mike and Iris had built a sound, information-based approach to estimating and controlling IT risk, some of the other company divisions used less empirical methods.

"I think we should come out of this okay," Iris told Mike. "After all, the main concern of the Audit Committee members is the newfound perception of their liability for IT security and the effects it has on the issues of privacy. We have a solid risk management plan in place that's working well, in my opinion."

Mike looked up from his notes and said, "It's not us I'm worried about. I'm afraid we may create some discomfort and unwanted attention for our peers after the board sees the wide variety of risk management approaches used in other divisions."

LEARNING OBJECTIVES

Upon completion of this material, you should be able to:

- Define risk management and its role in the organization
- Begin using risk management techniques to identify and prioritize risk factors for information assets
- Assess risk based on the likelihood of adverse events and the effects on information assets when events occur
- Begin to document the results of risk identification

INTRODUCTION

Information security departments exist primarily to manage information technology (IT) risk. Managing risk is one of the key responsibilities of every manager within the organization. In any well-developed risk management program, two formal processes are at work:

- The first, risk identification and assessment, is discussed in this chapter.
- The second, risk control, is the subject of the next chapter.

Each manager in the organization, regardless of his or her affiliation with one of the three communities of interest, should focus on reducing risk as follows:

- General management must structure the IT and information security functions in ways that will result in the successful defense of the organization's information assets, including data, hardware, software, procedures, and people.
- IT management must serve the information technology needs of the broader organization and at the same time exploit the special skills and insights of the information security community.
- Information security management must lead the way with skill, professionalism, and flexibility as it works with the other communities of interest to balance the constant trade-offs between information system utility and security.

> If you know the enemy and know yourself, you need not fear the result of a hundred battles. If you know yourself but not the enemy, for every victory gained you will also suffer a defeat. If you know neither the enemy nor yourself, you will succumb in every battle.[1]

Chinese general Sun Tzu's observation, made more than 2400 years ago, continues to have direct relevance to the philosophy of information security today. Information security strategy and tactics are in many ways similar to those employed in conventional warfare. Information security managers and technicians are the defenders of information. A myriad of threats constantly attacks the organization's information assets. A layered defense is the foundation of any information security program. So, as Sun Tzu recommends, to reduce risk an organization must (1) know itself and (2) know its enemy. This means that managers from all three communities of interest must locate the weaknesses of their organization's operations; understand how the organization's information is processed, stored, and transmitted; and identify what resources are available. Only then can any strategic plan of defense be developed.

Knowing Ourselves

When operating any kind of organization, a certain amount of risk is always involved. Risk is inherent in hiring, marketing products, and even in making decisions about where to place the building that houses the organization. Risk winds its way into the daily operations of every organization, and if it is not properly managed, can cause operational failures and even lead to complete collapse.

For an organization to manage risk properly, managers should understand how information is processed, stored, and transmitted. Armed with this knowledge, they can then initiate an in-depth risk management program. Note that the mere existence of a risk management program is not sufficient. Frequently, risk management mechanisms are implemented but not maintained and kept current. Risk management is a process, which means the safeguards and controls that are devised and implemented, as described in Chapter 8, are not install-and-forget devices.

Knowing the Enemy

Once an organization becomes aware of its weaknesses, managers can then take up Sun Tzu's second dictum: Know the enemy. This means identifying, examining, and understanding the *threats* facing the organization's information assets. Managers must be prepared fully to identify those threats that pose risks to the organization and the security of its information assets. **Risk management** is the process of discovering and assessing the risks to an organization's operations and determining how those risks can be controlled or mitigated. **Risk analysis** is the identification and assessment of levels of risk in the organization.

Accountability for Risk Management

All three communities of interest bear responsibility for the management of risks, and each has a particular strategic role to play.

- Information security: Because members of the information security community best understand the threats and attacks that introduce risk, they often take a leadership role in addressing risk.
- Information technology: This group must help to build secure systems and ensure their safe operation. For example, IT builds and operates information systems that are mindful of operational risks and have proper controls implemented to reduce risk.
- Management and users: When properly trained and kept aware of the threats faced by the organization, this group plays a part in the early detection and response process. Members of this community also ensure that sufficient resources (money and personnel) are allocated to the information security and information technology groups to meet the security needs of the organization. For example, business managers must ensure that supporting records for orders remain intact in case of data entry error or transaction corruption. Users must be made aware of threats to data and systems, and educated on practices that minimize those threats.

All three communities of interest must work together to address every level of risk, ranging from full-scale disasters (whether natural or human-made) to the smallest mistake made by an employee. To do so, they must be actively involved in the following activities:

- Evaluating the risk controls
- Determining which control options are cost effective
- Acquiring or installing the appropriate controls
- Overseeing processes to ensure that the controls remain effective
- Identifying risks, which includes:
  - Creating an inventory of information assets
  - Classifying and organizing those assets into meaningful groups
  - Assigning a value to each information asset
  - Identifying threats to the cataloged assets
  - Pinpointing vulnerable assets by tying specific threats to specific assets
- Assessing risks, which includes:
  - Determining the likelihood that vulnerable systems will be attacked by specific threats
  - Assessing the relative risk facing the organization's information assets, so that risk management and control activities can focus on assets that require the most urgent and immediate attention
  - Calculating the risks to which assets are exposed in their current setting
  - Looking in a general way at controls that might come into play for identified vulnerabilities and ways to control the risks that the assets face
  - Documenting the findings of risk identification and assessment
- Summarizing the findings, which involves stating the conclusions of the analysis stage of risk assessment in preparation for moving into the stage of controlling risk by exploring methods to mitigate risk

Figure 7-1 outlines the steps in the risk identification and assessment process.

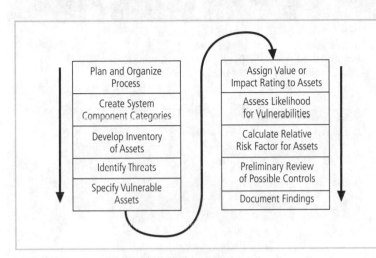

FIGURE 7-1   Risk Identification Process

RISK IDENTIFICATION

Risk identification begins with the process of self-examination. At this stage, managers *identify* the organization's information assets, classify them into useful groups, and *prioritize* them by their overall importance. This can be a daunting task, but it must be done to identify weaknesses and the threats they present.

Creating an Inventory of Information Assets

The risk identification process begins with the identification of information assets, including people, procedures, data, software, hardware, and networking elements. This step should be done without prejudging the value of each asset; values will be assigned later in the process. Table 7-1 is a model outline showing identified assets, which are subcategorized into risk management components.

TABLE 7-1 Organizational Assets Used in Systems

IT system components	Risk management components	
People	People inside an organization	Trusted employees Other staff
	People outside an organization	People at organizations we trust Strangers
Procedures	Procedures	IT and business standard procedures IT and business sensitive procedures
Data	Data/Information	Transmission Processing Storage
Software	Software	Applications Operating systems Security components
Hardware	Hardware	Systems and peripherals Security devices
Networking	Networking component	Intranet components Internet or Extranet components

Table 7-1 lists the standard IT system components (people, procedures, data, software, hardware, and networks) alongside a risk management breakdown of those components. More specifically:

- *People* are divided into insiders (employees) and outsiders (nonemployees). Insiders come in two categories: either they hold trusted roles and have correspondingly greater authority and accountability, or they are regular staff without any special privileges. The group of outsiders consists of other users who have access to the organization's information assets.

- *Procedures* are assets since they are used to create value for the organization. They are split into two categories: IT and business standard procedures, and IT and business sensitive procedures. Sensitive procedures have the potential to enable an attack or to otherwise introduce risk to the organization. For example, the procedures used by a telecommunications company to activate new circuits pose special risks because they reveal aspects of the inner workings of a critical process that can be subverted by outsiders for the purpose of obtaining unbilled, illicit services.

- *Data* components account for information in all states: transmission, processing, and storage. These categories expand the conventional use of the term "data," which is usually associated with databases, not the full range of information used by modern organizations.

- *Software* elements can be inventoried in one of three categories: applications, operating systems, or security components. Software components that provide security controls may fall into the operating systems or applications category, but are differentiated by the fact that they are part of the information security control environment and must be protected more thoroughly than other systems components.
- *Hardware* is split into two categories: the usual systems devices and their peripherals, and the devices that are part of information security control systems. The latter must be protected more thoroughly than the former.
- *Networking* components are extracted from software and hardware because networking subsystems are often the focal point of attacks against a system. Of course, most computer systems today include networking elements. You will have to determine whether a device is primarily a computer or primarily a networking device. A server computer that is used exclusively as a proxy server or bastion host may be classified as a networking component, while an identical server configured as a database server may be classified as hardware. For this reason, they should be considered separately, rather than combined with general hardware and software components.

Identifying Hardware, Software, and Network Assets

Many organizations use purchased asset inventory systems to keep track of their hardware, network, and perhaps software components. Numerous packages are available in the market today, and it is up to the CISO or CIO to determine which package best serves the needs of the organization. Organizations that do not use an automated inventory system must create an equivalent manual process.

Whether automated or manual, the inventory process requires a certain amount of planning. Most importantly, you must determine which attributes of each of these information assets should be tracked. That determination will depend on the needs of the organization and its risk management efforts, as well as the preferences and needs of the information security and information technology communities. When deciding which attributes to track for each information asset, consider the following list of potential attributes:

- Name: A list of all names commonly used for the device or program. Some organizations may have several names for the same product, and each of them should be cross-referenced in the inventory. This redundancy accommodates the usage across the organization and makes it accessible for everyone. No matter how many names you track or how you select a name, always provide a definition of the asset in question. Adopt naming standards that do not convey critical information to potential system attackers. For instance, a server named CASH1 or HQ_FINANCE may entice attackers.
- Asset Tag: Used to facilitate tracking of assets. Asset tags are unique numbers assigned to assets during the acquisition process.

- IP address: An attribute that is useful for network devices and servers but rarely applies to software. You can, however, use a relational database and track software instances on specific servers or networking devices. Many larger organizations use the Dynamic Host Control Protocol (DHCP) within TCP/IP, which reassigns IP numbers to devices as needed, making the use of IP numbers as part of the asset identification process very difficult.

- MAC address: Also called an electronic serial number or hardware address. As per the TCP/IP standard, all network interface hardware devices have a unique number. The network operating system uses this number to identify specific network devices. The client's network software uses it to recognize traffic that it needs to process. In most settings MAC addresses can be a useful way to track connectivity, but they can be spoofed by some hardware/software combinations.

- Asset type: An attribute that describes the function of each asset. For hardware assets, develop a list of possible asset types that includes servers, desktops, networking devices, and test equipment. For software assets, develop a list that includes operating systems, custom applications by type (accounting, human resources, or payroll, to name a few), and packaged applications and/or specialty application (such as firewall programs). The degree of specificity is determined by the needs of the organization. Asset types can be recorded at two or more levels of specificity by first recording one attribute that classifies the asset at a high level, and then adding attributes for more detail. For example, one server might be listed as follows:

  DeviceClass = S (server)
  DeviceOS = W2K (Windows 2000)
  DeviceCapacity = AS (Advanced Server)

  - Serial number: A number that uniquely identifies a specific device. Some software vendors also assign a software serial number to each instance of the program licensed by the organization.

- Manufacturer name: An attribute that can be useful for analyzing threat outbreaks when certain manufacturers announce specific vulnerabilities.

- Manufacturer's model or part number: A number that identifies exactly what the asset is. It can be very useful in later analysis of vulnerabilities, because some threats apply only to specific models of certain devices and/or software components.

- Software version, update revision, or FCO number: Current information about software and firmware versions and, for hardware devices, the current **field change order** (FCO) number. A field change order occurs when a manufacturer performs an upgrade to a hardware component at the customer's premises. Tracking this information is particularly important when inventorying networking devices that function mainly through the software running on them. For example, firewall devices often have three versions: an operating system version, a software version, and a Basic Input/Output System (BIOS) firmware version. Depending on an organization's needs, the inventory may have to track each of those version values for each asset.

- Physical location: An attribute that does not apply to software elements. Nevertheless, some organizations may have license terms that indicate where software can be used.
- Logical location: An attribute that specifies where an asset can be found on the organization's network. The logical location is most applicable to networking devices and indicates the logical network segment (sometimes labeled a VLAN) that houses the device.
- Controlling entity: The organizational unit that controls the asset. A remote location's on-site staff may sometimes be placed in control of network devices; at other organizations, a central corporate group may control all network devices. The inventory should determine which group controls each specific asset, as the controlling group will want a voice in determining how much risk that device can tolerate and how much expense it can sustain to add controls.

Identifying People, Procedures, and Data Assets

Unlike hardware and software, human resources, documentation, and data information assets are not as readily identified and documented. Responsibility for identifying, describing, and evaluating these information assets should be assigned to managers who possess the necessary knowledge, experience, and judgment. As these assets are identified, they should be recorded via a reliable data-handling process like the one used for hardware and software.

The record-keeping system should be flexible, allowing you to link assets to attributes based on the nature of the information asset being tracked. Some basic attributes for various classes of assets are:

People

- Position name/number/ID: Avoid names; use position titles, roles, or functions
- Supervisor name/number/ID: Avoid names; use position titles, roles, or functions
- Security clearance level
- Special skills

Procedures

- Description
- Intended purpose
- Software/hardware/networking elements to which it is tied
- Location where it is stored for reference
- Location where it is stored for update purposes

Data

- Classification
- Owner/creator/manager

- Size of data structure
- Data structure used: For example, sequential or relational
- Online or off-line
- Location
- Backup procedures

Consider carefully what should be tracked for specific assets. Often larger organizations find that that they can effectively track only a few valuable facts about the most critical information assets. For instance, a company may track only IP address, server name, and device type for its mission-critical servers. The organization might forgo additional attribute tracking on all devices, and completely omit the tracking of desktop or laptop systems.

Classifying and Categorizing Assets

Once the initial inventory is assembled, you must determine whether its asset categories are meaningful to the organization's risk management program. Such a review may cause managers to further subdivide the categories listed in Table 7-1 or to create new categories that better meet the needs of the risk management program. For example, if the category "Internet components" is deemed too general, it could be further divided into subcategories of servers, networking devices (routers, hubs, switches), protection devices (firewalls, proxies), and cabling.

The inventory should also reflect the sensitivity and security priority assigned to each information asset. A classification scheme should be developed (or reviewed, if already in place) that categorizes these information assets based on their sensitivity and security needs. Consider the following classification scheme for an information asset: *confidential, internal,* and *public.* Each of these classification categories designates the level of protection needed for a particular information asset. Some asset types, such as personnel, may require an alternative classification scheme that would identify the information security processes used by the asset type. For example, based on need-to-know and right-to-update, an employee might be given a certain level of security clearance, which identifies the level of information that individual is authorized to use. A more detailed discussion of classification schemes is provided later in this chapter in the section entitled "Data Classification Model."

Classification categories must be comprehensive and mutually exclusive. *Comprehensive* means that all inventoried assets fit into a category; *mutually exclusive* means that each asset is found in only one category. For example, an organization may have a public key infrastructure certificate authority, which is a software application that provides cryptographic key management services. Using a purely technical standard, a manager could categorize the application in the asset list of Table 7-1 as *software,* a general grouping with no special classification priority. Because the certificate authority must be carefully protected as part of the information security infrastructure, it should be categorized into a higher priority classification, such as *software/security component/cryptography,* and it should be verified that no overlapping category exists, such as *software/security component/PKI.*

Assessing Values for Information Assets

As each information asset is identified, categorized, and classified, a relative value must also be assigned to it. Relative values are comparative judgments intended to ensure that the most valuable information assets are given the highest priority when managing risk. It may be impossible to know in advance—in absolute economic terms—what losses will be incurred if an asset is compromised; however, a relative assessment helps to ensure that the higher-value assets are protected first.

As each information asset is assigned to its proper category, posing the following basic questions can help you develop the weighting criteria to be used for information asset valuation or impact evaluation. It may be useful to refer to the information collected in the BIA process (covered in Chapter 3) to help you assess a value for an asset. You can use a worksheet, such as the one shown in Figure 7-2, to collect the answers for later analysis.

System Name: __SLS E-Commerce__
Date Evaluated: __February 2003__
Evaluated By: __D. Jones__

Information assets	Data classification	Impact to profitability
Information Transmitted:		
EDI Document Set 1 — Logistics BOL to outsourcer (outbound)	Confidential	High
EDI Document Set 2 — Supplier orders (outbound)	Confidential	High
EDI Document Set 2 — Supplier fulfillment advice (inbound)	Confidential	Medium
Customer order via SSL (inbound)	Confidential	Critical
Customer service Request via e-maill (inbound)	Private	Medium
DMZ Assets:		
Edge Router	Public	Critical
Web server #1—home page and core site	Public	Critical
Web server #2—Application server	Private	Critical

Notes: BOL: Bill of Lading
    DMZ: Demilitarized Zone
    EDI: Electronic Data Interchange
    SSL: Secure Sockets Layer

FIGURE 7-2 Sample Asset Classification Worksheet

- **Which information asset is the most critical to the success of the organization?** When determining the relative importance of each information asset, refer to the organization's mission statement or statement of objectives. From this source, determine which assets are essential for meeting the organization's objectives, which assets support the objectives, and which are merely adjuncts. For example, a manufacturing company that makes aircraft engines may decide that the process control systems that control the machine tools on the assembly line are the first order of importance. While shipping and receiving data entry consoles are important to those functions, they may be less critical if alternatives are available or can be easily arranged. Another example is an online organization such as Amazon.com. The

Web servers that advertise the company's products and receive its orders 24 hours a day are essential, whereas the desktop systems used by the customer service department to answer customer e-mails are less critical.

- **Which information asset generates the most revenue?** The relative value of an information asset depends on how much revenue it generates—or, in the case of a nonprofit organization, how critical it is to service delivery. Some organizations have different systems in place for each line of business or service they offer. Which of these assets plays the biggest role in generating revenue or delivering services?

- **Which information asset generates the highest profitability?** Managers should evaluate how much profit depends on a particular asset. For instance, at Amazon. com, some servers support the book sales operations, others support the auction process, and still others support the customer book review database. Which of these servers contributes the most to the profitability of the business? Although important, the review database server does not directly generate profits. Note the distinction between revenues and profits: Some systems on which revenues depend operate on thin or nonexistent margins and do not generate profits. In nonprofit organizations, you can determine what percentage of the agency's clientele receives services from the information asset being evaluated.

- **Which information asset is the most expensive to replace?** Sometimes an information asset acquires special value because it is unique. If an enterprise still uses a Model-129 keypunch machine to create special punch-card entries for a critical batch run, for example, that machine may be worth more than its cost, because spare parts or service providers may no longer be available. Another example is a specialty device with a long delivery time frame because of manufacturing or transportation requirements. Organizations must control the risk of loss or damage to such unique assets—for example, by buying and storing a backup device.

- **Which information asset is the most expensive to protect?** Some assets are by their nature difficult to protect, and formulating a complete answer to this question may not be possible until after the risk identification phase is complete, because the costs of controls cannot be computed until the controls are identified. However, you can still make a preliminary assessment of the relative difficulty of establishing controls for each asset.

- **Which information asset's loss or compromise would be the most embarrassing or cause the greatest liability?** Almost every organization is aware of its image in the local, national, and international spheres. Loss or exposure of some assets would prove especially embarrassing. Microsoft's image, for example, was tarnished when an employee's computer system became a victim of the QAZ Trojan horse, and the latest version of Microsoft Office was stolen.[2]

You may also need to identify and add other institution-specific questions to the evaluation process.

Listing Assets in Order of Importance

The final step in the risk identification process is to list the assets in order of importance. This goal can be achieved by using a weighted factor analysis worksheet similar to the one shown in Table 7-2. In this process, each information asset is assigned a score for each critical factor. Table 7-2 uses the NIST SP 800-30 recommended values of 0.1 to 1.0. (NIST SP 800-30, *Risk Management for Information Technology Systems*, is published by the National Institute of Standards and Technology and is covered in detail in Chapter 8. Your organization may choose to use another weighting system.) Each criterion has an assigned weight, showing its relative importance in the organization.

TABLE 7-2 Example Weighted Factor Analysis Worksheet

Information Asset	Criterion 1: Impact on Revenue	Criterion 2: Impact on Profitability	Criterion 3: Impact on Public Image	Weighted Score
Criterion weight (1–100); must total 100	30	40	30	
EDI Document Set 1—Logistics bill of lading to outsourcer (outbound)	0.8	0.9	0.5	75
EDI Document Set 2—Supplier orders (outbound)	0.8	0.9	0.6	78
EDI Document Set 2—Supplier fulfillment advice (inbound)	0.4	0.5	0.3	41
Customer order via SSL (inbound)	1.0	1.0	1.0	100
Customer service request via e-mail (inbound)	0.4	0.4	0.9	55

EDI: Electronic Data Interchange
SSL: Secure Sockets Layer

A quick review of Table 7-2 shows that the Customer order via SSL (inbound) data flow is the most important asset on this worksheet, and that the EDI Document Set 2—Supplier fulfillment advice (inbound) is the least critical asset.

Data Classification Model

Corporate and military organizations use a variety of classification schemes. As you might expect, the **U.S. military classification scheme** relies on a more complex categorization system than the schemes of most corporations. The military is perhaps the best-known user of data classification schemes. It has invested heavily in information security (InfoSec), operations security (OpSec), and communications security (ComSec). In fact, many developments in data communications and information security are the result of military-sponsored research and development.

For most information, the U.S. military uses a five-level classification scheme, defined in Executive Order 12958 and presented below:[3]

- Unclassified data: Generally free for distribution to the public, and poses no threat to U.S. national interests.
- Sensitive but unclassified (SBU) data: "Any information of which the loss, misuse, or unauthorized access to, or modification of, might adversely affect U.S. national interests, the conduct of Department of Defense (DoD) programs, or the privacy of DoD personnel." Common designations include For Official Use Only, Not for Public Release, or For Internal Use Only.
- Confidential data: "Any information or material the unauthorized disclosure of which reasonably could be expected to cause damage to the national security. Examples of damage include the compromise of information that indicates strength of ground, air, and naval forces in the United States and overseas areas; disclosure of technical information used for training, maintenance, and inspection of classified munitions of war; and revelation of performance characteristics, test data, design, and production data on munitions of war."
- Secret data: "Any information or material the unauthorized disclosure of which reasonably could be expected to cause serious damage to the national security. Examples of serious damage include disruption of foreign relations significantly affecting the national security; significant impairment of a program or policy directly related to the national security; revelation of significant military plans or intelligence operations; compromise of significant military plans or intelligence operations; and compromise of significant scientific or technological developments relating to national security."
- Top secret data: "Any information or material the unauthorized disclosure of which reasonably could be expected to cause exceptionally grave damage to the national security. Examples of exceptionally grave damage include armed hostilities against the United States or its allies; disruption of foreign relations vitally affecting the national security; the compromise of vital national defense plans or complex cryptologic and communications intelligence systems; the revelation of sensitive intelligence operations; and the disclosure of scientific or technological developments vital to national security." This classification comes with the general expectation of "crib to grave" protection, meaning that individuals entrusted with top secret information are expected to honor the classification of the information for life, even after they are no longer employed in the role that originally allowed them to access the information.

The military also has some specialty classification ratings, such as Personnel Information and Evaluation Reports, to protect-related areas of information. Federal agencies such as the FBI and CIA also use specialty classification schemes, such as Need-to-Know and Named Projects. Obviously, Need-to-Know authorization allows access to information by individuals who need the information to perform their work. Named Projects are clearance levels based on a scheme similar to Need-to-Know. When an operation, project, or set of classified data is created, the project is assigned a code name. Next, a list of authorized individuals is created and assigned to either the Need-to-Know or the Named Projects category.

Most organizations do not need the detailed level of classification used by the military or federal agencies. Nevertheless, they may find it necessary to classify data to provide protection. Georgia-Pacific Corporation (G-P), for example, uses a corporate data classification scheme throughout the company that helps secure the confidentiality and integrity of its data. The G-P data classification scheme has three categories: confidential, internal, and external. Data owners must classify the information assets for which they are responsible. Data owners must review these classifications to ensure that the data are still classified correctly and the appropriate access controls are in place. G-P procedures call for this review to be done at least annually.

In G-P, information asset classifications are defined as follows:

- Confidential: The most sensitive G-P information assets that must be tightly controlled, even within the company. Access to information assets with this classification is strictly on a need-to-know basis or as required by the terms of a contract. Information assets with this classification may also be called "sensitive" or "proprietary."
- Internal: All internal information assets that do not meet the criteria for the confidential category. These assets can be viewed only by G-P employees, authorized contractors, and specific third parties.
- External: All information assets that have been approved by management for public release.[4]

A simple scheme can allow an organization to protect its sensitive information such as marketing or research data, personnel data, customer data, and general internal communications. A scheme such as the following could be adopted:

- Public: For general public dissemination, such as an advertisement or press release.
- For official use only: Not for public release but not particularly sensitive, such as internal communications.
- Sensitive: Important information that could embarrass the organization or cause loss of market share if compromised.
- Classified: Essential and confidential information, disclosure of which could severely damage the well-being of the organization.

Security Clearances

Another perspective on the data classification scheme is the personnel security clearance structure, in which each user of an information asset is assigned an authorization level that indicates the level of information classification he or she can access. This is usually accomplished by assigning each employee to a named role, such as data entry clerk, development programmer, information security analyst, or even CIO. Most organizations have developed a set of roles and corresponding security clearances, so that individuals are assigned authorization levels that correlate with the classifications of the information assets.

Beyond a simple reliance on the security clearance of the individual is the **need-to-know** principle. Regardless of one's security clearance, an individual is not allowed to view data simply because it falls within that individual's level of clearance. That is, after being granted a security clearance but before viewing a specific set of data, a person must also meet the need-to-know requirement. This extra requirement ensures that the confidentiality of information is properly maintained.

Management of the Classified Information Asset

Managing an information asset includes all aspects of its life cycle—from specification, design, acquisition, implementation, use, storage, distribution, backup, recovery, retirement, to destruction. An information asset, such as a report, that has a classification designation other than unclassified or public must be clearly marked as such. The U.S. government, for example, uses color-coordinated cover sheets to protect classified information from the casual observer. As shown in Figure 7-3, every classified document should also contain the appropriate security designation at the top and bottom of each page. Classified documents must be available only to authorized individuals, which usually require locking file cabinets, safes, or other such protective devices for hard copies and systems. When an individual carries a classified report, it should be inconspicuous and kept in a locked briefcase or portfolio, and in compliance with appropriate policies (for example, requirements for double-sealed envelopes, tamper-proof seals, etc.).

To maintain the confidentiality of classified documents, managers can implement a risk management policy control known as the clean desk policy. This policy usually meets with resistance because it requires each employee to secure all information in its appropriate storage container at the end of every business day.

When copies of classified information are no longer valuable or too many copies exist, care should be taken to destroy them properly, usually after double signature verification. Documents should be destroyed by means of shredding, burning, or transfer to a service offering authorized document destruction. Policy should ensure that no classified information is inappropriately disposed of in trash or recycling areas. Otherwise, people who engage in **dumpster diving** may retrieve information and thereby compromise the security of the organization's information assets.

Threat Identification

As mentioned at the beginning of this chapter, the ultimate goal of risk identification is to assess the circumstances and setting of each information asset to reveal any vulnerabilities. Armed with a properly classified inventory, you can assess potential weaknesses in each information asset—a process known as **threat identification**.

Any organization typically faces a wide variety of threats. If you assume that every threat can and will attack every information asset, then the project scope becomes too complex. To make the process less unwieldy, each step in the threat identification and

FIGURE 7-3 Military Data Classification Cover Sheets

vulnerability identification processes is managed separately and then coordinated at the end. At every step the manager is called on to exercise good judgment and draw on experience to make the process function smoothly.

Identify and Prioritize Threats and Threat Agents

Chapter 2 identified 12 categories of threats to information security, which are listed alphabetically in Table 7-3.

TABLE 7-3   Threats to Information Security

Threat	Example
Act of human error or failure	Accidents, employee mistakes
Compromises to intellectual property	Piracy, copyright infringement
Deliberate acts of espionage or trespass	Unauthorized access and/or data collection
Deliberate acts of information extortion	Blackmail for information disclosure
Deliberate acts of sabotage or vandalism	Destruction of systems or information
Deliberate acts of theft	Illegal confiscation of equipment or information
Deliberate software attacks	Viruses, worms, macros, denial-of-service
Deviations in quality of service by service provides	Power and WAN quality of service issues from service providers
Forces of nature	Fire, flood, earthquake, lightning
Technical hardware failures or errors	Equipment failure
Technical software failures or errors	Bugs, code problems, unknown loopholes
Technological obsolescence	Antiquated or outdated technologies

Source: ©2003 ACM, inc., included here by permission.

Each of these threats presents a unique challenge to information security and must be handled with specific controls that directly address the particular threat and the threat agent's attack strategy. Before threats can be assessed in the risk identification process, however, each threat must be further examined to determine its potential to affect the targeted information asset. In general, this process is referred to as threat assessment. Posing the following questions can help you understand the threat and its potential effects on an information asset:

- **Which threats present a danger to this organization's information assets in its current environment?** Not all threats endanger every organization, of course. Examine each of the categories in Table 7-3, and eliminate any that do not apply to your organization. While it is unlikely that you can eliminate an entire category of threats, if you can, it speeds the threat assessment process. The Offline feature entitled "Threats to Information Security" describes the threats that some CIOs of major companies identified for their organizations. Although the Offline feature directly addresses only information security, note that a weighted ranking of threats should be compiled for any information asset that is at risk. Once you have determined which threats apply to your organization, identify particular examples of threats within each category, eliminating those that are not relevant. For example, a company with offices on the 23rd floor of a high-rise building in Denver, Colorado, might not be subject to flooding. Similarly, a firm with an office in Oklahoma City, Oklahoma, might not be concerned with landslides.

- **Which threats represent the gravest danger to the organization's information assets?** The amount of danger posed by a threat is sometimes difficult to assess. It may be simply the probability of a threat attacking the organization, or it may reflect the amount of damage that the threat could create or the frequency with which an attack can occur. During this preliminary assessment phase, the analysis is limited to examining the existing level of preparedness and improving the strategy of information security. The results should give a quick overview of the components involved.

As you will discover in Chapter 8, you can use both quantitative and qualitative measures to rank values. Since information in this case is preliminary, the organization may want to rank threats subjectively in order of danger. Alternatively, it may simply rate each of the threats on a scale of 1 to 5, with 1 designating insignificant threats and 5 designating highly significant threats.

OFFLINE

Threats to Information Security: Survey of Industry

What are the threats to information security according to top computing executives? A study in the *Communications of the ACM* asked that very question. Based on the categories of threats presented earlier, more than 1000 top computing executives were asked to rate each threat category on a scale ranging from "not significant" to "very significant." The results were converted to a five-point scale, where 5 represented "very significant," and are shown under the heading "Mean" in the following table. Then the executives were also asked to identify the top five threats to their organization. Their responses were weighted, with five points assigned to a first-place vote and one point assigned to a fifth-place vote. The sum of weights is presented under the heading "Weight" in the table. The two ratings were then combined into a weighted rank.

Weighted Ranks of Threats to Information Security

	Threat	Mean	Standard Deviation	Weight	Weighted Rank
1.	Deliberate software attacks	3.99	1.03	546	2178.3
2.	Technical software failures or errors	3.16	1.13	358	1129.9
3.	Acts of human error or failure	3.15	1.11	350	1101.0
4.	Deliberate acts of espionage or trespass	3.22	1.37	324	1043.6
5.	Deliberate acts of sabotage or vandalism	3.15	1.37	306	962.6

continued

Risk Management: Identifying and Assessing Risk

Weighted Ranks of Threats to Information Security

	Threat	Mean	Standard Deviation	Weight	Weighted Rank
6.	Technical hardware failures or errors	3.00	1.18	314	942.0
7.	Deliberate acts of theft	3.07	1.30	226	694.5
8.	Forces of nature	2.80	1.09	218	610.9
9.	Compromises to intellectual property	2.72	1.21	182	494.8
10.	Quality-of-service deviations from service providers	2.65	1.06	164	433.9
11.	Technological obsolescence	2.71	1.11	158	427.9
12.	Deliberate acts of information extortion	2.45	1.42	92	225.2

Source: Adapted from M. E. Whitman. Enemy at the gates: Threats to information security. *Communications of the ACM,* August 2003 reprinted with permission.

Another popular study also examines threats to information security. The Computer Security Institute, in cooperation with the FBI, conduct an annual survey of computer users. The following table shows its results from the last eight years.

CSI/FBI Survey Results for Types of Attack or Misuse (1999–2006)

	Type of Attack or Misuse	2006	2005	2004	2003	2002	2001	2000	1999
1.	Virus	65%	74%	78%	82%	85%	94%	85%	90%
2.	Laptop/mobile theft	47%	48%	49%	59%	55%	64%	60%	69%
3.	Insider abuse of Net access	42%	48%	59%	80%	78%	91%	79%	97%
4.	Unauthorized access to information	32%	32%	37%	45%	38%	49%	71%	55%
5.	Denial of service	25%	32%	39%	42%	40%	36%	27%	31%
6.	System penetration	15%	14%	17%	36%	40%	40%	25%	30%

continued

CSI/FBI Survey Results for Types of Attack or Misuse (1999–2006)

	Type of Attack or Misuse	2006	2005	2004	2003	2002	2001	2000	1999
7.	Abuse of wireless network (New category–2004)	14%	17%	15%					
8.	Theft of proprietary information	9%	9%	10%	21%	20%	26%	20%	25%
9.	Financial fraud	9%	7%	5%	15%	12%	12%	11%	14%
10.	Telecommunications fraud	8%	10%	10%	10%	9%	10%	11%	17%
11.	Misuse of public Web applications (New category–2004)	6%	5%	10%					
12.	Web site defacement (New category–2004)	6%	5%	7%					
13.	Sabotage	3%	2%	5%	21%	8%	18%	17%	13%
14.	Telecomm eavesdropping (Category dropped–2004)				6%	6%	10%	7%	14%
15.	Active wiretap (Category dropped–2004)				1%	1%	2%	1%	2%

Source: CSI/FBI Computer Crime and Security Surveys (2001–2006). *Computer Security Issues & Trends* (http://gocsi.com).

Frequency of Attacks

Remarkably, detected attacks are decreasing. After a peak in 2000, the number of organizations reporting unauthorized use of computer systems has been declining steadily, while the amount reporting *no* unauthorized access has been increasing. Unfortunately, the number of organizations reporting that they just do not know is holding steady.[5] The fact is, almost every company has experienced an attack. Whether that attack was successful depends on the company's security efforts; whether the perpetrators were caught or the organization was willing to report the attack is another matter entirely.

- **How much would it cost to recover from a successful attack?** One of the calculations that guides corporate spending on controls is the cost of recovery operations if an attack occurs and is successful. At this preliminary phase, it is not necessary to conduct a detailed assessment of the costs associated with recovering from a particular attack. Instead, organizations often a create subjective ranking or listing of the threats based on recovery cost. Alternatively, you could assign a rating for each threat on a scale of 1 to 5, with 1 representing "not expensive at all" and 5 representing "extremely expensive." If the information is available, a raw value (e.g., $5000, $10,000, or $2 million) can be assigned. In other words, the goal at this phase is to provide a rough assessment of the cost to recover operations should the attack interrupt normal business operations.

- **Which threats would require the greatest expenditure to prevent?** Another factor that affects the danger posed by a particular threat is the amount it would cost to protect against that threat. Controlling some threats has a nominal cost, as in protections from malicious code, while other protective strategies are very expensive, as in protections from forces of nature. Here again the manager ranks, rates, or attempts to quantify the level of danger associated with protecting against a particular threat, by using the same techniques outlined earlier for calculating recovery costs. Look at the Offline feature on expenditure for threats to see how some top executives recently handled this issue.

This list of questions may not cover everything that affects risk identification. An organization's specific guidelines or policies should influence the process and will inevitably require that some additional questions be answered.

OFFLINE

Expenditures for Threats to Information Security

The CACM study mentioned earlier also asked computing executives to determine the priorities set in their organizations for expenditures geared toward threats to information security. Each executive responded by identifying his or her top five expenditures. These ratings were used to create a rank order of the expenses. The results are presented in the following table.

continued

Weighted Ranking of Threat-Driven Expenditures

Top Threat-Driven Expenses	Rating
1. Deliberate software attacks	12.7
2. Acts of human error or failure	7.6
3. Technical software failures or errors	7.0
4. Technical hardware failures or errors	6.0
5. Quality-of-service deviations from service providers	4.9
6. Deliberate acts of espionage or trespass	4.7
7. Deliberate acts of theft	4.1
8. Deliberate acts of sabotage or vandalism	4.0
9. Technological obsolescence	3.3
10. Forces of nature	3.0
11. Compromises to intellectual property	2.2
12. Deliberate acts of information extortion	1.0

Source: Adapted from M. E. Whitman. Enemy at the gates: Threats to information security. *Communications of the ACM*, August 2003 reprinted with permission.

Vulnerability Assessment

Once you have identified the information assets of the organization and documented some threat assessment criteria, you can begin to review every information asset for each threat. This review leads to the creation of a list of vulnerabilities that remain potential risks to the organization. What are vulnerabilities? They are specific avenues that threat agents can exploit to attack an information asset. In other words, they are chinks in the asset's armor—a flaw or weakness in an information asset, security procedure, design, or control that can be exploited accidentally or on purpose to breach security. For example, Table 7-4 analyzes the threats to and possible vulnerabilities of a DMZ router.

TABLE 7-4 Vulnerability Assessment of a DMZ Router

Threat	Possible Vulnerabilities
Acts of human error or failure	Employees or contractors may cause an outage if configuration errors are made
Compromises to intellectual property	Router has little intrinsic value, but other assets protected by this device could be attacked if it is compromised
Deliberate acts of espionage or trespass	Router has little intrinsic value, but other assets protected by this device could be attacked if it is compromised
Deliberate acts of information extortion	Router has little intrinsic value, but other assets protected by this device could be attacked if it is compromised
Deliberate acts of sabotage or vandalism	IP is vulnerable to denial-of-service attacks Device may be subject to defacement or cache poisoning
Deliberate acts of theft	Router has little intrinsic value, but other assets protected by this device could be attacked if it is compromised
Deliberate software attacks	Internet Protocol (IP) is vulnerable to denial-of-service attack Outsider IP fingerprinting activities can reveal sensitive information unless suitable controls are implemented
Forces of nature	All information assets in the organization are subject to forces of nature unless suitable controls are provided
Quality-of-service deviations from service providers	Unless suitable electrical power conditioning is provided, failure is probable over time
Technical hardware failures or errors	Hardware could fail and cause an outage Power system failures are always possible
Technical software failures or errors	Vendor-supplied routing software could fail and cause an outage
Technological obsolescence	If it is not reviewed and periodically updated, a device may fall too far behind its vendor support model to be kept in service

A list like the one in Table 7-4 must be created for each information asset to document its vulnerability to each possible or likely attack. This list is usually long and shows all the vulnerabilities of the information asset. Some threats manifest themselves in multiple ways, yielding multiple vulnerabilities for that asset–threat pair. Of necessity, the process of listing vulnerabilities is somewhat subjective and is based on the experience and knowledge of the people who create the list. Therefore, the process works best when groups of people with diverse backgrounds work together in a series of brainstorming sessions. For instance, the team that reviews the vulnerabilities for networking equipment should include networking specialists, the systems management team that operates the network, information security risk specialists, and even technically proficient users of the system.

The TVA Worksheet

At the end of the risk identification process, an organization should have a prioritized list of assets and their vulnerabilities. This list serves as the starting point (with its supporting documentation from the identification process) for the next step in the risk management process—risk assessment. Another list prioritizes threats facing the organization based on the weighted table discussed earlier. These two lists can be combined into a Threats-Vulnerabilities-Assets (TVA) worksheet, in preparation for the addition of vulnerability and control information during risk assessment. Along one axis lies the prioritized set of assets. Table 7-5 shows the placement of assets along the horizontal axis, with the most important asset at the left. The prioritized list of threats are placed along the vertical axis, with the most important or most dangerous threat listed at the top. The resulting grid provides a convenient method of examining the "exposure" of assets, allowing a simplistic vulnerability assessment. We now have a starting point for our risk assessment, along with the other documents and forms.

TABLE 7-5 Sample TVA Spreadsheet

	Asset 1	Asset 2	...	...	...	...	...	...	...	...	...	Asset n
Threat 1												
Threat 2												
...												
...												
...												
...												
...												
...												
...												
...												
...												
Threat n												
Priority of Controls	1		2	3		4		5		6		
These bands of controls should be continued through all asset–threat pairs.												

As you begin the risk assessment process, create a list of the TVA "triples" to facilitate your examination of the severity of the vulnerabilities. For example, between Threat 1 and Asset 1 there may or may not be a vulnerability. After all, not all threats pose risk to all assets. If a pharmaceutical company's most important asset is its research and development database, and that database resides on a stand-alone network (i.e., one that is not connected to the Internet), then there may be no vulnerability to external hackers. If the intersection of T1 and A1 has no vulnerability, then the risk assessment team simply crosses out that box. It is much more likely, however, that one or more vulnerabilities exist between the two, and as these vulnerabilities are identified, they are categorized as follows:

T1V1A1—Vulnerability 1 that exists between Threat 1 and Asset 1
T1V2A1—Vulnerability 1 that exists between Threat 1 and Asset 1
T1V2A1—Vulnerability 2 that exists between Threat 1 and Asset 1...
and so on.

In the risk assessment phase, discussed in the next section, not only are the vulnerabilities examined, but the assessment team also analyzes any existing controls that protect the asset from the threat, or mitigates the losses that may occur. Cataloging and categorizing these controls is the next step in the TVA spreadsheet.

VIEWPOINT

Getting at Risk

By George V. Hulme, an independent business and technology journalist who has covered information security for more than 10 years for such publications as *Information Week* and *Information Security Magazine*.

The risks that organizations face have never been higher. More systems are interconnected today than ever before, and there is only one constant to those systems: change. Aside from hackers, disgruntled employees, and corporate spies, a growing number of laws and regulations (such as Sarbanes-Oxley, Gramm-Leach-Bliley, and the Health Information Portability and Accountability Act) have forever changed the role of the information security professional as the gatekeeper of information and the manager of risk.

The role of the security professional is to help the organization manage risks poised against the confidentiality, integrity, and availability of its information assets. And the foundation of all information security programs begins and forever lives with the process of risk assessment. Risk isn't static. Rather, risk is fluid and evolves over time. A risk assessment conducted on the first day of the month can be quite different than the same assessment conducted several weeks later. The levels of risks for particular information systems can change as quickly as IT systems change. And geopolitical events such as war, economics, new employee hires, layoffs, and the steady introduction of new technologies all work to change the amount of risk faced by an organization.

continued

The first task in risk assessment is to identify, assess, classify, and then decide on the value of digital assets and systems. Many believe that the most difficult aspect of risk assessment is uncovering the myriad system and configuration vulnerabilities that place systems at risk, but that's not so: An abundance of tools is available that can help automate that task. It's really deciding, organization-wide, the value of information and intellectual property that poses one of the most daunting challenges for the security professional. How much is the research and development data worth? How much will it cost the organization if it loses access to the accounting, or customer relationship management, systems for a day? Without knowing the value of information, and the systems that ensure its flow, it's impossible to make reasonable decisions about how much can reasonably be spent protecting that information. It makes little sense to spend $200,000 annually to protect information that wouldn't cost an organization more than $25,000 if exposed or lost. In a perfect world, with unlimited budgets and resources in hand, everything could be protected all of the time. But we don't live in a perfect world, and tough decisions need to be made. That means bringing together management, legal, human resources, physical security, and other groups in the organization. In assessing risk, you must decide what needs to be protected and how much that information is worth. Only then can reasonable decisions be made as to how to mitigate risk by implementing defensive measures and sound policy.

During the risk assessment process, vulnerabilities to systems will inevitably be uncovered. The challenge here is to determine which ones pose the greatest threats to protected assets. It's a challenge that security professionals face every day. Does a low-risk vulnerability (something unlikely to be exploited) on a system holding highly valuable corporate information need to be remediated more quickly than a high-risk vulnerability (one that is easily, and likely to be, exploited) on a system holding information of little value? Maybe. It all depends. And each situation is different.

Risk can never be entirely eliminated; it can only be managed to levels that an organization can tolerate. The best way to keep risk low is to remain eternally vigilant by following a four-step process: (1) identify new assets, vulnerabilities, and threats; (2) assess and classify assets, vulnerabilities, and threats; (3) remediate and defend; and (4) return to Step 1.

RISK ASSESSMENT

Assessing the relative risk for each vulnerability is accomplished via a process called risk assessment. Risk assessment assigns a risk rating or score to each specific vulnerability. While this number does not mean anything in absolute terms, it enables you to gauge the relative risk associated with each vulnerable information asset, and it facilitates the creation of comparative ratings later in the risk control process.

Introduction to Risk Assessment

Figure 7-4 shows the factors that go into the risk-rating estimate for each of the vulnerabilities.

> **Risk is**
> The **likelihood** of the occurrence of a vulnerability
> **Multiplied by**
> The **value** of the information asset
> **Minus**
> The percentage of risk mitigated by **current controls**
> **Plus**
> The **uncertainty** of current knowledge of the vulnerability

FIGURE 7-4 Risk Identification Estimate Factors

The goal at this point is to create a method to evaluate the relative risk of each listed vulnerability. Chapter 8 describes how to determine more precise cost estimates for vulnerabilities as well as projected expenses for the controls that reduce the risks. For now, you can use the simpler risk model shown in Figure 7-4 to evaluate the risk for each information asset. The next section describes the factors used to calculate the relative risk for each vulnerability.

Likelihood

Likelihood is the overall rating—a numerical value on a defined scale—of the probability that a specific vulnerability will be exploited. In Special Publication 800-30, NIST recommends that vulnerabilities be assigned a likelihood rating between 0.1 (low) and 1.0 (high). For example, the likelihood of an employee or system being struck by a meteorite while indoors would be rated 0.1, while the likelihood of receiving at least one e-mail containing a virus or worm in the next year would be rated 1.0. You could also choose to use a number between 1 and 100, but not 0, since vulnerabilities with a 0 likelihood should have already been removed from the asset/vulnerability list. Whatever rating system you employ for assigning likelihood, use professionalism, experience, and judgment to determine the rating—and use it consistently. Whenever possible, use external references for likelihood values, after reviewing and adjusting them for your specific circumstances. For many asset/vulnerability combinations, existing sources have already determined their likelihood. For example,

- The likelihood of a fire has been estimated actuarially for each type of structure.
- The likelihood that any given e-mail will contain a virus or worm has been researched.
- The number of network attacks can be forecast depending on how many network addresses the organization has assigned.

Assessing Potential Loss

Using the information documented during the risk identification process, you can assign weighted scores based on the value of each information asset. The actual number used will vary according to the needs of the organization. Some groups use a scale of 1 to 100, with

100 being reserved for those information assets whose loss would stop company operations within a few minutes. Other recommended scales, including the one in NIST SP 800-30, use assigned weights in broad categories, with all-important assets having a value of 100, low-criticality assets having a value of 1, and all other assets having a medium value of 50. Still other scales employ weights from 1 to 10, or assigned values of 1, 3, and 5 to represent low-, medium-, and high-valued assets, respectively. Alternatively, you can create unique weight values customized to your organization's specific needs.

To be effective, the values must be assigned by asking the questions listed earlier in the section entitled "Identify and Prioritize Threats and Threat Agents." These questions are restated here for easy reference:

- Which threats present a danger to this organization's assets in its current environment?
- Which threats represent the gravest danger to the organization's information assets?
- How much would it cost to recover from a successful attack?
- Which threats would require the greatest expenditure to prevent?

After reconsidering these questions, use the background information from the risk identification process and add to that information by posing yet another question:

- Which of the aforementioned questions is the most important to the protection of information from threats within this organization?

The answer to this question determines the priorities used in the assessment of vulnerabilities. Which is the most important to the organization—the cost to recover from a threat attack or the cost to protect against a threat attack? More generally, which of the threats has the highest probability of successful attack? Recall that the purpose of risk assessment is to look at the threats an organization faces in its current state. Once these questions are answered, move to the next step in the process: examining how current controls can reduce the risk faced by specific vulnerabilities.

Percentage of Risk Mitigated by Current Controls

If a vulnerability is fully managed by an existing control, it can be set aside. If it is partially controlled, estimate what percentage of the vulnerability has been controlled.

Uncertainty

It is not possible to know everything about every vulnerability, such as how likely is an attack against an asset, or how great of an impact would a successful attack have on the organization. The degree to which a current control can reduce risk is also subject to estimation error. A factor that accounts for uncertainty must always be added to the equations; it consists of an estimate made by the manager using good judgment and experience.

Risk Determination

For the purpose of relative risk assessment, risk *equals* likelihood of vulnerability occurrence *times* value (or impact) *minus* percentage risk already controlled *plus* an element of uncertainty. To see how this equation works, consider the following scenario:

- Information asset A has a value score of 50 and one vulnerability: Vulnerability 1 has a likelihood of 1.0 with no current controls. You estimate that assumptions and data are 90% accurate.
- Information asset B has a value score of 100 and two vulnerabilities: Vulnerability 2 has a likelihood of 0.5 with a current control that addresses 50% of its risk; vulnerability 3 has a likelihood of 0.1 with no current controls. You estimate that assumptions and data are 80% accurate.

The resulting ranked list of risk ratings for the three vulnerabilities described above is as follows [(value times likelihood) minus risk mitigated plus uncertainty]:

- Asset A: Vulnerability 1 rated as 55 = (50×1.0) − ((50×1.0)2.2) + ((50×1.0)2.1)
- Asset B: Vulnerability 2 rated as 35 = (100×0.5) − ((100×0.5)2.5) + ((100×0.5)2.2)
- Asset B: Vulnerability 3 rated as 12 = (100×0.1) − ((100×0.5)2.0) + ((100×0.5)2.2)

Identify Possible Controls

For each threat and its associated vulnerabilities that have residual risk, create a preliminary list of control ideas. The purpose of this list, which begins with the identification of extant controls, is to identify areas of residual risk that may nor may not need to be reduced. Residual risk is the risk that remains even after the existing control has been applied. *Controls, safeguards,* and *countermeasures* are all terms used to describe security mechanisms, policies, and procedures. These mechanisms, policies, and procedures counter attacks, reduce risk, resolve vulnerabilities, and otherwise improve the general state of security within an organization.

Three general categories of controls exist: policies, programs, and technical controls. You learned about policies in Chapter 4. **Programs** are activities performed within the organization to improve security; they include security education, training, and awareness programs. Technical controls—also known as security technologies—are the technical implementations of the policies defined by the organization. These controls, whether in place or planned, should be added to the TVA worksheet as they are identified.

Access Controls

Access controls specifically address the admission of users into a trusted area of the organization. These areas can include information systems, physically restricted areas such as computer rooms, and even the organization in its entirety. Access controls usually consist of a combination of policies, programs, and technologies.

A number of approaches to, and categories of, access controls exist. They can be mandatory, nondiscretionary, or discretionary. Each category of controls regulates access to a particular type or collection of information, as explained below.

Mandatory Access Controls (MACs)

MACs are required—obviously—and are structured and coordinated with a data classification scheme. When MACs are implemented, users and data owners have limited control over their access to information resources. MACs use a data classification scheme that rates each collection of information. Each user is also rated to specify the level of information that he or she may access. These ratings are often referred to as sensitivity levels.

In a variation of this form of access control called **lattice-based access control**, users are assigned a matrix of authorizations for particular areas of access. The level of authorization may vary depending on the classification authorizations that individuals possess for each group of information assets or resources. The lattice structure contains subjects and objects, and the boundaries associated with each subject/object pair are clearly demarcated. Lattice-based access control then specifies the level of access each subject has to each object, if any. With this type of control, the column of attributes associated with a particular object (such as a printer) is referred to as an **access control list (ACL)**. The row of attributes associated with a particular subject (such as a user) is referred to as a **capabilities table**.

Nondiscretionary Controls

Nondiscretionary controls are determined by a central authority in the organization and can be based on roles—called **role-based controls**—or on a specified set of tasks—called **task-based controls**. Task-based controls can, in turn, be based on lists maintained on subjects or objects. Role-based controls are tied to the role that a particular user performs in an organization, whereas task-based controls are tied to a particular assignment or responsibility.

The role- and task-based controls make it easier to maintain controls and restrictions, especially if the individual performing the role or task changes often. Instead of constantly assigning and revoking the privileges of individuals who come and go, the administrator simply assigns the associated access rights to the role or task. When individuals are subsequently assigned to that role or task, they automatically receive the corresponding access. The administrator can easily remove individuals' associations with roles and tasks, thereby revoking their access.

Discretionary Access Controls (DACs)

DACs are implemented at the discretion or option of the data user. The ability to share resources in a peer-to-peer configuration allows users to control and possibly provide access to information or resources at their disposal. The users can allow general, unrestricted access, or they can allow specific individuals or sets of individuals to access these resources. As an example, suppose a user has a hard drive containing information to be shared with office coworkers. This user can elect to allow access to specific individuals by listing their names in the share control function.

DOCUMENTING THE RESULTS OF RISK ASSESSMENT

The goal of the risk management process so far has been to identify information assets and their vulnerabilities and to rank them according to the need for protection. In preparing this list, a wealth of factual information about the assets and the threats they face is collected. Also, information about the controls that are already in place is collected. The final summarized document is the ranked vulnerability risk worksheet, as shown in Table 7-6. This document is an extension of the TVA spreadsheet discussed earlier, showing only the assets and relevant vulnerabilities. A review of this worksheet reveals similarities to the weighted factor analysis worksheet depicted in Table 7-2. The columns in the worksheet shown in Table 7-6 are used as follows:

- Asset: List each vulnerable asset.
- Asset Impact: Show the results for this asset from the weighted factor analysis worksheet. In our example, this value is a number from 1 to 100.
- Vulnerability: List each uncontrolled vulnerability.
- Vulnerability Likelihood: State the likelihood of the realization of the vulnerability by a threat-agent as indicated in the vulnerability analysis step. In our example, the potential values range from 0.1 to 1.0.
- Risk-Rating Factor: Enter the figure calculated by multiplying the asset impact and its likelihood. In our example, the calculation yields a number ranging from 0.1 to 100.

TABLE 7-6 Ranked Vulnerability Risk Worksheet

Asset	Asset Impact	Vulnerability	Vulnerability Likelihood	Risk-Rating Factor
Customer service request via e-mail (inbound)	55	E-mail disruption due to hardware failure	0.2	11
Customer service request via e-mail (inbound)	55	E-mail disruption due to software failure	0.2	11
Customer order via Secure Sockets Layer (SSL) (inbound)	100	Lost orders due to Web server hardware failure	0.1	10
Customer order via SSL (inbound)	100	Lost orders due to Web server ISP service failure	0.1	10
Customer service request via e-mail (inbound)	55	E-mail disruption due to SMTP mail relay attack	0.1	5.5
Customer service request via e-mail (inbound)	55	E-mail disruption due to ISP service failure	0.1	5.5
Customer service request via e-mail (inbound)	55	E-mail disruption due to power failure	0.1	5.5
Customer order via SSL (inbound)	100	Lost orders due to Webserver denial-of-service attack	0.025	2.5

TABLE 7-6 Ranked Vulnerability Risk Worksheet (continued)

Asset	Asset Impact	Vulnerability	Vulnerability Likelihood	Risk-Rating Factor
Customer order via SSL (inbound)	100	Lost orders due to Web server software failure	0.01	1
Customer order via SSL (inbound)	100	Lost orders due to Web server buffer overrun attack	0.01	1

Looking at Table 7-6, you may be surprised that the most pressing risk requires making the mail server or servers more robust. Even though the impact rating of the information asset represented by the customer service e-mail is only 55, the relatively high likelihood of a hardware failure makes it the most pressing problem.

Now that the risk identification process is complete, what should the documentation package look like? In other words, what are the deliverables from this stage of the risk management project? The risk identification process should designate what function the reports serve, who is responsible for preparing them, and who reviews them. The ranked vulnerability risk worksheet is the initial working document for the next step in the risk management process: assessing and controlling risk. Table 7-7 shows an example list of the worksheets that should have been prepared by an information asset risk management team to this point.

TABLE 7-7 Risk Identification and Assessment Deliverables

Deliverable	Purpose
Information asset classification worksheet	Assembles information about information assets and their impact on or value to the organization
Weighted criteria analysis worksheet	Assigns a ranked value or impact weight to each information asset
TVA worksheet	Combines the output from the information asset identification and prioritization with the threat identification and prioritization and identifies potential vulnerabilities in the "triples"; also incorporates extant and planned controls
Ranked vulnerability risk worksheet	Assigns a risk-rating ranked value to each uncontrolled asset–vulnerability pair

In the last stage of the risk analysis (identification and assessment) process, you use the TVA worksheet, along with the other worksheets created, to develop a prioritized list of tasks. Obviously the presence of uncontrolled vulnerabilities in high ranking assets are the first priority for the implementation of new controls as part of the risk management process discussed in the next chapter. Before any additional controls are added, though, an organization must determine the levels of risk it is willing to accept, based on a cost benefit analyses—the subject of Chapter 8.

Chapter Summary

- Risk management examines and documents an organization's information assets. Management is responsible for identifying and controlling the risks that an organization encounters. In the modern organization, the information security group often plays a leadership role in risk management.

- A key component of a risk management strategy is the identification, classification, and prioritization of the organization's information assets.

- Assessment is the identification of assets, including all of the elements of an organization's system: people, procedures, data, software, hardware, and networking elements.

- The human resources, documentation, and data information assets of an organization are not as easily identified and documented as tangible assets, such as hardware and software. These more elusive assets should be identified and described using knowledge, experience, and judgment.

- You can use the answers to the following questions to develop weighting criteria for information assets:

  - Which information asset is the most critical to the success of the organization?
  - Which information asset generates the most revenue?
  - Which information asset generates the highest profitability?
  - Which information asset is the most expensive to replace?
  - Which information asset is the most expensive to protect?
  - Which information asset's loss or compromise would be the most embarrassing or cause the greatest liability?
  - What questions should be added to cover the needs of the specific organization and its environment?

- After identifying and performing a preliminary classification of information assets, the threats facing an organization should be examined. There are 12 general categories of threats to information security.

- Each threat must be examined during a threat assessment process that addresses the following questions: Which of these threats exist in this organization's environment? Are most dangerous to the organization's information? Require the greatest expenditure for recovery? Require the greatest expenditure for protection?

- Each information asset is evaluated for each threat it faces; the resulting information is used to create a list of the vulnerabilities that pose risks to the organization. This process results in an information asset and vulnerability list, which serves as the starting point for risk assessment.

- A Threat-Vulnerability-Asset (TVA) worksheet lists the assets in priority order along one axis, and the threats in priority order along the other axis. The resulting grid provides a convenient method of examining the "exposure" of assets, allowing a simple vulnerability assessment.

- The goal of risk assessment is the assignment of a risk rating or score that represents the relative risk for a specific vulnerability of a specific information asset.

- If any specific vulnerability is completely managed by an existing control, it no longer needs to be considered for additional controls.

- Controls, safeguards, and countermeasures should be identified for each threat and its associated vulnerabilities.

- In general, three categories of controls exist: policies, programs, and technologies.

- Access controls can be classified as mandatory, discretionary, or nondiscretionary.

- The risk identification process should designate what function the resulting reports serve, who is responsible for preparing them, and who reviews them. The TVA worksheet and the ranked vulnerability risk worksheet are the initial working documents for the next step in the risk management process: assessing and controlling risk.

Review Questions

1. What is risk management?
2. List and describe the key areas of concern for risk management.
3. Why is identification of risks, through a listing of assets and their vulnerabilities, so important to the risk management process?
4. According to Sun Tzu, what two things must be achieved to secure information assets successfully?
5. Who is responsible for risk management in an organization?
6. Which community of interest usually takes the lead in information asset risk management?
7. Which community of interest usually provides the resources used when undertaking information asset risk management?
8. In risk management strategies, why must periodic review be a part of the process?
9. Why do networking components need more examination from an information security perspective than from a systems development perspective?
10. What value would an automated asset inventory system have for the risk identification process?
11. Which information attributes are seldom or never applied to software elements?
12. Which information attribute is often of great value for networking equipment when DHCP is not used?
13. When you document procedures, why is it useful to know where the electronic versions are stored?
14. Which is more important to the information asset classification scheme, that it be comprehensive or that it be mutually exclusive?
15. What is the difference between an asset's ability to generate revenue and its ability to generate profit?
16. How many categories should a data classification scheme include? Why?
17. How many threat categories are listed in this chapter? Which do you think is the most common, and why?

18. What are vulnerabilities?

19. Describe the TVA worksheet. What is it used for?

20. Examine the simplest risk formula and the risk formula presented in this chapter. Do other formulas exist and, if so, when are they used?

Exercises

1. If an organization has three information assets to evaluate for risk management purposes as shown in the accompanying data, which vulnerability should be evaluated for additional controls first? Which vulnerability should be evaluated last?

    Data for Exercise 1

    - Switch L47 connects a network to the Internet. It has two vulnerabilities: (1) susceptibility to hardware failure, with a likelihood of 0.2, and (2) susceptibility to an SNMP buffer overflow attack, with a likelihood of 0.1. This switch has an impact rating of 90 and has no current controls in place. There is a 75% certainty of the assumptions and data.

    - Server WebSrv6 hosts a company Web site and performs e-commerce transactions. It has Web server software that is vulnerable to attack via invalid Unicode values. The likelihood of such an attack is estimated at 0.1. The server has been assigned an impact value of 100, and a control has been implemented that reduces the impact of the vulnerability by 75%. There is an 80% certainty of the assumptions and data.

    - Operators use the MGMT45 control console to monitor operations in the server room. It has no passwords and is susceptible to unlogged misuse by the operators. Estimates show the likelihood of misuse is 0.1. There are no controls in place on this asset, which has an impact rating of 5. There is a 90% certainty of the assumptions and data.

2. Using the Web, search for at least three tools to automate risk assessment. Collect information on automated risk assessment tools. What do they cost? What features do they provide? What are the advantages and disadvantages of each one?

3. Using the list of threats to information security presented in this chapter, identify and describe three instances of each threat not previously mentioned in the chapter.

4. Using the data classification scheme presented in this chapter, identify and classify the information contained in your personal computer or personal digital assistant. Based on the potential for misuse or embarrassment, what information is confidential, sensitive but unclassified, or suitable for public release?

5. Using the asset valuation method presented in this chapter, conduct a preliminary risk assessment on the information contained in your home. Answer each of the questions covered in the chapter. What would it cost if you lost all your data?

6. Using the Internet, locate the National Association of Corporate Directors' Web site. Describe its function and purpose. What does this association say about board member liability for information security issues?

Case Exercises

Mike and Iris were flying home from the meeting. The reaction of the Audit Committee members had not been as expected.

"I'm glad they understood the situation," Mike said to Iris. "I'd like you to start revising our risk management documentation to make it a little more general. It sounds like the board will want to take our approach company-wide soon."

Iris nodded and pulled out her notepad to make herself a to-do-list.

1. What will Iris have on her to-do-list?
2. What resources can Iris call on to assist her?

Endnotes

[1] Sun Tzu. *The Art of War*. Translation by Samuel B. Griffith. Oxford, UK: Oxford University Press, 1988.

[2] http://zdnet.com.com/2100-11-525083.html?legacy=zdnn.

[3] Executive Order 12958, *Classified National Security Information*. Accessed September 15, 2003. http://www.dss.mil/seclib/eo12958.htm.

[4] Adapted from the *Georgia-Pacific Corporation Practices Guide*.

[5] Lawrence A. Gordon, Martin P. Loeb, William Lucyshyn, and Robert Richardson. 2006 CSI/FBI Computer Crime and Security Survey. Accessed July 15, 2006. http://gocsi.com.

CHAPTER **8**

RISK MANAGEMENT: CONTROLLING RISK

QUOTE

Weakness is a better teacher than strength. Weakness must learn to understand the obstacles that strength brushes aside.

Mason Cooley, U.S. aphorist (1927–2002)

Iris went into the manager's lounge to get a soda. As she was leaving, she saw Jane Harris—accounting supervisor of RWW—at a table, poring over a spreadsheet that Iris recognized.

"Hi, Jane," she said. "Can I join you?"

"Sure, Iris," she said. "Perhaps you can help me with this form Mike wants us to fill out."

Jane was working on the asset valuation worksheet that Iris had sent to all of the company managers. The worksheet listed all of the information assets in Jane's department. Mike had asked each manager to provide three values for each item: its cost, its replacement value, its ranked criticality to the company's mission, with the most important item being ranked number one. Mike hoped that Iris and the rest of the risk management team could use the data to build a consensus about the relative importance of various assets.

"What's the problem?" Iris asked.

"I understand these first two columns. But how am I supposed to decide what's the most important?"

"Well," Iris began, "with your accounting background, you could base your answers on some of the data you collect about each of these information assets. For this quarter, what's more important to senior management—revenue or profitability?"

"Profitability is almost always more important," Jane replied. "We have some systems that have lots of revenue, but operate at a loss."

"Well, there you go," Iris said. "Why not calculate the profitability margin for each listed item and use that to rate and rank them?"

"Oh, okay, Iris. Thanks for the idea." Jane started to make notes on her copy of the form.

LEARNING OBJECTIVES

Upon completion of this material, you should be able to:

- Recognize and select from the risk mitigation strategy options used to control risk
- Evaluate risk controls and formulate a cost-benefit analysis using existing conceptual frameworks
- Understand how to maintain and perpetuate risk controls
- Understand the OCTAVE Method and other approaches to managing risk

INTRODUCTION

In the early days of information technology, corporations used information technology (IT) systems mainly to gain advantages over their competition. Managers discovered that establishing a competitive business model, method, or technique allowed an organization to provide a product or service that was superior in some decisive way, thus creating a **competitive advantage**. But this is no longer true. The current IT industry has evolved from this earlier model to one in which almost all competitors operate at a similar level of automation. Because IT is now readily available to almost all organizations willing to make the investment, they can all react quickly to changes in the market. In today's highly competitive environment, managers realize that investing in IT systems at a level that merely maintains the status quo is no longer sufficient to gain a competitive advantage. In fact, even the implementation of new technologies does not necessarily enable an organization to maintain a competitive lead. Instead, the concept of **competitive disadvantage**—the state of falling behind the competition—has emerged as a critical factor. Effective IT-enabled organizations now quickly absorb emerging technologies, not to gain or maintain the traditional competitive advantage, but rather to avoid the possibility of losing market share when faltering systems make it impossible to maintain the current standard of service.

To keep up with the competition, organizations must design and create a safe environment in which business processes and procedures can function effectively. This environment must maintain confidentiality and privacy and assure the integrity and availability of organizational data. These objectives are met via the application of the principles of risk management.

As discussed in Chapter 7, **risk management** is the process used by managers, auditors, and other professionals to identify vulnerabilities in an organization's information systems and to assure the confidentiality, integrity, and availability of all the components in the organization's information systems. When an organization depends on IT systems to remain viable, information security and the discipline of risk management move beyond theoretical discussions to become an integral part of the economic basis for making business decisions. These decisions are based on trade-offs between the costs of applying information systems controls and the benefits realized from the operation of secured, available systems.

This chapter builds on the concepts developed in Chapter 7, which focused on the *identification* of risk and the assessment of its relative impact from all identified vulnerabilities. This effort produces a list of documented vulnerabilities, ranked by criticality of impact. In this chapter, you will learn how to use such a list to *assess* options, estimate costs, weigh the relative merits of options, and gauge the benefits of various control approaches.

Controlling risk begins with an understanding of what risk mitigation strategies are and how to formulate them. The chosen strategy may include applying controls to some or all of the vulnerabilities from the ranked vulnerability worksheet prepared in the previous chapter. Chapter 8 explores a variety of control approaches, and then discusses how such approaches can be categorized. It also explains the critical concepts of cost-benefit analysis and residual risk, and describes control strategy assessment and maintenance.

RISK CONTROL STRATEGIES

When an organization's general management team determines that risks from information security threats are creating a competitive disadvantage, it empowers the information technology and information security communities of interest to control those risks. Once the project team for information security development has created the ranked vulnerability worksheet (see Chapter 7), the team must choose one of four basic strategies to control the risks that arise from these vulnerabilities:

- Avoidance: Applying safeguards that eliminate or reduce the remaining uncontrolled risks
- Transference: Shifting the risks to other areas or to outside entities
- Mitigation: Reducing the impact should an attacker successfully exploit the vulnerability
- Acceptance: Understanding the consequences and acknowledging the risk without any attempts at control or mitigation

Avoidance

Avoidance is the risk control strategy that attempts to prevent the exploitation of the vulnerability. It is the preferred approach, as it seeks to avoid risk rather than deal with it after it has been realized. Avoidance is accomplished through the following techniques:

- Application of policy: As discussed in Chapter 4, the application of policy allows all levels of management to mandate that certain procedures always be followed. For example, if the organization needs to control password use more tightly, it can implement a policy requiring passwords on all IT systems. But policy alone may not be enough. Effective management always couples changes in policy with the training and education of employees, or an application of technology, or both.

- Application of training and education: Communicating new or revised policy to employees may not be adequate to assure compliance. Awareness, training, and education are essential to creating a safer and more controlled organizational environment and to achieving the necessary changes in end-user behavior.

- Countering threats: Risks can be avoided by countering the threats facing an asset and by eliminating its exposure to threats. Eliminating a threat is difficult but possible. For example, if an organization is facing a threat of loss of files made available to trading partners in an unsecured FTP server, it can move to a more robust secure-shell or secure-FTP server and thus eliminate the threat to the unsecured files.

- Implementation of technical security controls and safeguards: In the everyday world of information security, technical solutions are often required to reduce risk effectively. For example, systems administrators can configure systems to use passwords where policy requires them and where the administrators are both aware of the requirement and trained to implement it.

OFFLINE

The Human Firewall Project

By The Human Firewall Council

A consortium of security experts from government, private industry, associations, and non-profit organizations known as the Human Firewall Council is directing the Human Firewall campaign. The goal of the Council is to help educate people in organizations on how to better protect information assets from the perspective of changing human behavior: creating a "human firewall" as a complement to the usual technical firewalls and other network security devices and software designed to safeguard the enterprise.

continued

Eight Essential Steps to Building a Human Firewall

1. Get top management buy-in and commitment. The Gartner Group has identified three major questions that executives and boards of directors need to answer
   when confronting information security issues:

   - Is our security policy enforced fairly, consistently, and legally across the
     organization?
   - Would our employees, contractors, and partners know if a security viola-
     tion were being committed?
   - Would they know what to do about it if they did recognize a security
     violation?

2. Assign and clarify roles and responsibilities.
3. Create an action plan with a budget.
4. Develop and/or update information security policies.
5. Develop an organization-wide security awareness/education program.
6. Measure the progress of your security awareness/education efforts.
7. Adapt and improve your security awareness/education programs according to
   progress/feedback.
8. Develop an information security incident response team and plan.

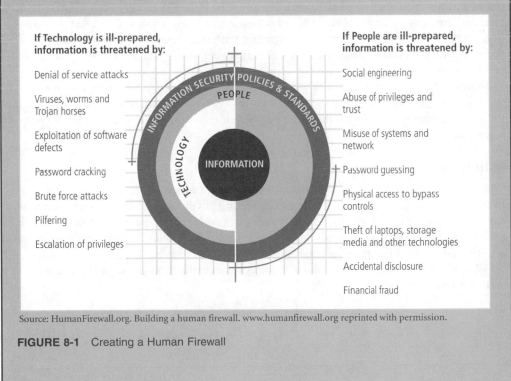

If Technology is ill-prepared, information is threatened by:

Denial of service attacks

Viruses, worms and Trojan horses

Exploitation of software defects

Password cracking

Brute force attacks

Pilfering

Escalation of privileges

If People are ill-prepared, information is threatened by:

Social engineering

Abuse of privileges and trust

Misuse of systems and network

Password guessing

Physical access to bypass controls

Theft of laptops, storage media and other technologies

Accidental disclosure

Financial fraud

Source: HumanFirewall.org. Building a human firewall. www.humanfirewall.org reprinted with permission.

FIGURE 8-1 Creating a Human Firewall

Transference

Transference is the control approach that attempts to shift the risk to other assets, other processes, or other organizations. This goal may be accomplished by rethinking how services are offered, revising deployment models, outsourcing to other organizations, purchasing insurance, or implementing service contracts with providers.

In the popular book *In Search of Excellence*, management consultants Tom Peters and Robert Waterman present a series of case studies of high-performing corporations. They assert that one of the eight characteristics of excellent organizations is that they "stick to their knitting. They stay reasonably close to the business they know."[1] What does this mean? It means that Kodak focuses on the manufacture of photographic equipment and chemicals, while General Motors focuses on the design and construction of cars and trucks. Neither company spends strategic energies on the technology for developing Web sites. They focus energy and resources on what they do best while relying on consultants or contractors for other types of expertise.

Organizations should consider this whenever they begin to expand their operations, including information and systems management, and even information security. If an organization does not have adequate security management and administration experience, it should hire individuals or firms that provide expertise in these areas. For example, many organizations want Web services, including Web presences, domain name registration, and domain and Web hosting. Rather than implementing their own servers, and hiring their own Webmasters, Web systems administrators, and even specialized security experts, savvy organizations hire ISPs or Web consulting organizations. This approach allows them to transfer the risk associated with the management of these complex systems to other organizations with more experience in dealing with those risks. A side benefit of specific contract arrangements is that the provider is responsible for disaster recovery and, through service-level agreements, for guaranteeing server and Web site availability.

Outsourcing, of course, is not without its own risks. It is up to the owner of the information asset, IT management, and the information security team to ensure that the disaster recovery requirements of the outsourcing contract are sufficient and have been met *before* they are needed.

Mitigation

Mitigation is the control approach that attempts to reduce, by means of planning and preparation, the damage caused by the exploitation of vulnerability. This approach includes three types of plans, which you learned about in Chapter 3: incident response (IR) plan, disaster recovery (DR) plan, and business continuity (BC) plan. Mitigation depends on the ability to detect and respond to an attack as quickly as possible.

Table 8-1 summarizes each of the three types of mitigation plans, including its characteristics and examples.

TABLE 8-1 Summaries of Mitigation Plans

Plan	Description	Example	When deployed	Timeframe
Incident Respond (IR) Plan	Actions an organization takes during incidents (attacks)	• List of steps to be taken during disaster • Intelligence gathering • Information analysis	As incident or disaster unfolds	Immediate and real-time reaction
Disaster Recovery (DR) Plan	• Preparations for recovery should a disaster occur • Strategies to limit losses before and during disaster • Step-by-step instructions to regain normalcy	• Procedures for the recovery of lost data • Procedures for the reestablishment of lost services • Shutdown procedures to protect systems and data	Immediately after the incident is labeled a disaster	Short-term recovery
Business Continuity (BC) Plan	Steps to ensure continuation of the overall business when the scale of a disaster exceeds the DRP's ability to quickly restore operations	• Preparation steps for activation of secondary data centers • Establishment of a hot site in a remote location	Immediately after the disaster is determined to affect the continued operations of the operation	Long-term organization

Acceptance

As described above, mitigation is a control approach that attempts to reduce the effects of an exploited vulnerability. In contrast, acceptance is the choice to do nothing to protect an information asset from risk, and to accept the outcome from any resulting exploitation. It may or may not be a conscious business decision. The only use of the acceptance strategy that industry practices recognize as valid occurs when the organization has done the following:

- Determined the level of risk posed to the information asset
- Assessed the probability of attack and the likelihood of a successful exploitation of a vulnerability
- Approximated the annual rate of occurrence of such an attack
- Estimated the potential loss that could result from attacks
- Performed a thorough cost-benefit analysis
- Evaluated controls using each appropriate type of feasibility analysis report
- Determined that the particular function, service, information, or asset did not justify the cost of protection

This control—or rather lack of control—assumes that it can be a prudent business decision to examine the alternatives and conclude that the cost of protecting an asset does not justify the security expenditure. Suppose it would cost an organization $100,000 a year to protect a server. The security assessment determines that for $10,000 the organization could replace the information contained in the server, replace the server itself, and cover associated recovery costs. Under those circumstances, management may be satisfied with taking its chances and saving the money that would otherwise be spent on protecting this particular asset.

An organization that decides on acceptance as a strategy for every identified risk of loss may in fact be unable to conduct proactive security activities, and may have an apathetic approach to security in general. It is not acceptable for an organization to plead ignorance and thus abdicate its legal responsibility to protect employees' and customers' information. It is also unacceptable for management to hope that if they do not try to protect information, the opposition will imagine that little will be gained by an attack. The risks far outweigh the benefits of this approach, which usually ends in regret, as the exploitation of the vulnerabilities causes a seemingly unending series of information security lapses.

MANAGING RISK

Risk appetite (also known as **risk tolerance**) describes the quantity and nature of risk that organizations are willing to accept, as they evaluate the trade-offs between perfect security and unlimited accessibility. For instance, a financial services company, regulated by government and conservative by nature, seeks to apply every reasonable control and even some invasive controls to protect its information assets. Other, less closely regulated organizations may also be conservative, and thus seek to avoid the negative publicity and perceived loss of integrity caused by the exploitation of a vulnerability. A firewall vendor might install a set of firewall rules that are far more stringent than necessary, simply because being hacked would jeopardize its market. Other organizations may take on dangerous risks because of ignorance. The reasoned approach to risk is one that balances the expense (in terms of finance and the usability of information assets) against the possible losses if exploited.

James Anderson Executive Consultant and Director at Emagined Security. formerly a senior executive with Inovant (the world's largest commercial processor of financial payment transactions), believes that information security in today's enterprise is a "well-informed sense of assurance that the information risks and controls are in balance." The key is for the organization to find balance in its decision-making processes and in its feasibility analyses, thereby assuring that its risk appetite is based on experience and facts, and not on ignorance or wishful thinking.

When vulnerabilities have been controlled as much as possible, there is often remaining risk that has not been completely removed, shifted, or planned for—in other words, residual risk. Expressed another way, "**Residual risk** is a combined function of (1) a threat less the effect of threat-reducing safeguards; (2) a vulnerability less the effect of vulnerability-reducing safeguards; and (3) an asset less the effect of asset value-reducing safeguards."[2] Figure 8-2 illustrates how residual risk persists even after safeguards are implemented.

Although it might seem counterintuitive, the goal of information security is not to bring residual risk to zero; rather, it is to bring residual risk in line with an organization's risk appetite. If decision makers have been informed of uncontrolled risks and the proper authority groups within the communities of interest decide to leave residual risk in place, then the information security program has accomplished its primary goal.

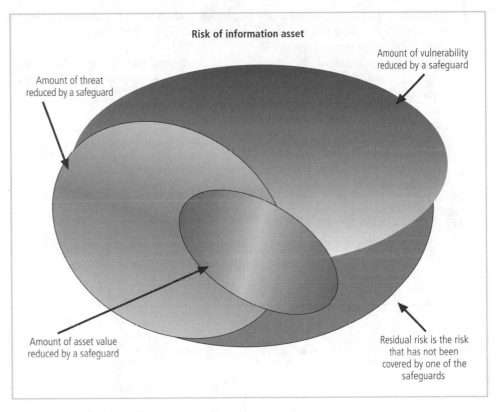

Risk of information asset

Amount of vulnerability
reduced by a safeguard

Amount of threat
reduced by a safeguard

Amount of asset value
reduced by a safeguard

Residual risk is the risk
that has not been
covered by one of the
safeguards

FIGURE 8-2   Residual Risk

Figure 8-3 illustrates the process by which an organization chooses from among the four risk control strategies. As shown in this flowchart, after the information system is designed, you must determine whether the system has vulnerabilities that can be exploited. If a viable threat exists, examine what an attacker would gain from a successful attack. Then, estimate the expected loss the organization will incur if the vulnerability is successfully exploited. If this loss is within the range of losses the organization can absorb, or if the attacker's gain is less than the likely cost of executing the attack, the organization may choose to accept the risk. Otherwise, you must select one of the other control strategies.

For further guidance, some rules of thumb on strategy selection are presented below. When weighing the benefits of the various strategies, keep in mind that the level of threat and the value of the asset should play a major role in strategy selection.

- When a vulnerability (flaw or weakness) exists: Implement security controls to reduce the likelihood of a vulnerability being exercised.
- When a vulnerability can be exploited: Apply layered protections, architectural designs, and administrative controls to minimize the risk or prevent the occurrence of an attack.

- When the attacker's potential gain is greater than the costs of attack: Apply protections to increase the attacker's cost, or reduce the attacker's gain, by using technical or managerial controls.
- When the potential loss is substantial: Apply design principles, architectural designs, and technical and nontechnical protections to limit the extent of the attack, thereby reducing the potential for loss.[3]

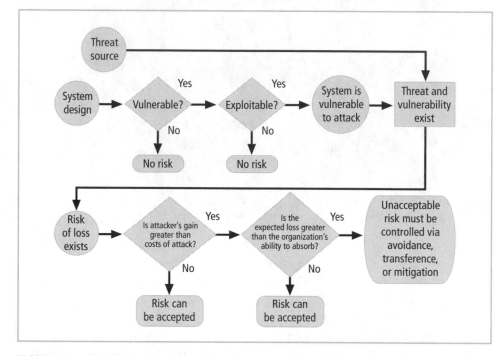

FIGURE 8-3 Risk-Handling Action Points

Once a control strategy has been selected and implemented, controls should be monitored and measured on an ongoing basis to determine their effectiveness and to estimate the remaining risk. Figure 8-4 shows how this cyclical process ensures that risks are controlled.

At a minimum, each information asset–threat pair should have a documented control strategy that clearly identifies any residual risk that remains after the proposed strategy has been executed. This control strategy articulates which of the four fundamental risk-reducing approaches will be used, how the various approaches might be combined, and justifies the findings by referencing the feasibility studies.

Some organizations document the outcome of the control strategy for each information asset–threat pair in an action plan. This action plan includes concrete tasks with accountability for each task being assigned to an organizational unit or to an individual. It may include hardware and software requirements, budget estimates, and detailed timelines.

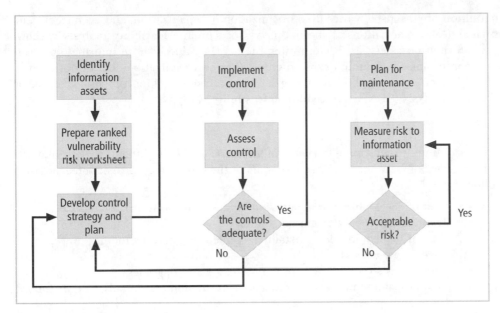

FIGURE 8-4   Risk Control Cycle

FEASIBILITY STUDIES AND COST-BENEFIT ANALYSIS

Before deciding on the strategy (avoidance, transference, mitigation, or acceptance) for a specific vulnerability, an organization must explore all readily accessible information about the economic and noneconomic consequences of the vulnerability. This exploration attempts to answer the question, "What are the actual and perceived advantages of implementing a control as opposed to the actual and perceived disadvantages of implementing the control?"

While the advantages of a specific control can be identified in a number of ways, the primary means is to determine the value of the information assets that it is designed to protect. There are also many ways to identify the disadvantages associated with specific risk controls. The following sections describe some of the more commonly used techniques for making these choices. Some of these techniques use dollar-denominated expenses and savings from economic cost avoidance, while others use noneconomic feasibility criteria. **Cost avoidance** is the money saved by avoiding, via the implementation of a control, the financial ramifications of an incident.

Cost-Benefit Analysis

The criterion most commonly used when evaluating a project that implements information security controls and safeguards is economic feasibility. While any number of alternatives may solve a particular problem, some are more expensive than others. Most organizations can spend only a reasonable amount of time and money on information security, and the definition of reasonable varies from organization to organization, and even from manager to manager. Organizations can begin this type of economic feasibility analysis by valuing the information assets, and determining the loss in value if those information assets become compromised. Common sense dictates that an organization should not spend more to protect an asset than it is worth. This decision-making process is called a **cost-benefit analysis (CBA)** or an **economic feasibility study**.

Cost

Just as it is difficult to determine the value of information, so it is difficult to determine the cost of safeguarding it. Among the items that affect the cost of a control or safeguard are the following:

- Cost of development or acquisition of hardware, software, and services
- Training fees (cost to train personnel)
- Cost of implementation (installing, configuring, and testing hardware, software, and services)
- Service costs (vendor fees for maintenance and upgrades)
- Cost of maintenance (labor expense to verify and continually test, maintain, train, and update)

Benefit

The **benefit** is the value to the organization of using controls to prevent losses associated with a specific vulnerability. It is usually determined by valuing the information asset or assets exposed by the vulnerability and then determining how much of that value is at risk, and how much risk exists for the asset. This result is expressed as the annualized loss expectancy, which is defined later in this chapter.

Asset Valuation

Asset valuation is the process of assigning financial value or worth to each information asset. As you learned in Chapter 7, the value of information differs within organizations and between organizations. Some argue that it is virtually impossible to determine accurately the true value of information and information-bearing assets, which is perhaps one reason why insurance underwriters currently have no definitive valuation tables for information assets. Asset valuation can draw on the assessment of information assets performed as part of the risk identification process you learned about in Chapter 7.

Asset valuation can involve the estimation of real or perceived costs. These costs can be selected from any or all of those associated with the design, development, installation, maintenance, protection, recovery, and defense against loss or litigation. Some costs are easily determined, such as the cost to replace a network switch, or the hardware needed for a specific class of server. Other costs are almost impossible to determine, such as the dollar value of the loss in market share if information on a firm's new product offerings were released prematurely and the company lost its competitive edge. A further complication is that some information assets acquire value over time that is beyond their **intrinsic value**—the essential worth—of the asset under consideration. This higher **acquired value** is the more appropriate value in most cases.

Asset valuation must account for the following:

- Value retained from the cost of creating the information asset: Information is created or acquired at a cost which can be calculated or estimated. For example, many organizations have developed extensive cost-accounting practices to capture the costs associated with collecting and processing data, as well as developing and maintaining software. Software development costs include the efforts of the many people involved in the systems development life cycle for each application and system. Although this effort draws mainly on IT personnel, it also includes the user and general management community and sometimes the information security staff. In today's marketplace, with high programmer salaries and even higher contractor expenses, the average cost to complete even a moderately sized application can quickly escalate. For example, multimedia-based training software that requires 350 hours of development for each hour of content will require the expenditure of as much as $10,000 per hour.

- Value retained from past maintenance of the information asset: It is estimated that for every dollar spent to develop an application or to acquire and process data, many more dollars are spent on maintenance over the useful life of the data or software. If actual costs have not been recorded, the cost can be estimated in terms of the human resources required to continually update, support, modify, and service the applications and systems.

- Value implied by the cost of replacing the information: The costs associated with replacing information should include the human and technical resources needed to reconstruct, restore, or regenerate the information from backups, independent transactions logs, or even hard copies of data sources. Most organizations rely on routine media backups to protect their information. When estimating recovery costs, keep in mind that you may have to hire contractors to carry out the regular workload that employees will be unable to perform during recovery efforts. Also, real-time information may not be recoverable from a tape backup, unless the system has built-in journaling capabilities. To restore this information, the various information sources may have to be reconstructed, and the data reentered into the system and validated for accuracy. This restoration can take longer than it took to create the data initially.

- Value from providing the information: Separate from the cost of developing or maintaining the information is the cost of providing the information to those users who need it. Such costs include the values associated with the delivery of the information through databases, networks, and hardware and software systems. They also include the cost of the infrastructure necessary to provide access to and control of the information.

- Value acquired from the cost of protecting the information: The value of an asset is based in part on the cost of protecting it, and the amount of money spent to protect an asset is based in part on the value of the asset. While this is a seemingly unending circle, estimating the value of protecting an information asset can help you to better understand the expense associated with its potential loss. The values listed previously are easy to calculate with some precision. This value and those that follow are likely to be estimates of cost.

- Value to owners: How much is your Social Security number worth to you? Or your telephone number? Placing a value on information can be quite a daunting task. A market researcher collects data from a company's sales figures and determines that a new product offering has a strong potential market appeal to members of a certain age group. While the cost of creating this new information may be small, how much is the new information actually worth? It could be worth millions if it successfully captures a new market share. Although estimating the value of information to an organization, or how what portion of revenue is directly attributable to that information, may be impossible, it is vital to understand the overall cost that could be a consequence of its loss so as to better realize its value. Here again, estimating value may be the only method possible.

- Value of intellectual property: The value of a new product or service to a customer may ultimately be unknowable. How much would a cancer patient pay for a cure? How much would a shopper pay for a new flavor of cheese? What is the value of a logo or advertising slogan? Related but separate are intellectual properties known as trade secrets. Intellectual information assets are the primary assets of some organizations.

- Value to adversaries: How much would it be worth to an organization to know what the competition is doing? Many organizations have established departments tasked with the assessment and estimation of the activities of their competition. Even organizations in traditionally nonprofit industries can benefit from knowing what is going on in political, business, and competitive organizations. Stories of industrial espionage abound, including the urban legend of Company A encouraging its employees to hire on as janitors at Company B. As custodial workers, the employees could snoop through open terminals, photograph and photocopy unsecured documents, and rifle through internal trash and recycling bins. Such legends support a widely accepted concept: Information can have extraordinary value to the right individuals. Similarly, stories are circulated of how disgruntled employees, soon to be terminated, might steal information and present it to competitive organizations to curry favor and land new employment. Those who hire such applicants in an effort to gain from their larceny should consider whether benefiting from such a tactic is wise. After all, such thieves could presumably repeat their activities when they become disgruntled with their newest employers.

- Loss of productivity while the information assets are unavailable: When a power failure occurs, effective use of UPS equipment can prevent data loss, but users cannot create additional information. Although this is not an example of an attack that damages information, it is an instance in which a threat (deviations in quality of service from service providers) affects an organization's productivity. The hours of wasted employee time, the cost of using alternatives, and the general lack of productivity will incur costs and can severely set back a critical operation or process.

- Loss of revenue while information assets are unavailable: Have you ever been in a retail store when your credit card would not scan? How many times did the salesperson rescan the card before resorting to entering the numbers manually? How long did it take to enter the numbers manually in contrast to the quick swipe? What if the credit card verification process was off-line? Did the organization have a manual process to validate or process credit card payment in the absence of the familiar approval system? Many organizations have all but abandoned manual backups for automated processes. Sometimes, businesses may even have to turn away customers because their automated payments systems are inoperative. Most grocery stores no longer label each item with the price, because the UPC scanners and the related databases calculate the costs and inventory levels dynamically. Without these systems, could your grocery store sell goods? How much would the store lose if it could not? It has been estimated that "43 percent of all businesses that close their doors due to a disaster or crisis, even for one day, never reopen them again. An additional 28 percent fail during the next three to five years."[4] Imagine, instead of a grocery store, an online book retailer such as Amazon.com suffering a power outage. The entire operation is instantly closed. Even if Amazon's offering system were operational, what if the payment systems were off-line? Customers could make selections, but could not complete their purchases. While dotcom businesses may be more susceptible to suffering a loss of revenue as a result of a loss of information, most organizations would be unable to conduct business if certain pieces of information were unavailable.

Once an organization has estimated the worth of various assets, it can begin to calculate the potential loss from the exploitation of vulnerability or a threat occurrence. This process yields the estimate of potential loss per risk. The questions that must be asked at this stage include the following:

- What damage could occur, and what financial impact would it have?
- What would it cost to recover from the attack, in addition to the financial impact of damage?
- What is the single loss expectancy for each risk?

A **single loss expectancy (SLE)** is the calculation of the value associated with the most likely loss from an attack. This calculation takes into account both the value of the asset and the expected percentage of loss that would occur from a particular attack:

SLE = asset value (AV) * exposure factor (EF)

where

EF = the percentage loss that would occur from a given vulnerability being exploited

For example, if a Web site has an estimated value of $1,000,000 (as determined by asset valuation), and a sabotage or vandalism (hacker defacement) scenario indicates that 10% of the Web site would be damaged or destroyed in such an attack (the exposure factor), the SLE for this Web site would be $1,000,000 × 0.10 = $100,000. This estimate is then used to calculate another value, annual loss expectancy, discussed below.

As difficult as it is to estimate the value of information, the estimation of the probability of a threat occurrence or attack is even more difficult. There are not always tables, books, or records that indicate the frequency or probability of any given attack, though some sources are available for certain asset–threat pairs. For instance, the likelihood of a tornado or thunderstorm destroying a building of a specific type of construction within a specified region of the country is available to insurance underwriters. In most cases, however, an organization can rely only on its internal information to calculate the security of its information assets. Even if the network, systems, and security administrators have been actively and accurately tracking these threat occurrences, the organization's information will be sketchy at best. As a result, this information is usually estimated.

Usually, the probability of a threat occurring is depicted as a table that indicates how frequently an attack from each threat type is likely to occur within a given time frame (for example, once every 10 years). This value is commonly referred to as the **annualized rate of occurrence (ARO)**. ARO simply indicates how often you expect a specific type of attack to occur. For example, if a successful act of sabotage or vandalism occurs about once every two years, then the ARO would be 50% (0.5). A network attack that can occur multiple times per second might be successful once each month and would have an ARO of 12.

Once you determine the loss from a single attack, and the likely frequency of successful attacks, you can calculate the overall loss potential per risk expressed as an **annualized loss expectancy (ALE)** using the values for the ARO and SLE from the previous sections.

ALE = SLE * ARO
To use our previous example, if SLE = $100,000 and ARO = 0.5, then
ALE = $100,00 × 0.5
ALE = $50,000

Thus, the organization can expect to lose $50,000 per year, every year, unless it increases its Web security. Now, armed with a figure to justify its expenditures for controls and safeguards, the information security design team can deliver a budgeted value for planning purposes. Sometimes noneconomic factors are considered in this process, so even when ALE amounts are not large, control budgets can be justified.

The Cost-Benefit Analysis Formula

CBA (or economic feasibility) determines whether a control alternative is worth its associated cost. Such analyses may be performed before implementing a control or safeguard, or after controls have been in place for a time. Observation over time adds precision to the evaluation of the benefits of the safeguard and the determination of whether the safeguard is functioning as intended. While many CBA techniques exist, it is most easily calculated using the ALE from earlier assessments.

CBA = ALE(pre-control) − ALE(post-control) − ACS
where
ALE(pre-control) = ALE of the risk before the implementation of the control
ALE(post-control) = ALE examined after the control has been in place for a period of time
ACS = annual cost of the safeguard

Once the controls are implemented, it is crucial to examine their benefits continuously to determine when they must be upgraded, supplemented, or replaced. As Frederick Avolio states in his article "Best Practices in Network Security":

> Security is an investment, not an expense. Investing in computer and network security measures that meet changing business requirements and risks makes it possible to satisfy changing business requirements without hurting the business's viability.[5]

Other Feasibility Studies

Earlier in this chapter, the concept of economic feasibility was employed to justify proposals for information security controls. The next step in measuring how ready an organization is for the introduction of these controls is to determine the proposal's organizational, operational, technical, and political feasibility.

Organizational Feasibility

Organizational feasibility analysis examines how well the proposed information security alternatives will contribute to the efficiency, effectiveness, and overall operation of an organization. In other words, the proposed control approach must contribute to the organization's strategic objectives. Does the implementation align well with the strategic planning for the information systems? Or does it require deviation from the planned expansion and management of the current systems? The organization should not invest in technology that changes its fundamental ability to explore certain avenues and opportunities. For example, suppose that a university decides to implement a new firewall. It takes a few months for the technology group to learn enough about the firewall to configure it completely. A few months after the implementation begins, it is discovered that the firewall as configured does not permit outgoing Web-streamed media. If one of the goals of the university is the pursuit of distance-learning opportunities, a firewall prevents that type of communication has not met the organizational feasibility requirement and should be modified or replaced.

Operational Feasibility

Operational feasibility refers to user acceptance and support, management acceptance and support, and the system's compatibility with the requirements of the organization's stakeholders. Operational feasibility is also known as **behavioral feasibility**. An important aspect of systems development is obtaining user buy-in on projects. If the users do not accept a new technology, policy, or program, it will inevitably fail. Users may not openly oppose a change, but if they do not support it, they will find ways to disable or otherwise circumvent it. One of the most common methods of obtaining user acceptance and support is via **user involvement**. User involvement can be achieved by means of three simple actions: communicate, educate, and involve.

Organizations should *communicate* with system users, sharing timetables and implementation schedules, plus the dates, times, and locations of upcoming briefings and training. Affected parties must know the purpose of the proposed changes and how they will enable everyone to work more securely.

In addition, users should be *educated* and trained on how to work under the new constraints while avoiding any negative performance consequences. A major frustration for users is the implementation of a new program that prevents them from accomplishing their duties, with only a promise of eventual training.

Finally, those making changes should *involve* users by asking them what they want, and what they will tolerate, from the new systems. One way to do so this is to include representatives from the various constituencies in the development process.

Communication, education, and involvement can reduce *resistance* to change, and build *resilience* for change—that ethereal quality that allows workers to not only tolerate constant change but also accept it as a necessary part of the job.

Technical Feasibility

Unfortunately, many organizations rush to acquire new safeguards, without thoroughly examining what is required to implement and use them effectively. Because the implementation of technological controls can be extremely complex, the project team must consider their **technical feasibility**; that is, examine whether the organization has or can acquire the technology necessary to implement and support them. For example, does the organization have the hardware and software necessary to support a new firewall system? If not, can it be obtained?

Technical feasibility analysis also examines whether the organization has the technological expertise needed to manage the new technology. Does the staff include individuals who are qualified (and possibly certified) to install and manage a new firewall system? If not, can staff be spared from their current obligations to attend formal training and education programs to prepare them to administer the new systems? Or must personnel be hired? In the current environment, how difficult is it to find qualified personnel?

Political Feasibility

Politics has been defined as "the art of the possible."[6] **Political feasibility** analysis considers what can and cannot occur based on the consensus and relationships among the communities of interest. The limits imposed by the information security controls must fit within the realm of the possible before they can be effectively implemented, and that realm includes the availability of staff resources.

In some cases, the information security community is assigned a budget, which they then allocate to activities and projects, making decisions about how to spend the money using their own judgment.

In other organizations, resources are first allocated to the IT community of interest, and the information security team must compete for these resources. Sometimes, the cost-benefit analysis and other forms of justification discussed in this chapter are used to make rational decisions about the relative merits of proposed activities and projects. Unfortunately, in other settings, these decisions are politically charged and do not focus on the pursuit of the greater organizational goals.

Another methodology for budget allocation requires the information security team to propose and justify use of the resources for activities and projects in the context of the entire organization. This approach requires that arguments for information security spending articulate the benefit of the expense for the whole organization, so that members of the organizational communities of interest can understand and perceive their value.

Alternatives to Feasibility Analysis

Rather than using cost-benefit analysis or some other feasibility reckoning to justify risk controls, an organization might look to alternative models. Many of these have been described in earlier chapters (especially in Chapter 6). A short list of alternatives is provided here:

- Benchmarking is the process of seeking out and studying the practices used in other organizations that produce the results you desire in your organization. When benchmarking, an organization typically uses either metrics-based or process-based measures.
- Due care and due diligence occur when an organization adopts a certain minimum level of security as what any *prudent* organization would do in similar circumstances.
- Best business practices are considered those thought to be among the best in the industry, balancing the need to access information with adequate protection.
- The gold standard is for those ambitious organizations in which the best business practices are not sufficient. They aspire to set the standard for their industry, and are thus said to be in pursuit of the gold standard.
- Government recommendations and best practices are useful for organizations that operate in industries regulated by governmental agencies. Government recommendations, which are, in effect, requirements, can also serve as excellent sources for information about what some organizations may be doing, or are required to do, to control information security risks.
- A baseline is derived by comparing measured actual performance against established standards for the measured category.

Risk Management

By Dr. Michael E. Whitman, CISSP

According to an IT saying, there are 10 types of people in the world: those who understand binary and those who do not. In the world of information security, there are three types of people: those who understand the importance of information security, those who don't, and those who think they do but really don't. The third group represents the highest risk to the security of information.

The first group, one hopes, is us—the protectors of the information, the defenders of the realm, the keepers of the gates. Those who get it know that information security is not really about technology, it's about people. More than 3000 years ago China defended itself from the nomadic barbarians to the north by building a massive wall. Legend has it that in the first 500 years of the wall's existence it was breached three times. Did these failures occur because the wall was not long enough, tall enough, or strong enough? No. In each instance, the invaders breached the Great Wall of China by bribing the gatekeeper.

Security has always been a people problem. In fact, the top five threats to information security are all people problems:

1. Deliberate software attacks, such as viruses, worms, and denial-of-service attacks. All of these attacks are instigated and propagated by people. Hackers write viruses, and, in almost all cases, the viruses are spread by individuals who open attachments, fail to scan disks for viruses, or commit some other breach of security common sense.

2. Technical software failures or errors. Most technical software failures or errors are the fault of software developers. The rush to market software has resulted in inadequate or incomplete controls. Most college programming classes teach fundamental security and emphasize thorough testing. You test lines of code, then modules of code, then entire applications, and finally interactions of applications. Today's companies tend to create three levels of testers: (1) alpha testers, programmers who examine the software in-house; (2) beta testers, outsiders who either are brought in for testing or receive the software to evaluate; and (3) gamma testers, unofficial software testers—users who buy the software and then contact tech support when something goes wrong. In the case of the gamma testers, tech support logs the problems and then programmers resolve them with patches and upgrades.

3. Acts of human error or failure. This threat is self-explanatory. Humans may fail to follow established policy or procedures, or make mistakes because other humans did not provide them with appropriate training, or make a mistake just because they are, after all, human.

4. Deliberate acts of espionage or trespass. It is hard enough to scratch out a meager profit, as many small to medium-sized companies do, without hackers trying to crash your e-business server, mangle your intranet servers, or worse.

5. Deliberate acts of sabotage or vandalism. Same as above.

continued

The second group, those who do not understand the importance of information security, make up the bulk of the population in the InfoSec world. Security education, training, and awareness (SETA) programs are designed to help educate and inform people in this group. We struggle to inform, communicate, and involve them in information security, but they are many and we are few. Nonetheless, a noble battle ensues.

The third group, those who think they know what is going on in information security but actually are misinformed or misguided, represent the biggest threat. Some members of this group claim that security is a technology problem, which can be solved by attending technical conferences. Others claim that the problem is overstated and that the threat is not that real; they are wrong. A manager at a major managed security services company recently told my class, "We tell our customers that an exposed server usually won't be on the Internet for more than 24 hours before it's scanned, hacked, infected, and/or crashed. In reality, it's about 4 hours!" And it's true; we ran a group of unprotected servers as a test, and all of them were infected with the Slammer worm before the day was over.

The people in the third group are the toughest to educate. They must be reeducated to dispel the bad information they currently hold on to. Until this reeducation happens, they pose the biggest threat to information security.

Here are a few words of wisdom:

Albert Einstein:

"Only two things are infinite, the universe and human stupidity, and I'm not sure about the former."

"Problems cannot be solved at the same level of awareness that created them."

Helen Keller:

"Science may have found a cure for most evils; but it has found no remedy for the worst of them all—the apathy of human beings."

"I am only one; but still I am one. I cannot do everything, but still I can do something; I will not refuse to do the something I can do."

RECOMMENDED RISK CONTROL PRACTICES

Assume that a risk assessment has determined it is necessary to protect a particular asset from a particular threat, at a cost up to $50,000. Unfortunately most budget authorities focus on the *up to,* and then try to cut a percentage of the total figure to save the organization money. This tendency underlines the importance of developing strong justifications for specific action plans and of providing concrete estimates in those plans.

Consider also that each control or safeguard affects more than one asset–threat pair. If a new $50,000 firewall is installed to protect the Internet connection infrastructure from hackers launching port-scanning attacks, the same firewall may also protect other information assets from other threats and attacks. The final choice may call for a balanced mixture of controls that provides the greatest value for as many asset–threat pairs as possible. This example reveals another facet of the problem: Information security professionals manage a dynamic matrix covering a broad range of threats, information assets, controls, and identified vulnerabilities. Each time a control is added to the matrix, it undoubtedly changes the ALE for the information asset vulnerability for which it has been designed, and it also may alter the ALE for other information asset vulnerabilities. To put it more simply, if you put in one safeguard, you decrease the risk associated with all subsequent control evaluations. To make matters worse, the action of implementing a control may change the values assigned or calculated in a prior estimate.

Between the difficult task of valuing information assets, and the dynamic nature of the ALE calculations, it is no wonder that organizations typically look for a more straightforward method of implementing controls. This preference has prompted an ongoing search for ways to design security architectures that go beyond the direct application of specific controls for specific information asset vulnerabilty. The following sections cover some of these alternatives.

Qualitative Measures

The steps described previously use actual values or estimates to create a **quantitative assessment**. In some cases, an organization might be unable to determine these values. Fortunately, risk assessment steps can be executed using estimates based on a **qualitative assessment**. For example, instead of placing a value of once every 10 years for the ARO, the organization might list all possible attacks on a particular set of information and rate each in terms of its probability of occurrence. This could be accomplished using scales, rather than specific estimates. For example, a scale might range from 0, representing no chance of occurrence, to 10, representing almost certain occurrence. Organizations may, of course, prefer other scales: 0–10, 1–5, 0–20. These same scales can be used in any situation requiring a value, even in asset valuation. For example, instead of estimating that a particular piece of information is worth $1,000,000, you might value information on a scale of 1–20; where 1 indicates relatively worthless information and 20 indicates extremely critical information, such as a certain soda manufacturer's secret recipe or the 11 herbs and spices of a popular chicken vendor.

Delphi Technique

How do you calculate the values and scales used in qualitative and quantitative assessment? An individual can pull the information together based on personal experience, but, as the saying goes, "two heads are better than one"—and a team of heads is better than two. The **Delphi technique**, named for the oracle at Delphi who predicted the future, is a process whereby a group rates or ranks a set of information. The individual responses are compiled and then returned to the group for another iteration. This process continues until the entire group is satisfied with the result. This technique can be applied to the development of scales, asset valuation, asset or threat ranking, or any scenario that can benefit from the input of more than one decision maker.

A Single-Source Approach to Risk Management

Until now, this book has presented a general treatment of risk management, synthesizing information and methods from many sources to present the customary or usual approaches that organizations use to manage risk. The next section presents an alternative, comprehensive approach to risk management that comes from a single source. The Operationally Critical Threat, Asset, and Vulnerability Evaluation (OCTAVE) Method is an InfoSec risk evaluation methodology that allows organizations to balance the protection of critical information assets against the costs of providing protective and detection controls. This process can enable an organization to measure itself against known or accepted good security practices, and then establish an organization-wide protection strategy and information security risk mitigation plan. (For more detailed information about the OCTAVE Method, you can download its implementation guide from www.cert.org/octave/omig.html.)

THE OCTAVE METHOD*

From Appendix D of OCTAVE Method Implementation Guide Version 2.0 *by C. Alberts and A. Dorofee , June 2001. Reprinted here with permission.*

The OCTAVE Method defines the essential components of a comprehensive, systematic, context-driven, self-directed information security risk evaluation.[7] By following the OCTAVE Method, an organization can make information-protection decisions based on risks to the confidentiality, integrity, and availability of critical information technology assets. The operational or business units and the IT department work together to address the information security needs of the organization.

Using a three-phase approach, the OCTAVE Method examines organizational and technology issues to assemble a comprehensive picture of the information security needs of an organization. The phases are described below:

- Phase 1: Build Asset-Based Threat Profiles. This is an organizational evaluation. Key areas of expertise within the organization are examined to elicit important knowledge about information assets, the threats to those assets, the security requirements of the assets, what the organization is currently doing to protect its information assets (current protection strategy practices), and weaknesses in organizational policies and practice (organizational vulnerabilities).

- Phase 2: Identify Infrastructure Vulnerabilities. This is an evaluation of the information infrastructure. The key operational components of the information technology infrastructure are examined for weaknesses (technology vulnerabilities) that can lead to unauthorized action.

- Phase 3: Develop Security Strategy and Plans. Risks are analyzed in this phase. The information generated by the organizational and information infrastructure evaluations (Phases 1 and 2) is analyzed to identify risks to the organization and to evaluate the risks based on their impact to the organization's mission. In addition, an organization protection strategy and risk mitigation plans for the highest priority risks are developed.

Important Aspects of the OCTAVE Method

1. The OCTAVE Method is *self-directed*. A small, interdisciplinary team of the organization's personnel (called the analysis team) manages the process and analyzes all information. Thus, the organization's personnel are actively involved in the decision-making process. When organizations outsource risk assessments, they often detach from making decisions.

2. The OCTAVE Method requires an *analysis team* to conduct the evaluation and to analyze the information. The analysis team is an interdisciplinary team comprising representatives from both the mission-related and information technology areas of the organization. Typically, the analysis team will contain a core membership of about three to five people, depending on the size of the overall organization and the scope of the evaluation. The basic tasks of the analysis team are:

   - To facilitate the knowledge elicitation workshops of Phase 1
   - To gather any supporting data that are necessary
   - To analyze threat and risk information
   - To develop a protection strategy for the organization
   - To develop mitigation plans to address the risks to the organization's critical assets

   Thus, the analysis team must have knowledge of the organization and its business processes (including mission-related processes and information technology processes), facilitation skills, and good communications skills. It is also important to note that the analysis team is responsible for analyzing information and for making decisions. The core members of the analysis team may not have all of the knowledge and skills needed during the evaluation. At each point in the process, the analysis team members must decide if they need to augment their knowledge and skills for a specific task. They can do so by including others in the organization or by using external experts.

3. The OCTAVE Method uses a *workshop-based approach* for gathering information and making decisions. In Phase 1, key areas of expertise within the organization are examined in facilitated workshops (also called knowledge elicitation workshops). The analysis team facilitates these workshops. The result is the identification of important information assets, the threats to those assets, the security requirements of the assets, what the organization is currently doing to protect its information assets (current protection strategy), and weaknesses in organizational policies and practice (organizational vulnerabilities). The remainder of Phase 1, as well as Phases 2 and 3, include consolidation and analysis workshops to consolidate and analyze the information gathered during the Phase 1 knowledge elicitation workshops. The consolidation and analysis workshops yield information such as the key operational components of the information infrastructure, the risks to the organization, the protection strategy for the organization, and mitigation plans for addressing the risks to the critical assets.

4. The OCTAVE Method relies upon the following major *catalogs of information*:

- Catalog of practices: A collection of good strategic and operational security practices
- Threat profile: The range of major sources of threats that an organization needs to consider
- Catalog of vulnerabilities: A collection of vulnerabilities based on platform and application

An organization that is conducting the OCTAVE Method evaluates itself against the above catalogs of information. During Phase 1, the organization uses the catalog of practices as a measure of what it is currently doing well with respect to security (its current protection strategy practices) as well as what it is not doing well (its organizational vulnerabilities). The analysis team also uses the catalog of practices when it creates the protection strategy for the organization during Phase 3. After the analysis team selects the critical assets for the organization, they use the threat profile to create the range of threat scenarios that affect each critical asset. This occurs at the end of Phase 1. The analysis team uses software tools to examine their information technology infrastructure for weaknesses (technology vulnerabilities) in Phase 2.

Phases, Processes, and Activities

Each phase of the OCTAVE Method contains two or more processes. Each process is made of activities. The following list highlights the phases and processes of OCTAVE:

- Preparing for the OCTAVE Method
- Phase 1: Build Asset-Based Threat Profiles
  - Process 1: Identify Senior Management Knowledge
  - Process 2: Identify Operational Area Management Knowledge
  - Process 3: Identify Staff Knowledge
  - Process 4: Create Threat Profiles
- Phase 2: Identify Infrastructure Vulnerabilities
  - Process 5: Identify Key Components
  - Process 6: Evaluate Selected Components
- Phase 3: Develop Security Strategy and Plans
  - Process 7: Conduct Risk Analysis
  - Process 8: Develop Protection Strategy

Each of these is described in more detail in the following sections.

Preparing for the OCTAVE Method

Preparing for the OCTAVE Method creates the foundation for a successful or unsuccessful evaluation. Getting senior management sponsorship, the selection of the analysis team, scoping of the project and the selection of the participats are all key to a successful evaluation: The preparation activities for the OCTAVE Method address the issues listed above. The following are the activities required when preparing to conduct the OCTAVE Method:

1. Obtain senior management sponsorship of OCTAVE.
2. Select analysis team members.
3. Train analysis team.
4. Select operational areas to participate in OCTAVE.
5. Select participants.
6. Coordinate logistics.
7. Brief all participants.

Once the preparation is completed, the organization is ready to start the evaluation.

Phase 1: Build Asset-Based Threat Profiles

The OCTAVE Method enables decision makers to develop relative priorities based on what is important to the organization. This involves examining both organizational practices and the installed technology base to identify risks to the organization's important information assets. A comprehensive information security risk evaluation, like the OCTAVE Method, involves the entire organization, including personnel from the information technology department and the business lines of the organization.[8]

The purpose of a risk evaluation is to help decision makers select cost-effective countermeasures by balancing the cost of addressing a risk with the benefit derived from avoiding a potential negative impact to the organization. The result of the evaluation is a mitigation plan for applying countermeasures designed to reduce the organization's risks.

In the OCTAVE Method, the analysis team conducts the evaluation. The analysis team is interdisciplinary in nature, including participants with various backgrounds and job roles. It is responsible for conducting workshops with the organization's staff, for analyzing the information that is elicited, and for ensuring that the evaluation process proceeds as scheduled.

During Phase 1, the analysis team facilitates workshop interviews with staff from multiple organizational levels. During these workshops, the participants identify important assets and discuss the impact on the organization if the assets are compromised. These knowledge elicitation workshops are held for the following organizational levels:

- Senior management
- Operational area management (middle management)
- Staff (including IT staff)

You should note that the organizational levels are not mixed during the workshops. In addition, the information technology staff normally participates in a separate workshop from the general staff members. The purpose of the knowledge elicitation workshops is to identify the following information from each organizational perspective:

- Important assets and their relative values
- Perceived threats to the assets

- Security requirements
- Current protection strategy practices
- Current organizational vulnerabilities

The OCTAVE Method requires workshop participants to examine the relative priority of assets based on the impact to the organization if the asset is lost. Participants are asked to examine threats to the highest-priority assets that they have identified. The participants create threat scenarios based on known sources of threat and typical threat outcomes (from the threat profile). Participants next examine security requirements. Security requirements outline the qualities of information assets that are important to an organization.

Process 1: Identify Senior Management Knowledge

The participants in this process are the organization's senior managers. The analysis team facilitates a knowledge elicitation activity with the managers in these activities:

- Identify assets and relative priorities.
- Identify areas of concern.
- Identify security requirements for the most important assets.
- Capture knowledge of protection strategy practices and organizational vulnerabilities.

Process 2: Identify Operational Area Management Knowledge

The participants in this process are the organization's operational area managers (middle managers). The analysis team facilitates a knowledge elicitation activity with the managers in these activities:

- Identify assets and relative priorities.
- Identify areas of concern.
- Identify security requirements for the most important assets.
- Capture knowledge of protection strategy practices and organizational vulnerabilities.

Process 3: Identify Staff Knowledge

The participants in this process are the organization's staff members. The analysis team facilitates a knowledge elicitation activity with them in these activities:

- Identify assets and relative priorities.
- Identify areas of concern.
- Identify security requirements for the most important assets.
- Capture knowledge of protection strategy practices and organizational vulnerabilities.

Process 4: Create Threat Profiles

The participants in this process are the analysis team members. During Process 4, the information elicited from the different organizational levels during the previous processes is grouped, critical assets are chosen, and a threat profile is created for each critical asset. The following are the activities of Process 4:

- Group assets, security requirements, and areas of concern by organizational level.
- Select critical assets.
- Refine security requirements for critical assets.
- Identify threats to critical assets.

After completion of the organization view, or Phase 1 of the OCTAVE Method, the organization is ready to move to the technological view. Phase 2 of the evaluation examines the organization's information technology infrastructure.

Phase 2: Identify Infrastructure Vulnerabilities

Each information technology system or component will have many specific technology vulnerabilities against which it can be benchmarked. The OCTAVE Method requires that technology be measured against a catalog of vulnerabilities. The Common Vulnerabilities and Exposures (CVE) is a list or dictionary that provides common names for publicly known vulnerabilities.[9] It enables open and shared information without any distribution restrictions.

Technology vulnerability evaluations target weaknesses in the installed technology base of the organization, including network services, architecture, operating systems, and applications. The following basic activities are performed during a technology vulnerability evaluation:

- Identify key information technology systems and components.
- Examine systems and components for technology weaknesses.

The focus of a vulnerability evaluation of systems and components is to identify and evaluate the configuration and strength of devices on the organization network(s). The following list includes examples of tests performed during a technology vulnerability evaluation:

- Reviewing firewall configuration
- Checking the security of public Web servers
- Performing a comprehensive review of all operating systems
- Identifying services running and/or available on hosts and systems
- Listing all system user accounts
- Identifying known vulnerabilities in routers, switches, remote access servers, operating systems, and specific services and applications
- Identifying configuration errors
- Looking for existing signs of intrusion (Trojan horses, backdoor programs, integrity checks of critical system files, etc.)
- Checking file ownership and permissions
- Testing password usage and strength

Process 5: Identify Key Components

The participants in this process are the analysis team and selected members of the information technology (IT) staff. Prior to the workshop, the analysis team must ensure that documentation of the present state of the computing infrastructure is available. The network topology diagrams used by the organization's IT group to conduct its business are sufficient for this activity. The key is that the network topology information must be current. During Process 5, components to be evaluated for technology vulnerabilities are selected using these activities:

- Identify system of interest.
- Identify key classes of components.
- Identify infrastructure components to examine.

Process 6: Evaluate Selected Components

The participants in this process are the analysis team and selected members of the IT staff. A technology vulnerability evaluation supported by software tools is conducted prior to the workshop. The analysis team and IT staff review the results of the evaluation during the workshop in these activities:

- Run vulnerability evaluation tools on selected infrastructure components.
- Review technology vulnerabilities and summarize results.

After the organization completes the technology view, or Phase 2 of the evaluation, it is ready to develop a protection strategy and mitigation plans. During Phase 3 of the OCTAVE Method, the analysis team identifies the risks to its critical assets, develops a protection strategy for the organization, and develops mitigation plans for the risks to the critical assets.

Phase 3: Develop Security Strategy and Plans

Once the assets, threats, and vulnerabilities have been identified, an organization is positioned to analyze the information and to identify the information security risks. The analysis team leads the risk analysis effort. The goal is to determine how specific threats affect specific assets. A risk is essentially a threat plus the resulting impacts to the organization based on these outcomes:

- Disclosure of a critical asset (a violation of confidentiality)
- Modification of a critical asset (a violation of integrity)
- Loss or destruction of a critical asset (a violation of availability)
- Interruption of a critical asset (a violation of availability)

The analysis of risks in the OCTAVE Method is based on scenario planning. The analysis team constructs a range of risk scenarios, or a risk profile, for each critical asset. The risk profile for a critical asset comprises the threat profile for the critical asset and a narrative description of the resulting impact(s) to the organization. Because data on threat probability are limited for the scenarios, the risks are assumed to be equally likely.[10] Thus, the analysis team establishes priorities based on the qualitative impact values assigned to the scenarios. After the risk analysis has been completed, the goal is to reduce risk through a combination of these actions:

- Implementing new security practices within the organization
- Taking the actions necessary to maintain the existing security practices
- Fixing identified vulnerabilities

Process 7: Conduct Risk Analysis

The participants in this process are the analysis team members. The goal of the process is to create a risk profile. The following are the activities of Process 7:

- Identify the impact of threats to critical assets.
- Create risk evaluation criteria.
- Evaluate the impact of threats to critical assets.

Process 8: Develop Protection Strategy

Process 8 consists of two workshops. The goal of Process 8 is to develop a protection strategy for the organization, mitigation plans for the risks to the critical assets, and an action list of near-term actions. The participants in the first workshop for Process 8 are the analysis team members and selected members of the organization. The following are the activities of the first workshop of Process 8:

- Consolidate protection strategy information.
- Create protection strategy.
- Create mitigation plans.
- Create an action list.

In the second workshop of Process 8, the analysis team presents the proposed protection strategy, mitigation plans, and action list to senior managers in the organization. The Senior managers review and revise the strategy and plans as necessary and then decide how the organization will build on the results of the evaluation. The following are the activities of the second workshop of Process 8:

- Review risk information.
- Review and refine protection strategy, mitigation plans, and action list.
- Create next steps.

After the organization has developed the protection strategy and risk mitigation plans, it is ready to implement them. This completes the OCTAVE Method.

MICROSOFT RISK MANAGEMENT APPROACH

Microsoft has recently updated its Security Risk Management Guide, located at: www.microsoft.com/technet/security/topics/complianceandpolicies/secrisk/srsgch03.mspx. The guide provides the company's approach to the risk management process. Since this version is comprehensive, easily scalable, and repeatable, it is summarized here with permission.[11]

Microsoft asserts that risk management is not a stand-alone subject, and should be part of a general governance program to allow the organizational general management community of interest to evaluate the organization's operations and make better, more informed decisions. The purpose of the risk management process is to prioritize and manage security risks. Microsoft presents four phases in its security risk management process:

1. Assessing risk
2. Conducting decision support
3. Implementing controls
4. Measuring program effectiveness

These four phases provide an overview of a program that is similar to the methods presented earlier in the text, including the OCTAVE Method. Microsoft, however, breaks the phases into fewer, more manageable pieces.

Assessing Risk

The first phase of the Microsoft Security Risk Management program is the same first step taken in both the OCTAVE Method and in Chapter 7: Risk assessment—the identification and prioritization of the risks facing the organization.

1. Plan data gathering. Discuss keys to success and preparation guidance.
2. Gather risk data. Outline the data collection process and analysis.
3. Prioritize risks. Outline prescriptive steps to qualify and quantify risks.

Conducting Decision Support

The second step is simply the identification and evaluation of controls available to the organization. Approaches used to evaluate the controls could include both the qualitative and quantitative methods discussed earlier, including cost-benefit analyses, which Microsoft stresses.

1. Define functional requirements. Create the necessary requirements to mitigate risks.
2. Select possible control solutions. Outline approach to identify mitigation solutions.
3. Review solution. Evaluate proposed controls against functional requirements.
4. Estimate risk reduction. Endeavor to understand reduced exposure or probability of risks.
5. Estimate solution cost. Evaluate direct and indirect costs associated with mitigation solutions.
6. Select mitigation strategy. Complete cost-benefit analysis to identify the most cost-effective mitigation solution.

Implementing Controls

The next step involves the deployments and operation of the controls selected from the cost-benefit analyses and other mitigating factors from the previous step.

1. Seek holistic approach. Incorporate people, process, and technology in mitigation solution.
2. Organize by defense-in-depth. Arrange mitigation solutions across the business.

Measuring Program Effectiveness

The last and first step in the rest of the program is the ongoing assessment of the effectiveness of the risk management program. As controls are used, and as the organization and its environment change and evolve, the process must be closely monitored to ensure the controls continue to provide the desired level of protection.

1. Develop risk scorecard. Understand risk posture and progress.
2. Measure program effectiveness. Evaluate the risk management program for opportunities to improve.

These steps are illustrated in Figure 8-5.

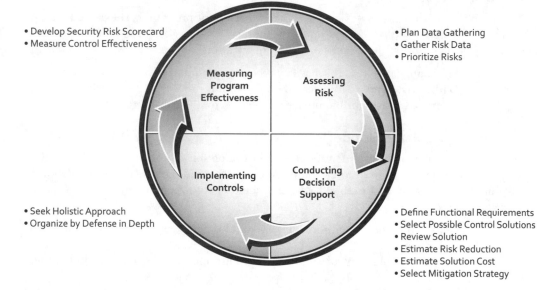

• Develop Security Risk Scorecard
• Measure Control Effectiveness

• Plan Data Gathering
• Gather Risk Data
• Prioritize Risks

Measuring Program Effectiveness

Assessing Risk

Implementing Controls

Conducting Decision Support

• Seek Holistic Approach
• Organize by Defense in Depth

• Define Functional Requirements
• Select Possible Control Solutions
• Review Solution
• Estimate Risk Reduction
• Estimate Solution Cost
• Select Mitigation Strategy

FIGURE 8-5   Security Risk Management Guide

Preliminary Tasks

Before beginning the risk management process, Microsoft suggests that the organization consider the level of effort involved, and the need to lay a good foundation As shown in Figure 8-6, while the amount of work involved in the early stages declines initially, as the organization enters the detailed risk analysis phase, the relative amount of work increases quickly, and could derail the program if the appropriate resources are not available.

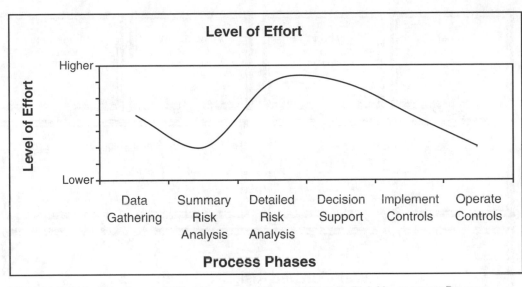

FIGURE 8-6   Relative Level of Effort During the Microsoft Security Risk Management Process

Laying a good foundation for risk management begins with ensuring everyone involved knows the difference between risk management and risk assessment. This subject is discussed in Chapter 7 and earlier in this chapter. A good foundation also involves clearly communicating what risk is and what it represents to the organization. Next comes determining the organization's "risk management maturity." Microsoft uses the concept of the "well-formed risk statement" in its work, and, as illustrated in Figure 8-7, this risk statement is based on both the probability and impact components of risk. While impact is based on the assets and threats facing those assets, probability in turn is based on vulnerabilities and any mitigation (e.g. controls) the organization currently employs. From this we can derive the Microsoft definition of risk as "the probability of a vulnerability being exploited in the current environment, leading to a degree of loss of confidentiality, integrity, or availability, of an asset."[12] Communicating the impact and probability of a risk can be accomplished using a complex metric; however a simple method of using high, moderate, or low, provides a more usable method. It is up to the organization's risk management team to define these.

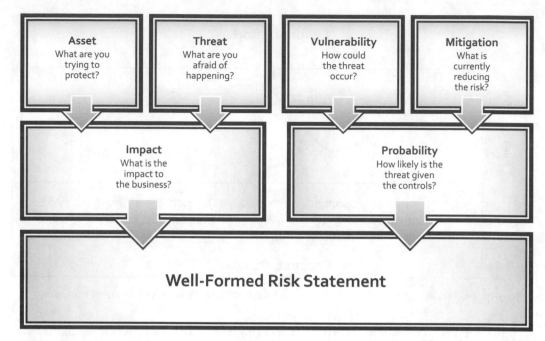

FIGURE 8-7 The Well-Formed Risk Statement

The organization's risk management maturity level describes the experience the organization has with risk management. If an organization previously implemented a different risk management process, this points to a general understanding of risk and risk management, as well as to the existence of policies and procedures. One method the organization can use to gauge its maturity is to refer to the COBIT method described in Chapter 6. COBIT includes an IT Governance Maturity Model method, which can be used here. The COBIT model includes six levels, as shown in Table 8-2.[13]

TABLE 8-2 COBIT IT Maturity Levels

Level 0	A lack of recognizable process, no recognition that there is even an issue to be addressed.
Level 1 "Ad-Hoc"	Evidence that the organization has recognized issues to be addressed. No standardized processes, ad-hoc approaches are applied on an individual or case-by-case basis.
Level 2 "Repeatable"	Awareness of issues. Performance indicators are being developed. Basic measurements have been identified, as have assessment methods and techniques.
Level 3 "Defined"	The need to act is understood and accepted. Procedures have been standardized, documented and implemented. Balanced scorecard ideas are being adopted by the organization.

TABLE 8-2 COBIT IT Maturity Levels (continued)

Level 4 "Managed"	Full understanding of issues on all levels. IT is fully aligned with the business strategy. Continuous improvement is addressed.
Level 5 "Optimized"	Continuous improvement, a forward-looking understanding of issues and solutions. Processes have been refined to a level of external best practice based on the results of continuous improvement and maturity modeling with other organizations.

Source: Weymeir, 2004.

To assess your organization's maturity, rate it on the issues presented in Table 8-3, which are based on ISO 17799. Scoring each response on a scale of 0 to 5 with the COBIT levels as a guide provides a maximum score of 85.

TABLE 8-3 Maturity Level Questions

Information security policies and procedures are clear, concise, well-documented, and complete.
All staff positions with job duties involving information security have clearly articulated and their roles and responsibilities are well understood.
Policies and procedures for securing third-party access to business data are well documented. For example, remote vendors performing application development for an internal business tool have sufficient access to network resources to collaborate and complete their work effectively, but they have only the minimum amount of access that they need.
An inventory of IT assets such as hardware, software, and data repositories is accurate and up to date.
Suitable controls are in place to protect business data from unauthorized access by both outsiders and insiders.
Effective user awareness programs, such as training and newsletters, regarding information security policies and practices are in place.
Physical access to the computer network and other information technology assets is restricted through the use of effective controls.
New computer systems are provisioned following organizational security standards in a consistent manner using automated tools such as disk imaging or build scripts.
An effective patch management system is able to deliver software updates automatically from most vendors to the vast majority of the computer systems in the organization.
An incident response team has been created and has developed and documented effective processes for dealing with and tracking security incidents. All incidents are investigated until the root cause is identified and any problems are resolved.
The organization has a comprehensive antivirus program, including multiple layers of defense, user awareness training, and effective processes for responding to virus outbreaks.
User-provisioning processes are well documented and at least partially automated so that new employees, vendors, and partners can be granted an appropriate level of access to the organization's information systems in a timely manner. These processes should also support the timely disabling and deletion of user accounts that are no longer needed.

TABLE 8-3 Maturity Level Questions (continued)

Computer and network access is controlled through user authentication and authorization, restrictive access control lists on data, and proactive monitoring for policy violations.
Application developers are provided with education and possess a clear awareness of security standards for software creation and quality assurance testing of code.
Business continuity and business continuity programs are clearly defined, well documented, and periodically tested through simulations and drills.
Programs have commenced and are effective for ensuring that all staff perform their work tasks in a manner compliant with legal requirements.
Third-party review and audits are used regularly to verify compliance with standard practices for security business assets.

Source: Microsoft, 2006.

According to Microsoft, a score of 51 or better means the organization is ready to implement the Microsoft process. If the organization scores 34–51, it should implement the process gradually, possibly as a pilot. Below that level, an organization should be very cautious in how it implements the risk management program, but it can still benefit from the process by implementing it in a small area over a short time. SP 800-26 can also be used to help the organization determine its maturity level by creating a subset of the questions provided over the same areas as the ISO example provided in Table 8-3.

Roles and Responsibilities

Microsoft's next step is the definition and assignment of the roles and responsibilities of individuals who will participate in the risk management process. The primary roles that are involved include many of the same players describe earlier, as shown in Table 8-4.

TABLE 8-4 Primary Roles and Responsibilities in the Microsoft Security Risk Management Process

Title	Primary Responsibility
Executive Sponsor	Sponsors all activities associated with managing risk to the business; for example, development, funding, authority, and support for the Security Risk Management Team. This role, which is usually filled by an executive such as the chief security officer or chief information officer, also serves as the last escalation point to define acceptable risk to the business.
Business Owner	Responsible for tangible and intangible assets to the business. Business owners are also accountable for prioritizing business assets and defining levels of impact to assets. Business owners are usually accountable for defining acceptable risk levels; however, the Executive Sponsor owns the final decision, which incorporates feedback from the Information Security Group.
Information Security Group	Owns the larger risk management process, including the Assessing Risk and Measuring Program Effectiveness phases. Also defines functional security requirements and measures IT controls and the overall effectiveness of the security risk management program.

TABLE 8-4 Primary Roles and Responsibilities in the Microsoft Security Risk Management Process (continued)

Title	Primary Responsibility
Information Technology Group	Includes IT architecture, engineering, and operations.
Security Risk Management Team	Responsible for driving the overall risk management program. Also responsible for the Assessing Risk phase and prioritizing risks to the business. At a minimum, the team is comprised of a facilitator and note taker.
Risk Assessment Facilitator	As lead role on the Security Risk Management Team, conducts the data-gathering discussions. This role may also lead the entire risk management process.
Risk Assessment Note Taker	Records detailed risk information during the data-gathering discussions.
Mitigation Owners	Responsible for implementing and sustaining control solutions to manage risk to an acceptable level. Includes the IT Group and, in some cases, Business Owners.
Security Steering Committee	Comprised of the Security Risk Management Team, representatives from the IT Group, and specific Business Owners. The Executive Sponsor usually chairs this committee. Responsible for selecting mitigation strategies and defining acceptable risk for the business.
Stakeholder	General term referring to direct and indirect participants in a given process or program; used throughout the Microsoft security risk management process. Stakeholders may also include groups outside IT, for example, finance, public relations, and human resources.

Source: Microsoft, 2006.

The first step is to ensure that everyone knows their roles and responsibilities in the risk management process. Even if some of these players were involved in previous efforts, the application of a different methodology requires a detailed discussion on what is expected.

To summarize, the Executive Sponsor is ultimately accountable for defining acceptable risk and provides guidance to the Security Risk Management Team in terms of ranking risks to the business. The Security Risk Management Team is responsible for assessing risk and defining functional requirements to mitigate risk to an acceptable level. The Security Risk Management Team then collaborates with the IT groups who own mitigation selection, implementation, and operations. The final relationship defined [in Figure 8-8] is the Security Risk Management Team's oversight of measuring control effectiveness. This usually occurs in the form of audit reports, which are also communicated to the Executive Sponsor.

Figure 8-8 illustrates the relationship between these individuals.

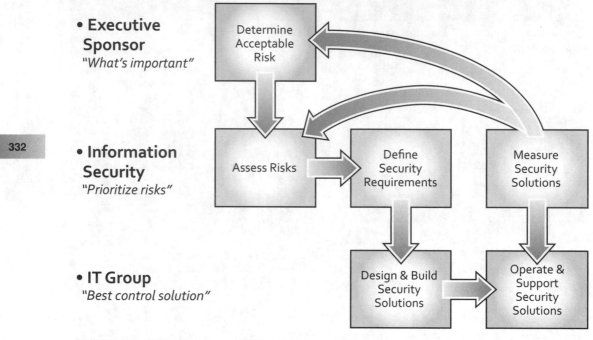

• Executive Sponsor
"What's important"

• Information Security
"Prioritize risks"

• IT Group
"Best control solution"

FIGURE 8-8 Risk Management Roles & Responsibilities

The Microsoft Risk Management process continues discussing the creation of the security risk management team, and the assignment of the various roles and responsibilities.

For additional information, refer to the complete document at www.microsoft.com/technet/security/topics/complianceandpolicies/secrisk/default.mspx.

Chapter Summary

- Once vulnerabilities are identified and ranked, a strategy to control the risks must be chosen. Four control strategies are avoidance, transference, mitigation, and acceptance.

- Economic feasibility studies determine and compare costs and benefits from potential controls (often called a cost-benefit analysis). Other forms of feasibility analysis include analyses based on organizational, operational, technical, and political factors.

- An organization must be able to place a dollar value on each collection of information and the information assets it owns. There are several methods an organization can use to calculate these values.

- Single loss expectancy (SLE) is calculated from the value of the asset and the expected percentage of loss that would occur from a single successful attack. Annualized loss expectancy (ALE) represents the potential loss per year.

- A specialized economic feasibility study known as a cost-benefit analysis (CBA) determines whether a control alternative is worth its associated cost. CBA calculations are based on costs before and after controls are implemented and the cost of the controls. Other feasibility analysis approaches can also be used.

- Organizations may choose alternatives to feasibility studies to justify applying information security controls, including: benchmarking with either metrics-based measures or process-based measures, due care and/or due diligence, best security practices up to and including the near-mythic gold standard, and/or baselining.

- Risk appetite defines the quantity and nature of risk that organizations are willing to accept, as they evaluate the trade-offs between perfect security and unlimited accessibility. Residual risk is the amount of risk unaccounted for after the application of controls.

- It is possible to repeat risk analysis using estimates based on a qualitative assessment. Delphi techniques can be used to obtain group consensus on risk assessment values.

- Once a control strategy has been implemented, the effectiveness of controls should be monitored and measured.

- The OCTAVE Method provides a methodology to risk management that represents an alternative to the approaches presented in Chapter 7 and this chapter.

- The Microsoft risk management approach offers another risk management methodology.

Review Questions

1. What is competitive advantage? How has it changed over the years since the IT industry began?
2. What is competitive disadvantage? Why has it emerged as a factor?
3. What are the four risk control strategies?
4. Describe the strategy of risk avoidance.
5. Describe the strategy of risk transference.
6. Describe the strategy of risk mitigation.

7. Describe the strategy of risk acceptance.

8. Describe residual risk.

9. What four types of controls or applications can be used to avoid risk?

10. Describe how outsourcing can be used for risk transference.

11. What conditions must be met to ensure that risk acceptance has been used properly?

12. What is risk appetite? Explain why risk appetite varies from organization to organization.

13. What is a cost-benefit analysis?

14. What is the difference between intrinsic value and acquired value?

15. What is single loss expectancy? What is annual loss expectancy?

16. What is the difference between benchmarking and baselining? What is the difference between due diligence and due care?

17. What is the difference between organizational feasibility and operational feasibility?

18. What is the difference between qualitative measurement and quantitative measurement?

19. What is the OCTAVE Method? What does it provide to those who adopt it?

20. How does Microsoft define risk management? What phases are used in its approach?

Exercises

1. Using the following table, calculate the SLE, ARO, and ALE for each threat category listed.

XYZ Software Company, Major Threat Categories for New Applications Development (Asset value: $1,200,000 in projected revenues)		
	Cost per Incident	Frequency of Occurrence
Programmer Mistakes	$5000	1 per week
Loss of Intellectual Property	$75,000	1 per year
Software Piracy	$500	1 per week
Theft of Information (Hacker)	$2500	1 per quarter
Theft of Information (Employee)	$5000	1 per 6 months
Web Defacement	$500	1 per month
Theft of Equipment	$5000	1 per year
Viruses, Worms, Trojan Horses	$1500	1 per week
Denial-of-Service Attack	$2500	1 per quarter
Earthquake	$250,000	1 per 20 years
Flood	$250,000	1 per 10 years
Fire	$500,000	1 per 10 years

2. How did the XYZ Software Company arrive at the values in the table in Exercise 1? For each entry, describe the process of determining the cost per incident and the frequency of occurrence.

3. How do the values in the table in Exercise 1 differ from the calculations presented in the text? How can we determine SLE if there is no percentage given? Which method is easier for determining the SLE: a percentage of value lost or cost per incident?

4. Assume a year has passed and XYZ has improved its security. Using the following table, calculate the SLE, ARO, and ALE for each threat category listed.

335

XYZ Software Company, Major Threat Categories for New Applications Development (Asset value: $1,200,000 in projected revenues)				
	Cost per Incident	Frequency of Occurrence	Cost of Controls	Type of Control
Programmer Mistakes	$5000	1 per month	$20,000	Training
Loss of Intellectual Property	$75,000	1 per 2 years	$15,000	Firewall/IDS
Software Piracy	$500	1 per month	$30,000	Firewall/IDS
Theft of Information (Hacker)	$2500	1 per 6 months	$15,000	Firewall/IDS
Theft of Information (Employee)	$5000	1 per year	$15,000	Physical Security
Web Defacement	$500	1 per quarter	$10,000	Firewall
Theft of Equipment	$5000	1 per 2 year	$15,000	Physical Security
Viruses, Worms, Trojan Horses	$1500	1 per month	$15,000	Antivirus
Denial-of-Service Attack	$2500	1 per 6 months	$10,000	Firewall
Earthquake	$250,000	1 per 20 years	$5000	Insurance/ Backups
Flood	$50,000	1 per 10 years	$10,000	Insurance/ Backups
Fire	$100,000	1 per 10 years	$10,000	Insurance/ Backups

Why have some values changed in the following columns: Cost per Incident and Frequency of Occurrence? How could a control affect one but not the other?

5. Assume the costs of controls presented in the table for Exercise 4 were unique costs directly associated with protecting against that threat. In other words, do not worry about overlapping costs between threats. Calculate the CBA for each control. Are they worth the costs listed?

Risk Management: Controlling Risk

6. Using the Web, research the costs associated with the following items:
   - Managed antivirus software licenses for 500 workstations
   - FW-1 firewall
   - Tripwire host–based IDS for 10 servers
   - Java programming continuing education training program for 10 employees
   - Checkpoint Firewall solutions

Case Exercises

Mike and Iris were reviewing the asset valuation worksheets that had been collected from all of the company managers. After a few minutes of review, Mike said, "Iris, the problem as I see it is that no two managers used the same criteria to assess the asset values or rank the priority of their asset lists."

Iris nodded and said, "I agree. Some of the worksheets have only one of the four asset valuations filled in. This is going to be very difficult to merge into a single, uniform list of information assets. We're going to have to visit each manager and figure out what basis was used and how the assets were ranked."

1. If you could have spoken to Mike Edwards before he distributed the asset valuation worksheets, what advice would you have given him to make the consolidation process easier?

2. How would you advise Mike and Iris to proceed with the worksheets they already have in hand?

Endnotes

[1] Thomas J. Peters and Robert H. Waterman. *In Search of Excellence: Lessons from America's Best-Run Companies.* New York: Harper and Row, 1982.

[2] Gamma Secure Systems. First measure your risk. *Gamma Online*, January 2, 2002. Accessed June 19, 2002. www.gammassl.co.uk/inforisk/.

[3] National Institute of Standards and Technology. *Risk Management Guide for Information Technology Systems.* SP 800-30. January 2002.

[4] Peter Gourlay. Playing it safe. *U.S. Business Review Online*, December 2001. Accessed June 19, 2002. www.usbusiness-review.com/0112/02.html.

[5] Frederick M. Avolio. Best practices in network security. *Network Computing*, March 20, 2000, 60–66.

[6] Thomas Mann. Politics is often defined as the art of the possible. Speech in the Library of Congress, Washington, DC, May 29, 1945.

[7] Christopher J. Alberts, Sandra G. Behrens, Richard D. Pethia, and William R. Wilson. *Operationally Critical Threat, Asset, and Vulnerability Evaluation (OCTAVE) Framework, Version 1.0* (CMU/SEI-99-TR-017, ADA 367718). Pittsburgh, PA: Software Engineering Institute, Carnegie Mellon University, June 1999.

[8] U.S. General Accounting Office. *Executive Guide: Information Security Management* (GAO/AIMD-98-68). Washington, DC: GAO, May 1998.

[9] M. S. Merkow and J. Breithaupt. *The Complete Guide to Internet Security.* New York: AMACOM, American Management Association, 2000: 95–109.

[10] Kees Van der Heijden. *Scenarios: The Art of Strategic Conversation.* Chichester, UK: John Wiley & Sons, 1997.

[11] Microsoft Security Risk Management Guide. March 15, 2006. Accessed August 15, 2006. www.microsoft.com/technet/security/topics/complianceandpolicies/secrisk/srsgch03.mspx.

[12] Microsoft, Security Risk Management Guide: Chapter 3: Security Risk Management Overview. March 15, 2006. Accessed August 15, 2006. www.microsoft.com/technet/security/topics/complianceandpolicies/secrisk/srsgch03.mspx.

[13] M. J. Weymeir. Part 4 Project Performance—Get on the path to continuous improvement. May 26, 2004. Accessed August 20, 2006. wistechnology.com/article.php?id=859.

[14] Special permission to reproduce "OCTAVE™ Method Implemention Guide: Appendix D," © 2001 by Carnegie Mellon University, is granted by the Software Engineering Institute.

PROTECTION MECHANISMS

One night toward the end of his shift, a technician at RWW, Inc., received a call from his wife. One of their children was ill, and she wanted the technician to pick up some medicine on his way home from work. He decided to leave a few minutes early.

Like all watch-standing employees in the operations center, he had a procedures manual, which was organized sequentially. He used the checklists for everyday purposes, and had an index to look up anything else he needed. Only one unchecked box remained on the checklist when he snapped the binder closed and hurriedly secured his workstation.

Since he was the second-shift operator and RWW did not have a third shift in its data center, the technician carefully reviewed the shutdown checklist next to the door, making sure all the room's environmental, safety, and security systems were set correctly. He activated the burglar alarm, exited the room and the building, and was soon on his way to the drugstore.

At about the same time, a 10th-grader in San Diego was up late, sitting at her computer. Her parents assumed that she was listening to music while "chatting" with school friends online. In fact, she had become bored with chatting and had discovered some new friends on the Internet—friends who shared her interest in programming and Perl script writing. One of these new friends had sent the girl a link to a new warez (illegally copied software) site.

From this site the teenager downloaded a kit called Blendo, which helps hackers create attack programs that combine a mass e-mailer with a worm, a macro virus, and a network scanner. She clicked her way through the configuration options, clicked a button labeled "custom scripts," and then pasted in a script that one of her new friends had e-mailed to her. This script was built to exploit a brand-new vulnerability (announced only a few hours before). Although she didn't know it, the anonymous high-schooler had created new malware that was soon to bring the Internet to a standstill. She exported the attack script, attached it to an e-mail, and sent it out to an anonymous remailer service to be forwarded to as many e-mail accounts as possible. She had naively set up a mailback option to an anonymous e-mail account so she could track the progress of her creation. Thirty minutes later she checked that anonymous e-mail account and saw that she had more than 8000 new messages, and her mailbox was full.

Back at RWW, the e-mail gateway was sorting and forwarding all of the incoming e-mail. The account sales@rww.biz always received a lot of traffic, as did service@rww.biz. Tonight was no exception. Unfortunately for RWW, and for the second-shift operator who had failed to install the patch download that fixed the new vulnerability announced by the vendor, the young hacker's attack code tricked the RWW mail server into running the program. The RWW mail server, with its high-performance server and high-bandwidth Internet connection, began to do three things at once: It sent an infected e-mail to everyone with whom RWW had ever traded e-mail; it infected every RWW server that the e-mail server could reach; and it started deleting files, randomly, from every folder on each infected server.

Within seconds, the network intrusion detection system had determined that something was afoot. By then, it was too late to stop the infection, but, just before it sputtered into silence, the system sent a message to Iris's PDA.

LEARNING OBJECTIVES

Upon completion of this material, you should be able to:

- Describe the various access control approaches, including authentication, authorization, and biometric access controls
- Identify the various types of firewalls and the common approaches to firewall implementation
- Recognize the current issues in dial-up access and protection
- Identify and describe the types of intrusion detection systems and the two strategies on which they are based
- Explain cryptography and the encryption process, and compare and contrast symmetric and asymmetric encryption

INTRODUCTION

Information security is a discipline that combines the efforts of people, policy, education, training, awareness, procedures, and technology to improve the confidentiality, integrity, and availability of an organization's information assets. Technical controls alone cannot secure an IT environment, but they are usually an essential part of information security programs. Managing the development and use of technical controls requires some knowledge and familiarity with the technology that enables them. Technical controls, when properly managed, enhance the confidentiality, integrity, and availability of information in each of its three states (storage, transit, and processing). In this chapter, you will learn about firewalls, intrusion detection systems, encryption-based systems, and some other widely used security technologies. The chapter is designed to help you evaluate and manage the technical controls for use in information security programs. If you are seeking expertise in the configuration and maintenance of technical control systems, you will need additional education and training beyond the overview presented here.

Technical controls can enable policy enforcement where human behavior is difficult to regulate. A password policy that specifies composition requirements (for example, mixed case) and periodic password changes, and that prohibits the reuse of passwords, is difficult to enforce on an employee-by-employee basis, but can usually be enforced by the implementation of common operating system software controls.

Figure 9-1 illustrates how technical controls can be implemented at a number of points in the technical infrastructure. The technical controls that defend against threats from outside the organization are shown on the left side of the diagram. The controls that defend against threats from within the organization are shown on the right side of the diagram. Because individuals inside an organization often have direct access to the information, they can circumvent many of the most potent technical controls. Controls that can be applied to this human element are also shown on the right side of the diagram.

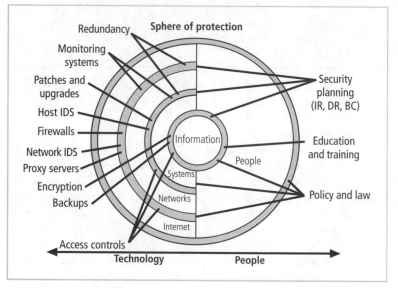

Sphere of protection

Redundancy
Monitoring systems
Patches and upgrades
Host IDS
Firewalls
Network IDS
Proxy servers
Encryption
Backups

Security planning (IR, DR, BC)
Education and training
Policy and law

Information
People
Systems
Networks
Internet

Access controls

Technology   People

FIGURE 9-1   Sphere of Security

ACCESS CONTROLS

Access control encompasses four processes: obtaining the identity of the entity request-ing access to a logical or physical area (**identification**), confirming the identity of the entity seeking access to a logical or physical area (**authentication**), determining which actions that entity can perform in that physical or logical area (**authorization**), and finally docu-menting the activities of the authorized individual and systems (**accountability**). A suc-cessful access control approach—whether intended to control physical access or logical access—always incorporates all four of these elements.

Identification

Identification is a mechanism that provides information about an unverified entity—called a **supplicant**—that wants to be granted access to a known entity. The label applied to the supplicant is called an identifier (ID). The identifier must be a unique value that can be mapped to one and only one entity within the security domain being administered. Some organizations use composite identifiers, concatenating elements—department codes, ran-dom numbers, or special characters—to make unique identifiers within the security domain. Most organizations use a single piece of unique information, such as name, or first initial and surname.

Authentication

Authentication is the process of validating a supplicant's purported identity. It ensures that the entity requesting access is the entity claimed. There are four types of authentication mechanisms:

- Something you *know* (for example, passwords and passphrases)

- Something you *have* (such as cryptographic tokens and smart cards)
- Something you *are* (this includes fingerprints, palm prints, hand topography, hand geometry, and retina and iris scans)
- Something you *produce* (such as voice and signature pattern recognition)

Certain critical logical or physical areas require higher levels of access controls and, therefore, use **strong authentication**—at minimum two different authentication mechanisms (usually something you have and something you know). For example, access to a bank's ATM requires a banking card plus a personal identification number (PIN). Such systems are called two-factor authentication, because two separate mechanisms are used. Strong authentication requires that one of the mechanisms be something other than what you know.

The following sections describe each of the four authentication mechanisms.

Something You Know

This authentication mechanism verifies the user's identity by means of a password, passphrase, or other unique authentication code, such as a PIN.

The technical infrastructure for something you know is built into commonly used computer and network operating systems software, and is in use unless it has been deliberately disabled. In some older client operating systems, such as Windows 95 and Windows 98, password systems are widely known to be insecure. Implementing other authentication mechanisms often requires separate supplemental physical devices. Some product vendors offer these hardware controls as built-in features; for example, some laptop vendors include thumbprint readers on certain models.

A **password** is a private word or combination of characters that only the user should know. One of the biggest debates in security focuses on the complexity of passwords. A password should be difficult to guess, which means it cannot be a word that is easily associated with the user, such as the name of a spouse, child, or pet. Nor should it be a series of numbers easily associated with the user, such as a phone number, Social Security number, or birth date. At the same time, the password must be something the user can easily remember, which means it should be short or have an association the user can remember but that is not accessible to others.

A **passphrase** is a plain-language phrase, typically longer than a password, from which a **virtual password** is derived. For example, while a typical password might be 23skedoo, a passphrase could be *May The Force Be With You Always*, from which the virtual password *MTFBWYA* is derived. Another way to create a virtual password is to use a set of construction rules applied to facts you know very well, such as the first three letters of your last name, a hyphen, the first two letters of your first name, an underscore, the first two letters of your mother's maiden name, a hyphen, and the first four letters of the city in which you were born. This may sound complicated, but once memorized, the construction rules are easy to use. If you add another rule to substitute numeric digits for certain letters—1 for L, 0 for O, and 3 for E, and capitalize the first letter of each section, then you have a very powerful virtual password that you can easily reconstruct. Using the preceding rules would create a virtual password for Charlie Moody (born in Atlanta, mother's maiden name Meredith) of *M00-Cha_M3-Atlu*, a very strong password.

Another method for creating strong passwords is to use a password memory support device such as the PassWheel from Surelock Security Products. The PassWheel, as shown in Figure 9-2, allows the user to create a complex password by using the multialphabet dials. You simply use a reference word (e.g., MIKE), align the four wheels to spell that word, move the marker a predetermined number of letters to the left or right of the reference word, and then read 4–12 letters on the other side. Using the PassWheel, you can change common letters to numbers and mix capitalization. The result is a complex, powerful password that cannot be easily broken, even if someone found the PassWheel device (as long as you scramble it after use).

Source: Surelock Security Products Pty Ltd

FIGURE 9-2   PassWheel Password Generator

How important is it to have a long, not obvious password? As shown in Table 9-1, the longer the password, the lower the odds of it being guessed in a brute-force attack using random bit combinations (you will learn more about such attacks later in this chapter). A good rule of thumb is to require that passwords be at least eight characters long and contain at least one number and one special character.

TABLE 9-1 Password Power

Case-Insensitive Passwords		
Number of Characters	Odds of Cracking: 1 in	Estimated Time to Crack*
1	68	0.000009 second
2	4624	0.0006 second
3	314,432	0.04 second
4	21,381,376	2.7 seconds
5	1,453,933,568	3 minutes, 2 seconds
6	98,867,482,624	3 hours, 26 minutes
7	6,722,988,818,432	9 days, 17 hours, 26 minutes
8	457,163,239,653,376	1 year, 10 months, 1 day
9	31,087,100,296,429,600	124 years, 11 months, 5 days
10	2,113,922,820,157,210,000	8495 years, 4 months, 17 days
Case-Sensitive Passwords		
Number of Characters	Odds of Cracking: 1 in	Estimated Time to Crack*
1	94	0.00001 second
2	8836	0.011 second
3	830,584	0.1 second
4	78,074,896	9.8 seconds
5	7,339,040,224	15 minutes, 17 seconds
6	689,869,781,056	23 hours, 57 minutes, 14 seconds
7	64,847,759,419,264	3 months, 3 days, 19 hours
8	6,095,689,385,410,820	24 years, 6 months
9	572,994,802,228,617,000	2302 years, 8 months, 9 days
10	53,861,511,409,490,000,000	216,457 years, 4 months

*Estimated Time to Crack is based on a Pentium 4 computer performing 8 million guesses per second. The estimates take into consideration all keyboard characters, some of which are not allowed by some systems.

Something You Have

This authentication mechanism makes use of something (a card, key, or token) that the user or the system has. While there are many implementations of this mechanism, one example is a **dumb card**, a category that includes ID and ATM cards with magnetic strips containing the digital (and often encrypted) PIN against which user input is compared. A more capable object is the **smart card**, which contains a computer chip that can verify and validate other information in addition to PINs. Another often-used device is the crypto-graphic token, a computer chip in a card that has a display. This device contains a built-in seed number that uses a formula or a clock to calculate a number that can be used to perform a remote login authentication. Tokens may be either synchronous or asynchronous. Once **synchronous tokens** are synchronized with a server, each device (server and token) uses the time to generate the authentication number that is entered during the user login. **Asynchronous tokens** use a challenge-response system in which the server challenges the user with a number. That is, the user enters the challenge number into the token, which in turn calculates a response number. The user then enters the response number into the system to gain access. Only a person who has the correct token can calculate the correct response number and thus log into the system. This system does not require synchronization and does not suffer from mistiming issues. Figure 9-3 shows two examples of access control tokens.

Source: RSA Security

FIGURE 9-3 Access Control Tokens

Something You Are

This authentication mechanism takes advantage of something inherent in the user that is evaluated using biometrics, which you will learn more about later in this chapter. Biometric authentication methods include the following:

- Fingerprints
- ID cards (face representation)
- Palm scan
- Facial recognition
- Hand geometry
- Retina scan
- Hand topology
- Iris scan

Most of the technologies that scan human characteristics convert these images to obtain some form of **minutiae**; that is, unique points of reference that are digitized and stored. Some technologies encrypt the minutiae to make them more resistant to tampering. Each subsequent scan is also digitized and then compared with the encoded value to determine whether users are who they claim to be. One limitation of this technique is that some human characteristics can change over time, due to normal development, injury, or illness. Among the human characteristics currently employed for authentication purposes, only three are considered truly unique:

- Fingerprints
- Retina (blood vessel pattern)
- Iris (random pattern of features found in the iris, including freckles, pits, striations, vasculature, and coronas)

DNA or genetic authentication would be included in this category if it ever becomes a cost-effective and socially accepted technology.

Something You Produce

This type of authentication makes use of something the user performs or produces; for example, a signature or voice pattern. (In some authentication methodologies, this type of authentication is placed within the "something you are" category, since it is sometimes difficult to differentiate biometric output from the biometric feature.) Signature recognition is commonplace. Many retail stores use signature recognition, or at least signature capture, for authentication during a purchase. Customers sign a special pad, using a stylus; the signatures are then digitized and either compared to a database for validation or simply saved. Signature capture is much more widely accepted than signature comparison, because signatures can vary due to a number of factors, including age, fatigue, and the speed with which they are written.

Voice recognition for authentication captures the analog waveforms of human speech, and compares these waveforms to a stored version. Voice recognition systems provide the user with a phrase that they must read; for example, "My voice is my password, please verify me. Thank you."

Another pattern-based approach is keystroke pattern recognition. This authentication method relies on the timing between key signals when a user types in a known sequence of keystrokes. When measured with sufficient precision, this pattern can provide a unique identification.

Figure 9-4 depicts some of these biometric and other human recognition characteristics.

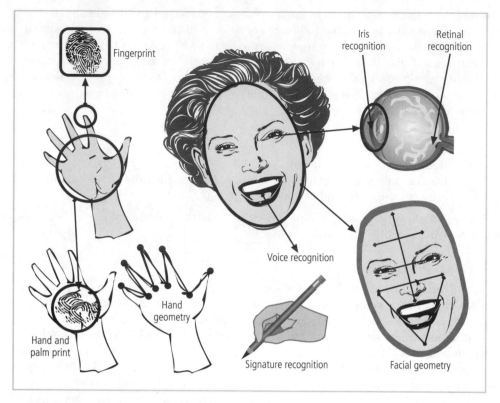

FIGURE 9-4 Recognition Characteristics

Authorization

The authorization process begins with an authenticated entity—a person, or a virtual identity such as another computer program. In general, authorization can be handled in one of three ways:

- Authorization for each authenticated user, in which the system performs an authentication process to verify each entity and then grants access to resources for only that entity. This quickly becomes a complex and resource-intensive process in a computer system environment.
- Authorization for members of a group, in which the system matches authenticated entities to a list of group memberships, and then grants access to resources based on the group's access rights. This is the most common authorization method.
- Authorization across multiple systems, in which a central authentication and authorization system verifies entity identity and grants a set of credentials to the verified entity. These credentials (sometimes called an **authorization ticket**) are honored by all systems within the authentication domain. Sometimes called single sign-on (SSO) or reduced sign-on, this approach is becoming more common and is frequently enabled using a shared directory structure such as the Lightweight Directory Access protocol (LDAP).

Accountability

Accountability assures that all actions on a system can be attributed to an authenticated identity. These actions could be ones that the entity is authorized for, such as looking up or modifying certain data, or might include unauthorized attempts to escalate privileges, or to look at or modify data that is beyond its access level. Accountability is most often accomplished by implementing system logs and database journals, and the auditing of these records. **Systems logs** are records maintained by a particular system that has been configured to record specific information, such as failed access attempts and systems modifications. Logs have many uses, such as intrusion detection, determining the root cause of a system failure, or simply tracking the use of a particular resource. Table 9-2 lists some of the items that logs can track.

TABLE 9-2 Log Data Category and Types of Data

Category	Types of Data
Network performance	• Total traffic load in and out over time (packet, byte, and connection counts) and by event (new product or service release) • Traffic load (percentage of packets, bytes, connections) in and out over time sorted by protocol, source address, destination address, other packet header data • Error counts on all network interfaces
Other network data	• Service initiation requests • Name of the user/host requesting the service • Network traffic (packet headers) • Successful connections and connection attempts (protocol, port, source, destination, time) • Connection duration • Connection flow (sequence of packets from initiation to termination) • States associated with network interfaces (up, down) • Network sockets currently open • Mode of network interface card (promiscuous or not) • Network probes and scans • Results of administrator probes
System performance	• Total resource use over time (CPU, memory [used, free], disk [used, free]) • Status and errors reported by systems and hardware devices • Changes in system status, including shutdowns and restarts • File system status (where mounted, free space by partition, open files, biggest file) over time and at specific times • File system warnings (low free space, too many open files, file exceeding allocated size) • Disk counters (input/output, queue lengths) over time and at specific times • Hardware availability (modems, network interface cards, memory)
Other system data	• Actions requiring special privileges • Successful and failed logins • Modem activities • Presence of new services and devices • Configuration of resources and devices

TABLE 9-2 Log Data Category and Types of Data (continued)

Process performance	• Amount of resources used (CPU, memory, disk, time) by specific processes over time; top resource-consuming processes • System and user processes and services executing at any given time
Other process data	• User executing the process • Process start-up time, arguments, filenames • Process exit status, time, duration, resources consumed • Means by which each process is normally initiated (administrator, other users, other programs or processes) with what authorization and privileges • Devices used by specific processes • Files currently open by specific processes
Files and directories	• List of files, directories, attributes • Cryptographic checksums for all files and directories • Accesses (open, create, modify, execute, delete), time, date • Changes to sizes, contents, protections, types, locations • Changes to access control lists on system tools • Additions and deletions of files and directories • Results of virus scanners
Users	• Login/logout information (location, time): successful attempts, failed attempts, attempted logins to privileged accounts • Login/logout information on remote access servers that appears in modem logs • Changes in user identity • Changes in authentication status (such as enabling privileges) • Failed attempts to access restricted information (such as password files) • Keystroke monitoring logs • Violations of user quotas
Applications and services	• Application information (such as network traffic [packet content], mail logs, FTP logs, Web server logs, modem logs, firewall logs, SNMP logs, DNS logs, intrusion detection system logs, database management system logs) • FTP file transfers and connection statistics • Web connection statistics, including pages accessed, credentials of the requestor, user requests over time, most requested pages, and identities of requestors • Mail sender, receiver, size, and tracing information for mail requests • Mail server statistics, including number of messages over time and number of queued messages • DNS questions, answers, and zone transfers • File server transfers over time • Database server transactions over time

Some systems are configured to record a common set of data by default; other systems must be configured to be activated. To protect the log data, you must ensure that the servers that create and store the logs are secure. Also, you must actively manage log recording systems as follows:

- Make sure that data stores can handle the amount of data generated by the configured logging activities. Some systems may generate multiple gigabytes of data for each hour of operation.
- Rotate logs when unlimited data storage is not possible. Some systems overwrite older log entries with newer entries to accommodate space limitations. Log rotation settings must be configured for your system, which may require modifying the default settings.
- Archive logs. Log systems can copy logs periodically to remote storage locations. Security administrators disagree about how long log files should be retained. Some argue that log files may be subpoenaed during legal proceedings and thus should be routinely destroyed to prevent unwanted disclosure. Others argue that the information gained from analyzing legacy and archival logs outweighs the risk. Still others aggregate the log information, then destroy the individual entries. Regardless of the method employed, some plan must be in place to handle these files or risk loss.
- Secure logs. Archives logs should be encrypted when stored to prevent unwanted disclosure if the log data store is compromised.
- Destroy logs. Once log data has outlived its usefulness, it should be securely destroyed.[1]

The process of reviewing the information collected in logs to detect misuse or attempted intrusion is part of a larger process called auditing. Logs are of no value to an organization if their contents are not reviewed periodically and included as part of the records trail used for auditing. Auditing can combine automated and manual mechanisms and can be done internally in an organization or part of an external review that may or may not include financial auditing procedures.

Evaluating Biometrics

Two of the four authentication mechanisms (something you are and something you produce) are **biometric**, which literally means life measurement. Biometric technologies are generally evaluated according to three basic criteria:

- False reject rate: the percentage of authorized users who are denied access
- False accept rate: the percentage of unauthorized users who are allowed access
- Crossover error rate: the point at which the number of false rejections equals the false acceptances

False Reject Rate

The **false reject rate** is the rate at which authentic users are denied or prevented access to authorized areas, as a result of a failure in the biometric device. This failure is also known as a Type I error or a false negative. Rejection of an authorized individual represents not a threat to security but an impedance to legitimate use. Consequently, it is often not seen as a serious problem until the rate increases is high enough to irritate users.

False Accept Rate

The **false accept rate** is the rate at which fraudulent users or nonusers are allowed access to systems or areas, as a result of a failure in the biometric device. This failure, known as a Type II error or a false positive, represents a serious security breach. Often, multiple authentication measures must be used to back up a device whose failure would otherwise result in erroneous authorization.

Crossover Error Rate

The **crossover error rate (CER)**, also called the equal error rate, is the point at which the rate of false rejections equals the rate of false acceptances. It is the optimal outcome for biometrics-based systems. CERs are used to compare various biometrics and may vary by manufacturer. A biometric device that provides a CER of 1% is considered to be superior to one with a CER of 5%, for example.

Acceptability of Biometrics

A balance must be struck between the acceptability of a system to its users and the effectiveness of the same system. Many of the reliable, effective biometric systems are perceived as being somewhat intrusive by users. Organizations implementing biometrics must carefully balance a system's effectiveness against its perceived intrusiveness and acceptability to users. The rated effectiveness of a system is roughly inverse to its acceptability, as shown in Table 9-3.

TABLE 9-3   Orders of Effectiveness and Acceptance

Effectiveness of Biometric Authentication Systems Ranking from Most Secure to Least Secure	Acceptance of Biometric Authentication Systems Ranking from Most Accepted to Least Accepted
• Retina pattern recognition	• Keystroke pattern recognition
• Fingerprint recognition	• Signature recognition
• Handprint recognition	• Voice pattern recognition
• Voice pattern recognition	• Handprint recognition
• Keystroke pattern recognition	• Fingerprint recognition
• Signature recognition	• Retina pattern recognition

Source: Harold F. Tipton and Micki Krause. *Handbook of Information Security Management.* Boca Raton, FL: CRC Press, 1998: 39–41.

Managing Access Controls

To appropriately manage access controls, an organization must have in place a formal **access control policy**, which determines how access rights are granted to entities and groups. This policy must include provisions for periodically reviewing all access rights, granting access rights to new employees, changing access rights when job roles change, and revoking access rights as appropriate. Without an access control policy, systems administrators may implement access controls in a way that is inconsistent with the organization's overall philosophy. Once a policy is in place, implementing access controls becomes a technical issue.

FIREWALLS

A physical firewall in a building is a concrete or masonry wall running from the basement through the roof to prevent fire from spreading. In the aircraft and automotive industries, a firewall is an insulated metal barrier that keeps the hot and dangerous moving parts of the motor separate from the interior where the passengers sit. In information security, a **firewall** is any device that prevents a specific type of information from moving between the outside world, known as the **untrusted network** (e.g., the Internet), and the inside world, known as the **trusted network**. The firewall may be a separate computer system, a service running on an existing router or server, or a separate network containing a number of supporting devices.

The Development of Firewalls

Firewalls have made significant advances since their earliest implementations. The first generation of firewalls, **packet filtering firewalls**, are simple networking devices that filter packets by examining every incoming and outgoing packet header. They can selectively filter packets based on values in the packet header, accepting or rejecting packets as needed. These devices can be configured to filter based on IP address, type of packet, port request, and/or other elements present in the packet. The filtering process examines packets for compliance with or violation of rules configured into the firewall's database. The rules most commonly implemented in packet filtering firewalls are based on a combination of IP source and destination address, direction (inbound or outbound), and/or source and destination port requests. Figure 9-5 shows how such a firewall typically works.

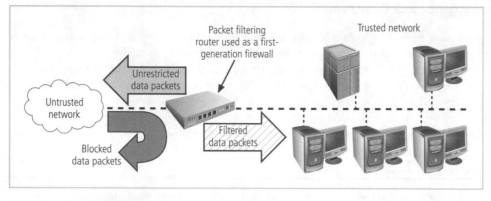

FIGURE 9-5   Packet Filtering Firewall

The ability to restrict a specific service is now considered standard in most modern routers, and is invisible to the user. Unfortunately, these systems are unable to detect whether packet headers have been modified, as occurs in IP spoofing attacks.

Early firewall models examined one aspect of the packet header: the destination address and the source address. For example, consider the rules listed in Table 9-4.

TABLE 9-4   Packet Filtering Example Rules

Source Address	Destination Address	Service Port	Action
10.10.x.x	172.16.126.x	Any	Deny
192.168.x.x	10.10.x.x	Any	Deny
172.16.121.1	10.10.10.22	FTP	Allow
10.10.x.x	x.x.x.x	HTTP	Allow
x.x.x.x	10.10.10.25	HTTP	Allow
x.x.x.x	10.10.10.x	Any	Deny

Notes: These rules apply to a network at 10.10.x.x.

This table uses special, nonroutable IP addresses in the rules for this example. In reality, a firewall that connects to a public network will use real address ranges.

With the rules shown in Table 9-4, attempts to make a connection from any computers or network devices in the 10.10.x.x address range is blocked from all services offered at the network with the address 172.16.126.x. This first rule might be used to block objectionable content found at that particular address, for example. At the same time, the fourth rule allows all other 10.10 addresses to access any HTTP services at any other address. The second rule blocks any devices in the 192.168 network from any access to the 10.10 network, effectively blacklisting that external network from connecting to this network. The third rule allows a specific computer found at 172.16.121.1 to access a certain FTP server found at 10.10.10.22. The fourth rule allows all internal users to browse the entire Internet, unless blocked by an earlier rule, and the fifth rule allows any outside user to access the Web server at 10.10.10.25 unless otherwise blocked by an earlier rule. The final rule enforces an exclusionary policy that blocks all access not specifically allowed.

The second generation of firewalls, known as **application-level firewalls**, often consists of dedicated computers kept separate from the first filtering router (called an edge router); they are commonly used in conjunction with a second or internal filtering router. This second router is often called a **proxy server**, because it serves as a proxy for external service requests to internal services.

With this configuration, the proxy server, rather than the Web server, is exposed to the outside world from within a network segment called the **demilitarized zone (DMZ)**. The DMZ is an intermediate area between a trusted network and an untrusted network (see Figure 9-8 later in this chapter). Using this model, additional filtering routers are placed between the proxy server and internal systems, thereby restricting access to internal systems to the proxy server alone. If these servers store the most recently accessed pages in their internal caches, they may also be called **cache servers**.

Suppose an external user wanted to view a Web page from an organization's Web server. Rather than expose the Web server to direct traffic from the users and potential attackers, the organization can install a proxy server, configured with the registered domain's URL. This proxy server receives Web page requests, accesses the Web server on behalf of external clients, and then returns the requested pages to users.

The primary disadvantage of application-level firewalls is that they are designed for a specific protocol, and cannot easily be reconfigured to work with other protocols.

The third generation of firewalls, **stateful inspection firewalls**, keeps track of each network connection established between internal and external systems using a **state table**. State tables track the state and context of each exchanged packet by recording which station sent which packet and when. Like first-generation firewalls, stateful inspection firewalls perform packet filtering, but where simple packet filtering firewalls merely allow or deny certain packets based on their addresses, a stateful inspection firewall can restrict incoming packets by restricting access to packets that constitute responses to internal requests. If the stateful inspection firewall receives an incoming packet that it cannot match in its state table, then it defaults to its ACL to determine whether to allow the packet to pass.

The primary disadvantage of this type of firewall is the additional processing requirements of managing and verifying packets against the state table, which can expose the system to a DoS attack. In such an attack, the firewall is subjected to a large number of external packets, slowing it down as it attempts to compare all of the incoming packets first to the state table and then to the ACL. On the positive side, these firewalls can track connectionless packet traffic such as User Datagram Protocol (UDP) and remote procedure call (RPC) traffic.

Whereas static filtering firewalls, such as those in the first and third generations, allow entire sets of one type of packet to enter in response to authorized requests, a fourth-generation firewall, called a **dynamic packet filtering firewall**, allows only a particular packet with a specific source, destination, and port address to pass through the firewall. It does so by understanding how the protocol functions, and by opening and closing "doors" in the firewall based on the information contained in the packet header.[2] Dynamic packet filters are an intermediate form between traditional static packet filters and application proxies.

Firewall Architectures

Each of the firewall generations can be implemented in a number of architectural configurations. These configurations are sometimes mutually exclusive but sometimes can be combined. The configuration that works best for a particular organization depends on the uses of its network, the organization's ability to develop and implement the architectures, and the available budget. Although literally hundreds of variations exist, four architectural implementations of firewalls are especially common: packet filtering routers, screened-host firewalls, dual-homed host firewalls, and screened-subnet firewalls.

Packet Filtering Routers

Most organizations with an Internet connection use some form of router between their internal networks and the external service provider. Many of these routers can be configured to block packets that the organization does not allow into the network. This is a simple but effective means of lowering the organization's risk of external attack. Such an architecture lacks auditing and strong authentication, and the complexity of the access control lists used to filter the packets can grow and degrade network performance. Figure 9-5 shows an example of this type of architecture.

Screened-Host Firewall Systems

Screened-host firewall systems combine the packet filtering router with a separate, dedicated firewall such as an application proxy server. This approach allows the router to screen packets to minimize the network traffic and load on the internal proxy. The application proxy examines an application layer protocol, such as HTTP, and performs the proxy services. This separate host, which is often referred to as a **bastion host**, represents a single, rich target for external attacks, and should be very thoroughly secured. Because it stands as a sole defender on the network perimeter, it is also commonly referred to as the **sacrificial host**.

Even though the bastion host/application proxy actually contains only cached copies of the internal Web documents, it can still present a promising target. An attacker that infiltrates the bastion host can discover the configuration of internal networks and possibly provide external sources with internal information. To its advantage, the proxy requires the external attack to compromise two separate systems before the attack can access internal data. As a consequence, the bastion host protects the data more fully than the router alone. Figure 9-6 shows a typical configuration of a screened-host architectural approach.

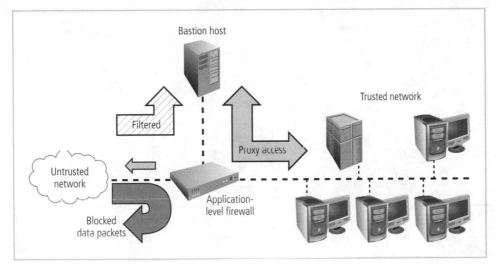

FIGURE 9-6 Screened-Host Firewall

Dual-Homed Host Firewalls

The next step up in firewall architectural complexity is the dual-homed host. In this configuration, the bastion host contains two network interfaces: one that is connected to the external network, and one that is connected to the internal network. All traffic *must* go through the firewall to move between the internal and external networks.

A technology known as **network–address translation (NAT)** is often implemented with this architecture. NAT is a method of converting multiple real, valid, external IP addresses to special ranges of internal IP addresses. A related approach called port-address translation (PAT) converts a single real, valid, external IP addresses to special ranges of internal IP addresses. Both of these approaches create a barrier to internal intrusion because these internal addresses cannot be routed over the public network. These special, nonroutable addresses have three possible ranges:

- Organizations that need very large numbers of local addresses can use the 10.x. x.x range, which has more than 16.5 million usable addresses.
- Organizations that need a moderate number of addresses can use the 192.168. x.x range, which has more than 65,500 addresses.
- Organizations with smaller needs can use the 172.16.0.0 to 172.16.15.0 range, which has approximately 4000 usable addresses.

Taking advantage of NAT prevents external attacks from reaching internal machines with addresses in specified ranges. This type of translation works by dynamically assigning addresses to internal communications and tracking the conversations with sessions to determine which incoming message is a response to which outgoing traffic. Figure 9-7 shows a typical configuration of a dual-homed host firewall that uses NAT and proxy access to protect the internal network.

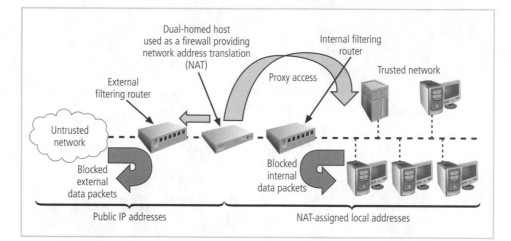

FIGURE 9-7 Dual-Homed Host Firewall

A dual-homed host is able to translate between the protocols of two different data link layers, such as Ethernet, Token Ring, Fiber Distributed Data Interface (FDDI), and asynchronous transfer method (ATM). This approach has two disadvantages, however:

- If the dual-homed host is compromised, it can take out the connection to the external network.
- As traffic volume increases, the dual-homed host can become overloaded.

Overall, however, this architecture provides strong protection with minimal expense compared to more complex solutions.

Screened-Subnet Firewalls (with DMZ)

The screened-subnet firewall consists of one or more internal bastion hosts located behind a packet filtering router, with each host protecting the trusted network. Many variants of the screened-subnet architecture exist. The first general model uses two filtering routers, with one or more dual-homed bastion hosts between them. In the second general model, as illustrated in Figure 9-8, the connections are routed as follows:

- Connections from the outside or untrusted network are routed through an external filtering router.
- Connections from the outside or untrusted network are routed into—and then out of—a routing firewall to the separate network segment known as the DMZ.
- Connections into the trusted internal network are allowed only from the DMZ bastion host servers.

As depicted in Figure 9-8, the screened subnet is an entire network segment that performs two functions: It protects the DMZ systems and information from outside threats, and it protects the internal networks by limiting how external connections can gain access to internal systems. Although extremely secure, the screened subnet can be expensive to implement and complex to configure and manage; the value of the information it protects must justify the cost.

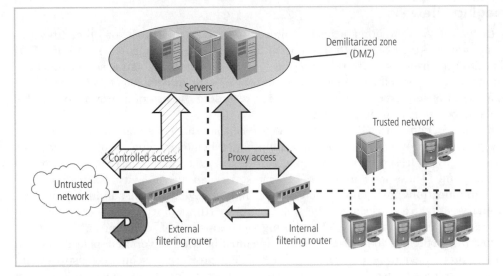

FIGURE 9-8   Screened Subnet (DMZ)

The screened-subnet firewall architecture provides an intermediate area between the trusted network and the untrusted network; that is, a DMZ. This DMZ can be a dedicated port on the firewall device linking a single bastion host, or it can be connected to a screened subnet or DMZ as shown in Figure 9-8. Until recently, servers providing services via the untrusted network were commonly placed in the DMZ. Examples include Web servers, File Transfer Protocol (FTP) servers, and certain database servers. More recent strategies utilizing proxy servers have provided much more secure solutions.

Selecting the Right Firewall

When evaluating a firewall for your networks, ask the following questions:[3]

1. What type of firewall technology offers the right balance between protection and cost for the needs of the organization?
2. What features are included in the base price? What features are available at extra cost? Are all cost factors known?
3. How easy is it to set up and configure the firewall? How accessible are the staff technicians who can competently configure the firewall?
4. Can the candidate firewall adapt to the growing network in the target organization?

Question 2 addresses the second most important issue—cost. The cost of a firewall may put a certain make, model, or type out of reach for a particular security solution. As with all security decisions, the budgetary constraints stipulated by management must be taken into account.

Managing Firewalls

Any firewall device—whether a packet filtering router, bastion host, or other firewall implementation—must have its own set of configuration rules that regulate its actions. With packet filtering firewalls, these rules may be simple statements regulating source and destination addresses, specific protocol or port usage requests, or decisions to allow or deny certain types of requests. In all cases, a policy regarding the use of a firewall should be articulated before it is made operable.

In practice, configuring firewall rule sets can be something of a nightmare. Logic errors in the preparation of the rules can cause unintended behavior, such as allowing access instead of denying it, specifying the wrong port or service type, or causing the network to misroute traffic. These and a myriad of other mistakes can turn a device designed to protect communications into a choke point. For example, a novice firewall administrator might improperly configure a virus screening e-mail gateway (think of it as a type of e-mail firewall), resulting in the blocking of all incoming e-mail, instead of screening only e-mail that contains malicious code. Each firewall rule must be carefully crafted, placed into the list in the proper sequence, debugged, and tested. The proper rule sequence ensures that the most resource-intensive actions are performed after the most restrictive ones, thereby reducing the number of packets that undergo intense scrutiny.

The ever-present need to balance performance against restrictions imposed by security practices is very obvious in the use of firewalls. If users cannot work due to a security restriction, then the security administration will most likely be told by management to remove it. Organizations are much more willing to live with a potential risk than certain failure.

Using a computer to protect a computer is fraught with problems that must be managed by careful preparation and continuous evaluation. Automated control systems, including firewalls, for the most part cannot learn from mistakes, and they cannot adapt to changing situations. They are limited by the constraints of their programming and rule sets in the following ways:

- Firewalls are not creative and cannot make sense of human actions outside the range of their programmed responses.
- Firewalls deal strictly with defined patterns of measured observation. These patterns are known to possible attackers and can be used to their benefit in an attack.
- Firewalls are computers themselves and are thus prone to programming errors, flaws in rule sets, and inherent vulnerabilities.
- Firewalls are designed to function within limits of hardware capacity and thus can only respond to patterns of events that happen in an expected and reasonably simultaneous sequence.
- Firewalls are designed, implemented, configured and operated by people and are subject to the expected series of mistakes from human error.[4]

There are also a number of management challenges to administering firewalls:

1. No training. Most managers think of a firewall as just another device, more or less similar to the computers already buzzing in the rack [...] if you get time to read manuals, you are lucky.

2. Firewalls are quite different. You have mastered your firewall and now every new configuration requirement is just a matter of a few clicks in the Telnet window; however, the new e-commerce project just brought you a new firewall running on a different OS.

3. Responsible for security. Since you are the firewall guy, suddenly everyone assumes that anything to do with computer security is your responsibility.

4. Daily administration tasks. Being a firewall administrator for a medium or large organization should be a full-time job by itself; however, that's hardly ever the case.[5]

Some of the best practices for firewall use are described below:[6]

- All traffic from the trusted network is allowed out. This allows members of the organization to access the services they need. Filtering and logging outbound traffic is possible when indicated by specific organizational policy goals.

- The firewall device is never accessible directly from the public network. Almost all access to the firewall device is denied to internal users as well. Only authorized firewall administrators access the device via secure authentication mechanisms, with preference for a method based on cryptographically strong authentication using two-factor access control techniques.

- Simple Mail Transport Protocol (SMTP) data is allowed to pass through the firewall, but all of it is routed to a well-configured SMTP gateway to filter and route messaging traffic securely.

- All Internet Control Message Protocol (ICMP) data is denied. Known as the ping service, it is a common method for hacker reconnaissance and should be turned off to prevent snooping.

- Telnet (terminal emulation) access to all internal servers from the public networks is blocked. At the very least, Telnet access to the organization's Domain Name Service (DNS) server should be blocked to prevent illegal zone transfers, and to prevent hackers from taking down the organization's entire network. If internal users need to reach an organization's network from outside the firewall, use a virtual private network (VPN) client or other secure authentication system to allow this kind of access.

- When Web services are offered outside the firewall, HTTP traffic is prevented from reaching your internal networks via the implementation of some form of proxy access or DMZ architecture. That way, if any employees are running Web servers for internal use on their desktops, the services will be invisible to the outside Internet. If your Web server is located behind the firewall, you need to allow HTTP or HTTPS (SHTTP) data through for the Internet at large to view it. The best solution is to place the Web servers containing critical data inside the network and to use proxy services from a DMZ (screened network segment). It is also advisable to restrict incoming HTTP traffic to internal network addresses such that the traffic must be responding to requests originating at internal addresses. This restriction can be accomplished through NAT or firewalls that can support stateful inspection or are directed at the proxy server itself. All other incoming HTTP traffic should be blocked. If the Web servers contain only advertising, they should be placed in the DMZ and rebuilt when (not if) they are compromised.

INTRUSION DETECTION SYSTEMS

Information security **intrusion detection systems (IDSs)** work like burglar alarms. When the system detects a violation—the IT equivalent of an opened or broken window—it activates the alarm. This alarm can be audible and visible (noise and lights), or it can be a silent alarm that sends a message to a monitoring company. With almost all IDSs, administrators can choose the configuration and alarm levels. Many IDSs can be configured to notify administrators via e-mail and numerical or text paging. The systems can also be configured to notify an external information security service organization, just as burglar alarms do. Like firewall systems, IDSs require complex configurations to provide the level of detection and response desired. These systems are either network based to protect network information assets, or host based to protect server or host information assets. IDSs use one of two detection methods: signature based or statistical anomaly based. Figure 9-9 depicts two typical approaches to intrusion detection where IDSs are used to monitor both network connection activity and current information states on host servers.

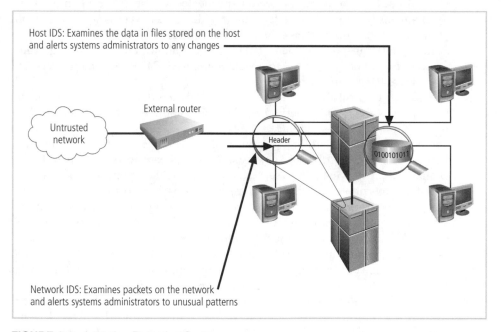

FIGURE 9-9   Intrusion Detection Systems

Host-Based IDS

A **host-based IDS** works by configuring and classifying various categories of systems and data files. In many cases, IDSs provide only a few general levels of alert notification. For example, an administrator might configure an IDS to report changes to certain folders, such as system folders (e.g., C:\Windows or C:\WINNT), security-related applications (C:\Tripwire), or critical data folders; at the same time, the IDS might be instructed to ignore changes to other files (e.g., C:\Program Files\Office). Administrators might configure the system to instantly page or e-mail them for high-priority alerts, but to simply record other lower-priority activity. Most administrators are concerned only if unauthorized changes occur in sensitive areas. After all, applications frequently modify their internal files, such as dictionaries and configuration templates, and users constantly update their data files. Unless the IDS is precisely configured, these benign actions can generate a large volume of false alarms. Some organizations will use a variable degree of reporting and recording detail. During times of routine operation, the system will provide alerting only for a few urgent reasons and recording only for exceptions. During periods of increased threat, however, it may send alerts on suspicious activity and record all activity for later analysis.

Host-based IDSs can monitor multiple computers simultaneously. They do so by storing a client file on each monitored host and then making that host report back to the master console, which is usually located on the system administrator's computer. This master console monitors the information from the managed clients and notifies the administrator when predetermined attack conditions occur.

Network-Based IDS

In contrast to host-based IDSs, which reside on a host (or hosts) and monitor only activities on the host, **network-based IDSs** monitor network traffic. When a predefined condition occurs, the network-based IDS notifies the appropriate administrator. Whereas host-based IDSs look for changes in file attributes (create, modify, delete), the network-based IDS looks for patterns of network traffic, such as large collections of related traffic that can indicate a denial-of-service attack or a series of related packets that could indicate a port scan in progress. Consequently, network IDSs require a much more complex configuration and maintenance program than do host-based IDSs. Network IDSs must match known and unknown attack strategies against their knowledge base to determine whether an attack has occurred. These systems yield many more false-positive readings than do host-based IDSs, because they are attempting to read the network activity pattern to determine what is normal and what is not.

Most organizations that implement an IDS solution install data collections sensors that are both host-based and network-based. A system of this type is called a hybrid-IDS and it also usually includes a provision to concentrate the event notifications from all sensors into a central repository for analysis. The analysis makes use of either signature-based or statistical anomaly-based detection techniques.

Signature-Based IDS

IDSs that use signature-based methods work like antivirus software. In fact, antivirus software can be classified as a form of signature-based IDS. A **signature-based IDS** or **knowledge-based IDS** examines data traffic for something that matches the signatures, which comprise preconfigured, predetermined attack patterns. The problem with this approach is that the signatures must be continually updated, as new attack strategies emerge. Failure to stay current allows attacks using new strategies to succeed. Another weakness of this method is the time frame over which attacks occur. If attackers are slow and methodical, they may slip undetected through the IDS, as their actions may not match a signature that includes factors based on duration of the events. The only way to resolve this dilemma is to collect and analyze data over longer periods of time, which requires substantially larger data storage ability and additional processing capacity.

Statistical Anomaly-Based IDS

Another popular type of IDS is the **statistical anomaly-based IDS (stat IDS)** or **behavior-based IDS**. The stat IDS first collects data from normal traffic and establishes a baseline. It then periodically samples network activity, using statistical methods, and compares the samples to the baseline. When the activity falls outside the baseline parameters (known as the **clipping level**), the IDS notifies the administrator. The baseline variables can include a host's memory or CPU usage, network packet types, and packet quantities.

The advantage of this approach is that the system is able to detect new types of attacks because it looks for abnormal activity of any type. Unfortunately, these IDSs require much more overhead and processing capacity than do signature-based versions because they must constantly attempt to pattern matched activity to the baseline. In addition, they may not detect minor changes to system variables and may generate many false-positive warnings. If the actions of the users or systems on the network vary widely, with unpredictable periods of low and high activity levels, this type of IDS may not be suitable, as dramatic swings from one level to another will almost certainly generate false alarms. As a result, this type of IDS is less commonly used than the signature-based approach.

Intrusion Prevention Systems

A recent development in the field of intrusion management is an approach called intrusion prevention systems. **Intrusion prevention systems (IPSs)** combine the ability to respond to known methods of attack with the ability to create adaptive responses to previously unknown attacks. This technology is closely aligned with so-called application defenses that use an understanding of what and how an application functions to make informed defensive decisions.

Because it is an extension of existing technological controls (making use of the existing capabilities of NIDS, HIDS, proxy-based firewalls, and multiprotocol firewall technologies), IPS is seen by many industry observers as an evolutionary approach that provides layered defenses. While some vendors market IPS as a new technology, it is more accurate to emphasize that it is the integration of existing detection and countermeasure technologies. IPS should be viewed as a mature version of the defense in-depth model.

The biggest challenge when configuring an IPS is the tuning of the automated responses. While an IDS simply identifies an intrusion, the IPS is designed to prevent or react to one. Therefore, one mechanism the IPS may have at its disposal is the severance of the communications circuit. This extreme measure may be justified when the organization is hit with a massive DDoS or malware-laden attack, but false positives that terminate the organization's connection can create bigger problems than potential attacks. Therefore, care should be taken when selecting, implementing, and tuning an IPS.

Managing Intrusion Detection Systems

Just as with any alarm system, if there is no response to an IDS alert, then it does no good. An IDS does not remove or deny access to a system by default and, unless it is programmed to take an action, merely records the events that trigger it. IDSs must be configured using technical knowledge and adequate business and security knowledge to differentiate between routine circumstances and low, moderate, or severe threats to the security of the organization's information assets.

A properly configured IDS can translate a security alert into different types of notification—for example, log entries for low-level alerts, e-mails for moderate-level alerts, and text messages or paging for severe alerts. Some organizations may configure systems to automatically take action in response to IDS alerts, although this technique should be carefully considered and undertaken only by organizations with experienced staff and well-constructed information security procedures. A poorly configured IDS may yield either information overload—causing the IDS administrator to shut off the pager—or failure to detect an actual attack. When a system is configured to take unsupervised action without obtaining human approval first, then the organization must be prepared to take accountability for these IDS actions.

The human response to false alarm can lead to behavior that can be exploited by attackers. For example, consider the following tactic: One possible car theft strategy exploits human intolerance for technological glitches that cause false alarms. In the early morning hours—say, 2:00 a.m.—a thief deliberately sets off the target car alarm, and then retreats to a safe distance. The owner comes out, resets the alarm, and goes back to bed. Twenty to thirty minutes later, the thief does it again, and then again. After the third or fourth time, the owner assumes that the alarm is faulty and turns it off, leaving the vehicle unprotected. The thief is then free to steal the car without having to deal with the now disabled alarm.

Most IDSs monitor systems by means of agents. An **agent** is a piece of software that resides on a system and reports back to a management server. If this piece of software is not properly configured and does not use a secure transmission channel to communicate with its manager, then an attacker could compromise and subsequently exploit the agent or the information from the agent.

A valuable tool in managing an IDS is the consolidated enterprise manager. This software allows the security professional to collect data from multiple host- and network-based IDSs and look for patterns across systems and subnetworks. An attacker might potentially probe one network segment or computer host, and then move on to another target before the first system's IDS caught on. The centralized manager not only collects responses from all IDSs, thereby providing one central monitoring station, but also can be used to identify these cross-system probes and intrusions.

REMOTE ACCESS PROTECTION

Before the Internet emerged as a public network, organizations created private networks and allowed individuals and other organizations to connect to them using dial-up or leased-line connections. In the current networking environment, firewalls are used to safeguard the connection between an organization and its Internet (public network) connection. The equivalent level of protection is necessary to protect connections when using private networks that allow dial-up access. While large organizations have replaced much of their dial-up capacity with Internet-enabled VPN connectivity, the maintenance and protection of dial-up connections from users' homes and in small offices remains a concern for many organizations.

Unsecured dial-up access represents a substantial exposure to attack. An attacker who suspects that an organization has dial-up lines can use a device called a **war-dialer** to locate the connection points. A war-dialer is an automatic phone-dialing program that dials every number in a configured range (e.g., 555–1000 to 555–2000), and checks whether a person, answering machine, or modem picks up. If a modem answers, the war-dialer program makes a note of the number and then moves to the next target number. The attacker then attempts to hack into the network through the identified modem connection using a variety of techniques.

Dial-up connections are usually much simpler and less sophisticated than Internet connections. For the most part, simple user name and password schemes are the only means of authentication. Some newer technologies have improved this process, including RADIUS systems, Challenge Handshake Authentication Protocol (CHAP) systems, and even systems that use strong encryption. The most prominent of these approaches are RADIUS and TACACS.

RADIUS and TACACS

RADIUS and TACACS are systems that authenticate the credentials of users who are trying to access an organization's network via a dial-up device or a secured network session. Typical remote access systems place the responsibility for the authentication of users on the system directly connected to the modems. If the dial-up system includes multiple points of entry, such an authentication scheme is difficult to manage. The **Remote Authentication Dial-In User Service (RADIUS)** system centralizes the management of user authentication by placing the responsibility for authenticating each user in the central RADIUS server. When a remote access server (RAS) receives a request for a network connection from a dial-up client, it passes the request along with the user's credentials to the RADIUS server. RADIUS then validates the credentials and passes the resulting decision (accept or deny) back to the accepting RAS. Figure 9-10 shows the typical configuration of a Microsoft Remote Access Server (RAS) system making use of RADIUS authentication.

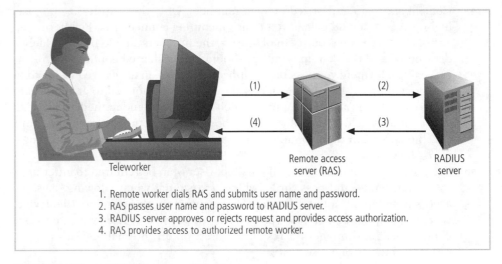

1. Remote worker dials RAS and submits user name and password.
2. RAS passes user name and password to RADIUS server.
3. RADIUS server approves or rejects request and provides access authorization.
4. RAS provides access to authorized remote worker.

FIGURE 9-10   RADIUS Configuration

Similar in function to the RADIUS system is the **Terminal Access Controller Access Control System (TACACS)**. This remote access authorization system is based on a client/server configuration. It makes use of a centralized data service, such as the one provided by a RADIUS server, and validates the user's credentials at the TACACS server. Three versions of TACACS exist: TACACS, Extended TACACS, and TACACS+. The original version combines authentication and authorization services. The extended version authenticates and authorizes in two separate steps, and records the access attempt and the requestor's identity. The plus version uses dynamic passwords and incorporates two-factor authentication.[7]

Managing Dial-Up Connections

Many organizations that once operated large dial-up access pools are now reducing the number of telephone lines they support, in favor of Internet access secured by VPNs. An organization that continues to offer dial-up remote access must:

- Determine how many dial-up connections it has. Many organizations do not even realize they have dial-up access, or they leave telephone connections in place long after they have stopped fully using them. This creates two potential problems: (1) The organization continues to pay for telecommunications circuits it is not using; and (2) these circuits may remain connected, permitting unmonitored access to the networks. For example, an employee may have installed a modem on an office computer to do a little telecommuting without management's knowledge. The organization should periodically scan its internal phone networks with special software to detect available connections. It should also integrate risk assessment and risk approval into the telephone service ordering process.

- Control access to authorized modem numbers. Only those authorized to use dial-up access should be allowed to use incoming connections. Furthermore, although there is no security in obscurity, the numbers should not be widely distributed and the dial-up numbers should be considered confidential.
- Use call-back whenever possible. Call-back requires an access requestor to be at a preconfigured location, which is essential for authorized telecommuting. Users call into the access computer, which disconnects and immediately calls the requestor back. If the caller is an authorized user at the preconfigured number, the caller can then connect. This solution is not so useful for traveling users, however.
- Use token authentication if at all possible. Users can be required to enter more than user names and passwords, which is essential when allowing dial-up access from laptops and other remote computers. In this scheme, the device accepts an input number, often provided by the computer from which access is requested, and provides a response based on an internal algorithm. The result is much stronger security.

WIRELESS NETWORKING PROTECTION

The use of wireless network technology is an area of concern for information security professionals. Most organizations that make use of wireless networks use an implementation based on the IEEE 802.11 protocol. A wireless network provides a low-cost alternative to a wired network because it does not require the difficult and often expensive installation of cable in an existing structure. The downside is the management of the wireless network **footprint**—the geographic area within which there is sufficient signal strength to make a network connection. The size of the footprint depends on the amount of power the transmitter/receiver **wireless access points (WAPs)** emit. Sufficient power must exist to ensure quality connections within the intended area, but not so much as to allow those outside the footprint to receive them.

Just as war-dialers represent a threat to dial-up communications, so does war driving for wireless. **War driving** is moving through a geographic area or building, actively scanning for open or unsecured WAPs. In some cities, groups of war-drivers move through an urban area, marking locations with unsecured wireless access with chalk ("war-chalking"). A number of encryption protocols can be used to secure wireless networks. The most common are the Wired Equivalent Privacy (WEP) and Wi-Fi Protected Access (WPA) families of protocols.

Wired Equivalent Privacy (WEP)

Wired Equivalent Privacy (WEP) is part of the IEEE 802.11 wireless networking standard. WEP is designed to provide a basic level of security protection to these radio networks, to prevent unauthorized access or eavesdropping. However, WEP, like a traditional wired network, does not protect users from each other; it only protects the network from unauthorized users. In the early 2000s, cryptologists found several fundamental flaws in WEP, resulting in vulnerabilities that can be exploited to gain access. These vulnerabilities ultimately led to the replacement of WEP as the industry standard with WPA. However, for the average home or small office user, for whom the risk of attack is low, WEP may be sufficient.

Wi-Fi Protected Access (WPA)

Wi-Fi Protected Access (WPA) is a family of protocols used to secure wireless networks that was created by the Wi-Fi Alliance industry group. The protocols were developed as an intermediate solution until the IEEE 802.11i standards were fully developed. **IEEE 802.11i** has been implemented in products such as **WPA2**. This is an amendment to the 802.11 standard published in June 2004 specifying security protocols for wireless networks. While WPA works with virtually all wireless network cards, it is not compatible with some older WAPs. WPA2, on the other hand, has compatibility issues with some older wireless network cards. WPA and WPA2 provide increased capabilities for authentication, encryption, and increased throughput as compared to WEP.

Unlike WEP, both WPA and WPA2 can use an IEEE 802.1X authentication server, similar to the RADIUS servers mentioned in the previous section. This type of authentication server can issue keys to authenticated users. The alternative is to allow all users to share a key. Use of these **pre-shared keys** is quite convenient but is not secure compared to other authentication techniques. WPA also uses a Message Integrity Code, a type of message authentication code to prevent certain types of attacks. WPA was the strongest possible mechanism that was backwardly compatible with the older systems. WPA2 introduced newer, more robust security protocols based on the Advanced Encryption Standard (discussed in the cryptography section of this chapter) to improve greatly the protection of wireless networks. The WPA2 standard is currently incorporated in virtually all Wi-Fi devices.

Wi-Max

The next generation of wireless networking is Wi-Max, or WirelessMAN, essentially an improvement on the technology developed for cellular telephones and modems. Wi-Max, developed as part of the IEEE 802.16 standard, is a certification mark that stands for *Worldwide Interoperability for Microwave Access.* As noted by the WiMAX Forum,

> WiMAX is not a technology *per se*, but rather a certification mark, or 'stamp of approval' given to equipment that meets certain conformity and interoperability tests for the IEEE 802.16 family of standards. A similar confusion surrounds the term Wi-Fi (Wireless Fidelity), which like WiMAX, is a certification mark for equipment based on a different set of IEEE standards from the 802.11 working group for wireless local area networks (WLAN). Neither WiMAX, nor Wi-Fi, is a technology but their names have been adopted in popular usage to denote the technologies behind them. This is likely due to the difficulty of using terms like 'IEEE 802.16' in common speech and writing.[8]

Managing Wireless Connections

Users and organizations can use a number of measures to implement a secure wireless network. These safeguards include the wireless security protocols mentioned earlier, VPNs, and firewalls. It is also possible to restrict access to the network to a preapproved set of wireless network card MAC addresses. This is especially easy in small or personal networks where all possible users are known.

One of the first management requirements is to regulate the size of the wireless network footprint. The initial step is to determine the best locations for placement of the WAPs. In addition, by using radio-strength meters, network administrators can adjust the power of the broadcast antennae to provide sufficient but not excessive overage. This is especially important in areas where public access is possible.

WEP is usually the first choice in network installation, and there may be a natural tendency to select this option. While this is fine in a home or small office/home office (SOHO) setting, for most professional installations WPA or WPA2 is preferred. The setups of wireless networks are also slightly different than what many users are familiar with. Most smaller wireless networks require the use of a preshared key, which is a specific length password. WEP networks require a 5- or 13-character passphrase. In WPA and WPA2 settings, the passphrase can be any length, with longer being more secure. On some older equipment, the preshared key must be converted into a string of hexadecimal characters that is entered into both the configuration software used to set up the wireless access point, and each associated wireless network access card. This can quickly turn into a labor-intensive process for all but the smallest of networks.

SCANNING AND ANALYSIS TOOLS

Although they are not always perceived as defensive tools, scanners, sniffers, and other analysis tools enable security administrators to see what an attacker sees. Scanner and analysis tools can find vulnerabilities in systems, holes in security components, and other unsecured points in the network. Unfortunately, they cannot detect the unpredictable behavior of people.

Some of these devices are extremely complex; others are very simple. Some are expensive commercial products; others are available for free from their creators. Conscientious administrators will have several hacking Web sites bookmarked, and should frequently browse for discussions about new vulnerabilities, recent conquests, and favorite assault techniques. There is nothing wrong with security administrators using the tools used by hackers to examine their own defenses and search out areas of vulnerability. A word of caution: Many of these tools have distinct signatures, and some ISPs scan for these signatures. If the ISP discovers someone using hacker tools, it may choose to deny access to that customer and discontinue service. It is best to establish a working relationship with the ISP and notify it before using such tools.

Scanning tools collect the information that an attacker needs to succeed. Collecting information about a potential target is known as footprinting. **Footprinting** is the organized research of the Internet addresses owned or controlled by a target organization. Attackers may use public Internet data sources to perform keyword searches to identify the network addresses of the organization. They may also use the organization's Web page to find information that can be used in social engineering attacks. For example, the Reveal Source option on most popular Web browsers allows users to see the source code behind the graphics on a Web page. A number of clues can provide additional insight into the configuration of an internal network: the locations and directories for Common Gateway Interface (CGI) script bins, and the names and possibly addresses of computers and servers.

A scanner can be used to augment the data collected by a common browser. A Web scanner, such as Sam Spade (www.samspade.org), can scan entire Web sites for valuable information, such as server names and e-mail addresses. It can also do a number of other common information collection activities, such as sending multiple ICMP information requests (pings), attempting to retrieve multiple and cross-zoned DNS queries, and performing common network analysis queries—all powerful diagnostic and/or hacking activities. Sam Spade is not usually considered to be hackerware (or hacker-oriented software), but it is a useful utility for network administrators and potential attackers alike.

The next phase of the preattack data gathering process, **fingerprinting**, entails the systematic examination of all of the organization's Internet addresses (collected during the footprinting phase). By means of the tools described in the following section, fingerprinting yields a detailed network analysis that provides useful information about the targets of the planned attack. The tool discussions here are necessarily brief; to attain true expertise in the use and configuration of these tools, you will need more specific education and training.

Port Scanners

Port scanning utilities (or **port scanners**) can identify (or fingerprint) computers that are active on a network, as well as the active ports and services on those computers, the functions and roles fulfilled by the machines, and other useful information. These tools can scan for specific types of computers, protocols, or resources, or they can conduct generic scans. It is helpful to understand your network environment, so that you can select the best tool for the job. The more specific the scanner is, the more detailed and useful the information it provides. However, you should keep a generic, broad-based scanner in your toolbox as well, to help locate and identify rogue nodes on the network of which administrators may not be aware.

A **port** is a network channel or connection point in a data communications system. Within the TCP/IP networking protocol, TCP and UDP port numbers differentiate among the multiple communication channels used to connect to network services that are offered on the same network device.[9] Each service within the TCP/IP protocol suite has either a unique default port number or a user-selected port number. Table 9-5 shows some of the commonly used port numbers. In total, there are 65,536 port numbers in use. The well-known ports are those from 0 through 1023. The registered ports are those from 1024 through 49151, and the dynamic and private ports are those from 49152 through 65535.

TABLE 9-5 Commonly Used Port Numbers

Port Numbers	Description
20 and 21	File Transfer Protocol (FTP)
25	Simple Mail Transfer Protocol (SMTP)
53	Domain Name Services (DNS)
67 and 68	Dynamic Host Configuration Protocol (DHCP)
80	Hypertext Transfer Protocol (HTTP)
110	Post Office Protocol (POP3)
161	Simple Network Management Protocol (SNMP)
194	IRC Chat port (used for device sharing)
443	HTTP over SSL
8080	Proxy services

The first order of business in securing a system is to secure open ports. Why? Simply put, an **open port** can be used to send commands to a computer, gain access to a server, and exert control over a networking device. As a general rule, you should secure all ports, and remove from service any ports not required for essential functions. For instance, if an organization does not host Web services, there is no need for port 80 to be available in its network or on its servers.

Vulnerability Scanners

Vulnerability scanners, which are variants of port scanners, are capable of scanning networks for very detailed information. As a class, they identify exposed user names and groups, show open network shares, and expose configuration problems and other server vulnerabilities. One vulnerability scanner is Nmap, a professional freeware utility available from www.insecure.org/nmap. Nmap identifies the systems available on a network, the services (ports) each system is offering, the operating system and operating system version they are running, the type of packet filters and firewalls in use, and dozens of other characteristics. LANguard Network Scanner is another vulnerability scanner. Several commercial vulnerability scanners are available as well, including products from ISS, Inc. and NetIQ, Inc.

Packet Sniffers

A **packet sniffer** is a network tool that collects and analyzes copies of packets from the network. It can provide a network administrator with valuable information to help diagnose and resolve networking issues. In the wrong hands, it can be used to eavesdrop on network traffic. The commercially available and open-source sniffers include Sniffer (a commercial product) and Snort (open-source software). An excellent free network protocol analyzer is Ethereal (www.ethereal.com), which allows administrators to examine both live network traffic and previously captured data. Ethereal offers a variety of features, including a language filter and TCP session reconstruction utility.

Typically, to use a packet sniffer effectively, you must be connected directly to a local network from an internal location. Simply tapping into any public Internet connection will flood you with more data than you can process, and technically constitutes a violation of wiretapping laws. To use a packet sniffer legally, you must satisfy the following criteria: (1) be on a network that the organization owns, not leases; (2) be under the direct authorization of the network's owners; (3) have the knowledge and consent of the content creators (users); and (4) have a justifiable business reason for doing so. If all four conditions are met, you can selectively collect and analyze packets to identify and diagnose problems on the network. Conditions 1 and 2 are self-explanatory, and condition 3 is usually a stipulation for using the company network. Incidentally, these conditions are the same as for employee monitoring in general.

Content Filters

Another type of tool that effectively protects the organization's systems from misuse and unintentional denial-of-service conditions is the **content filter**. Technically not a firewall, a content filter is a software program or a hardware/software appliance that allows administrators to restrict content that comes into a network. The most common application of a content filter is the restriction of access to Web sites with nonbusiness-related material, such as pornography or entertainment. Another application is the restriction of spam e-mail from outside sources. Content filters can consist of small add-on software for the home or office, such as NetNanny or SurfControl, or major corporate applications, such as Novell's Border Manager.

Content filters ensure that employees are not using network resources inappropriately. Unfortunately, these systems require extensive configuration and constant updating of the list of unacceptable destinations or incoming restricted e-mail source addresses. Some newer content filtering applications update the restricted database automatically, in the same way that some antivirus programs do. These applications match either a list of disapproved or approved Web sites, for example, or key content words, such as "nude" and "sex." Content creators, of course, work to bypass such restrictions by suppressing these trip words, creating additional problems for networking and security professionals.

Trap and Trace

Another set of technologies, trap and trace applications, are growing in popularity. Trap function software entices individuals who are illegally perusing the internal areas of a network to determine who they are. These individuals discover or find indicators of rich content areas on the network, which are actually set up to attract potential attackers. Better known as **honey pots**, these directories or servers distract the attacker while the software notifies the administrator of the intrusion.

The newest accompaniment to the trap is the trace. Similar in concept to telephone Caller ID service, the trace is a process by which the organization attempts to determine the identity of someone discovered in unauthorized areas of the network or systems.

Managing Scanning and Analysis Tools

It is vitally important that the security manager be able to see the organization's systems and networks from the viewpoint of potential attackers. Therefore the security manager should develop a program, using in-house resources, contractors, or an outsourced service provider, to scan the organization's systems and networks periodically for vulnerabilities with the same tools that a typical hacker might use.

There are a number of drawbacks to using scanners and analysis tools, content filters, and trap and trace tools:

- These tools are not human and thus cannot simulate the more creative behavior of a human attacker.
- Most tools function by pattern recognition, so only previously known issues can be detected. New approaches, modifications to well-known attack patterns, and the randomness of human behavior can cause them to misdiagnose the situation, thereby allowing vulnerabilities to go undetected or threats to go unchallenged.
- Most of these tools are computer-based software or hardware, and so are prone to errors, flaws, and vulnerabilities of their own.
- All of these tools are designed, configured, and operated by humans and are subject to human errors.[10]
- You get what you pay for. Use of hackerware may actually infect a system with a virus, or open the system to outside attacks or other unintended consequences. Always view a hacker kit skeptically before using it and especially before connecting it to the Internet. Never put anything valuable on the computer that houses the hacker tools. Consider segregating it from other network segments and disconnect it from the network when not in use.
- Some governments, agencies, institutions, and universities have established policies or laws that protect the individual user's right to access content, especially if it is necessary for the conduct of his or her job. There are also situations where an entire class of content has been proscribed and mere possession of that content is a criminal act, for example, child pornography.
- Tool usage and configuration must comply with an explicitly articulated policy, and the policy must provide for valid exceptions. This mandate prevents administrators from becoming arbiters of morality as they create a filter rule set.

CRYPTOGRAPHY

Although it is not a specific application or security tool, cryptography represents a sophisticated element of control that is often included in other information security controls. In fact, many security-related tools use embedded encryption technologies to protect sensitive information. The use of the proper cryptographic tools can ensure confidentiality by keeping private information concealed from those who do not need to see it. Other cryptographic methods can provide increased information integrity by providing a mechanism to guarantee that a message in transit has not been altered by using a process that creates a secure message digest, or hash. In e-commerce situations, some cryptographic tools can be used to assure that parties to the transaction are authentic, so that they cannot later deny having participated in a transaction, a feature often called **nonrepudiation**.

Encryption is the process of converting an original message into a form that cannot be used by unauthorized individuals. That way, anyone without the tools and knowledge to convert an encrypted message back to its original format will be unable to interpret it. The science of encryption, known as **cryptology**, actually encompasses two disciplines: cryptography and cryptanalysis. **Cryptography**—from the Greek words *kryptos,* meaning "hidden," and *graphein,* meaning "to write"—is the processes involved in encoding and decoding messages so that others cannot understand them. **Cryptanalysis**—from *analyein,* meaning "to break up"—is the process of deciphering the original message (or **plaintext**) from an encrypted message (or **ciphertext**), without knowing the algorithms and keys used to perform the encryption.

Cryptology is a very complex field based on advanced mathematical concepts. The following sections provide a brief overview of the foundations of encryption and a short discussion of some of the related issues and tools in the field of information security. For more information about cryptography, you should refer to two books by Bruce Schneier: *Applied Cryptography: Protocols, Algorithms, and Source Code in C,* which provides a technical tutorial in the discipline, and *Secrets and Lies: Digital Security in a Networked World,* which discusses many of the theoretical and practical considerations in the use of cryptographic systems.

ENCRYPTION DEFINITIONS

You can better understand the tools and functions popular in encryption security solutions if you know some basic terminology:

- Algorithm: The mathematical formula or method used to convert an unencrypted message into an encrypted message
- Cipher: The transformation of the individual components (characters, bytes, or bits) of an unencrypted message into encrypted components
- Ciphertext or cryptogram: The unintelligible encrypted or encoded message resulting from an encryption
- Cryptosystem: The set of transformations necessary to convert an unencrypted message into an encrypted message
- Decipher: To decrypt or convert ciphertext to plaintext
- Encipher: To encrypt or convert plaintext to ciphertext
- Key: The information used in conjunction with the algorithm to create the ciphertext from the plaintext; it can be a series of bits used in a mathematical algorithm, or the knowledge of how to manipulate the plaintext
- Keyspace: The entire range of values that can possibly be used to construct an individual key
- Plaintext: The original unencrypted message that is encrypted and results from successful decryption
- Steganography: The process of hiding messages; for example, if messages are hidden within the digital encoding of a picture or graphic, it becomes almost impossible to detect that the hidden messages even exist
- Work factor: The amount of effort (usually expressed in units of time) required to perform cryptanalysis on an encoded message

Encryption Operations

Encryption is accomplished by using algorithms to manipulate the plaintext into the ciphertext for transmission. Some widely used encryption operations are explained in the sections that follow.

Common Ciphers

In encryption the most commonly used algorithms include three functions: substitution, transposition, and XOR. In a **substitution cipher**, you substitute one value for another. For example, using the line labeled "input text," you can substitute the message character with the character three values to the right in the alphabet by looking at the aligned text in the line labeled "output text."

```
Input text:     ABCDEFGHIJKLMNOPQRSTUVWXYZ
Output text:    DEFGHIJKLMNOPQRSTUVWXYZABC
```

Thus a plaintext of BERLIN becomes EHUOLQ.

This is a simple enough method by itself, but it becomes very powerful if combined with other operations. Incidentally, this type of substitution is based on a **monoalphabetic substitution**, as it uses only one alphabet. More advanced substitution ciphers use two or more alphabets and are called **polyalphabetic substitutions**. To continue the previous example, consider the following block of text:

```
Input text:              ABCDEFGHIJKLMNOPQRSTUVWXYZ
Substitution cipher 1:   DEFGHIJKLMNOPQRSTUVWXYZABC
Substitution cipher 2:   GHIJKLMNOPQRSTUVWXYZABCDEF
Substitution cipher 3:   JKLMNOPQRSTUVWXYZABCDEFGHI
Substitution cipher 4:   MNOPQRSTUVWXYZABCDEFGHIJKL
```

Here the plaintext is matched character by character to the input text row. The next four lines are four sets of substitution ciphers. In this example, you can encode the word TEXT as WKGF, as you select letters from the second row for the first letter, letters from the third row for the second letter, and so on. This type of encryption is substantially more difficult to decipher without the algorithm (rows of ciphers) and key (use of the second row for the first letter, the third row for the second letter, and so on). It is also easy to randomize the cipher rows completely to create more complex substitution operations.

Another simple example of the substitution cipher is the daily cryptogram in your local newspaper, or the well-known Little Orphan Annie decoder ring. Julius Caesar reportedly used a three-character shift to the right (using the Roman alphabet), in which A becomes D and so on, giving that particular substitution cipher his name—the Caesar cipher. Like the substitution operation, transposition is simple to understand but can be complex to decipher if properly used. Unlike the substitution cipher, the **transposition cipher** (or **permutation cipher**) simply rearranges the values within a block to create the ciphertext. This can be done at the bit or byte (character) level. Here is an example:

```
Plaintext: 001001010110101110010101010101001001
Key:       1 > 3,2 > 6,3 > 8,4 > 1,5 > 4,6 > 7,7 > 5,8 > 2
```

(Read as bit 1 moves to position 4, and so on, with bit position 1 being the rightmost bit.)

The following shows the plaintext broken into 8-bit blocks (for ease of discussion) and the corresponding ciphertext, based on the application of the preceding key to the plaintext:

```
Plaintext 8-bit blocks:      00100101   01101011   10010101   01010100
Ciphertext:                  11000100   01110101   10001110   10011000
```

To make this easier to follow, consider the following example in character transposition:

```
Plaintext:MY DOG HAS FLEAS. (Spaces count as characters.)
Key:  Same key as above but characters are transposed, rather than bits.
      (Note that spaces are transposed as well.)
      Plaintext 8-character blocks:  MY DOG H    AS FLEAS
      Ciphertext:                    G  YDHMO    E ASFSAL
```

Transposition ciphers and substitution ciphers can be used together in multiple combinations to create a very secure encryption process. To make the encryption stronger (more difficult to cryptanalyze), the keys and block sizes can be made much larger (64-bit or 128-bit), resulting in substantially more complex substitutions or transpositions.

In the **XOR cipher conversion**, the bit stream is subjected to a Boolean XOR function against some other data stream, typically a key stream. The symbol commonly used to represent the XOR function is "^". XOR works as follows:

```
'0'  XOR'ed  with '0' results in a '0'. (0 ^ 0 = 0)
'0'  XOR'ed  with '1' results in a '1'. (0 ^ 1 = 1)
'1'  XOR'ed  with '0' results in a '1'. (1 ^ 0 = 1)
'1'  XOR'ed  with '1' results in a '0'. (1 ^ 1 = 0)
```

Simply put, if the two values are the same, you get "0"; if not, you get "1". Suppose you have a data stream in which the first byte is 01000001. If you have a key stream in which the first "byte" is '0101 1010', and you XOR them:

```
      '0100 0001' Plaintext
^     '0101 1010' Key stream
      '0001 1011' Ciphertext
```

This process is reversible. That is, if you XOR the ciphertext with the key stream, you get the plaintext.

Vernam Cipher

Also known as the one-time pad, the Vernam cipher was developed at AT&T and uses a set of characters for encryption operations only one time and then discards it. The values from this one-time pad are added to the block of text, and the resulting sum is converted to text. When the two sets of values are added, if the resulting values exceed 26, 26 is subtracted from the total (a process called modulo 26). The corresponding results are then converted back to text. The following example demonstrates how the Vernam cipher works:

Plaintext	M	Y	D	O	G	H	A	S	F	L	E	A	S
Corresponding values	13	25	04	15	07	08	01	19	06	12	05	01	19
One-time pad	F	P	Q	R	N	S	B	I	E	H	T	Z	L
Pad corresponding values	06	16	17	18	14	19	02	09	05	08	20	26	12

Results

Plaintext		13	25	4	15	7	8	1	19	6	12	5	1	19
One-time pad		6	16	17	18	14	19	2	9	5	8	20	26	12
Sum		19	41	21	33	21	27	3	28	11	20	25	27	31
Subtraction (modulo 26)			15		7		1		2				1	5
Ciphertext		P	O	U	G	U	A	C	B	K	T	Y	A	E

Book or Running Key Cipher

Another method, one seen in the occasional spy movie, is the use of text in a book as the algorithm to decrypt a message. The key relies on two components: (1) knowing which book to use, and (2) having a list of codes representing the page number, line number, and word number of the plaintext word. For example, using a copy of a particular popular novel, one might send the following message: 67,3,1;145,9,4;375,7,4;394,17,3. Dictionaries and thesauruses are the most popular sources as they provide every needed word, although almost any book will suffice. If the receiver knows which book is used for the preceding example, he or she goes to page 67, line 3, and selects the first word from that line; then goes to page 145, line 9, and uses the fourth word; and so forth. The resulting message `cancel operation target compromised` can then be deciphered. When using dictionaries, it is necessary to use only a page and word number. An even more sophisticated version of this cipher can use multiple books, with a new book in a particular sequence for each word or phrase.

Symmetric Encryption

Each of the aforementioned encryption and decryption methods requires the same algorithm and key—a **secret key**—to be used to both encipher and decipher the message. This is known as **private key encryption**, or **symmetric encryption**. Symmetric encryption is efficient and easy to process, as long as both the sender and the receiver possess the encryption key. Of course, if either copy of the key becomes compromised, an intermediary can decrypt and read the messages. One challenge in symmetric key encryption is getting a copy of the key to the receiver, a process that must be conducted out-of-band (that is, through a different channel or band than the one carrying the ciphertext) to avoid interception. Figure 9-11 illustrates the concept of symmetric encryption.

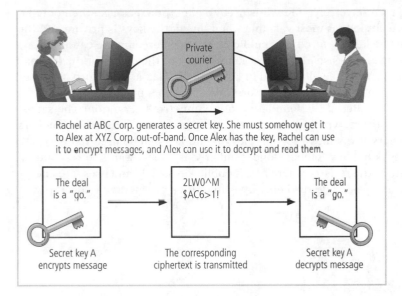

Rachel at ABC Corp. generates a secret key. She must somehow get it to Alex at XYZ Corp. out-of-band. Once Alex has the key, Rachel can use it to encrypt messages, and Alex can use it to decrypt and read them.

The deal is a "go."   →   2LWO^M $AC6>1!   →   The deal is a "go."

Secret key A encrypts message | The corresponding ciphertext is transmitted | Secret key A decrypts message

FIGURE 9-11   Symmetric Encryption

A number of popular symmetric encryption cryptosystems are available. One of the most familiar is Data Encryption Standard (DES). DES was developed in 1977 by IBM and is based on the Data Encryption Algorithm (DEA), which uses a 64-bit block size and a 56-bit key. With a 56-bit key, the algorithm has 256 (more than 72 quadrillion) possible keys.

DES is a federally approved standard for nonclassified data (see Federal Information Processing Standards Publication 46-2 at www.itl.nist.gov/fipspubs/fip46-2.htm). It was cracked in 1997 when the developers of a new algorithm, Rivest-Shamir-Aldeman (RSA), which you will learn about later in this chapter, offered a $10,000 reward for the first person or team to crack the algorithm. Fourteen thousand users collaborated over the Internet to break the encryption! **Triple DES (3DES)** was developed as an improvement to DES and uses as many as three keys in succession. It is substantially more secure than DES, not only because it uses as many as three keys instead of one, but also because it performs three different encryption operations.

The successor to 3DES is **Advanced Encryption Standard (AES)**. It is based on the Rinjndael Block Cipher, which features a variable block length and a key length of either 128, 192, or 256 bits. In 1998, it took a special computer designed by the Electronic Freedom Frontier (www.eff.org) more than 56 hours to crack DES. It would take the same computer approximately 4,698,864 quintillion years (4,698,864,000,000,000,000,000) to crack AES.

Asymmetric Encryption

Another encryption technique is **asymmetric encryption**, also known as **public key encryption**. Whereas symmetric encryption systems use a single key both to encrypt and decrypt a message, asymmetric encryption uses two different keys. Either key can be used to encrypt or decrypt the message. However, if Key A is used to encrypt the message, then only Key B can decrypt it; conversely, if Key B is used to encrypt a message, then only Key A can decrypt it. This technique is most valuable when one of the keys is private and the other is public. The public key is stored in a public location, where anyone can use it. The private key, as its name suggests, is a secret known only to the owner of the key pair.

Consider the following example, illustrated in Figure 9-12. Alex at XYZ Corp. wants to send an encrypted message to Rachel at ABC Corp. Alex goes to a public key registry and obtains Rachel's public key. Recall the foundation of asymmetric encryption: The same key cannot be used to both encrypt and decrypt the same message. Thus, when Rachel's public key is used to encrypt the message, only her private key can be used to decrypt it—and that private key is held by Rachel alone. Similarly, if Rachel wants to respond to Alex's message, she goes to the registry where Alex's public key is held and uses it to encrypt her message, which of course can be read only by using Alex's private key to decrypt it.

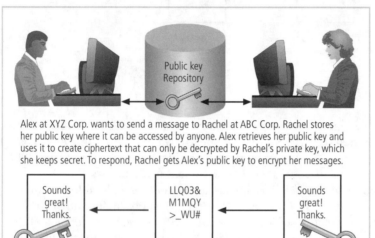

Alex at XYZ Corp. wants to send a message to Rachel at ABC Corp. Rachel stores her public key where it can be accessed by anyone. Alex retrieves her public key and uses it to create ciphertext that can only be decrypted by Rachel's private key, which she keeps secret. To respond, Rachel gets Alex's public key to encrypt her messages.

FIGURE 9-12   Public Key Encryption

The problem with asymmetric encryption is that it requires four keys to hold a single conversation between two parties. If four organizations want to exchange messages frequently, each must manage its private key and four public keys. It can be confusing to determine which public key is needed to encrypt a particular message. With more organizations in the loop, the problem grows. Also, asymmetric encryption is not as efficient in its use of CPU resources as symmetric encryptions when performing the extensive mathematical calculations. As a result, the hybrid system described in the section "Public Key Infrastructure" (later in this chapter) is more commonly used.

Digital Signatures

When the asymmetric process is reversed—the private key encrypts a (usually short) message, and the public key decrypts it—the fact that the message was sent by the organization that owns the private key cannot be refuted. This **nonrepudiation** is the foundation of digital signatures. **Digital signatures** are encrypted messages that can be independently verified by a central facility (registry) as authentic, but can also be used to prove certain characteristics of the message or file with which they are associated. They are often used in Internet software updates (see Figure 9-13). A pop-up window shows that the downloaded files did, in fact, come from the purported agency and thus can be trusted. A **digital certificate** is a block of data similar to a digital signature, attached to a file certifying that the file is from the organization it claims to be from and has not been modified from the original format. A **certificate authority (CA)** is an agency that manages the issuance of certificates and serves as the electronic notary public to verify their origin and integrity.

FIGURE 9-13   Digital Signature

RSA

One of the most popular public key cryptosystems is a proprietary model named Rivest-Shamir-Aldeman (RSA) after the surnames of its developers. It is the first public key encryption algorithm developed for commercial use. RSA is very popular and has been integrated into both Microsoft Internet Explorer and Netscape Navigator. A number of extensions to the RSA algorithm exist, including RSA Encryption Scheme—Optimal Asymmetric Encryption Padding (RSAES-OAEP) and RSA Signature Scheme with Appendix—Probabilistic Signature Scheme (RSASSA-PSS).

Public Key Infrastructure

A public key infrastructure (PKI) is the entire set of hardware, software, and cryptosystems necessary to implement public key encryption. PKI systems are based on public key cryptosystems and include digital certificates and certificate authorities. Common implementations of PKI include:

- Systems to issue digital certificates to users and servers
- Encryption enrollment
- Key-issuing systems
- Tools for managing the key issuance
- Verification and return of certificates
- Key revocation services
- Other services associated with PKI that vendors bundle into their products

The use of cryptographic tools is made more manageable when using PKI. PKI can increase the capabilities of an organization in protecting its information assets by providing the following services:[11]

- Authentication: Digital certificates in a PKI system permit individuals, organizations, and Web servers to authenticate the identity of each of the parties in an Internet transaction.
- Integrity: Digital certificates assert that the content signed by the certificate has not been altered while in transit.
- Confidentiality: PKI keeps information confidential by ensuring that it is not intercepted during transmission over the Internet.
- Authorization: Digital certificates issued in a PKI environment can replace user IDs and passwords, enhance security, and reduce some of the overhead for authorization processes and controlling access privileges for specific transactions.
- Nonrepudiation: Digital certificates can validate actions, making it less likely that customers or partners can later repudiate a digitally signed transaction, such as an online purchase.

Hybrid Systems

Pure asymmetric key encryption is not widely used except in the area of certificates. For other purposes, it is typically employed in conjunction with symmetric key encryption, creating a hybrid system. The hybrid process in current use is based on the **Diffie-Hellman key exchange method**, which provides a way to exchange private keys without exposure to any third parties. In this method, asymmetric encryption is used to exchange symmetric keys so that two organizations can conduct quick, efficient, secure communications based on symmetric encryption. Diffie-Hellman is the foundation for subsequent developments in public key encryption.

The process, which is illustrated in Figure 9-14, works like this: Because symmetric encryption is more efficient than asymmetric encryption for sending messages, and because asymmetric encryption does not require out-of-band key exchange, asymmetric encryption can be used to transmit symmetric keys in a hybrid approach. Suppose Alex at XYZ Corp. wants to communicate with Rachel at ABC Corp. First, Alex creates a **session key**, a symmetric key for limited-use, temporary communications. Alex encrypts a message with the session key, and then gets Rachel's public key. He uses her public key to encrypt both the session key and the message that is already encrypted. Alex transmits the entire package to Rachel, who uses her private key to decrypt the package containing the session key and the encrypted message, and then uses the session key to decrypt the message. Rachel can then continue the electronic conversation using only the more efficient symmetric session key.

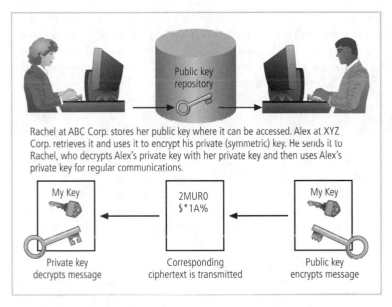

Rachel at ABC Corp. stores her public key where it can be accessed. Alex at XYZ Corp. retrieves it and uses it to encrypt his private (symmetric) key. He sends it to Rachel, who decrypts Alex's private key with her private key and then uses Alex's private key for regular communications.

FIGURE 9-14   Hybrid Encryption

Using Cryptographic Controls

Cryptographic controls are often misunderstood by those new to the area of information security. While modem cryptosystems can certainly generate unbreakable ciphertext, that is possible only when the proper key management infrastructure has been constructed and when the cryptosystems are operated and managed correctly. As in many InfoSec endeavors, the technical control is valuable, as long it remains within programs that are founded on sound policy and managed with an awareness of the fundamental objectives of the organization. Unfortunately, many vendors of cryptographic controls have sold products to organizations that were not able to deploy them to improve their security programs. This may have been due to poor project planning, errors in executing the implementation plans, or failures to put sound policies in place before acquiring the controls. Whatever the causes, many organizations have failed to make full use of their investment in cryptographic controls.

Organizations with the need and the ability to use cryptographic controls can use them to support several aspects of the business:

- Confidentiality and integrity of e-mail and its attachments
- Authentication, confidentiality, integrity, and nonrepudiation of e-commerce transactions

- Authentication and confidentiality of remote access through VPN connections
- A higher standard of authentication when used to supplement access control systems

E-Mail Security

A number of cryptosystems have been adapted to help secure e-mail, a notoriously insecure method of communication. Some of the more popular adaptations include Secure Multipurpose Internet Mail Extensions, Privacy Enhanced Mail, and Pretty Good Privacy.

Secure Multipurpose Internet Mail Extensions (S/MIME) builds on the Multipurpose Internet Mail Extensions (MIME) encoding format by adding encryption and authentication via digital signatures based on public key cryptosystems. **Privacy Enhanced Mail (PEM)** has been proposed by the Internet Engineering Task Force (IETF) as a standard that will function with public key cryptosystems. PEM uses 3DES symmetric key encryption and RSA for key exchanges and digital signatures. **Pretty Good Privacy (PGP)** was developed by Phil Zimmerman and uses the IDEA Cipher, a 128-bit symmetric key block encryption algorithm with 64-bit blocks for message encoding. Like PEM, it uses RSA for symmetric key exchange and to support digital signatures. PGP relies on a "web of trust" model to allow its users to share key information easily, albeit with some loss in the degree of control and trust in the key information. With PGP, if user A has established a trusting relationship with user B, and user B has a trusting relationship with user C, then user A is presumed to have a trusting relationship with user C and can exchange encrypted information with that user.

Securing the Web

Just as PGP, PEM, and S/MIME help to secure e-mail operations, a number of cryptosystems help to secure Web activity, especially transactions between customers' browsers and the Web servers at electronic commerce sites. Among the protocols used for this purpose are Secure Electronic Transactions, Secure Sockets Layer, Secure Hypertext Transfer Protocol, Secure Shell, and IP Security.

Secure Electronic Transactions (SET) was developed by MasterCard and VISA in 1997 to provide protection from electronic payment fraud. It works by encrypting the credit card transfers with DES for encryption and RSA for key exchange, much as other algorithms do. SET provides the security for both Internet-based credit card transactions and the encryption of card swipe systems in retail stores.

Secure Sockets Layer (SSL) was developed by Netscape in 1994 to provide security for online electronic commerce transactions. It uses a number of algorithms, but mainly relies on RSA for key transfer and on IDEA, DES, or 3DES for encrypted symmetric key-based data transfer. Figure 9-13 shows the certificate and SSL information that are displayed when you check out of an e-commerce site. If the Web connection does not automatically display the certificate, you can right-click in the window and select Properties to view the connection encryption and certificate properties.

Secure Hypertext Transfer Protocol (SHTTP) is an encrypted solution to the unsecured version of HTTP. It provides an alternative to the aforementioned protocols and can provide secure e-commerce transactions as well as encrypted Web pages for secure data transfer over the Web, using a number of different algorithms.

Secure Shell (SSH) is a popular extension to the TCP/IP protocol suite. Sponsored by the IETF, SSH provides security for remote access connections over public networks by creating a secure and persistent connection. It provides authentication services between a client and a server and is used to secure replacement tools for terminal emulation, remote management, and file transfer applications.

IP Security (IPSec) is the primary and now dominant cryptographic authentication and encryption product of the IETF's IP Protocol Security Working Group. It is used to support a variety of applications, just as SSH does. A framework for security development within the TCP/IP family of protocol standards, IPSec provides application support for all uses within TCP/IP, including VPNs. This protocol combines several different cryptosystems:

- Diffie-Hellman key exchange for deriving key material between peers on a public network
- Public key cryptography for signing the Diffie-Hellman exchanges to guarantee the identity of the two parties
- Bulk encryption algorithms, such as DES, for encrypting the data
- Digital certificates signed by a certificate authority to act as digital ID cards[12]

IPSec has two components: (1) the IP Security protocol itself, which specifies the information to be added to an IP packet and indicates how to encrypt packet data; and (2) the Internet Key Exchange (IKE), which uses asymmetric key exchange and negotiates the security associations.

IPSec works in two modes of operation: transport and tunnel. In **transport mode**, only the IP data is encrypted—not the IP headers themselves. This allows intermediate nodes to read the source and destination addresses. In **tunnel mode**, the entire IP packet is encrypted and inserted as the payload in another IP packet. This requires other systems at the beginning and end of the tunnel to act as proxies to send and receive the encrypted packets. These systems then transmit the decrypted packets to their true destinations.

IPSec and other cryptographic extensions to TCP/IP are often used to support a **virtual private network (VPN)**. A VPN is a private, secure network operated over a public and insecure network. It keeps the contents of the network messages hidden from observers who may have access to public traffic. Using the VPN tunneling approach described earlier, an individual or organization can set up a network connection on the Internet and send encrypted data back and forth, using the IP-packet-within-an-IP-packet method to deliver the data safely and securely. VPN support is built into most Microsoft Server software, including Windows 2000, and client support for VPN services is included in Windows XP. While true private network services can cost hundreds of thousands of dollars to lease, configure, and maintain, a VPN can be established for much less.

Securing Authentication

Cryptosystems can also be used to provide enhanced and secure authentication. One approach to this issue is provided by **Kerberos**, named after the three-headed dog of Greek mythology (*Cerberus* in Latin) that guarded the gates to the underworld. Kerberos uses symmetric key encryption to validate an individual user's access to various network resources. It keeps a database containing the private keys of clients and servers that are in the authentication domain it supervises. Network services running on the servers in the shared authentication domain register with Kerberos, as do clients that want to use those services.[13] The Kerberos system recognizes these private keys and can authenticate one network node (client or server) to another. For example, it can authenticate a client to a print service. To understand Kerberos, think of a typical multiscreen cinema. You acquire your ticket at the box office, and the ticket-taker then lets you in to the proper screen based on the contents of your ticket. Kerberos also generates temporary session keys; that is, private keys given to the two parties in a conversation. The session key is used to encrypt all communications between these two parties. Typically, a user logs into the network, is authenticated to the Kerberos system, and is then authenticated by the Kerberos system to other resources on the network.

Kerberos consists of three interacting services, all of which rely on a database library:

- Authentication Server (AS), which is a Kerberos server that authenticates clients and servers.
- Key Distribution Center (KDC), which generates and issues session keys.
- Kerberos Ticket Granting Service (TGS), which provides tickets to clients who request services. An authorization ticket is an identification card for a particular client that verifies to the server that the client is requesting services and that the client is a valid member of the Kerberos system and, therefore, authorized to receive services. The ticket consists of the client's name and network address, a ticket validation starting and ending time, and the session key, all encrypted in the private key of the target server.

Kerberos operates according to the following principles:

1. The KDC knows the secret keys of all clients and servers on the network.
2. The KDC initially exchanges information with the client and server by using the secret keys.
3. Kerberos authenticates a client to a requested service on a server through TGS and by issuing temporary session keys for communications between the client and the KDC, the server and the KDC, and the client and the server.
4. Communications take place between the client and server using the temporary session keys.[14]

Kerberos may be obtained free of charge from MIT at itinfo.mit.edu/product.php?name=kerberos. If you decide to use it, however, be aware of some concerns. If the Kerberos servers are subjected to denial-of-service attacks, no client can request (or receive) any services. If the Kerberos servers, service providers, or clients' machines become compromised, their private key information may also be compromised.

Managing Cryptographic Controls

Cryptographic controls require close management attention. Some of the more important managerial issues are as follows:

- Don't lose your keys. Any key-based system is contingent upon the physical security of its keys. If the keys are compromised, so is all communication. If the keys are lost, any data encrypted with those keys may be lost as well. Unlike your car keys, which the dealer can replace, cryptographic keys are not known to the software vendors and are usually not recoverable. The purpose of the encryption algorithm is to prevent unauthorized entities from viewing the data. Unless your organization has made an investment in a key management solution that enables key recovery, if you lose your key, you may lose your data or the service being protected. Loss of unrecoverable keys will deny access to everyone. Given the current state of cryptographic technology, breaking the code is very likely impossible.

- Know who you are communicating with. One of the most popular encryption-based attacks is the man-in-the-middle attack, in which the attacker pretends to be the second party in a conversation and relays the traffic to the actual second party. The attacker collects, decrypts, reads, possibly modifies, reencrypts, and transmits the information. This type of operation is possible only if the attacker is involved in the initial key exchange. Always verify the public keys in a public key exchange.

- It may be illegal to use a specific encryption technique when communicating to some nations. Federal export regulation still restricts the countries with which you can share strong encryption. Check the U.S. Department of Commerce's export FAQs for more information (www.bis.doc.gov/Encryption/default.htm).

- Every cryptosystem has weaknesses. Make sure you can live with the weaknesses of any system you choose. Research your selection before trusting any cryptosystem.

- Give access only to those users, systems, and servers with a business need, a principle known as least privilege. Do not load cryptosystems on systems that can be easily compromised.

- When placing trust into a certificate authority, ask the following question: *Quis custodiet ipsos custodes?* That is, who watches the watchers? CAs do not assume any liability for the accuracy of their information, which is strange given that their purpose is to validate the identity of a third party. However, if you read the fine print on the CA agreement, you will most likely find statements to that effect.

- There is no security in obscurity. Just because a system is secret does not mean it is safe. It is better to put your trust in a tried-and-true tested solution.

Security protocols and the cryptosystems they use are subject to the same limitations as firewalls and IDSs. They are all installed and configured by humans, and are only as secure as their configuration allows. VPNs are particularly vulnerable to direct attacks; compromise of the remote client can directly result in compromise of the trusted system. Home-computing users frequently use the Windows "remember passwords" function, which could present a real problem if these systems are compromised. Don't let telecommuters use this option.

As with all other information security program components, make sure that your organization's use of cryptography is based on well-constructed policy and supported with sound management procedures. The tools themselves may work exactly as advertised, but if they are not used correctly and managed diligently, your organization's secrets may soon be public knowledge.

VIEWPOINT

Leveraging Protection Mechanisms to Provide Defense in Depth

By Todd E. Tucker, CISSP, Director, Chief Security Strategist, NetIQ Solutions by Attachmate

Defense in depth is a protection strategy with a long history. It is characterized by layers of protection that, while not impenetrable, provide the advantage of increasing the time and resources necessary to penetrate through every layer of defense. Perhaps the best-known physical example of defense in depth comes from the archetypical fortress, built with high walls, manned by armed guards, and placed behind a protective moat.

In information security, protection mechanisms are essential for providing defense in depth. Each mechanism, when considered alone, may provide little protection against today's sophisticated attacks. However, information security architects build systems and networks by implementing layers of protection. For example, architects leverage a secured physical perimeter to protect media and hardware, implement firewalls to secure the internal networks from untrusted ones, install antivirus applications to detect and eradicate malicious code, implement intrusion detection and prevention systems to identify and inhibit attacks, and harden critical platforms to reduce vulnerabilities. These protection mechanisms become the walls, guards, and moats of today's electronic fortresses and effectively provide defense in depth.

Defense in depth provides several advantages to organizations. The obvious benefit is the added security that results from requiring an attacker to spend more time and resources to break in. Another benefit is the flexibility it provides in responding to specific threats. For example, consider a worm that exploits databases via a specific TCP port. The options for responding to the threat include shutting down the port the worm uses, hardening the database directly, or perhaps setting intrusion detection rules to spot and terminate an attack. Flexibility is important in production environments, where one action may adversely impact mission critical systems, requiring other actions to be considered.

Defense in depth provides a major disadvantage, too—complexity. Defense in depth increases the number of protection mechanisms implemented. It requires architects and administrators to consider the overall design of the network. Moreover, they must consider all the protection mechanisms to ensure they adequately protect against threats and do not conflict with one another.

As you learn about protection mechanisms, think not just about their technical aspects and the security they provide. Think about their ability to work with other mechanisms to provide defense in depth. How can they work together to increase the overall security of the system? Also, consider the management implications of each mechanism. Remember that these mechanisms are often implemented on a large scale and each one requires maintenance, administration, and monitoring. One of the greatest challenges in information security today is in managing the protection mechanisms on an enterprise-scale and effectively leveraging them to provide defense in depth.

Chapter Summary

- Identification is a mechanism that provides basic information about an unknown entity to the known entity that it wants to communicate with.

- Authentication is the validation of a user's identity. Authentication devices can depend on one or more of four factors: what you know, what you have, what you are, and what you produce.

- Authorization is the process of determining which actions an authenticated entity can perform in a particular physical or logical area.

- Accountability is the documentation of actions on a system and the tracing of those actions to a user, who can then be held responsible for those actions. Accountability is performed using system logs and auditing.

- To obtain strong authentication, a system must use two or more authentication methods.

- Biometric technologies are evaluated on three criteria: false reject rate, false accept rate, and crossover error rate.

- A firewall in an information security program is any device that prevents a specific type of information from moving between the outside world (the untrusted network) and the inside world (the trusted network).

- Types of firewalls include packet filtering firewalls, application-level firewalls, stateful inspection firewalls, and dynamic packet filtering firewalls. There are four common architectural implementations of firewalls: packet filtering routers, screened-host firewalls, dual-homed firewalls, and screened-subnet firewalls.

- A host-based IDS resides on a particular computer or server and monitors activity on that system. A network-based IDS monitors network traffic; when a predefined condition occurs, it responds and notifies the appropriate administrator.

- A signature-based IDS, also known as a knowledge-based IDS, examines data traffic for activity that matches signatures, which are preconfigured, predetermined attack patterns. A statistical anomaly-based IDS (also known as a behavior-based IDS) collects data from normal traffic and establishes a baseline. When the activity is outside the baseline parameters (called the clipping level), the IDS notifies the administrator.

- The science of encryption, known as cryptology, encompasses cryptography and cryptanalysis. Cryptanalysis is the process of obtaining the original message from an encrypted code, without the use of the original algorithms and keys.

- In encryption, the most commonly used algorithms employ either substitution or transposition. A substitution cipher substitutes one value for another. A transposition cipher (or permutation cipher) rearranges the values within a block to create the ciphertext.

- Symmetric encryption uses the same key, also known as a secret key, to both encrypt and decrypt a message. Asymmetric encryption (public key encryption) uses two different keys for these purposes.

- A public key infrastructure (PKI) encompasses the entire set of hardware, software, and cryptosystems necessary to implement public key encryption.

- A digital certificate is a block of data similar to a digital signature, attached to a file, certifying that the file is from the organization it claims to be from and has not been modified.

- A number of cryptosystems have been developed to make e-mail more secure. Examples include Pretty Good Privacy (PGP), Secure Multipurpose Internet Mail Extensions (S/MIME), and Privacy Enhanced Mail (PEM).

- A number of cryptosystems work to secure Web browsers, including Secure Electronic Transactions (SET), Secure Sockets Layer (SSL), Secure Hypertext Transfer Protocol (SHTTP), Secure Shell (SSH), and IP Security (IPSec).

Review Questions

1. What is the difference between authentication and authorization? Can a system permit authorization without authentication? Why or why not?

2. What is the most widely accepted biometric authorization technology? Why do you think this is the case?

3. What is the most effective biometric authorization technology? Why do you think this is the case?

4. What is the typical relationship between the untrusted network, the firewall, and the trusted network?

5. How is an application layer firewall different from a packet filtering firewall? Why is an application layer firewall sometimes called a proxy server?

6. What special function does a cache server perform? Why does this function have value for larger organizations?

7. How does screened-host firewall architecture differ from screened-subnet firewall architecture? Which offers more security for the information assets that remain on the trusted network?

8. What is a DMZ? Is this really a good name for the function that this type of subnet performs?

9. What is RADIUS? What advantage does it have over TACACS?

10. How does a network-based IDS differ from a host-based IDS?

11. What is network footprinting? What is network fingerprinting? How are they related?

12. Why do many organizations ban port scanning activities on their internal networks? Why would ISPs ban outbound port scanning by their customers?

13. Why is TCP port 80 always of critical importance when securing an organization's network?

14. What kind of data and information can be found using a packet sniffer?

15. What are the main components of cryptology?

16. Explain the relationship between plaintext and ciphertext.

17. Define steganography. Why would it be of interest to information security professionals?

18. One tenet of cryptography is that increasing the work factor to break a code increases the security of that code. Why is that true?

19. Explain the key differences between symmetric and asymmetric encryption. Which can the computer process faster? Which lowers the costs associated with key management?

20. What is a VPN? Why are VPNs widely used?

Exercises

1. Create a spreadsheet that takes eight values input into eight different cells and then applies a transposition cipher to them. Next, create a row that takes the results and applies a substitution cipher to them (substitute 0 for 5, 1 for 6, 2 for 7, 3 for 8, 4 for 9, and vice versa).

2. Search the Internet for information about a technology called personal firewalls. Examine the various alternatives and compare their functionality, cost, features, and type of protection.

3. Go to the Web site of VeriSign, one of the market leaders in digital certificates. Determine whether VeriSign serves as a registration authority, certificate authority, or both. Download its free guide to PKI and summarize VeriSign's services.

4. Go to csrc.nist.gov and locate Federal Information Processing Standard (FIPS) 197. What encryption standard does this address use? Examine the contents of this publication and describe the algorithm discussed. How strong is it? How does it encrypt plaintext?

5. Search the Internet for vendors of biometric products. Find one vendor with a product designed to examine each characteristic mentioned in Figure 9-4. What is the CER associated with each product? Which would be more acceptable to users? Which would be preferred by security administrators?

Case Exercises

Iris's PDA beeped. Frowning, she glanced at the screen, expecting to see another junk e-mail. "We've really got to do something about the spam!" she muttered to herself. She scanned the header of the message.

"Uh-oh!" She glimpsed at her watch, grabbed her cell phone, and while looking at her incident response pocket card, dialed the home number of the on-call systems administrator. When he answered, she asked "Seen the alert yet? What's up?"

"Wish I knew—some sort of virus," he replied. "A user must have opened an infected attachment."

Iris made a mental note to remind the awareness program manager to restart the refresher training program for virus control. Her users should know better, but some new employees had not been trained yet.

"Why didn't the firewall catch it?" Iris asked.

"It must be a new one," he replied. "It slipped by the pattern filters."

"What are we doing now?" Iris was growing more nervous by the minute.

"I'm ready to cut our Internet connection remotely, then drive down to the office and start our planned recovery operations—shut down infected systems, clean up any infected servers, recover data from tape backups, and notify our peers that they may receive this virus from us in our e-mail. I just need your go-ahead." The admin sounded uneasy. This was not a trivial operation, and he was facing a long night of intense work.

"Do it. I'll activate the incident response plan and start working the notification call list to get some extra hands in to help." Iris knew this situation would be the main topic at the weekly CIO's meeting. She just hoped her colleagues would be able to restore the systems to safe operation quickly. She looked at her watch: 12:35 a.m.

1. What can be done to minimize the risk of the situation recurring? Can these types of situations be completely avoided?

2. If you were in Iris's position, how would you approach your interaction with the second-shift operator?

3. How should RWW go about notifying its peers? What other procedures should Iris have the technician perform?

4. When would be the appropriate time to begin the forensic data collection process to analyze the root cause of this incident? Why?

Endnotes

1 CERT, "Managing Logging and Other Data Collection Mechanisms," CERT Security Improvement Modules. Accessed May 29, 2005. www.cert.org/security-improvement/practices/p092.html.

2 Fred Avolio and Chris Blask. Application gateways and stateful inspection: a brief note comparing and contrasting. *Avolio Consulting Online,* January 22, 1998. Accessed November 22, 2006. www.avolio.com/papers/apgw+spf.html.

3 Elron Software, Inc. Choosing the best firewall for your growing network. April 22, 2002. Accessed November 22, 2006. www.e-consultancy.com/knowledge/whitepapers/77864/choosing-the-best-firewall-for-your-growing-network.html.

4 Kevin Day. *Inside the Security Mind: Making the Tough Decisions.* Upper Saddle River, NJ: Prentice-Hall, 2003: 220.

5 Adrian Grigorof. Challenges in managing firewalls. Accessed November 22, 2006. www.eventid.net/show.asp?DocId=18.

6 Laura Taylor. Guidelines for configuring your firewall rule-set. *Tech Update Online,* April 12, 2001. Accessed November 22, 2006. techupdate.zdnet.com/techupdate/stories/main/0,14179,2707159,00.html.

7 Shon Harris. *CISSP Certification: All in One Exam Guide.* Berkeley, CA: Osborne McGraw-Hill, 2001:163.

8 OECD, The Implications of Wimax for Competition and Regulation. Accessed November 22, 2006. www.oecd.org/dataoecd/32/7/36218739.pdf.

9 FOLDOC. Port. *FOLDOC Online,* June 19, 2002. Accessed November 22, 2006. wombat.doc.ic.ac.uk/foldoc/foldoc.cgi?query=port&action=Search.

10 Kevin Day. *Inside the Security Mind: Making the Tough Decisions.* Upper Saddle River, NJ: Prentice-Hall, 2003: 225.

11 VeriSign. Understanding PKI. *VeriSign Online.* Accessed November 22, 2006. verisign.netscape.com/security/pki/understanding.html.

12 Cisco Systems, Inc. White Paper: IPSec. *Cisco Online,* November 21, 2000. Accessed November 22, 2006. www.cisco.com/en/US/tech/tk827/tk369/tech_white_papers_list.html.

13 Jennifer G. Steiner, Clifford Neuman, and Jeffrey I. Schiller. An authentication service for open network systems. Paper presented for Project Athena, March 30, 1988. Accessed November 22, 2006. www.scs.stanford.edu/nyu/05sp/sched/readings/kerberos.pdf.

14 Ronald L. Krutz and Russell Dean Vines. *The CISSP Prep Guide: Mastering the Ten Domains of Computer Security.* New York: John Wiley and Sons, 2001: 40.

PERSONNEL AND SECURITY

Mike Edwards stuck his head into Iris's office and asked, "Iris, are you free for the next hour or so?"

Iris glanced at her calendar and said, "Sure. What's up?"

Mike was standing in the hall with Erik Paulson, the manager of RWW's help desk. Both men looked grave. Mike said, "Can you bring the human resources policy manual with you?"

Without asking any further questions, Iris pulled the manual from her bookshelf and joined the pair. As they walked down the hall, Mike filled her in on the brewing situation.

In the meeting room that adjoined the CEO's office, three people were already seated. Mike and Paul took seats at the table, and Iris took a chair along the wall. Robin Gateere, RWW's CEO, cleared her throat and said, "Okay. Let's get started."

Jerry Martin from Legal was facilitating the meeting. Also in the room was Gloria Simpson, Senior Vice President of Human Resources. Mike had asked Iris to join this upper-level management meeting because of her familiarity with human resources policy regarding information security.

Jerry began, "Recent events have caused us to revisit our hiring policies. Last week, one of our employees was arrested, and our company name was plastered all over the newspapers and on television. It turns out that the employee was on parole for sexual assault. He was hired into our IT department to work at the help desk. The police have discovered that he is running a Web-based pornography site. His parole was revoked, and he's now in state prison. The questions are, how did he come to be an employee of this company in the first place, and what do we do now?"

Robin said, "As to the second question, we terminated his employment for cause since he did not report to work because he is in jail. As to the first question, ..." She looked pointedly at Erik and said, "What do you know?"

Erik looked uneasy. He said, "This is the first time I became aware that Sam had trouble with the law. As a matter of fact, I was the hiring manger who recruited him, and all of this is news to me. Of course, we followed the usual human resources procedures when we hired him, although I have always wondered why hiring managers don't get to see the whole personnel file for new hires."

Gloria spoke up. "I agree that practice seems odd in light of this case. According to his file, Sam did write about his conviction and parole status on his application. In fact, we did an identity check and received a criminal background report that confirmed the conviction and his parole status. He didn't lie on his application, but it's beyond me how Erik was ever cleared to make him a job offer."

Erik lifted the folder he was holding. "Here's the whole manager's file on Sam. The standard clearance to extend an offer is right here." He slid the folder down the table to Gloria, who looked at the approval signature on the form.

Iris realized several things: Some of the archaic practices in human resources were about to change, somebody in human resources was in lot of trouble, and it was time for her to revisit all of the company's personnel information security policies.

LEARNING OBJECTIVES

Upon completion of this material, you should be able to:

- Identify the skills and requirements for information security positions
- Recognize the various information security professional certifications, and identify which skills are encompassed by each
- Understand and implement information security constraints on the general hiring processes
- Understand the role of information security in employee terminations
- Describe the security practices used to control employee behavior and prevent misuse of information

INTRODUCTION

Maintaining a secure environment requires that the InfoSec department be carefully structured and staffed with appropriately skilled and screened personnel. It also requires that the proper procedures be integrated into all human resources activities, including hiring, training, promotion, and termination practices.

The first part of this chapter discusses information security personnel hiring issues and practices, including information about the most sought-after professional certification credentials. Some aspects of managing InfoSec personnel—such as the placement of the information security department within the organization—were covered in Chapter 5. This chapter provides more details about the proper staffing (or adjusting the staffing plan) of the information security function. It also describes how to adjust IT job descriptions and documented practices to fulfill information security requirements throughout the organization.

The second part of this chapter presents strategies for integrating information security policies into an organization's general hiring practices. This effort requires collaboration between the general management community of interest and information security professionals.

STAFFING THE SECURITY FUNCTION

Selecting an effective mix of information security personnel for a given organization requires that you consider a number of criteria. Some of these criteria are within the control of the organization; others are not, such as the supply and demand of varied skills and experience levels. In general, when the demand for any commodity—including personnel with critical information security technical or managerial skills—rises quickly, the initial supply often fails to meet it. As demand becomes known, professionals entering the job market or refocusing their job skills seek to gain the required skills, experience, and credentials. Until this new supply can meet the demand, however, competition for the scarce resource will continue to drive up costs. Once the supply is level with or higher than demand, organizations can become more selective, and no longer need to pay a premium for those skills.

This process swings back and forth like a clock pendulum, because the real economy, unlike an econometric model, is seldom in a state of equilibrium. For example, there was excess demand for experienced Enterprise Resource Planning (ERP) professionals in the 1990s, and for experienced COBOL programmers at the turn of the 21st century, because of concerns about Y2K issues. At the time of this writing, the outlook is good for experienced security professionals and many new entrants to the field are able to find work. But funding priorities have precluded massive hiring to meet this predicted need for skilled information security professionals. Many economic forecasters expect this deferred demand to become active as organizations seek to meet the perceived demand for information security workers.

Qualifications and Requirements

Due to the relatively recent emergence of information security as a distinct discipline, many organizations are not certain which qualifications competent information security personnel should have. In many cases, the information security staff lacks established roles and responsibilities. To move the information security discipline forward, organizations should take the following steps:

- The general management community of interest should learn more about the requirements and qualifications for both information security positions and relevant IT positions.
- Upper management should learn more about information security budgetary and personnel needs.
- The IT and general management communities of interest must grant the information security function—in particular, the chief information security officer—an appropriate level of influence and prestige.

In most cases, organizations look for a technically qualified information security generalist, with a solid understanding of how organizations operate. In many other fields, the more specialized professionals become, the more marketable they are. In information security, overspecialization can actually be a drawback.

When hiring information security professionals at all levels, organizations frequently look for individuals able to:

- Understand how organizations are structured and operated
- Recognize that information security is a management task that cannot be handled with technology alone
- Work well with people in general, including users, and communicate effectively using both strong written and verbal communication skills
- Acknowledge the role of policy in guiding security efforts
- Understand the essential role of information security education and training, which helps make users part of the solution, rather than part of the problem
- Perceive the threats facing an organization, understand how these threats can become transformed into attacks, and safeguard the organization from information security attacks
- Understand how technical controls (e.g., firewalls, IDSs, and antivirus software) can be applied to solve specific information security problems
- Demonstrate familiarity with the mainstream information technologies, including Disk Operating System (DOS) and/or the Windows command-line, Windows NT/2000, Linux, and UNIX
- Understand IT and InfoSec terminology and concepts

Entering the Information Security Profession

Many information security professionals enter the field after having prior careers in law enforcement or the military, or careers in other IT areas, such as networking, programming, database administration, or systems administration. Recently, college graduates who have tailored their degree programs to specialize in information security have begun to enter the field in appreciable numbers. Figure 10-1 illustrates these possible career paths.

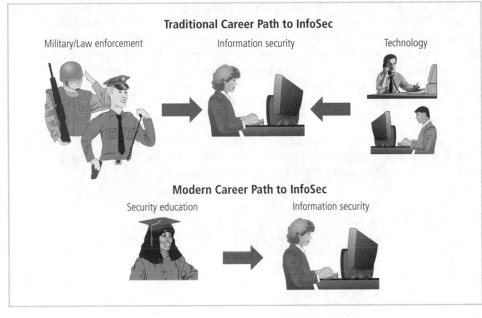

Traditional Career Path to InfoSec

Military/Law enforcement   Information security   Technology

Modern Career Path to InfoSec

Security education   Information security

FIGURE 10-1 Information Security Career Paths

Many information technologists believe that information security professionals must have an established track record in some other IT specialty. However, IT professionals who move into information security tend to focus on technical problems and solutions, to the exclusion of general information security issues. Organizations can foster greater professionalism in the information security discipline by clearly defining their expectations and establishing explicit position descriptions.

Information Security Positions

Standardizing job descriptions can increase the degree of professionalism in the field of information security, as well as improve the consistency of roles and responsibilities among organizations. Organizations can find complete information security job descriptions in Charles Cresson Wood's book *Information Security Roles and Responsibilities Made Easy*. Excerpts from this book are provided later in this chapter.[1]

As you learned in Chapter 5, Schwartz et al. found that information security positions can be classified into one of three areas: those that *define*, those that *build*, and those that *administer*.

> Definers provide the policies, guidelines, and standards ... They're the people who do the consulting and the risk assessment, who develop the product and technical architectures. These are senior people with a lot of broad knowledge, but often not a lot of depth. Then you have the builders. They're the real techies, who create and install security solutions. ... Finally, you have the

people who operate and [administer] the security tools, the security monitoring function, and the people who continuously improve the processes. This is where all the day-to-day, hard work is done. What I find is we often try to use the same people for all of these roles. We use builders all the time ... If you break your InfoSec professionals into these three groups, you can recruit them more efficiently, with the policy people being the more senior people, the builders being more technical, and the operating people being those you can train to do a specific task.[2]

One could find a number of position titles that fit these three roles. The following sections discuss some specific job titles that follow this model. Figure 10-2 shows typical information security job positions and the departmental hierarchy.

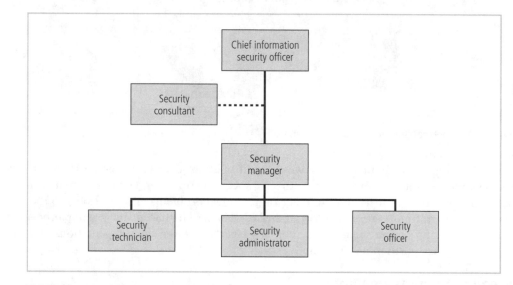

FIGURE 10-2 Possible Information Security Positions and Reporting Relationships

Chief Information Security Officer (CISO)

The CISO is often considered the top information security officer in the organization. As you learned earlier in this book, the CISO is usually not an executive-level position and frequently reports to the CIO. Although CISOs are business managers first and technologists second, they must be conversant in all areas of information security, including technology, planning, and policy. The CISO is expected to draft or approve a range of information security policies. He or she works with the CIO on strategic planning, develops tactical plans, and works with security managers on operational planning. The CISO also develops information security budgets based on available funding, and makes decisions or recommendations about purchasing, project and technology implementation, and the recruiting, hiring, and firing of security staff. This individual is the spokesperson for the security team and is responsible for the overall information security program.

Qualifications and Position Requirements.   The most common qualification for the CISO is the Certified Information Systems Security Professional (CISSP), which is described later in this chapter. A graduate degree in criminal justice, business, technology, or another related field is usually required as well. A candidate for this position should have experience as a security manager, as well as in planning, policy, and budgets. As mentioned earlier, some organizations prefer to hire individuals with law enforcement experience.

Charles Cresson Wood's *Information Security Roles and Responsibilities Made Easy* defines and describes the CISO position, which he calls the Information Security Department Manager, as follows:

Information Security Department Manager

Job Title: Information Security Department Manager [also known as Information Security Manager, Chief Information Security Officer (CISO), or in high-tech firms, simply Chief Security Officer (CSO)]

Reports to: Chief Information Officer (CIO)

Dotted Line: Board of Directors Audit Committee

Summary: The Information Security Department Manager directs, coordinates, plans, and organizes information security activities throughout Company X. He or she acts as the focal point for all communications related to information security, both with internal staff and third parties. The Manager works with a wide variety of people from different internal organizational units, bringing them together to manifest controls that reflect workable compromises as well as proactive responses to current and future information security risks.

Responsibilities and Duties: The Information Security Department Manager is responsible for envisioning and taking steps to implement the controls needed to protect both Company X information as well as information that has been entrusted to Company X by third parties. The position involves overall Company X responsibility for information security regardless of the form that the information takes (paper, blueprint, floppy disk, audio tape, embedded in products or processes, etc.), the information handling technology employed (mainframes, microcomputers, fax machines, telephones, local area networks, file cabinets, etc.), or the people involved (contractors, consultants, employees, vendors, outsourcing firms, etc.).

Threats to information and information systems addressed by the Information Security Department Manager and his or her staff include, but are not limited to: information unavailability, information corruption, unauthorized information destruction, unauthorized information modification, unauthorized information usage, and unauthorized information disclosure. These threats to information and information systems include consideration of physical security matters only if a certain level of physical security is necessary to achieve a certain level of information security (for example, as is necessary to prevent theft of portable computers).

- Acts as the central point of contact within Company X when it comes to all communications dealing with information security problems, issues, and concerns

- Establishes and maintains strong working relationships with the Company X groups involved with information security matters (Legal, Internal Audit, Physical Security, Information Security Management Committee, etc.)
- Establishes, manages, and maintains organizational structures and communications channels with those responsible for information security; these responsible parties include individuals within Company X departments (such as Local Information Security Coordinators) as well as Company X business partners (outsourcing firms, consulting firms, etc.)
- Assists with the clarification of individual information security responsibility and accountability so that necessary information security activities are performed as needed, according to pre-established polices and standards
- Coordinates the information security efforts of all internal groups that have one or more information security-related responsibilities, to ensure that organization-wide information security efforts are consistent across the organization, and that duplication of effort is avoided [this is a shared responsibility with the Physical Security Department Manager]
- Coordinates all multi-application or multi-system information security improvement projects at Company X [a good example would be converting all operating system access control systems to a standard minimum password length]
- Represents Company X and its information security-related interests at industry standards committee meetings, technical conferences, and the like [smaller or less visible organizations will generally dispense with this duty]
- Investigates the ways that information security-related technologies, requirements statements, internal processes, and organizational structures can be used to achieve the goals found in the Company X strategic plan [this effort should include consideration of the long-range information systems plan, which in turn should be an intermediate link between the business strategic plan and the information security plan]
- Creates a strategic information security plan with a vision for the future of information security at Company X (utilizing evolving information security technology, this vision meets a variety of objectives such as management's fiduciary and legal responsibilities, customer expectations for secure modern business practices, and the competitive requirements of the marketplace)
- Understands the fundamental business activities performed by Company X, and based on this understanding, suggests appropriate information security solutions that uniquely protect these activities
- Develops action plans, schedules, budgets, status reports, and other top management communications intended to improve the status of information security at Company X
- Obtains top management approval and ongoing support for all major information security initiatives at Company X (or supervises others in their efforts with these proceedings)

- Brings pressing information security vulnerabilities to top management's attention so that immediate remedial action can be taken
- Performs and/or oversees the performance of periodic Company X risk assessments that identify current and future security vulnerabilities, determines what level of risk is acceptable to management, and identifies the best ways to reduce information security risks to this acceptable level [in a general sense, the Information Security Department Manager performs information security risk management or else establishes a management structure that has others (such as line managers) perform this function]
- Examines information security from a cross-organizational viewpoint including Company X's participation in extranets, electronic data interchange (EDI) trading networks, ad hoc Internet commerce relationships, and other new business structures, and makes related recommendations to protect Company X information and information systems [the prior item discussing risk assessments deals with internal information systems, while this paragraph is advisable whenever new multi-organizational networks are contemplated or deployed]
- Directs the development of or originates self-assessment questionnaires and other tools that assist user department managers and other members of the management team in their efforts to determine the degree of compliance with information security requirements within their respective organizational units
- Periodically initiates quality measurement studies to determine whether the information security function at Company X operates in a manner consistent with standard industry practices (these include customer satisfaction surveys, benchmarking studies, peer comparison efforts, and internal tests)
- Coordinates and directs the development, management approval, implementation, and promulgation of objectives, goals, policies, standards, guidelines, and other requirements needed to support information security throughout Company X as well as within Company X business networks (such as extranets)
- Provides managerial guidance on the development of local, system-specific, and application-specific information security policies, guidelines, standards, and procedures
- Assists with the establishment and refinement of procedures for the identification of Company X information assets as well as the classification of these information assets with respect to criticality, sensitivity, and value [...]
- Coordinates internal staff in their efforts to determine Company X information security obligations according to external requirements (contractual, regulatory, legal, ethical, etc.)
- Closely monitors changes in society's information security-related ethics, values, morals, and attitudes with an eye toward changes that Company X should make in response to these developments

- Designs and manages business processes for the detection, investigation, correction, disciplinary action, and/or prosecution related to information security breaches, violations, and incidents [these efforts would include an intrusion detection system, also known as an IDS]
- Manages internal Company X activities pertaining to the investigation, correction, prosecution, and disciplinary action needed for the resolution of information security breaches, violations, and incidents (whether actual or alleged)
- Prepares post-mortem analyses of information security breaches, violations, and incidents to illuminate what happened and how this type of problem can be prevented in the future
- Directs the preparation of information systems contingency plans and manages worker groups (such as Computer Emergency Response Teams or CERTs) that respond to information security relevant events (hacker intrusions, virus infections, denial-of-service attacks, etc.)
- Works with public relations and top management to develop suitable public responses to information security incidents, violations, and problems
- Acts as an external representative for Company X in the event of a hacker break-in or some other information security relevant event [this may involve news media interviews, discussions with concerned customers, etc.]
- Acts as an expert witness in information security-related legal proceedings involving Company X
- Initiates and manages special projects related to information security that may be needed to appropriately respond to ad hoc or unexpected information security events
- Provides technical support consulting services on matters related to information security such as the criteria to use when selecting information security products
- Performs management and personnel administration functions associated with Company X's Information Security Department (coaches employees, hires and fires employees, disciplines employees, reviews employee performance, recommends salary increases and promotions, counsels employees, establishes employee task lists and schedules, trains staff, etc.)
- Acts as the primary liaison and decision maker regarding the work of information security consultants, contractors, temporaries, and outsourcing firms
- Provides technical information security consulting assistance for Company X staff disciplinary measures, civil suits, and criminal prosecutions
- Stays informed about the latest developments in the information security field, including new products and services, through online news services, technical magazines, professional association memberships, industry conferences, special training seminars, and other methods[3]

In addition to taking on these roles and responsibilities, the CISO must demonstrate competency in a number of areas, as shown in Table 10-1.

TABLE 10-1 Job Competencies for the CISO

1. Job-Specific Competency: Provides organization information security oversight.
   - Maintains current and appropriate body of knowledge necessary to perform the information security management function.
   - Effectively applies information security management knowledge to enhance the security of the open network and associated systems and services.
   - Maintains working knowledge of external legislative and regulatory initiatives. Interprets and translates requirements for implementation.
   - Develops appropriate information security policies, standards, guidelines, and procedures.
   - Works effectively with other organization information security personnel and the committee process.
   - Provides meaningful input, prepares effective presentations, and communicates information security objectives.
   - Participates in short- and long-term planning.
   - Monitors information security program compliance and effectiveness.
   - Works with committees and management professionals to accomplish information security goals.
   - Coordinates and prioritizes activities of the Office of Information Security in support of the mission.
   - Acts as a resource for matters of information security. Provides pertinent and useful information.
   - Oversees and conducts information security reviews and liaison visits to organization [system practices]. Makes recommendations and reports to Regional Practice Administration.
   - Coordinates and performs reviews of contracts, projects, and proposals. Assists information technology proponents with standards compliance.
   - Oversees the conduct of investigations of information security violations and computer crimes. Works effectively with management and external law enforcement to resolve these instances.
   - Reviews instances of noncompliance and works effectively and tactfully to correct deficiencies.

2. Job-Specific Competency: Manages Office of Information Security personnel.
   - Determines positions and personnel necessary to accomplish information security goals. Requests positions, screens personnel, and takes the lead in the interviewing and hiring process.
   - Develops meaningful job descriptions. Communicates expectations and actively coaches personnel for success.
   - Prioritizes and assigns tasks. Reviews work performed. Challenges staff to better themselves and advance the level of service provided.
   - Provides meaningful feedback to staff on an ongoing basis and formally appraises performance annually.
   - Assists information technology proponents with standards compliance.
   - Conducts investigations of information security violations and computer crimes. Works effectively with management and external law enforcement to resolve these instances.
   - Reviews instances of noncompliance and works effectively and tactfully to correct deficiencies.

Source: AAMC-GASP. *Job Descriptions.* Accessed October 14, 2006. http://www.aamc.org/members/gir/gasp/jobdescriptions.pdf.

Security Manager

Security managers are accountable for the day-to-day operation of the information security program. They accomplish objectives identified by the CISO and resolve issues identified by the technicians. Security managers are often assigned specific managerial duties by the CISO, including policy development, risk assessment, contingency planning, and operational and tactical planning for the security function. They often liaise with managers from other departments and divisions in joint planning and development sections, such as security functions in human resources hiring and termination procedures, plant operations in environmental controls, and physical security design.

Management of technology requires an understanding of the technology administered, but not necessarily proficiency in its configuration, operation, or fault resolution. Management of a technology or area is very different from administration of it. For example, systems administrators are expected to be very technically proficient in the technology used by the systems under their control, and are responsible for ensuring that systems are used in compliance with the organization's policies. They may have some management functions, but they are not held accountable as managers. Within the information security community, security managers are those true managers given responsibility for specific tasks, assigned resources to control and apply to those tasks, and held responsible and accountable for the accomplishment of those tasks.

Qualifications and Position Requirements. It is not uncommon for a security manager to have a CISSP. These individuals must have experience in traditional business activities, including budgeting, project management, personnel management, and hiring and firing, and they must be able to draft middle- and lower-level policies as well as standards and guidelines. Experience with business continuity planning is usually considered a plus. There are several types of information security managers, and the people who fill these roles tend to be much more specialized than CISOs. For instance, a Risk Manager performs a different role than a manager hired to administer the SETA program. A careful reading of the job description can identify exactly what a particular employer is looking for.

Wood's job description for the Information Security Department Manager (provided earlier in this chapter) assumes that a single management-level professional performs all the organization's information security management functions. In such a case, the security manager and the CISO are the same person. However, larger organizations that require 24-7 management oversight generally have several positions that collaborate to fulfill the functions that Wood describes. For example, an information security manager-of-managers—the CISO—may supervise managers who are accountable for specialized areas. These managers directly supervise the analysts, technicians, and support staff, and often have additional managerial responsibilities.

Security Technician

Security technicians are technically qualified individuals who configure firewalls and IDSs, implement security software, diagnose and troubleshoot problems, and coordinate with systems and network administrators to ensure that security technology is properly implemented. The role of security technician is the typical information security entry-level position, albeit a technical one. One dilemma for those seeking employment in the field is that it does require a certain level of technical skill, which can be difficult to obtain without experience. As a result, security technicians are likely to be information technology technicians who have adopted a different career path.

Like network technicians, security technicians tend to be specialized, focusing on one major security technology group (firewalls, IDS, servers, routers, and software), and then further specializing in one particular software or hardware package within the group (e.g., Checkpoint firewalls, Nokia firewalls, or Tripwire IDS). These areas are sufficiently complex to warrant this level of specialization. Security technicians who want to move up in the corporate hierarchy must expand their technical knowledge horizontally, and obtain an understanding of the general organizational side of information security as well as all technical areas.

Qualifications and Position Requirements. The technical qualifications and position requirements for a security technician vary. Organizations typically prefer expert, certified, proficient technicians. Job requirements usually include some level of experience with a particular hardware and software package. Sometimes familiarity with a particular technology is enough to secure an applicant an interview; however, experience using the technology is usually required.

Information Security Engineer

Job Title: Information Security Engineer

Reports to: Information Security Department Manager

Summary: An Information Security Engineer provides technical assistance with the design, installation, operation, service, and maintenance of a variety of multiuser information security systems such as virtual private networks (VPNs). A hands-on technical specialist, an Engineer handles the complex and detailed technical work necessary to establish security systems such as firewalls and encryption-based digital signatures. An Engineer configures and sets up information security systems such as firewalls, or else trains Access Control System Administrators, Systems Administrators, Network Administrators, and/or Database Administrators to do these tasks themselves.

Responsibilities and Duties:

- Provides hands-on technical consulting services to teams of technical specialists working on integrating either centralized or networked systems that will offer enhanced levels of information security [examples include an active data dictionary, a data warehouse, or a data mart]
- Provides technical assistance with the initial set-up and secure deployment of systems that support information security, including virus detection systems, firewall content filtering systems, and software license management systems
- Offers technical information security consulting services to distributed personnel who are responsible for one or more information security systems; these people include Network Administrators, Systems Administrators, and Database Administrators
- Evaluates information system bug reports, security exploit reports, and other information security notices issued by information system vendors, government agencies, universities, professional associations, and other organizations, and as needed, makes recommendations to internal management to take precautionary steps [an example of these notices is the periodic reports issued by the CERT at Carnegie Mellon University]
- Runs or works with others who periodically run vulnerability identification software packages and related tools to highlight errors in systems configuration immediately, the need for the application of fixes and patches, and other security-related changes [to leave this task solely to Systems Administrators introduces a conflict of interest because the results of such software will often indicate that Systems Administrators need to perform additional work]

- With management authorization, collects, securely stores, and utilizes software that is able to decrypt encrypted files, automatically guess user passwords, copy software that has been copy-protected, or otherwise circumvent information security measures
- Maintains and, as necessary, documents a collection of software that is able to trace the source of and otherwise investigate attacks on Company X systems
- Conducts selected tests of information security measures in accordance with specific instructions provided by the Information Security Department Manager [this effort usually includes penetration attacks]
- Interprets information security policies, standards, and other requirements as they relate to a specific internal information system, and assists with the implementation of these and other information security requirements
- Redesigns and reengineers internal information handling processes so that information is appropriately protected from a wide variety of problems, including unauthorized disclosure, unauthorized use, inappropriate modification, premature deletion, and unavailability
- Regularly attends conferences, professional association meetings, and technical symposia to remain aware of the latest information security technological developments[4]

Other Position Titles

Organizations often find that many (if not all) noninformation security job descriptions must define information security roles and responsibilities. The following list of positions with information security elements is drawn from *Information Security Roles and Responsibilities Made Easy* and shows the breadth of job titles that may be affected. The job description elements have been grouped according to the community of interest.

Information Security Community:

- InfoSec Department Manager
- Access Control System Administrator
- Internal InfoSec Consultant
- InfoSec Engineer
- InfoSec Documentation Specialist
- InfoSys Contingency Planner
- Local InfoSec Coordinator

IT Community:

- Chief Information Officer
- InfoSys Analyst/Business Analyst
- Systems Programmer
- Business Applications Programmer
- Computer Operations Manager
- Computer Operator
- InfoSys Quality Assurance Analyst
- Help Desk Associate

- Archives Manager/Records Manager
- Telecommunications Manager
- Systems Administrator/Network Administrator
- Web Site Administrator/Commerce Site Administrator
- Database Administrator
- Data Administration Manager

General Business Community:

- Physical Security Department Manager
- Physical Asset Protection Specialist
- Building and Facilities Guard
- Office Maintenance Worker
- Internal Audit Department Manager
- EDP Auditor
- Internal Intellectual Property Attorney
- Human Resources Department Manager
- Human Resources Consultant
- Receptionist
- Outsourcing Contract Administrator
- In-House Trainer
- Insurance and Risk Management Department Manager
- Insurance and Risk Management Analyst
- Business Contingency Planner
- Public Relations Manager
- Chief Financial Officer
- Purchasing Agent
- Chief Executive Officer[5]

INFORMATION SECURITY PROFESSIONAL CREDENTIALS

As you learned in Chapter 2, many organizations rely to some extent on professional certifications to ascertain the level of proficiency possessed by any given candidate. Many of the certification programs are relatively new, and consequently their precise value is not fully understood by most hiring organizations. The certifying bodies work diligently to educate their constituent communities on the value and qualifications of their certificate recipients. Employers struggle to match certifications to position requirements, while potential information security workers try to determine which certification programs will help them in the job market. This section identifies widely recognized information security certification programs and describes their test contents and methodologies.

Certified Information Systems Security Professional (CISSP) and Systems Security Certified Practitioner (SSCP)

Considered the most prestigious certification for security managers and CISOs, the CISSP is one of two certifications offered by the International Information Systems Security Certification Consortium [(ISC)^2; www.isc2.org]; SSCP is the other. The CISSP certification recognizes mastery of an internationally identified common body of knowledge (CBK) in information security. To sit for the CISSP exam, the candidate must have at least three years of direct, full-time security professional work experience in one or more of 10 domains (see below).

The CISSP exam consists of 250 multiple-choice questions and must be completed within six hours. It covers 10 domains of information security knowledge:

- Access control systems and methodology
- Applications and systems development
- Business continuity planning
- Cryptography
- Law, investigation, and ethics
- Operations security
- Physical security
- Security architecture and models
- Security management practices
- Telecommunications, network, and Internet security

CISSP certification requires both successful completion of the exam and, to ensure that the applicant meets the experience requirement, endorsement by a qualified third party (typically another CISSP, the candidate's employer, or another licensed, certified, or commissioned professional). The breadth and depth covered in each of the 10 domains makes it one of the most challenging information security certifications to obtain. Holders of the CISSP must earn a specific number of continuing education credits every three years to retain the certification.

Because it is difficult to master all 10 domains covered on the CISSP exam, many security professionals seek other less rigorous certifications, such as (ISC)²'s SSCP certification. Like the CISSP, the SSCP certification is more applicable to the security manager than the technician, as the bulk of its questions focus on the operational nature of information security. The SSCP focuses on practices, roles, and responsibilities as defined by experts from major IS industries.[6] Nevertheless, the information security technician seeking advancement can benefit from this certification.

The SSCP exam consists of 125 multiple-choice questions and must be completed within three hours. It covers seven domains:

- Access controls
- Administration
- Audit and monitoring
- Risk, response, and recovery
- Cryptography
- Data communications
- Malicious code/malware

Many consider the SSCP to be the little brother of the CISSP. The seven domains are not a subset of the CISSP domains, but rather contain slightly more technical content. Just as with the CISSP, a SSCP holder must earn continuing education credits to retain the certification, or else retake the exam.

(ISC)² also has an innovative approach to the experience requirement in its certification program, the (ISC)² Associate. This program is geared toward individuals who want to take the CISSP or SSCP exams before obtaining the requisite experience for certification. "The Associate of (ISC)^2 program is a mechanism for information security professionals, who are still in the process of acquiring the necessary experience to become CISSPs or SSCPs, to become associated with (ISC)^2 and obtain career-related support during this early period in his or her information security career."[7]

CISSP Concentrations

In addition, to the major certifications that (ISC)^2 offers, a number of concentrations are available for CISSPs to demonstrate advanced knowledge beyond the CISSP CKB. Each concentration requires that the applicant be a CISSP in good standing, pass a separate examination, and maintain the certification in good standing through ongoing continuing professional education. These concentrations and their respective areas of knowledge are presented here:[8]

ISSAP®: Information Systems Security Architecture Professional

- Access control systems and methodology
- Telecommunications and network security
- Cryptography
- Requirements analysis and security standards, guidelines, criteria
- Technology-related business continuity planning and disaster recovery planning
- Physical security integration

ISSEP®: Information Systems Security Engineering Professional

- Systems security engineering
- Certification and accreditation
- Technical management
- U.S. government information assurance regulations

ISSMP®: Information Systems Security Management Professional Enterprise Security Management Practices

- Enterprise-wide system development security
- Overseeing compliance of operations security
- Understanding business continuity planning, disaster recovery planning, and continuity of operations planning
- Law, investigations, forensics, and ethics

Certified Information Systems Auditor (CISA) and Certified Information Security Manager (CISM)

The Certified Information Systems Auditor certification, while not specifically a security certification, does include many information security components. The Information Systems Audit and Control Association and Foundation (ISACA), the sponsoring organization for the CISA, touts the certification as being appropriate for auditing, networking, and security professionals. CISA requirements are as follows:

- Successful completion of the CISA examination

- Experience as an information systems auditor, with a minimum of five years' professional experience in information systems auditing, control, or security
- Agreement to the Code of Professional Ethics
- Payment of maintenance fees, a minimum of 20 contact hours of continuing education annually, and a minimum of 120 contact hours during a fixed three-year period
- Adherence to the Information Systems Auditing Standards

The exam covers the following areas of information systems auditing:

- IS audit process (10 percent)
- IT governance (15 percent)
- Systems and infrastructure lifecycle management (16 percent)
- IT service delivery and support (14 percent)
- Protection of information assets (31 percent)
- Business continuity and disaster recovery (14 percent)

The CISA exam is offered only once a year, so planning in advance is a must.

The Certified Information Security Manager certification program is also offered by ISACA. The CISM credential is geared toward experienced information security managers and others who may have information security management responsibilities. The CISM can assure executive management that a candidate has the required background knowledge needed for effective security management and consulting. This exam is also offered annually. The CISM examination covers the following practice areas:

Information Security Governance (21%)—Establish and maintain a framework to provide assurance that information security strategies are aligned with business objectives and consistent with applicable laws and regulations.

Risk Management (21%)—Identify and manage information security risks to achieve business objectives.

Information Security Program(me) Management (21%)—Design, develop, and manage an information security program(me) to implement the information security governance framework.

Information Security Management (24%)—Oversee and direct information security activities to execute the information security program(me).

Response Management (13%)—Develop and manage a capability to respond to and recover from disruptive and destructive information security events.[9]

To be certified, the applicant must:

- Pass the examination
- Adhere to a code of ethics promulgated by ISACA
- Pursue continuing education as specified
- Complete five years of information security work experience with at least three years in information security management in three or more of the defined areas of practice

Global Information Assurance Certification (GIAC)

In 1999, the System Administration, Networking and Security Organization (SANS; www.sans.org) developed a series of technical security certifications known as the Global Information Assurance Certification (www.giac.org). At the time, no other technical security certifications existed. Those working in the technical security field could only obtain networking or computing certifications like the Microsoft Certified Systems Engineer (MCSE) or Certified Novell Engineer (CNE).

GIAC certifications not only test for knowledge, but also require candidates to demonstrate application of that knowledge. While a growing number of entry-level certifications are available, GIAC currently offers the only advanced technical certifications. The GIAC family of certifications can be pursued independently or combined to earn a comprehensive certification called GIAC Security Engineer (GSE). The GIAC Information Security Officer (GISO) is an overview certification that combines basic technical knowledge with an understanding of threats, risks, and best practices, similar to the SSCP. Unlike other certifications, the GIAC certifications require the applicant to complete a written practical assignment that tests the applicant's ability to apply skills and knowledge. These assignments are submitted to the SANS Information Security Reading Room for review by security practitioners, potential certificate applicants, and others with an interest in information security. Only when the practical assignment is complete is the candidate allowed to take the online exam.

> GIAC now offers two types of certification: Silver and Gold. The requirements for Silver certification are the completion of exam(s). Full certifications require two exams; certificates require a single exam. After earning Silver certification, a candidate can apply for Gold certification which requires a technical paper. The technical paper demonstrates real-world, hands-on mastery of security skills. Passing technical papers will be posted to the GIAC List of Certified Professionals pages and to the SANS Information Security Reading Room to share candidates' knowledge and research, and to further educate the security community.[10]

The individual GIAC certificates and certifications are as follows:

- GIAC Information Security Fundamentals (GISF)
- Stay Sharp Program-Computer and Network Security Awareness (SSP-CNSA)
- Stay Sharp Program-Mastering Packet Analysis (SSP-MPA)
- GIAC Security Essentials Certification (GSEC)
- Securing Solaris-The Gold Standard (GGSC-0200)
- Securing Windows 2000-The Gold Standard (GGSC-0100)
- Auditing Cisco Routers-The Gold Standard (GGSC-0400)
- Stay Sharp Program-Defeating Rogue Access Points (SSP-DRAP)
- GIAC Certified Firewall Analyst (GCFW)
- GIAC Certified Intrusion Analyst (GCIA)
- GIAC Certified Incident Handler (GCIH)
- GIAC Certified Windows Security Administrator (GCWN)
- GIAC Certified UNIX Security Administrator (GCUX)
- GIAC Certified Forensics Analyst (GCFA)

- GIAC Securing Oracle Certification (GSOC)
- GIAC Intrusion Prevention (GIPS)
- GIAC Cutting Edge Hacking Techniques (GHTQ)
- GIAC Web Application Security (GWAS)
- Stay Sharp Program-Google Hacking and Defense (SSP-GHD)
- GIAC Reverse Engineering Malware (GREM)
- GIAC Secure Internet Presence (GSIP)
- GIAC .Net (GNET)
- GIAC Assessing Wireless Networks (GAWN)

Most GIAC certifications are offered in conjunction with SANS training. For more information on the GIAC security-related certification requirements, visit http://www.giac.org/certifications/security/.

The GIAC Security Expert is considered the pinnacle of GIAC security-related certifications.

> Before a person can attempt the GSE, they must successfully complete three GIAC certifications (GSEC, GCIA and GCIH) with GIAC Gold in at least two. In addition, you must pass a proctored GSEC exam with an average score of 80 between the two exams before being allowed to attend the onsite examination.[11]

Security Certified Program (SCP)

One of the newest certifications in the information security discipline is the Security Certified Program (www.securitycertified.net). The SCP offers two tracks: the Security Certified Network Professional (SCNP) and the Security Certified Network Architect (SCNA). Both are designed for the security technician and emphasize technical knowledge; the latter also includes authentication principles. The tests focus on network security, rather than on general networking concepts, making them distinct from the MSCE and the CNE. The SCNP track targets firewalls and intrusion detection, and requires two exams:[12]

- Hardening The Infrastructure (HTI)
- Network Defense and Countermeasures (NDC)

The SCNA program includes the following:

- Enterprise Security Implementation (ESI) which covers:
  - Advanced Security Implementation (ASI)
  - Enterprise Security Solutions (ESS)
- The Solution Exam (TSE) covering all facets of the SCP courses

While not as detailed as the GIAC certifications, these programs provide a useful way for a professional to demonstrate the knowledge needed to work in new areas of security, while developing a vendor-neutral core of practitioner knowledge evaluation.

Security+

From CompTIA (www.comptia.com)—the organization that offered the first vendor-neutral professional IT certifications, the A+ series—comes another certification program, the Security+ certification.

The CompTIA Security+ certification tests for security knowledge mastery of an individual with two years on-the-job networking experience, with emphasis on security. The exam covers industrywide topics including communication security, infrastructure security, cryptography, access control, authentication, external attack, and operational and organization security. CompTIA Security+ curricula are being taught at colleges, universities, and commercial training centers around the globe. CompTIA Security+ is being used as an elective or prerequisite to advanced vendor-specific and vendor-neutral security certifications.[13]

The exam covers five domains, as shown in Table 10-2.

TABLE 10-2 Domains Covered in the CompTIA Security+ Exam

Domain	Percentage of Exam
1.0 General Security Concepts	30%
2.0 Communication Security	20%
3.0 Infrastructure Security	20%
4.0 Basics of Cryptography	15%
5.0 Operational/Organizational Security	15%

Source: CompTIA. *CompTIA Security+ Certification.* Accessed July 17, 2003. www.comptia.com/certification/security/default.asp.

Certified Computer Examiner (CCE)

The Certified Computer Examiner (CCE)® certification is a computer forensics certification provided by the International Society of Forensic Computer Examiners (http://www.isfce.com/). To complete the CCE certification process, the applicant must:

- Have no criminal record
- Meet minimum experience, training, or self-training requirements
- Abide by the certification's code of ethical standards
- Pass an online examination
- Successfully perform actual forensic examinations on three test media

The CCE certification process covers the following areas:

- Acquisition, marking, handling, and storage of evidence procedures
- Chain of custody
- Essential "core" forensic computer examination procedures
- The "rules of evidence" as they relate to computer examinations
- Basic PC hardware construction and theory
- Very basic networking theory
- Basic data recovery techniques
- Authenticating MS Word documents and accessing and interpreting metadata

- Basic optical recording processes and accessing data on optical media
- Basic password recovery techniques
- Basic Internet issues

This certification also has concentrations/endorsements corresponding to the various operations systems present in the current business environments. A CCE who earns three or more of these endorsements qualifies as Master Certified Computer Examiners (MCCE).[14]

Certified Information Forensics Investigator (CIFI)

The Information Security Forensics Association (IFSA; www.infoforensics.org) is developing an examination for a Certified Information Systems Forensics Investigator. This program will evaluate expertise in the tasks and responsibilities of a security administrator or security manager, including incident response, working with law enforcement, and auditing. Although the certification exam has not been finalized yet, the body of knowledge has been tentatively defined to include the following aspects of information security:

- Countermeasures
- Auditing
- Incident response teams
- Law enforcement and investigation
- Traceback
- Tools and techniques

Certification Costs

Certifications cost money, and the preferred certifications can be expensive. Individual certification exams can cost as much as $500, and certifications that require multiple exams can cost thousands of dollars. In addition, the cost for formal training to prepare for the certification exams can be significant. While you should not wholly rely on certification preparation courses as groundwork for a real-world position, they can help you round out your knowledge and fill in gaps. Some certification exams, such as the CISSP, are very broad; others, such as the components of the GIAC, are very technical. Given the nature of the knowledge needed to pass the examinations, most experienced professionals find it difficult to do well on them without at least some review. Many prospective certificate holders engage in individual or group study sessions, and purchase one of the many excellent exam review books on the subject.

Certifications are designed to recognize experts in their respective fields, and the cost of certification deters those who might otherwise take the exam just to see if they can pass. Most examinations require between two and three years of work experience, and they are often structured to reward candidates who have significant hands-on experience. Some certification programs require that candidates document certain minimum experience requirements before they are permitted to sit for the exams. Before attempting a certification exam, do your homework. Look into the exam's stated body of knowledge as well as its purpose and requirements to ensure that the time and energy spent pursuing the certification are well spent. Figure 10-3 shows several approaches to preparing for security certification.

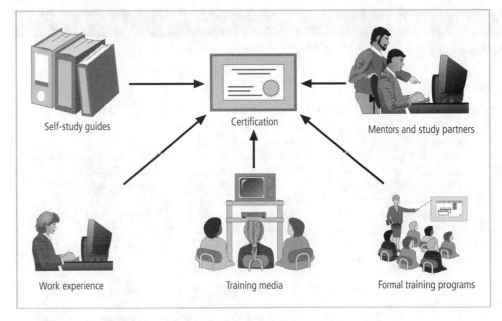

Self-study guides

Certification

Mentors and study partners

Work experience

Training media

Formal training programs

FIGURE 10-3 Preparing for Security Certification

In regard to professional certification for information security practitioners, Charles Cresson Wood reports:

> With résumé fraud on the rise, one of the sure-fire methods for employers to be sure that the people they hire are indeed familiar with the essentials of the field is to insist that they have certain certifications. The certifications can then be checked with the issuing organizations to make sure that they have indeed been conferred on the applicant for employment.
>
> The [...] professional certifications are relevant primarily to centralized information security positions. They are not generally relevant to staff working in decentralized information security positions, unless these individuals intend to become information security specialists. You may also look for these certifications on the résumés of consultants and contractors working in the information security field.
>
> You may wish to list these designations in help wanted advertisements, look for them on résumés, and ask about them during interviews. Automatic résumé scanning software can also be set up to search for these strings of characters.[15]

VIEWPOINT

Finding Your Path

By Herb Mattord, CDP, CISSP

I started my IT career in 1977 programming in COBOL on a mainframe. I had a good academic record, a good attitude, many aspirations, and lots of hope for the future. But I did not foresee a path leading to a career as a university professor and author.

I learned early in my career that certification is an important part of the IT profession. My first certification was the Certificate in Data Processing, which I earned in 1979. While that certification was never the single most critical factor in my career, it helped me understand the power of external validation. That's why in the 1990s I pursued the Microsoft Certified Systems Engineer (MCSE) credential. I took most of the required exams, yet always managed to stay one exam short of certification, and then my career took a different turn.

Inexorable corporate forces drew me to information security in the late 1990s. To gain skills and to demonstrate my professionalism, I decided to pursue another certification, the Certified Information Systems Security Professional (CISSP). A quick look at my byline shows that I was successful in that pursuit.

I take my credentials seriously, finding ways to contribute to the success of my own career and to the future of the profession. When I began the CISSP certification program, I hoped for a positive performance review and another career credential. In fact, I gained a lot more than that: I started on a trail that led me out of corporate information security and into academia. Now, I am privileged to teach and stress the value of quality certifications to my students.

How did the CISSP come to redirect my career path? I suppose the only answer comes from Joseph Campbell. He said:

> If you follow your bliss, you put yourself on a kind of track that has been there all the while, waiting for you, and the life that you ought to be living is the one you are living. Wherever you are—if you are following your bliss, you are enjoying that refreshment, that life within you, all the time.[16]

The CISSP gave me the opportunity and the courage to follow my own sense of what gives me fulfillment. This pursuit of satisfaction is truly what Campbell had in mind when he said to follow your bliss.

As you progress in your own career, look for opportunities, and be aware that they may be very well camouflaged. What looks like a precipice might just be the springboard for your dreams.

EMPLOYMENT POLICIES AND PRACTICES

The general management community of interest should integrate solid information security concepts across all of the organization's employment policies and practices. The following sections examine important concepts associated with recruiting, hiring, firing, managing, and releasing human resources. Including information security responsibilities into every employee's job description and subsequent performance reviews can make an entire organization take information security more seriously.

Hiring

From an information security perspective, the hiring of employees is laden with potential security pitfalls. The CISO, in cooperation with the CIO and relevant information security managers, should establish a dialogue with human resources personnel so that information security considerations become part of the hiring process. Figure 10-4 highlights some of the hiring concerns.

Background checks

Certifications

Policies

Covenants and agreements

Contracts

FIGURE 10-4   Hiring Issues

Job Descriptions

Integrating information security into the hiring process begins with reviewing and updating job descriptions to include information security responsibilities. Organizations that provide complete job descriptions when advertising open positions should omit the elements of the job description that describe access privileges.

Interviews

Some interviews are conducted by members of the human resources staff; others include members of the department that the employee will eventually join. When a position within the information security department opens up, the security manager can take the opportunity to educate human resources personnel on the various certifications, the specific experience each credential requires, and the qualifications of a good candidate. In general, information security should advise human resources to limit the information provided to the candidates on the access rights of the position. When an interview includes a site visit, the tour should avoid secure and restricted sites because the visitor could observe enough information about the operations or information security functions to represent a potential threat to the organization.

New Hire Orientation

New employees should receive, as part of their orientation, an extensive information security briefing. This orientation should cover policies, security procedures, access levels, and training on the secure use of information systems. By the time employees are ready to report to their positions, they should be thoroughly briefed on the security component of their particular jobs, as well as the rights and responsibilities of all personnel in the organization.

On-the-Job Security Training

Organizations should conduct the periodic security awareness and training activities described in Chapter 5 to keep security at the forefront of employees' minds and minimize employee mistakes. Formal external and informal internal seminars also increase the level of security awareness for all employees, but especially for InfoSec employees.

Security Checks

A background check should be conducted before the organization extends an offer to any candidate, regardless of job level. A background check can uncover past criminal behavior or other information that suggests a potential for future misconduct or a vulnerability that might render a candidate susceptible to coercion or blackmail. A number of regulations govern which areas organizations are permitted to investigate and how the information gathered can influence the hiring decision. The security and human resources managers should discuss these matters with legal counsel to determine which local and state regulations apply.

Background checks differ in their levels of detail and depth. In the military, background checks are used to help determine the individual's security clearance. In the business world, the thoroughness of a background check can vary with the level of trust required for the position being filled. Candidates for information security positions should expect to undergo a reasonably detailed and thorough background check. Those applying for jobs in law enforcement or high-security positions may be required to submit to polygraph tests. Some of the common types of background checks are as follows:

- Identity checks: personal identity validation
- Education and credential checks: institutions attended, degrees and certifications earned, and certification status
- Previous employment verification: where candidates worked, why they left, what they did, and for how long
- Reference checks: validity of references and integrity of reference sources
- Worker's compensation history: claims from worker's compensation
- Motor vehicle records: driving records, suspensions, and other items noted in the applicant's public record
- Drug history: drug screening and drug usage, past and present
- Medical history: current and previous medical conditions, usually associated with physical capability to perform the work in the specified position

- Credit history: credit problems, financial problems, and bankruptcy
- Civil court history: involvement as the plaintiff or defendant in civil suits
- Criminal court history: criminal background, arrests, convictions, and time served

Organizations must comply with federal regulations regarding the use of personal information in employment practices. Among those is the Fair Credit Reporting Act (FCRA), enacted in 1970, which governs the activities of consumer credit reporting agencies as well as the uses of the information procured from these agencies.[17] Credit reports contain information on a job candidate's credit history, employment history, and other personal data.

Among other things, FCRA prohibits employers from obtaining a credit report unless the candidate gives written permission for such a report to be released. This regulation also allows the candidate to request information on the nature and type of reporting used in making the employment decision, and to know the content of these reports and how they were used in making the hiring decision. FCRA restricts the time period that these reports can address. Unless the candidate earns more than $75,000 per year, they can contain only seven years of adverse information.[18]

Contracts and Employment

Once a candidate has accepted a job offer, the employment contract becomes an important security instrument. Many of the policies discussed in Chapter 6 require an employee to agree in writing to monitoring and nondisclosure agreements. It is important to have these contracts and agreements in place at the time of the hire because existing employees cannot necessarily be compelled to sign, nor can they be denied access to the systems that enable them to perform their duties. Job candidates, on the other hand, can be offered "employment contingent upon agreement," whereby they are not offered a position unless they agree to the binding organizational policies. While such a policy may seem harsh, it is a necessary component of the security process. Once candidates sign the security agreements, the remainder of the employment contracts may be executed.

Security as Part of Performance Evaluation

To heighten information security awareness and change workplace behavior, organizations should incorporate information security components into employee performance evaluations. Employees pay close attention to job performance evaluations, and including information security tasks in them will motivate employees to take more care when performing these tasks.

Termination Issues

An organization can downsize, be bought out, be taken over, shut down, go out of business, or simply lay off, fire, or relocate its workforce. In any event, when an employee leaves an organization, a number of security-related concerns arise. Chief among these is the continuity of protection for all information to which the employee had access. When an employee leaves an organization, the following tasks must be performed:

- The former employee's access to the organization's systems must be disabled.
- The former employee must return all removable media.

- The former employee's hard drives must be secured.
- File cabinet locks must be changed.
- Office door locks must be changed.
- The former employee's keycard access must be revoked.
- The former employee's personal effects must be removed from the premises.
- The former employee should be escorted from the premises, once keys, keycards, and other business property have been turned over.

In addition to performing these tasks, many organizations conduct an **exit interview** to remind the employee of any contractual obligations, such as nondisclosure agreements, and to obtain feedback on the employee's tenure in the organization. At this time, the employee should be reminded that failure to comply with contractual obligations could lead to civil or criminal action.

Of course, most employees are allowed to clean out their own offices and collect their personal belongings, and are simply asked to return their keys. From a security standpoint, however, regardless of the level of trust in the employee or the level of cordiality in the office environment, voluntary or involuntary termination inevitably brings a risk of exposure of organizational information.

Some organizations adopt a policy of immediate severance for all employees, or for employees in certain positions or areas of trust. These organizations have examined the risks of the customary two-week notice model, and choose to pay two weeks severance but ask the employee to leave the facility immediately.

Two methods for handling employee outprocessing, depending on the employee's reasons for leaving, are as follows:

- Hostile departure (usually involuntary), including termination, downsizing, lay-off, or quitting: Security cuts off all logical and keycard access, before the employee is terminated. As soon as the employee reports for work, he or she is escorted into the supervisor's office to receive the bad news. The individual is then escorted from the workplace and informed that his or her personal property will be forwarded, or is escorted to his or her office, cubicle, or personal area to collect personal effects under supervision. No organizational property is allowed to leave the premises, including disks, pens, papers, or books. Terminated employees can submit, in writing, a list of the property they want to retain, stating their reasons for doing so. Once personal property has been gathered, the employee is asked to surrender all keys, keycards, and other organizational identification and access devices, PDAs, pagers, cell phones, and all remaining company property, and is then escorted from the building.
- Friendly departure (voluntary) for retirement, promotion, or relocation: The employee may have tendered notice well in advance of the actual departure date, which can make it much more difficult for security to maintain positive control over the employee's access and information usage. Employee accounts are usually allowed to continue, with a new expiration date. The employee can come and go at will and usually collects any belongings and leaves without escort. The employee is asked to drop off all organizational property before departing.

In either circumstance, the offices and information used by departing employees must be inventoried, their files stored or destroyed, and all property returned to organizational stores. It is possible in either situation that departing employees have collected organizational information and taken home files, reports, data from databases, and anything else that could be valuable in their future employment. This outcome may be impossible to prevent. Only by scrutinizing system logs during the transition period and after the employee has departed, and sorting out authorized actions from system misuse or information theft, can the organization determine whether a breach of policy or a loss of information has occurred. If information has been illegally copied or stolen, it should be treated as an incident and the appropriate policy followed. Figure 10-5 illustrates some termination concerns and procedures.

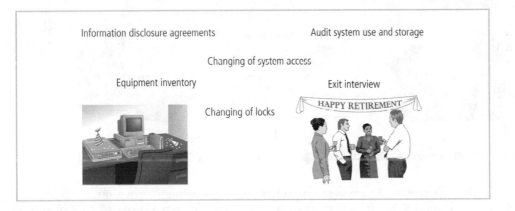

FIGURE 10-5 Termination Issues

Personnel Security Practices

There are various ways of monitoring and controlling employees to minimize their opportunities to misuse information. **Separation of duties** is used to make it difficult for an individual to violate information security and breach the confidentiality, integrity, or availability of information. This control is particularly important in financial matters. For example, banks typically require two employees to issue a cashier's check. The first is authorized to prepare the check, acquire the numbered financial document, and ready the check for signature. The second, usually a supervisor, is authorized to sign the check. If one person has the authority to do both tasks, then that person can prepare checks made out to coconspirators, sign them, and steal large sums from the bank.

Separation of duties can also be applied to critical information and information systems. For example, one programmer might update the software in the systems, and a supervisor or coworker might then apply the tested update to the production system following the procedures of the change management process. Alternatively, one employee might be authorized to initiate backups to the system, while another mounts and dismounts the physical media. This checks-and-balances method requires two or more people to conspire to commit a theft or other misadventure, which is known as **collusion.** The odds that two people will be able to collaborate successfully to misuse the system are much lower than the odds of one person doing so. A practice similar to separation of duties, known as **two-person control**, requires that two individuals review and approve each other's work before the task is considered complete. Figure 10-6 illustrates separation of duties and two-person control.

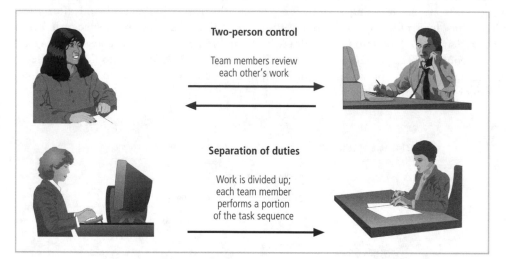

FIGURE 10-6   Personnel Security Controls

Another control used to prevent personnel from misusing information assets is job rotation. **Job rotation** requires that every employee be able to perform the work of at least one other employee. If that approach is not feasible, an alternative is **task rotation**, in which all critical tasks can be performed by multiple individuals. Both job rotation and task rotation ensure that no one employee is performing actions that cannot be knowledgeably reviewed by another employee. In general, this overlap of knowledge is just good business sense. Among the many threats to an organization's information, a major concern is the inability to perform the tasks of an employee who is unable or unwilling to perform them. If everyone knows at least part of another person's job (a human RAID system), the organization can survive the loss of any single employee.

For similar reasons, each employee should be required to take a **mandatory vacation**, of at least one week per year. This policy gives the organization a chance to perform a detailed review of everyone's work. Employees who are stealing from an organization or otherwise misusing information or systems are reluctant to take vacations; for fear that their actions will be detected if they are not present to conceal them.

Finally, another important way to minimize opportunities for employee misuse information is to limit access to information. That is, employees should be able to access only the information they need, and only for the period required to perform their tasks. This idea is referred to as the principle of **least privilege**. Similar to the need-to-know concept, least privilege ensures that no unnecessary access to data occurs. If all employees can access all the organization's data all the time, it is almost certain that abuses—possibly leading to losses in confidentiality, integrity, and availability—will occur.

Security of Personnel and Personal Data

Organizations are required by law to protect sensitive or personal employee information, including personally identifying facts such as employee addresses, phone numbers, Social Security numbers, medical conditions, and even names and addresses of family members. This responsibility also extends to customers, patients, and anyone with whom the organization has business relationships. While personnel data is, in principle, no different than other data that information security is expected to protect, certainly more regulations cover its protection. As a result, information security procedures should ensure that this data receives at least the same level of protection as the other important data in the organization. You will learn more about privacy and information security in Chapter 11.

Security Considerations for Nonemployees

People who are not employees often have access to sensitive organizational information. Relationships with people in this category should be carefully managed to prevent threats to information assets from materializing. Some of the categories of nonemployees, and the security considerations specific to them, are discussed in the sections that follow.

Temporary Workers

Temporary workers—often called temps—are brought in by organizations to fill positions temporarily or to supplement the existing workforce. In many cases, they are actually employees of a temp agency, a company that is paid to supply specially qualified individuals to an organization. Temps frequently provide secretarial or administrative support but can be used to fill almost any position in an organization, including executives. These workers are often exposed to a wide range of information as they perform their assigned duties. Because they are not employed by the organization for which they are working, however, they may not be subject to the contractual obligations or general policies that govern other employees. Therefore, if a temp violates a policy or causes a problem, the strongest action that the host organization can take is to terminate the relationship with the individual and request that he or she be censured. The employing agency is under no contractual obligation to do so, but may want to accommodate a powerful or lucrative client. Unless specified in its contract with the organization, the temp agency may not be liable for losses caused by its workers.

From a security standpoint, temporary workers' access to information should be limited to what is necessary to perform their duties. The organization can attempt to have temps sign nondisclosure agreements and fair use policies, but the temp agency may refuse to go along, forcing the host organization to either dismiss the temp workers or allow them to work without such agreements. This can create an awkward—and potentially dangerous—situation. It may be impossible to limit a temp's access to information that is beyond the scope of his or her assigned tasks. The only way to combat this threat is to ensure that employees who are supervising temporary workers restrict their access to information, and to make sure that all workers—whether employees or temps—follow good security practices, especially clean desk policies and securing classified data. Temps can provide great benefits to organizations, but they should not be employed at the cost of sacrificing information security.

Contract Employees

Contract employees—often called contractors—are typically hired to perform specific services for the organization. In many cases, they are hired via a third-party organization. Typical contract employees include groundskeepers, maintenance services staff, electricians, mechanics, and other repair people, but can include professionals such as attorneys, technical consultants, and IT specialists.

While professional contractors may require access to virtually all areas of the organization to do their jobs, service contractors usually need access only to specific facilities, and should not be allowed to wander freely in and out of buildings. In a secure facility, all service contractors are escorted from room to room, and into and out of the facility. When these employees report for maintenance or repair services, someone must verify that services are actually scheduled or requested. As mentioned earlier in this book, attackers have been known to dress up as telephone repairers, maintenance technicians, or janitors to gain physical access to a building; therefore, direct oversight is a necessity. Any service agreements or contracts should contain the following regulations: The facility requires 24 to 48 hours' notice of a maintenance visit; the facility requires all on-site personnel to undergo background checks; and the facility requires advance notice for cancellation or rescheduling of a maintenance visit.

Consultants

Organizations sometimes hire self-employed or agent contractors—typically called consultants—for specific tasks or projects. Consultants have their own security requirements and contractual obligations; their contracts should specify their rights of access to information and facilities. Security and technology consultants must be prescreened, escorted, and subjected to nondisclosure agreements to protect the organization from intentional or accidental breaches of confidentiality. Consultants tend to brag about the complexity of a particular job or an outstanding service provided to another client. If the organization does not want a consultant to make the relationship public or to disclose any detail, however small, about its particular system configuration, the organization must write these restrictions into the contract. Although these professionals typically request permission to include the business relationship on their résumés or promotional materials, the hiring organization is not obligated to grant this permission and can explicitly deny it.

Just because you pay security consultants, it does not mean that protecting your information is their number one priority. Always remember to apply the principle of least privilege when working with consultants.

Business Partners

Businesses sometimes engage in strategic alliances with other organizations to exchange information, integrate systems, or enjoy some other mutual advantage. In these situations, a prior business agreement must specify the levels of exposure that both organizations are willing to tolerate. Sometimes one division of an organization enters a strategic partnership with another organization that directly competes with one of its own divisions. If the strategic partnership evolves into an integration of the systems of both companies, competing groups may be provided with information that neither parent organization expected. For this reason, there must be a meticulous, deliberate process of determining what information is to be exchanged, in which format, and to whom. Nondisclosure agreements are an important part of any such collaborative effort. The level of security of both systems must be examined before any physical integration takes place, as system connection means that vulnerability on one system becomes vulnerability for all linked systems.

OFFLINE

Social Engineering

The most nontechnical attack involves people. For this reason, this book dedicates a great deal of space to reinforcing the concept that security is a people problem, not a technological one. Every day thousands of systems are attacked successfully by individuals who take advantage of the natural gullibility of people. This gullibility is usually the result of a simple lack of computing knowledge and experience.

Social engineering (SE) uses persuasive techniques to gain the confidence of an individual in an effort to obtain information. Contrary to popular myth, most social engineering attacks don't come in as a phone call from "Joe in technology services" asking for your user name and password to fix your computer problem. Most attacks are subtle, and involve the collection of small bits of seemingly innocuous information until a base of insider knowledge is built and then deployed to gain access to systems or information. According to the infamous Kevin Mitnick, who used social engineering as the primary means of gaining access to an organization's systems: "'(As) the media characterizes social engineering, hackers will call up and ask for a password,' Mitnick said. 'I have never asked anyone for their password.'"[19] The former superhacker turned security consultant served five years for his crimes. How do you succeed at SE attacks? "You try to make an emotional connection with the person on the other side to create a sense of trust," he said. "That is the whole idea: to create a sense of trust and then exploit it."[20]

Some forms of SE attacks are so prevalent that there are formal warnings about them:

CERT/CC has received reports of social engineering attacks on users of Internet Relay Chat (IRC) and Instant Messaging (IM) services. Intruders trick unsuspecting users into downloading and executing malicious software, which allows the intruders to use the systems as attack platforms for launching distributed denial-of-service (DDoS) attacks. The reports to the CERT/CC indicate that tens of thousands of systems continue to be compromised in this and other manners. Other reports indicate that Trojan horse and backdoor programs are being propagated via similar techniques. Here is an example of one such message:

You are infected with a virus that lets hackers get into your machine and read your files, etc. I suggest you download [malicious URL] and clean your infected machine. Otherwise, you will be banned from [IRC network].[21]

Many people recognize these types of e-mails, IMs, and pop-ups for what they are. However, people with little computer experience may fail to discriminate between legitimate virus warnings and SE attacks.

continued

Personnel and Security

A similar attack has been conducted recently to propagate viruses. An e-mail arrives, apparently from Microsoft (see Figure 10-7), insisting that the user immediately download a critical patch or upgrade to avoid leaving his or her system open to attack. Because Microsoft does not e-mail individuals directly, experienced computer users simply delete the message. To the untrained eye, the message appears legitimate, however, and consequently it may be activated.

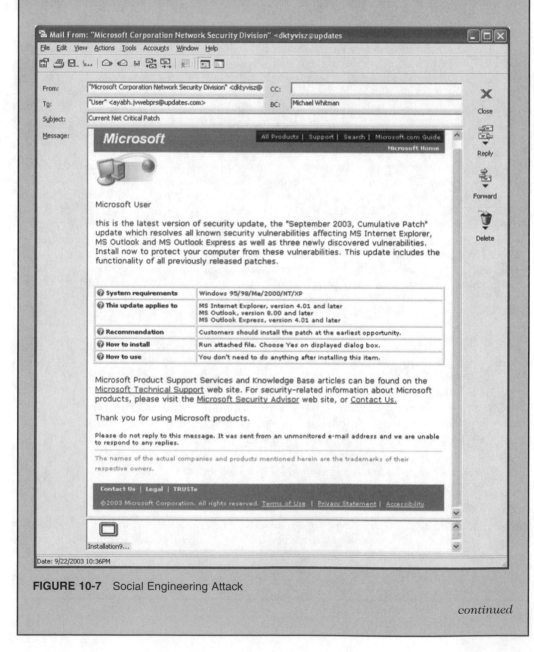

FIGURE 10-7 Social Engineering Attack

continued

SE Attack Detection

It can be quite difficult to detect a social engineering attack. Indeed, attackers are becoming increasingly sophisticated. Sometimes they ask for seemingly innocuous information, such as the name or telephone number of a coworker. Many employees may have given this information out routinely, without a second thought, allowing an attacker to begin building a story to get more information from the next person. To detect an SE attack, employees should be trained to detect anomalies in a conversation, e-mail, or pop-up window. These anomalies include "refusal to give contact information, rushing, name-dropping, intimidation, small mistakes (misspellings, misnomers, odd questions), and requesting forbidden information. Look for things that don't quite add up."[22]

SE Attack Prevention

The best method of preventing SE attacks is preparation. All employees must be trained and aware of the potential for these types of attacks. Security education, training, and awareness programs that focus on SE attacks can provide the organization with invaluable preparation and prevention techniques. Some additional prevention methods, along with the attacks they intend to thwart, are presented in Table 10-3.

TABLE 10-3 Social Engineering Tactics and Strategies

Area of Risk	Hacker Tactic	Combat Strategy
Phone (help desk)	Impersonation and persuasion	Train employees and help desk personnel to never give out passwords or other confidential information by phone
Building entrance	Unauthorized physical access	Use tight badge security, provide employee training, and have security officers present
Office	Shoulder surfing	Do not type in passwords with anyone else present (if you must, do it quickly!)
Phone (help desk)	Impersonation on help desk calls	Assign all employees a PIN specific to help desk support
Office	Wandering through halls looking for open offices	Require all guests to be escorted
Mailroom	Insertion of forged memos	Lock and monitor the mailroom
Machine room/ phone closet	Attempting to gain access, remove equipment, and/or attach a protocol analyzer to grab confidential data	Keep phone closets, server rooms, and other facilities locked at all times and keep an updated inventory of equipment

continued

TABLE 10-3 Social Engineering Tactics and Strategies (continued)

Area of Risk	Hacker Tactic	Combat Strategy
Phone and PBX	Stealing phone toll access	Control overseas and long-distance calls, trace calls, and refuse transfers
Dumpsters	Dumpster diving	Keep all trash in secured, monitored areas, shred important data, and erase magnetic media
Intranet-Internet	Creation and insertion of mock software on intranet or Internet to steal passwords	Maintain continual awareness of system and network changes, and provide training on password use
Office	Stealing sensitive documents	Mark documents as confidential and require them to be locked
General–psychological	Impersonation and persuasion	Keep employees on their toes through continued awareness and training programs

Source: S. Granger. *Social Engineering Fundamentals, Part II: Combat Strategies Security Focus.* January 9, 2002. Accessed October 14, 2006. www.securityfocus.com/infocus/1533.

SE Attack Defense

The first thing an employee must do to defend against an SE attack is to tell someone. The organization should have an established procedure for reporting suspected SE attacks. If the organization uses some form of caller ID, the number of the suspected SE attacker should be documented and reported. The organization's incident response team should log these attacks and treat them no differently than any other form of attack.

A paper by David Gragg overviews a multilayered defense against SE. In this paper, Gragg defines the following layers of defense:[23]

Foundational Level: Security Policy Addressing Social Engineering
Parameter Level: Security Awareness Training for All Users
Fortress Level: Resistance Training for Key Personnel
Persistence Level: Ongoing Reminders
Gotcha Level: Social Engineering Land Mines (SELM)

- The Justified Know-It-All
- Centralized Security Log
- Call Backs by Policy
- Key Questions
- "Please Hold" by Policy

Offensive Level: Incident Response

It is not difficult to protect against SE attacks, but employees must first know what they are and how they are conducted. Through these educational efforts, SE attacks can become your least dangerous threat, rather than the most dangerous one.

Chapter Summary

- The hiring of information security personnel is affected by a number of factors, among them the law of supply and demand. In most cases, organizations look for a technically qualified information security generalist, with a solid understanding of how the organization conducts its business, to serve as the chief information security officer.

- Many organizations rely on certifications to document the qualifications of current and/or prospective employees, recognizing that a professional association's assessment of skills and knowledge is a valid way of assessing the quality of these individuals.

- Many information security professionals enter the field through one of two career paths: (1) as former members of law enforcement or the military, or (2) as IT professionals. A relatively new trend is the emergence of university-trained information security specialists.

- During the hiring process, applying standard job descriptions can increase the degree of professionalism in the information security field and improve the consistency of roles and responsibilities among organizations.

- Many organizations use recognizable certifications to identify the level of proficiency associated with the various security positions.

- Management should integrate information security concepts and practices into the organization's employment activities.

- Organizations need the special services of nonemployees—temps, contractors, and consultants—and these relationships must be carefully managed to prevent information security breaches.

- Separation of duties, two-man control, job and task rotation, mandatory vacations, and least privilege are among the practices and methods recommended to minimize employees' opportunities to misuse information.

- Government-mandated requirements for the privacy and security of personnel and personal data must be met by the organization's information security program.

Review Questions

1. When an organization undertakes an information security-driven review of job descriptions, which job descriptions must be reviewed? Which IT jobs not directly associated with information security should be reviewed?

2. List and describe the criteria for selecting information security personnel.

3. What are some of the factors that influence an organization's hiring decisions?

4. What attributes do organizations seek in a candidate when hiring information security professionals? Prioritize this list of attributes and justify your ranking.

5. What are the critical issues that management must consider when dismissing an employee? Do these issues change based on whether the departure is friendly or hostile?

6. How do the security considerations for temporary or contract workers differ from those for regular employees?

7. Which two career paths are often used as entrees into the information security discipline? Are there other paths? If so, describe them.

8. Why is it important to have a body of standard job descriptions for hiring information security professionals?

9. What functions does the CISO perform, and what are the key qualifications and requirements for the position?

10. What functions does the security manager perform, and what are the key qualifications and requirements for the position?

11. What functions does the security technician perform, and what are the key qualifications and requirements for the position?

12. What functions does the internal security consultant perform, and what are the key qualifications and requirements for the position?

13. What is the rationale for acquiring professional credentials?

14. List and describe the certification credentials available to information security professionals.

15. In your opinion, who should pay for the expenses of certification? Under what circumstances would your answer be different? Why?

16. List and describe the standard personnel practices that are part of the information security function. What happens to these practices when they are integrated with information security concepts?

17. Why shouldn't you show a job candidate secure areas during interviews?

18. List and describe the types of nonemployee workers often used by organizations. What special security considerations apply to such workers, and why are they significant?

19. What is separation of duties? How can this method be used to improve an organization's information security practices?

20. What is least privilege? Why is implementing least privilege important?

Exercises

1. Using the Internet, find at least five job postings for security administrators. What qualifications do the listings have in common?

2. Go to the (ISC)² Web site (www.isc2.org). Research the body of knowledge requirements for the CISSP and the SSCP. Which required areas are *not* covered in this text?

3. Using the Internet, search for three different employee hiring and termination policies. Review each and look carefully for inconsistencies. Does each have a section addressing security of information requirements? What clauses should a termination policy contain to prevent disclosure of the organization's information? Create your own variant of either a hiring or a termination policy.

4. Using your local telephone directory, locate a service that offers background checks. Select one at random and call to determine the costs of conducting such checks. How much should an organization spend on conducting these checks if it interviews dozens of potential employees?

5. Using the descriptions given in the chapter, write a job description for Iris's new position, described in the following Case Exercises. What qualifications and responsibilities should be associated with this position?

Case Exercises

Iris reviewed the scant stack of applications for the newly created security manager position and frowned. There should have been many more than just three applicants for the position.

After the human resources incident earlier in the month, she had been extremely careful in crafting the job description, and was elated when Mike Edwards approved the creation of the position and the plan to hire. The new security manager was to assist in the drafting of security policies and plans, a need that had been highlighted by the recent problem.

Iris called Gloria in human resources. "I'm worried about the number of applicants we've had," she said. "I really thought there would be more than three given the way the local economy is right now."

Gloria replied, "Oh, there were dozens, but I prescreened them for you."

"What do you mean?" Iris asked. "Prescreened how?"

Gloria elaborated. "Well, we pass on only the most qualified applicants. According to our criteria, applicants for information security positions must have a CISA certification or some level of GIAD."

"Since I'm not aware of such a certification as a GIAD, you must mean GIAC?" Iris asked, her uneasiness building.

"No, the file says GIAD," Gloria replied confidently.

"Well, for this position we need a CISSP or CISM, not a GIAD or CISA. Those certifications don't match the job description I wrote, and I don't remember specifying any required certifications."

"You don't have to," Gloria said. "We've determined that the best people for the jobs are the ones who have the most certifications. We don't really look at anyone who isn't certified. Is there a problem?"

1. If you were Iris, how would reply to Gloria's question?
2. What, if anything, is wrong with the human resources focus depicted here? Examine the relationship between certifications and experience. Do certifications alone identify the job candidates with the most appropriate expertise and work experience?

Endnotes

1 Charles Cresson Wood. *Information Security Roles and Responsibilities Made Easy.* Houston: PentaSafe, 2002: 55–94.

2 Eddie Schwartz, Dan Erwin, Vincent Weafer, and Andy Briney. Roundtable: Infosec staffing help wanted! *Information Security Magazine Online,* April 2001. [Cited October 14, 2006]. www.infosecuritymag.com/articles/april01/features_roundtable.shtml.

3 Charles Cresson Wood. *Information Security Roles and Responsibilities Made Easy.* Houston: PentaSafe, 2002: 57–59.

4 Charles Cresson Wood. *Information Security Roles and Responsibilities Made Easy.* Houston: PentaSafe, 2002: 63.

5 Charles Cresson Wood. *Information Security Roles and Responsibilities Made Easy.* Houston: PentaSafe, 2002: Table of contents.

6. International Information Systems Security Certification Consortium. About SSCP certification. *ISC² Online.* Accessed October 14, 2006. www.isc2.org/cgi-bin/content.cgi?category=1192.

7. ISC². *The Associate ISC² Program.* Accessed December 14, 2006 from www.isc2.org/cgi-bin/content.cgi?page=824.

8. ISC². *ISC² Concentrations.* Accessed October 14, 2006. www.isc2.org/cgi-bin/content.cgi?category=99.

9. ISACA.. *CISM Examination Content Areas.* Accessed October 14, 2006. www.isaca.org/Content/NavigationMenu/Security/CISM_Certification/Exam_Information1/Content_Areas1/CISM_Certification_Content_Areas.htm.

10. GIAC. *GIAC Certifications.* Accessed October 14, 2006. www.giac.org/certifications/.

11. GIAC. *GIAC Security Expert.* Accessed October 14, 2006. www.giac.org/certifications/gse.php.

12. Security Certified Programs. Certifications. *Ascendant Learning, LLC Online.* Accessed October 14, 2006. www.securitycertified.net/certifications.htm.

13. CompTIA. *CompTIA Security+ Certification.* Accessed July 17, 2003. www.comptia.com/certification/security/default.asp.

14. ISFCE. *The Certified Computer Examiner Content Areas.* Accessed October 14, 2006. www.certified-computer-examiner.com/.

15. Charles Cresson Wood. *Information Security Roles and Responsibilities Made Easy.* Houston: PentaSafe, 2002: 169.

16. Joseph Campbell and Bill Moyer. *The Power of Myth*, p. 113. New York: Doubleday, 1988.

17. Background Check International. *BCI Online.* Accessed October 14, 2006. www.bcint.com/legal.html.

18. Privacy Rights Clearinghouse. *Employment Background Checks: A Guide for Small Business Owners.* Accessed October 14, 2006. www.privacyrights.org/fs/fs16b-smallbus.htm.

19. R. Lemos. Mitnick teaches "social engineering." *Ziff-Davis News Net.* July 17, 2000. Accessed October 14, 2006. news.zdnet.com/2100-9595_22-522261.html.

20. R. Lemos. Mitnick teaches "social engineering." *Ziff-Davis News Net.* July 17, 2000. Accessed October 14, 2006. news.zdnet.com/2100-9595_22-522261.html.

21. CERT. *Social Engineering Attacks via IRC and Instant Messaging.* CERT Incident Note IN-2002-03, March 19, 2002. Accessed October 14, 2006. www.cert.org/incident_notes/IN-2002-03.html.

22. S. Granger. *Social Engineering Fundamentals, Part II: Combat Strategies Security Focus.* January 9, 2002. Accessed October 14, 2006. www.securityfocus.com/infocus/1533.

23. D. Gragg. A multi-level defense against social engineering. *SANS Institute.* December 2002. Accessed October 14, 2006. www.sans.org/reading_room/whitepapers/engineering/920.php.

LAW AND ETHICS

Iris was just over halfway through her morning e-mail ritual when she came to a message that caught her attention. Just a few weeks ago RWW had set up a new Web server that allowed anyone, anywhere, to send anonymous e-mail to the company's most senior executive. The message had in fact been sent by the CEO's executive assistant. It read as follows:

```
To: Iris Majwabu

From: Cassandra Wilmington

Date: 2007-11-18 07:45 AM

Subject: FW: Anonymous Ethics Report - 2007-11-17 02:46 AM

    Iris, you better look at this. I pulled the text out and encrypted it. I
am briefing a special executive meeting with Robin, Jerry, and Mike at 10:00
this morning. You should be there too.

    Meeting invitation follows...

    — Cassandra
```

Iris opened her safe and mounted her secure document drive, then exported the file to it. She opened the decryption program, fumbling with her badge carrier to read the encrypted key from her security token. The text of the anonymous e-mail appeared on her screen:

```
To: RWW Anonymous Ethics Mailbox

From: A Friend

Date: 2007-11-17 02:46 AM

Subject: Anonymous Ethics Report - 2007-11-17 02:46 AM
```

You might want to look at the nile.com auction site at www.nile.com/
auctions/ref=19085769340

Iris opened her browser window and typed in the URL. She saw:

Item #19085769340

RWW, Inc. Customer and key accounts list

Starting bid: US $10,000.00

Time left: 2 days 22 hours 50 mins 3-day listing

History: 0 bids

Location: Cityville, WI

Iris reached for her incident response plan binder. She knew it was going to be a busy morning, and a busy afternoon, too.

LEARNING OBJECTIVES

Upon completion of this material, you should be able to:

- Differentiate between law and ethics
- Identify major national and international laws that relate to the practice of information security
- Understand the role of culture as it applies to ethics in information security
- Access current information on laws, regulations, and relevant professional organizations

INTRODUCTION

This chapter covers information security law and ethics. Although the two topics are intertwined, the first part of this chapter focuses on legislation and regulations concerning the management of information in an organization. The second part of the chapter discusses ethics and information security and offers a summary guide to professional organizations with established ethical codes. You can use this chapter both as a reference guide to the legal aspects of information security and as an aid in planning your professional career.

As a future information security professional, it is vital that you understand the scope of an organization's legal and ethical responsibilities. The information security professional should play an important role in an organization's approach to controlling liability for privacy and security risks. In the modern litigious societies of the world, sometimes laws are enforced in civil courts, and plaintiffs are awarded large payments for damages or to punish defendants. To minimize these liabilities the information security practitioner must understand the current legal environment and keep apprised of new laws, regulations, and ethical issues as they emerge. By educating employees and management about their legal and ethical obligations and the proper use of information technology and information security, security professionals can keep their organizations focused on their primary objectives.

LAW AND ETHICS IN INFORMATION SECURITY

Within modern society, individuals elect to trade some aspects of personal freedom for social order. As Jean Jacques Rousseau explains in *The Social Contract Or Principles Of Political Right* [1] (1762), the rules the members of a society create to balance the individual's right to self-determination with the needs of the whole are called laws. **Laws** are rules adopted and enforced by governments to codify expected behavior in modern society. Laws are largely drawn from the **ethics** of a culture, which define socially acceptable behaviors that conform to the widely held principles of the members of that society. The key difference between law and ethics is that law carries the sanction of a governing authority and ethics do not. Ethics are based on **cultural mores**: relatively fixed moral attitudes or customs of a societal group. Some ethics are thought to be universal. For example, murder, theft, and assault are actions that deviate from ethical and legal codes in most, if not all, the world's cultures.

THE LEGAL ENVIRONMENT

Information security professionals, and managers involved in information security, must possess a rudimentary grasp of the legal framework within which their organizations operate. This legal environment can influence the organization to a greater or lesser extent, depending on the nature of the organization and the scale on which it operates. The following pages outline, in general terms, the current legal environment.

Types of Law

There are a number of ways to categorize laws. **Civil law** embodies a wide variety of laws pertaining to relationships between and among individuals and organizations. **Criminal law** addresses violations harmful to society and is actively enforced and prosecuted by the state. **Tort law** is a subset of civil law, which allows individuals to seek recourse against others in the event of personal, physical, or financial injury. Tort law is pursued in civil court, and is not prosecuted by the state.

Legislation that affects the individual in the workplace can be categorized as private law or public law. **Private law** regulates the relationships among individuals and among individuals and organizations, and encompasses family law, commercial law, and labor law. **Public law** regulates the structure and administration of government agencies and their relationships with citizens, employees, and other governments. Public law includes criminal, administrative, and constitutional law.

Relevant U.S. Laws

The United States has led the development and implementation of information security legislation to prevent misuse and exploitation of information and information technology. The development of information security legislation promotes the general welfare and creates a stable environment for a solid economy. In its capacity as a global leader, the United States has demonstrated a clear understanding of the problems facing the information security field and has identified necessary penalties for the individuals and organizations that fail to follow the requirements set forth in the U.S. civil statutes. Table 11-1 summarizes the U.S. federal laws relevant to information security.

TABLE 11-1   Key U.S. Laws of Interest to Information Security Professionals

Area	Act	Date	Web Resource Location	Description
Threats to computers	Computer Fraud and Abuse Act (also known as Fraud and Related Activity in Connection with Computers (18 U.S.C. 1030)	1986 (amended, 1996, 2001, and 2006)	www.usdoj.gov/ criminal/cybercrime/ 1030_new.html	Defines and formalizes laws to counter threats from computer-related acts and offenses
Criminal intent	National Information Infrastructure Protection Act of 1996 (update to 18 U.S.C. 1030)	1996	www.usdoj.gov/ criminal/cybercrime/ ccpolicy.html#NIFPA	Categorizes crimes based on defendant's authority to access a protected computer system and criminal intent
Terrorism	USA PATRIOT Act of 2001 (update to 18 U.S.C. 1030)	2001	thomas.loc.gov/cgi-bin/ bdquery/z?d107: H.R.3162:	Defines stiffer penalties for prosecution of terrorist crimes
Terrorism and Extreme Drug Trafficking	USA PATRIOT Improvement and Reauthorization Act of 2005 (update to 18 U.S.C. 1030)	2006	homas.loc.gov/cgi-bin/ cpquery/R?cp109: FLD010:@1(hr333)	Renews critical sections of the USA PATRIOT Act
Telecommunications	Telecommunications Deregulation and Competition Act of 1996—Update to Communications Act of 1934 (47 U.S.C. 151 et seq.)	1934 (amended 1996 and 2001)	thomas.loc.gov/cgi-bin/ bdquery/z?d104: SN00652: @@@L&summ2=m&	Regulates interstate and foreign telecommunications

TABLE 11-1 Key U.S. Laws of Interest to Information Security Professionals (continued)

Area	Act	Date	Web Resource Location	Description
Federal agency information security	Computer Security Act of 1987	1987	www.cio.gov/archive/ computer_security_act_ jan_1998.html	Requires all federal computer systems that contain classified information to have surety plans in place, and requires periodic security training for all individuals who operate, design, or manage such systems
Privacy	Federal Privacy Act of 1974	1974	www.justice.gov/oip/ privstat.htm	Governs federal agency use of personal information
Cryptography	Electronic Communications Privacy Act of 1986(Update to 18 USC)	1986	homas.loc.gov/cgi-bin/ bdquery/z?d099: HR04952: @@@L&summ2=m&	Regulates interception and disclosure of electronic information; also referred to as the Federal Wiretapping Act
Banking	Gramm-Leach-Bliley Act of 1999 (GLB) or the Financial Services Modernization Act	1999	banking.senate.gov/ conf/	Repeals the restrictions on banks affiliating with insurance and securities firms. It has significant impact on the privacy of personal information used by these industries.
Trade secrets	Economic Espionage Act of 1996	1996	www.usdoj.gov/ criminal/cybercrime/ eea.html	Prevents abuse of information gained while employed elsewhere
Accountability	Sarbanes-Oxley Act of 2002 (SOX) or Public Company Accounting Reform and Investor Protection Act	2002	www.sec.gov/spotlight/ sarbanes-oxley.htm	Enforces accountability for executives at publicly traded companies. This law is having ripple effects throughout the accounting, IT, and related units of many organizations.
Copyright	Copyright Act of 1976 Update to U.S. Copyright Law (17 USC)	1976	www.copyright.gov/ title17/	Protects intellectual property, including publications and software

Area	Act	Date	Web Resource Location	Description
Copy Protection	Digital Millennium Copyright Act (update to 17 USC §101)	1998	www.copyright.gov/ legislation/dmca.pdf	Provides specific penalties for removing copyright protection from media
Personal Health Information Protection	Health Insurance Portability and Accountability Act of 1996 (HIPAA)	1996	aspe.hhs.gov/ admnsimp/ pl104191.htm	Requires medical practices to ensure the privacy of personal medical information
Freedom of Information	Freedom of Information Act (FOIA)	1966	www.usdoj.gov/oip/ index.html	Allows for the disclosure of previously unreleased information and documents controlled by the U.S. Government.
Encryption and Digital Signatures	Security and Freedom through Encryption Act of 1997	1997	www.epic.org/crypto/ legislation/safe_bill_ 106.html	Affirmed the rights of persons in the United States to use and sell products that include encryption and to relax export controls on such products.

General Computer Crime Laws

Several key laws are relevant to the field of information security. The Computer Fraud and Abuse Act of 1986 (CFA Act) is the cornerstone of many computer-related federal laws and enforcement efforts. It was amended in October 1996 by the National Information Infrastructure Protection Act of 1996, which modified several sections of the previous act, and increased the penalties for selected crimes. Punishment for offenses prosecuted under this statute varies from fines to imprisonment up to 20 years, or both. The penalty depends on the value of the information obtained and whether the offense is judged to have been committed for one of the following reasons:

- For purposes of commercial advantage
- For private financial gain
- In furtherance of a criminal act

COMPUTER FRAUD AND ABUSE ACT OF 1986

(Section 1030, Chapter 47, Title 18 USC)

Fraud and Related Activity in Connection with Computers.

Whoever having knowingly accessed a computer without authorization or exceeding authorized access, and by means of such conduct having obtained information that has been determined by the United States Government ... to require protection against unauthorized disclosure for reasons of national defense or foreign relations, or any restricted data ... with reason to believe that such information so obtained could be used to the injury of the United States, or to the advantage of any foreign nation, willfully communicates, delivers, transmits, or causes to be communicated, delivered, or transmitted, or attempts to communicate, deliver, transmit or cause to be communicated, delivered, or transmitted the same to any person not entitled to receive it, or willfully retains the same and fails to deliver it to the officer or employee of the United States entitled to receive it; intentionally accesses a computer without authorization or exceeds authorized access, and thereby obtains information contained in a financial record of a financial institution, or of a card issuer ... , or contained in a file of a consumer reporting agency on a consumer ...; information from any department or agency of the United States; or information from any protected computer if the conduct involved an interstate or foreign communication; intentionally, without authorization to access any nonpublic computer of a department or agency of the United States, accesses such a computer of that department or agency that is exclusively for the use of the Government of the United States or, in the case of a computer not exclusively for such use, is used by or for the Government of the United States and such conduct affects that use by or for the Government of the United States; knowingly and with intent to defraud, accesses a protected computer without authorization, or exceeds authorized access, and by means of such conduct furthers the intended fraud and obtains anything of value, unless the object of the fraud and the thing obtained consists only of the use of the computer and the value of such use is not more than $5,000 in any 1-year period; knowingly causes the transmission of a program, information, code, or command, and as a result of such conduct, intentionally causes damage without authorization, to a protected computer; intentionally accesses a protected computer without authorization, and as a result of such conduct, recklessly causes damage; or intentionally accesses a protected computer without authorization, and as a result of such conduct, causes damage; knowingly and with intent to defraud traffics ... in any password or similar information through which a computer may be accessed without authorization, if such trafficking affects interstate or foreign commerce; or such computer is used by or for the Government of the United States; with intent to extort from any person, firm, association, educational institution, financial institution, government entity, or other legal entity, any money or other thing of value, transmits in interstate or foreign commerce any communication containing any threat to cause damage to a protected computer.

The CFA Act was further modified by the USA PATRIOT Act of 2001—the abbreviated name for "Uniting and Strengthening America Act by Providing Appropriate Tools Required to Intercept and Obstruct Terrorism Act of 2001," which provides law enforcement agencies with broader latitude to combat terrorism-related activities. Some of the laws modified by the Patriot Act are among the earliest laws created to deal with electronic technology.

Authority to Intercept Voice Communications in Computer Hacking Investigations. Under previous law, investigators could not obtain a wiretap order to intercept wire voice communications for violations of the Computer Fraud and Abuse Act. The Patriot Act identifies specific crimes under which investigators may obtain a wiretap order for wire communications by adding felony violations of the Computer Fraud and Abuse Act to the list of offenses. This authority was set to sunset December 31, 2005.

Obtaining Voice-mail and Other Stored Voice Communications. Previously, the Electronic Communications Privacy Act (ECPA) governed law enforcement access to stored electronic communications like e-mail, but not stored wire voice communications (voice mail). Instead, the wiretap act regulated these actions primarily because the definition of "wire communication" included stored voice communications; therefore, investigators were required to obtain a wiretap order from a judge to confiscate and review voice mail or answering machine messages. What was not envisioned when the original ECPA was developed was the creation of hybrid systems that stored voice communications as digital messages (digital voice mail). The Patriot Act alters the way that the wiretap statute and ECPA apply to stored voice communications. The amendments delete "electronic storage" of wire communications from the definition of "wire communication" and insert language to ensure that stored wire communications are covered under the same rules as stored electronic communications, allowing investigators to search these messages using standard search warrants, rather than wiretap orders. Sunset: December 31, 2005.

Emergency Disclosures by Communications Providers. Previous law relating to voluntary disclosures by communication service providers (like ISPs) contained no special provision allowing providers to disclose customer records or communications in emergencies. If an ISP voluntarily provided account information or subscriber information to law enforcement officials, it risked being subject to civil suit, even if the information pointed to a potential crime or terrorist attack.

This Patriot Act permits, but does not require, ISPs to disclose customer information if it suspects an immediate risk of death or serious physical injury to any person. ISPs are also allowed to disclose such information to protect their property and rights.

Intercepting the Communications of Computer Trespassers. The wiretapping act permits owners of computers and computer systems to monitor their systems to protect rights and property. However, it does not provide clear guidance as to what extent these owners can ask for assistance in this monitoring from the law enforcement community. The Patriot Act allows computer system owners to monitor trespassers on their systems and obtain support from law enforcement officials in conducting this monitoring. This provision also stipulates that *if* the owners or operators of the system authorize law enforcement to monitor a suspected trespassers traffic, *and* the individual intercepting the traffic is engaged in a lawful investigation, *and* the investigator has reason to suspect that the intercepted traffic is vital to the investigation, *and* only those communications conducted by the trespasser will be intercepted, *then* it is legal to intercept the wire or electronic communications of a computer trespasser—even if acting "under color of law" or

continued

440

as an agent of the law. A computer trespasser is defined as "any person who accesses a protected computer without authorization." The definition explicitly excludes individuals "known by the owner or operator of the protected computer to have an existing contractual relationship with the owner or operator for access to all or part of the computer." Sunset: December 31, 2005.

Nationwide Search Warrants for E-mail. Current law requires the government to use a search warrant to compel a provider to disclose unopened e-mail less than six months old. Changes resulting from the Patriot Act allow investigators to obtain warrants for computer records outside their native jurisdiction. Sunset December 31, 2005.

Deterrence and Prevention of Cyberterrorism. This section makes a number of changes to the Computer Fraud and Abuse Act, increasing penalties for hackers from 10 to 20 years and clarifying the definition of intent to make explicit that a hacker need only intend damage. It creates new offenses for special types of computer crime, such as those targeting national security or the criminal justice system. It also allows aggregation of computer criminal offenses to meet some of the minimum requirements for stiffer penalties.

Development and Support of Cybersecurity Forensic Capabilities. This section requires the Attorney General to establish and fund a number of regional computer forensic laboratories as well as provide support for existing labs.

In 2005, with the signing of the USA PATRIOT Improvement and Reauthorization Act of 2005, several key sections were reauthorized and enhanced. Some of the provisions of this act were previously known by the following names:

- Combat Methamphetamine Epidemic Act of 2005
- Combating Terrorism Financing Act of 2005
- Reducing Crime and Terrorism at America's Seaports Act of 2005
- Secret Service Authorization and Technical Modification Act of 2005
- Terrorist Death Penalty Enhancement Act of 2005

Among its other provisions, it:

- Makes permanent 14 of the 16 USA PATRIOT Act sections scheduled to expire at the end of 2005.
- Provides for greater congressional and judicial oversight of section 215 Foreign Intelligence Surveillance Act (FISA) business records orders and section 206 FISA roving wiretaps and calls for both sections to sunset at the end of 2009.
- Expands law enforcement wiretap authority to cover more than 20 federal crimes.
- Establishes judicial review and enforcement procedures for national security letters.
- Revises federal criminal provisions relating to seaport and maritime security.
- Reinforces federal money laundering and forfeiture authority particularly in connection with terrorist offenses.
- Intensifies federal regulation of foreign and domestic commerce in methamphetamine precursors.

continued

441

- Foregoes all but technical modifications in federal capital punishment procedures.
- Makes organization adjustments in the Department of Justice and Secret Service.[2]

The major sections of the act are as follows:

TITLE I—USA PATRIOT IMPROVEMENT AND REAUTHORIZATION ACT

TITLE II—TERRORIST DEATH PENALTY ENHANCEMENT

    Subtitle A—Terrorist Penalties Enhancement Act

    Subtitle B—Federal Death Penalty Procedures

TITLE III—REDUCING CRIME AND TERRORISM AT AMERICA'S SEAPORTS

TITLE IV—COMBATING TERRORISM FINANCING

TITLE V—MISCELLANEOUS PROVISIONS

TITLE VI—SECRET SERVICE

TITLE VII—COMBAT METHAMPHETAMINE EPIDEMIC ACT OF 2005

    Subtitle A—Domestic Regulation of Precursor Chemicals

    Subtitle B—International Regulation of Precursor Chemicals

    Subtitle C—Enhanced Criminal Penalties for Methamphetamine Production and Trafficking

    Subtitle D—Enhanced Environmental Regulation of Methamphetamine Byproducts

    Subtitle E—Additional Programs and Activities

COMMUNICATIONS DECENCY ACT

The Communications Act of 1934 was revised by the Telecommunications Deregulation and Competition Act of 1996, which attempts to modernize the archaic terminology of the older act. Some of these much-needed updates included the Communications Decency Act (CDA) as Title V the broader Telecommunications Deregulation and Competition Act of 1996. The CDA was immediately ensnared in a thorny legal challenge on First Amendment grounds over the attempt to define indecency, which through major efforts sponsored by the Internet Blue Ribbon Campaign and by the Electronic Freedom Frontier (www.eff.org), quickly reached the Supreme Court. The subsequent Supreme Court ruling left weak and ineffective controls in place of the more aggressive and ambitious ones originally intended, still leaving unclear the ability to enforce offenses such as harassment through fax or e-mail.

Whoever in interstate or foreign communications by means of a telecommunications device knowingly makes, creates, or solicits, and initiates the transmission of, any comment, request, suggestion, proposal, image, or other communication which is obscene, lewd, lascivious, filthy, or indecent, with intent to annoy, abuse, threaten, or

continued

harass another person; by means of a telecommunications device knowingly makes, creates, or solicits, and initiates the transmission of any comment, request, suggestion, proposal, image, or other communication which is obscene or indecent, knowing that the recipient of the communication is under 18 years of age regardless of whether the maker of such communication placed the call or initiated the communication; makes a telephone call or utilizes a telecommunications device, whether or not conversation or communication ensues, without disclosing his identity and with intent to annoy, abuse, threaten, or harass any person at the called number or who receives the communications; makes or causes the telephone of another repeatedly or continuously to ring, with intent to harass any person at the called number; or makes repeated telephone calls or repeatedly initiates communication with a telecommunications device, during which conversation or communication ensues, solely to harass any person at the called number or who receives the communication; or knowingly permits any telecommunications facility under his control to be used for any activity prohibited; with the intent that it be used for such activity, shall be fined or imprisoned not more than two years, or both.

Whoever knowingly within the United States, by means of telephone, makes (directly or by recording device) any obscene communication for commercial purposes to any person, regardless of whether the maker of such communication placed the call; or permits any telephone facility under such person's control to be used for an activity prohibited; shall be fined, or imprisoned not more than two years, or both.

Whoever knowingly within the United States, by means of telephone, makes (directly or by recording device) any indecent communication for commercial purposes which is available to any person under 18 years of age or to any other person without that person's consent, regardless of whether the maker of such communication placed the call; or permits any telephone facility under such person's control to be used for an activity prohibited; shall be fined not more than $50,000 or imprisoned not more than six months, or both.

Whoever in interstate or foreign communications knowingly uses an interactive computer service to send to a specific person or persons under 18 years of age, or uses any interactive computer service to display in a manner available to a person under 18 years of age, any comment, request, suggestion, proposal, image, or other communication that, in context, depicts or describes, in terms patently offensive as measured by contemporary community standards, sexual or excretory activities or organs, regardless of whether the user of such service placed the call or initiated the communication; or knowingly permits any telecommunications facility under such person's control to be used for an activity prohibited, with the intent that it be used for such activity, shall be fined, or imprisoned not more than two years, or both.

Another law of critical importance to information security professionals is the Computer Security Act of 1987. This legislation was one of the first attempts to protect federal computer systems by establishing minimum acceptable security practices. The Computer Security Act of 1987 charged the National Bureau of Standards, in cooperation with the National Security Agency, with the development of:

- Standards, guidelines, and associated methods and techniques for computer systems
- Uniform standards and guidelines for most federal computer systems

- Technical, management, physical, and administrative standards and guidelines for the cost-effective security and privacy of sensitive information in federal computer systems
- Guidelines for use by operators of federal computer systems that contain sensitive information in training their employees in security awareness and accepted security practice
- Validation procedures for, and evaluation of the effectiveness of, standards and guidelines through research and liaison with other government and private agencies[3]

The Computer Security Act also established a Computer System Security and Privacy Advisory Board within the Department of Commerce. This board identifies emerging managerial, technical, administrative, and physical safety issues relative to computer systems security and privacy, and it advises the Bureau of Standards and the Secretary of Commerce on security and privacy issues pertaining to federal computer systems. The board reports to the Secretary of Commerce, the Director of the Office of Management and Budget, the Director of the National Security Agency, and the appropriate committees of Congress.

The Computer Security Act of 1987 also amended the Federal Property and Administrative Services Act of 1949. The amendments required the National Bureau of Standards to distribute standards and guidelines pertaining to federal computer systems, making such standards compulsory and binding to the extent to which the secretary determines necessary to improve the efficiency of operation or security and privacy of federal computer systems. It also permitted the head of any federal agency to employ more stringent standards than those distributed.

Another provision of the Computer Security Act requires mandatory periodic training in computer security awareness and accepted computer security practice for all employees who are involved with the management, use, or operation of each federal computer system. This training for federal employees is intended to enhance their awareness of the threats to, and vulnerability of, computer systems and to encourage the use of good computer security practices. It also informs federal agencies who is responsible for computer systems security and privacy, requires the identification of systems that contain sensitive information, and outlines the requirements for formal security plans.

Privacy Laws

Many organizations collect, trade, and sell personal information as a commodity, and many people are becoming aware of these practices, and are looking to governments to protect their privacy. In the past it was not possible to create databases that contained personal information collected from multiple sources. Today, the aggregation of data from multiple sources permits unethical organizations to build databases with alarming quantities of personal information.

The number of statutes addressing individual privacy rights has grown; however, **privacy** in this context is not absolute freedom from observation, but rather is defined as the "state of being free from unsanctioned intrusion."[4] It is possible to track this freedom from intrusion to the Fourth Amendment to the U.S. Constitution, which states:

> The right of the people to be secure in their persons, houses, papers, and effects, against unreasonable searches and seizures, shall not be violated, and no Warrants shall issue, but upon probable cause, supported by Oath or affirmation, and particularly describing the place to be searched, and the persons or things to be seized.[5]

The origins of this right can be traced to a 1772 document titled *The Rights of the Colonists and a List of Infringements and Violations of Rights* by Samuel Adams. This document in turn has its roots in a 1604 ruling by a British court that upheld the rights of a man to refuse entry to the king's men without royal warrant, or at least to restrict search to items listed in a warrant.[6]

To better understand this rapidly evolving issue, some of the more relevant privacy laws and regulations are presented in the pages that follow.

The Privacy of Customer Information in section 222 of USC TITLE 47, CHAPTER 5, SUBCHAPTER II, Part I covering common carriers[7] (organizations that process or move data for hire) specifies that any proprietary information shall be used explicitly for providing services, and not for any marketing purposes. It also stipulates that carriers cannot disclose this information except when necessary to provide its services, or by customer request, and then the disclosure is restricted to that customer's information only. This law does permit the use of aggregate information (which is created by combining nonprivate data elements) as long as the same information is provided to all common carriers, and the carrier in question conducts business with fair competition. The use of aggregate information raises privacy concerns because an organization could assemble data from a variety of sources in ways that would allow correlation of seemingly innocuous information into something more intrusive. For example, the mapping of a government census database with telephone directory information, cross-indexed to bankruptcy court records, could be used to facilitate marketing efforts to people experiencing financial difficulties.

While this common carrier regulation controls public carrier's use of private data, the Federal Privacy Act of 1974 regulates the government's use of private information. The Federal Privacy Act was created to ensure that government agencies protect the privacy of individuals' and businesses' information, and holds those agencies responsible if any portion of this information is released without permission. The act states, "No agency shall disclose any record which is contained in a system of records by any means of communication to any person, or to another agency, except pursuant to a written request by, or with the prior written consent of, the individual to whom the record pertains...."[8] The following entities are exempt from some of the regulations so that they can perform their duties:

- Bureau of the Census
- National Archives and Records Administration
- U.S. Congress
- Comptroller General
- Certain court orders
- Credit agencies

Also, individuals can access information controlled by others if they can demonstrate that it is necessary to protect their health or safety.

The Electronic Communications Privacy Act of 1986 is a collection of statutes that regulates the interception of wire, electronic, and oral communications. These statutes are frequently referred to as the federal wiretapping acts. They address the following areas:[9]

- Interception and disclosure of wire, oral, or electronic communications
- Manufacture, distribution, possession, and advertising of wire, oral, or electronic communication intercepting devices
- Confiscation of wire, oral, or electronic communication intercepting devices
- Evidentiary use of intercepted wire or oral communications
- Authorization for interception of wire, oral, or electronic communications
- Authorization for disclosure and use of intercepted wire, oral, or electronic communications
- Procedure for interception of wire, oral, or electronic communications
- Reports concerning intercepted wire, oral, or electronic communications
- Injunction against illegal interception

The Health Insurance Portability and Accountability Act of 1996 (HIPAA), also known as the Kennedy-Kassebaum Act, attempts to protect the confidentiality and security of health care data by establishing and enforcing standards and by standardizing electronic data interchange. HIPAA affects all health care organizations, including small medical practices, health clinics, life insurers, and universities, as well as some organizations that have self-insured employee health programs. It provides for stiff penalties for organizations that fail to comply with the law, with up to $250,000 and/or 10 years imprisonment for knowingly misusing client information. Organizations were required to comply with the act as of April 14, 2003.[10]

HIPAA affects the field of information security in a number of ways. It requires organizations that retain health care information to use information security mechanisms to protect this information, as well as policies and procedures to maintain them. It also requires a comprehensive assessment of the organization's information security systems, policies, and procedures. HIPAA provides guidelines for the use of electronic signatures based on security standards ensuring message integrity, user authentication, and nonrepudiation. There is no specification of particular security technologies for each of the security requirements; only that security must be implemented to ensure the privacy of the health care information.

The privacy standards of HIPAA severely restrict the dissemination and distribution of private health information without documented consent. The standards provide patients the right to know who has access to their information and who has accessed it. The privacy standards also restrict the use of health information to the minimum required for the health care services required.

HIPAA has five fundamental privacy principles:

1. Consumer control of medical information
2. Boundaries on the use of medical information
3. Accountability for the privacy of private information

4. Balance of public responsibility for the use of medical information for the greater good measured against impact to the individual
5. Security of health information

The Financial Services Modernization Act or Gramm-Leach-Bliley Act of 1999 contains a number of provisions that affect banks, securities firms, and insurance companies. This act requires all financial institutions to disclose their privacy policies, describing how they share nonpublic personal information, and describing how customers can request that their information not be shared with third parties. It also ensures that the privacy policies in effect in an organization are fully disclosed when a customer initiates a business relationship, and distributed at least annually for the duration of the professional association.

Export and Espionage Laws

The need to protect national security, trade secrets, and a variety of other state and private assets has led to several laws affecting what information and information management and security resources may be exported from the United States (see, for example, Figure 11-1). These laws attempt to stem the theft of information by establishing strong penalties for related crimes.

To protect intellectual property and competitive advantage, Congress passed the Economic Espionage Act (EEA) in 1996. This law attempts to protect trade secrets "from the foreign government that uses its classic espionage apparatus to spy on a company, to the two American companies that are attempting to uncover each other's bid proposals, or to the disgruntled former employee who walks out of his former company with a computer diskette full of engineering schematics."[11]

The Security and Freedom through Encryption Act of 1997 provides guidance on the use of encryption, and institutes measures of public protection from government intervention. Specifically, the act:

- Reinforces an individual's right to use or sell encryption algorithms, without concern for the impact of other regulations requiring some form of key registration. Key registration is when a cryptographic key (or its text equivalent) is stored with another party to be used to break the encryption of the data under some circumstances. This is often called key escrow.
- Prohibits the federal government from requiring the use of encryption for contracts, grants, and other official documents, and correspondence.
- States that the use of encryption is not probable cause to suspect criminal activity.
- Relaxes export restrictions by amending the Export Administration Act of 1979.
- Provides additional penalties for the use of encryption in the commission of a criminal act.

U.S. Copyright Law

U.S. copyright law extends protection to intellectual property, which includes words published in electronic formats. The doctrine of fair use allows material to be quoted for the purpose of news reporting, teaching, scholarship, and a number of other related activities, so long as the purpose is educational and not for profit, and the usage is not excessive. Proper acknowledgement must be provided to the author and/or copyright holder of such

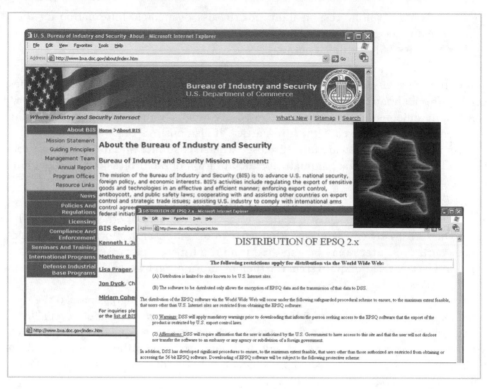

FIGURE 11-1 Export Restrictions

works, including a description of the location of source materials by using a recognized form of citation.

Freedom of Information Act of 1966 (FOIA)

All federal agencies are required under the Freedom of Information Act (FOIA) to disclose records requested in writing by any person. However, agencies may withhold information pursuant to nine exemptions and three exclusions contained in the statute. The FOIA applies only to federal agencies and does not create a right of access to records held by Congress, the courts, or by state or local government agencies. Each state has its own public access laws that should be consulted for access to state and local records.

Sarbanes-Oxley Act of 2002

In the wake of the Enron and WorldCom financial scandals and the damage on financial markets from criminal violations of the federal securities laws, the U.S. Congress enacted a law designed to enforce accountability for the financial record keeping and reporting at publicly traded corporations. While this law on its face would not seem to affect information security or even general IT functions, in fact its effects are being felt throughout the organizations to which it applies.

The law requires that the CEO and chief financial officer (CFO) assume direct and personal accountability for the completeness and accuracy of a publicly traded organization's financial reporting and record-keeping systems. As these executives attempt to ensure that the reporting and recording systems are sound—often relying upon the expertise of CIOs and CISOs to do so—they also must maintain the availability and confidentiality of information.

The provisions include:

- Creation of the Public Company Accounting Oversight Board (PCAOB)
- A requirement that public companies evaluate and disclose the effectiveness of their internal controls as they relate to financial reporting, and that independent auditors for such companies "attest" (i.e., agree, or qualify) to such disclosure
- Certification of financial reports by chief executive officers and chief financial officers
- Auditor independence, including outright bans on certain types of work for audit clients and precertification by the company's Audit Committee of all other nonaudit work
- A requirement that companies listed on stock exchanges have fully independent audit committees that oversee the relationship between the company and its auditor
- Ban on most personal loans to any executive officer or director
- Accelerated reporting of trades by insiders
- Prohibition on insider trades during pension fund blackout periods
- Additional disclosure
- Enhanced criminal and civil penalties for violations of securities law
- Significantly longer maximum jail sentences and larger fines for corporate executives who knowingly and willfully misstate financial statements, although maximum sentences are largely irrelevant because judges generally follow the Federal Sentencing Guidelines in setting actual sentences
- Employee protections allowing those corporate fraud whistleblowers who file complaints with OSHA within 90 days, to win reinstatement, back pay and benefits, compensatory damages, abatement orders, and reasonable attorney fees and costs

Since CIOs are responsible for the *security*, accuracy, and reliability of the systems that manage and report the financial data, they are inextricably linked to the overall financial reporting process and need to be assessed, along with other important processes for compliance with the Sarbanes-Oxley Act. Although the act signals a fundamental change in business operations and financial reporting, and places responsibility in corporate financial reporting on the CEO and CFO, the CIO plays a significant role in the signoff of financial statements.[12]

International Laws and Legal Bodies

IT professionals and information security practitioners must realize that when their organizations do business on the Internet, they do business globally. Many domestic laws and customs do not apply to international trade, which is governed by international treaties and

449

trade agreements. It may seem obvious, but it is often overlooked, that there are a variety of laws and ethical practices in place in other parts of the world. Different security bodies and laws are described in the following sections. Because of the political complexities of the relationships among nations and cultural differences, currently few international laws relate to privacy and information security. Therefore, these international security bodies and regulations are sometimes limited in scope and enforceability.

European Council Cyber-Crime Convention

The Council of Europe drafted the European Council Cyber-Crime Convention, which empowers an international task force to oversee a range of Internet security functions, and to standardize technology laws across international borders. It also attempts to improve the effectiveness of international investigations into breaches of technology law. This convention is well received by advocates of intellectual property rights, since it provides for copyright infringement prosecution.

As with any complex international legislation, the Cyber-Crime Convention lacks any realistic provisions for enforcement. The goal of the convention is to simplify the acquisition of information for law enforcement agents in certain types of international crimes, as well as the extradition process. The convention has more than its share of skeptics who see it as an attempt by the European community to exert undue influence to control a complex problem. Critics of the convention say that it could create more problems than it resolves. As the product of a number of governments, the convention tends to favor the interests of national agencies over the rights of businesses, organizations, and individuals.

Digital Millennium Copyright Act (DMCA)

The Digital Millennium Copyright Act (DMCA) is a U.S.-based international effort to reduce the impact of copyright, trademark, and privacy infringement especially via the removal of technological copyright protection measures. The European Union also put forward Directive 95/46/EC of the European Parliament and of the Council of 24 October 1995 that increases individual rights to process and freely move personal data. The United Kingdom has already implemented a version of this directive called the Database Right.

State and Local Regulations

Each state or locality may have a number of laws and regulations that affect the use of computer technology. It is the responsibility of information security professionals to understand state laws and regulations and ensure that their organization's security policies and procedures comply with the laws and regulations.

For example, the State of Georgia passed the Georgia Computer Systems Protection Act, which has various computer security provisions, and establishes specific penalties for use of information technology to attack or exploit information systems in organizations.

These laws do not affect individuals outside the state unless they do business or have offices in the state. Key provisions of this law are as follows:

GEORGIA COMPUTER SYSTEMS PROTECTION ACT

(Section 90 et seq., Chapter 9, Title 16, Official Code of Georgia Annotated)

Computer Theft. Any person who uses a computer or computer network with knowledge that such use is without authority and with the intention of: Taking or appropriating any property of another, whether or not with the intention of depriving the owner of possession; Obtaining property by any deceitful means or artful practice; or Converting property to such person's use in violation of an agreement or other known legal obligation to make a specified application or disposition of such property shall be guilty of the crime of computer theft.

Computer Trespass. Any person who uses a computer or computer network with knowledge that such use is without authority and with the intention of; deleting or in any way removing, either temporarily or permanently, any computer program or data from a computer or computer network; obstructing, interrupting, or in any way interfering with the use of a computer program or data; or altering, damaging, or in any way causing the malfunction of a computer, computer network, or computer program, regardless of how long the alteration, damage, or malfunction persists shall be guilty of the crime of computer trespass.

Computer Invasion of Privacy. Any person who uses a computer or computer network with the intention of examining any employment, medical, salary, credit, or any other financial or personal data relating to any other person with knowledge that such examination is without authority shall be guilty of the crime of computer invasion of privacy.

Computer Forgery. Any person who creates, alters, or deletes any data contained in any computer or computer network, who, if such person had created, altered, or deleted a tangible document or instrument would have committed forgery under Article 1 of this chapter, shall be guilty of the crime of computer forgery. The absence of a tangible writing directly created or altered by the offender shall not be a defense to the crime of computer forgery if a creation, alteration, or deletion of data was involved in lieu of a tangible document or instrument.

Computer Password Disclosure. Any person who discloses a number, code, password, or other means of access to a computer or computer network knowing that such disclosure is without authority and which results in damages (including the fair market value of any services used and victim expenditure) to the owner of the computer or computer network in excess of $500.00 shall be guilty of the crime of computer password disclosure.

Penalties. Any person convicted of the crime of computer theft, computer trespass, computer invasion of privacy, or computer forgery shall be fined not more than $50,000.00 or imprisoned not more than 15 years, or both. Any person convicted of computer password disclosure shall be fined not more than $5,000.00 or incarcerated for a period not to exceed one year, or both.

Computer Trademark Infringement. It shall be unlawful for any person, any organization, or any representative of any organization knowingly to transmit any data through a computer network or over the transmission facilities or through the network facilities of a local telephone network for the purpose of setting up, maintaining, operating, or

continued

> exchanging data with an electronic mailbox, home page, or any other electronic information storage bank or point of access to electronic information if such data uses any individual name, trade name, registered trademark, logo, legal or official seal, or copyrighted symbol to falsely identify the person, organization, or representative transmitting such data or which would falsely state or imply that such person, organization, or representative has permission or is legally authorized to use such trade name, registered trademark, logo, legal or official seal, or copyrighted symbol for such purpose when such permission or authorization has not been obtained; provided, however, that no telecommunications company or Internet access provider shall violate this Code section solely as a result of carrying or transmitting such data for its customers.[13]

The Georgia legislature also passed the Georgia Identity Theft Law in 1998 (Section 120 et seq., Chapter 9, Title 16, Official Code of Georgia Annotated). This law prohibits a business from discarding a record containing personal information unless it:

1. Shreds the customer's record before discarding the record;
2. Erases the personal information contained in the customer's record before discarding the record;
3. Modifies the customer's record to make the personal information unreadable before discarding the record; or
4. Takes actions that it reasonably believes will ensure that no unauthorized person will have access to the personal information contained in the customer's record for the period between the record's disposal and the record's destruction.[14]

Personal information is defined as:

- Personally identifiable data about a customer's medical condition, if the data are not generally considered to be public knowledge;
- Personally identifiable data that contain a customer's account or identification number, account balance, balance owing, credit balance, or credit limit, if the data relate to a customer's account or transaction with a business;
- Personally identifiable data provided by a customer to a business upon opening an account or applying for a loan or credit; or
- Personally identifiable data about a customer's federal, state, or local income tax return.[15]

Failure to dispose of customer information properly can result in a fine of $500 per instance up to a total of $10,000.

"Consumer victim" means any individual whose personal identifying information has been obtained, compromised, used or recorded in any manner without the permission of that individual.

"Identifying information" includes, but is not limited to:

- Current or former names
- Social Security numbers
- Driver's license numbers
- Checking account numbers

- Savings account numbers
- Credit and other financial transaction card numbers
- Debit card numbers
- Personal identification numbers
- Electronic identification numbers
- Digital or electronic signatures
- Medical identification numbers
- Birth dates
- Mother's maiden name
- Selected personal identification numbers
- Tax identification numbers
- State identification card numbers
- Any numbers or information that can be used to access a person's or entity's resources

Policy versus Law

Most organizations develop and formalize descriptions of acceptable and unacceptable employee behavior, which are called policies (covered in detail in Chapter 4). Properly defined and enforced policies function in an organization the same way as laws, complete with penalties, judicial practices, and sanctions. Because policies function like laws, they must be crafted with the same care as laws to ensure that the policies are complete, appropriate, and fairly applied to everyone in the workplace. The key difference between policy and law is that ignorance of policy is a viable defense, and therefore policies must be:

- Distributed to all individuals who are expected to comply with them
- Readily available for employee reference
- Easily understood, with multilingual translations and translations for visually impaired or low-literacy employees
- Acknowledged by the employee, usually by means of a signed consent form

Only when all of these conditions are met does the organization have the reasonable expectation that policy violations can be appropriately penalized without fear of legal retribution.

VIEWPOINT

Law, Ethics, and Information Security: Setting a Higher Standard

By Lee Imrey, IT Security Architect (CISSP, CISA, CPP), U.S. Department of Justice

What if a speeding driver loses control of a car, and he and his passengers die in an accident? Or the captain of an ocean liner fails to read the weather report, and hits an iceberg? Or a pharmaceutical manufacturer mislabels the dosage on a shipment of medication?

continued

Each of these is an example of a critical lapse in judgment, yet the impact of each is markedly different. Each successive example either affects, or has the potential to affect, a substantially greater number of people.

What if an insurance provider fails to protect the sensitive data of half a million people adequately?

If the address, telephone numbers, and names of family members are compromised, how does the impact of that lapse in judgment compare to that of the previous examples?

As we place increasing reliance on computers to manage sensitive information, it is incumbent upon us that we place appropriately effective controls on the systems. In most business environments, the information system controls are managed by information security professionals. In those environments that lack an information security specialist, the role is generally assumed by network and system administrators. In either case, the information system controls can frequently be bypassed by those who installed them.

How do we mitigate the risk that these *trusted parties* will abuse our trust? We do this by applying legal and ethical requirements to those we trust to secure our information.

We hope that our information security professionals will not abuse the power with which we entrust them, in much the same way that we trust that law enforcement professionals will not abuse their power. Yet we know from experience that not all professionals live up to their professed ethical standards.

Setting ethical expectations is not enough. Society needs another layer of assurance. This is provided by the adaptation of current legal code to the unique environment of information systems, and by the creation of new laws where existing law is not applicable.

Legal systems of various nations and states are all struggling to keep up with our rapidly changing environment. However, the ubiquitous and global nature of our information systems render many of the individual laws unenforceable, in any practical sense. Even acts of corporate espionage, incidents of computer hacking, and the writing of computer viruses and worms are judged by varying standards, depending on the circumstances and the forum.

Given the complex and fluid environment in which information security decisions are made, and the critical nature of these decisions, it is imperative that we be able to rely on the advice of our information security advisor. For this reason, we must hold these professionals to higher legal and ethical standards. There's too much at stake not to.

ETHICAL CONCEPTS IN INFORMATION SECURITY

Some consider ethics to be the organized study of how humans ought to act. Others consider ethics to be a consideration of rules we should live by. The student of information security is not expected to study ethics in a vacuum, but within a larger ethical framework. However, information security professionals may be expected to be more articulate about the topic than others in the organization, and often must withstand a higher degree of scrutiny. The Ten Commandments of Computer Ethics (see the following Offline) are a useful guide to the field's ethical standards.

The Ten Commandments of Computer Ethics

—from The Computer Ethics Institute[16]

1. Thou shalt not use a computer to harm other people.
2. Thou shalt not interfere with other people's computer work.
3. Thou shalt not snoop around in other people's computer files.
4. Thou shalt not use a computer to steal.
5. Thou shalt not use a computer to bear false witness.
6. Thou shalt not copy or use proprietary software for which you have not paid.
7. Thou shalt not use other people's computer resources without authorization or proper compensation.
8. Thou shalt not appropriate other people's intellectual output.
9. Thou shalt think about the social consequences of the program you are writing or the system you are designing.
10. Thou shalt always use a computer in ways that ensure consideration and respect for your fellow humans.

Differences in Ethical Concepts

Studies reveal that individuals of different nationalities have different views on the ethics of computer use. Difficulties arise when one nationality's ethical behavior does not correspond to that of another national group. For example, Westerners view some of the ways in which Asians use computer technology as software copyright piracy.[17] This conflict arises from Asian traditions of collective ownership, which clashes with the Western notions of intellectual property.

In a study of computer-use ethics among countries such as Singapore, Hong Kong, the United States, Great Britain, Australia, Sweden, Wales, and the Netherlands, researchers selected a number of computer-use vignettes (see Offline: The Use of Scenarios in Computer Ethics Studies later in this chapter) and presented them to students in universities in these countries. This study did not categorize or classify the responses as ethical or unethical, but indicated a degree of "ethical sensitivity" about the performance of the individuals in the short case studies. The results were grouped into three categories of ethical computer use: software license infringement, illicit use, and misuse of resources. The following sections are taken from the study, "Cross-National Differences In Computer-Use Ethics: A Nine Country Study," published in *The Journal of International Business Studies*.[18]

Software License Infringement

Overall, most of the countries studied had similar outlooks toward software piracy. Statistically speaking, only the United States and the Netherlands had attitudes that differed substantially from the other countries examined. The United States was significantly less tolerant of piracy, while the Netherlands was significantly more permissive. Although a number of studies have reported that the Pacific Rim countries of Singapore and Hong Kong are software piracy hotbeds, the study found their tolerance for copyright infringement to be moderate, as were the attitudes of Great Britain, Australia, and Sweden. This could mean that the individuals surveyed understood what software license infringement was, but either felt their use was not piracy, or that their society permitted it anyway. Peer pressure, lack of legal disincentives, lack of punitive measures, or any one of a number of other reasons could also explain why these reported piracy centers were not oblivious to intellectual property laws.

Although the Netherlands displayed a more permissive attitude toward piracy, which reflects its general culture, it only ranked third in piracy rates of the countries represented in this study.

Illicit Use

All of the individuals studied condemned viruses, hacking, and other forms of system abuse as unacceptable behavior. There were, however, differences in groups as to just how tolerant individuals were. Singapore and Hong Kong proved to be significantly more tolerant than the United States, Wales, Great Britain, and Australia. Sweden and the Netherlands were also significantly more tolerant than Wales and Australia and significantly less tolerant than Hong Kong. The low overall degree of tolerance for illicit system use may be a function of the easy association between the common crimes of breaking and entering, trespassing, theft, and destruction of property to their computer-related counterparts.

Misuse of Corporate Resources

The scenarios used to examine the levels of tolerance in this category each represented different kinds of personal use of corporate assets, with no indication of established policy toward personal use of company resources. In general, individuals displayed a rather lenient view of personal use of company equipment. Only Singapore and Hong Kong view personal use of company equipment as unethical. There were several substantial national differences in this category, with the Netherlands reporting the most lenient view. Regardless of cultural background, many individuals feel that if an organization does not specifically forbid the use of its computing resources for personal use, then such use is acceptable. In fact, only the two Asian samples, Singapore and Hong Kong, reported generally intolerant attitudes toward personal use of organizational computing resources. The reasons behind this are unknown. Perhaps the formal Asian work ethic provides stricter guidance on duty to the company versus personal rights and privileges.

Overall, the researchers found that there is a general agreement among nationalities as to what is acceptable or unacceptable computer use. There is however, a range of degrees of tolerance of unethical behavior.

Thus, the results of this study underscore inter-cultural similarities as much as they describe inter-cultural differences. The study also found little to support, from an ethical perspective, the popular media's portrayal of Asians as 'digital bandits'. In fact, the Hong Kong and Singapore respondents were not consistently the most permissive nationalities among those studied. As noted earlier, the higher piracy rates in Singapore and Hong Kong may be less a function of ethical difference and more a function of the lack of legal and financial disincentive to engage in software copyright infringement. The only country that consistently ranked as 'most tolerant' was the Netherlands. However, this level of tolerance does not seem to have completely manifested itself in action; although the Netherlands has a higher piracy rate than the United States, Australia, Wales, England, and Sweden, it still ranks behind Singapore and Hong Kong.[19]

OFFLINE

The Use of Scenarios in Computer Ethics Studies

The following vignettes can be used in an open and frank discussion of computer ethics. Review each scenario carefully and respond to each question using the following statement, choosing the description you feel most appropriate. Then, justify your response. *I feel the actions of this individual were (very ethical/ethical/neither ethical nor unethical/unethical/very unethical).*

Ethical Decision Evaluation

1. A scientist developed a theory that required proof through the construction of a computer model. He hired a computer programmer to build the model, and the theory was shown to be correct. The scientist won several awards for the development of the theory, but he never acknowledged the contribution of the computer programmer.

   The scientist's failure to acknowledge the computer programmer was:

2. The owner of a small business needed a computer-based accounting system. He identified the various inputs and outputs he felt were required to satisfy his needs, showed his design to a computer programmer, and asked the programmer if she could implement such a system. The programmer knew she could implement the system because she had developed much more sophisticated systems in the past. In fact, she felt this design was rather crude and would soon need several major revisions. But she didn't say anything about the design flaws because the business owner didn't ask her and she thought she might be the one hired to implement the needed revisions later.

   The programmer's decision not to point out the design flaws was:

continued

3. A student suspected and found a loophole in the university computer's security system that allowed him access to other students' records. He told the system administrator about the loophole, but continued to access other records until the problem was corrected two weeks later.

   The student's action in searching for the loophole was:

   The student's action in continuing to access others' record for two weeks was:

   The system administrator's failure to correct the problem sooner was:

4. A computer user called a mail-order computer program store to order a particular accounting system. When he received his order, he found that the store had accidentally sent him a very expensive word-processing program as well as the accounting package that he had ordered. The invoice listed only the accounting package. The user decided to keep the word-processing program.

   The user's decision to keep the word-processing program was:

5. A programmer at a bank realized that he had accidentally overdrawn his checking account. He made a small adjustment in the bank's accounting system so that his account would not have an additional service charge assessed. As soon as he deposited funds that made his balance positive again, he corrected the bank's accounting system.

   The programmer's modification of the accounting system was:

6. A computer programmer enjoyed building small computer systems (programs) to give to his friends. He would frequently go to his office on Saturday when no one was working and use his employer's computer to develop systems. He did not hide the fact that he was going into the building; he had to sign a register at a security desk each time he entered.

   The programmer's use of the company computer was:

   If the programmer sold the programs his actions would have been:

7. A student enrolled in a computer class was also employed at a local business part-time. Frequently her homework in the class involved using popular word-processing and spreadsheet packages. Occasionally she worked on her homework on the office computer at her part-time job, on her coffee or meal breaks.

   The student's use of the company computer was:

   If the student had worked on her homework during "company time" (not during a break), the student's use of the company computer would have been:

8. A student at a university learned to use an expensive spreadsheet program in her accounting class. The student would go to the university microcomputer lab and use the software to complete her assignment. Signs were posted in the lab indicating that copying software was forbidden. One day, she decided to copy the software anyway to complete her work assignments at home.

continued

> *If the student destroyed her copy of the software at the end of the term, her action in copying the software was:*
>
> *If the student forgot to destroy her copy of the software at the end of the term, her action in copying the software was:*
>
> *If the student never intended to destroy her copy of the software at the end of the term, her action in copying the software was:*
>
> 9. A student at a university found out that one of the local computer bulletin boards contained a "pirate" section (a section containing a collection of illegally copied software programs). He subscribed to the board, and proceeded to download several games and professional programs, which he then distributed to several of his friends.
>
>   *The student's actions in downloading the games were:*
>
>   *The student's actions in downloading the programs were:*
>
>   *The student's actions in sharing the programs and games with his friends were:*

Ethics and Education

Differences in computer use ethics are not exclusively cultural. Differences are found among individuals within the same country, within the same social class, and within the same company. Key studies reveal that the overriding factor in leveling the ethical perceptions within a small population is education. Employees must be trained and kept up to date on information security topics, including the expected behaviors of an ethical employee. This is especially important in areas of information security, as many employees may not have the formal technical training to understand that their behavior is unethical or even illegal. Proper ethical and legal training is vital to creating an informed, well-prepared, and low-risk system user.

Deterring Unethical and Illegal Behavior

It is the responsibility of information security personnel to deter unethical and illegal acts, using policy, education and training, and technology as controls or safeguards to protect the information and systems. Many security professionals understand technological means of protection, but many underestimate the value of policy.

There are three general categories of unethical behavior that organizations and society should seek to eliminate:

- Ignorance: As you learned earlier, ignorance of the law is no excuse, but ignorance of policies and procedures is. The first method of deterrence is education. Organizations must design, publish, and disseminate organizational policies and relevant laws, and employees must explicitly agree to abide by them. Reminders and training and awareness programs support retention, and, one hopes, compliance.

- Accident: Individuals with authorization and privileges to manage information within the organization have the greatest opportunity to cause harm or damage by accident. Careful placement of controls can help prevent accidental modification to systems and data.
- Intent: Criminal or unethical intent refers to the state of mind of the individual committing the infraction. A legal defense can be built on whether the accused acted out of ignorance, by accident, or with the intent to cause harm or damage. Deterring those with criminal intent is best done by means of litigation, prosecution, and technical controls. As you learned in Chapter 2, intent is only one of several factors to consider when determining whether a computer-related crime has occurred.

Deterrence is the best method for preventing an illegal or unethical activity. Laws, policies, and technical controls are all examples of deterrents. However, laws and policies and their associated penalties only deter if three conditions are present.

- Fear of penalty: Threats of informal reprimand or verbal warnings may not have the same impact as the threat of imprisonment or forfeiture of pay.
- Probability of being caught: There must be a strong possibility that perpetrators of illegal or unethical acts will be caught.
- Probability of penalty being administered: The organization must be willing and able to impose the penalty.

PROFESSIONAL ORGANIZATIONS AND THEIR CODES OF ETHICS

A number of professional organizations have established codes of conduct and/or codes of ethics that members are expected to follow. Codes of ethics can have a positive effect on an individual's judgment regarding computer use.[20] Unfortunately, many employers do not encourage their employees to join these professional organizations. The loss of accreditation or certification due to a violation of a code of conduct can be a deterrent, as it can dramatically reduce the individual's marketability and earning power.

In general, research has shown that some certifications have little impact on the long-term earning potential of practitioners, while other certifications, notably those in information security, have a lingering effect on the economic prospects of certificate holders.[21] The long-term value of an information security certification adds leverage to the certification-granting authority to exert influence over its members, including influence in matters of ethical responsibility.

It remains the individual responsibility of security professionals to act ethically and according to the policies and procedures of their employers, their professional organizations, and the laws of society. It is likewise the organization's responsibility to develop, disseminate, and enforce its policies. The following sections describe several of the relevant professional associations.

Association of Computing Machinery (ACM)

The **ACM** (www.acm.org), a well-respected professional society, was originally established in 1947 as the world's first educational and scientific computing society. It is one of the few organizations that strongly promotes education, and provides discounted membership for students. The ACM's code of ethics requires members to perform their duties in a manner befitting an ethical computing professional. The code contains specific references to protecting the confidentiality of information, causing no harm (with specific references to viruses), protecting the privacy of others, and respecting the intellectual property and copyrights of others. The ACM also publishes a wide variety of professional computing publications, including the highly regarded *Communications of the ACM*.

International Information Systems Security Certification Consortium, Inc. (ISC)^2

The **(ISC)^2** (www.isc2.org) is not a professional association in the strictest sense, and has no member or membership services. It is a nonprofit organization that focuses on the development and implementation of information security certifications and credentials. The (ISC)^2 manages a body of knowledge on information security and administers and evaluates examinations for information security certifications. The code of ethics put forth by (ISC)^2 is primarily designed for information security professionals who have earned one of their certifications. This code includes four mandatory canons:

- Protect society, the commonwealth, and the infrastructure
- Act honorably, honestly, justly, responsibly, and legally
- Provide diligent and competent service to principals
- Advance and protect the profession[22]

Through this code, (ISC)^2 seeks to provide sound guidance that will enable reliance on the ethicality and trustworthiness of the information security professional as the guardian of the information and systems.

System Administration, Networking, and Security Institute (SANS)

Founded in 1989, **SANS** (www.sans.org) is a professional research and education cooperative organization. The organization, which enjoys a large professional membership, is dedicated to the protection of information and systems. Individuals who seek one of SANS's many GIAC certifications, must agree to comply with the organization's code of ethics:

Respect for the Public
- I will accept responsibility in making decisions with consideration for the security and welfare of the community.
- I will not engage in or be a party to unethical or unlawful acts that negatively affect the community, my professional reputation, or the information security discipline.

Respect for the Certification
- I will not share, disseminate, or otherwise distribute confidential or proprietary information pertaining to the GIAC certification process.
- I will not use my certification, or objects or information associated with my certification (such as certificates or logos), to represent any individual or entity other than myself as being certified by GIAC.

Respect for My Employer

- I will deliver capable service that is consistent with the expectations of my certification and position.
- I will protect confidential and proprietary information with which I come into contact.
- I will minimize risks to the confidentiality, integrity, or availability of an information technology solution, consistent with risk management practice.

Respect for Myself

- I will avoid conflicts of interest.
- I will not misuse any information or privileges I am afforded as part of my responsibilities.
- I will not misrepresent my abilities or my work to the community, my employer, or my peers.[23]

Information Systems Audit and Control Association (ISACA)

ISACA (www.isaca.org) is a professional association with a focus on auditing, control, and security. Its membership comprises both technical and managerial professionals. ISACA focuses on providing IT control practices and standards. The organization offers the Certified Information Systems Auditor (CISA) certification, which does not focus exclusively on information security but does contain many information security components.

The ISACA abides by the following code of ethics:

Members and ISACA certification holders shall:

1. Support the implementation of, and encourage compliance with, appropriate standards, procedures and controls for information systems.
2. Perform their duties with objectivity, due diligence and professional care, in accordance with professional standards and best practices.
3. Serve in the interest of stakeholders in a lawful and honest manner, while maintaining high standards of conduct and character, and not engage in acts discreditable to the profession.
4. Maintain the privacy and confidentiality of information obtained in the course of their duties unless disclosure is required by legal authority. Such information shall not be used for personal benefit or released to inappropriate parties.
5. Maintain competency in their respective fields and agree to undertake only those activities, that they can reasonably expect to complete with professional competence.
6. Inform appropriate parties of the results of work performed; revealing all significant facts known to them.
7. Support the professional education of stakeholders in enhancing their understanding of information systems security and control.[24]

Information Systems Security Association (ISSA)

The ISSA (www.issa.org) is a nonprofit society of information security professionals. Its primary mission is to bring together qualified practitioners of information security for information exchange and educational development. ISSA provides conferences, meetings, publications, and information resources to promote information security awareness and education.[25] ISSA also supports a code of ethics, similar to those of (ISC)[2], ISACA, and the ACM, for "promoting management practices that will ensure the confidentiality, integrity, and availability of organizational information resources."[26]

I have in the past and will in the future:

- Perform all professional activities and duties in accordance with all applicable laws and the highest ethical principles;
- Promote generally accepted information security current best practices and standards;
- Maintain appropriate confidentiality of proprietary or otherwise sensitive information encountered in the course of professional activities;
- Discharge professional responsibilities with diligence and honesty;
- Refrain from any activities that might constitute a conflict of interest or otherwise damage the reputation of employers, the information security profession, or the Association; and
- Not intentionally injure or impugn the professional reputation or practice of colleagues, clients, or employers.[27]

ORGANIZATIONAL LIABILITY AND THE NEED FOR COUNSEL

What if an organization does not support or even encourage strong ethical conduct on the part of its employees? What if an organization does not behave ethically? Even if there is no criminal conduct, there can be liability. **Liability**—an entity's legal obligation—can be applied to conduct even when no law or contract has been breached. Liability for a wrongful act includes the obligation to make payment or **restitution**—compensation for the wrong. If an employee, acting with or without the authorization, performs an illegal or unethical act, causing some degree of harm, the organization can be held financially liable for that action. An organization increases its liability if it refuses to take measures—**due care**—to make sure that every employee knows what is acceptable and what is not, and the consequences of illegal or unethical actions. **Due diligence** requires that an organization make a valid and ongoing effort to protect others. Because of the Internet, it is possible that a person wronged by an organization's members could be anywhere, in any state, or any country, around the world. Under the U.S. legal system, any court can impose its authority over an individual or organization if it can establish **jurisdiction**—a court's right to hear a case if the act was committed in its territory or involving its citizenry. This is sometimes referred to as **long-arm jurisdiction**, as the long arm of the law reaches across the country or around the world to bring the accused into its court systems. Trying a case in the injured party's home area usually favors the injured party or parties, as it creates a home court advantage.[28]

Key Law Enforcement Agencies

Sometimes organizations need assistance from law enforcement. While local law enforcement may be the first point of contact, and is capable of handling physical security threats or employee problems, it is usually ill equipped to handle electronic crimes. Most states have law enforcement and investigation agencies. For example, the Georgia State Patrol and the Georgia Bureau of Investigation have separate structures and missions, but do work together and with local law enforcement to assist organizations and individuals.

In addition, a number of key federal agencies are charged with the protection of U.S. information resources, and the investigation of threats to, or attacks on, these resources. Among them are the Federal Bureau of Investigation's National Infrastructure Protection Center, the National Security Administration, and the U.S. Secret Service.

What was originally the Federal Bureau of Investigation's **National Infrastructure Protection Center (NIPC)** was established in 1998 and served as the U.S. government's focal point for threat assessment and the warning, investigation, and response to threats or attacks against critical U.S. infrastructures. The NIPC was folded into the Department of Homeland Security (DHS) after the 2001 terrorist attacks to increase communications and focus the department's efforts in cyber defense. It is now a part of the National Interagency Coordination Center.[29]

Established in January 2001, the **National InfraGard Program** began as a cooperative effort between the FBI's Cleveland field office and local technology professionals. The FBI sought assistance in establishing a more effective method of protecting critical national information resources. The resulting cooperative formed the first InfraGard chapter as a formal effort to combat both cyber and physical threats. Today, every FBI field office has established an InfraGard chapter and collaborates with public and private organizations and the academic community to share information about attacks, vulnerabilities, and threats. The National InfraGard Program serves its members using the following tools:

- Intrusion alert network using encrypted e-mail
- Secure Web site for communication about suspicious activity or intrusions
- Local chapter activities
- Help desk for questions

InfraGard's primary contribution is the free exchange of information to and from the private sector in the subject areas of threats and attacks on information resources.[30]

Another key federal agency is the **National Security Agency (NSA)**. As the nation's cryptologic organization, the NSA coordinates, directs, and performs highly specialized activities to protect U.S. information systems and produce foreign intelligence information. It is also one of the government's most important centers of foreign language analysis and research.[31]

The NSA is responsible for the security of communications and information systems at many federal government agencies associated with national security. The NSA's Information Assurance Directorate (IAD) provides information security "solutions including the technologies, specifications and criteria, products, product configurations, tools, standards, operational doctrine and support activities needed to implement the protect, detect and report, and respond elements of cyber defense."[32] The IAD also develops and promotes an Information Assurance Framework Forum in cooperation with commercial organizations and academic researchers. This framework provides strategic guidance as well as technical specifications for security solutions. IAD's Common Criteria is a set of standards designed to promote understanding of information security.

Prominent among the NSA's information security efforts and activities are its information security outreach programs. The NSA recognizes universities that offer information security education opportunities, and that integrate information security philosophies and efforts into their internal operations. These recognized Centers of Excellence in Information Assurance Education can display this recognition on their Web sites and in other materials, and are named on the NSA's Web site. Additionally, the NSA has an information security curriculum certification program. The Information Assurance Courseware Evaluation process reviews an institution's information security course offerings, and gives three-year accreditation to those that meet its standards. Graduates of these programs receive certificates recognizing this accreditation.

In addition to its well-known mission to protect key members of the U.S. government, the **U.S. Secret Service** is also charged with the detection and arrest of any person committing a U.S. federal offense relating to computer fraud, as well as false identification crimes.[33] This is an extension of its original duty to protect U.S. currency. After all, the communications networks of the U.S. carry more funds, in the form of electronic data, than all of the armored cars in the world combined. Protect the networks, protect the data, and you protect money, stocks, and other financial transactions.

The USA PATRIOT Act and subsequent PATRIOT Improvement and Reauthorization Act increased the Secret Service's role in investigating fraud and related activity in connection with computers. In addition, these acts authorized the director of the Secret Service to establish nationwide electronic crimes task forces to assist law enforcement, the private sector, and academia in detecting and suppressing computer-based crime. The acts increase the statutory penalties for the manufacturing, possession, dealing and passing of counterfeit U.S. or foreign obligations; and they allow enforcement action to be taken to protect our financial payment systems while combating transnational financial crimes directed by terrorists or other criminals.

The Secret Service was transferred from the Department of the Treasury to the Department of Homeland Security effective March 1, 2003. Since that time, DHS has added to its critical infrastructure defense strategies the protection of the nation's cyber-infrastructures. To directly support the public, DHS promotes individual emergency preparedness through its READY Campaign and Citizen Corp (http://ready.gov). This site has content dedicated to cyber defense (see, for example, http://www.ready.gov/business/protect/cybersecurity.html).

Chapter Summary

- Laws are formally adopted rules for acceptable behavior in modern society. Ethics are socially acceptable behaviors. The key difference between laws and ethics is that laws bear the sanction of a governing authority and ethics do not.

- Organizations formalize desired behaviors in documents called policies. Unlike laws, policies must be read and explicitly agreed to by employees before they are binding.

- Civil law encompasses a wide variety of laws that regulate relationships between and among individuals and organizations. Criminal law addresses violations that harm society and that are prosecuted by the state. Tort law is a subset of civil law that deals with lawsuits by individuals rather than criminal prosecution by the state.

- The desire to protect national security, trade secrets, and a variety of other state and private assets has led to several laws affecting what information and information management and security resources may be exported from the United States.

- U.S. copyright law extends intellectual property rights to the published word, including electronic publication.

- Studies of ethical sensitivity to computer use have determined that individuals of different nationalities have various perspectives on the ethics of computer use.

- Deterrence can prevent an illegal or unethical activity from occurring. Successful deterrence requires the institution of severe penalties, the probability of apprehension, and an expectation that penalties will be enforced.

- As part of an effort to sponsor positive ethics, a number of professional organizations have established codes of conduct or codes of ethics that their members are expected to follow.

- A number of key U.S. federal agencies charged with the protection of American information resources, and the investigation of threats to, or attacks on, these resources.

Review Questions

1. What is the difference between criminal law and civil law?
2. What is tort law and what does it permit an individual to do?
3. What are the primary examples of public law?
4. Which law amended the Computer Fraud and Abuse Act of 1986, and what did it change?
5. Which organization led the efforts to overturn the Computer Decency Act? What happened to the law it opposed?
6. What is privacy, in the context of information security?
7. What is another name for the Kennedy-Kassebaum Act (1996), and why is it important to organizations that are not in the health care industry?
8. If you work for a financial service organization (such as a bank or credit union) which law from 1999 affects your use of customer data? What other effects does it have?
9. Which 1997 law provides guidance on the use of encryption?

10. What is intellectual property? Is it offered the same protection in every country? What laws currently protect intellectual property in the United States and Europe?

11. What is a policy? How does it differ from a law?

12. What are the three general categories of unethical and illegal behavior?

13. What is the best method for preventing an illegal or unethical activity?

14. Of the professional organizations listed in this chapter, which has been established for the longest time? When was it founded?

15. Of the professional organizations listed in this chapter, which is focused on auditing and control?

16. What is the stated purpose of the SANS organization? In what ways is it involved in professional certification for information security professionals?

17. Which U.S. federal agency sponsors the InfraGard program? Which agency has taken control of the overall National Infrastructure Protection mission?

18. What is due care? Why would an organization want to make sure it exercises due care in its usual course of operations?

19. What can be done to deter someone from committing a crime?

20. How does due diligence differ from due care? Why are both important?

Exercises

1. What does CISSP stand for? Using the Internet, find out what continuing education is required for the holder of a CISSP to remain current and in good standing.

2. For what kind of information security jobs does the NSA recruit? Use the Internet to visit its Web page and find a listing.

3. Using the resources available in your library, find out what laws your state has passed to prosecute computer crime.

4. Using the Web, go to www.eff.org. What are the current top concerns of this organization?

5. Using the ethical scenarios presented in the chapter, answer each question, and bring your answers to class to compare them with those of your peers.

Case Exercises

Iris was a little unsure of what to do next. She had just left the meeting with the other executives of RWW, Inc. At the meeting they confirmed the need for action on the matter of the critical information offered for sale on a public auction site. That was the last point of agreement. This was a risk they had simply not planned for and they were completely unprepared.

Just before the meeting broke up, they had made assignments to various people in the meeting. Robin, the CEO, was going to contact the members of the Board of Directors to brief them so that if the story became public, they would not be surprised. Jerry, the corporate counsel, was going to start an intensive effort to discover what peer companies had done in situations like this. Mike, the CIO, was assigned to contact the auction site to get the auction shut down and lay the groundwork for working with whatever authorities were brought in for the criminal aspects of the case.

Iris was assigned to investigate which law enforcement agency should be involved in the investigation. She reached for her business card box and began thumbing through the contacts she had.

1. Do you think the response of the company so far indicates any errors in the matter of this incident?

2. With which agency do you think Iris should start? On what factors do you base that recommendation?

3. What criminal acts do you think are involved in this situation? What do you think the relationship of the perpetrator to RWW, Inc., might be?

Endnotes

[1] J. B. Noone. *Rousseau's Social Contract: A Conceptual Analysis.* University of Georgia Press, 1981.

[2] Brian T. Yeh and Charles Doyle. *USA PATRIOT Improvement and Reauthorization Act of 2005 (H.R. 3199)*: A Brief Look. Accessed August 26, 2006. www.fas.org/sgp/crs/intel/RS22348.pdf.

[3] Epic. Computer Security Act of 1987. Accessed October 14, 2006. www.epic.org/crypto/csa/csa.html.

[4] *The American Heritage Dictionary of the English Language.* 4th ed. 2000.

[5] U.S. Constitution, Fourth Amendment. Accessed August 28, 2006. www.archives.gov/national-archives-experience/charters/bill_of_rights_transcript.html.

[6] Findlaw. Search and Seizure: History and Scope of the Amendment. Accessed August 28, 2006. caselaw.lp.findlaw.com/data/constitution/amendment04/01.html#t2.

[7] Cornell Law School. Title 47, Chapter 5, Subchapter II, Part I, § 222. Accessed October 14, 2006. www4.law.cornell.edu/uscode/47/222.html.

[8] U. S. Department of Justice, The Privacy Act of 1974. Accessed October 14, 2006. from www.usdoj.gov/foia/privstat.htm.

[9] Cornell Law School. Title 18, Part I, Chapter 119. Accessed October 14, 2006. www4.law.cornell.edu/uscode/18/pIch119.html.

[10] HIPAA Advisory. HIPAA Regulations. Accessed October 14, 2006. www.hipaadvisory.com/regs/.

[11] U.S. Department of Justice. *The Economic Espionage Act of 1996: An Overview*. Accessed October 14, 2006. www.cybercrime.gov/usamay2001_6.htm.

[12] Wikipedia: The Free Encyclopedia. Information Technology and SOX. Accessed August 28, 2006. en.wikipedia.org/wiki/Sarbanes-Oxley_Act#Information_technology_and_SOX_404.

[13] Georgia Institute of Technology. Georgia Computer Systems Protection Act. Accessed October 14, 2006. www.security.gatech.edu/policy/law_library/gcspa.html.

[14] OCGA. Official Code of Georgia Annotated §10-15-1. Definitions.

[15] OCGA. Official Code of Georgia Annotated §10-15-2. Business must properly dispose of identifying information.

16. Computer Professionals for Social Responsibility. *The Ten Commandments of Computer Ethics*. Referenced October 14, 2006. Available on the World Wide Web at www.cpsr.org/issues/ethics/cei.

17. Mike Magee. Software piracy in Asia exposed. *The Inquirer*. Accessed October 14, 2006. www.theinquirer.net/default.aspx?article=2385.

18. M. E. Whitman, A. M. Townsend, and A. R. Hendrickson. Cross-National Differences in Computer-Use Ethics: A Nine Country Study. *The Journal of International Business Studies*, 30(4), 1999, 673–687.

19. M. E. Whitman, A. M. Townsend, and A. R. Hendrickson. Cross-National Differences In Computer-Use Ethics: A Nine Country Study. *The Journal of International Business Studies*, 30(4), 1999, 673–687.

20. S. J. Harrington. The Effects of Codes of Ethics and Personal Denial of Responsibility on Computer Abuse Judgment and Intentions. *MIS Quarterly*, September 1996, 257–278.

21. Foote Partners, LLC. Press Release. August 18, 2003, New Canaan, CT.

22. (ISC)². Code of Ethics. Accessed October 14, 2006. www.isc2.org/cgi-bin/content.cgi?category=12.

23. GIAC. Code of Ethics. Accessed August 28, 2006. www.giac.org/overview/ethics.php.

24. ISACA. Code of Ethics. Accessed August 28, 2006. www.isaca.org/Template.cfm?Section=Code_of_Professional_Ethics.

25. ISSA. What Is ISSA? Accessed October 14, 2006. http://www.issa.org/aboutissa.html.

26. ISSA. Code of Ethics. Accessed October 14, 2006. www.issa.org/codeofethics.html.

27. ISSA. Code of Ethics. Accessed August 28, 2006. www.issa.org/codeofethics.html.

28. R. J. Alberts, A. M. Townsend, and M. E. Whitman. The Threat of Long-arm Jurisdiction to Electronic Commerce. *Communications of the ACM*, 41(12), December 1998, 15–20.

29. National Interagency Coordination Center. Accessed October 14, 2006. www.nifc.gov/nicc/.

30. U.S. Federal Bureau of Investigation. Press Release. Accessed October 14, 2006. www.fbi.gov/pressrel/pressrel01/infragard.htm.

31. U.S. National Security Agency. Introduction to NSA/CSS. Accessed October 14, 2006. www.nsa.gov/about/index.cfm.

32. U.S. National Security Agency. Information Assurance. Accessed October 14, 2006. www.nsa.gov/ia/index.cfm.

33. U.S. Secret Service. Mission Statement. Accessed October 14, 2006. www.secretservice.gov/mission.shtml.

## CHAPTER 12

INFORMATION SECURITY PROJECT MANAGEMENT

QUOTE

I find that the harder I work, the more luck I seem to have.

Thomas Jefferson (1743–1826)

"Come in," said Iris to Maria Rodriguez, one of the technicians in the Information Security department. "Have a seat, please." As Iris closed her office door, Maria settled at the small table by the window.

Iris began. "Maria, we've been working together since I joined RWW. I've been very happy with your work as the team leader for the network vulnerability assessment team. You and the others have done a good job finding holes and fixing them across the company. I know how much collaboration and teamwork goes into that process. Now I'm ready to offer you another opportunity in a different part of the security group. Are you ready for some new challenges?"

"Yes!" said Maria.

"Great." Iris continued. "I think it would be good for you to start training Marion on the vulnerability team to be the team leader while we get you started as project manager for the deployment of our upgraded intrusion detection system."

Maria said, "I don't have any experience with project management, but I'm willing to learn."

Iris nodded. "Maria, you have a great track record as a developer and a system administrator here at RWW. You've got the right attitude for this job, and I'm here to make sure you get the right skills. I would like you to take the next week to work out the transition of your team lead role, and then you'll spend a week at a project management class that I asked the RWW Training Department to arrange for you. I've already ordered you a license for Microsoft Project, which is the software that you'll need for the class."

Maria thought about it for just a second, and then said, "I'm ready."

INTRODUCTION

The need for project management skills within the practice of information security may not at first be self-evident. It has been emphasized throughout this book that information security is a process, not a project. However, each element of an information security program must be managed as a project, even if it is an ongoing one. Organizations routinely require technically skilled IT or information security experts to lead projects, or they assign experienced project and general managers to lead information security projects. Some organizations use both approaches simultaneously, sometimes assigning project management tasks to technical managers and sometimes assigning those tasks to a general manager, so that all elements of the information security program are completed with quality deliverables, on a timely basis, and within budget.

The job posting shown in Figure 12-1 shows the typical requirements for an information security analyst.

While it is not certain that project management and organizational skills will be part of every information security analyst position description, many employers seek employees who couple their information security focus and skills with strong project management skills. Many consulting firms now offer information security services in conjunction with, or in the context of, project management.

How can information security be both a process and a project? It is, in fact, a continuous series, or chain, of projects. As illustrated in Figure 12-2, each link in this chain could be a specific project, and each of these projects would be guided by the security systems development life cycle (SecSDLC).

To be sure, some aspects of information security are not project based; rather, they are managed processes. These managed processes include the monitoring of the external and internal environments during incident response, ongoing risk assessments of routine operations, and continuous vulnerability assessment and vulnerability repair. These activities are called **operations** and are ongoing.

Projects, on the other hand, are discrete sequences of activities with starting points and defined completion points. In other words, a "project is a temporary endeavor undertaken to create a unique product or service."[1] Although each individual information security project has an end point, larger organizations never completely finish the information security improvement process; they periodically review progress and realign planning to

Information Security Analyst

The Information Security Analyst will be responsible for managing and performing end-to-end technical security reviews, solutions, and implementations for all applications and interfaces within Google. Works with the members of the security team to provide product development input, and assure the security of the company's Infrastructure. This is a highly technical hands-on role. Review existing service offerings and suggest improvements. Perform security architectural reviews of existing/planned IT and production infrastructure. Act as a resource to internal departments (Engineering, Operations, Product Development, HR, QA) for security related topics.

Responsibilities:

- Conduct information security risk assessments and risk management services throughout the company, providing security risk evaluation, mitigation and solutions to projects and initiatives.
- Stay abreast of industry best practices in risk management techniques and integrate new methods and tools as appropriate.
- Coordinate efforts between the Information Security and development and production teams.
- Work with the members of the security team to develop and implement strategies to balance security recommendations with business needs.
- Provide guidance and consultation for security related questions from users, developers, and managers.
- Provide technical support for corporate security initiatives such as intrusion detection, virus and malicious code protection, operating systems (Windows XP and Linux) security support, networking, and firewall administration.

Requirements:

- Bachelor's degree, preferably in a technical discipline; or equivalent.
- Expert knowledge and experience of Information Security best practices and business controls.
- Experienced in facilitating Information Security risk assessments for major processes, systems and projects.
- Excellent verbal and written communication skills, including facilitation and team leadership skills.
- Strong project management and organization skills.
- Teamwork/interpersonal ability to gain agreement effectively.
- Results oriented, high energy, self-motivated.
- Knowledge of computer applications design, software and network architectures, protocols, and standards.
- Technical knowledge and demonstrated technical expertise in at least two of the following areas: operating systems, networking, database, client server and web technologies.
- Minimum of 4 years experience in Information Security or IT auditing related fields.

Source: Association of American Medical Colleges. Reprinted with permission.

FIGURE 12-1   Position Posting for an Information Security Analyst

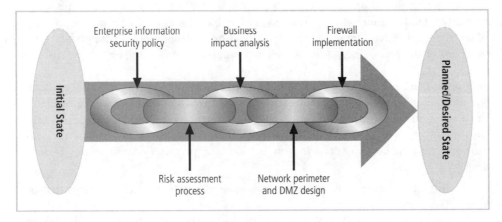

FIGURE 12-2   The Information Security Program Chain

meet business and IT objectives. This realignment can lead to new goals and projects, as well as the modification, cancellation, or reprioritization of existing projects.

PROJECT MANAGEMENT

The *Guide to the Project Management Body of Knowledge* by W. R. Duncan (hereafter called the *PMBoK*) defines **project management** as:

> the application of knowledge, skills, tools, and techniques to project activities to meet project requirements. Project management is accomplished through the use of processes such as: initiating, planning, executing, controlling, and closing.[2]

In other words, project management—which makes use of many of the approaches discussed in the management sections of Chapter 1—is focused on achieving the objectives of the project.

Unlike ongoing operations, project management involves the temporary assemblage of a group that completes the project, and whose members are then released, and perhaps assigned to other projects. Projects are sometimes seen as development opportunities that enable employees and managers to extend their skills in readiness for promotion to larger opportunities. This can lead to one of the common pitfalls in organizations that have operations groups and project teams: the *prima donna* effect, where certain groups are perceived as elite or more skilled than others. This effect is often seen when workers in operations support roles or software maintenance are seen as less dynamic or capable than their project-focused peers.

Although project management is focused on projects that have end points, this does not mean these projects are one-time occurrences. Some projects are iterative, and occur regularly. Budgeting processes, for example, are iterative projects. Each year the budget committee meets, designs a proposed budget for the following year, and then presents it to the appropriate manager. The committee may not meet again for six to nine months until the next budget cycle. Another common practice is the creation of a sequence of projects, with periodic submission of grouped deliverables. Each project phase has a defined set of objectives and deliverables, and the authorization to progress to future phases is tied to the success of the preceding phase as well as availability of funding or other critical resources.

Some organizational cultures have a long record of relying on project management and have put in place training programs and reward structures to develop a cadre of highly skilled project managers and a corresponding group of trained technical personnel. Other organizations implement each project from scratch, and define the process as they go. Organizations that make project management skills a priority accrue many benefits, including:

- Implementation of a methodology—such as the SecSDLC—ensures that no steps are missed.
- Creation of a detailed blueprint of project activities serves as a common reference tool, and makes all project team members more productive by shortening the learning curve when getting projects underway.
- Identification of specific responsibilities for all involved personnel lessens ambiguity and reduces confusion when individuals are assigned to new or different projects.

- Clear definition of project constraints, including time frame, budget, and minimum-quality requirements increases the likelihood that the project stays within them.
- Establishing measures of performance and creation of project milestones simplifies project monitoring.
- Early identification of deviations in quality, time, or budget enables early correction.

Successful project management relies on careful and realistic project planning coupled with aggressive proactive control. The project success may be defined differently in each organization, but in general a project is deemed a success when:

- It is completed on time or early.
- It comes in at or below the expenditures planned for in the baseline budget.
- It meets all specifications outlined in the approved project definition, and the deliverables are accepted by the end user and/or assigning entity.

APPLYING PROJECT MANAGEMENT TO SECURITY

To apply project management to information security, you must first select an established project management methodology. Just as information security systems analysts use the SecSDLC, information security project managers often follow methodologies based on the Project Management Body of Knowledge (PMBoK), a methodology promoted by the Project Management Institute. While other project management approaches exist, the PMBoK is considered the industry best practice. In the following sections, the PMBoK is examined in the context of information security project management.

PMBoK Knowledge Areas

The PMBoK identifies the project management knowledge areas shown in Table 12-1. Each of these areas is discussed in the following sections.

TABLE 12-1 Project Management Knowledge Areas

Knowledge Area	Focus	Processes
Integration	Elements are coordinated	• Project plan development • Project plan execution • Overall change control
Scope	Including all necessary work	• Initiation • Scope planning • Scope definition • Scope verification
Time	On-time completion	• Activity definition • Activity sequencing • Activity duration estimating • Schedule development • Schedule control

TABLE 12-1 Project Management Knowledge Areas (continued)

Knowledge Area	Focus	Processes
Cost	Completion within budget	• Resource planning • Cost estimating • Cost budgeting • Cost control
Quality	Satisfying target needs	• Quality planning • Quality assurance • Quality control
Human Resource	Effectively using workers	• Organizational planning • Staff acquisition • Team development
Communications	Efficiently processing information	• Communications planning • Information distribution • Performance reporting • Administrative closure
Risk	Minimizing impact of adverse occurrences	• Risk identification • Risk quantification • Risk response development • Risk response control
Procurement	Acquiring needed resources	• Procurement planning • Solicitation planning • Solicitation • Source selection • Contract administration • Contract closeout

Project Integration Management

Project integration management includes the processes required to ensure that effective coordination occurs within and between the project's many components, including personnel. Most projects include a wide variety of elements: people, time, information, financial resources, internal coordination units (other departments), outside coordination units (regulatory agencies, standards organizations), computing resources, and physical resources (meeting rooms), to name a few.

Major elements of the project management effort that require integration include:

- Development of the initial project plan
- Monitoring of progress as the project plan is executed
- Control of the revisions to the project plan as well as control of the changes made to resource allocations as measured performance causes adjustments to the project plan

Project plan development is the process of integrating all of the project elements into a cohesive plan with the goal of completing the project within the allotted work time using no more than the allotted project resources. As shown in Figure 12-3, these three elements—work time, resources, and project deliverables—are core components used in the creation of the project plan. Changing any one element usually affects the accuracy and reliability of the estimates of the other two, and likely means that the project plan must be revised. For instance, changing the quality or quantity of project deliverables requires changes in work time or resource allocations for the project plan to remain realistic.

FIGURE 12-3   Project Plan Inputs

When integrating the disparate elements of a complex information security project, complications are likely to arise. Among these complications are:

Conflicts among Communities of Interest.   When business units do not perceive the need or purpose of an information security project, they may not fully support the project. When IT staff are not completely aligned with the objectives of the information security project, or do not fully understand its impact or criticality, they may be less than fully supportive and may make less than a complete effort toward ensuring its success. The information security community must educate and inform the other communities so that information security projects are afforded the same support as other IT and non-IT projects.

Far-reaching Impact.   Many information security projects span the enterprise and may affect every user of an organization's IT systems. Some parts of the organization may not have the same degree of motivation to participate and, in fact, may be opposed to the goals of the project. The project manager may have to build consensus across the organization and must allow for any necessary education, training, and systems integration efforts when estimating work time and resource demands.

New Technology.   Information security projects often introduce new technologies. Depending on an organization's appetite for risk, a project may deploy technology-based controls that are new to the industry as well as to the organization. Sometimes the disparate constituencies that are needed to make a project successful are not open to new or different technologies and the project manager becomes engaged in debates about technology selections, or is required to build consensus around technology choices. Project team members, as well as other workers in the organization, may require special training when new technologies are introduced. This increases the risk of human resource turnover because personnel trained in a new, high-demand skill are more likely to leave the organization for opportunities elsewhere. Proactive steps, such as retention bonuses or gainsharing arrangements, may help mitigate this risk, but the project plan should include contingency plans for personnel turnover.

VIEWPOINT

Okay, Go Ahead and Do It

By Henry Bonin, Consultant, Adromeda Sciences

Congratulations! You made it this far learning about the various components of information security management. Now it's time to sew all the pieces together to make information security actually happen.

You and your team have gone through all the steps of planning and analyzing your concept for some element of an information security system, and you have presented a proposal to the decision maker. You convinced the boss that this is the right thing to do, and he or she has just given you the go-ahead. Is your response "Yikes!" or "Cool!"?

The last step is to demonstrate (prove) that this portion of the information security system can be installed and configured to do the things you claimed it would. That's what this final chapter is about. This last step will have as profound an effect on your information security project and total information security program as will the technology you have selected, the process you have designed, and the personnel you have chosen. Failure here will have no less an impact than a failure of the technology itself.

Projects can have high failure rates, and failure is usually traceable to a failure to follow an accepted methodology or a lack of experience in project management. Information security projects introduce a third reason for possible failure: the incorrect assumption that information security projects are just another IT project. They are not, as you are learning in this chapter.

I just left one of the many conferences I attend every year put on by one of the major IT vendors. At this conference, the theme was low-cost computing. Rosy pictures of some future state or end points were shown—the future of your organization, if you implement the ideas presented at the conference. Most of the presentations avoid illustrating the less picturesque process of getting from here to there. That process is project management. By practicing and mastering the project management methods described in this chapter, the journey between here and there will be a smoother one.

Project Scope Management

Project scope management includes ensuring that the project plan includes those activities—and only those activities—necessary to complete it. One issue that undermines many projects once they are underway is a phenomenon known as scope creep. **Scope creep** occurs when the quantity or quality of project deliverables is expanded from the original project plan. Stopping scope creep can pose a challenge to many project managers, who seek to meet the objectives expressed to them by project sponsors. Experienced project managers, exposed to project scope creep in the past, are prepared to ask for a corresponding expansion of project work time or project resources or both.

Major processes of this stage include:

- Scope planning
- Scope definition
- Scope verification

In addition to these three processes, another process is often added by practitioners in the field, that of change control for all requests for change in scope in order to gain more control of the planning process after the project is underway.

Project Time Management

Project time management entails ensuring that the project is finished by the identified completion date while meeting its objectives. Failure to meet project deadlines is one of the most frequently cited failures in project management. Many completion deadlines are tied to such external requirements as market demands, business alliances, or government regulations. Missing a deadline can sometimes make project completion moot.

Many missed deadlines are the result of poor planning. While poor performance by project managers and project resources can cause missed deadlines, it is more often the case that project planners impose unrealistic and often impossible deadlines. The hope that the gap between realistic and unrealistic planning can be closed by hard work may be realized from time to time, but far too often projects that begin with unrealistic timetables only get worse. An experienced project manager becomes adept at estimating the time and resources required to complete projects. Such a project manager, with a track record of success, is in a position to stick to accurate and realistic estimates in the face of management resistance.

The fact is that a given result (the deliverable of the project) requires a certain amount of time and resources (money, people, equipment, and so on) to accomplish. Management wants notwithstanding, trimming time or resources from these amounts requires reducing the quantity or quality of the deliverables. Some believe that most of the projects that fail do so in the planning phase, when management underestimates the necessary time and resources, or overestimates the quantity and quality of project deliverables given the available resources.

This management area includes the following processes:

- Activity definition
- Activity sequencing
- Activity duration estimating
- Schedule development
- Schedule control

Project Cost Management

Project cost management includes the processes required to ensure that a project is completed within the resource constraints placed on it. Some projects are planned using only a financial budget from which all resources—personnel, equipment, supplies, and so forth—must be procured (see the section entitled Project Procurement Management later in this chapter). Other projects have a variety of resources cobbled together, with no real financial support, just whatever the managers can scrounge.

The earlier description of the components of planning—deliverables, work time, and resources—emphasizes the interrelated nature of these three components. Beyond this level of interdependence, note that project work time directly influences the consumption of resources. Some resources have associated costs based on reserved time, regardless of whether they are actually used. If a project manager arranges for 20 computer workstations, but only has five developers at work, cost of the unused workstations is wasted. Planning for resource usage is among the more complex processes in project management, and many project management tools (covered later in this chapter) focus on the development of efficient resource planning.

This management area includes the following processes:

- Resource planning
- Cost estimating
- Cost budgeting
- Cost control

Project Quality Management

Project quality management includes the processes required to ensure that the project adequately meets the project specifications. The common use of the word "quality" may seem vague—what is a quality product to one person may not be to another. In fact, the definition of quality is quite clear: If the project deliverables meet the requirements specified in the project plan, the project has met its quality objective; if they do not, it has not met its quality objectives. Unfortunately, far too often, poorly planned projects do not provide clear descriptions of what the project is to deliver, whether it is a product, a service, or a revised process. As the quotation from Yogi Berra that opened Chapter 2 said, "You got to be careful if you don't know where you're going, because you might not get there."

A good plan defines project deliverables in unambiguous terms against which actual results are easily compared. This enables the project team to determine at each step along the way whether all components are being developed to the original specifications. As noted above in the section on scope management, changes made along the way can threaten the overall success of the project. Any change to the definition of project deliverables must be codified, and then the other two areas of project planning—work time and resources—must be reconciled to the changes.

This focus of management includes the following processes:

- Quality planning
- Quality assurance
- Quality control

Project Human Resource Management

Project human resource management includes the processes necessary to ensure the personnel assigned to a project are effectively employed. Staffing a project requires careful estimates of the number of worker hours required. Too few people working on a project almost guarantees it will not be completed on time. Too many people working on a project may be an inefficient use of resources, and may cause the project to exceed its resource limits.

In general, human resource management faces some complications, including:

- Not all workers operate at the same level of efficiency; in fact, wide variance in the productivity of individuals is the norm. Project managers must accommodate the work style of each project resource while encouraging every worker to be as efficient as possible.
- Not all workers begin the project assignment with the same degree of skill. An astute project manager attempts to evaluate the skill level of some or all of the assigned resources to better match them to the needs of the project plan.
- Skill mixtures among actual project workers seldom match the needs of the project plan. This means that in some circumstances workers may be asked to perform tasks for which they are not necessarily well suited, and those tasks take longer and/or cost more than planned.
- Some tasks may require skills that are not available from resources on hand. This might require the project manager to go outside normal channels for a key skill, which almost always results in delays and higher costs.

Managing human resources in information security projects has additional complexities, including:

- Extended clearances may be required. Since some information security projects involve working in sensitive areas of the organization, project managers may have restrictions placed on which resource can be used (for example, only those with the requisite clearances). While this is not yet a common restriction in most commercial organizations, it does affect organizations in the financial sector (banking and brokerage) as well as many government agencies.
- Often, information security projects deploy technology controls that are new to the organization, and so there is not a pool of skilled resources in that area from which to draw. This can occur in any project that faces a skill shortage, but is more likely in an information security project than in a routine development project.

Major processes that take place in this management area include:

- Organizational planning
- Staff acquisition
- Team development

Project Communications Management

Project communications management includes the processes necessary to convey the details of activities associated with the project to all involved parties. This includes the creation, distribution, classification, storage, and ultimately destruction of documents, messages, and other associated project information.

Overcoming resistance to change may be more of a challenge in information security projects than in traditional development projects. In some cases, users and IT partners may be uncertain about the reasons for the project and wary of its effect on their work lives. In extreme cases, a project may face hostility from the future users of the system. The only way to change this situation is to initiate education, training, and awareness programs. The project manager, usually working in conjunction with the SETA program within the Information Security department, should communicate the need for the project as early as possible, and should answer any questions about the effect on users of the deployment of the project deliverables.

Major processes associated with this area of project management include:

- Communications planning
- Information distribution
- Performance reporting
- Administrative closure

Project Risk Management

Project risk management includes the processes necessary to assess, mitigate, manage, and reduce the impact of adverse occurrences on the project. Project risk management is very similar to normal security risk management, except the scope and scale are usually much smaller because the area to be protected is the individual project and not the entire organization. In many cases, simply identifying and rating the threats facing the project and assessing the probability of the occurrence of these threats is sufficient. The usual purpose of this component is to identify large risks and to plan the mitigation of adverse events should the risks manifest themselves.

Information security projects do face risks that may be different from other types of projects, as noted in the preceding sections. Those projects that face higher than normal risks should include appropriate planning, and perhaps preemptive action to mitigate these risks.

Major processes involved in this area are:

- Risk identification
- Risk quantification
- Risk response development
- Risk response control

Project Procurement Management

Project procurement management includes the processes necessary to acquire needed resources to complete the project. Depending on the common practices of the organization, project managers may simply requisition human resources, hardware, software, or supplies from the organization's stocks. Or, they may have to specify the required resources, request and evaluate bids, and then negotiate contracts for them.

Information security projects may have more complex procurement needs than other types of projects because they are more likely than other projects to need different software or hardware products and/or differently skilled human resources than other common types of IT projects.

Major processes involved in this area of project management are:

- Procurement planning
- Solicitation planning
- Solicitation
- Source selection
- Contract administration
- Contract closeout

Additional Project Planning Considerations

The sections below discuss important considerations for project planners as they decide what to include in the project plan, how to break tasks into subtasks and action steps, and how to accomplish the objectives of the project.

Financial Considerations

Regardless of the information security needs within the organization, the effort that can be expended depends on the funds available. A cost-benefit analysis (CBA), usually prepared early in the project planning effort, must be verified prior to the finalization of the project plan. The CBA identifies the impact that a specific technology or approach can have on the organization's information assets, and what it may cost.

Each organization has its own approach to the creation and management of budgets and expenses. In many cases, the information security budget is a subsection of the overall IT budget. In some organizations, information security is a separate budget category that may have parity with the IT budget. Regardless of where information security is located in the budget, monetary constraints determine what can be accomplished. Both public and private organizations have budgetary constraints, albeit of a different nature.

Publicly funded organizations (notably government agencies) are the most predictable in their budget processes. Based on the results of legislative budget meetings, they usually know in advance the amount of the next fiscal year's budget. If during a fiscal year additional funding is needed for operations such as information security, the funds must come from a different spending category. In addition, some public organizations rely on temporary or renewable grants. The expenses must be determined when the grants are written. If new expenses arise, funds must be requested in new grant applications. Grant expenditures are usually audited and cannot be misspent. Also, many public institutions have a budget requirement that is rarely present in the private sector: all budgeted funds must be spent in one fiscal year. If not, the budget is reduced by that amount the next fiscal year. The result can be an "end-of-fiscal-year spend-a-thon." This is often the best time to acquire that remaining piece of information security technology.

Nonprofit organizations face many of the same regulatory and financial complications of publicly funded organizations, but in addition also face a perennial shortage of reliable funding and the need to find contributors for most activities that do not directly address the core mission of the organization. Information security activities are rarely construed as contributing to the core mission.

Profit-driven (for-profit) organizations have different budgetary constraints that are governed by the marketplace, not a legislative body. If a for-profit organization does not generate adequate revenue, there is often no funding available for discretionary information security expenditures.

When a for-profit organization needs to fund a project to improve security, the funding comes from the company's capital and expense budgets. Each for-profit organization determines its capital budget and the rules for managing capital spending and expenses differently, but in any case, the budget significantly guides the implementation of information security. For example, a less desirable technology or solution may be chosen over the preferred one simply because it is more affordable.

To justify a budget for a security project in either a public or for-profit organization, it may be useful to benchmark expenses of similar organizations. Most for-profit organizations publish the components of their expense reports. Publicly funded organizations are generally required to show how funds were spent. The savvy security project manager can find a number of similarly sized organizations with larger expenditures for security and use these as justification for planned expenditures. While such tactics may not improve this year's budget, they could improve the budget in future years. Attacks can also help to justify the information security budget. If, during the year, attacks have successfully compromised secured information systems, management may be more willing to support the information security budget.

Priority Considerations

In general, the most important information security controls in the project plan should be scheduled first. As with budgetary constraints, however, there are also constraints when assigning priorities. As discussed in Chapters 7 and 8, risk management is the procedure used to identify controls applied to the information assets that are threatened. A control that costs a little more and is a little lower on the prioritization list but addresses many more vulnerabilities and threats may be implemented before a less expensive, higher priority component that only addresses one particular vulnerability (such as encryption).

Time and Scheduling Considerations

Time is another constraint that has a broad impact on the development of the project plan. Time can affect a project plan at dozens of points in its development, including the following: time to order and receive a security control; time to install and configure the control; time to train the users; and time to realize the return on investment of the control. If a control must be in place before a new electronic commerce product can be implemented, the selection of a technology may be influenced by differences in acquisition and implementation time lines.

Staffing Considerations

The lack of qualified, trained, and available personnel also constrains the project plan. Experienced staff is often needed to implement available technologies and to develop and implement policies and training programs. For instance, if no staff members are trained to configure a firewall that is being purchased, someone must be trained, or someone must be hired who is experienced with that technology.

Scope Considerations

The project plan should not attempt to implement the entire security system at one time. In addition to the difficulty of handling so many complex tasks at one time, there are interrelated conflicts between the installation of information security controls and the daily operations of the organization. Also, new information security controls may conflict with existing controls. For example, installing a new packet filtering router and a new application proxy firewall at the same time can cause a conflict between the controls, and as a result, the organization's users could be blocked from accessing the Web. Which technology caused the conflict? Was it the router, firewall, or an interaction between the two? As this example shows, it is best to limit the scope of implementation to manageable tasks. This does not mean that the project can allow change to only one component at a time; it does mean that it is prudent to cut back on the number of planned simultaneous tasks in a single department.

Procurement Considerations

There are a number of constraints on the selection process of equipment and services in most organizations, specifically in the selection of certain service vendors or products from manufacturers and suppliers. For example, in a recent situation, a lab administrator was considering an automated risk analysis software package. The leading candidate promised to deliver a solution that met all requirements at a cost within the budget limits. Unfortunately, the vendor was not authorized by the organization's procurement unit and could not be qualified in the time remaining before the budget authorization expired.

Organizational Feasibility Considerations

New policies require time to develop and new technologies must be installed, configured, and tested. In addition, employees need training on both the new policies and new technology components. Employees need to understand how the new information security program affects their working lives. Changes to security components should be transparent to systems users, unless the new technology necessitates changes to procedures, such as requiring additional authentication or verification. The organization must develop and conduct training sessions that minimize the impact of the changes before the new technologies come online. Waiting until the processes are in place can create tension and resistance, and possibly undermine security operations. Unless properly trained, users may develop ways to work around difficult or unfamiliar security procedures, bypassing controls and creating additional vulnerabilities. Conversely, users should not be prepared so far in advance that they forget the new training techniques and requirements. The optimal time is usually one to three weeks before the new policies and technologies come online.

Training and Indoctrination Considerations

The size of the organization and the normal conduct of business may preclude a single large training program covering new security procedures or technologies. Therefore, the organization should conduct a pilot approach to implementation—roll-out training for one department at a time, or conduct the training in phases. To implement policies, it may be sufficient to brief all supervisors and assign them the task of updating users in regularly scheduled meetings. All employees should receive compliance documents, and be required to read, understand, and agree to the new policies.

Technology Governance and Change Control Considerations

Other factors that determine the success of an organization's IT and information security programs are technology governance and change control processes. Technology governance is a complex process that organizations use to manage the effects and costs of technology implementation, innovation, and obsolescence. This process determines how frequently technical systems are updated, and how technical updates are approved and funded. Technology governance also facilitates communication about technical advances and issues across the organization.

Medium-sized or large organizations deal with the impact of technical change on operations by means of a change control process. By managing the process of change the organization can:

- Improve communication about change across the organization.
- Enhance coordination among groups within the organization as change is scheduled and completed.
- Reduce unintended consequences by having a process to resolve potential conflicts and disruptions that uncoordinated change can introduce.
- Improve quality of service as potential failures are eliminated and groups work together.
- Assure management that all groups are complying with the organization's policies regarding technology governance, procurement, accounting, and information security.

Effective change control is an essential part of the IT operation in all but the smallest organizations. The information security group can also use the change control process to ensure that essential process steps, which assure confidentiality, integrity, and availability, are followed as systems are upgraded across the organization.

Controlling the Project

Once a project plan has been defined and all of the preparatory actions are complete, the project gets underway. The following sections discuss project supervision and execution.

Supervising Implementation

Some organizations may choose to designate a champion from the general management community of interest to supervise the information security project. In this case, groups of tasks are delegated to individuals or teams from the IT and information security communities of interest. Other organizations will designate a senior IT manager or the CIO of the organization to lead the implementation. In this case, the detailed work is delegated to cross-functional teams. The optimal approach is usually to designate a suitable person from the information security community of interest. Each organization must find the leadership that best suits its specific needs and the personalities and politics of the organizational culture.

Executing the Plan

Once a project is underway, it is managed using a process known as a **negative feedback** loop or cybernetic loop, which ensures that progress is measured periodically. The measured results are compared to expected results. When significant deviation occurs, corrective action is taken to bring the task that is deviating from plan back into compliance with the projection, or else the estimate is revised in light of new information. Figure 12-4 illustrates this process.

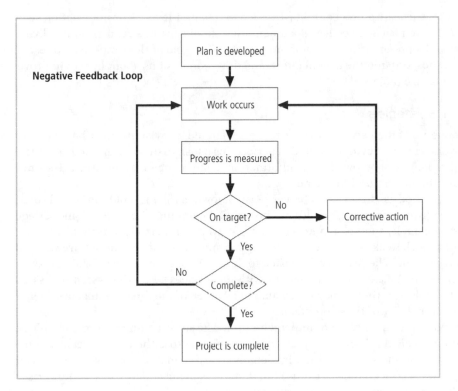

FIGURE 12-4   Negative Feedback Loop

Corrective action is required in two basic situations: the estimate is flawed or performance has lagged. When an estimate is flawed, as when an incorrect estimate of effort-hours is made, the plan should be corrected and downstream tasks updated to reflect the change. When performance has lagged, perhaps because of a high turnover of skilled employees, correction is accomplished by adding resources, lengthening the schedule, or reducing the quality or quantity of the deliverable. These corrective actions are usually expressed in terms of trade-offs.

Often a project manager can adjust one of the three following planning parameters:

- Effort and money allocated
- Elapsed time or scheduling impact
- Quality or quantity of the deliverable

When too much effort and money is being expended, you can either slow down and take longer, or lower the deliverable quality or quantity. If the task is taking too long to complete, you can add more resources in staff time or money, or else lower the quality or quantity of the deliverable. If quality is too low, you can add more staff time or money, or take longer to complete the task. Of course, these simplistic solutions do not serve in all cases, but this simple trade-off model can help a project manager to analyze available options.

Wrap-Up

Project wrap-up is usually a procedural task assigned to a mid-level IT or information security manager. These managers collect documentation, finalize status reports, and deliver a final report and a presentation at a wrap-up meeting. The goal of the wrap-up is to resolve any pending issues, critique the overall effort, and draw conclusions about how to improve the process in future projects.

Conversion Strategies

As the components of the new security system are planned, provisions must be made for the changeover from the previous method of performing a task to the new method. There are four basic approaches—borrowed from information systems changeover strategies—to changing from the old method to the new.

The first method is **direct changeover**. Also known as going cold turkey, direct changeover involves stopping the old method and beginning the new. Some direct changeovers are simple, such as requiring a new password with stronger authentication at the start of a work week; some are more complex, such as disabling an old firewall and activating the new one. The primary drawback to direct changeover is that if the new system fails or needs modification, users may be without services while the system's bugs are worked out. Complete testing of the new system in advance of the direct changeover helps to reduce the probability of these problems.

The second approach is **phased implementation**. The most common approach, phase implementation involves rolling out a piece of the system across the entire organization. This could mean that the security group implements only a small portion of the new security profile, giving users a chance to get used to it, and resolving small issues as they arise. This is usually the best approach to security rollouts.

The next strategy is **pilot implementation**. This strategy involves implementing all security improvements in a single office, department, or division, and resolving issues within that group before expanding to the rest of the organization. Pilot implementation works well when an isolated group can serve as a guinea pig without dramatically affecting the performance of the organization as a whole. Implementing security improvements in a research and development group, for example, may not affect the real-time operations of the organization and could assist security in resolving issues that emerge.

The final strategy, **parallel operation**, involves running the new methods alongside the old methods. In information systems, this means running two systems concurrently. Although parallel operation may be too complex for general use when deploying information systems, in security it may be justifiable. For instance, it can involve running two firewalls concurrently, and allowing the old systems to back up the new systems if they fail or are compromised. Drawbacks to parallel operation usually include the need to manage both systems and having to maintain two sets of procedures.

To Outsource or Not

Not every organization needs to develop project management capability within its Information Security department. Just as some organizations outsource part of or all of their IT operations, so too can organizations outsource part of or all of their information security programs, especially developmental projects. The expense and time it takes to develop effective information security project management skills may be beyond the reach—as well as the needs—of some organizations, and it is in their best interest to hire competent professional services.

When an organization has outsourced most or all of its IT services, information security should be part of the contract arrangement with the service provider. When an organization retains its own IT department, it may choose to outsource some of the more specialized information security projects. It is not at all unusual for small and medium-sized organizations to hire outside consultants for penetration testing and information security program audits in addition to information security deployment projects. It is also common for organizations of all sizes to outsource monitoring the quality of service of the network and monitoring the network for intrusions.

Because of the complex nature of outsourcing—whether for IT, information security, or other infrastructure and corporate services—organizations should hire the best available specialists, and then obtain capable legal counsel to negotiate and verify the contract.

Dealing with Change

The prospect of change, shifting the familiar to the unfamiliar, can cause employees to be unconsciously or consciously resistant. Whether the changes are perceived as good, such as information security implementations, or bad, such as a downsizing or massive restructuring, employees prefer the old way of doing things. Even when employees embrace changes, the stress of making changes and adjusting to the new procedures can increase the probability of mistakes or create vulnerabilities in systems. By understanding and applying some of the basic tenets of change management, you can lower the resistance to change, and even build resilience for change, thus making ongoing change more palatable to the entire organization.

Change management must take into account the fundamental culture of the organization. Changes that disrupt this culture must be managed to minimize their effects. One of the most widely accepted models of change management is the Lewin change model, which consists of:[3]

- Unfreezing
- Moving
- Refreezing

Unfreezing is the thawing of hard and fast habits and established procedures. Moving is the transition between the old way and the new. Refreezing is the integration of the new methods into the organizational culture, by creating an atmosphere in which the changes are accepted as the preferred way of accomplishing tasks.

Unfreezing

Unfreezing can be broken down into three subprocesses, each of which must be effective for employees to feel ready and motivated to change:

1. Disconfirmation: You must instill the belief among employees that unless they change to the new standards, they will fail to achieve their goals (survival anxiety), or to perform their duties to their own satisfaction (survival guilt). This is a necessary part of getting employees to break with their old habits.

2. Induction of survival guilt or survival anxiety: To reinforce these feelings, employees must feel that the reasons behind their survival guilt are valid. The validity of these feelings can be thwarted by learning anxiety—the fear that you must change because you are imperfect or flawed (learning anxiety). Learning anxiety can promote fear and lead to a loss of self-esteem or effectiveness. The change process can accommodate this risk by creating some degree of psychological safety as planning for change occurs.

3. Creation of psychological safety or overcoming learning anxiety: "The key to effective change management, then, becomes the ability to balance the amount of threat produced by disconfirming data with enough psychological safety to allow the change target to accept the information, feel the survival anxiety, and become motivated to change."[4]

Moving

Moving is composed of three subprocesses:

1. Cognitive redefinition: Moving is the process of enabling the employees to realize that there is no loss of honor in accepting the new learning. Cognitive redefinition is when a group of individuals redefine what are acceptable and desirable behaviors. Cognitive redefinition results in cognitive restructuring, also known as frame breaking or reframing. Restructuring occurs when new information enables employees to accept the new way of doing things.

2. Imitation and positive or defensive identification with a role model: The easiest way to get employees to accept new procedures is to use role models. An organization can designate as a role model an employee who is respected by others, who adopts the new methods, and demonstrates that the new methods do not threaten status or well-being. If no positive role models exist, then you have to create the environment for scanning.

3. Scanning (also called insight or trial-and-error learning): Scanning is the process whereby employees learn by examining their environment, talking to coworkers, and generally learning new methods on their own. Scanning can result in employees assimilating poor or negative reinforcement. Change agents—trained employees or consultants—can support scanning, if they meet with employees in training sessions and demonstrate the positive results of the change process. Once the new learning has occurred, employees go through a period of trial and error, during which the learning must be reinforced to avoid the commencement of a new, erroneous scanning process.

Refreezing

For change to become permanent, it must be refrozen through personal and relational refreezing. Personal refreezing occurs when each employee comes to understand that the new way of doing things is the best way. Relational refreezing occurs when a group comes to a similar decision. Both can be accomplished by means of group training in the new procedures and methods. Each individual applies the new training in the work environment, reinforcing the group learning, and solidifying the personal refreezing.

Considerations for Organizational Change

Steps can be taken to make an organization more amenable to change. These steps reduce resistance to change at the beginning of the planning process and help the organization to be more flexible as changes occur during project implementation.

Reducing Resistance to Change from the Start

The more ingrained the previous methods and behaviors, the more difficult the change. It is best to establish the interaction between the affected members of the organization and the project planners early in the project. The interaction between these groups is improved through a three-step process: communication, education, and involvement.

Communication is the first and most crucial step. You should notify employees that a new security process is being considered, and solicit their feedback. You should also update employees on the progress of the project and provide information on the expected completion dates. This ongoing series of updates prevents the process from being a surprise, and helps employees to accept the change when it finally arrives.

Updates should also educate employees on exactly how the proposed changes will affect them, both individually and across the organization. While detailed information may not be available in earlier stages, as the project progresses, more details become available. Education also involves teaching employees how to use the new systems once they are in place. This means a high-quality training program delivered at the appropriate times.

Finally, involvement means getting key representatives from user groups to serve as members of the development team. In systems development this is referred to as joint application development (JAD). Users who are part of the development team report to their coworkers on the progress of the project, and report to the project team on the concerns of their coworkers. This representative approach serves the team well in early planning stages, when potential problems accepting the project are addressed.

Developing a Culture that Supports Change

An ideal organization fosters resilience to change. This resilience means the organization accepts that change is a necessary part of the culture, and that embracing change is more productive than fighting it. A resilient culture can be either cultivated or undermined by management's approach. Strong management support for change, with a clear executive-level champion, enables others in the organization to recognize the necessity and strategic importance of change. Weak management support, with delegated responsibility and no champion, sentences projects to certain failure, as employees perceive and mirror this weak support.

PROJECT MANAGEMENT TOOLS

There are many tools that support the management of the diverse resources in complex projects. Some of these tools are modeling approaches, such as PERT or CPM, and others involve the use of software. Most project managers combine software tools that implement one or more of the dominant modeling approaches. A few of the more common models are discussed here. If you are planning to become a project manager, seek out the proper level of training to acquire the needed skills and background to be successful. The most successful project managers gain sufficient skill and experience to earn a certificate in project management.

The Project Management Institute (PMI) is project management's leading global professional association, and sponsors two certificate programs, which it describes as follows:

- The Project Management Professional (PMP): PMP certification is the profession's most globally recognized and respected certification credential. The PMP designation following your name tells current and potential employers that you have a solid foundation of project management knowledge that can be readily applied in the workplace. To be eligible for the PMP certification, you must first meet specific education and experience requirements and agree to adhere to a code of professional conduct. The final step in becoming a PMP is passing a multiple-choice examination designed to objectively assess and measure your project management knowledge.
- Certified Associate in Project Management (CAPM): A logical stepping stone to the PMP, and a boon to your overall professional development, is the CAPM. The CAPM is intended for those practitioners who provide project management services but are relatively new to the profession. ...Like the PMP, CAPM candidates must first meet specific education and experience requirements and then pass an examination.[5]

Most project managers engaged in the execution of project plans that are nontrivial in scope use tools to facilitate scheduling and execution of the project. A project manager usually determines that certain tasks cannot be performed until prerequisite tasks are complete. It is almost always advantageous to determine in what order tasks must be performed. It is equally important to determine what tasks must not be delayed to avoid holding up the entire project.

Using complex project management tools often results in a complication called projectitis—a common pitfall of IT and information security projects. **Projectitis** occurs when the project manager spends more time documenting project tasks, collecting performance measurements, recording project task information, and updating project completion forecasts than accomplishing meaningful project work. The development of an overly elegant, microscopically detailed plan before gaining consensus for the work and related coordinated activities that it requires may be a precursor to projectitis. However, the proper use of project tools can help project managers organize and coordinate project activities, and can enhance communication among the project team.

The following sections discuss some of the more commonly used project management tools.

Work Breakdown Structure

A project plan can be created using a very simple planning tool, such as the **work breakdown structure (WBS)** shown in Table 12-2. The WBS can be prepared with a simple desktop PC spreadsheet program, as well as with more complex project management software tools.

In the WBS approach, the project plan is first broken down into a few major tasks. Each of these major tasks is placed on the WBS task list. The minimum attributes that should be determined for each task are:

- The work to be accomplished (activities and deliverables)
- Estimated amount of effort required for completion in hours or workdays
- The common or specialty skills needed to perform the task
- Task interdependencies

As the project plan develops, additional attributes can be added, including:

- Estimated capital expenses for the task
- Estimated noncapital expenses for the task
- Task assignment according to specific skills
- Start and end dates, once tasks have been sequenced and dates projected

Each major task on the WBS is then further divided into either smaller tasks or specific action steps. For simplicity, the sample WBS later in this chapter divides each task only into action steps. In an actual project plan, tasks are often more complex; you may need to subdivide major tasks before action steps can be determined and assigned. Although there are few hard-and-fast rules as to the appropriate level of detail, generally a task or subtask becomes an action step when it can be completed by one individual or skill set, and when it includes a single deliverable, as defined later.

Work To Be Accomplished

The first step in the WBS is to identify the work to be accomplished in the task or task area; that is, the activities and deliverables. A deliverable is a completed document or program module that is either the beginning point for a later task or an element of the finished project. Ideally, the project planner provides a label for the task followed by a thorough description. The description should be complete enough to avoid ambiguity during the later tracking process, but not so detailed as to make the WBS unwieldy. For instance, if the task is to write firewall specifications for the preparation of a request for proposal (RFP), the planner would note that the deliverable is a specification document suitable for distribution to vendors.

Amount of Effort

Planners need to estimate the effort required to complete each task, subtask, or action step. Estimating effort hours for technical work is a complex process. Even when an organization has formal governance, technical review processes, and change control procedures, it is always good practice to ask the individuals who are most familiar with the work or with similar types of work to make the estimates. Then, those assigned to action steps should review the estimated effort hours, understand the tasks, and agree with the estimates.

Skill Sets/Human Resources

The project planner should describe the skill set or person (often called a human resource) needed to accomplish the task. Naming individuals should be avoided in the early planning efforts. Instead, the plan should focus on roles or known skill sets. For example, if any of the engineers in the networks group can write the specifications for a router, the assigned resource would be "network engineer" on the WBS. As planning progresses to a more detailed level, however, the specific tasks and action steps should be assigned to specific people. For example, when only the manager of the networks group can evaluate the responses to the RFP and make an award for a contract, the planner identifies the network manager by name as the resource.

Task Dependencies

Planners should note wherever possible when a task or action step is dependent on other tasks or actions steps. Tasks or action steps that come before a particular task are called predecessors; tasks or action steps that come after a particular task are called successors. There is more than one type of dependency; most courses on project management cover this subject in detail.

Estimated Capital Expenses

Planners need to estimate the expected capital expenses for the completion of each task, subtask, or action item. While each organization budgets and expends capital according to its own established procedures, most differentiate between expenses for durable assets and expenses for other purposes. Be sure to determine the practices in place at the organization where the plan is to be used. For example, a firewall device costing $5,000 may be a capital expense for a given organization, but the same organization might not consider a $5,000 software package to be a capital expense.

Estimated Noncapital Expenses

Planners need to estimate the expected noncapital expenses for the completion of each task, subtask, or action item. Some organizations require that this cost include a recovery charge for staff time, while others exclude employee time and only plan contract or consulting time as a noncapital expense. Organizations follow their own established procedures in classifying different kinds of expenses as being capital or noncapital. As mentioned earlier, it is important to determine the practices in place at the organization where the plan is to be used. For example, an information security management program costing $600,000 may be considered a noncapital expense, but a network router that costs $600 may be considered a capital expense.

Start and End Dates

In the early stages of planning, the project planner should focus on determining completion dates only for major milestones within the project. A milestone is a specific task completion point in the project plan that has a noticeable effect on the progress of the project plan as a whole. For example, the date for sending the final RFP to vendors is considered a milestone, because it signals that all RFP preparation work is complete. Early in the planning process, assigning too many dates to too many tasks can be a symptom of projectitis. By assigning only key or milestone start and end dates early in the process, planners can avoid this pitfall. Later in the planning process, additional start and end dates can be added as needed.

An example project plan is provided below to help you better understand the process of creating one. The project is to design and implement a firewall for a single small office. The hardware is a standard organizational product and will be installed at a location that already has a network connection. The first step is to list the major tasks:

1. Contact field office and confirm network assumptions
2. Purchase standard firewall hardware.
3. Configure firewall.
4. Package and ship firewall to field office.
5. Work with local technical resource to install and test.
6. Completion of the vulnerability assessment by the penetration test team.
7. Get remote office sign-off and update all network drawings and documentation.

TABLE 12-2 Early Draft Work Breakdown Structure

Task	Effort (hours)	Skill	Dependencies
1. Contact field office and confirm network assumptions	2	Network architect	
2. Purchase standard firewall hardware	4	Network architect and purchasing group	1
3. Configure firewall	8	Network architect	2
4. Package and ship firewall to field office	2	Intern	3
5. Work with local technical resource to install and test	6	Network architect	4
6. Complete network vulnerability assessment	12	Network architect and penetration test team	5
7. Get remote office sign-off and update all network drawings and documentation	8	Network architect	6

After the project manager has compiled the draft WBS and consulted with specific participants of the project team, additional detail is added and more dates are assigned to tasks. Another, more detailed version emerges, as shown in Table 12-3. The project plan has been further developed and illustrates the breakdown of tasks 2 and 6 into action steps.

TABLE 12-3 Later Draft Work Breakdown Structure

Task	Effort (hours)	Skill	Dependencies	Capital expenses	Noncapital expenses	Start and end dates
1. Contact field office and confirm network assumptions; notify penetration test team of intent for test	2	Network architect		0	200	S:9/22 E:9/22
2. Purchase standard firewall hardware						
2.1 Order firewall through purchasing group	1	Network architect	1	4500	100	S:9/23 E:9/23
2.2 Order firewall from group manufacturer	2	Purchasing group	2.1		100	S:9/24 E:9/24
2.3 Firewall delivered	1	Purchasing group	2.2		50	E:10/3
3. Configure firewall	8	Network architect	2.3		800	S:10/3 E:10/5
4. Package and ship firewall to field office	2	Intern	3		85	S:10/6 E:10/15
5. Work with local technical resource to install and test	6	Network architect	4		600	S:10/22 E:10/31
6. Penetration test						
6.1 Request penetration test	1	Network architect	5		100	S:11/1 E:11/1
6.2 Perform penetration test	9	Penetration test team	6.1		900	S:11/2 E:11/12
6.3 Verify results of penetration test	2	Network architect	6.2		200	S:11/13 E:11/15
7. Get remote office sign-off and update all network drawings and documentation	8	Network architect	6.3		800	S:11/16 E:11/30

Once the project manager has completed the WBS by breaking tasks into subtasks, estimating effort, and forecasting the necessary resources, the work phase—during which the project deliverables are prepared—may begin. A more complex project may require the use of more complex models to complete the task-sequencing effort.

Task-Sequencing Approaches

Sequencing tasks and subtasks in a large and complex project can be truly daunting. Once a project reaches even a relatively modest size, say a few dozen tasks, there can be almost innumerable possibilities for task assignment and scheduling. Fortunately, a number of approaches are available to assist the project manager in this sequencing effort.

Network Scheduling

One method for sequencing tasks and subtasks in a project plan is known as network scheduling. The word "network" in this context does not refer in any way to computer networks; rather, it refers to the web of possible pathways to project completion from the beginning task to the ending task. For example, activity A must occur before activity B, which in turn must occur before activity C; a network diagram illustrating this network dependency is shown in Figure 12-5.

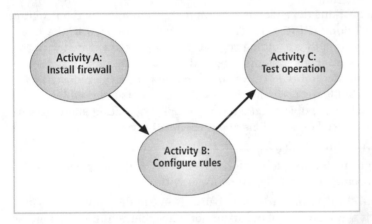

FIGURE 12-5   Simple Network Dependency

While this illustration is very simple, the method of depiction gains value as the number of tasks and subtasks increases and information is added about the effort and type of resources necessary to complete each activity. If multiple activities can be completed concurrently, this can be shown in the diagram. If a single activity has two or more prerequisites, or is the common prerequisite for two or more activities, this can also be depicted, as shown in Figure 12-6.

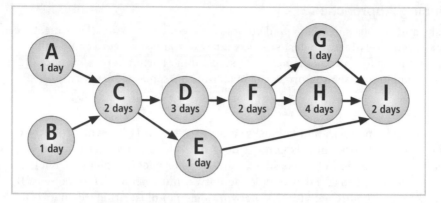

FIGURE 12-6 Complex Network Dependency

The most popular of networking dependency diagramming techniques is the **Program Evaluation and Review Technique (PERT)**. PERT was originally developed in the late 1950s to meet the needs of the rapidly expanding engineering projects associated with government acquisitions, such as weapons systems. About the same time, a similar technique, called the **Critical Path Method (CPM)**, was being developed in the industry. The PERT diagram, as illustrated in Figure 12-7, shows a number of events followed by key activities and their duration. It is possible to take a very complex operation and diagram it in PERT if you can answer three key questions about each activity:

1. How long will this activity take?
2. What activity occurs immediately before this activity can take place?
3. What activity occurs immediately after this activity?

By determining the path through the various activities, you can determine the critical path. The **critical path** is the sequence of events or activities that requires the longest duration to complete, and that therefore cannot be delayed without delaying the entire project. The difference in time between the critical path and any other path is called **slack time**. All tasks not on the critical path have slack time, and thus can be delayed or postponed, within the limits of their slack time, without delaying the entire project. In Figure 12-7, the critical path is the sequence of events A → C → G as shown by the heavier arrows. A project can have more than one critical path, if two or more paths have the same total time requirement. In the example shown in Figure 12-7, the noncritical path A → D → F → G has one day of slack time. This path can incur a delay of up to one day without adversely affecting the overall completion of the project.

Among the advantages to the PERT method are that it:

- Makes planning large projects easier by facilitating the identification of pre- and post activities.
- Allows planning to determine the probability of meeting requirements (i.e., timely delivery through calculation of critical paths).
- Anticipates the impact of changes on the system. Should a delay in one area occur, how does it affect the overall project schedule?

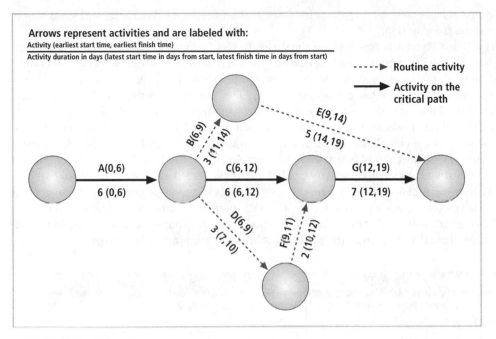

Arrows represent activities and are labeled with:
Activity (earliest start time, earliest finish time)
Activity duration in days (latest start time in days from start, latest finish time in days from start)

- - - - -▶ Routine activity

────▶ Activity on the critical path

A(0,6)
6 (0,6)

B(6,9)
3 (11,14)

E(9,14)
5 (14,19)

C(6,12)
6 (6,12)

G(12,19)
7 (12,19)

D(6,9)
3 (7,10)

F(9,11)
2 (10,12)

FIGURE 12-7 PERT Example

- Presents information in a straightforward format that both technical and non-technical managers can understand and refer to in planning discussions.
- Requires no formal training. After a brief explanation most people understand it thoroughly.

Disadvantages of the PERT method include:

- Diagrams can become awkward and cumbersome, especially in very large projects.
- Diagrams can become expensive to develop and maintain due to the complexities of some project development processes.
- It can be difficult to place an accurate "time to complete" on some tasks, especially in the initial construction of a project; inaccurate estimates invalidate any close critical path calculations.

The Critical Path Method is similar in design to the PERT method. CPM relies on a scheduling process designed to identify the sequence of tasks that make up the shortest elapsed time to complete the project. Other tasks may then be scheduled in ways that do not lengthen the total time of the project. In most other ways CPM is very similar to PERT.

Gantt Chart

Another popular project management tool is the bar or Gantt chart, named for Henry Gantt, who developed this method in the early 1900s. Like network diagrams, Gantt charts are simple to read and understand, and thus easy to present to management. These simple bar charts are even easier to design and implement than the PERT diagrams, and yield much of the same information.

The Gantt chart lists activities on the vertical axis of a bar chart, and provides a simple time line on the horizontal axis. A bar represents each activity, with its starting and ending points coinciding with the appropriate points on the time line. The length of the bar thus represents the duration of that particular phase. Activities that overlap can be performed concurrently. Those that do not must be performed sequentially. A vertical reference line can be used to evaluate the current date. Some implementations of the Gantt chart use a fill method to show percentage completion of particular activities. As shown in Figure 12-8, the Gantt chart can provide a wealth of information in a simple format. Activity A has been completed; Activity B is ahead of schedule; Activity C is behind schedule. Milestones can be added to individual activities, and are usually represented by a numbered triangle just above the bar. These milestones might include the completion of a key report, or a component that requires outside interventions. Whatever the case, this method of tracking has proven so simple to use, yet so effective, that it is frequently the preferred method of tracking project progress.

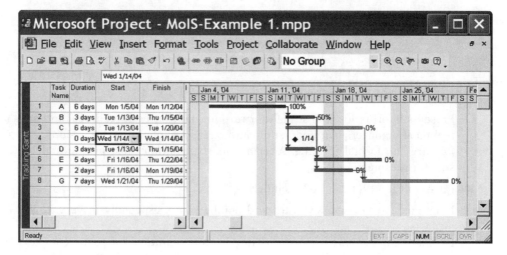

FIGURE 12-8 Project Gantt Chart

Automated Project Tools

Microsoft Project is a commonly used project management tool. While it is not the only automated project management tool (there are quite few), and is not universally perceived as the best (that is matter of heated opinion among project managers), it is generally acknowledged to be the most widely used. If you are considering using an automated project management tool, keep the following in mind:

- A software program cannot take the place of a skilled and experienced project manager who understands how to define tasks, allocate scarce resources, and manage the resources that are assigned. While an automated tool can be powerful in the hands of someone who knows how to use it, it can temporarily disguise the shortcomings of an unprepared project manager.

- A software tool can get in the way of the work. A project manager who spends more than a small amount of time using a tool to record progress and forecast options is on the way to projectitis. Sufferers of this condition spend many hours tweaking project details and calculating trade-offs without making any measurable progress toward completing the project. When project workers must use unfamiliar procedures to report progress in minute detail, they may not be as productive as possible. When status meetings turn into multihour slideshows detailing each aspect of progress, experienced project managers will wonder why everyone is not working on their assigned tasks.

- Choose a tool that you can use effectively. Any project manager is better served using a tool they know than an overly complex tool they cannot use to good effect. Multimillion dollar projects have been brought in on time and under budget using nothing more than a simple spreadsheet and lots of hard work. On the other hand, a project manager using state-of-the-art tools can trim weeks from a schedule and save thousands of dollars while meeting every deliverable requirement.

Chapter Summary

- Employers looking for security personnel often seek individuals who couple their information security mindset and skills with strong project management skills.

- Operations are activities that are ongoing events without discernable end. Projects are discrete sequences of activities with known starting points and defined completion points.

- Each link in a chain of projects accomplishes a specific goal toward the completion of the overall objective of information security program improvement.

- Project management is the application of knowledge, skills, tools, and techniques to project activities to meet project requirements. Project management is accomplished through the use of processes that include initiation, planning, execution, controlling, and closing.

- Nine areas make up the component process of project management: integration, scope, time, cost, quality, human resource, communications, risk, and procurement.

- The amount of effort that can be expended on information security programs depends on the funds available. All organizations have budgetary constraints of one kind or another.

- Once a project is underway, it is managed using a negative feedback loop, which ensures that progress is measured periodically. Corrective action is taken if the estimate was flawed or performance has lagged.

- Provisions must be made for the changeover from the previous method of performing a task to the new method. There are four changeover methods: direct changeover, phased implementation, pilot implementation, and parallel operation.

- Organizations can choose to outsource part or all of their information security programs, and are more likely to outsource developmental projects.

- Change management can lower resistance to, and build resilience for, change.

- One of the oldest models of change is the Lewin change model, which consists of unfreezing, moving, and refreezing.

- The creation of a project plan can be accomplished using a very simple planning tool, such as the work breakdown structure (WBS).

- A set of methods that can be used to sequence the tasks and subtasks in a project plan is known as network scheduling. Popular techniques include the Program Evaluation and Review Technique (PERT), the Critical Path Method, and the Gantt chart.

- Automated project management tools can assist experienced project managers in the complexities of managing a large project, but may get in the way when used by novice project managers or when used on simple projects.

Review Questions

1. Why are project management skills important to the information security professional?
2. How can security be both a project and a process?
3. What is an operation, and how does it differ from a project?

4. What are the benefits to an organization that emphasizes project management skills?

5. What are the nine areas that make up the component process of project management?

6. What complications can information security projects face in complex projects?

7. What are the respective drawbacks of having too many or too few people working on a project?

8. What differences between publicly funded and for-profit institutions affect how projects are budgeted?

9. Why is change management important in organizations?

10. What benefits can organizations gain by actively managing change?

11. What is a negative feedback loop and how is it used to keep a project in control?

12. What are the three planning parameters that can be adjusted when a project is not being executed according to plan?

13. What are the risks and benefits of outsourcing an information security program?

14. What are the three stages of the Lewin change model?

15. What is resilience to change?

16. Name three tools that can be used to help manage projects.

17. What is a work breakdown structure and why is it important?

18. What is projectitis and how can it be prevented?

19. List the various approaches to task sequencing.

20. How do PERT/CPM methods help to manage a project?

Exercises

1. Using a Web search engine, search for the terms "information security" *and* "project management." What information can you find that incorporates both search terms?

2. Using only pencil and paper, draft a Gantt chart outlining the process of registering for classes. Identify key resources needed and constraints on the process.

3. Draft a work breakdown structure for the task of implementing and using a PC-based virus detection program (one that is not centrally managed).

4. Your instructor has been provided with an Instructor Resources Kit that includes several MS Project files. If you have access to MS Project and can access the file MoIS_12_01.mpp, you can perform this exercise.

   Open the project file. Make a note of the project completion date as shown in the Gantt chart. (You can easily see this date by selecting Project | Project Information from the menu bar.) Now, change the predecessors in task G from 3, 7 to 3, 6. Check the completion date again. What happened? Why?

5. Your instructor has been provided with an Instructor Resources Kit that includes several MS Project files. If you have access to MS Project and can access the file MoIS_12_02.mpp, you can perform this exercise.

   Open the project file. When is the project scheduled to begin? When will it be completed? Which phase will take the longest to complete?

Case Exercises

Charlie Moody looked up from his coffee as Iris sat down across from him. "How's it going?" he asked.

"I don't know how much longer I'll be able to squeeze time in for these coffee meetings," she replied, looking exhausted.

"Why's that?" Charlie asked.

"It seems I spend all my time in meetings, and when I'm not in a meeting I'm explaining some aspect of the job to one of my security managers."

"Really?" Charlie asked, concealing a smile.

"Really!" Iris replied. "Just today I spent half an hour with Maria going over the basics of project management, much of which I had to dredge up from my old college textbook. I mean, I know how to manage a project, but I don't remember all of the technical components."

"A project management text? What in the world are you doing that requires a project management text?" Charlie asked.

"I've assigned Maria to head the deployment of our new IDS. I felt it was a perfect opportunity for her to show me what she can do, and complete some of her background education at the same time."

"So you're the master now, Grasshopper?" Charlie laughed.

Iris looked confused, and then began to laugh. "Yes, sensei...and my Kung Fu is strong."

For the next hour Iris explained how she integrated project management techniques into the development and implementation of key security components. Before long Charlie pulled out a yellow pad and began scribbling notes. Iris was proud that she had mastered the lessons offered by her former boss and was now able to teach him something in return.

1. What other components of information security could Iris have used project management techniques to control?

2. How could Charlie have made it as far as he has in the IT and information security industry without any formal project management education?

Endnotes

[1] W. R. Duncan. *A Guide to the Project Management Body of Knowledge.* 1996, Project Management Institute, 3.

[2] W. R. Duncan. *A Guide to the Project Management Body of Knowledge. 1996,* Project Management Institute, 6.

[3] Edgar H. Schein. Kurt Lewin's Change Theory in the Field and in the Classroom: Notes Toward a Model of Managed Learning. *Systemic Practice and Action Research.* February 1996. Springer Netherlands.

[4] Edgar H. Schein. Kurt Lewin's Change Theory in the Field and in the Classroom: Notes Toward a Model of Managed Learning. *Systemic Practice and Action Research.* February 1996. Springer Netherlands.

[5] H. Kerzner. *Project Management: A Systems Approach to Planning, Scheduling, and Controlling*, 6th ed. New York: Van Nostrand Reinhold Publishing, 1999: 646.

NIST SP 800-26, SECURITY SELF-ASSESSMENT GUIDE FOR INFORMATION TECHNOLOGY SYSTEMS, AND ISO 17799:2005 OVERVIEW

NIST SP 800-26, SECURITY SELF-ASSESSMENT GUIDE FOR INFORMATION TECHNOLOGY SYSTEMS

The self-assessment questionnaire contains three sections: a cover sheet, questions, and notes. The cover sheet requires descriptive information about the major application, general support system, or group of interconnected systems being assessed.

The questions take a hierarchical approach to assessing a system by examining critical elements and subordinate questions. The critical element level is determined by the answers to the subordinate questions. The critical elements are derived primarily from OMB Circular A-130. The subordinate questions address the control objectives and techniques that can be implemented to satisfy the critical elements. Assessors will need to carefully review the levels of subordinate control objectives and techniques to determine which level has been reached for the related critical element. The control objectives were obtained from the list of source documents given in Appendix B. Note that there is some flexibility in implementing the control objectives and techniques. In some cases, not all control objectives and techniques may be needed to achieve the critical element.

The questionnaire section may be customized by the organization. An organization can add questions, require more descriptive information, and even pre-mark certain questions if applicable. For example, many agencies have personnel security procedures that apply to all systems within the agency. The level 1 and level 2 columns in the questionnaire can be pre-marked to reflect the standard personnel procedures in place. Additional columns may be added to reflect the status of the control (i.e., planned action date, not applicable, or location of documentation). The questionnaire should not have questions removed or questions modified to reduce the effectiveness of the control.

After each question, there is a comment field and an initial field. The comment field can be used to note the reference to supporting documentation that is attached to the questionnaire or is obtainable for that question. The initial field can be used when a risk-based decision is made not to implement a control or if the control does not apply to the system.

At the end of each set of questions, there is also an area provided for notes. This area may be used to denote where in a system security plan specific sections should be modified. It can be used to document why a particular control objective is not being implemented fully or why it is overly rigorous. The notes section may be a good place to mark where follow-up work is needed or where additional testing (e.g., penetration testing or product evaluations) should be initiated. Additionally, the section may reference supporting documentation on how the control objectives and techniques were tested and a summary of findings.

Utilizing the Completed Questionnaire

The questionnaire can be used for two purposes. First, agency managers who know their agency's systems and security controls can use it to quickly gain a general understanding of where security for a system, group of systems, or the entire agency needs improvement. Second, the questionnaire can serve as a guide for thoroughly evaluating the status of security for a system. The results of such comprehensive reviews provide a much more reliable measure of security effectiveness and may be used to fulfill reporting requirements, prepare for audits, and identify resource needs.

Questionnaire Analysis

Because this questionnaire is a self-assessment, ideally the individuals who are assessing the system will be the owners of the system or will be responsible for operating or administering it. The same individuals who completed the assessment can conduct the analysis of the completed questionnaire. Alternatively, a centralized group, such as an agency's Information System Security Program Office, can conduct the analysis as long as the supporting documentation is sufficient. The results of the analysis should be placed in an action plan, and the system security plan should be created or updated to reflect each control objective and technique decision.

Action Plans

How the critical element will be implemented—that is, specific procedures, equipment installed and tested, and personnel trained—should be documented in an action plan. This action plan must contain projected dates, an allocation of resources, and follow-up reviews to ensure that remedial actions have been effective. Routine reports should be submitted to senior management on weaknesses identified, status of the action plans, and resources still needed.

The results from the completed questionnaires' 17 control topic areas can be used to summarize an agency's implementation of management, operational, and technical controls. For the report to give an accurate picture, these results must be summarized by system type, rather than being compiled into an overall agency grade level. As an example, suppose ten systems were assessed using the questionnaire. Five of the ten systems assessed were major applications; the other five were general support systems. The summary should then separate the systems into general support systems and major applications.

By further separating the systems and control objectives into groups according to criticality, the report stresses which ones require more attention based on their sensitivity and criticality. Not all systems require the same level of protection, of course; the report should reflect that diversity. The use of percentages for describing compliance (i.e., 50% of the major applications and 25% of the general support systems that are deemed high in criticality have complete system security plans that were developed within the past three years) can be used as long as a distinct division is made between the types of systems being reported.

All, or a sampling of, the completed questionnaires can be analyzed to determine which controls, if implemented, would affect the most systems. For example, if viruses frequently plague systems, then a stricter firewall policy that prohibits attached files in e-mail may be a solution. Also, systemic problems should be culled out. If an agency sees an influx of poor password management controls in the questionnaire results, then possibly password checkers should be used, awareness material issued, and password-aging software installed.

The report should conclude with a summary of planned IT security initiatives. This summary should include goals, actions needed to meet those goals, projected resources, and anticipated dates of completion.

Questionnaire Cover Sheet

The cover sheet provides instruction on completing the questionnaire, standardizing how the completed evaluation should be marked, indicating how systems are named, and labeling the criticality of the system.

All completed questionnaires should be marked, handled, and controlled at the level of sensitivity determined by organizational policy. Note that the information contained in a completed questionnaire could easily identify where the system or group of systems is most vulnerable.

The cover sheet of the questionnaire begins with the name and title of the system to be evaluated. As explained in NIST SP 800-18, each major application or general support system should be assigned a unique name/identifier. The purpose and objectives of the assessment should be identified as well. The names, titles, and sponsoring organizations of the individuals who will perform the assessment should also be listed, and the organization should customize the cover page accordingly. Finally, the start and completion dates of the evaluation should appear on the cover sheet.

Criticality of Information

The level of sensitivity of information as determined by the program official or system owner should be documented using the table on the questionnaire cover sheet. The premise behind formulating the level of sensitivity is that systems supporting higher-risk operations would be expected to have more stringent controls than those supporting lower-risk operations.

The questions are separated into three major control areas: management controls, operational controls, and technical controls. The division of control areas in this manner complements three other NIST Special Publications: NIST SP 800-12, An Introduction to Computer Security: The NIST Handbook (Handbook); NIST SP 800-14, Generally Accepted Principles and Practices for Securing Information Technology Systems (Principles and Practices); and NIST SP 800-18, Guide for Developing Security Plans for Information Technology Systems (Planning Guide).

The method for answering the questions can be based primarily on an examination of relevant documentation and a rigorous examination and test of the controls. The five levels describing the state of the control objective provide a picture of each operational control; the determination of how well each one of these control objectives is met, however, is subjective. Criteria have been established for each of the five levels that should be applied when determining whether the control objective has fully reached one or more of these levels.

As stated previously, the critical elements are required to be implemented; the control objectives and techniques, however, tend to be more detailed and leave room for reasonable subjective decisions. If a particular control does not reasonably apply to the system, then "not applicable" or "NA" can be entered next to the question. Note that management controls focus on the management of the IT security system and the management of risk for a system; these techniques and concerns are normally addressed by management.

The Self-Assessment Guide Questions

To measure the progress of effectively implementing the needed security control, five levels of effectiveness are provided for each answer to the security control question:

- Level 1: control objective is documented in a security policy
- Level 2: security controls have been documented as procedures
- Level 3: procedures have been implemented
- Level 4: procedures and security controls are tested and reviewed
- Level 5: procedures and security controls are fully integrated into a comprehensive program

Each of the items shown in the following checklist is evaluated on this scale. Individuals using the guide will check the level that corresponds to their current readiness level.

Specific Control Objectives and Techniques	Level 1	Level 2	Level 3	Level 4	Level 5	Risk-Based Decision Made	Comments	Initials
Management Controls								
1. Risk Management								
1.1 Critical Element: Is risk periodically assessed?								
1.1.1 Is the current system configuration documented, including links to other systems?								
1.1.2 Are risk assessments performed and documented on a regular basis or whenever the system, facilities, or other conditions change?								
1.1.3 Has data sensitivity and integrity of the data been considered?								
1.1.4 Have threat sources, both natural and manmade, been identified?								
1.1.5 Has a list of known system vulnerabilities, system flaws, or weaknesses that could be exploited by the threat sources been developed and maintained current?								
1.1.6 Has an analysis been conducted that determines whether the security requirements in place adequately mitigate vulnerabilities?								
1.2 Critical Element: Do program officials understand the risk to systems under their control and determine the acceptable level of risk?								

NIST SP 800-26, Security Self-Assessment Guide

Specific Control Objectives and Techniques	Level 1	Level 2	Level 3	Level 4	Level 5	Risk-Based Decision Made	Comments	Initials
1.2.1 Are final risk determinations and related management approvals documented and maintained on file?								
1.2.2 Has a mission/business impact analysis been conducted?								
1.2.3 Have additional controls been identified to sufficiently mitigate identified risks?								
2. Review of Security Controls								
2.1 Critical Element: Have the security controls of the system and interconnected systems been reviewed?								
2.1.1 Has the system and all network boundaries been subjected to periodic reviews?								
2.1.2 Has an independent review been performed when a significant change occurred?								
2.1.3 Are routine self-assessments conducted?								
2.1.4 Are tests and examinations of key controls routinely made i.e., network scans, analyses of router and switch settings, penetration testing?								
2.1.5 Are security alerts and security incidents analyzed and remedial actions taken?								
2.2 Critical Element: Does management ensure that corrective actions are effectively implemented?								
2.2.1 Is there an effective and timely process for reporting significant weaknesses and ensuring effective remedial actions?								

Appendix A

Specific Control Objectives and Techniques	Level 1	Level 2	Level 3	Level 4	Leve 5	Risk-Based Decis on Made	Comments	Initials
3. Life Cycle								
3.1 Critical Element: Has a system development life-cycle methodology been developed?								
Initiation Phase								
3.1.1 Is the sensitivity of the system determined?								
3.1.2 Does the business case document the resources required for adequately securing the system?								
3.1.3 Does the Investment Review Board ensure any investment request includes the security resources needed?								
3.1.4 Are authorizations for software modifications documented and maintained?								
3.1.5 Does the budget request include the security resources required for the system?								
Development/Acquisition Phase								
3.1.6 During the system design, are security requirements identified?								
3.1.7 Was an initial risk assessment performed to determine security requirements?								
3.1.8 Is there a written agreement with program officials on the security controls employed and residual risk?								

Specific Control Objectives and Techniques	Level 1	Level 2	Level 3	Level 4	Level 5	Risk-Based Decision Made	Comments	Initials
3.1.9 Are security controls consistent with and an integral part of the IT architecture of the agency?								
3.1.10 Are the appropriate security controls with associated evaluation and test procedures developed before the procurement action?								
3.1.11 Do the solicitation documents (e.g., request for proposals) include security requirements and evaluation/test procedures?								
3.1.12 Do the requirements in the solicitation documents permit updating security controls as new threats/vulnerabilities are identified and as new technologies are implemented?								
Implementation Phase								
3.2 Critical Element: Are changes controlled as programs progress through testing to final approval?								
3.2.1 Are design reviews and system tests run prior to placing the system in production?								
3.2.2 Are the test results documented?								
3.2.3 Is certification testing of security controls conducted and documented?								
3.2.4 If security controls were added since development, has the system documentation been modified to include them?								

Specific Control Objectives and Techniques	Level 1	Level 2	Level 3	Level 4	Level 5	Risk-Based Decision Made	Comments	Initials
3.2.5 If security controls were added since development, have the security controls been tested and the system recertified?								
3.2.6 Has the application undergone a technical evaluation to ensure that it meets applicable federal laws, regulations, policies, guidelines, and standards?								
3.2.7 Does the system have written authorization to operate either on an interim basis with planned corrective action or full authorization?								
Operation/Maintenance Phase								
3.2.8 Has a system security plan been developed and approved?								
3.2.9 If the system connects to other systems, have controls been established and disseminated to the owners of the interconnected systems?								
3.2.10 Is the system security plan kept current?								
Disposal Phase								
3.2.11 Are official electronic records properly disposed/archived?								
3.2.12 Is information or media purged, over-written, degaussed, or destroyed when disposed or used elsewhere?								
3.2.13 Is a record kept of who implemented the disposal actions and verified that the information or media was sanitized?								

NIST SP 800-26, Security Self-Assessment Guide

Specific Control Objectives and Techniques	Level 1	Level 2	Level 3	Level 4	Level 5	Risk-Based Decision Made	Comments	Initials
4. Authorize Processing (Certification and Accreditation)								
4.1 Critical Element: Has the system been certified/recertified and authorized to process (accredited)?								
4.1.1 Has a technical and/or security evaluation been completed or conducted when a significant change occurred?								
4.1.2 Has a risk assessment been conducted when a significant change occurred?								
4.1.3 Have rules of behavior been established and signed by users?								
4.1.4 Has a contingency plan been developed and tested?								
4.1.5 Has a system security plan been developed, updated, and reviewed?								
4.1.6 Are in-place controls operating as intended?								
4.1.7 Are the planned and in-place controls consistent with the identified risks and the system and data sensitivity?								
4.1.8 Has management authorized interconnections to all systems (including systems owned and operated by another program, agency, organization, or contractor)?								
4.2 Critical Element: Is the system operating on an interim authority to process in accordance with specified agency procedures?								

Specific Control Objectives and Techniques	Level 1	Level 2	Level 3	Level 4	Level 5	Risk-Based Decision Made	Comments	Initials
4.2.1 Has management initiated prompt action to correct deficiencies?								
5. System Security Plan								
5.1 Critical Element: Is a system security plan documented for the system and all interconnected systems if the boundary controls are ineffective?								
5.1.1 Is the system security plan approved by key affected parties and management?								
5.1.2 Does the plan contain the topics prescribed in NIST Special Publication 800-18?								
5.1.3 Is a summary of the plan incorporated into the strategic IRM plan?								
5.2 Critical Element: Is the plan kept current?								
5.2.1 Is the plan reviewed periodically and adjusted to reflect current conditions and risks?								
Operational Controls								
6. Personnel Security								
6.1 Critical Element: Are duties separated to ensure least privilege and individual accountability?								
6.1.1 Are all positions reviewed for sensitivity level?								
6.1.2 Are there documented job descriptions that accurately reflect assigned duties and responsibilities and that segregate duties?								

NIST SP 800-26, Security Self-Assessment Guide

Appendix A

Specific Control Objectives and Techniques	Level 1	Level 2	Level 3	Level 4	Level 5	Risk-Based Decision Made	Comments	Initials
6.1.3 Are sensitive functions divided among different individuals?								
6.1.4 Are distinct systems support functions performed by different individuals?								
6.1.5 Are mechanisms in place for holding users responsible for their actions?								
6.1.6 Are regularly scheduled vacations and periodic job/shift rotations required?								
6.1.7 Are hiring, transfer, and termination procedures established?								
6.1.8 Is there a process for requesting, establishing, issuing, and closing user accounts?								
6.2 Critical Element: Is appropriate background screening for assigned positions completed prior to granting access?								
6.2.1 Are individuals who are authorized to bypass significant technical and operational controls screened prior to access and periodically thereafter?								
6.2.2 Are confidentiality or security agreements required for employees assigned to work with sensitive information?								
6.2.3 When controls cannot adequately protect the information, are individuals screened prior to access?								
6.2.4 Are there conditions for allowing system access prior to completion of screening?								
7. Physical and Environmental Protection								

Specific Control Objectives and Techniques	Level 1	Level 2	Level 3	Level 4	Leve 5	Risk-Based Decision Made	Comments	Initials
7.1 Critical Element: Have adequate physical security controls been implemented that are commensurate with the risks of physical damage or access?								
7.1.1 Is access to facilities controlled through the use of guards, identification badges, or entry devices such as key cards or biometrics?								
7.1.2 Does management regularly review the list of persons with physical access to sensitive facilities?								
7.1.3 Are deposits and withdrawals of tapes and other storage media from the library authorized and logged?								
7.1.4 Are keys or other access devices needed to enter the computer room and tape/media library?								
7.1.5 Are unused keys or other entry devices secured?								
7.1.6 Do emergency exit and reentry procedures ensure that only authorized personnel are allowed to reenter after fire drills, etc?								
7.1.7 Are visitors to sensitive areas signed in and escorted?								
7.1.8 Are entry codes changed periodically?								
7.1.9 Are physical accesses monitored through audit trails and apparent security violations investigated and remedial action taken?								
7.1.10 Is suspicious access activity investigated and appropriate action taken?								

NIST SP 800-26, Security Self-Assessment Guide

Specific Control Objectives and Techniques	Level 1	Level 2	Level 3	Level 4	Level 5	Risk-Based Decision Made	Comments	Initials
7.1.11 Are visitors, contractors, and maintenance personnel authenticated through the use of preplanned appointments and identification checks?								
Fire Safety Factors								
7.1.12 Are appropriate fire suppression and prevention devices installed and working?								
7.1.13 Are fire ignition sources, such as failures of electronic devices or wiring, improper storage materials, and the possibility of arson, reviewed periodically?								
Supporting Utilities								
7.1.14 Are heating and air-conditioning systems regularly maintained?								
7.1.15 Is there a redundant air-cooling system?								
7.1.16 Are electric power distribution, heating plants, water, sewage, and other utilities periodically reviewed for risk of failure?								
7.1.17 Are building plumbing lines known and do not endanger system?								

Specific Control Objectives and Techniques	Level 1	Level 2	Level 3	Level 4	Level 5	Risk-Based Decision Made	Comments	Initials
7.1.18 Has an uninterruptible power supply or backup generator been provided?								
7.1.19 Have controls been implemented to mitigate other disasters, such as floods, earthquakes, etc.?								
Interception of Data								
7.2 Critical Element: Is data protected from interception?								
7.2.1 Are computer monitors located to eliminate viewing by unauthorized persons?								
7.2.2 Is physical access to data transmission lines controlled?								
Mobile and Portable Systems								
7.3 Critical Element: Are mobile and portable systems protected?								
7.3.1 Are sensitive data files encrypted on all portable systems? (NIST SP 800-14)								
7.3.2 Are portable systems stored securely? (NIST SP 800-14)								
8. Production, Input/Output Controls								
8.1 Critical Element: Is there user support?								
8.1.1 Is there a help desk or group that offers advice?								
8.2 Critical Element: Are there media controls?								

Specific Control Objectives and Techniques	Level 1	Level 2	Level 3	Level 4	Level 5	Risk-Based Decision Made	Comments	Initials
8.2.1 Are there processes to ensure that unauthorized individuals cannot read, copy, alter, or steal printed or electronic information?								
8.2.2 Are there processes for ensuring that only authorized users pick up, receive, or deliver input and output information and media?								
8.2.3 Are audit trails used for receipt of sensitive inputs/outputs?								
8.2.4 Are controls in place for transporting or mailing media or printed output?								
8.2.5 Is there internal/external labeling for sensitivity?								
8.2.6 Is there external labeling with special handling instructions?								
8.2.7 Are audit trails kept for inventory management?								
8.2.8 Is media sanitized for reuse?								
8.2.9 Is damaged media stored and/or destroyed?								
8.2.10 Is hardcopy media shredded or destroyed when no longer needed?								
9. Contingency Planning								
9.1 Critical Element: Have the most critical and sensitive operations and their supporting computer resources been identified?								

Specific Control Objectives and Techniques	Level 1	Level 2	Level 3	Level 4	Level 5	Risk-Based Decision Made	Comments	Initials
9.1.1 Are critical data files and operations identified and the frequency of file backup documented?								
9.1.2 Are resources supporting critical operations identified?								
9.1.3 Have processing priorities been established and approved by management?								
9.2 Critical Element: Has a comprehensive contingency plan been developed and documented?								
9.2.1 Is the plan approved by key affected parties?								
9.2.2 Are responsibilities for recovery assigned?								
9.2.3 Are there detailed instructions for restoring operations?								
9.2.4 Is there an alternate processing site; if so, is there a contract or interagency agreement in place?								
9.2.5 Is the location of stored backups identified?								
9.2.6 Are backup files created on a prescribed basis and rotated off-site often enough to avoid disruption if current files are damaged?								
9.2.7 Is system and application documentation maintained at the off-site location?								

NIST SP 800-26, Security Self-Assessment Guide

Specific Control Objectives and Techniques	Level 1	Level 2	Level 3	Level 4	Level 5	Risk-Based Decision Made	Comments	Initials
9.2.8 Are all system defaults reset after being restored from a backup?								
9.2.9 Are the backup storage site and alternate site geographically removed from the primary site and physically protected?								
9.2.10 Has the contingency plan been distributed to all appropriate personnel?								t
9.3 Critical Element: Are tested contingency/disaster recovery plans in place?								
9.3.1 Is an up-to-date copy of the plan stored securely off-site?								
9.3.2 Are employees trained in their roles and responsibilities?								
9.3.3 Is the plan periodically tested and readjusted as appropriate?								
10. Hardware and System Software Maintenance								
10.1 Critical Element: Is access limited to system software and hardware?								
10.1.1 Are restrictions in place on who performs maintenance and repair activities?								
10.1.2 Is access to all program libraries restricted and controlled?								

Specific Control Objectives and Techniques	Level 1	Level 2	Level 3	Level 4	Level 5	Risk-Based Decision Made	Comments	Initials
10.1.3 Are there on-site and off-site maintenance procedures (e.g., escort of maintenance personnel, sanitization of devices removed from the site)?								
10.1.4 Is the operating system configured to prevent circumvention of the security software and application controls?								
10.1.5 Are up-to-date procedures in place for using and monitoring use of system utilities?								
10.2 Critical Element: Are all new and revised hardware and software authorized, tested, and approved before implementation?								
10.2.1 Is an impact analysis conducted to determine the effect of proposed changes on existing security controls, including the required training needed to implement the control?								
10.2.2 Are system components tested, documented, and approved (operating system, utility, applications) prior to promotion to production?								
10.2.3 Are software change request forms used to document requests and related approvals?								
10.2.4 Are there detailed system specifications prepared and reviewed by management?								

NIST SP 800-26, Security Self-Assessment Guide

Specific Control Objectives and Techniques	Level 1	Level 2	Level 3	Level 4	Level 5	Risk-Based Decision Made	Comments	Initials
10.2.5 Is the type of test data to be used specified, i.e., live or made up?								
10.2.6 Are default settings of security features set to the most restrictive mode?								
10.2.7 Are there software distribution implementation orders including effective date provided to all locations?								
10.2.8 Is there version control?								
10.2.9 Are programs labeled and inventoried?								
10.2.10 Are the distribution and implementation of new or revised software documented and reviewed?								
10.2.11 Are emergency change procedures documented and approved by management, either prior to the change or after the fact?								
10.2.12 Are contingency plans and other associated documentation updated to reflect system changes?								
10.2.13 Is the use of copyrighted software or shareware and personally owned software/equipment documented?								
10.3 Critical Element: Are systems managed to reduce vulnerabilities?								

Specific Control Objectives and Techniques	Level 1	Level 2	Level 3	Level 4	Level 5	Risk-Based Decision Made	Comments	Initials
10.3.1 Are systems periodically reviewed to identify and, when possible, eliminate unnecessary services (e.g., FTP, HTTP, mainframe supervisor calls)?								
10.3.2 Are systems periodically reviewed for known vulnerabilities and software patches promptly installed?								
11. Data Integrity								
11.1 Critical Element: Is virus detection and elimination software installed and activated?								
11.1.1 Are virus signature files routinely updated?								
11.1.2 Are virus scans automatic?								
11.2 Critical Element: Are data integrity and validation controls used to provide assurance that the information has not been altered and the system functions as intended?								
11.2.1 Are reconciliation routines used by applications, i.e., checksums, hash totals, record counts?								
11.2.2 Is inappropriate or unusual activity reported, investigated, and appropriate actions taken?								
11.2.3 Are procedures in place to determine compliance with password policies?								

NIST SP 800-26, Security Self-Assessment Guide

Specific Control Objectives and Techniques	Level 1	Level 2	Level 3	Level 4	Level 5	Risk-Based Decision Made	Comments	Initials
11.2.4 Are integrity verification programs used by applications to look for evidence of data tampering, errors, and omissions?								
11.2.5 Are intrusion detection tools installed on the system?								
11.2.6 Are the intrusion detection reports routinely reviewed and suspected incidents handled accordingly?								
11.2.7 Is system performance monitoring used to analyze system performance logs in real time to look for availability problems, including active attacks?								
11.2.8 Is penetration testing performed on the system?								
11.2.9 Is message authentication used?								
12. Documentation								
12.1 Critical Element: Is there sufficient documentation that explains how software/hardware is to be used?								
12.1.1 Is there vendor-supplied documentation of purchased software?								
12.1.2 Is there vendor-supplied documentation of purchased hardware?								
12.1.3 Is there application documentation for in-house applications?								

Appendix A

Specific Control Objectives and Techniques	Level 1	Level 2	Level 3	Level 4	Level 5	Risk-Based Decision Made	Comments	Initials
12.1.4 Are there network diagrams and documentation on setups of routers and switches?								
12.1.5 Are there software and hardware testing procedures and results?								
12.1.6 Are there standard operating procedures for all the topic areas covered in this document?								
12.1.7 Are there user manuals?								
12.1.8 Are there emergency procedures?								
12.1.9 Are there backup procedures?								
12.2 Critical Element: Are there formal security and operational procedures documented?								
12.2.1 Is there a system security plan? FISCAM SP-2.1								
12.2.2 Is there a contingency plan?								
12.2.3 Are there written agreements regarding how data is shared between interconnected systems?								
12.2.4 Are there risk assessment reports?								
12.2.5 Are there certification and accreditation documents and a statement authorizing the system to process?								

NIST SP 800-26, Security Self-Assessment Guide

Specific Control Objectives and Techniques	Level 1	Level 2	Level 3	Level 4	Level 5	Risk-Based Decision Made	Comments	Initials
13. Security Awareness, Training, and Education								
13.1 Critical Element: Have employees received adequate training to fulfill their security responsibilities?								
13.1.1 Have employees received a copy of the rules of behavior?								
13.1.2 Are employee training and professional development documented and monitored? FISCAM SP-4.2								
13.1.3 Is there mandatory annual refresher training?								
13.1.4 Are methods employed to make employees aware of security, i.e., posters, booklets?								
13.1.5 Have employees received a copy of or have easy access to agency security procedures and policies?								
14. Incident Response Capability								
14.1 Critical Element: Is there a capability to provide help to users when a security incident occurs in the system?								
14.1.1 Is a formal incident response capability available?								

Specific Control Objectives and Techniques	Level 1	Level 2	Level 3	Level 4	Level 5	Risk-Based Decision Made	Comments	Initials
14.1.2 Is there a process for reporting incidents?								
14.1.3 Are incidents monitored and tracked until resolved?								
14.1.4 Are personnel trained to recognize and handle incidents?								
14.1.5 Are alerts/advisories received and responded to?								
14.1.6 Is there a process to modify incident handling procedures and control techniques after an incident occurs?								
14.2 Critical Element: Is incident-related information shared with appropriate organizations?								
14.2.1 Is incident information and common vulnerabilities or threats shared with owners of interconnected systems?								
14.2.2 Is incident information shared with FedCIRC concerning incidents and common vulnerabilities and threats?								
14.2.3 Is incident information reported to FedCIRC, NIPC4, and local law enforcement when necessary?								
Technical Controls								
15. Identification and Authentication								

NIST SP 800-26, Security Self-Assessment Guide

Specific Control Objectives and Techniques	Level 1	Level 2	Level 3	Level 4	Level 5	Risk-Based Decision Made	Comments	Initials
15.1 Critical Element: Are users individually authenticated via passwords, tokens, or other devices?								
15.1.1 Is a current list maintained and approved of authorized users and their access?								
15.1.2 Are digital signatures used and conform to FIPS 186-2?								
15.1.3 Are access scripts with embedded passwords prohibited?								
15.1.4 Is emergency and temporary access authorized?								
15.1.5 Are personnel files matched with user accounts to ensure that terminated or transferred individuals do not retain system access?								
15.1.6 Are passwords changed at least every 90 days or earlier if needed?								
15.1.7 Are passwords unique and difficult to guess (e.g., do passwords require alpha numeric, upper/lower case, and special characters)?								
15.1.8 Are inactive user identifications disabled after a specified period of time?								
15.1.9 Are passwords not displayed when entered?								

Specific Control Objectives and Techniques	Level 1	Level 2	Level 3	Level 4	Level 5	Risk-Based Decision Made	Comments	Initials
15.1.10 Are there procedures in place for handling lost and compromised passwords?								
15.1.11 Are passwords distributed securely and users informed not to reveal their passwords to anyone (social engineering)?								
15.1.12 Are passwords transmitted and stored using secure protocols/algorithms?								
15.1.13 Are vendor-supplied passwords replaced immediately?								
15.1.14 Is there a limit to the number of invalid access attempts that may occur for a given user?								
15.2 Critical Element: Are access controls enforcing segregation of duties?								
15.2.1 Does the system correlate actions to users?								
15.2.2 Do data owners periodically review access authorizations to determine whether they remain appropriate?								
16. Logical Access Controls								
16.1 Critical Element: Do the logical access controls restrict users to authorized transactions and functions?								
16.1.1 Can the security controls detect unauthorized access attempts?								

NIST SP 800-26, Security Self-Assessment Guide

Specific Control Objectives and Techniques	Level 1	Level 2	Level 3	Level 4	Level 5	Risk-Based Decision Made	Comments	Initials
16.1.2 Is there access control software that prevents an individual from having all necessary authority or information access to allow fraudulent activity without collusion?								
16.1.3 Is access to security software restricted to security administrators?								
16.1.4 Do workstations disconnect or screen savers lock the system after a specific period of inactivity?								
16.1.5 Are inactive users' accounts monitored and removed when not needed?								
16.1.6 Are internal security labels (naming conventions) used to control access to specific information types or files?								
16.1.7 If encryption is used, does it meet federal standards?								
16.1.8 If encryption is used, are there procedures for key generation, distribution, storage, use, destruction, and archiving?								
16.1.9 Is access restricted to files at the logical view or field?								
16.1.10 Is access monitored to identify apparent security violations and are such events investigated?								
16.2 Critical Element: Are there logical controls over network access?								

Specific Control Objectives and Techniques	Level 1	Level 2	Level 3	Level 4	Level 5	Risk-Based Decision Made	Comments	Initials
16.2.1 Has communication software been implemented to restrict access through specific terminals?								
16.2.2 Are insecure protocols (e.g., UDP, FTP) disabled?								
16.2.3 Have all vendor-supplied default security parameters been reinitialized to more secure settings?								
16.2.4 Are there controls that restrict remote access to the system?								
16.2.5 Are network activity logs maintained and reviewed?								
16.2.6 Does the network connection automatically disconnect at the end of a session?								
16.2.7 Are trust relationships among hosts and external entities appropriately restricted?								
16.2.8 Is dial-in access monitored?								
16.2.9 Is access to telecommunications hardware or facilities restricted and monitored?								
16.2.10 Are firewalls or secure gateways installed?								
16.2.11 If firewalls are installed, do they comply with firewall policy and rules?								
16.2.12 Are guest and anonymous accounts authorized and monitored?								

Specific Control Objectives and Techniques	Level 1	Level 2	Level 3	Level 4	Level 5	Risk-Based Decision Made	Comments	Initials
16.2.13 Is an approved standardized logon banner displayed on the system warning unauthorized users that they have accessed a U.S. Government system and can be punished?								
16.2.14 Are sensitive data transmissions encrypted?								
16.2.15 Is access to tables defining network options, resources, and operator profiles restricted?								
16.3 Critical Element: If the public accesses the system, are there controls implemented to protect the integrity of the application and the confidence of the public?								
16.3.1 Is a privacy policy posted on the Web site?								
17. Audit Trails								
17.1 Critical Element: Is activity involving access to and modification of sensitive or critical files logged, monitored, and possible security violations investigated?								
17.1.1 Does the audit trail provide a trace of user actions?								
17.1.2 Can the audit trail support after-the-fact investigations of how, when, and why normal operations ceased?								

Specific Control Objectives and Techniques	Level 1	Level 2	Level 3	Level 4	Level 5	Risk-Based Decision Made	Comments	Initials
17.1.3 Is access to online audit logs strictly controlled?								
17.1.4 Are off-line storage of audit logs retained for a period of time, and, if so, is access to audit logs strictly controlled?								
17.1.5 Is there separation of duties between security personnel who administer the access control function and those who administer the audit trail?								
17.1.6 Are audit trails reviewed frequently?								
17.1.7 Are automated tools used to review audit records in real time or near real time?								
17.1.8 Is suspicious activity investigated and appropriate action taken?								
17.1.9 Is keystroke monitoring used? If so, are users notified?								

ISO 17799: 2005 Scoring Methodology

This scoring methodology is designed to assess an organization's management practices using a framework based on ISO 17799. The respondent is asked to assess the organization's implementation of security objectives for security standards across the domains of ISO 17799:2005. For each objective, a respondent may choose one of the following degrees of compliance:

- Fully compliant: The standard objective has been fully implemented at the organization. Results in a score of 10 for the objective.
- Partially compliant: The standard objective has been partially implemented at the organization. Results in a score of 5 for the objective.
- Planned: The organization has made definite plans to implement the standard objective. Results in a score of 2 for the objective.
- Not compliant or planned: The standard objective has not been implemented (even partly) and there are no plans to implement it. Results in a score of 0 for the objective.
- Not applicable: The objective does not appear to apply to the organization. No score is given and the potential score of 10 is not incorporated in the calculation of the total score, as if the objective was not included in the index.

The scoring methodology is designed to illustrate a great benefit from implementing minimum and basic security standards, although implementation of all standards are required for a score of 100%. Individuals should review each low-level standard (i.e., 5.1.1) and assess their performance against a maximum score of 10 per item, as described above (1320 points max—if all low-level standards are applicable). Scores of 80% or higher indicate a strong performance against the standard. Scores of 60–79% indicate progress, but additional effort is required to become more compliant. Scores below 60% indicate that several areas are out of compliance and an overall strategic plan to improve general security management should be undertaken.

Praxiom's ISO/IEC 17799 2005 Information Security Standard In Plain English (Source: http://www.praxiom.com/iso-17799-2005.htm, reprinted here with permission)

5. Security Policy Management

5.1   Establish a comprehensive information security policy
        5.1.1   Develop an information security policy document
        5.1.2   Review your information security policy

6. Corporate Security Management

6.1   Establish an internal security organization
        6.1.1   Make an active commitment to information security
        6.1.2   Coordinate information security implementation

7. Organizational Asset Management

8. Human Resource Security Management

9. Physical and Environmental Security Management

10. Communications and Operations Management

10.10.4   Log system administrator and operator activities
10.10.5   Log information processing and communication faults
10.10.6   Synchronize your system clocks

11. Information Access Control Management

11.1   Control access to information
    11.1.1   Develop a policy to control access to information
11.2   Manage user access rights
    11.2.1   Establish a user access control procedure
    11.2.2   Control the management of system privileges
    11.2.3   Establish a process to manage passwords
    11.2.4   Review user access rights and privileges
11.3   Encourage good access practices
    11.3.1   Expect users to protect their passwords
    11.3.2   Expect users to protect their equipment
    11.3.3   Establish a cleardesk and clearscreen policy
11.4   Control access to networked services
    11.4.1   Formulate a policy on the use of networks
    11.4.2   Authenticate remote user connections
    11.4.3   Use automatic equipment identification methods
    11.4.4   Control access to diagnostic and configuration ports
    11.4.5   Use segregation methods to protect your networks
    11.4.6   Restrict connection to shared networks
    11.4.7   Establish network routing controls
11.5   Control access to operating systems
    11.5.1   Establish secure logon procedures
    11.5.2   Identify and authenticate all users
    11.5.3   Establish a password management system
    11.5.4   Control the use of all system utilities
    11.5.5   Use session timeouts to protect information
    11.5.6   Restrict connection times in highrisk areas
11.6   Control access to applications and information
    11.6.1   Restrict access by users and support personnel
    11.6.2   Isolate sensitive application systems
11.7   Protect mobile and teleworking facilities
    11.7.1   Protect mobile computing and communications
    11.7.2   Protect and control teleworking activities

12. Information Systems Security Management

12.1   Identify information system security requirements
    12.1.1   Identify security controls and requirements
12.2   Make sure applications process information correctly
    12.2.1   Validate data input into your applications
    12.2.2   Use validation checks to control processing

15.2   Perform security compliance reviews
    15.2.1   Review compliance with security policies and standards
    15.2.2   Review technical security compliance
15.3   Carry out controlled information system audits
    15.3.1   Control the audit of information systems
    15.3.2   Protect information system audit tools

Note: No organization should attempt a 17799 audit solely on the basis of this document. While the underlying methodology is sound, the level of detail is insufficient to successfully complete a meaningful assessment of the organization's information security management strategies. This information is presented for academic discussion and should only be used as such.

3DES Synonymous with Triple DES. An enhancement to the Data Encryption Standard (DES). An algorithm that uses up to three keys to perform three different encryption operations.

access The ability to use, manipulate, modify, or affect an object.

access control A security measure such as a badge reader that admits or prohibits users from entering sensitive areas.

access control list (ACL) A list of people or other entities permitted to access a computer resource.

accountability Characteristic of information that exists when every activity involving the information can be attributed to a named person or automated process.

accreditation The state of having been reviewed by an authority and being recognized as having approved processes, programs, or skills. Individual persons are often accredited via certification testing and the fulfillment of experience requirements. The term can also be used to describe the requirement to demonstrate that processes or programs comply with government sanctioned rules before an IT system is authorized to process, store, or transmit information.

acquired value The value an asset has gained over time within an organization.

Advanced Encryption Standard (AES) A Federal Information Processing Standard (FIPS) specified cryptographic algorithm for use within the U.S. government to protect unclassified information.

after-action review A detailed examination of the events that occur from the first detection of a security breach to the final recovery.

agent A piece of software that resides on a system and reports back to a management server.

alert message A scripted description of a security breach that points the recipient to a specific section of a response plan for immediate action.

alert roster A document containing contact information for the individuals to be notified in the event of a security breach.

analysis phase The portion of the SDLC that assesses the organization's readiness, its current systems status, and its capability to implement and then support the proposed systems.

annualized loss expectancy (ALE) The element of a formula for calculating the overall loss an organization could incur from the specified threat over the course of an entire year. ALE=SLE X ARO (annualized loss expectancy equals single loss expectancy times annualized rate of occurrence).

annualized rate of occurrence (ARO) The element of a formula for calculating the overall loss an organization could incur from a potential risk that represents the anticipated rate of occurrence of a loss from the specified threat. ALE=SLE X ARO (annualized loss expectancy equals single loss expectancy times annualized rate of occurrence).

application-level firewall A device, typically a computer, that provides a defense between a network inside the firewall and a network outside the firewall (the Internet) that could pose a threat to the inside network. All traffic to and from the network must pass through the firewall, so that unauthorized traffic can be blocked.

asset valuation The process of assigning financial value or worth to each information asset.

asymmetric encryption Synonymous with public key encryption. A method of communicating on a network using two different but related keys, one to encrypt and the other to decrypt messages.

asynchronous token A device that uses a challenge-response method, in which a server challenges a user during login with a numerical sequence. The user places the sequence into a token, which generates a response that is entered to gain access.

attack An act that is an intentional or unintentional attempt to compromise the information and/or the systems that support it.

attack profile A detailed description of the activities that occur during an attack.

attack scenario end case The summary that describes an attack, the most likely outcome from that attack, and the associated costs from that outcome.

authentication Validation that the claimed identity of supplicant is indeed the person or entity requesting authorized access to a system or facility.

authorization Permission granted to properly identified and validated supplicant by an authority to access, update, or delete the contents of an information asset.

authorization ticket In a client/server environment, a token issued to a particular client that verifies to a server that the client is requesting services on behalf of an authorized user and that the client is a valid member of a system and therefore authorized to receive services.

availability A quality or state of information characterized by being accessible and correctly formatted for use without interference or obstruction.

avoidance The risk control strategy that attempts to prevent the exploitation of the vulnerability.

baseline A value or profile of a performance metric against which changes in the performance metric can be usefully compared.

bastion host A dedicated server that receives screened network traffic, which is usually prepared with extra attention to detail and hardened for use in an unsecured or limited security zone. Sometimes referred to as a sacrificial host.

behavior-based intrusion detection system (IDS) Synonymous with statistical anomaly-based IDS. A device that collects data from normal traffic to establish a baseline. The IDS compares periodic data samples with the baseline to highlight irregularities.

behavioral feasibility Synonymous with operational feasibility. The examination of user acceptance of proposed security measures.

benchmarking The process of seeking out and studying the organizational practices that produce desired results.

benefit The value that an organization recognizes by using controls to prevent losses associated with a specific vulnerability.

best business practices Synonymous with best practices and recommended practices. Procedures that provide a superior level of security for an organization's information.

best security practices Security efforts that seek to provide a superior level of performance in the protection of information.

blueprint The basis for the design, selection, and implementation of security controls.

bottom-up approach A method of establishing security policies that begins as a grassroots effort in which systems administrators attempt to improve the security of their systems.

British Standard BS 7799 A code of practice adopted as an international standard framework for information security by the International Organization for Standardization (ISO) and the International Electrotechnical Commission (IEC) as ISO/IEC 17799 in 2000.

bull's-eye model An implementation model in which information security issues are addressed from the general to the specific, always starting with policy.

business continuity planning (BCP) A program designed to assure the continuation of business activities if a catastrophic event occurs, such as the unrecoverable loss of an entire database, building, or operations center, usually involving operations at an alternate location.

business impact analysis (BIA) The first phase in the continuity planning process. It extends the activities of the risk assessment process to determine the priority for controlling risks in the area of information security or for establishing relative priority of various systems for the resumption of business activities.

business resumption plan (BR plan) A single planning approach and supporting documentation that combines the disaster recovery and business continuity processes.

cache server The server used by proxy servers to temporarily store frequently accessed pages.

capabilities table A list that specifies data items or physical devices (for example printers) that users are authorized to access.

CERT Coordination Center A center of Internet security expertise located at the Software Engineering Institute, a federally funded research and development center operated by Carnegie Mellon University.

certificate authority (CA) An agency that manages the issuance of digital certificates and serves as the electronic notary public to verify their worth and integrity.

certification The process of reviewing processes, programs, or skills for compliance with a standard or expected level of performance. Individuals achieve certification by means of testing and the fulfillment of experience requirements. Organizations can obtain certification by demonstrating that processes or programs comply with government or other sanctioned rules.

Certified Information Security Manager (CISM) A credential sponsored by The Information Systems Audit and Control Association and Foundation (ISACA) that requires mastery in specified information security management skills and attainment of the required number of years of experience.

Certified Information Systems Auditor (CISA) A credential sponsored by The Information Systems Audit and Control Association and Foundation (ISACA) for individuals that can demonstrate the specified information system auditing skills and who possess the required number of years of experience.

champion An executive with sufficient influence and interest who supports a security project and pushes for its acceptance throughout the organization.

Chief Information Officer (CIO) The senior technology officer responsible for aligning the strategic efforts of the organization into action plans for the information systems or data processing division of the organization.

Chief Information Security Officer (CISO) The senior security officer responsible for the assessment, management, and implementation of securing the information in the organization.

C.I.A. triangle The industry standard for computer security since the development of the mainframe. It is based on three characteristics that describe the utility of information: confidentiality, integrity, and availability.

ciphertext A message that is formed when plaintext data is encrypted by a cryptosystem.

civil law A wide variety of laws that are recorded in volumes of legal code available for review by any citizen.

clipping level As detected by an intrusion detection system, a level of network activity that is higher than an established baseline and therefore suspect.

cold site An alternate site that can be used by an organization if a disaster occurs at the home site. Contains rudimentary services and facilities.

collusion The act of conspiring to circumvent laws, policies, or information security controls.

communications security The protection of an organization's communications media, technology, and content, and its ability to use these tools to achieve the organization's objectives.

community of interest A group of individuals united by shared interests or values within an organization.

competitive advantage The leverage gained by an organization that supplies superior products or services. Establishing a competitive business model, method, or technique allows an organization to provide a product or service that is superior to others in the marketplace.

competitive disadvantage The leverage lost by an organization that supplies products or services perceived to be inferior to other organizations.

Computer Security Division (CSD) of the National Institute of Standards and Technology An organization that raises the awareness of issues on information security, especially on new and emerging technologies.

confidentiality The quality or state of information that prevents disclosure or exposure to unauthorized individuals or systems.

consultant A self-employed individual who is hired for a specific, one-time purpose. Sometimes used as a senior position title for very experienced employees within large organizations.

content filter A software device that allows administrators to work within a network to restrict accessibility to information.

contingency planning (CP) The program developed to prepare for, react to, and recover from events that threaten the security of the information assets of an organization.

control Synonymous with safeguard and countermeasure. A security mechanism, policy, or procedure that can counter system attack, reduce risks, limit losses, and resolve vulnerabilities.

Committee of Sponsoring Organizations of the Treadway Commission (COSO) A U.S. private-sector initiative, formed in 1985 with the major objective to identify the factors that cause fraudulent financial reporting and to make recommendations to reduce its incidence. The report of the commission serves as a control-based model for information security program design.

cost avoidance The money saved by using a control to avoid the financial impact of an incident.

cost benefit analysis (CBA) Synonymous with economic feasibility study. The comparison of the cost of protecting an asset with the worth of the asset or the costs of the compromise of an asset.

criminal law Laws that address violations harmful to society and that are actively enforced through prosecution by the state.

crisis management The actions taken during and after a disaster.

critical path The sequence of project events/activities that requires the longest duration to complete; it identifies the series of events/activities that cannot be delayed without delaying the entire project.

Critical Path Method A networking dependency project diagramming technique similar to PERT.

crossover error rate (CER) Evaluation criteria for biometric technologies, the crossover rate is the point at which the number of false rejections (denial-of-access to authorized users) equals the number of the false acceptances (granting of access to unauthorized users).

cryptanalysis The methodologies used to obtain information from encoded messages when the cryptographic algorithm and/or keys are unknown.

cryptography From the Greek work *kryptos*, meaning hidden, and *graphein*, meaning to write. The enciphering and deciphering of coded messages.

cryptology The science of encryption; a field of study that encompasses cryptography and cryptanalysis.

cultural mores Fixed moral attitudes or customs of a particular group.

cyberactivism The use of computer-related technologies to advance a political agenda.

cybernetic control The process of monitoring progress toward completion, and making necessary adjustments to achieve desired objectives.

cyberterrorist The act of hacking to conduct terrorist activities via network or Internet pathways.

data custodian Individual responsible for the storage, maintenance, and protection of information.

data owner   Individual who determines the level of classification associated with data.

data user   Synonymous with end user. An individual who uses computer applications for his daily work.

database shadowing   A process that duplicates data in real-time using databases at a remote site or to multiple servers.

decisional role   Management role that involves selecting from among alternative approaches, and resolving conflicts, dilemmas, or challenges.

Delphi technique   Named for the oracle at Delphi, a process in which a group rates or ranks asset values or threats to assets.

demilitarized zone (DMZ)   An intermediate area between a trusted network and an untrusted network.

denial-of-service (DoS)   An attack in which the abuser sends a large number of connection or information requests to overwhelm and cripple a target.

Desk check   A validation process where the steps of a plan or computer program are validated by people reviewing it in sequence to identify error or omissions.

detective control   A measure that warns organizations of violations of security principles, organizational policies, or of attempts to exploit vulnerabilities.

deterrence   Discouraging illegal or unethical activity by punishing violators of laws, policies, and technical controls.

Diffie-Hellman key exchange method   A method for exchanging private keys using public key encryption.

digital certificate   An electronic document attached to a file that certifies the file is from the organization it claims to be from and has not been modified from the original format.

digital signature   An encrypted message that is independently verified as authentic by a central facility (registry).

direct changeover   A modification to work practices that involves stopping the old method and beginning the new.

disaster recovery planning (DRP)   A program to limit losses during a disaster and resume business processes afterwards at the original site.

due care   The actions that demonstrate that an organization makes sure that every employee knows what is acceptable or not acceptable behavior, and knows the consequences of illegal or unethical actions.

due diligence   The actions that demonstrate that an organization has made a valid effort to protect others.

dumb cards   ID cards or ATM cards with magnetic stripes containing the digital (and often encrypted) user personal identification number (PIN) against which a user input is compared; performs no computation as contrasted with smart cards, which can perform some computations using an onboard processor.

dumpster diving   The retrieval of information from refuse that could prove embarrassing to the company or could compromise the security of information.

Dynamic Host Control Protocol (DHCP)   A standard within TCP/IP that reassigns IP numbers to devices as needed, making the use of IP numbers as part of the asset identification process very difficult.

dynamic packet filtering firewall   A firewall that allows only a particular packet with a particular source, destination, and port address to enter through the firewall.

economic feasibility study   Synonymous with cost benefit analysis. The comparison of the cost of protecting an asset with the worth of the asset or the costs if the asset is compromised.

electronic vaulting   The transfer of large batches of data to an off-site facility.

encryption   The process of converting an original message into a form that is unreadable by unauthorized individuals.

end user   Synonymous with data user. An individual who uses computer applications for his daily work.

enterprise information security policy (EISP)   A policy document that establishes the strategic direction, scope, and tone for all of an organization's security efforts.

ethical hacker   Synonymous with tiger team, white-hat hacker, and red team. Consultants or outsourced contractors who are hired to perform controlled attacks to compromise or disrupt systems by using documented vulnerabilities.

ethics   Behaviors that are socially acceptable.

event-driven   The impetus to begin a SDLC-based project that is in response to some event in the business community, inside the organization, or within the ranks of employees, customers, or other stakeholders.

exit interview   A discussion at the end of employment that reminds an employee of contractual obligations, such as nondisclosure agreements, and obtains feedback on the employee's tenure in the organization.

exploit   A technique used to compromise a system. Usually a documented way to circumvent controls or take advantage of weaknesses in control systems.

false accept rate   The percentage or value associated with the rate at which fraudulent users or nonusers are allowed access to systems or areas as a result of a failure in the biometric device.

false reject rate   The percentage or value associated with the rate at which authentic users are denied or prevented access to authorized areas as a result of a failure in the biometric device.

field change order (FCO)   An authorization issued by an organization for the repair, modification, or update of a piece of equipment.

file hashing   Method for ensuring information validity. Involves a file being read by a special algorithm that uses the value of the bits in the file to compute a single large number called a hash value.

fingerprinting   A data-gathering process that discovers the assets that can be accessed from a network, usually performed in advance of a planned attack. It is the systematic examination of the entire set of Internet addresses of the organization.

firewall   Synonymous with application firewall and application-level firewall. A computer that provides a defense between a network inside the firewall and a network outside the firewall (the Internet) that could pose a threat to the inside network. All traffic to and from the network must pass through the firewall, so that unauthorized data can be blocked.

footprint   The geographic area within which a wireless access point provides sufficient signal strength to maintain a connection.

footprinting   The identification of the Internet addresses that are owned or controlled by an organization.

framework   The outline from which a detailed security blueprint evolves.

Full-interruption testing   The testing of a plan by halting production and then using the actual workplace and all its systems to test the plan.

general business community   A group of nontechnical business managers and professionals within an organization.

Global Information Assurance Certification (GIAC)   A professional qualification consisting of twelve individual technical certifications that can be tied into six tracks, or culminate in the GIAC Security Engineer certification.

goal   The end result of a planning process.

guidelines   Instructions to employees that explain how to comply with organizational policy.

hacktivist   Synonymous with cyberactivist. An individual who uses technology as a tool for civil disobedience.

hash value   Synonymous with message digest. A single large number created when a file is read by a special algorithm that uses the value of the bits in the file to compute the number. The hash value ensures information validity.

hierarchical roster   A list of names of people who are called in the case of an emergency. Each person in turn calls an assigned group from the next level of the roster.

honeypot   A computer server configured to misdirect hackers by resembling a production system that contains substantial information.

host-based intrusion detection system (IDS)   Device that is installed on a computer system to monitor the status of files stored on that system and protect them from security breaches.

hot site   Synonymous with business recovery site. A remote location with systems identical or similar to a home site for use after a disaster.

identification   The ability of an information system to recognize individual users.

implementation phase   The portion of the SDLC during which the organization develops, acquires, and integrates necessary software.

incident   An attack on an organization's information assets.

incident candidate   An event that may or may not be an attack on an organization's information systems.

incident classification   The process of determining whether an incident candidate is an actual incident or is some other phenomenon.

incident response (IR)   Activities taken to plan for, detect, and correct the impact of an incident on information assets.

incident response plan (IR Plan)   A documented set of processes and procedures that comprise a detailed set of actions than anticipate, detect and mitigate the effects of an unexpected event.

incident response planning (IRP)   A process to establish procedures an organization's staff would follow if it were attacked.

information security (InfoSec)   The protection of information and the systems and hardware that use, store, and transmit that information.

information security community   Those members of an organization who are assigned to protect the information and the systems that process it.

information security policy   A set of rules designed to protect the information assets of an organization.

information security program   The structure and organization of the effort that strives to contain the risks to the information assets of the organization.

Information Systems Audit and Control Association (ISACA)   A professional association focused on auditing, control, and security.

Information Systems Audit and Control Association's Certified Information Systems Auditor (CISA)   A certificate that focuses on auditing information security, business process analysis, and information security planning.

Information Systems Audit and Control Association's Certified Information Security Manager (CISM)   A certificate that focuses on information security management practices.

Information Systems Security Association (ISSA)   A nonprofit society of information security professionals.

information technology community Those technology professionals that supports the business objectives of the organization by supplying and supporting information technology.

information warfare An offensive organized and lawful operation conducted by a sovereign state that involves the use of information technology.

informational role A management role that seeks to collect, process, and evaluate information that can affect decisions and outcomes.

integrity The quality or state of being whole, complete, and uncorrupted.

International Information Systems Security Certification Consortium (ISC)^2, Systems Security Certified Professional (SSCP) An international consortium dedicated to improving the quality of security professionals.

International Standard Organization (ISO) model An approach that provides a five-layer structure to the administration and management of networks and systems.

Internet Engineering Task Force (IETF) A group of professionals in the fields of computing, networking, and telecommunications who develop the Internet's technical foundations.

Internet Society (ISOC) A nonprofit, nongovernmental, international professional organization that promotes the development and implementation of education, standards, policy, and education and training to promote the Internet.

Internet vulnerability assessment The process of finding and documenting the vulnerabilities that may be present in the public-facing network of an organization.

interpersonal role A management role that includes interacting with superiors, subordinates, outside stakeholders, and others that influence or are influenced.

intrinsic value The essential worth of an asset.

intrusion detection systems (IDSs) Devices that inspect data communication flows to identify patterns that may indicate that hacking is underway.

IP Security (IPSec) The primary and now dominant cryptographic authentication and encryption product of the IETF's IP Protocol Security Working Group.

investigation phase The portion of the SDLC that identifies the problem that the system being developed is to solve.

ISO/IEC 17799:2002 The assigned reference number for the Information Technology—Security Techniques—Code of Practice for Information Security Management standard, one of the most widely referenced and often discussed security models. It is based on the British Standard 7799.

ISO/IEC 27001:2005 The assigned reference number for the Information Technology—Security Techniques—Information Security Management Systems—Requirements standard. This document provides implementation details for the standards espoused in ISO/IEC 17799:2002 and is the foundation for third-party certification of that standard.

issue-specific security policy A program that addresses specific areas of technology and contains a statement on the organization's position on each specific issue.

job rotation Synonymous with task rotation. A security check that requires that every employee is trained to perform the work of another employee.

Joint application Development (JAD) A IT systems development methodology that integrates IT developers, system users and subject matter experts (such as InfoSec or Networking) to speed the development of systems and improve overall system quality.

jurisdiction A court's right to hear a case because a wrong was committed in its territory or involving its citizenry.

Kerberos A cryptosystem that uses symmetric key encryption to validate an individual user to various network resources.

knowledge-based intrusion detection system (IDS) Synonymous with signature-based IDS. A device that examines data traffic for signature matches with predefined, preconfigured attack patterns.

lattice-based access control A matrix of authorizations that control access to data.

laws Rules adopted by society for determining expected behavior; drawn from ethics.

leadership A management role that addresses the direction and motivation of human resources.

least privilege A security measure by which employees are provided access to the minimum amount of information for the least duration of time necessary for them to perform their duties.

liability The legal obligation of an entity that includes responsibility for a wrongful act and the legal obligation to make restitution.

logical design phase Portion of the SDLC in which the information obtained during the analysis phase is used to create a proposed system-based solution for the business problem.

long arm jurisdiction A law that reaches across the country or around the world to pull an accused individual into its court systems.

maintenance phase Portion of the SDLC during which tasks necessary to support and modify the system for the remainder of its useful life cycle are executed.

management The process of achieving objectives using a given set of resources.

manager A member of an organization who coordinates the work of employees order to accomplish organizational goals.

management controls Synonymous with managerial controls. Organizational processes that are designed and implemented to reduce risk to the organization by using the role of the manager to enforce policy compliance.

managerial controls Synonymous with management controls. Organizational processes that are designed and implemented to reduce risk to the organization by using the role of the manager to enforce policy compliance.

mandatory vacation A policy requiring that all employees take at least one week of vacation per year.

methodology A formal approach to solving a problem based on a structured sequence of procedures.

minutiae In biometrics, unique points of reference that are digitized and stored in an encrypted format for comparison with scanned human characteristics.

mission statement A written declaration of an organization's purpose and its intended areas of operations.

mitigation A control approach that attempts to reduce the impact caused by the exploitation of vulnerability through planning and preparation.

monoalphabetic substitution In encryption, the substitution of one value for another using a single alphabet.

mutual agreement A contract between two or more organizations that specifies how each assists the other in the event of a disaster.

National InfraGard Program A cooperative effort of the FBI and local technology professionals to protect critical national information.

National Infrastructure Protection Center (NIPC) An organization that serves as the U.S. government's center for threat assessment, warning, investigation, and response to threats or attacks against critical U.S. infrastructures.

National Security Agency (NSA) The organization responsible for signal intelligence and information system security.

need-to-know A principle within a data classification scheme that limits individuals' access to information to that which is required to perform their jobs.

negative feedback loop Synonymous with cybernetic loop. A process to manage a project that insures that progress is measured periodically and that measured results are compared to expected results.

network address translation (NAT) A method of mapping real, valid, external IP addresses to special ranges of internal IP addresses, creating a barrier to internal intrusion.

network-based intrusion detection systems (IDSs) Devices that are installed on networks to monitor patterns of network traffic to detect unusual and therefore threatening activity.

network review board Synonymous with technical architecture team. A group that directs the orderly introduction of change in information technology across the organization.

network security The protection of an organization's data networking devices, connections, and contents, and the ability to use the network to accomplish the organization's data communication functions.

nonrepudiation A message characteristic wherein the fact that a message was sent by a particular entity cannot be refuted.

objective An intermediate point at which you can measure progress toward a goal.

open port A network channel or device used to send commands to a computer, gain access to a server, and exert control over a networking device.

operational controls Measures that deal with the operational functionality of security in an organization.

operational feasibility Synonymous with behavioral feasibility. The examination of user acceptance of proposed security measures.

operations Managed, ongoing processes.

operations security The safeguarding of the organization's ability to fulfill operational activities without interruption or compromise.

organization The management principle dedicated to the structuring of resources to support the accomplishment of objectives. Also, a group of people who work together to accomplish objectives such as a business, government agency or not-for-profit group.

organizational feasibility A comparison of how proposed information security alternatives contribute to the efficiency, effectiveness, and overall operation of an organization.

packet filtering firewall Networking devices that filter data packets based on their headers as they travel in and out of an organization's network.

packet sniffer A network tool that collects copies of packets from the network and analyzes them.

parallel operations A method of modifying work practices that involves using the new methods alongside the old methods.

parallel testing A method of testing a plan that involves using the actual workplace to follow the planned process steps without disrupting normal operation.

passphrase A series of characters, typically longer than a password, from which a virtual password is derived.

password A private word or combination of characters that only the user knows.

penetration testing An attempt to compromise a control system performed by security personnel attempting to access a system without authorization or disrupt operations by exploiting documented vulnerabilities. Must be done with prior authorization from system owners to avoid being considered an attack.

permutation cipher Synonymous with transposition cipher. The rearranging of values within a block to create coded information.

personal security The protection of the people within an organization.

phased implementation An approach to implementing new security systems that involves rolling out a piece of a new system across the entire organization.

physical design phase Portion of the SDLC during which the team selects specific technologies that support the alternatives identified and evaluated in the logical design phase.

physical security An aspect of information security that addresses the design, implementation, and maintenance of countermeasures that protect the physical resources of an organization.

pilot implementation The changing of work practices that involves implementing all security improvements in a single office, department, or division, and resolving issues within that group before expanding to the rest of the organization.

plaintext Synonymous with cleartext. The unencrypted message that will be encrypted into ciphertext for transmission over an unsecured channel.

plan-driven The impetus for a project that is the result of a carefully developed planning strategy.

planning The process that develops, creates, and implements strategies for the accomplishment of objectives.

policy The set of organizational guidelines that describe acceptable and unacceptable behaviors of employees in the workplace.

political feasibility An examination of the acceptability of limits placed on an organization and its employees' actions or behaviors.

polyalphabetic substitutions In encryption, the substitution of one value for another, using two or more alphabets.

port A network channel or connection point in a data communications system.

port scanners The tools used to identify (or fingerprint) computers that are active on a network.

practices Methods or processes used by an organization to accomplish its objectives.

Pretty Good Privacy (PGP) A hybrid cryptosystem that combines some of the best available cryptographic algorithms. PGP is the open source *de facto* standard for encryption and authentication of e-mail and file storage applications.

pre-shared key A technique of using a cryptographic variable or an equivalent pass phrase known to both parties in a communications channel prior to the establishment of a connection. Knowledge of the key is required to establish the channel.

preventive control The implementation of an organizational policy or a security principle, such as authentication or confidentiality, to protect a vulnerability.

privacy The state of being free from unauthorized observation, or as defined in information security, the ability to exercise control over how others use personal information collected from individuals.

Privacy Enhanced Mail (PEM) A standard proposed by the Internet Engineering Task Force (IETF) that will function with public key cryptosystems. PEM uses 3DES symmetric key encryption and RSA for key exchanges and digital signatures.

private key encryption Synonymous with symmetric encryption. A method of communicating on a network using a single key to both encrypt and decrypt a message.

private law Laws that regulate the relationship between the individual and the organization, and that encompass family law, commercial law, and labor law.

procedures Methods or processes, usually detailed, put in place by an organization in order to accomplish its objectives.

program A collection of steps, often many of them being projects, performed within the organization to improve security.

project management The application of knowledge, skills, tools, and techniques to meet planned objectives.

projectitis The phenomenon of becoming so engrossed in project administration that meaningful project work is neglected.

proxy server Synonymous with proxy firewall. A server that is configured to look like a Web server, and which performs actions on behalf of that server to protect it from hacking.

public key encryption Synonymous with asymmetric encryption. A method of communicating on a network using two different keys, one to encrypt and the other to decrypt a message.

public law Laws that regulate the structure and administration of government agencies and their relationships with citizens, employees, and other governments.

qualitative assessment The evaluation of an organization's assets using their relative values to the organization.

quantitative assessment The evaluation of an organization's assets using actual values or estimates.

rapid onset disasters Episodes—often natural disasters—that occur suddenly, with little warning, taking the lives of people, and destroying the means of production.

readiness and review The domain of the security maintenance model concerned with keeping the information security program functioning as designed and keeping it continuously improving over time.

recommended practices Synonymous with best practices and best business practices. Procedures that provide a superior level of security for an organization's information.

recovery time objective (RTO) The amount of time that passes before an infrastructure is available once the need for BC is declared.

recovery point objective (RPO) The point in the past to which the recovered applications and data at the alternate infrastructure will be restored.

red team Synonymous with ethical hacker, tiger team, and white-hat hacker. Consultants or outsourced contractors who are hired to perform controlled attacks to compromise or disrupt systems by using documented vulnerabilities.

Remote Authentication Dial-in User Service (RADIUS) A system that authenticates the credentials of users who are trying to access an organization's network through a dial-up connection.

remote journaling The transfer of live transactions to an off-site facility.

residual risk The risk that remains to an information asset after an existing control has been applied.

resource An individual or skill set whose function is detailed in a project plan.

restitution The compensation for a misdeed.

risk The probability that something can happen. Also, used to express the potential for loss.

risk analysis Synonymous with risk assessment. An analysis of the probability of loss faced by an information asset within its own situational context.

risk appetite The quantity and nature of risk that organizations are willing to accept.

risk assessment Synonymous with risk analysis. An assessment of the probability of loss faced by an information asset within its own situational context.

risk management The process of identifying vulnerabilities in an organization's information system and taking steps to assure that losses experienced by the systems are within the acceptable loss limits (risk appetite) of the organization. In the context of InfoSec it is usually associated with assessing risks and then implementing or repairing controls to assure the confidentiality, integrity, and availability of information.

role-based control A type of access control in which individuals are allowed to use data based on their positions in an organization.

sacrificial host Synonymous with bastion host. A dedicated firewall that enables a router to prescreen data packets to minimize the network traffic and load on a proxy server.

safeguard Synonymous with control and countermeasure. A security mechanism, policy, or procedure that can counter system attacks, reduce risks, and resolve vulnerabilities.

scope creep A project phenomenon that occurs when the quantity or quality of project deliverables is expanded from the original project plan.

secret key In symmetric encryption, the single key shared by both parties. In asymmetric encryption, the private key retained by the owner for use in decrypting messages encrypted with owner's public key.

Secure Electronic Transactions (SET) A standard developed by MasterCard and VISA in 1997 to provide protection from electronic payment fraud. It works by encrypting the credit card transfers with DES for encryption and RSA for key exchange.

Secure Hypertext Transfer Protocol (SHTTP) A protocol designed to enable secure communications across the Internet. SHTTP is the application of SSL over HTTP, which allows the encryption of all information passing between two computers through a protected and secure virtual connection.

Secure Multipurpose Internet Mail Extensions (S/MIME) A specification developed to increase the security of e-mail that adds encryption and user authentication.

Secure Shell (SSH) A popular extension to the TCP/IP protocol suite, sponsored by the IETF. It provides authentication services between a client and a server and is used to secure replacement tools for terminal emulation, remote management, and file transfer applications.

Secure Sockets Layer (SSL) A protocol for transmitting private information securely over the Internet.

security To be protected from the threat of loss; protection from that which would do harm, intentionally or otherwise.

security education, training, and awareness (SETA) program An education program designed to reduce the number of security breaches that occur through a lack of employee security awareness.

security incident response team (SIRT) The group of persons assigned to carry out the actions specified in the IR Plan. The SIRT is sometimes identified as CSIRT or computer security incident response team.

Security Management Index (SMI) A survey developed by the Human Firewall Council that gathers information on how organizations manage security.

security manager A member of an organization accountable for the day-to-day operation of the information security program, accomplishing the objectives identified by the CISO, and resolving issues identified by technicians.

security model   A collection of security rules that represents the implementation of a security policy.

security systems development life cycle (SecSDLC)   A methodology for the design and implementation of security for information systems.

security technician   The technically qualified individual who configures firewalls and IDSs, implements security software, diagnoses and troubleshoots problems, and coordinates with systems and network administrators to ensure that security technology is properly implemented.

separation of duties   A control used to reduce the chance of an individual violating information security and breaching the confidentiality, integrity, or availability of the information.

sequential roster   A list of people who are called, in sequential order, by a single operative in the case of an emergency.

service bureau   A service agency that provides a service for a fee.

session key   A limited-use symmetric key for encrypting electronic communication.

signature-based intrusion detection system (IDS)   Synonymous with knowledge-based IDS. A device that examines data traffic for signature matches with predefined, preconfigured attack patterns.

simulation   A testing regime where each person works individually, rather than in a group setting, to simulate the performance of each task. The simulation stops short of performing the actual physical tasks required.

single loss expectancy (SLE)   The calculation of the cost incurred in a single instance when a specific asset within an organization is attacked.

slack time   The difference in time between the critical path and any other path. It identifies how much time is available for starting a non-critical task without delaying the project as a whole.

slow onset disasters   Episodes that occur over time and slowly deteriorate the capacity of an organization to withstand their effects.

smart card   A device that contains memory and a processor that can verify and validate a number of pieces of information about an individual beyond recording facts.

standard   A detailed statement of what employees of an organization must do to comply with a policy.

standard of due care   Organizational assurance that its actions demonstrate that every employee knows what is acceptable or not acceptable behavior, and knows the consequences of illegal or unethical actions.

state table   A process used by a server that tracks the state and context of each connection to authenticate the exchange of packets by recording which host sent which packet, when, and to which remote host.

stateful inspection firewall   Devices that track network connections that are established between internal and external systems.

statistical anomaly-based intrusion detection system (IDS)   Synonymous with behavior-based IDS. A device that collects data from normal traffic to establish a baseline. The IDS compares periodic data samples with the baseline to highlight irregularities.

strategic planning   Synonymous with strategy. The process of moving an organization towards its vision by accomplishing its mission.

strategy   Synonymous with strategic planning. The process of moving an organization towards its vision by accomplishing its mission.

strong authentication   The use of two or more authentication mechanism types to authenticate a single transaction or session; for example, the use of something you have and something you know as occurs when making an ATM banking transaction.

structured review   Synonymous with structured walk-through. A process that reviews a systems development plan or an element of a plan using an orderly process of review to verify essential processes have been followed and all needed components are present.

structured walk-through   Synonymous with structured review. A process that reviews a systems development plan or an element of a plan using an orderly process of review to verify essential processes have been followed and all needed components are present.

substitution cipher   In encryption, the substitution of one value for another.

supplicant   An entity requesting access to a controlled system. May be a person or other entity attempting to gain access to an information or other system.

symmetric encryption   Synonymous with private key encryption. Symmetric encryption is a method of communicating on a network using a single key to both encrypt and decrypt a message.

synchronous tokens   Authentication devices that are synchronized with a server so that each device (server and token) uses the time or a time-based database to generate a number that is entered during the user login phase.

systems development life cycle (SDLC)   A methodology for the design and implementation of an information system.

Systems Security Certified Professional (SSCP)   A certification for operational planning for information security with an operational focus on seven domains of information security.

systems-specific policy (SysSP)   A policy document that addresses the particular use of certain systems. This could include firewall configuration policies, systems access policies, and other technical configuration areas.

task rotation Synonymous with job rotation. A security check that requires that every employee is trained to perform the work of another employee.

task-based control A type of data access control in which individuals are allowed to use data, based on their job responsibilities.

technical controls Control measures that use or implement a technical solution to reduce risk of loss in an organization, as well as issues related to examining and selecting the technologies appropriate to protecting information.

technical feasibility An examination of whether an organization has or can acquire the technology and expertise necessary to implement and support specific control alternatives.

Terminal Access Controller Access Control System (TACACS) A remote access system that validates a user's credentials.

threat An object, person, or other entity that represents a risk or potential for loss to an asset.

threat agent A specific instance or component that represents a danger to an organization's assets. Threat agents can be environmental or human, for example, lightning strikes or malicious code authors.

threat identification The examination of a danger to assess its potential to impact an organization.

tiger team Synonymous with ethical hacker, white-hat hacker, and red team. Consultants or outsourced contractors who are hired to perform controlled attacks to compromise or disrupt systems by using documented vulnerabilities.

timeshare A site that is leased by an organization in conjunction with a business partner for use if a disaster occurs at the home site.

top-down approach A methodology of establishing security policies that is initiated by upper management.

tort law The body of law that allow individuals to seek recourse against others in the event of personal, physical, or financial injury.

transference The control approach used by an organization to shift the risks from one asset to another.

transport mode One of the two modes of operation of the IP Security Protocol. In transport mode, only the IP data is encrypted, not the IP headers.

transposition cipher Synonymous with permutation cipher. The rearranging of values within a block to create coded information.

triple DES Synonymous with 3DES. An enhancement to the Data Encryption Standard (DES). An algorithm that uses up to three keys to perform three different encryption operations.

trusted network A network segment that has had some degree of protection established (such as an intranet that is inside an organization's firewall) and is therefore perceived as being less susceptible to attack or loss.

tunnel mode One of the two modes of operation of the IP Security Protocol. In tunnel mode, the entire IP packet is encrypted and placed as payload into another IP packet.

two-man control A security check that requires that two individuals review and approve each other's work in order to complete a task.

U.S. military classification scheme A categorization method used by the U.S. Department of Defense to assign key documents to groups based on sensitivity levels.

U.S. Secret Service A unit within the Department of the Treasury that provides protective services for key members of the U.S. government and has enforcement responsibility for certain criminal acts, including crimes involving U.S. currency (counterfeiting) and some aspects of computer and technology crimes.

untrusted network A network segment perceived as uncontrolled, such as the Internet.

user involvement The inclusion of users in the organizational process of developing security systems.

values statement A formal set of organizational principles, standards, and qualities.

virtual password A password calculated or extracted from a passphrase that meets system storage requirements.

virtual private networks (VPNs) A network within a network that typically allows a user to use the Internet as a private network.

vision statement A written declaration of the organization's long-term goals.

vulnerability A weakness or fault in a system or protection mechanism that exposes information to attack or damage.

vulnerability assessment The process of identifying and documenting specific and provable flaws in the organization's information asset environment.

vulnerability scanner A device that scans servers to identify exposed usernames, shows open network shares, and exposes configuration problems and other vulnerabilities.

war dialer An automatic phone-dialing program that dials every number on a list or in a configured range (e.g., 555-1000 to 555-2000), and checks to see if a person, answering machine, or modem picks up.

war driving A technique used to determine the location of wireless access points and then assess that access point's security requirements with the intent to determine if an unauthorized connection is possible.

warm site An alternate site that can be used by an organization if a disaster occurs at the home site. Frequently includes computing equipment and peripherals with servers but not client workstations.

white-hat hacker Synonymous with ethical hacker, tiger team, and red team. Consultants or outsourced contractors who are hired to perform controlled attacks to compromise or disrupt systems by using documented vulnerabilities.

Wi-Fi Protected Access (WPA) A family of protocols used to secure wireless networks. It was initially developed as an intermediate solution known as WPA. Currently known as WPA2, it incorporates the IEEE 802.11i standards.

Wired Equivalent Privacy (WEP) Part of the IEEE 802.11 wireless networking standard designed to provide a basic level of security protection to these radio networks with an intent to prevent unauthorized access or eavesdropping.

wireless access point (WAP) A radio transceiver device that enables radio-frequency network access to a local area network.

work breakdown structure (WBS) A planning approach that breaks a project plan into specific action steps.

XOR cipher conversion A programming algorithm that uses the Boolean XOR function to combine binary digits from two data streams, one with a clear text and the other with an encryption key, to produce an encrypted data stream.

INDEX

C

D

E

F

O

P

S

X

Z